COMPLETE
BIRDS
OF BRITAIN AND EUROPE

RSPB COMPLETE BIRDS
OF BRITAIN AND EUROPE

Rob Hume

DK

DORLING KINDERSLEY

LONDON, NEW YORK, MUNICH,
MELBOURNE, AND DELHI

DK LONDON
Senior Art Editor Ina Stradins
Senior Editor Angeles Gavira
Designer Kirsten Cashman
DTP Designer John Goldsmid
Production Controller Linda Dare,
Elizabeth Cherry, Inderjit Bhullar
Managing Art Editor Phil Ormerod
Managing Editors Sarah Larter,
Liz Wheeler
Art Director Bryn Walls
Publisher Jonathan Metcalf

Picture Editor Chris Gomersall
Illustrator Andrew Mackay

DK DELHI
Managing Art Editor Shuka Jain
Project Designer Shefali Upadhyay
Designer Pallavi Narain
Design Assistance Elizabeth Thomas,
Sukanto Bhattacharjya, Suresh Kumar
DTP Designer Umesh Aggarwal
Managing Editor Ira Pande
Project Editor Atanu Raychaudhuri
Editor Rimli Borooah

REVISED EDITIONS
Project Designer Shefali Upadhyay
Project Editor Pankhoori Sinha,
Rohan Sinha
DTP Designer Sunil Sharma

First published in Great Britain in 2002
by Dorling Kindersley Limited
80 Strand, London WC2R 0RL
Copyright © 2002, 2007
Dorling Kindersley Limited
A Penguin Company

ISBN: 9781405322287

Reproduced by Colourscan, Singapore
Printed and bound in China by Toppan
Printing Co. (Shenzhan), Ltd

see our complete catalogue at
www.dk.com

CD TRACK LISTING

Track	Species	Sound	Page
1	Black-throated Diver	Display calls	57
2	Little Grebe	i Call	59
		ii Winter call	
3	Fulmar	Calls at nest	65
4	Bittern	Booming call	75
5	Grey Heron	i Flight call	82
	Grey Heron	ii Adult call	
6	Mute Swan	i Threatened call	92
		ii Chicks call	
7	Whooper Swan	Call	91
8	Bewick's Swan	Call	90
9	Pink-footed Goose	Call	95
10	Greylag Goose	Call	96
11	Canada Goose	i Call	97
		ii Call of a flock	
12	Brent Goose	Call	99
13	Mallard	i Female quacks	101
		ii Chicks call	
14	Wigeon	i Male call	105
		ii Female call	
15	Peregrine Falcon	i Call	143
		ii Alarm calls at nest	
16	Grey Partridge	i Male song	153
		ii Call	
17	Quail	Male song	154
18	Pheasant	Call	155
19	Corncrake	Song	157
20	Moorhen	Call	160
21	Coot	i Call	161
		ii Young call	
22	Oystercatcher	i Piping display call	166
		ii Call	
23	Ringed Plover	Flight call	170
24	Grey Plover	Call	175
25	Golden Plover	i Call	174
		ii Summer call	
26	Lapwing	i Male flight call	176
		ii Call	
27	Dunlin	i Call	178
		ii Adult, young calls	
28	Common Sandpiper	Call	186
29	Green Sandpiper	i Call	188
		ii Flight call	
30	Redshank	Flight call	190
31	Greenshank	Call	192
32	Curlew	i Call	196
		ii Song	
33	Snipe	i Drumming	200
		ii Flight call	
34	Black-headed Gull	i Call of a flock	208
		ii Call	
35	Herring Gull	Call	211
36	Kittiwake	Calls at colony	215
37	Common Tern	i Call	222
		ii Adult, young calls	
38	Stock Dove	Song	235
39	Woodpigeon	Song	236
40	Collared Dove	Song	237
41	Turtle Dove	Song	238

Track	Species	Sound	Page
42	Tawny Owl	i Song	241
		ii Call	
43	Barn Owl	Call	249
44	Nightjar	Song	250
45	Swift	Call	254
46	Hoopoe	Song	259
47	Green Woodpecker	Call	262
48	Great Spotted Woodpecker	i Drumming, calls	265
		ii Flight call	
49	Skylark	i Song	270
		ii Call	
50	Crested Lark	Call	271
51	Woodlark	Song	273
52	Swallow	Song	280
53	Meadow Pipit	Song	286
54	Tree Pipit	Song	287
55	White/Pied Wagtail	Call	290
56	Yellow Wagtail	Call	291
57	Grey Wagtail	Call	292
58	Wren	Song	294
59	Dunnock	Song	297
60	Robin	i Song	300
		ii Call	
61	Nightingale	Song	303
62	Black Redstart	Song	305
63	Stonechat	Call	310
64	Song Thrush	Song	313
65	Mistle Thrush	Song	315
66	Blackbird	Song	317
67	Garden Warbler	Song	320
68	Blackcap	Song	322
69	Sedge Warbler	Song	328
70	Reed Warbler	Song	330
71	Great Reed Warbler	Song	332
72	Cetti's Warbler	Song	336
73	Willow Warbler	Song	339
74	Chiffchaff	Song	342
75	Goldcrest	Song	343
76	Great Tit	Song	348
77	Coal Tit	Song	349
78	Blue Tit	Song	350
79	Willow Tit	Call	352
80	Marsh Tit	Call	353
81	Long-tailed Tit	Call	354
82	Nuthatch	Call	358
83	Golden Oriole	Song	367
84	Magpie	Call	369
85	Jay	Call	370
86	Jackdaw	Call	375
87	Rook	Call	376
88	Carrion Crow	Call	377
89	Raven	Call	379
90	Starling	Song	380
91	House Sparrow	Call	383
92	Chaffinch	Song	388
93	Linnet	Flight call	390
94	Goldfinch	Call	393
95	Greenfinch	Song	394
96	Bullfinch	Call	398
97	Crossbill	Call	400
98	Yellowhammer	Song	408
99	Corn Bunting	Song	413

CONTENTS

HOW THIS BOOK WORKS

This guide covers just under 800 bird species from the Western Palearctic region (Europe, the Middle East, and North Africa). The species are organized into three sections: the first profiles common European species, with each given detailed, full-page treatment; the second covers over 190 rarer birds in concise, quarter-page entries; the third section consists of a list of rare visitors (vagrants) as well as birds that live in North Africa and the Middle East.

▽ INTRODUCTION

The species are organized conventionally by order and family. This means related birds appear together, with a group introduction.

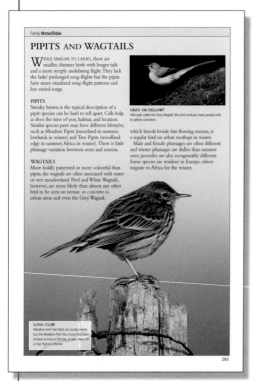

Family **Motacillidae**

PIPITS AND WAGTAILS

WHILE SIMILAR TO LARKS, these are smaller, slimmer birds with longer tails and a more steeply undulating flight. They lack the larks' prolonged song-flights but the pipits have more ritualized song-flight patterns and less varied songs.

PIPITS
Streaky brown is the typical description of a pipit: species can be hard to tell apart. Calls help, as does the time of year, habitat, and location. Similar species pairs may have different lifestyles, such as Meadow Pipit (moorland in summer, lowlands in winter) and Tree Pipits (woodland edge in summer, Africa in winter). There is little plumage variation between sexes and seasons.

WAGTAILS
More boldly patterned or more colourful than pipits, the wagtails are often associated with water or wet meadowland. Pied and White Wagtails, however, are more likely than almost any other bird to be seen on tarmac or concrete in urban areas and even the Grey Wagtail,

GREY OR YELLOW?
Although called the Grey Wagtail, this bird confuses many people with its yellow coloration.

which breeds beside fast-flowing streams, is a regular bird on urban rooftops in winter.
Male and female plumages are often different and winter plumages are duller than summer ones; juveniles are also recognizably different. Some species are resident in Europe, others migrate to Africa for the winter.

LONG CLAW
Meadow and Tree Pipits are closely similar, but the Meadow Pipit has a long hind claw, at least as long as the toe, as seen here; on a Tree Pipit it is shorter.

283

MAPS

Each profile includes a map showing the range of the species, with colours reflecting seasonal movements. Migration ranges are not always mapped, as some migrants simply leave one site, turn up in another, and are not seen in between.

KEY
- ■ Summer distribution
- ■ Resident all year
- ■ Winter distribution
- ■ Seen on migration

COLOUR BAND
The information bands at the top and bottom of each entry are colour-coded for each family.

COMMON NAME

IN FLIGHT
Illustrations show the bird in flight, from above and/or below (note that differences of season, age, or sex are not always visible in flight).

DESCRIPTION
Conveys the main features and essential character of the species including:

VOICE: *a description of the species' calls and songs.*

NESTING: *the type of nest and its usual location; the number of eggs in a clutch; the number of broods in a year; the breeding season.*

FEEDING: *how, where, and what the species feeds on.*

HABITAT/BEHAVIOUR
Additional photographs show the species displaying typical behaviour in one of its preferred habitats.

LENGTH, WINGSPAN AND WEIGHT: *length is tip of tail to tip of bill; measurements are averages or ranges.*

SOCIAL: *the social unit the species is usually found in.*

LIFESPAN: *the average or maximum life expectancy.*

STATUS: *the conservation status of the species; the symbol † means the data available can only suggest a provisional status.*

▽ COMMON SPECIES

The main section of the book features the 330 most commonly seen European bird species. Each entry follows the same easy-to-access structure.

| Order **Passeriformes** | Family **Motacillidae** |

Yellow Wagtail

two white bars on blackish wings

bright yellow stripe over eye

MALE (SPRING)

green back

IN FLIGHT

MALE (SPRING)

white sides to black tail

long, spindly black legs

Elegant and colourful, the Yellow Wagtail, particularly the male, is a highly distinctive bird. However, autumn birds, especially juveniles, cause confusion with rarer species and also juvenile Pied Wagtails, which can appear strongly yellowish. The call always helps to identify it. In summer, it lives around pools and reservoirs and damp, grassy fields where horses and cattle disturb the insects it eats. In winter, it is found near big mammal herds on African plains.
VOICE Call distinctive, loud, full, flat, or rising *tsli*, or *tsweep* or *tswi-eep*; song repetition of brief, chirping phrases.
NESTING Grassy cup in vegetation on ground; 5 or 6 eggs; 2 broods; May–July.
FEEDING Forages on ground, skipping and leaping after flies in short flycatching sallies; eats insects and other invertebrates.

SIMILAR SPECIES	
longer tail	greyer back
shorter, pale legs	longer tail
GREY WAGTAIL ♂ ♀; see p.292	**PIED WAGTAIL** juvenile, similar to juvenile; see p.290

| Length **17cm (6½in)** | Wingspan **23–27cm (9–** |
| Social **Small flocks** | Lifespan **Up to 5 years** |

SIMILAR SPECIES
Similar-looking species are identified and the key differences pointed out.
♂ = male, ♀ = female

SUBSPECIES
Panels show significan[t] subspecies, together with distribution and distinguishing feature[s]

CLASSIFICATION
The top band of each entry provides the scientific order, family, and species names (see p.463 for full definitions of these terms).

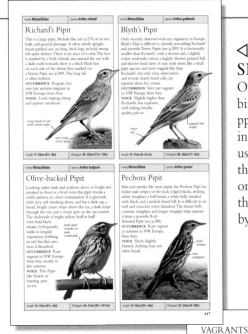

Family Motacillidae   Species *Anthus richardi*

Richard's Pipit
This is a large pipit, Skylark-like (see p.270) in size, bulk, and general plumage. It often stands upright, breast pushed out on, long, thick legs, its bold, strong bill quite distinct. There is no trace of a crest. The face is marked by a bold whitish area around the eye with a dark mark beneath; there is a thick black line on each side of the throat (less marked on a Tawny Pipit, see p.289). The long tail is often bobbed.
OCCURRENCE Regular, but rare, late autumn migrant in NW Europe, from Asia.
VOICE Loud, rasping *sheep* and quieter variations.

long blackish tail with white sides

very long hind claw

Length 17–20cm (6½–8in)   Wingspan 29–34cm (11½–13in)

Family Motacillidae   Species *Anthus godlewskii*

Blyth's Pipit
Only recently observed with any regularity in Europe, Blyth's Pipit is difficult to identify, resembling Richard's and juvenile Tawny Pipits (see p.289). It is fractionally smaller than Richard's, with a shorter tail, a slightly richer underside colour, a slightly shorter, pointed bill, and shorter hind claws. It may look more like a small pipit species and more wagtail-like than Richard's, but only close observation and several clearly heard calls can separate them for certain.
OCCURRENCE Very rare vagrant in NW Europe, from Asia.
VOICE Slightly higher than Richard's, less explosive, with fading, breathy quality, *puh-ee.*

short tail

wagtail-like shape

Length 15–17cm (6–6½in)   Wingspan 28–30cm (11–12in)

Family Motacillidae   Species *Anthus hodgsoni*

Olive-backed Pipit
Looking rather dark and uniform above or bright and streaked in front in a brief view, this pipit reveals a subtle pattern on closer examination. It is greenish, with very soft streaking above, and has a dark cap, a broad, bright cream stripe above the eye, a dark stripe through the eye, and a cream spot on the ear coverts. The underside is bright yellow-buff to buff with bold black streaks. It frequently walks in longish vegetation, bobbing its tail, but flies into trees if disturbed.
OCCURRENCE Rare vagrant in NW Europe from Asia, mostly in late autumn.
VOICE Tree Pipit-like hoarse or buzzing *speee* or *tees.*

bold dark streaks on pale underside

Length 14–15cm (5½–6in)   Wingspan 24–27cm (9½–10½in)

Family Motacillidae   Species *Anthus gustavi*

Pechora Pipit
Slim and streaky like most pipits, the Pechora Pipit has bolder pale stripes on the back (edged black), striking white wingbars, a buff breast, a white belly streaked with black, and a pinkish-based bill. It is difficult to see well and crouches when disturbed. The breast-belly contrast, wingbars, and longer wingtips help separate it from a juvenile Red-throated Pipit (see p.288).
OCCURRENCE Rare vagrant in autumn in NW Europe, from Asia.
VOICE Short, slightly buzzed, clicking *dzep*, not often heard.

bold streaks

two wingbars

Length 14–15cm (5½–6in)   Wingspan 23–25cm (9–10in)

447

GROUP NAME
The common name of the group the species belongs to is at the top of each page.

Over 190 less common birds are presented on pp. 414–462. Arranged in the same group order used in the main section, these entries consist of one clear photograph of the species accompanied by a focused description.

PIPITS AND WAGTAILS

Species **Motacilla flava**

pale stripe over eye

white lines on wings

buff underside

JUVENILE (AUTUMN)

pale line over eye

grey-green back

FEMALE (SPRING)

FLIGHT: strong but undulating, with long, sweeping bounds; flurries of quick wingbeats.

FEEDING
The Yellow Wagtail is usually found around livestock in damp fields and pastures: it eats insects dislodged from the grass by the grazing cattle and horses.

long white stripe over eye

OCCURRENCE
Widespread in summer, breeding throughout Europe except for Ireland and Iceland. Often near water, in wet fields and pastures with livestock. Migrant flocks often on muddy reservoir edges or adjacent grass.

Seen in the UK
J F **M A M J J A S O** N D

Weight **16–22g (9/16–13/16 oz)**

Status **Secure**

291

PHOTOGRAPHS
These illustrate the species in different views and plumage variations. Significant differences relating to age, sex, and season are shown and the images labelled accordingly; if there is no variation, the images have no label. Unless stated otherwise, the bird shown is an adult.

FLIGHT PATTERNS
This feature illustrates and briefly describes the way the species flies. See panel below.

MAPS
See panel on p.6

VAGRANTS

The list that follows consists of birds that occur only very rarely in Europe, known as vagrants or accidentals. It also looks a little further beyond Europe, to list those birds whose normal range is the Middle East and North Africa, so covering a total faunal area known as the Western Palearctic.
Vagrants to Europe arrive from Asia and North America (and fewer from Africa). Western Europe, especially the UK, is well placed to receive birds that are blown off course from eastern North America and cross the Atlantic. It was thought that such birds cross the ocean on board ship, but it is now accepted that even small birds can, with a following wind, survive a flight across the Atlantic, although they probably do not survive long afterwards. Larger species, however, such as some wildfowl, may live for years in Europe and a few (that have been trapped, ringed, and released in order to follow their movements) have even returned to North America in subsequent years. These are not, in any true sense, European birds, but are included here to complete the range of species that have been recorded. Many appear again, others may not: by their nature these "accidentals" are unpredictable.

Common Name	Scientific Name	Family/Scientific Name	Description
Ostrich			
Ostrich	*Struthio camelus*	Ratites/Struthidae	Vagrant in North Africa, from southern Africa
Albatrosses			
Shy Albatross	*Diomedea cauta*	Albatrosses/Diomedeidae	Large seabird from southern oceans
Yellow-nosed Albatross	*Diomedea chlororhynchos*	Albatrosses/Diomedeidae	Large seabird from southern oceans
Black-browed Albatross	*Diomedea melanophris*	Albatrosses/Diomedeidae	Long-winged seabird from South Atlantic
Wandering Albatross	*Diomedea exulans*	Albatrosses/Diomedeidae	Large seabird from southern oceans
Petrels and Shearwaters			
Black-capped Petrel	*Pterodroma hasitata*	Petrels and Shearwaters/Procellariidae	Large petrel from Caribbean
Atlantic Petrel	*Pterodroma incerta*	Petrels and Shearwaters/Procellariidae	Large petrel from South Atlantic
Soft-plumaged Petrel	*Pterodroma mollis*	Petrels and Shearwaters/Procellariidae	Large petrel from South Atlantic
Fea's Petrel	*Pterodroma feae*	Petrels and Shearwaters/Procellariidae	Large, rare petrel from Madeira
Zino's Petrel	*Pterodroma madeira*	Petrels and Shearwaters/Procellariidae	Large, rare petrel from Madeira
Bulwer's Petrel	*Bulweria bulwerii*	Petrels and Shearwaters/Procellariidae	Dark, long-tailed petrel from mid-Atlantic islands
Streaked Shearwater	*Calonectris leucomelas*	Petrels and Shearwaters/Procellariidae	Vagrant in Middle East, from tropical oceans
Flesh-footed Shearwater	*Puffinus carneipes*	Petrels and Shearwaters/Procellariidae	All-dark shearwater from Indian Ocean
Audubon's Shearwater	*Puffinus lherminieri*	Petrels and Shearwaters/Procellariidae	Small shearwater from Indian Ocean

463

▷ VAGRANTS
Very rare visitors and peripheral species are listed at the back of the book with a brief description, including where the species is from.

SEEN IN THE UK
Specifies the months in which the species is found in the UK.
J Bird is present
J Bird not present

FLIGHT PATTERNS

Simple diagrams are used to illustrate the seven basic flight patterns. The broadly horizontal lines indicate whether the species has a level, swooping, or undulating flight, with the wingbeats represented by up and down strokes to indicate bursts of wingbeats, regular flaps, and speed.

wingbeats

Woodpecker-like: bursts of wingbeats between deeply undulating glides.

Finch-like: light, bouncy action with flurries of wingbeats between deep, undulating glides.

Sparrowhawk-like: straight, with several quick, deep beats between short, flat glides.

Gull-like: continually flapping, with slow, steady wingbeats

Duck-like: continually flapping, with fast wingbeats.

Kite-like: deep, slow wingbeats between soaring glides.

Swallow-like: swooping, with burst of wingbeats between glides.

EVOLUTION

Most scientists believe birds evolved from dinosaurs. Whether the first birds climbed trees and began to glide back to the ground, or ran along the ground and learned to lift off, is still debated. What we do know is that, over hundreds of millions of years, birds spread over the globe and adapted to exploit every habitat except deep underwater. Some species are still evolving separate subspecies today.

ANCIENT BIRDS
Gamebirds are ancient, but have changed little over millions of years. One group, the grouse, are adapted to survival on a very simple diet in demanding habitats.

THE MISSING LINK

In 1861 a series of fossils were found in limestone beds in Germany that pointed to the relationship between dinosaurs and birds. The fossilized creature, named *Archaeopteryx*, is now viewed as the "missing link" because it is very bird-like in appearance, with well-developed feathers that are just like those of a modern bird, and yet still has many reptilian features such as teeth in its jaws and a long, flexible, bony tail.

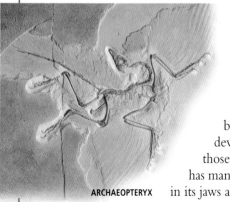

ARCHAEOPTERYX

SPECIALIZED SPECIES
There are only five species of divers worldwide, all found on northern lakes and sea coasts. They have a very specialized aquatic lifestyle.

BIRD ANCESTRY

This table shows the relationships between modern birds (all within the sub-class Neornithes), and their age. Using the branches of the evolutionary tree we can see how different groups split from common ancestors. Songbirds divided off from the rest more than 100 million years ago.

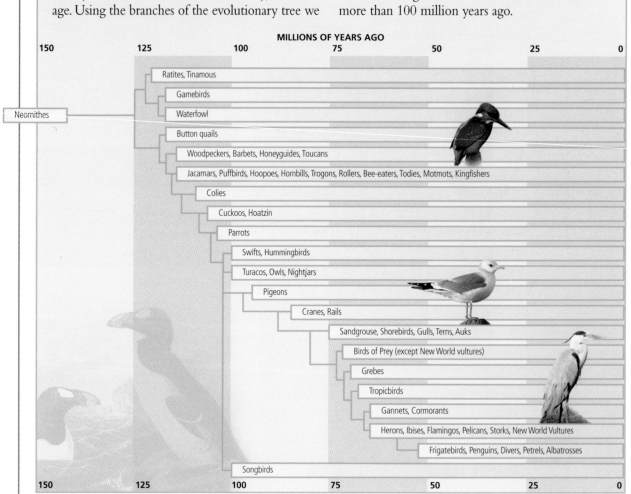

MILLIONS OF YEARS AGO

150	125	100	75	50	25	0

Neornithes

- Ratites, Tinamous
- Gamebirds
- Waterfowl
- Button quails
- Woodpeckers, Barbets, Honeyguides, Toucans
- Jacamars, Puffbirds, Hoopoes, Hornbills, Trogons, Rollers, Bee-eaters, Todies, Motmots, Kingfishers
- Colies
- Cuckoos, Hoatzin
- Parrots
- Swifts, Hummingbirds
- Turacos, Owls, Nightjars
- Pigeons
- Cranes, Rails
- Sandgrouse, Shorebirds, Gulls, Terns, Auks
- Birds of Prey (except New World vultures)
- Grebes
- Tropicbirds
- Gannets, Cormorants
- Herons, Ibises, Flamingos, Pelicans, Storks, New World Vultures
- Frigatebirds, Penguins, Divers, Petrels, Albatrosses
- Songbirds

150	125	100	75	50	25	0

NATURAL SELECTION

"Only the fittest survive." That is the theory of natural selection and it is true that the birds best adapted to an environment have an advantage over the rest and produce offspring that perpetuate their own genetic make-up. There are many ways in which a species may evolve in response to changing habitats or food. If such a change happens in only one part of a species' range, and the birds in that area remain separate, they may change so much that they can no longer interbreed. The result is two species instead of one. There is a halfway stage: two groups may differ in size or colour, but can still interbreed. At this point they are called "subspecies" or "races".

CHAFFINCH

BRAMBLING

PERSISTENT STARLING
The common Starling is successful through most of Europe but does not breed in Iberia and North Africa, where the Spotless Starling replaces it. This latter species must have evolved in isolation but has persisted despite an influx of common Starlings into Spain every winter.

EVOLUTION THROUGH ISOLATION
Two finches in the family Fringillidae are alike in size, shape, pattern, and even in their behaviour and calls. The Chaffinch and the Brambling evolved as two species from one ancestor. The Ice Age forced one population (later the Chaffinch) southwest, the other (which became the Brambling) southeast. Ice caps on mountains in the centre separated them for millennia.

EXTINCTION

Extinction is forever: the total loss of a species from the world. Modern rates of extinction are exceptionally high and still accelerating. In Europe, however, we have lost only one species in historical times: the Great Auk. This large, flightless relative of the Razorbill bred in Scotland but was hunted until few remained; the final survivors were killed by collectors of stuffed birds. The last pair to be seen alive were then killed off Iceland in 1844.

CLASSIFYING BIRDS

The purpose of classifying birds is to indicate the relationship between them while at the same time giving each species a unique name. Birds are grouped into "orders", each with one or more "families". The next subdivision is the "genus", which has one or more "species" (denoted by a two-part name). Some species are split into "subspecies", indicated by a third name.

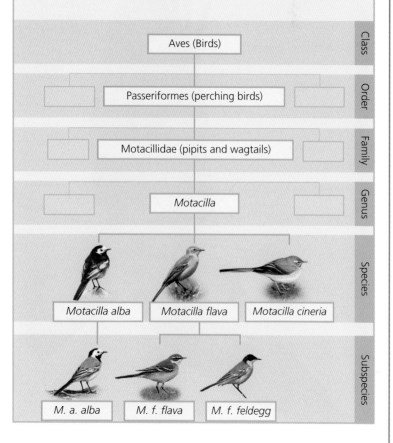

Aves (Birds)		Class
Passeriformes (perching birds)		Order
Motacillidae (pipits and wagtails)		Family
Motacilla		Genus
Motacilla alba	Motacilla flava	Motacilla cineria	Species
M. a. alba	M. f. flava	M. f. feldegg	Subspecies

ANATOMY

Although there is a huge diversity in shape, size, and outer appearance, all birds have a similar internal structure. They are vertebrates, so have a jointed internal skeleton with two forelimbs and two hindlimbs, just like fish, reptiles, and mammals – including humans.

Their bones are like ours, but the proportions are very different. For example, the wing bones are like a human arm; the "inner wing" equivalent to our forearm, and the "outer wing" like the bones of our hand. What makes them unique is that they are the only animals with feathers.

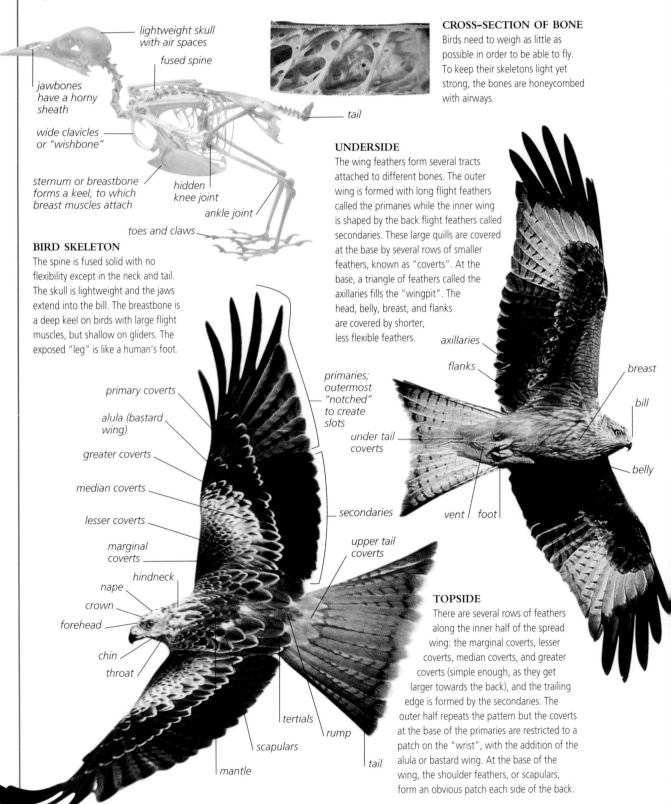

lightweight skull
with air spaces

fused spine

jawbones
have a horny
sheath

wide clavicles
or "wishbone"

sternum or breastbone
forms a keel, to which
breast muscles attach

hidden
knee joint

ankle joint

toes and claws

tail

CROSS–SECTION OF BONE
Birds need to weigh as little as possible in order to be able to fly. To keep their skeletons light yet strong, the bones are honeycombed with airways.

UNDERSIDE
The wing feathers form several tracts attached to different bones. The outer wing is formed with long flight feathers called the primaries while the inner wing is shaped by the back flight feathers called secondaries. These large quills are covered at the base by several rows of smaller feathers, known as "coverts". At the base, a triangle of feathers called the axillaries fills the "wingpit". The head, belly, breast, and flanks are covered by shorter, less flexible feathers.

axillaries

flanks

breast

bill

belly

vent | foot

BIRD SKELETON
The spine is fused solid with no flexibility except in the neck and tail. The skull is lightweight and the jaws extend into the bill. The breastbone is a deep keel on birds with large flight muscles, but shallow on gliders. The exposed "leg" is like a human's foot.

primary coverts

alula (bastard
wing)

greater coverts

median coverts

lesser coverts

marginal
coverts

hindneck

nape

crown

forehead

chin

throat

primaries;
outermost
"notched"
to create
slots

under tail
coverts

secondaries

upper tail
coverts

tertials

rump

scapulars

mantle

tail

TOPSIDE
There are several rows of feathers along the inner half of the spread wing: the marginal coverts, lesser coverts, median coverts, and greater coverts (simple enough, as they get larger towards the back), and the trailing edge is formed by the secondaries. The outer half repeats the pattern but the coverts at the base of the primaries are restricted to a patch on the "wrist", with the addition of the alula or bastard wing. At the base of the wing, the shoulder feathers, or scapulars, form an obvious patch each side of the back.

WING MARKINGS

Look at the feather tracts on a bird when perched and in flight. On some species most feathers are visible on the closed wing. On others, such as this Gull-billed Tern, the primaries and secondaries are hidden: all we can see are the primary tips. A large area between the back and the wingtips is formed by rounded, plain grey feathers called the tertials. On some birds these are large and obvious but in flight, as the wings straighten, they may slide out of sight under the scapulars. Therefore what is a prominent feature at rest may disappear in flight.

"wrist"

tertials hidden in flight

"elbow"

secondaries now visible on spread wing

full length of primaries revealed on open wing

OPEN AND CLOSED WINGS
This Gull-billed Tern has very long, tapered, pointed wings that reach well beyond its tail when folded but extend to reveal the obvious "wrist" (or carpal) joint and the elbow joint closer to the body. Only the fore edge of the inner half of the wing has any solid muscle; the rest is just feathers.

scapulars

primary tips

tertials cover half of primaries

wing coverts cover secondaries

FEET

The shape of the feet indicates the lifestyle of a bird. For example, webbed feet or toes with broad lobes each side aid swimming, while feathered feet help prevent heat loss. There are variations, but below are four of the main shapes and details of the actions they enable.

WALKING
The long hind claw is typical of small birds, such as pipits, that run or walk in grassy places.

CLIMBING
Two backward-facing toes and strong claws allow climbing birds to grip onto a branch.

HUNTING
Sharp, hooked claws grasp live prey; a strong grip makes the hind claw a lethal weapon.

SWIMMING
Webbed feet provide extra thrust under the water's surface, which is ideal for swimming.

FEATHERS

Feathers not only allow flight and keep a bird warm and dry, but they also add a variety of colour, pattern, and shape. Some develop purely for decoration, while others provide cryptic patterns to help the bird avoid predators. The large, stiff quills that support a bird in the air, the "flight feathers", and the equally large tail feathers, are usually wider on one side than the other to create the aerofoil shape that gives a bird extra lift. They are overlain at the base by smaller "coverts". The feathers that smooth the shape of a bird's body are the contour feathers, while loose down feathers form an insulating underlayer.

COMPLEX STRUCTURE
Feathers are amazingly complex. This close-up shows that the vanes each side of the central shaft "zip" together with minute hooks and barbs.

outer web

inner web

shaft

DOWN FEATHER   CONTOUR FEATHER   PRIMARY COVERT   TAIL FEATHER

LIFE CYCLE

A bird's appearance can vary significantly as a result of age or seasonal change. Newly hatched, chicks may be naked or downy. The down is quickly replaced by a first set of feathers, called the juvenile plumage. In autumn, some of these feathers are moulted and replaced (the wing and tail feathers are usually retained) to produce a first winter plumage. In the following spring, a partial moult produces the first summer plumage. From late summer onwards, all the feathers are replaced in a complete moult. Smaller birds may now be in their adult plumage; larger species, such as many of the gulls and birds of prey, have more intermediate (immature) stages: second winter, second summer, third winter,

third summer, and so on (as illustrated here by the Black-headed Gull, whose sequence of plumages is related to the seasons). There are variations on the theme. For example, while most birds have their brightest plumage in summer, wildfowl are at their best while pairing up in midwinter; the males become dull in summer, in an "eclipse" plumage.

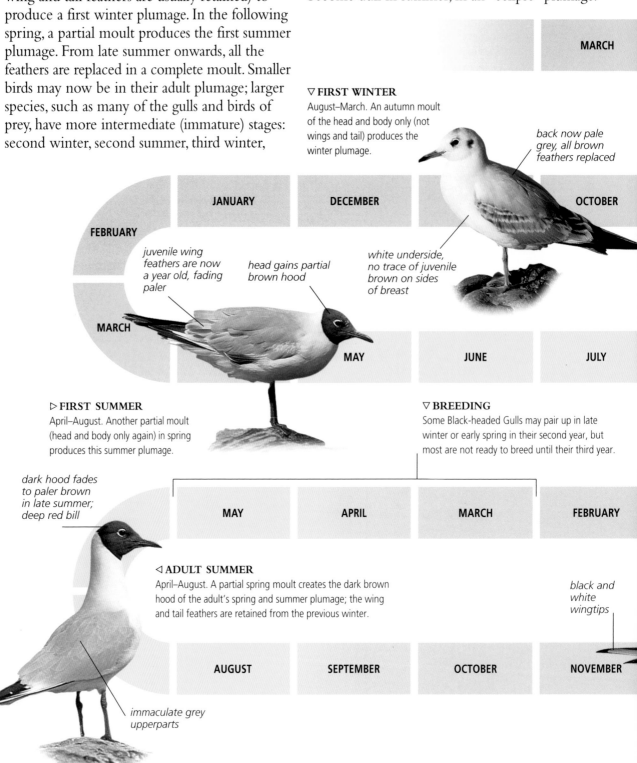

MARCH

▽ **FIRST WINTER**
August–March. An autumn moult of the head and body only (not wings and tail) produces the winter plumage.

back now pale grey, all brown feathers replaced

JANUARY

DECEMBER

OCTOBER

FEBRUARY

juvenile wing feathers are now a year old, fading paler

head gains partial brown hood

white underside, no trace of juvenile brown on sides of breast

MARCH

MAY

JUNE

JULY

▷ **FIRST SUMMER**
April–August. Another partial moult (head and body only again) in spring produces this summer plumage.

▽ **BREEDING**
Some Black-headed Gulls may pair up in late winter or early spring in their second year, but most are not ready to breed until their third year.

dark hood fades to paler brown in late summer; deep red bill

MAY

APRIL

MARCH

FEBRUARY

◁ **ADULT SUMMER**
April–August. A partial spring moult creates the dark brown hood of the adult's spring and summer plumage; the wing and tail feathers are retained from the previous winter.

black and white wingtips

AUGUST

SEPTEMBER

OCTOBER

NOVEMBER

immaculate grey upperparts

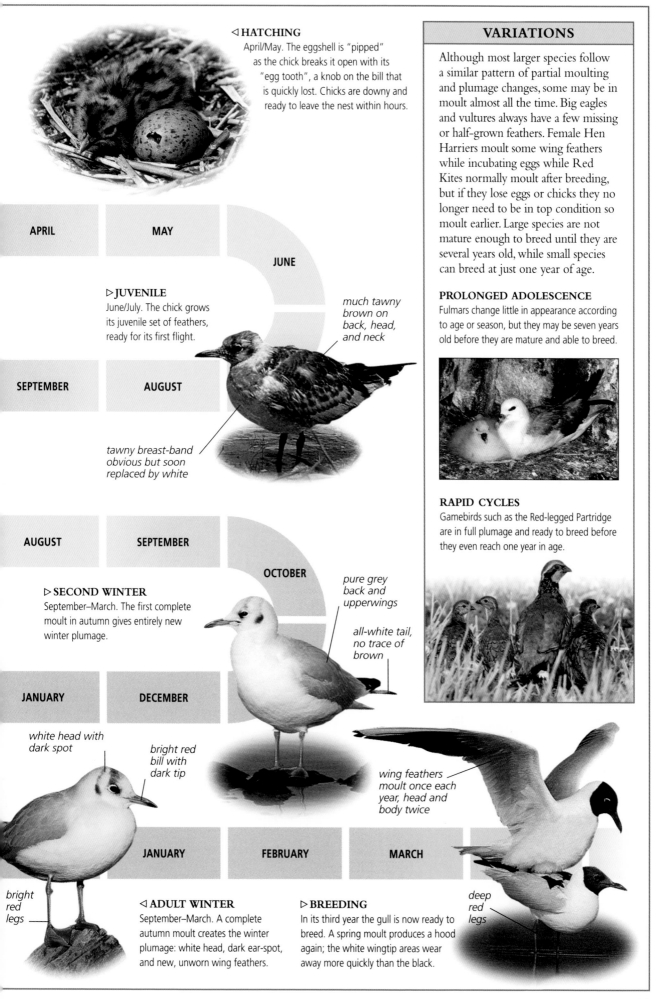

◁ **HATCHING**
April/May. The eggshell is "pipped" as the chick breaks it open with its "egg tooth", a knob on the bill that is quickly lost. Chicks are downy and ready to leave the nest within hours.

APRIL

MAY

JUNE

▷ **JUVENILE**
June/July. The chick grows its juvenile set of feathers, ready for its first flight.

much tawny brown on back, head, and neck

SEPTEMBER

AUGUST

tawny breast-band obvious but soon replaced by white

AUGUST

SEPTEMBER

OCTOBER

pure grey back and upperwings

▷ **SECOND WINTER**
September–March. The first complete moult in autumn gives entirely new winter plumage.

all-white tail, no trace of brown

JANUARY

DECEMBER

white head with dark spot

bright red bill with dark tip

wing feathers moult once each year, head and body twice

JANUARY

FEBRUARY

MARCH

bright red legs

◁ **ADULT WINTER**
September–March. A complete autumn moult creates the winter plumage: white head, dark ear-spot, and new, unworn wing feathers.

▷ **BREEDING**
In its third year the gull is now ready to breed. A spring moult produces a hood again; the white wingtip areas wear away more quickly than the black.

deep red legs

VARIATIONS

Although most larger species follow a similar pattern of partial moulting and plumage changes, some may be in moult almost all the time. Big eagles and vultures always have a few missing or half-grown feathers. Female Hen Harriers moult some wing feathers while incubating eggs while Red Kites normally moult after breeding, but if they lose eggs or chicks they no longer need to be in top condition so moult earlier. Large species are not mature enough to breed until they are several years old, while small species can breed at just one year of age.

PROLONGED ADOLESCENCE
Fulmars change little in appearance according to age or season, but they may be seven years old before they are mature and able to breed.

RAPID CYCLES
Gamebirds such as the Red-legged Partridge are in full plumage and ready to breed before they even reach one year in age.

COURTSHIP AND MATING

Birds spend most of their time keeping their distance from each other. To breed, they must break down barriers so that they can come into contact, if only briefly. Those that rear young together as pairs need a stronger, longer-lasting pair bond, so that they can rely on one another to risk their lives for the sake of their young. Courtship must help foster this trust.

COURTSHIP

Courtship has two functions. It bonds pairs together in a lasting partnership but, initially, it also helps the female to choose which male to mate with. A female is impressed by the size, colour, ability of a male to perform complex courtship rituals, and sometimes even his competence at fighting off other males. These attributes indicate that a male is fit, strong, and efficient. A female will invest a huge amount of time and energy into the rearing of her chicks and therefore must make the right decision when choosing which male to breed with.

MUTUAL DISPLAY
Gannet's ritualized postures reinforce their commitment to their nest and to each other. They "fence" with raised bills in greeting and bow with open wings to show "ownership" of the nest. Fencing develops into nape nibbling, mutual preening, and mating.

CHASE AND DISPLAY
A male Redshank is determined to mate with the hen of his choice and must impress her with his persistence and colourful displays. She will eventually give in to him if she is suitably interested. Courtship displays continue for some weeks as the pair learn to trust each other and accept close contact in order to mate and share parental duties.

FIT TO BREED
Wildfowl have ritualized calls and displays specific to their species. This male Ruddy Duck is literally blowing bubbles to impress: he rattles his bill against his breast feathers, forcing air from between them into the water.

THE LEK
A lek is a communal display ground where males of some species, such as these Black Grouse, have mock battles. The outcome is serious, though: females choose the strongest, most dominant males to mate with.

TOP MALE
A male Pheasant calls and thrashes his wings, raising his tail to make himself look as big as he can. He does this in order to dominate other males and attract a hen. Once he has her attention, he will tilt towards her, drooping his nearside wing and spreading his tail, to show himself off to best advantage.

BREEDING

When it comes to reproducing, there isn't just one favoured strategy. Even within some species there is variation. The Dunnock may form a simple pair that stays together all summer, but some males have more than one mate and, indeed, so do some females. Even within apparently monogamous species, fidelity is not always the norm, and should one of the pair die, the survivor usually has little difficulty finding a new mate. Unless the population is in decline, there is usually a healthy surplus.

MATING

The act of mating is brief, but can be frequent. Ospreys mate scores of times during the egg-laying period, but a single mating is enough to fertilize a whole clutch of eggs. Most birds mate on the ground or a perch. However, Swifts may mate in the air whereas ducks, such as these Goldeneyes, mate on water.

MONOGAMOUS BONDS

Most birds are monogamous, although many are quick to seize the chance to mate with a passing stranger. It seems that an extra mate is viewed as insurance against possible failure, as it doubles the chance of finding a fit and successful partner. Some species, such as the Mute Swan, however, pair for life and maintain a year-round bond that is rarely broken.

MUTUAL PREENING

Strengthening the bond between a male and female bird takes many forms. These Guillemots are preening each other; such intimate contact means that all the usual barriers that keep individuals apart have been broken down while they are rearing their offspring.

PROMISCUITY

The male Capercaillie mates with many hens. This gives him as many chances as possible to sire healthy offspring. Afterwards, he has nothing more to do with the hens.

REVERSAL OF ROLES

In a few species, such as the Dotterel, the female is larger and brighter than the male. She lays a clutch of eggs for him to incubate, then goes off to find another male.

NESTS AND EGGS

A bird's life, behaviour, and appearance revolves around finding a mate and producing eggs in order to ensure the survival of its genes. The nest is a safe place to lay those eggs, incubate them, and raise the resulting brood, so individuals will spend time locating and building the perfect nest for their situation.

BUILDING A NEST

The birds within a species will create nests that are remarkably constant in terms of size, shape, structure, and the materials from which they are made; building such nests seems to be instinctive. However, different birds use an extraordinary variety of techniques to create a whole range of structures. Some of these are little more than scrapes in the ground with a few pebbles or shells as lining. Others are hugely complex, and some are masterpieces of construction and effective camouflage.

COLLECTING MATERIAL
Puffins line their burrows with grass and scraps of vegetation from nearby slopes.

CUP NEST

Most small birds make an open, cup-shaped nest that has a rough base, a neat superstructure, and a fine, soft, warm lining for the eggs and chicks. This kind of nest can take a week or more to build.

DUPING

Some species habitually lay their eggs in other birds' nests and leave them to rear their young. Not all of these birds remain parasites at all times. Many ducks, and even Swallows and Starlings, lay eggs in other nests while still incubating a clutch in their own.

CUCKOO
The Cuckoo never makes its own nest. Once hatched in a foster-parent's nest, its chick throws all other eggs out to gain their sole attention.

EGGS AND HATCHING

TYPES OF EGGS

While most eggs are oval and have a camouflage pattern, there are variations (some examples pictured). Eggs laid out of sight in dark holes, for example, are white. Gamebirds and owls lay spherical eggs, while wading birds lay pear-shaped eggs. Aerial species such as Swifts have narrow bodies so they lay longitudinal eggs. The pear shape of the Guillemot's egg prevents it from rolling off the narrow cliff ledge it is laid on.

ELLIPTICAL **LONGITUDINAL**

PEAR SHAPED

OVAL **SPHERICAL** **CONICAL**

NEAT ARRANGEMENT
Waders lay four eggs that fit neatly under the sitting bird's body. The pointed ends also accommodate the long, folded legs of chicks that can run within hours of hatching.

THE HATCHING PROCESS

Chicks call to each other and to their parents from within the egg, helping to co-ordinate their hatching. They use a tiny "egg tooth" on the bill tip to break the shell and then struggle until they push the two ends apart.

CRACKING **FORCING** **BREAKING OUT**

NEST SITES FOR ALL PURPOSES

Most nests are vulnerable to predators, which may eat the eggs, chicks, and sometimes even the adult that is within the nest. Even wooden nestboxes may be raided by woodpeckers. So birds think about the safest place to locate their nests. Small birds tend to hide their nests away in thick bushes, or suspend them beneath the long branches of conifers. Many species nest inside holes that they either stumble across or excavate themselves in trees or earth banks. Larger species may rely on inaccessibility and make large nests of sticks in plain sight at the tops of trees.

TUNNELLING INTO SAND

Sand Martins dig a metre into a solid earth or soft sandstone cliff with their feet. The inner end of the tunnel then broadens out into a nest chamber that will house four or five chicks.

NO NEST

The Little Ringed Plover makes a shallow scrape in sand for its eggs, giving it little or no lining. When disturbed, the bird runs off and relies on the eggs' camouflage pattern to save them. While hawks and eagles make large nests, falcons never do: they lay their eggs straight onto a bare ledge.

PLASTERWORK

The Nuthatch uses a woodpecker's hole or a natural hole in a tree. It plasters the entrance with mud to get a perfect fit – just big enough for it to squeeze inside – which should protect the nest from predators.

TREE HOLE

Woodpeckers, such as this Lesser Spotted Woodpecker, excavate holes in living trees, using their chisel-like bills. The nest chamber is left unlined apart from a few chippings.

FLOATING NEST

Black-necked Grebes build floating heaps of weed that are anchored to the bottom. If they have to leave the site, they cover their eggs with a few scraps of weed in order to hide them from predators.

NESTING ON BUILDINGS

White Storks have long nested on buildings, especially on church towers, although some still use trees. In parts of Europe they use telegraph poles. In Spain, poles with cartwheels are provided specially for them.

COMPLEX STRUCTURE

The Long-tailed Tit's nest is a masterpiece of spiders' webs, moss, lichens, and feathers. It is hard to see, and stretches as the chicks grow bigger.

PLUMAGE

Feathers are unique to birds. They keep them warm, are lightweight, and add aerodynamics that allow flight. They also provide colours and patterns that are used for camouflage, display, and communication. Feathers are renewed at least every year by a process of moult, but older ones can look slightly worn and faded. All birds keep their plumage in as good a condition as possible by frequent preening and bathing in water or sometimes in dust.

MARKINGS

Feathers create complex patterns but these usually have regular structures. On the head, the crown may have a central stripe and darker sides; above the eye may be a superciliary stripe, while through the eye there could be an eye-stripe. Wings may have wingbars across the tips of the coverts or along the base of the flight feathers. There may be streaks, spots, or bars on the body. Each of these marks helps us to distinguish individual species.

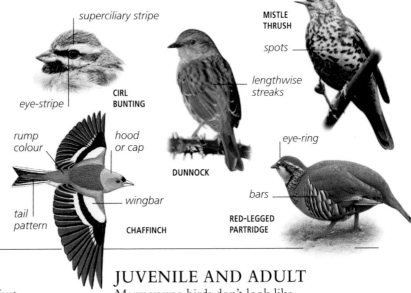

superciliary stripe

eye-stripe

CIRL BUNTING

MISTLE THRUSH

spots

lengthwise streaks

rump colour

hood or cap

DUNNOCK

eye-ring

wingbar

tail pattern

CHAFFINCH

bars

RED-LEGGED PARTRIDGE

MALE AND FEMALE

Plumage differences between sexes may just be focused on the colour or pattern. However, they are often structural too as a lot of males are bigger than the females.

fanned tail to impress females

CAPERCAILLIE

Female

camouflage pattern protects from predators

Male

JUVENILE AND ADULT

Many young birds don't look like their parents. This is because young have no need to impress possible mates. It is more important for them to be camouflaged from predators and to avoid being mistaken for an intruding adult.

Juvenile

HERRING GULL

Adult

dark plumage prevents mistaken attack by territorial parent

white body gives long-distance visual contact when feeding

SUMMER AND WINTER

Summer plumage is intended to look good, to show off to other males and females. In winter this is less important – camouflage is a better option to keep safe from predators.

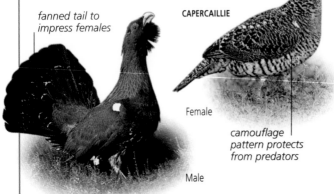

camouflaged, not needing to display

Summer

SNOW BUNTING

Winter

male at his most striking in summer

SUBSPECIES

Subspecies or races occupy isolated areas and may look subtly different. Birds tend to be larger in cold areas to reduce heat loss. The Wheatear found in Greenland, for example, is bigger than the European race.

browner above, brighter below

clean grey and pale buff

Greenland race

WHEATEAR

European race

ABERRATIONS AND VARIATIONS

Not all birds are perfect examples of their species. Some are "aberrant", because of some genetic deficiency. "Albinos" are all-white, "albinistic" birds are partly white, and "leucistic" birds look pale and washed out through lack of pigment. "Melanistic" individuals have too much pigment, and look exceptionally dark. Other variations are a normal part of everyday life. For example, feathers naturally bleach and fade in the sun and wear away at the tips during the course of months of wear.

WHITE BLACKBIRD
The normally black Blackbird quite often throws up partly white variants. This is a minor genetic flaw; such birds are "albinistic" or "partial albinos".

WEAR AND TEAR
This gull has gaps in its wings and tail. Some feathers have been shed and not yet replaced while others are simply worn and faded, which alters the wing pattern.

MOULTING

Moult is a well-ordered process. Each worn feather is pushed out when a new one grows through the skin at its base. The new feather begins as a tiny bump – a "goose bump" – on the skin and grows as a shiny sheath that bursts open at the tip to reveal the soft webs. On most birds moult is not easy to see, but on some larger ones it is possible to spot gaps where feathers are missing. Old feathers usually become paler and pure colours, such as grey and green, tend to turn browner as the feathers age. These contrasts can sometimes be seen on a bird at close range, or in a photograph, but most studies of moult rely on trained bird ringers, who catch birds and examine their stage of moult before releasing them.

BAR-TAILED GODWIT IN MOULT
The stretched wing reveals five old outermost primaries (the longest wingtip feathers), a gap where several have been shed, and a few new inner ones. Some missing wing coverts also reveal spaces in the neat rows of white feathers. This is the complete autumn moult, so this bird is changing from summer to winter plumage, probably in August or September.

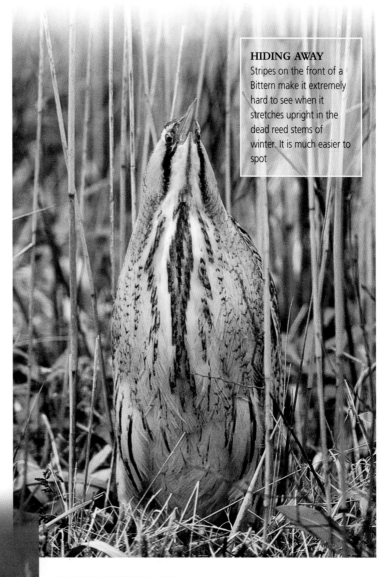

HIDING AWAY
Stripes on the front of a Bittern make it extremely hard to see when it stretches upright in the dead reed stems of winter. It is much easier to spot

CAMOUFLAGE

A major function of plumage pattern is to break up the shape of a bird so it is hard to see. Both predators and prey use camouflage: one to get close to its meal, the other to avoid detection. For example, Oystercatcher flocks confuse predators with a mass of dazzling white patches.

FLIGHT

All the birds that are found within Europe can fly. It is this ability that allows them to travel the globe, moving far and wide to exploit seasonal abundances of food while escaping any shortages. It is fascinating that these small creatures are able to fly across oceans, mountains, and deserts, although such journeys often tax them to the limit. Their most significant features, which provide them with the means to fly and control the direction of that flight, are their wings and tail.

HOVERING LESSER KESTREL
Birds of prey can hover while they search for food. To do this, they position their head into the wind, flicker their wings, and fan their tail.

WING AND TAIL SHAPE

The shape of wings varies from species to species (as shown below), and is largely dependent on the type of flight used. Generally, long, narrow wings (such as a Swallow's) are most efficient for sustained, fluent, manoeuvrable flight. Long, broad wings enable many birds to ride the winds using little energy. Short, round wings allow for shorter bursts of rapid, whirring beats and provide fast acceleration – useful for ground-dwelling birds escaping predators. Tails are used for balance, steering, and braking; a long, stiff tail ensures good balance while a forked tail or long tail that can open and close like a fan acts as a rudder and a brake.

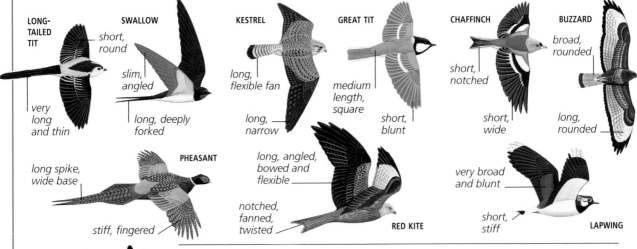

LONG-TAILED TIT — *short, round* — SWALLOW — KESTREL — GREAT TIT — CHAFFINCH — BUZZARD

slim, angled
very long and thin
long, deeply forked
long, flexible fan
long, narrow
medium length, square
short, blunt
short, notched
short, wide
broad, rounded
long, rounded

long spike, wide base
PHEASANT
long, angled, bowed and flexible
very broad and blunt

stiff, fingered
notched, fanned, twisted
RED KITE
short, stiff
LAPWING

EXPERT EAGLE
A White-tailed Eagle raises its wings, separates the wingtip feathers to allow air to slip through, fans its tail as a brake, then swings forward to strike with its feet. It uses powerful wing flaps to climb away from the water with its load.

BALANCE AND CONTROL

Large birds such as eagles and buzzards have a delicacy in the air that belies their size and shape. Their fingered primary feathers are "notched" on each side, creating slots at the wingtip to increase stability within flight and reduce turbulence. Their remarkable balance and precise control in flight allow them to home in on and catch their prey.

TAKING OFF

Getting airborne uses a lot of energy. Many birds take off into the wind from dry land, flapping their wings hard in a figure of eight pattern to create lift and forward propulsion; others jump from a clifftop or tree, moving forwards into the air. Most water birds need to run along the surface of the water in order to build up the necessary momentum.

TAKING OFF FROM LAND
This Grey Heron stretches forwards, pushes down as hard as it can with its wings, and leaps up with a powerful spring of its legs to rise into the air.

LANDING

Birds fly surprisingly fast and so have to reduce their speed quickly before landing. Most birds swing their bodies backwards and fan their tails to assist braking, flapping their wings against the direction of flight. Just before impact they thrust their feet forward to act as shock absorbers.

HEAVYWEIGHT SWAN
The Mute Swan is close to the upper weight limit for flight. It needs to run along the water to get aloft: its legs are too short to give much of a leap from dry land.

TAIL BRAKE
This Woodpigeon (below) has its head up, feet ready to push down, and its wings well back. Its broad tail, when fully spread, acts as an air brake and enables a safe landing.

CO-ORDINATION AND SPEED

Travelling in flocks requires great co-ordination. Each bird takes its cue from the bird ahead or to one side of it, so the decision of the leading bird to turn, rise, or fall carries fluidly through the flock. Many birds can fly at speed, but sustaining this is costly in energy.

SHORT BURSTS OF SPEED
Grey Partridges have deep breast muscles and short wings, which allow bursts of low, fast flight.

SETTLING ON WATER
Water cushions this Mallard's landing, while its webbed feet act as skis. Its wings beat forward and back to reduce the overall speed.

CO-ORDINATION
A mixed flock of Oystercatchers and Knots makes a remarkable sight in the air as it turns and twists like smoke, without a single collision. Such birds have super-quick reactions and tight control.

FEEDING

Birds eat a wide range of items from a variety of sources; some, for example, perch to eat berries while others dive into water to fish. The overall shape of a bird is a strong indication of what it eats and how it obtains its food. This is most obviously revealed in the shape of its bill, but there are also clues in its head and neck shape, and the length and shape of its legs and feet.

BLACKBIRD — forages for worms and berries

BLUE TIT — pecks at tiny insects and seeds

REED WARBLER — picks up insects

CHAFFINCH — cracks seeds and picks up caterpillars

BILL SHAPE

There are many subtle variations in bill shape, but there are a few basic forms that perform specific functions. For example, long, thin bills probe into soft mud and sand to grab worms, and thick beaks crack seeds or pluck grass. Hooked bills, on the other hand, can tear flesh, while saw-toothed bills are able to grasp and hold on to slippery fish.

CURLEW — probes for worms in deep mud

AVOCET — sweeps sideways for tiny shrimps in water

GREY HERON — grasps fish

GREYLAG GOOSE — tears grass and roots

MALLARD — dabbles for seeds from water

GOLDEN EAGLE — tears meat

DABBLING

"Dabbling" involves opening the beak while skimming it across the surface of the water. Dabblers filter water through a fine mesh at the sides of their bill in order to trap tiny seeds and organisms that they then swallow.

WATER FEEDERS

Birds use various methods to obtain food from water. Some wade or swim in order to pick insects from the surface and shore line. Others dive headlong into the water to catch fish. Razorbills actually dive as deep down as 100m (330ft) underwater, using their wings to propel them downwards. Grebes, divers, cormorants, and diving ducks are able to dive underwater from their sitting position on the surface, while other birds, such as swans, reach the bottom by "upending" and using their long necks.

UPENDING

This Shelduck is unable to reach the bottom by just dipping its head under the water's surface, so it gets a little deeper by swinging its whole body over and stretching its neck.

FISHING

A Kingfisher catches fish by grabbing them, not stabbing, despite its sharp bill. It usually drops from a perch, then flies back up with a fish in its beak. It will then beat the fish against a branch before swallowing it.

PROBING

The long bill of a Godwit is the ideal tool for pushing deep into soft mud in order to probe for worms and molluscs. However, if the ground is too hard it cannot feed.

LAND FEEDERS

Birds of all shapes and sizes are land feeders. Many, such as pigeons and finches, feed on the ground as well as in trees, depending on the time of year. Geese, some waders, and pipits are, on the other hand, exclusively ground birds; some birds, such as bustards and cranes, are so big that they have no option but to stay on the ground. Others, such as woodpeckers, prefer trees, and chip away at bark to locate insects. The type of food that they eat affects the way that bird communities feed. Some take in food that is spread over a wide area but is not very abundant, so they disperse themselves in order to avoid competing with each other. Others eat food, such as seeds, that is only located in a few places. It is often in plentiful supply, however, which allows them to feed in sociable flocks.

BERRY EATERS

Redwings and other thrushes gorge themselves in the autumn and early winter if the berry crop is good. If the crop fails then they must turn to worms and other food, or fly great distances in search of berries and fruit elsewhere.

TEARING FLESH

Birds of prey catch food with their feet, which have incredibly sharp talons. However, they often kill the prey and rip it apart using their hooked bills.

TEARING GRASS
Geese use their broad bills to tear at grass, shoots, and roots. This type of food is easy to find, so they are able to feed together without needing to defend their territories to gain sole use of the food supply.

PROBING IN THE GROUND
The Hoopoe uses its slim, faintly curved bill to probe into loose soil and under clumps of earth or roots to reach worms, grubs, and a variety of insects.

AERIAL FEEDERS

Catching insects in flight is a skilful operation, and is undertaken in different ways. Nightjars have tiny bills but wide mouths that are fringed with bristles – these allow them to catch flying moths after dark. Swifts catch tiny insects high in the sky by day while swallows chase bigger flies low down over meadows. Hobbies also catch bigger insects, as well as small birds, but use their feet to do so. All of these examples eat their prey in mid-air. Flycatchers and many warblers, however, return to a perch once they have snapped up their prey.

FLY-CATCHING EXPERT
The Spotted Flycatcher sits alert and upright on a perch until it spots a small moth or a fly. It darts out, twisting and turning with great agility, to catch the prey in its bill with a loud "snap", then returns to the same perch to eat its meal at leisure.

KLEPTOPARASITISM

Many birds are quick to take advantage of smaller, weaker species by stealing their food. This is called kleptoparasitism. For example, Great Black-backed Gulls harry Puffins returning to their burrows with fish while Black-headed Gulls chase lapwings in fields, forcing them to drop juicy worms. Sometimes even one bird of prey will rob another.

POWERFUL SKUAS
Great Skuas not only kill birds but also force down and steal food from other seabirds such as Kittiwakes, Fulmars, and even Gannets.

SONG AND CALLS

B irds' voices are remarkably far-carrying and can
convey a variety of messages to other birds. A bird
will use many vocal sounds but each type is normally
constant within a species. This helps us to use song and
calls to identify individual birds. Usually it is the males
that sing to attract females for mating and to repel
other males from their nesting area.

UNIQUE INSTRUMENTS

Birds have no voice box or larynx, but
a muscular organ called the syrinx at
the base of the windpipe. A series of
membranes are stretched and relaxed by
bunches of muscles, and vibrate as air
passes across them. Some birds have a
simple syrinx so produce little variety
of song. But complex ones produce
great variations in pitch and quality.

trachea

muscle

cartilage rings

membrane

SYRINX
A bird can use the
muscles within the syrinx,
which are attached to
rings of cartilage,
to change the sound
that is produced.

KEEPING IN TOUCH
Many calls are contact notes,
which are used by birds as
they go about their everyday
lives. Such calls help to keep
flocks and family groups
together as they feed or
move about, even when
they are within thick cover.

VARYING FUNCTIONS

It can be difficult to distinguish between a
song and a call but basically they have different
functions. A song is primarily used to attract a
mate or to defend a territory. It can be varied
and intricate, made up of a complex set of
notes. Calls are usually simpler and are used to
pass on information – such as an alarm call
warning of a predator. Such calls are high and
thin, to penetrate through dense woods. Birds
also call in flight, purely to keep in touch.

AGGRESSIVE DEFENCE
Loud, harsh cries are given by terns, gulls, and
skuas, such as this Long-tailed Skua, when they
chase intruders that venture too close to their
nests. Their alarm notes have an obvious urgency,
sounding hysterical if their chicks are threatened.

CONSTANT REPETITION
The Song Thrush is easy to identify when in song.
It sings a few notes – mellow or loud and
challenging – in a short phrase. Each quick burst
of notes is repeated two or three times before
another theme is introduced.

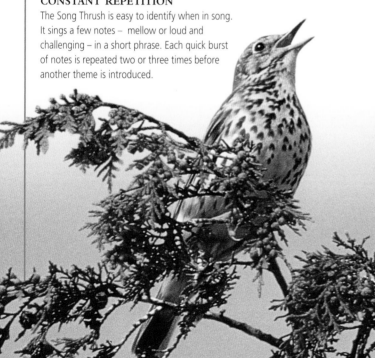

UNMUSICAL PERFORMANCE
The Fulmar sits on its nesting ledge and greets its
mate as it flies by, or settles alongside it, with a burst of
raucous, throaty cackling. To us the calls are coarse and
unmusical, but they probably help Fulmars to identify
each other and are an important part of courtship.

SCREAMING DISPLAY
Swifts form high-speed "screaming parties" that dash around in the sky calling loudly. This practice seems to have a social significance within the breeding colony. They call as they approach the nest, too, alerting their partner to their imminent arrival.

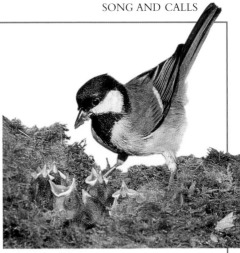

HUNGER CALL
Baby birds stimulate their parents to feed them by calling loudly, just like a human baby cries for attention. They risk attracting a predator, so the parent is forced to provide food to keep them quiet.

WHERE ARE YOU?
Young birds in large colonies may wander away from the nest and can easily be lost. Only their own parents feed them. Loud, whining calls help these young gulls to keep in touch with their parents.

MECHANICAL SOUNDS
Not all sounds that birds create are vocal. Some species produce distinctive mechanical sounds during their display that have the same function as song, communicating with other birds within their species over long distances. The Snipe combines its bleating sound with a visual display, using a steeply undulating, switchback flight. Some pigeons clap their wings together in display but also use this same movement to raise an alarm. Certain owls and nightjars do a similar thing, clapping their wings beneath their bodies in display flights. The woodpecker uses a purely mechanical sound (see below).

DAWN CHORUS

No-one is really sure why so many birds sing most persistently at dawn. It is a wonderful experience, especially in a large wood just as the sky brightens on a spring morning. Suddenly all the territorial birds for miles around sing loudly together; but the performance is short-lived and the song becomes erratic.

EARLY PERFORMER
In most areas the Robin is one of the dominant songsters in the dawn chorus. It also sings under street lights at night, apparently fooled by the artificial lighting.

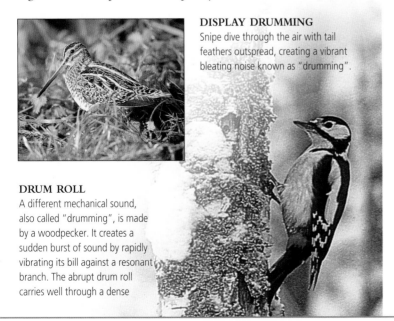

DISPLAY DRUMMING
Snipe dive through the air with tail feathers outspread, creating a vibrant bleating noise known as "drumming".

DRUM ROLL
A different mechanical sound, also called "drumming", is made by a woodpecker. It creates a sudden burst of sound by rapidly vibrating its bill against a resonant branch. The abrupt drum roll carries well through a dense

MIGRATION

Northern Europe is full of insect food in summer, when long days allow birds time to feed both themselves and their young. Such resources are too good to miss, but few birds can survive in the far north in winter when the days become short and cold. Only by huge movements of millions of birds can they exploit feeding opportunities to the full. The regular rhythms of migration are an essential part of many species' existence.

INSTINCTIVE MOVE

Birds migrate by instinct. In many species adults and young birds migrate separately, but the youngsters are somehow programmed to move at the right time and to follow the right routes. Some gather into large flocks and migrate together. Others simply slip away one night alone, embarking on a journey that remains one of nature's most magical and dramatic undertakings. Before proceeding with such a journey a bird needs to ensure that it is in tiptop condition – this often requires some careful preparation.

A SIGN OF THE SEASONS
Migrating geese make a marvellous spectacle and sound. In parts of northern Europe they are a visible sign of the changing seasons as they migrate south in autumn and north in spring.

Canadian Arctic islands

PUTTING ON WEIGHT
Small warblers such as the Sedge Warbler double their weight before they migrate. Sedge Warblers eat aphids in reedbeds before flying across the Sahara in one flight that may last four days. Others feast on rich, sugary berries before they migrate. Such birds quickly put on layers of fat: essential fuel for their journeys.

North America

WHEN TO DEPART
Changing day length in spring and autumn is more of a clue that the time is right to migrate than changes in temperature. A bird's internal clock takes note of the seasonal changes and stimulates a restlessness at migration time. It also starts off the hormonal changes that make physical adjustments, such as the accumulation of extra fat for long-distance journeys.

MAKING THEIR WAY

Birds navigate in a number of ways. They certainly use the sun and the stars and may also see polarized light, which allows them to judge where the sun is even on cloudy days. They probably have a magnetic sense too, and may even be able to detect the position of the poles as they refer to the sky, which would indicate their latitude. What we still don't understand is how they know which way they should fly.

OVERLAND FLIGHTS
Broad-winged birds such as White Storks use up too much energy in flapping flight so must glide over long distances. To do this, they must be able to gain height, which they do by riding thermals or "bubbles" of warm, rising air. These only form over land, so the birds must cross the sea at the narrowest points, such as Gibraltar and

NIGHT MIGRANTS
Many songbirds, such as Goldcrests, migrate at night, relying on the stars to find their way. A sudden onset of cloud and fog may "ground" thousands of them along a coast, making exciting birdwatching the next morning.

READY TO GO
Swallows and House Martins migrate by day, feeding on insects as they go. They gather in large flocks in autumn, before making a move together towards Africa.

GLOBETROTTERS

Waders and wildfowl are amazing travellers but so are some small, familiar birds. For example, Swallows from the United Kingdom travel to the far south of Africa in winter. Barnacle Geese fly north in spring to breed around the Arctic. Such birds that breed in the far north remain in the south till late in May, when the Arctic snows begin to melt. The map below shows three examples of long-distance migration.

DASH FOR THE NORTH
The Arctic Tern is one of the greatest globetrotters. It breeds in 24 hours of daylight in the Arctic, then spends the northern winter in 24-hour daylight, flying over southern oceans before making the journey north again.

SWEEPING SOUTH
West Europe is on the great East Atlantic flyway, which is a migration route for birds from vast areas of the Arctic and northern Europe. The path of waders such as Knots makes a huge sweep southwards, emptying regions on both sides of

KEY
▬	Arctic Terns
▬	Knots
▬	Fieldfares

Map labels: ARCTIC OCEAN · Franz Joseph Island · Greenland · Svalbard · Novaya Zemlya · Jan Mayan · KARA SEA · BARENTS SEA · Iceland · NORTH ATLANTIC · Europe · BLACK SEA · CASPIAN SEA · Azores · Madeira · MEDITERRANEAN SEA · ATLANTIC OCEAN · Canary Islands · Sahara Desert · Cape Verde Islands · Africa · South America · SOUTH ATLANTIC · 2,000km · 2,000 miles

WINTER WANDERERS
Fieldfares move south and west in winter to avoid cold weather. In midwinter they may be forced to travel further still if there is severe cold or snow, but they return as soon as conditions improve. Several species are nomadic, wandering wherever there is food during the winter months.

PARTIAL MIGRANTS

Some species are resident, remaining in the same area all year round. Others are what are called partial migrants. This means that part of the the species population is resident, inhabiting an area that can sustain them year round, while the other part lives in less hospitable areas and so needs to migrate south during the winter months to find food.

summer range

resident all year

winter range | seen on migration

MEADOW PIPIT
Meadow Pipits are summer visitors in some areas, resident in others. Those that breed in the north go south for winter (see map).

27

WESTERN PALEARCTIC

Europe, North Africa, and Asia (north of the Himalayas) form one large entity, called the Palearctic. It is identified by a characteristic set of plants and animals, which adhere to natural rather than political boundaries. This book focuses on the western part of this region – west of the Ural Mountains – giving an overview of the birdlife in an area extending slightly beyond Europe.

BEWICK'S SWAN
A number of species breed widely around the Arctic and move to western Europe in winter to escape severe weather conditions. The Bewick's Swan is typical of these.

SONG THRUSH
Thrushes are found almost worldwide, but form a distinctive part of Western Palearctic birdlife. They include some of the best known songbirds in Europe, such as the Blackbird, and widely travelled migrants, such as this Song Thrush.

ROBIN
Robins are related to thrushes and evolved in Western Palearctic forests. They adapted to forest life, finding worms and insects in earth turned up by moles and foraging wild boars. More recently they have turned to garden habitats.

DIFFERENT ENVIRONMENTS

"Palearctic" refers to the arctic conditions endured by much of the region in the Ice Ages; the legacy of this remains, with several species still moving back to areas from which they were driven by the ice. The Western Palearctic is claearly delimited by the sea in the west and the Sahara in the south, but its eastern boundary is harder to draw. Within this region, the habitats available to birds are amazingly varied. Arctic and Siberian habitats provide tundra and a belt of dense forest. There are also grasslands and steppes and a mixed European zone with temperate forests, wetlands, and mountains. The Mediterranean has distinctive hot, dry summers and cooler winters, while North Africa and the Middle East are hot and arid but also have snow-capped mountain peaks. Birds have adapted in many ways to this great range of challenges and opportunities.

DARTFORD WARBLER
Warblers include many typical Palearctic forms. The Dartford Warbler is one of several centred on Mediterranean heathland.

WHEATEAR
The Wheatear is an exceptionally widespread representative of its family, breeding from Africa to the Arctic. Other wheatears prefer to stay in more southerly regions, in hot, often semi-arid, habitats.

DISTRIBUTION

Various distribution patterns occur in the region. Birds such as the Kestrel breed across Europe, Africa, and Asia. Others, such as the Long-eared Owl, breed in North America, Europe, and Asia. Species found across Europe and Asia are labelled "Palearctic", while the Robin is solely "European", and the Dartford Warbler "Mediterranean".

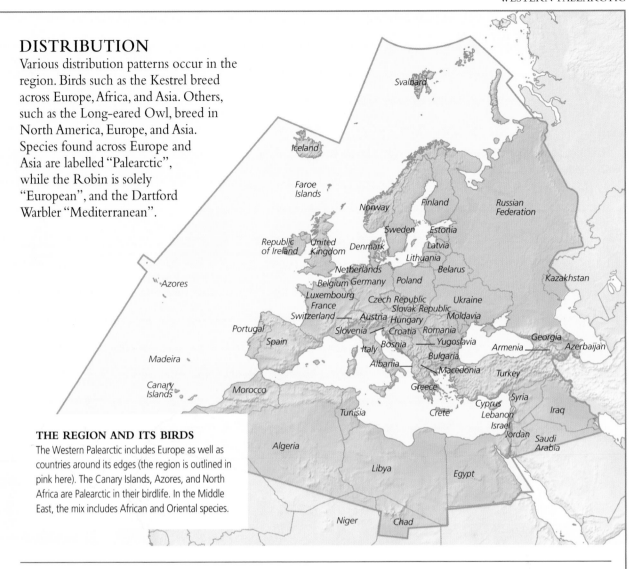

THE REGION AND ITS BIRDS
The Western Palearctic includes Europe as well as countries around its edges (the region is outlined in pink here). The Canary Islands, Azores, and North Africa are Palearctic in their birdlife. In the Middle East, the mix includes African and Oriental species.

PALEARCTIC BIRDS

Most Palearctic birds are unique to the region. Of the hundreds of Palearctic songbirds, for example, only 16 also occur in the Americas. Of the rest of the bird species in the region, just 100 are found in the Americas. There is more of an overlap with the Orient and Africa, but there are still 65 genera that are only ever found in the Palearctic. However, the Western Palearctic has only half as many species as the Eastern Palearctic.

A SELECT FEW
While there are just three species of kingfisher in the Western Palearctic, and only one occurs in Europe, there are 88 worldwide. In some ways the Palearctic is more easily defined by what it lacks than by what it has. What it does have, nonetheless, is a unique combination of birdlife.

HABITAT RANGE
Western Palearctic habitats create a variety of bird communities. Those living in deserts, which have hot days and cold nights, face quite different challenges to those in northern forests and on high ground.

WETLANDS

Wetlands include a range of watery habitats, from the edge of the sea to lakes, reservoirs and lagoons, rivers, marshes, and seasonal floods. Water means just one thing to birds – abundant food, in the form of fish, invertebrates, and plant material. Wetland birds exploit these food stocks in innumerable ways: swimming on or under water, wading into it, flying over it, or living in the dense, upright stems of plants found alongside the edge. Unfortunately, many of these habitats have been reduced by centuries of drainage and some wetland habitats and their birds are under serious threat today.

SALINE SPECIALIST
Greater Flamingos require salty water full of tiny invertebrates and algae. They sweep their odd bills upside down through the water to filter out food.

LOWLAND FLOODS AND WASHES

Wet grasslands with scattered pools are great places for breeding waders in spring. In winter, the areas flood and become magnets for waterfowl. Many of the best areas are managed as nature reserves; by controlling water levels and grazing livestock the best conditions for birds can be produced.

SWANS ON WET PASTURE
Bewick's and Whooper Swans are wild, migrant swans from the north that travel to wet grassland areas in northwest Europe each winter.

WETLAND FEAST
Flood plains and low-lying river valleys flood during heavy rainfall. Worms, insects, seeds, and other vegetable matter float to the surface or are washed up at the water's edge for waterfowl to feed on.

MARSH HARRIER
This bird of prey flies low over the reeds looking for prey, such as young waterbirds.

FRESHWATER MARSHES

Bitterns, Marsh Harriers, Reed Warblers, and Bearded Tits all depend on areas of reed growing up from the shallow water found within freshwater marshes. They build their nests in the safety of dense reeds, using the stems and leaves as nest materials. Bitterns need wet reedbeds, so they can catch fish without going into the open. Bearded Tits feed on both insects and seeds in the reeds.

REED WARBLER
Small patches of reed are perfect for this songbird. Its strong feet provide a good grip on upright perches. It weaves its deep, cup-shaped nest around several stems.

RESERVOIRS AND LAKES

Huge numbers of water birds penetrate far inland to take advantage of lakes, which add variety to birdlife in otherwise dry areas. Reservoirs with natural shores are excellent, especially if the water level falls, as the mud attracts migrant waders. Flooded gravel workings have steep shores and so few waders, but are ideal for ducks. The dragonflies found there are food for Hobbies.

WILDFOWL BONANZA
Lowland reservoirs have great concentrations of wildfowl. In winter, huge roosts of gulls appear as lakes freeze over.

LITTLE EGRET
With a changing climate, this egret has spread north in western Europe. It is attracted to lakes and open shores.

ADAPTATIONS

■ **Fine mesh** located at the sides of their bills allow dabbling ducks to sieve seeds from water. They skim their opened beaks across the surface to take in water before filtering it.

DABBLING TEAL

■ **The distinctively long toes** of Egrets, Moorhens, and Bitterns spread their weight and support them as they walk on floating vegetation. Coots and grebes have long, lobed toes, which aid propulsion when they are in water.
■ **The uniquely flattened and round-tipped bill** of the Spoonbill sweeps sideways, half-open, through the shallow water, until it touches a fish. It then quickly snaps its bill shut in order to feed.

flattened bill tip

SPOONBILL

WHERE TO WATCH

❶ LAKE MYVATN, ICELAND

This northern lake sees an abundance of birds including Common Scoters, Long-tailed Ducks, Wigeon, Barrow's Goldeneyes, Harlequin Ducks, Red-necked Phalaropes, Whooper Swans, and Ptarmigan.

❷ OUSE WASHES, UK

This is made up of pools and low-lying grassy fields that often flood. Breeding birds include Snipe and Black-tailed Godwit; migrant waders and terns are frequent; and in winter there are Wigeon, Pintail, and Bewick's and Whooper Swans.

❸ COTO DOÑANA, SPAIN

This vast coastal wetland sees Spanish Imperial Eagles, Black Kites, White Storks, Little and Cattle Egrets, Purple and Night Herons, Black-Winged Stilts, Avocets, Ruffs, Spoonbills, and Whiskered Terns as well as an abundance of waders, ducks, and geese throughout the winter months.

❹ CAMARGUE, FRANCE

A huge southern delta complex full of rice fields and lagoons – breeding sites for egrets, herons, Greater Flamingos, and Avocets.

GREATER FLAMINGOS

❺ ALBUFERA MARSHES, MAJORCA

This large reedbed with small open lagoons and ditches is an excellent place in summer for Great Reed and Moustached Warblers and Eleonora's Falcons.

❻ NEUSIEDLER SEE, AUSTRIA

A lake and reedy marsh complex, this area has a great variety of egrets, herons, Little Bitterns, Whiskered Terns, Ferruginous Ducks, and River Warblers.

❼ DANUBE DELTA, ROMANIA

This magnificent, huge wetland complex, leading to the Black Sea, is a vital habitat for Dalmatian and White Pelicans and Pygmy Cormorants. There is also an abundance of herons, egrets, spoonbills, Glossy Ibises, Black-Tailed Godwits, Whiskered Terns, Penduline Tits, Red-footed Falcons, and White-tailed Eagles here.

■ *Wetland areas*

LITTLE EGRET

❽ PORTO LAGO, GREECE

This lake and coastal marsh attracts Dalmatian and White Pelicans, Great White and Little Egrets, and a host of other wetland birds.

ESTUARIES AND LOW-LYING COASTS

A river broadening towards the sea deposits mud and
silt over vast areas that are exposed at low tide. The
sides of such an estuary and other stretches of soft coast
consolidate into salt marshes, where muddy creeks
wind through green swards of salt-tolerant vegetation.
Sand dunes, shingle spits, shell banks, and sand or pebble
beaches all provide habitats for birds on low-lying shores.

ESTUARIES

A muddy estuary is an excellent
source of food for numerous birds
as fish, tiny snails, worms, shellfish,
and other invertebrates are very
abundant. The twice-daily flow of
the tides also enriches the inter-
tidal mud and sand with nutrients.
Birds from vast areas of northern
Europe and Asia rely on such estuaries
from autumn right through to late spring
as they rarely freeze over. During those
seasons swimmers, divers, waders, probers,
and aerial feeders all exploit the food that
is to be found in the mud, sand, and
shallow water. In the summertime, gulls,
terns, ducks, larks, and pipits also breed on
the firmer salt marshes that are situated all
the way around the edge of an estuary.

**SLAVONIAN
GREBE**
Grebes breed on
freshwater lakes but
move to the sea in the
autumn. Slavonian
Grebes, such as this one
in its winter plumage,
can often be seen
drifting into an estuary
with the rising tide.

**DUNES AND
LAGOONS**
Sand consolidates into tall,
grassy dunes with damp
hollows ideal for waders,
Skylarks, and Meadow
Pipits. Shallow lagoons
above high tides offer
feeding areas for gulls,
Shelducks, and Ringed
Plovers, while dry sand
spits are nest sites for
terns and waders.

FLOCKING TO THE BEACH
Black-headed Gulls find safe refuge on offshore bars
and beaches, resting between feeding sessions.

SAND AND SHINGLE

Harder beaches, which are made up of
sand and gravel, are not as good as soft
mud for long-billed, probing waders.
However, these beaches are used by
short-billed waders, such as plovers,
that can pick food from the surface
or from between stones. Seaweed and
other debris washed up at high tide
form a "tidewrack" or strandline, along
which other birds, including some land
birds such as Starlings, can feed on tiny
sand hoppers and other
small creatures.

SWEEPING AVOCET
An Avocet sweeps its upcurved bill
sideways through shallow water,
catching tiny crustaceans.

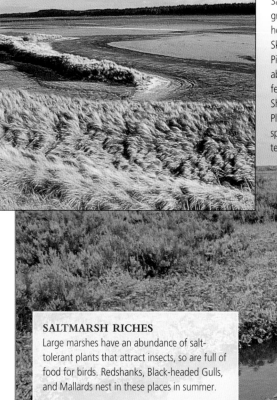

SALTMARSH RICHES
Large marshes have an abundance of salt-
tolerant plants that attract insects, so are full of
food for birds. Redshanks, Black-headed Gulls,
and Mallards nest in these places in summer.

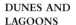

ADAPTATIONS

■ **The curved bill** of the Curlew is strong enough to catch and break up crabs.

■ **With flattened, chisel-shaped bills**, Oystercatchers prise shellfish off rocks and break into them.

■ **The camouflage patterning of the Little Tern's eggs** allows it to lay them straight onto sand or shingle without building a nest. They are perfectly camouflaged against the beach so are usually safe even when unattended.

LITTLE TERN

■ **Broad, flattened bills with rough edges** are swept in semi-circular directions across soft mud and shallow water by Shelducks. This enables them to gather up tiny snails, which they then feed on.

■ **Long legs** allow waders, such as Knots, to stand upright in water, while their long toes stop them sinking into the sticky mud. Their sensitive bill tips allow them to probe for worms. The length of the bill is a good clue to the depth to which a species will probe and the size of food they take.

SHELDUCK

KNOTS

WADERS FLOCK TO SAFE ROOSTS AT HIGH TIDE

❶ MORECAMBE BAY, ENGLAND

This is a vast estuary complex with mostly sandy flats fringed with extensive salt marshes and sand dunes. Firm banks above the high tide mark offer refuges for wildfowl and waders to roost at high tide. The area attracts Oystercatchers, Bar-tailed Godwits, Knots, Dunlins, Curlews, Shelducks, Redshanks, Ringed Plovers, and Turnstones.

❷ THE WASH, ENGLAND

The wash is a huge enclosed estuary that opens out onto the North Sea. Most of it is muddy, but there are sand banks at the mouth and extensive saltmarshes around the edges. It sees big flocks of Knots, Dunlins, Bar-tailed Godwits, and Grey Plovers. In winter it attracts tens of thousands of Pink-footed Geese, Brent Geese, and Wigeon.

PINK-FOOTED GEESE

❸ IJSSELMEER, NETHERLANDS

This enclosed and part-reclaimed estuary sees migrant gulls, terns, and waders in spring and autumn while in winter it has great numbers of Tufted Ducks, Pochards, Scaup, Wigeon, Goosanders, and Smews.

❹ WATTENMEER, GERMANY

This is the eastern end of the Netherlands' Waddenzee – a vast, shallow area of estuarine character where over a million water birds appear in spring and autumn.

AVOCETS

❺ EBRO DELTA, SPAIN

This area is half reclaimed but is still great for birds; in summer it has the world's biggest colony of Audouin's Gulls as well as Gull-billed Terns, Kentish Plovers, and Pratincoles. In autumn and winter Greater Flamingos and many wildfowl and waders can be seen.

■ Low-lying coasts

ROCKY COASTS, ISLANDS, AND THE OPEN SEA

M ost of the European coastline is a "hard" coast of some kind, with rocks or cliffs and stony beaches. The majority of these shores are less attractive to birds than soft estuaries and marshes, but seabirds must still come to land on cliffs and islands in order to breed.

ROCKY AND STONY SHORES

Stony beaches and wave-washed rocks do see some waders from autumn to spring. Typical rocky shore waders are short-billed species such as Turnstones and Purple Sandpipers, which feed on invertebrate food found among weedy, barnacle-encrusted rocks right at the edge of the waves. Knots, Dunlins, Curlews, even migrant Common Sandpipers, however, often feed around flatter rocks by the shoreline. Nearby higher rocks and isolated islets out of reach of predators offer solid sites for nesting gulls and terns.

SHELLFISH EATER
Oystercatchers hammer open mussels on seaweedy rocks.

HIGH TIDE REFUGE
Even though they feed on muddy estuaries, waders may move to nearby higher rocks when the tide covers the mudflats. The Dunlins shown here may be joined by Redshanks, Knots, Bar-tailed Godwits, and Curlews.

ROCKY ISLANDS, OFFSHORE STACKS, AND CLIFFS

Within western Europe, some of the rocky islands, offshore stacks, and mainland coasts that have sheer cliffs see birds in huge numbers. Most seabirds nest in colonies and so choose the best of these sites, at which Gannets, Fulmars, Herring Gulls, Kittiwakes, Guillemots, Razorbills, and Puffins create some of Europe's finest bird spectacles. Different island areas see particular seabirds coming in to nest in burrows created in crevices in rocks or cliffs, old rabbit burrows in soil, or burrows they dig out themselves. Mediterranean and Cory's Shearwaters, for example, prefer the Mediterranean, while Manx Shearwaters nest around Britain and Ireland; Black Guillemots and Arctic Terns prefer to nest on low, rocky islets, while Shags and Cormorants like broad ledges on larger cliffs.

CLIFF NEST
Cliff ledges are out of reach of predators, so attract seabirds. They are difficult places though: seabirds' chicks would fall to their deaths if they didn't have the natural instinct to keep still on a tiny ledge. Shags build big nests of sticks and weed, Kittiwakes create a nest on the tiniest outcrop, while Guillemots do not make nests at all.

NOCTURNAL VISITOR
Storm Petrels spend most of their time at sea but must come to land to nest. As they are easily captured by gulls, they will only land after dark.

OPEN SEA

Many birds live at sea outside the breeding season. Gannets, Fulmars, Puffins, petrels, and shearwaters stay way out in the middle of the Atlantic. Migrants from much farther south pass European coasts on their ocean wanderings, including shearwaters from the southern hemisphere that appear west of Europe in late summer and autumn. All of these birds occasionally come close inshore during gales but prefer life on the open sea, where there is an abundance of food such as fish, jellyfish, and plankton. But this food source is not uniformly distributed: ocean currents and seasonal changes mean the birds have to travel great distances in order to locate food, often far from the cliffs that offer them nest sites.

SEA RESIDENT
The Kittiwake spends months in the middle of the ocean. It is attracted to fishing boats, where it feeds on discarded, undersized fish.

GUILLEMOTS
Guillemots dive from the water's surface for fish such as sandeels; they rarely feed close to land.

ADAPTATIONS

■ **A cushioned skull and air sacs** on the head and neck help the Gannet to survive its spectacular 30m (100ft) plunges into the sea for fish.

■ **Tubular nostrils** on shearwaters and petrels – known as "tubenoses" – help them to excrete excess salt. (necessary because they mainly drink salt water from the sea).

■ **The pyramidal shape of Guillemots' eggs** helps them to incubate one egg under a wing and also stops the eggs from rolling off a narrow ledge.

GANNETS

■ **Narrow wings** form stiff "paddles" that Razorbills and Puffins use to "fly" acrobatically deep underwater when they are in pursuit of fish.

■ **A special bill** with a fleshy "rosette" at the base helps the Puffin to keep the edges of its mandibles parallel as it opens them, so that it can carry a line of fish neatly held tight with its tongue.

PUFFIN

WHERE TO WATCH

❶ ROST, NORWAY

This island group houses many seabird colonies, including hundreds of thousands of Puffins as well as guillemots, Razorbills, Storm Petrels, and Leach's Petrels.

❷ ORKNEY ISLANDS, UK

A spectacular archipelago with Fulmars, Guillemots, Razorbills, Kittiwakes, Arctic Terns, Arctic Skuas, and Great Skuas.

❸ BASS ROCK, UK

This has a stunning Gannet colony that reaches more than 40,000 pairs. Also sees guillemots, Puffins, Kittiwakes, and other gulls and is easily reached by boat.

BASS ROCK

❹ BEMPTON CLIFFS, UK

These cliffs house an unusual mainland Gannet colony (most are found on islands), and one of the easiest large seabird colonies to see in the UK, with safe viewing platforms above sheer cliffs. There are many Kittiwakes and guillemots, Razorbills, Puffins, Herring Gulls, Fulmars, and some Shags and Cormorants. It is a good place to view offshore seabird migration.

❺ BERLENGO, PORTUGAL

This island attracts thousands of Yellow-legged Gulls, Cory's Shearwaters, Shags, and guillemots.

❻ GREEK ISLANDS

Many Greek islands have Yellow-legged Gulls, Cory's Shearwaters, and Mediterranean Shearwaters. Some have breeding Eleonora's Falcons and Audouin's and Mediterranean Gulls, as well as an excellent selection of land birds such as shrikes and warblers, including migrants in autumn.

❼ MAJORCA, SPAIN

The Balearic Islands in general are rocky and have many cliffs where seabirds can nest. They are good places to view Cory's and Mediterranean Shearwaters, often close inshore, as well as Yellow-legged Gulls. In late summer Eleonora's Falcons nest locally, preying on migrant songbirds. Some islets and headlands have the rare and local Audouin's Gull.

▨ *Rocky coasts*

CORY'S SHEARWATERS

THE FAR NORTH

In the winter, the far north is a dark, frozen, and barren place. However, by late spring the snow is melting, the days are starting to get very long, and insects and their larvae abound in myriad pools. These far northern regions, with their summer food bonanza, attract millions of birds. They are all dependent on the Arctic during the summertime but are unable to survive there at other times of the year. Only such hardy species as the Ptarmigan can remain in the far north all year round, the rest will appear farther south as migrants or winter visitors.

PTARMIGAN
In winter the Ptarmigan turns white to match its surroundings. Its feet are densely feathered to help it to avoid heat loss; they also act as "snow shoes".

THE COAST AND OPEN SEA

The sea is rich in invertebrate food and fish so seabirds and ducks abound on many of the northern coasts. This is an exciting area, as birds that are rare in Europe head north and east into Siberia in spring, and others that are essentially Arctic species appear in a handful of sheltered bays on the fringes of their normal range. In Europe, this is the one small patch of land and sea that has the character of the Arctic, so it sees some of its great birds.

FULMAR
Fulmars nest on cliffs, occupying small, earthy ledges. They need access to the open sea, where they often feed around fishing boats.

ARCTIC TUNDRA

Open tundra is bleak and exposed as it is beyond the northern limits of tree growth. It is a very tough environment for birds but its dwarf shrubs provide seeds and shoots as food for Ptarmigan, which are widespread on broad, rocky ridges. These ridges are also nesting places for Snowy Owls. Small cliffs may have nesting birds of prey, which survive on rodents and birds, but they usually have to move south in winter. Skuas that nest around the Arctic, feeding mostly on lemmings, are purely summer visitors. It is the ability to feed in perpetual summer daylight, and the close proximity of many pools, that draws geese and waders to nest on the higher ridges.

ARCTIC TERN
The broad, stony tundra slopes of larger islands and headlands are ideal for nesting Arctic Terns.

WHOOPER SWANS
This is the swan of northern lakes, bogs, and river deltas. The Bewick's Swan, on the other hand, breeds around more open, exposed tundra pools.

NORTHERN FJORDS
Sheltered bays and cold water full of fish offer security and food for seabirds and wildfowl in what is otherwise the bleak and windswept far northern tip of Europe.

POOLS

From autumn until May or early June the pools of the tundra are frozen and covered with snow. Waders, ducks, and geese that breed up here are still in their wintering areas until May; slightly south, larger lakes on the tundra fringe see birds in early spring. Once the short summer is under way, the pools are alive with insects and their larvae. Long-tailed Ducks and Red-necked Phalaropes gorge themselves on the thick rime of insect life found on some northern lakes. Downy chicks of waders and ducks can feed themselves within hours of hatching and find life easy with so much food; but they also face a barrage of hungry predators.

STELLER'S EIDER

In spring and summer. a few hundred spectacular Steller's Eiders form dense flocks offshore in food-rich seas off the extreme north of Norway.

ADAPTATIONS

■ **Thickly feathered legs** like those of the Rough-legged Buzzard provide invaluable added warmth for life in northern areas.

feathered legs

ROUGH-LEGGED BUZZARD

■ **The thick, strong bill** of the Long-tailed Skua is also hard and hooked at the tip. This allows it to catch small rodents and some small birds more easily as it only uses its bill, not its feet, when hunting.

■ **White plumage** helps vulnerable birds such as Willow Grouse stay hidden, but also allows predators such as the Snowy Owl to get close to them unseen.

SNOWY OWL

WHERE TO WATCH

❶ ICELAND

Harlequin Ducks and Barrow's Goldeneyes are not found anywhere else in Europe, while Red-necked and Grey Phalaropes, Brunnich's Guillemots, Glaucous Gulls, Little Auks, Puffins, White-tailed Eagles, and Gyr Falcons are also specialities of Iceland. Thousands of pairs of Pink-Footed Geese and Whooper Swans, Black-tailed Godwits, Long-tailed Ducks, and Common Scoters breed in the area, and Iceland Gulls are regular visitors to the region during the winter months.

WHOOPER SWANS

❷ VARANGER FJORD, NORWAY

The area around Varanger in Norway is exceptionally rich in birds during spring and summer. Offshore migrants include Long-tailed and Pomarine Skuas and White-billed Divers, while Steller's and King Eiders are regular visitors. A large range of exciting breeding birds includes Red-necked Phalaropes and Black-throated Divers.

BLACK-THROATED DIVER

■ Tundra areas

NORTHERN MOUNTAINS AND MOORLANDS

These are tough habitats for wildlife, and many birds are only summer visitors to the uplands, breeding when insects or other small birds are available as prey. In winter, snow and exposure to gales and rain make life impossible for all but a few hardy species. Some birds survive on a very restricted diet, in areas that offer little variety. Nevertheless, these are imposing and often inspiring places that do see exciting birds.

NORTHERN MOUNTAINS

These mountains reproduce the cold, windswept, and barren conditions of far northern lowlands, and so winter sees most birds journeying south or moving to lowland areas. In summer, however, these same habitats offer greater possibilities for migrants, as insect and plant life has a brief period of abundance and small rodents multiply quickly in the grasslands, providing food for predators. The rocky gullies and crags provide nest sites for birds and good feeding opportunities.

DOTTEREL
Dotterels like broad, rolling ridges and stony plateaux at high altitude, where they feed on insect life in summer.

EXPOSED MOUNTAIN REGIONS
On high, exposed ground the tundra-like conditions, which include sparse vegetation, cliffs, and screes, are exploited by only a small selection of hardy sub-Arctic birds.

MOORLAND

Moorland forms on peaty ground where conditions are cold and wet for much of the year. This means dead plant material is slow to rot, so it builds up into thick layers of peat. Where this becomes waterlogged, extensive blanket bog forms. This is a rare habitat worldwide, but is well represented in northwest Europe. Such places are impoverished in wildlife terms, but still attract a small selection of birds. Some of these birds, such as Skylarks, are widespread elsewhere, while others are upland moor and bog specialists. For example, Dunlins prefer wet bogs, while Golden Plovers choose more open spaces of grassy moors or heather for feeding and nesting.

RED GROUSE
Red Grouse can be scarce on heathery moors. Only where the habitat is managed for them do they appear in large numbers. They feed almost exclusively on heather shoots and seeds.

WHINCHAT
The Whinchat likes gentle slopes with bracken and heather, or young conifer plantations.

CONIFER PLANTATIONS
Many moorlands have been planted with alien conifers. These provide temporary homes for Black Grouse, Hen Harriers, and Whinchats until they grow too tall and dense. Chaffinches, Robins, and Coal Tits may then move in.

ADAPTATIONS

■ **Camouflage** helps Dotterels, Golden Plovers, and other breeding birds to blend in to barren surroundings.
■ **Ptarmigan turn white in winter**, helping them to hide in the snow. Their feet are feathered to reduce winter heat loss.

feathered legs

PTARMIGAN

■ **The long, fine-tipped bills** of Dunlin are ideal for picking insects and small worms from moss-covered bogs in summer, and for probing in mud for worms during winter.
■ **Open moors** have few perches so birds such as Golden Plovers and Skylarks sing in flight to claim their territorial rights and attract females.
■ **Muscular gizzards and elongated intestines** allow grouse to swallow grit to help grind up the shoots of tough, heathery plants.

SKYLARK

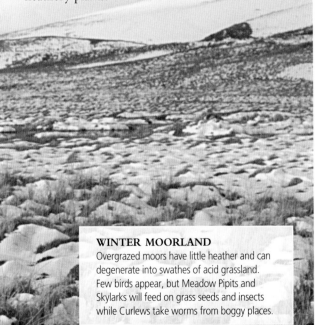

WINTER MOORLAND
Overgrazed moors have little heather and can degenerate into swathes of acid grassland. Few birds appear, but Meadow Pipits and Skylarks will feed on grass seeds and insects while Curlews take worms from boggy places.

THE CAIRNGORMS

❶ VATNA JOKULL, ICELAND

The high central plateau of Iceland is bleak and forbidding. Even in summertime, it has a thick central ice cap that is almost devoid of birdlife. Around it is a spectacular landscape that sees a small range of birds. Bare ground provides habitat for Ptarmigans, Snow Buntings, and rare Gyr Falcons and Snowy Owls. Locally, Pink-footed Geese and Purple Sandpipers breed.

PURPLE SANDPIPER

❷ DOVREFJELL, NORWAY

This national park has a mix of bogs, lakes, woodland, snowfields, and mountain peaks and plateaux. Here there are Rough-legged Buzzards, Cranes, Dotterels, Temminck's Stints, Red-necked Phalaropes, Shore Larks, Bramblings, and Lapland and Snow Buntings in summer.

❸ CAIRNGORMS, SCOTLAND

A unique area in the UK with extensive boulder fields, screes, and cliffs in a very high plateau, where Dotterels, Ptarmigan, a few Snow Buntings, Ravens, and Golden Eagles breed.

❹ NORTH PENNINES, ENGLAND

This is rolling moorland with heather and limestone grassland, dissected by wooded valleys and rocky gulleys with tumbling streams. Many Golden Plovers, Curlews, Wheatears, Snipe, Meadow Pipits, and Skylarks breed, as well as a few Merlins, Short-eared Owls, Dunlins, Dippers, Twites, Whinchats, Stonechats, and Ring Ouzels.

CURLEW

■ Mountains and moorland in northern Europe

SOUTHERN MOUNTAINS AND CRAGS

The highest, harshest, snowiest peaks of southern European mountains are little different from their counterparts in the north, but many others are snow-free and characterized by big, bare crags, dizzying cliffs, and deep gorges with rushing rivers. Forests of beech, oak, and pine climb high on the mountain slopes, creating conditions that attract woodland species more characteristic of northern Europe. The southern influence, however, remains strong, with the presence of birds of prey hunting overhead, and, in the valleys, many other species that are not found farther north.

HABITAT MIXTURE

With their peaks, high pastures, and valleys, mountainous areas bring together a variety of habitats within a small area. From one spot it is possible to see riverside birds, woodland birds, and those characteristic of grassy pastures and hedgerows, as well as species that prefer cliffs and crags. Slightly further up the hillside, alpine species can be heard or seen flying across the valleys or over the highest peaks. Superimposed upon this natural diversity there are regional differences. For example, some species, including various eagles and other birds of prey, are more easterly and so are found in the Balkans but not within Iberia. Birds of prey have also been wiped out of some areas due to centuries of persecution, although they remain numerous in Spain. Some species – such as eagles, vultures, buzzards, and falcons – occupy different "niches", exploiting particular foods and nest sites. This may allow them to live close together without competing against each other. Alternatively, it may mean that species remain apart, each inhabiting an area that meets its particular requirements.

COASTAL CLIFFS
Several mountain birds also breed on crags by the sea that offer safe nesting sites.

BLACK WHEATEAR
Warmer, south-facing stony slopes and crags in Iberia attract this eyecatching wheatear, as well as Black-eared Wheatears and Stonechats.

CLIFFTOP THRUSH
Limestone crags are the favoured haunt of the Blackbird-sized Blue Rock Thrush, which ventures anywhere from sea level to high in the mountains.

STUNNING PEAKS
High mountain peaks with deep gorges and shady valleys have a great range of birds of prey, many of which nest lower down but move up each day to hunt over high ground. Cliff faces have their own unique birds – some move out to feed on high-altitude grassy meadows.

WHERE TO WATCH

❶ MASSIF CENTRAL, FRANCE

This famous mountainous region in France has seen the reintroduction of Griffon and Black Vultures. It also has natural populations of Red Kites, Egyptian Vultures, Short-toed, Booted, and Golden Eagles, Eagle Owls, and Alpine Accentors.

TYPICAL LIMESTONE CRAGS

❷ PYRENEES

Straddling France and Spain, the Pyrenees offer wonderful birds in spectacular settings. There is a great range of eagles, vultures, and Kites, as well as alpine and cliff birds such as Ptarmigan, Wallcreepers, Alpine Choughs, Alpine Swifts, Alpine Accentors, Snowfinches, and other birds that thrive in mountains and forests.

❸ SIERRA DE GUADARAMA, SPAIN

This is a superb area for Black, Griffon, and Egyptian Vultures, as well as eagles and a variety of upland species such as the Rock Thrush, Blue Rock Thrush, Black Redstart, Rock Bunting and Citril Finch. The local Black Stork also breeds in a few locations within the Sierra de Guadarama.

GOLDEN EAGLE

❹ SIERRA NEVADA, SPAIN

Although not so rich in birds of prey as some northern ranges, this big range of hills still sees Griffon and Egyptian Vultures, Golden, Booted, and Bonelli's Eagles, and Peregrines. It is a good place to spot Alpine Accentors, Black and Black-eared Wheatears, Rock Thrushes, and Alpine Swifts.

❺ PUIG MAYOR, MAJORCA

The mountains and valleys of Majorca have some remote and spectacular sites that attract Black Vultures, which are rare and local. In summer, many cliffs have Eleonora's Falcons, Red Kites, Ospreys, Blue Rock Thrushes, Black-eared Wheatears, Rock Buntings, Alpine and Pallid Swifts, and Crag Martins. Alpine Accentors only visit in the wintertime.

 Mountainous areas in southern Europe

❻ EVROS MOUNTAINS, GREECE

Greece no longer has the rich populations of birds of prey that used to be there, but in the extreme northeast the mountains attract specially conserved Black Vultures as well as Imperial, Lesser Spotted, and White-tailed Eagles, Lanners, Long-legged Buzzards, and Levant Sparrowhawks.

ADAPTATIONS

■ **Big, soaring birds** are attracted to more southerly areas rather than northwest Europe, which lacks the warm, rising air currents that offer them so much lift. These species have evolved to make the best use of air currents, including cold winds on the high tops. This enables them to travel long distances and search for widely scattered food (such as animal carcasses) over vast areas – with the least expenditure of energy. To aid them in this, they also have exceptional eyesight.

■ **The fine bill** of the Wallcreeper probes for insect food in damp recesses, under dark overhangs on cliff faces, and deep inside shady gorges.

■ **The strong, curved bill** of the Chough can overturn animal droppings and prise cushions of grass and lichens from rocks to expose invertebrates.

■ **The exceptionally tough oesophagus** of the Lammergeier has developed in order to cope with sharp-ended fragments of shattered bone, which it feeds on. The bird drops large bones onto rocks to break them into pieces small enough to swallow.

GRIFFON VULTURE IN SOARING FLIGHT

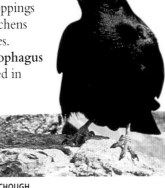

CHOUGH

LOWLAND HEATH AND MEDITERRANEAN SCRUB

In Northwest Europe lowland heath is a rare and restricted habitat. It is often found in a thin strip along a rocky coast but also in special regions with sandy or acid soils, such as the New Forest and Brecklands in England and a few areas of the Netherlands and northern France. In southern Europe, however, much larger areas of rough ground with short, aromatic shrubs and evergreen bushes cover sunny slopes.

MEDITERRANEAN SIZZLER
A typical bird found in Mediterranean scrub is the Serin, whose jingling, sizzling song is a familiar summer sound.

HEATHLAND
Coastal heath bordering an estuary provides a unique habitat.

COASTAL DUNES
A lack of water and erosion by the wind create harsh conditions for most birds. However, Crested Larks feed in the open spaces.

LOWLAND HEATHS

These are habitats for a few specialist species that require the mixture of open space and patchy scrub, which is often maintained by grazing animals and periodic fires. Dartford Warblers are resident in such areas while Nightjars are summer visitors to them. In the summertime a variety of birds take advantage of the insect food and nesting opportunities found in dense heather and gorse. Some thickets have Nightingales that prefer dense vegetation down to ground level, while open spaces see nesting Stone-curlews and Woodlarks, which need bare earth to pick up insects from. Dragonflies breed where there are pools in boggy valleys and attract hunting Hobbies.

MEDITERRANEAN SCRUB

Mediterranean slopes have bare rocks, patches of short grass, cushions of short, spiny herbs, and taller, thick, evergreen bushes. This is the "garrigue" or "maquis" habitat, wonderful for birds such as Rollers, Great Grey Shrikes, and Lesser Kestrels that take large insects and lizards from the ground. Overhead, many kinds of birds of prey may be seen, while on the bush tops are shrikes, which are small bird- and insect eaters. Ground feeders as varied as Red-legged Partridges, Hoopoes, larks, pipits, and buntings are attracted to the scrubland while the bushes have an exciting array of small warblers, mostly restricted to the Mediterranean region in Europe. There are some habitats that are found in just a few scattered locations and are home to specific species. For example, patches of introduced cactus attract Rufous Bush Robins and rocky gullies are perfect nesting sites for Rock Sparrows.

RUFOUS BUSH ROBIN
This large chat is one of an essentially African family that prefers dry, sandy gullies, small cliffs, and patches of prickly pear cactus.

ADAPTATIONS

■ **Enormous pupils** allow the Stone-curlew to feed at dawn and dusk; its large eyes are ideal for maximum light gathering. They shrink to pinpoints by day.

■ **The long, slender tail** of the Sardinian Warbler helps it to balance as it tips up to dive head first into a bush; the tail is also used to warn others of potential danger.

■ **Big eyes and very short, wide bills fringed with bristles** characterize the Red-necked Nightjar and Nightjar. Both these adaptations allow them to feed after dark, catching flying moths in their mouths in mid-air.

SARDINIAN WARBLER

■ **The hooked bills of Shrikes** allows the birds to tear at their prey, but their feet are not especially strong. Instead, they impale large prey such as lizards, small birds, and beetles on thorns, so that they can tear at them easily.

NIGHTJAR

BOOTED EAGLE

A small eagle, this species hunts other birds and small mammals that are plentiful on bushy slopes and heaths.

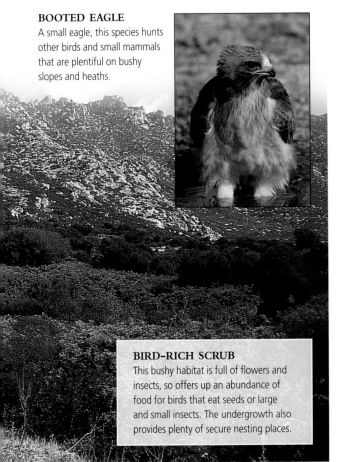

BIRD-RICH SCRUB

This bushy habitat is full of flowers and insects, so offers up an abundance of food for birds that eat seeds or large and small insects. The undergrowth also provides plenty of secure nesting places.

WHERE TO WATCH

HEATH AND WOODLAND IN THE NEW FOREST

❶ NEW FOREST, UK

This is a large, rolling tract of heath and forest. The grass is kept close-cropped by ponies, which makes the area ideal for Woodlarks. The gorse and heather areas attract Dartford Warblers. Snipe and Curlews nest in damp patches, while Hobbies feed over open heath.

DARTFORD WARBLER

❷ BRECKLAND, UK

Woodlarks and Nightjars breed in felled conifer plantations on the dry, sandy soil in this area, while Stone-curlews nest on the grassy heaths and nearby fields. The grassland also attracts Wheatears, Stonechats, and Curlews.

❸ LA CRAU, FRANCE

An area of very dry, stony plains, with Little Bustards, Pin-tailed Sandgrouse, Rollers, Stone-curlews, and various larks.

❹ MAJORCA

This has many areas of heathland worth exploring to see local Marmora's and Spectacled Warblers as well as Subalpine and Sardinian Warblers. It is also good for Thekla Larks and Short-toed Larks. Some areas also attract Stone-curlews, Rock Sparrows, Woodchat Shrikes, and Rock Thrushes.

❺ ALGARVE, PORTUGAL

This part of Iberia has a mixture of sand dunes, open woodland, wetland, and rich Mediterranean scrub. Birds to be found here include Short-toed, Crested, and Thekla Larks, Great Spotted Cuckoo, and Sardinian, Subalpine, and Spectacled Warblers.

SUBALPINE WARBLER

▨ *Heath and scrub areas*

FARMLAND AND GRASSLAND

Natural grassland habitats have been almost eliminated from most of Europe by millennia of agricultural development. Those remaining are now rare and fragile. They host a collection of wildlife, including birds whose requirements are very specific, and which are often shy and easily disturbed by human activity. Change of any kind, including irrigation, ploughing, over-grazing, and encroachment by trees, spells disaster for them.

GREAT BUSTARDS
These birds are among Europe's most threatened, as they face pressure from agriculture.

FOLLOWING THE PLOUGH
Not all birds avoid farming activities: Lapwings, Black-headed Gulls, Jackdaws, and Rooks find food on ploughed fields.

FARMLAND

Agricultural land is naturally rich and full of birds but intensification, especially change from mixed farming to a dry, unvarying monoculture, removes birds from vast areas of countryside. However, arable land that is ploughed for growing a variety of crops does offer feeding opportunities – a wealth of invertebrate food when the earth is turned over and insect food in growing crops. Old, unimproved grassland, which is grazed by animals, has a wide range of plants and insects and many safe nest sites.

GRASSLAND

Dry grassy steppes have species that are adapted to living within semi-arid environments, including bustards, sandgrouse, and larks. They survive in such places by foraging within the short vegetation, but irrigation and development schemes have ruined a lot of these habitats and threaten many more, including the last great steppe lands in Eastern Europe. Other grassy habitats, such as the cold, wet northern moorlands through to hot Mediterranean scrub are "farmed" by being grazed by millions of sheep. They would not look the same nor have the same birds if such usage changed as the areas would quickly be invaded by scrub. On the other hand, too many sheep and goats reduce the variety of plants and destroy the structure of the vegetation, so grazing at just the right intensity is vital to the survival of birds and other wildlife.

LESSER KESTREL
This handsome falcon has suffered a long-term decline. This may be due to the pesticides that have reduced its insect prey in both Europe and Africa, where it spends the winter.

WHITE STORK
White Storks survive on farmland unless it is intensively cultivated and drained. They eat frogs and small rodents, which require marshy ground or tall, rich grassland.

ABUNDANT FOOD SUPPLIES
Grassland in northern and western Europe has periodic increases in vole populations, which attracts Short-eared Owls and Kestrels in large numbers.

NORTHERN VISITORS
Huge numbers of geese from far northern breeding areas, including Pink-footed, Barnacle, and White-fronted Geese, have come to rely on European farmland in winter – feeding on grass and waste crops.

ADAPTATION

■ **Skylarks and Calandra Larks** have no perches to sing from in open fields: they pour out prolonged songs from high-level song flights instead.

■ **Lapwings and Stone-curlews** are happy to adapt to farmland habitats so long as there is a mixture of pasture on which they can situate their nests, and bare earth where their growing chicks can forage for insects.

PIN-TAILED SANDGROUSE

■ **Sandgrouse** are able to survive on one drink a day and they fly huge distances to get it. They also carry water to their nestlings, holding it in their belly feathers.

■ **Geese** have changed their eating habits and now enjoy feasting on waste crops, such as sugar beet tops and carrots.

■ **Choughs** feed in old pastures, probing for ants with their long, curved bills.

CHOUGH

WHERE TO WATCH

❶ ISLAY, SCOTLAND

In summer, the damp fields here see breeding Snipe, Lapwings, Redshanks, and Curlews. Choughs, Twites, and Rock Doves feed in the fields and along the field margins. In winter, huge flocks of Barnacle and Greenland White-fronted Geese feed on grassy pastures.

❷ SALISBURY PLAIN, ENGLAND

This is an exceptional area of chalk downland, which has especially large numbers of Skylarks as well as other widespread farm birds such as Yellowhammers and Linnets. It also attracts some Stone-curlew and Grey Partridges.

❸ TEXEL, NETHERLANDS

A wonderful island to visit all year round, it sees breeding Black-tailed Godwits, Ruffs, and Redshanks on wetter nature reserves in summer. In winter, large numbers of Lapwings, Snipe, Oystercatchers, Golden Plovers, Brent, Bean, and White-fronted Geese, Wigeon, Mallards, Shovelers, other wildfowl, birds of prey, and finches, including Twites, visit the area.

TWITES

❹ BELCHITE, SPAIN

These semi-arid northern Spanish steppes have a nature reserve area in which can be found Dupont's, Crested, Lesser Short-toed, Short-toed, and Thekla Larks as well as Stone-curlews, Pin-tailed Sandgrouse, various warblers, Hobbies, Lesser Kestrels, and other birds of prey.

CRESTED LARK

❺ BIEBRZA MARSHES, POLAND

This farmed wetland and grassland region has rare Aquatic Warblers and Great Snipes as well as a great variety of other exciting species – from Black and White Storks to Cranes, Corncrakes, Greater Spotted Eagles, and White-winged Black Terns.

❻ HORTOBAGY, HUNGARY

This is a huge area of farmland and semi-natural steppe, which attracts Red-footed Falcons, Great Bustards, Aquatic Warblers, Rollers, Bee-Eaters, and Lesser Grey Shrikes in summer. Tens of thousands of Cranes pass by on their migration route and White-tailed Eagles visit in winter.

■ Grassland areas

FOREST AND WOODLAND

Most of Europe would naturally be covered with forest, but human activities have destroyed many areas and left others impoverished. Even so, Europe's forests and woodlands still include such varied types as Mediterranean evergreen oak and ancient Scots pine forest.

OAK AND BEECH WOODS
Oak woods (below) let in more light than beech (right), so have a thicker, more varied shrub layer beneath and consequently a greater variety of birds.

DECIDUOUS WOODS

The character of deciduous woods changes greatly with the seasons, so offers different opportunities and challenges to birds. Deciduous trees lose their leaves in winter to survive the cold. Insects are abundant and active in summer, but many of them survive the winter as cocoons or eggs, or hibernate, so insect-eating birds are forced to migrate unless they can turn to seeds in winter. In contrast, many seed-eating species are year-round woodland residents. The gnarled trunks of deciduous trees have many crevices for birds to nest in.

PIED FLYCATCHER
Pied Flycatchers need holes for nesting, most easily found in mature deciduous trees.

EVERGREEN FORESTS

Evergreen trees – mostly conifers – keep their leaves year-round. Conifers tend to be smoother and straighter than many deciduous trees, and have fewer holes for nesting birds. Their insect food is more uniform through the seasons but their seed production tends to fluctuate, resulting in a few good years between several poor ones. Some birds breed well in such forests during the good years but move out in a nomadic search for food when the seeds run out. Conifers have tough needle-leaves and their dense foliage casts a deep shade, so few plants can grow underneath them. This reduces the variety of feeding and nesting possibilities for birds.

CROSSBILLS
Cones have nutritious seeds but are protected by tough, overlapping scales. Crossbills have evolved a special, cross-tipped bill that can prise these apart. They reach the seeds inside using their tongues.

CONIFERS
Conifers suit a wide variety of birds as the trees mature. Old trees and open glades at the edge of a forest create a light, accessible area.

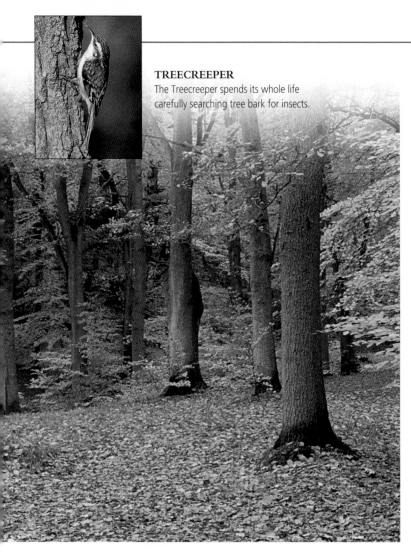

TREECREEPER
The Treecreeper spends its whole life carefully searching tree bark for insects.

ADAPTATIONS

■ **An elongated, backward-pointing outer toe and a stiff tail** provide the Green Woodpecker with a sure grip as it perches on broad branches.

GREEN WOODPECKER

■ **The stout, dagger-like bill** of the Nuthatch is used for breaking into nuts and seeds, which it wedges into crevices in bark.

■ **A Woodcock's dead-leaf camouflage** is perfect for nesting on the forest floor.

■ **A Sparrowhawk's long tail** helps it twist and turn quickly in tight spaces between trees when chasing prey.

SPARROWHAWK

WHERE TO WATCH

❶ ABERNETHY, SCOTLAND

A magnificent area of rolling moor and ancient pine forest (the largest remaining tract of native pine forest in Britain) with dense bilberry, crowberry, heather, and juniper – ideal for rare Capercaillies. The mature trees are good for Crested Tits as well as Parrot, Scottish, and Two-barred Crossbills. Younger plantations have Black Grouse.

YOUNG CONIFER PLANTATION

❷ FONTAINEBLEAU, FRANCE

This is an excellent area of deciduous and mixed forest and parkland, which has great possibilities for many woodland species such as interesting birds of prey, six species of woodpeckers – including Black, Middle Spotted, and Grey-headed – as well as a good selection of warblers in summer.

❸ PICOS DE EUROPA, SPAIN

A fine mountain range in northwest Spain, often cloudy and wet but with spectacular forested peaks and gorges and some extensive hillside oak and pine woods, where there are Griffon Vultures, Bonelli's, Short-toed, Booted, and Golden Eagles, Black Woodpeckers, Crested Tits, Goshawks, and Bonelli's Warblers.

CRESTED TIT

❹ EXTREMADURA, SPAIN

Woodlands in this region are mixed or of open cork oak. It sees a superb selection of forest and woodland-glade birds exploiting the nesting and feeding opportunities, including Great Spotted Cuckoos, Azure-winged Magpies, and Rollers.

Woodland areas

GARDENS, PARKS, AND TOWNS

Gardens vary greatly according to their location: some are little more than enclosed pieces of Mediterranean scrub while others represent woodland habitats in miniature. Urban gardens bring birds right into cities and tend to have a selection (though limited) of woodland birds but lack most of the bigger, shyer, or more demanding species. Artificial food in gardens is a lifeline to huge numbers of birds – and not just in winter. Spring is an important period when birds are trying to build up energy levels to begin nesting but many natural foods are running short. Town parks provide birds with shrubberies, lawns, and mature trees, while a park lake will attract wetland species.

PUBLIC SPACES

Town and city centres attract few species but spilled food and scraps and the abundance of ledges and cavities in buildings offer food and nest sites for an increasing number. Town and city parks are often much better areas for birds, especially if there is a lake or pond, and some shy species become surprisingly tame if they are not disturbed. Town or feral pigeons, which are derived from wild Rock Doves, are abundant in towns, while large lakes attract various ducks, coots, and gulls that forage for scraps. Few birds feed on roads, paved areas, and rooftops but wagtails often do so, finding insects trapped in rainwater puddles. The large numbers of town pigeons are increasingly attracting predatory peregrines into city centres and onto tall buildings in industrial areas. As towns are warmer than the surrounding countryside in winter, some species fly in specially to roost in city trees or on buildings.

BLACK REDSTART
In much of Europe Black Redstarts nest in cavities in buildings, which take the place of natural cliff habitats.

URBAN SECRETS
Dunnocks display to one another in town parks and gardens. Their sober appearance belies a complex social life: males and females often have more than one mate and can frequently be seen in "wing-waving displays".

ROOSTING WAGTAILS
Pied Wagtails feed on roofs, tarmac-covered footpaths, car parks, and town centre riverbanks, and each evening come together in large roosts for warmth and protection. They often choose ornamental trees for this, but equally seek out glasshouses and industrial sites in towns.

SUBURBAN SURPRISES
Industrial areas and roads on urban outskirts often see birds, such as these Lapwings, flocking in large numbers.

PRIVATE GARDENS

Ordinary suburban and rural gardens are becoming increasingly important wildlife havens. If there are thick shrubberies, flowerbeds with freshly turned earth, patches of lawn, and perhaps a few garden ponds, a suburban area can be almost as rich as a piece of natural woodland. These small habitats offer a range of feeding opportunities for all kinds of birds, some of which live permanently in the gardens while others just visit from nearby woods and streams. Even the shy Kingfisher and Grey Heron may make an early morning raid on a goldfish pond. Gardens are far poorer for birds, however, if they are too regimented and over-tidy.

GARDEN FEEDER
Robins are among many woodland birds that have become garden inhabitants. They like thick hedges and shrubs, close to pieces of bare ground and short grass where they can forage for worms and insects.

BERRY EATERS
Many birds eat berries, especially in autumn when they provide much needed energy. To attract birds like the Song Thrush, plant shrubs such as elderberry and cotoneaster.

EXPLOITING THE GARDENER
Blackbirds and Robins are well known for their bold and fearless behaviour, especially when a gardener is turning over soil and they get a good chance of grabbing a worm.

BIRD-TABLES
By placing food on a bird-table each day we are giving birds regular meals when natural food may be lacking. As an added bonus, we can watch them as they eat.

ADAPTATIONS

The most successful urban birds are species that can find habitats and food that resemble their more natural requirements out of town.

■ **Starlings** have strong muscles that can open their bills when they probe into a lawn for a leatherjacket. Their eyes are able to swivel backwards, so that they can watch for predators without having to stop searching for food.

■ **House Martins** naturally nest on cliff faces, but long ago learned to come into town and nest under the eaves of buildings. They do have problems when dry weather makes finding mud difficult.

HOUSE MARTIN

■ **Old buildings** provide all kinds of holes and cavities for birds to nest in, and Kestrels through to House Sparrows and Starlings exploit these. Swifts are now almost entirely reliant on buildings. However, as old buildings are being knocked down and new houses and office blocks go up that offer no nest sites, such birds may find life more difficult.

■ **Woodpigeons and town pigeons** can see a broader range of light than humans can. Grains and seeds, which we find difficult to find on gravel, stand out to their eyes as different colours and are quickly pecked up with great precision.

WOODPIGEON

WATCHING BIRDS

There are a vast number of opportunities to birdwatch – whether you visit a different country specifically for that purpose, go to a nature reserve, or simply look at the species that can be found every day in your garden or on your journey to work. You will find that there are a huge range of birds to see and the more you look, the more you will want to learn about the differences there are between them so that you can start to identify individual species.

WINTER ROBIN
In winter, putting out food or leaving apples unpicked on a tree will attract Robins and thrushes to your garden.

BIRD BOXES
Most gardens have food but no natural nest sites for hole-nesting birds such as sparrows, tits, and Starlings. Artificial boxes give them a chance to nest where you can watch them.

GETTING STARTED

It can be difficult to get close enough to birds to identify them as they tend to perch high on trees or far out on lakes. Don't let this put you off, however, as with practice and experience you will learn how to pick out unique characteristics from afar. The better you get, the more you will enjoy birdwatching. To help with this process, buy yourself an identification guide, a pair of binoculars, and a notebook – a knowledgeable friend is a great asset too.

BINOCULARS AND TELESCOPES

Binoculars are essential for birdwatching. They are described by figures, such as 10 x 40 or 8 x 30. The first is the magnification while the second is the diameter of the large lens. Higher magnification means larger images, but the lenses are also larger, making it harder to hold the binoculars steady; the field of view is also narrower and the image duller. You will need to compromise. There are top-quality binoculars that give really bright images but they are still heavy and expensive. It is best to opt for a magnification between 7 and 10. If you want to look at birds far away and need more power, consider buying a telescope. It will magnify 20 or 30 times but you will need a 60 or 80mm wide lens to let in enough light.

THE ESSENTIALS
Choose binoculars that you can handle easily, and buy the best you can afford. A camera and telescope can also be useful in the field.

BINOCULARS

focusing wheel

the "object lens" described by its diameter in millimetres

USING A NOTEBOOK

Notebooks are really invaluable for novice and experienced birdwatchers alike. Note down what you see if you want to keep records at home: it is much better than trying to rely on shaky memories later. If you come across a bird that is new to you, or has an unusual plumage, try to take a description – you will need to look closely at the bird in order to do this. It is a useful discipline, for example, to look at the colour of the bill, legs, and any special markings. Also write down the calls you hear and try to make a few sketches, however rough they are.

focus wheel

TELESCOPE

adjustable angle

objective lens

tripod

SLR CAMERA

use a camera with a long lens to capture detail

CODE OF CONDUCT

There is one simple rule for birdwatchers to follow: the welfare of the bird comes first. It is easy to get carried away, and to inch forward while trying to see a bird that you think might be rare or is one that you have not seen before. It may be tempting to chase a bird if it starts to move away, or to try flushing a bird out one last time, but all you will do is scare it away. Most birds are not bothered too much by everyday disturbance, but use your common sense. Don't disturb birds while they are at their nests, as you may put them in danger, and never be tempted to handle eggs. Keep all types of disturbance to a minimum – for the sake of the birds, other people, and your own view.

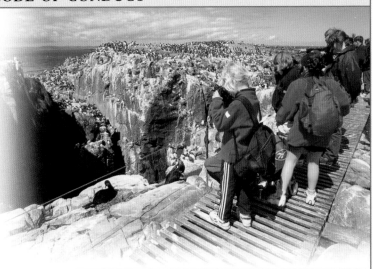

VIEWING CONDITIONS

Viewing conditions are an important consideration. It may seem obvious but many people forget that a white bird will look dark against a bright sky, while a dark brown bird may look remarkably pale against a ploughed field or winter hedgerow. White gulls lit by low, evening light may look orange on the sunlit side and quite blue on the shaded side; in strong sunlight they simply look brilliant white and dark grey. Dull light in rain or snow may reveal the subtleties of their greys and whites much better.

DAWN
Low, weak, misty light with an orange glow, which is not good for revealing detail.

MISTY MORNING
Mist may make a bird look large but it hides detail of colour and pattern, or even shape.

MORNING LIGHT
Low light may exaggerate contrast, but the brightness is perfect for seeing detail.

MIDDAY
Overhead sun can cast surprisingly deep shadows and "washes out" the colours on the upperside.

INTO THE SUN
Looking into bright light makes it difficult to see much more than a silhouette, even on a pale bird.

EVENING LIGHT
Lovely soft, warm light, but beware a rather orange cast to many colours.

USING BINOCULARS
If you see a bird that you want to view close-up, keep your eyes on it as you lift your binoculars.

USING A TRIPOD
Modern telescopes are short and need support, preferably on a good, firm tripod. This is a clumsy, heavy combination but the reward is unbelievably close views.

CONSERVATION

Conservation is simply wise management, which aims to maintain or enhance the numbers and variety of wild species and the habitats on which they depend. The birdlife in most parts of Europe has undergone dramatic changes almost everywhere over several centuries: little of Europe is now "natural", apart from the far north, some forests, mountains, and seas. It is therefore difficult to say that the present birdlife is "as it should be", and that all change must be resisted. Most people would, however, agree that we should at least try to maintain the variety of birds that we do have now. Every effort should be made to ensure that we do not lose any species from the European avifauna.

GREAT BUSTARD
The loss of grassland habitat, particularly to intensive farming, now threatens the last few thousand Great Bustards more severely than ever before.

CROWDED COASTS
Waders such as Redshanks use estuaries and other coastal habitats. Unfortunately for them, coasts are also ideal for various developments, from ports and industry to sport and leisure. Even people using beaches may disturb feeding or roosting flocks. Estuary birds face many threats.

THREATENED HABITATS

Conserving birds is not usually a case of preventing persecution or over-hunting. Most threats arise because birds' habitats are being damaged or destroyed. No wild creature can survive unless its needs for food, breeding sites, and safe refuges from predators are met. Protecting habitats usually involves planning and managing human activity, especially farming, forestry, drainage of marshes, and other large-scale changes. Local developments such as building roads and airports or urban housing expansion also affect the habitats. Food and habitat protection is often a political matter. A clear example of this is the farming and fishery policies, which affect countryside birds and seabirds across the whole of Europe.

DEGRADED RIVERS
Many rivers are dredged and straightened, which removes the habitat for riverside birds that prefer muddy shallows, sheltered bays, or beds of reed and sedges. Erosion eats into banks used by Kingfishers, while pollution, especially the acidification of rivers, affects the food supply – from tiny aquatic invertebrates to fish. An increased frequency of summer drought also affects river birds.

GLOBAL WARMING
Wading birds, wildfowl, gulls, and terns that use low-lying sea coasts and nearby lagoons for feeding and nesting face severe threats from the effects of global warming and sea-level rise. This presents many challenges to coastal conservation, not least finding sensitive ways to protect the coast.

FINDING SOLUTIONS

Conservation is complicated, and to achieve a political solution to some of the more intractable problems conservationists must have hard facts and figures. There is no substitute for good, reliable research to give a solid and well-respected backing to any conservation argument. Once the problems and their causes are understood, it is possible to have a more organized and objective approach to finding practical and economic solutions which other people, such as farmers, foresters, and gamekeepers, then put into practice.

RADIO TAGGING

This Black Grouse is being fitted with a minute radio transmitter so that its movements can be followed. Black Grouse have declined rapidly so finding out more about them and their problems is essential if solutions are to be found.

CORNCRAKE

In some countries, farmers are paid to maintain uncut field corners that provide early spring cover for Corncrakes, and to continue growing hay and cutting it late in the season. Such schemes are essential for the bird's survival.

GANNET PROBLEMS

Pollution and discarded waste, especially at sea, may cause unexpected problems for birds. Gannets build their nests out of discarded nylon twine and other debris that can entangle their growing chicks. Greater awareness and improved rules for the disposal of waste at ports rather than overboard at sea would help solve such problems.

RECORD KEEPING

Conservation in Europe relies on collating facts and figures, following trends, and identifying sudden changes in numbers and distributions of birds. This has a proud tradition of extensive amateur involvement, as thousands of people add their own records to the national and international data upon which our collective knowledge depends.

CONSERVATION GROUPS

Bird and habitat conservation groups worldwide work together in a global federation called BirdLife International. Each country has a BirdLife "partner". The largest is the RSPB in the UK. The RSPB works for a healthy environment that is rich in birds and other wildlife. It relies on the support and generosity of others to make a difference. Without members and other supporters it would lack the finance to do its work. When it does find and advocate solutions to problems faced by birds in the countryside, it relies on the willingness of decision-makers, landowners, and others to take notice, and act upon its advice. There are many other bird conservation bodies, bird clubs, and local groups that also play a vital role in conservation. Contact your country's BirdLife partner for further details of societies and groups near you if you would like to get involved.

THREATENED LESSER KESTREL

SPECIES
GUIDE

Families **Gaviidae, Podicipedidae**

DIVERS AND GREBES

ENTIRELY WATER BIRDS except when nesting, these sleek, dagger-billed birds have thick plumage, narrow wings, short tails, and legs set very far back on the body. This makes it difficult for them to move on land: they merely shuffle on their bellies, pushing with their feet, onto the nest and off again into water. Their feet are not webbed, but have broad lobes along each toe (the hind toe is very small). These lobes fold together as the foot is pushed forwards through water, reducing drag, but open out when pushed against it to give greater propulsion.

DIVERS
These are bigger and longer-bodied than grebes, flying more often (indeed, the Red-throated Diver flies from its nesting lake to feed in the sea) and more northerly in their distribution in summer. They have loud, wailing calls.

WINTER DABCHICK
Like most grebes, the Little Grebe, often known as the Dabchick, loses its bright colours in winter, but has rich rufous cheeks in summer. A pale spot near the base of the bill is distinctive in all seasons.

GREBES
Round-bodied but long-necked, grebes are widespread in Europe, breeding on rivers, marshes, and larger lakes. They have barking, croaking, or trilling calls, less wild and dramatic than the divers' vocalizations. They characteristically cover their eggs with waterweed whenever they leave the nest, in an effort to deter predators.

RED THROAT IN SUMMER
Divers have distinctive plumages when breeding, such as this Red-throated Diver, but in winter they become more anonymous in dark brown and white.

GRACEFUL DISPLAY
Black-necked Grebes show off their dramatic plumage in courtship displays; the sexes look alike.

Order **Gaviiformes**	Family **Gaviidae**	Species *Gavia stellata*

Red-throated Diver

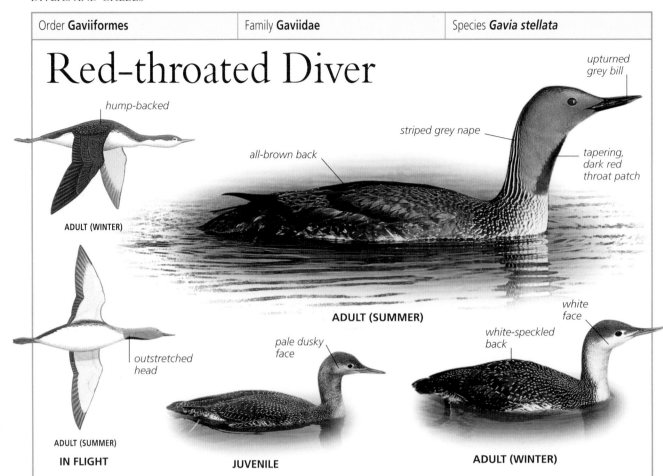

hump-backed

ADULT (WINTER)

all-brown back

upturned grey bill

striped grey nape

tapering, dark red throat patch

ADULT (SUMMER)

outstretched head

ADULT (SUMMER)

IN FLIGHT

pale dusky face

JUVENILE

white-speckled back

white face

ADULT (WINTER)

A low-profile, swimming bird, rarely found on land except at the nest, this diver is distinguished by its slim, tapered bill held angled upwards. Red-throated Divers nest on small freshwater pools but fly off to feed at the coast. They are typically found flying high overhead to and from the sea in summer, calling loudly. In winter, they are mostly marine birds. Brown-backed and grey-headed with a dark red throat patch in summer, the plumage of the Red-throated Diver is less distinctive in winter.

VOICE Loud, high wail and fast, staccato quacking (in flight) in summer; quiet in winter.
NESTING Scrape almost on shoreline, in danger of flooding; 2 eggs; 1 brood; April–July.
FEEDING Dives for fish and other aquatic creatures; underwater for long periods, reappears at some distance from point of dive.

FLIGHT: low and straight over sea, head outstretched, legs slightly drooped; steady, strong wingbeats.

CALL POSTURE
Red-throated Divers, like other divers, use several strange, ritualized postures while calling on breeding pools in summer.

SIMILAR SPECIES

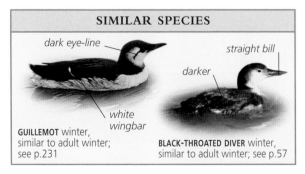

dark eye-line

straight bill

darker

white wingbar

GUILLEMOT winter, similar to adult winter; see p.231

BLACK-THROATED DIVER winter, similar to adult winter; see p.57

OCCURRENCE
Breeds on small, remote moorland pools and lakes in north, but feeds on sea in N Scotland, Iceland, and Scandinavia. In winter, more widespread around W European shores on open coasts and estuaries, but very rare inland.

Seen in the UK
J F M A M J J A S O N D

Length **50–60cm (20–23½ in)**	Wingspan **1.06–1.16m (3½–3¾ft)**	Weight **1.2–1.6kg (2¾–3½lb)**
Social **Winter flocks**	Lifespan **Up to 20 years**	Status **Vulnerable**

| Order **Gaviiformes** | Family **Gaviidae** | Species *Gavia arctica* |

Black-throated Diver 🔊 1

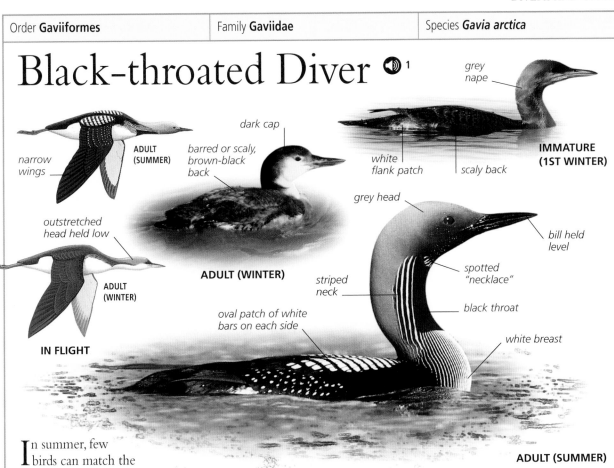

grey nape

IMMATURE (1ST WINTER)

narrow wings

ADULT (SUMMER)

dark cap

barred or scaly, brown-black back

white flank patch

scaly back

grey head

bill held level

spotted "necklace"

striped neck

black throat

outstretched head held low

ADULT (WINTER)

oval patch of white bars on each side

white breast

ADULT (WINTER)

IN FLIGHT

ADULT (SUMMER)

In summer, few birds can match the exquisite patterning of the Black-throated Diver. In winter, it is duller and harder to tell from a Great Northern or Red-throated Diver, but the slightly bulbous head, slim, straight bill, and narrow body are distinctive, along with the greyish nape, paler than the back. Small parties of Black-throated Divers gather in coastal bays in summer. However, this bird is generally solitary, swimming low on the sea.

VOICE Wild, loud wailing notes in summer; silent in winter.

NESTING Shallow scoop near water's edge on island (or raft) in lake; 2 eggs; 1 brood; April–July.

FEEDING Dives long and deep for fish, reappearing far away; slides evenly head-first into water with barely a ripple.

FLIGHT: head low, outstretched, legs trailed; narrow wings have slightly whip-like action.

SUMMER GATHERING
Black-throated Divers gather in impressive groups, swimming close together with heads raised.

NESTING ON RAFT
Black-throated Diver nests are often subject to flooding or left high and dry; artificial nest rafts ensure greater breeding success.

SIMILAR SPECIES

chequered back

black head

RED-THROATED DIVER
winter, similar to adult winter; see p.56

whiter face

GREAT NORTHERN DIVER
summer, similar to adult summer; see p.58

OCCURRENCE
Breeds on large lakes with small islands in remote areas of N Scotland and Scandinavia. In winter, more widespread but scarce on coasts of NW Europe. Often in larger estuaries or broad sandy bays; rare inland.

| Seen in the UK |
| J F M A M J J A S O N D |

| Length **60–70cm (23½–28in)** | Wingspan **1.1–1.3m (3½–4¼ft)** | Weight **2–3kg (4½–6½lb)** |
| Social **Small summer flocks** | Lifespan **Up to 20 years** | Status **Vulnerable** |

Order **Gaviiformes**	Family **Gaviidae**	Species *Gavia immer*

Great Northern Diver

drooped neck

ADULT (SUMMER)

dark crown

long, heavy bill

blackish hindneck

broad body

black neck-band

white face

ADULT (MOULTING TO WINTER)

trailing legs

slender wings

ADULT (WINTER)

IN FLIGHT

nape darker than back

barred back

dark collar

JUVENILE

evenly white-chequered back

black head

striped white collar

ADULT (SUMMER)

One of the largest divers, the Great Northern Diver has a heavy, dagger-like bill, and often an angular head shape with a "bump" on the forehead. It is a splendidly chequered bird in breeding plumage. In winter, its large size, very broad body, heavy bill, and dark nape (while the barred back is paler) are distinguishing features. A young Cormorant might be taken for it, or vice versa, in a poor view. The Great Northern Diver typically swims very low, back often awash.

VOICE Wolf-like wailing and tremulous laughing notes in summer; silent in winter.

NESTING Shallow scrape on water's edge; 2 eggs; 1 brood; April–June.

FEEDING Feeds on large fish, crabs, and other aquatic life, often bringing big flatfish to surface after long dive.

FLIGHT: flies low and direct; typical long, slender wings of diver, legs trailing, neck drooped.

FLAPPING WINGS
The Great Northern Diver, like most other divers, often sits up on the water and flaps its wings, revealing its white underparts.

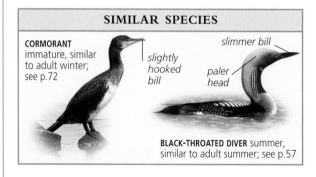

SIMILAR SPECIES

CORMORANT immature, similar to adult winter; see p.72

slightly hooked bill

slimmer bill

paler head

BLACK-THROATED DIVER summer, similar to adult summer; see p.57

OCCURRENCE
Breeds on larger lakes in Iceland. Scarce in winter but widespread on wide estuaries, in broad, sandy coastal bays, and also on wilder, open water in W Europe; rare inland on bigger reservoirs or flooded pits.

Seen in the UK

J	F	M	A	M	J	J	A	S	O	N	D

Length **70–80cm (28–32in)**	Wingspan **1.27–1.47m (4¼–4¾ft)**	Weight **3–4kg (6½–8¾lb)**
Social **Solitary**	Lifespan **10–20 years**	Status **Secure†**

| Order **Podicipediformes** | Family **Podicipedidae** | Species *Tachybaptus ruficollis* |

Little Grebe 🔊 2.1, 2.11

trailing feet

ADULT (WINTER)

dark wings

IN FLIGHT

buffish face

ADULT (WINTER)

buff foreneck

JUVENILE

rounded body

rufous face

blackish cap

straight, pointed bill

pale yellow spot at base of bill

blunt buff tail

ADULT (SUMMER)

Little Grebes are small, dark, short-billed, and round as a ball, their near lack of tail rendering them especially buoyant on freshwater rivers, lakes, and ponds. Their loud, trilling or whinnying calls ring around marshes in summer. In winter, they often move to larger waters, less prone to freeze, and more rarely to the coast. They may then mix loosely with other species of waterfowl but tend to keep in little groups, slightly dispersed, in their own corner of the lake.

VOICE High, loud, rapid trill that fades away; silent in winter.

NESTING Floating mound of wet weed, anchored to stem or branch; 4–6 eggs, which the bird covers if it leaves the nest; 1 brood; April–June.

FEEDING Dives for small fish, aquatic insects, and molluscs, often diving under with a little leap and reappearing like a cork.

FLIGHT: flies little, usually very low, skittering over water on small wings.

ALERT ON WATER
When alarmed, the Little Grebe looks larger-necked and less dumpy, and in winter, can look surprisingly like a Black-necked Grebe.

SIMILAR SPECIES

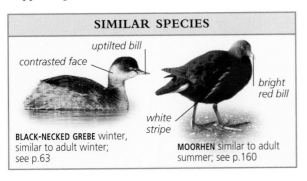

uptilted bill

contrasted face

bright red bill

white stripe

BLACK-NECKED GREBE winter, similar to adult winter; see p.63

MOORHEN similar to adult summer; see p.160

OCCURRENCE
Widespread in summer except in N Europe, breeding on broad rivers and canals, freshwater pools, and flooded pits. Dispersal to larger waters in W Europe in autumn also takes them onto sea at times, in sheltered areas.

Seen in the UK
J F M A M J J A S O N D

| Length **25–29cm (10–11½in)** | Wingspan **40–45cm (16–18in)** | Weight **100–120g (3⅝–4oz)** |
| Social **Small flocks** | Lifespan **10–15 years** | Status **Secure†** |

Order **Podicipediformes**	Family **Podicipedidae**	Species **Podiceps grisegena**

Red-necked Grebe

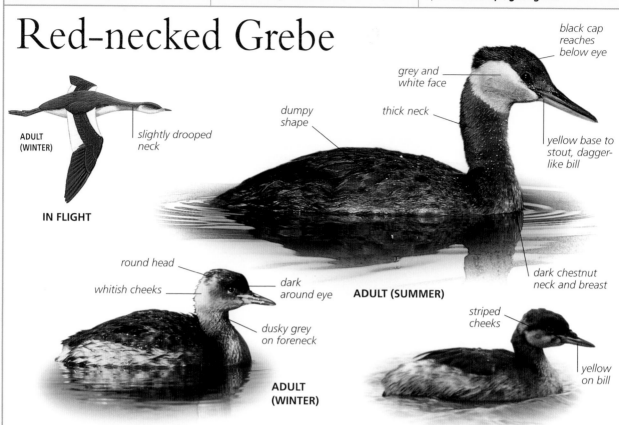

ADULT (WINTER)
slightly drooped neck

IN FLIGHT

black cap reaches below eye

grey and white face

dumpy shape

thick neck

yellow base to stout, dagger-like bill

dark chestnut neck and breast

ADULT (SUMMER)

round head

whitish cheeks

dark around eye

dusky grey on foreneck

ADULT (WINTER)

striped cheeks

yellow on bill

JUVENILE

/\

FLIGHT: low, straight, heavy, with slightly drooped neck and legs.

In much of northeast Europe, this is a typical bird of large, well-vegetated lakes; in Great Britain, it is mostly a late summer and winter visitor and never common. Like other grebes it can look dumpy, squat, and thickset, or rather slim, according to conditions and intent: an active, feeding bird looks much more slim and alert than a resting one. Such changes in shape can make judgement of size, especially at a distance on open water, very difficult, but this is a large grebe, along with the Great Crested Grebe, compared with the small grebes such as Slavonian and Black-necked Grebes.
VOICE Various growling notes; silent in winter.
NESTING Typical grebe nest: heap of waterweed with shallow depression on top, semi-floating on fresh water amongst vegetation; 3 or 4 eggs; 1 brood; April–June.
FEEDING Dives for food, mostly fish, but also feeds on various crustaceans and insects in summer.

A STRUGGLE ON LAND
Grebes are unable to walk on land, and use an ungainly shuffle to leave the nest. They are adept swimmers.

SIMILAR SPECIES

slimmer bill never yellow

whiter foreneck

longer neck

smaller bill

GREAT CRESTED GREBE winter, similar to adult winter; see p.61

SLAVONIAN GREBE winter, similar to adult winter; see p.62

OCCURRENCE
Breeds on reedy lakes and broad rivers in E Europe. In autumn and winter, moves west, mostly on quiet estuaries and sheltered coastal bays; scarce on inland waters such as flooded gravel pits and reservoirs.

Seen in the UK
| J | F | M | A | M | J | J | A | S | O | N | D |

Length **40–46cm (16–18in)**	Wingspan **77–85cm (30–34in)**	Weight **700–900g (25–32oz)**
Social **Small flocks**	Lifespan **Up to 10 years**	Status **Secure**

Order **Podicipediformes**	Family **Podicipedidae**	Species **Podiceps cristatus**

Great Crested Grebe

IN FLIGHT

ADULT
(WINTER)

- drooping neck
- legs below body level
- bold white wing patches

- black head plumes
- white face
- unique ruff
- dagger-like pink bill
- slender neck
- dull, dark back
- white neck and breast

ADULT (SUMMER)

- striped head
- pale greyish body

JUVENILE

- white over eye
- pink bill
- white breast
- tailless shape
- dark back

ADULT (WINTER)

The upright, slender neck with a silky white front and bright white breast are always characteristic of this large, dagger-billed grebe. In summer, its black cap extends into a double, backward-facing tuft and a frill of chestnut appears on the face, used in face-to-face head-wagging displays by breeding pairs. Small groups breed close together and larger flocks form on more open water, such as large reservoirs, in winter.

VOICE Various loud barks and growling notes in summer; juveniles make loud, fluty whistles.

NESTING Pile of weed on water, anchored to vegetation; 3 or 4 white eggs; 1 brood; February–June.

FEEDING Dives from surface, staying under for lengthy periods in search of fish and large aquatic invertebrates.

/\

FLIGHT: low, direct; head and trailing legs drooped below body level.

OCCURRENCE
Widespread except in far N Europe. Mostly breeds on flooded gravel pits, large lakes, and reservoirs; also on larger rivers. In winter, mostly on bigger reservoirs and sheltered coastal waters in W Europe; autumn migrants often on sea.

Seen in the UK
J F M A M J J A S O N D

SIMILAR SPECIES

- stubbier bill
- stockier and deeper

RED-NECKED GREBE winter, similar to adult winter; see p.60

COURTING
Pairs of Great Crested Grebes perform complex courting rituals, diving underwater and surfacing with weeds that they offer each other.

Length **46–51cm (18–20in)**	Wingspan **85–90cm (34–35in)**	Weight **800–1000g (29–36oz)**
Social **Flocks**	Lifespan **10–15 years**	Status **Secure**

Order **Podicipediformes**	Family **Podicipedidae**	Species *Podiceps auritus*

Slavonian Grebe

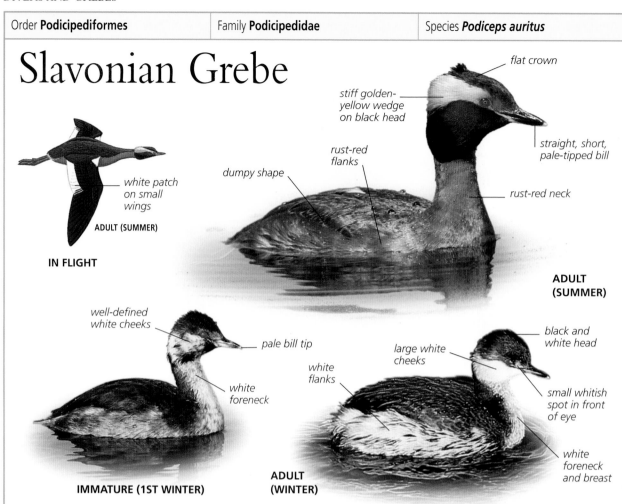

flat crown

stiff golden-yellow wedge on black head

rust-red flanks

dumpy shape

straight, short, pale-tipped bill

rust-red neck

white patch on small wings

ADULT (SUMMER)

IN FLIGHT

ADULT (SUMMER)

well-defined white cheeks

pale bill tip

white foreneck

IMMATURE (1ST WINTER)

large white cheeks

white flanks

black and white head

small whitish spot in front of eye

white foreneck and breast

ADULT (WINTER)

A bird of remote, upland, northern pools in summer, the Slavonian Grebe is then easy to identify. Its complex head pattern and plumes are used in display: like other grebes, the sexes are alike. In winter, in stark black and white plumage, it is much more like some other grebes. It typically breeds in loose groups of three or four pairs, and spends the winter in twos and threes at most. These may be seen near Black-necked Grebes in favoured spots.

VOICE High, fast, whistling trills in summer; usually silent in winter.

NESTING Pile of weeds anchored to reed or sedge stem; 4 or 5 eggs; 1 brood; April–July.

FEEDING Dives to find small fish; in summer, mostly feeds on insects and various aquatic crustaceans.

FLIGHT: low, quick; may patter across water surface.

NEST BUILDING
Slavonian Grebes build soggy heaps of water weeds in which to lay their eggs, covering them for safety when they leave the nest.

SIMILAR SPECIES

BLACK-NECKED GREBE winter, similar to adult winter; see p.63

yellow bill-base

duskier cheeks

uptilted bill

dusky foreneck

RED-NECKED GREBE winter, similar to adult winter; see p.60

OCCURRENCE
Breeds in cool, wild pools with some fringing vegetation in Iceland, N Scotland, and N and E Europe. In winter, mostly on sea in NW Europe, especially on muddy estuaries, more rarely on reservoirs and pits inland.

Seen in the UK
J F M A M J J A S O N D

Length **31–38cm (12–15in)**	Wingspan **59–65cm (23–26in)**	Weight **375–450g (13–16oz)**
Social **Pairs/Small flocks**	Lifespan **Up to 10 years**	Status **Secure†**

Order **Podicipediformes**	Family **Podicipedidae**	Species *Podiceps nigricollis*

Black-necked Grebe

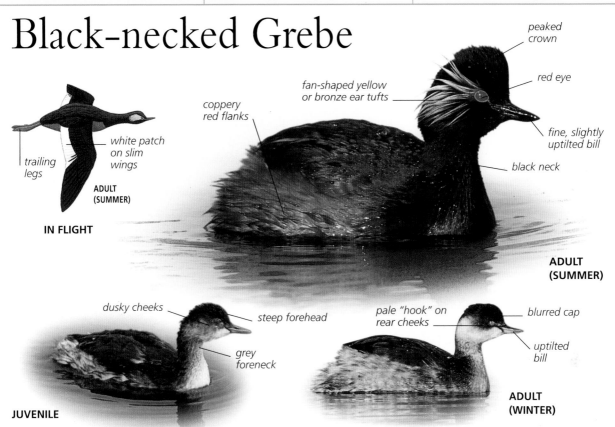

IN FLIGHT

trailing legs

white patch on slim wings

ADULT (SUMMER)

coppery red flanks

fan-shaped yellow or bronze ear tufts

peaked crown

red eye

fine, slightly uptilted bill

black neck

ADULT (SUMMER)

dusky cheeks

steep forehead

grey foreneck

JUVENILE

pale "hook" on rear cheeks

blurred cap

uptilted bill

ADULT (WINTER)

More restricted to richer, lower-lying lakes than the Slavonian Grebe as a breeding bird, the Black-necked Grebe is more frequent on fresh water in winter. It is characterized by a slim, slightly uptilted bill and round head with a peaked crown. Although it is one of the smallest grebes, barely bigger than a Little Grebe, in breeding plumage, with head erect, it can look quite large out on a still, gleaming lake. Ones and twos may be seen on estuaries in winter, swimming very buoyantly, drifting in and out with the tide. Black-necked Grebes often mix loosely with other grebe species, usually outnumbering Slavonian Grebes.

VOICE Chattering and high-pitched whistling notes; silent in winter.

NESTING Pile of wet water weeds; 3 or 4 eggs; 1 brood; March–July.

FEEDING Catches insects, molluscs, and a few fish, in lengthy dives underwater.

FLIGHT: low, weak, fluttery; head extended, legs trail.

NEST OF WEEDS
The Black-necked Grebe builds a typical grebe nest by piling up water weeds. The only time it is not on water is when it is at the nest.

SIMILAR SPECIES

sharper contrast on face

straight bill

LITTLE GREBE winter, similar to adult winter; see p.59

browner face

SLAVONIAN GREBE winter, similar to adult winter; see p.62

OCCURRENCE
Widespread but very local; breeds on pools with large amounts of reeds and other vegetation. In winter, on estuaries and in coastal bays, reservoirs, and flooded pits; in spring, often on sea in Mediterranean.

Seen in the UK
| J | F | M | A | M | J | J | A | S | O | N | D |

Length **28–34cm (11–13½in)**	Wingspan **56–60cm (22–23½in)**	Weight **250–350g (9–13oz)**
Social **Small flocks**	Lifespan **Up to 10 years**	Status **Secure**

Families **Procellariidae, Hydrobatidae**

PETRELS AND SHEARWATERS

S O SUPREMELY ADAPTED to life at sea that they are cumbersome and vulnerable on land, petrels and shearwaters (with the exception of the cliff-nesting Fulmar) come to land only to breed and then do so only under the cover of darkness. By far the best chance of seeing most of them is from a ship at sea.

PETRELS

Like shearwaters and albatrosses, petrels' tubular nostrils excrete excess salt, and these birds are known collectively as "tubenoses". They breed in burrows or cavities, staying out of sight all day. Returning birds follow calls from their mates on the nests and use scent to find the right burrow in pitch dark.

Petrels are mostly small and insignificant over the open sea, but are dainty fliers, coping with the most ferocious gales as they skim the wave crests. They are sometimes driven close inshore and may then find it difficult to get back out to sea, sometimes ending up, exhausted, inland. Several species, especially the Storm Petrel, follow ships to feed on organisms that are disturbed in the wake.

The Fulmar is a larger bird, easily seen on its open cliff ledge nest or flying beside cliff tops during the day.

SHEARWATERS

Superb fliers, using air currents over the waves, shearwaters are almost helpless ashore and in danger from predatory gulls and skuas when returning to their colonies. They fly with stiffly outstretched wings and long glides between brief periods of wingbeats. In still air, they look rather heavy but with a wind become wonderfully capable, banking steeply over onto one wingtip then to the other, showing alternately dark upperparts and light underparts as they fly past far offshore. Young birds may be exhausted and blown inland by autumn gales.

GREAT SHEARWATER
An ocean-going migrant, this species breeds in the northern winter on islands in the South Atlantic.

FULMAR
The tubular nostrils are easy to see on the thick bill of this Fulmar, as it soars in the wind above a coastal cliff.

STORM PETREL
Swallow-like in its actions, the Storm Petrel feeds on tiny plankton and oily waste out at sea.

Order **Procellariiformes**	Family **Procellariidae**	Species *Fulmarus glacialis*

Fulmar 🔊 3

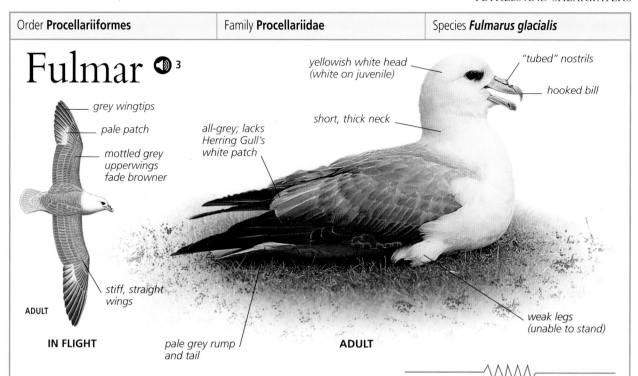

grey wingtips

pale patch

mottled grey
upperwings
fade browner

yellowish white head
(white on juvenile)

"tubed" nostrils

hooked bill

short, thick neck

all-grey; lacks
Herring Gull's
white patch

stiff, straight
wings

ADULT

IN FLIGHT

pale grey rump
and tail

weak legs
(unable to stand)

ADULT

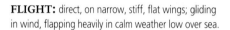

FLIGHT: direct, on narrow, stiff, flat wings; gliding in wind, flapping heavily in calm weather low over sea.

Gliding very low over the open sea or along clifftops, the Fulmar is a strong flier. Superficially gull-like, it is a "tubenose" (having large, raised nasal tubes) more closely related to albatrosses. Some Fulmars spend much of the year visiting breeding cliffs, even in winter, and can be viewed at close range as they sail by on the wind currents. Their real home, however, is over the wildest, windswept seas of the North Atlantic. Large flocks, often mixed with Gannets, gulls, and skuas, follow fishing fleets: Fulmar numbers have increased in the past century with far more food made available from these vessels.

VOICE Loud, harsh, throaty cackling.

NESTING On rocky or earth ledge, rarely ledges on buildings; 1 egg; 1 brood; April–June.

FEEDING Feeds mostly on fish offal from trawlers, small fish, jellyfish, squid, and other marine organisms.

SWIMMING IN SEA
Drinking saltwater, while swimming in the sea, is normal for "tube-noses" such as the Fulmar. Excess salt is excreted through the nostrils.

BREEDING
The Fulmar breeds in loose colonies on ledges on steep coastal cliffs or in burrows on inaccessible slopes, but also locally on buildings.

SIMILAR SPECIES

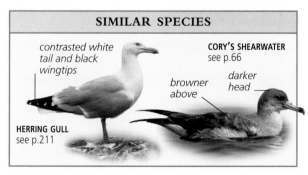

contrasted white
tail and black
wingtips

CORY'S SHEARWATER
see p.66

browner
above

darker
head

HERRING GULL
see p.211

OCCURRENCE
Breeds in NW Europe on cliffs, earth ledges, and even buildings or, where abundant, on grassy banks, usually close to sea. Out on open sea, sometimes mouths of estuaries or smaller bays.

Seen in the UK
J F M A M J J A S O N D

Length **45–50cm (18–20in)**	Wingspan **1–1.12m (3¼–3¾ft)**	Weight **700–900g (25–32oz)**
Social **Flocks**	Lifespan **20–30 years**	Status **Secure**

Order **Procellariiformes**	Family **Procellariidae**	Species **Calonectris diomedea**

Cory's Shearwater

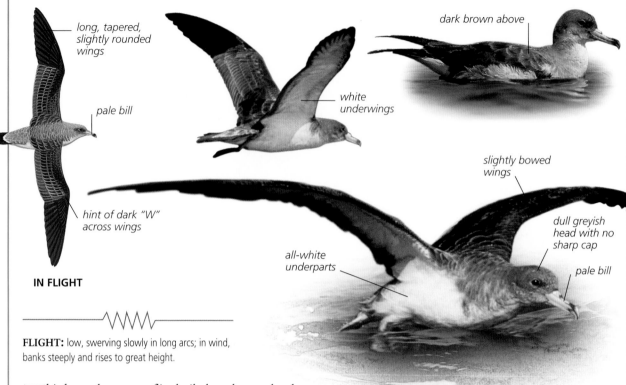

long, tapered, slightly rounded wings

pale bill

white underwings

dark brown above

slightly bowed wings

dull greyish head with no sharp cap

pale bill

all-white underparts

hint of dark "W" across wings

IN FLIGHT

FLIGHT: low, swerving slowly in long arcs; in wind, banks steeply and rises to great height.

This large shearwater flies lazily by – low and rather heavily – sometimes quite close inshore, in small groups; however, strong winds allow it to show great mastery in the air. In southern Europe and off northwest Africa, this is an abundant seabird. In the Mediterranean, it is quite frequently seen in summer from many islands and headlands. Near nesting areas, birds flying to their burrows after dark make loud, strange calls, even over towns, such as Funchal in Madeira.

VOICE Loud, varied, wailing sounds near breeding sites; mostly silent at sea.

NESTING Hole among rocks in scree and on cliff, or burrow on steep slope; used only at night; 1 egg; 1 brood; March–July.

FEEDING Takes fish, squid, shrimps, jellyfish, and waste from fishing vessels in shallow dives from surface of sea.

LIGHT AND SHADE
Strong light gives these swimming Cory's Shearwaters a pale-napped appearance, with unusually dark faces and contrasting upperparts.

SIMILAR SPECIES

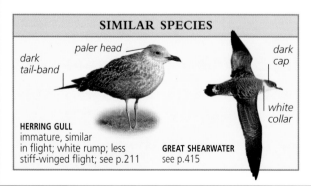

paler head

dark tail-band

HERRING GULL
immature, similar in flight; white rump; less stiff-winged flight; see p.211

dark cap

white collar

GREAT SHEARWATER
see p.415

OCCURRENCE
Mostly out at sea, but sometimes in broad bays or close inshore off headlands and islands. Outside breeding season, in western approaches off Ireland, N France, and SW England.

Seen in the UK
J F M A M J **J A S** O N D

Length **45–56cm (18–22in)**	Wingspan **1–1.25m (3¼–4 ft)**	Weight **700–800g (25–29oz)**
Social **Flocks**	Lifespan **Up to 20 years**	Status **Vulnerable†**

Order **Procellariiformes**	Family **Procellariidae**	Species *Puffinus puffinus*

Manx Shearwater

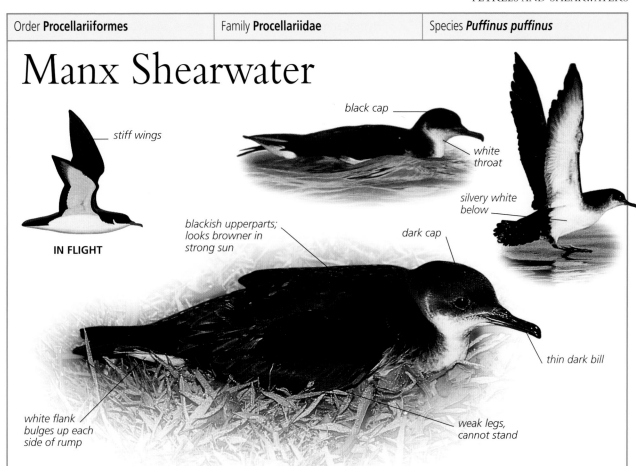

stiff wings

IN FLIGHT

black cap

white throat

silvery white below

blackish upperparts; looks browner in strong sun

dark cap

thin dark bill

white flank bulges up each side of rump

weak legs, cannot stand

Nesting sites of Manx Shearwaters are relatively localized, nearly all on islands; these seabirds are commonly seen on surrounding seas and are sometimes very numerous, especially in the evenings as they gather prior to going ashore. In autumn, large numbers are seen close to the shore during gales and a few are blown inland each year. Like other shearwaters and storm petrels, they only go to the nest in the cover of darkness, but many are still caught and killed by gulls. They are ungainly on land, moving with a shuffle, using legs, wings, and bill to scramble over rough ground.

VOICE Loud, strangled wailing and chortling sounds at night around breeding colony.
NESTING Uses rabbit or Puffin burrow or similar tunnel, or hole in scree; 1 egg; 1 brood; April–July.
FEEDING Flocks gather over fish or small squid, diving from surface or after short plunge from air.

FLIGHT: fast, especially downwind, with long, swerving glides, banking on one wingtip then wheeling over onto other; wingbeats fast, stiff, flickering.

FLAP AND GLIDE
In calm air, shearwaters fly low over the water with many more deep wingbeats and short, flat glides.

OCCURRENCE
Over open sea, except when breeding. Large colonies on islands, sometimes high up on rocky mountain peaks, more often in burrows in turf on lower slopes, in NW Europe. In autumn, widespread off coasts.

Seen in the UK
J F **M A M J J A S O** N D

SIMILAR SPECIES

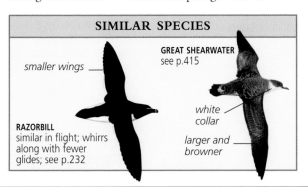

smaller wings

GREAT SHEARWATER
see p.415

RAZORBILL
similar in flight; whirrs along with fewer glides; see p.232

white collar

larger and browner

Length **30–38cm (12–15in)**	Wingspan **76–82cm (30–32in)**	Weight **350–450g (13–16oz)**
Social **Flocks**	Lifespan **25–30 years**	Status **Localized†**

Order **Procellariiformes**	Family **Hydrobatidae**	Species *Hydrobates pelagicus*

Storm Petrel

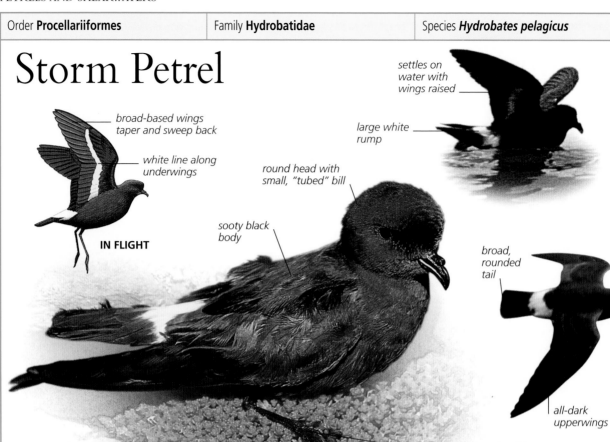

broad-based wings taper and sweep back

white line along underwings

IN FLIGHT

settles on water with wings raised

large white rump

round head with small, "tubed" bill

sooty black body

broad, rounded tail

all-dark upperwings

short legs (unable to stand)

FLIGHT: constant, easy, relaxed wingbeats, rolling from side to side or turning and dipping to feed.

It is quite remarkable that such tiny, delicate creatures as Storm Petrels spend months on end far out at sea, surviving the most difficult weather. They return to islands, more rarely headlands, to breed, coming to land only at night for fear of predation by gulls and skuas. At sea, they fly slightly erratically but quite strongly, low over waves, pattering at times, or swooping like Swallows over the surface, but they are often able to overtake ferries and other ships at surprising speed.

VOICE Soft purring trill with abrupt ending, at nest.
NESTING Hole amongst rocks or in old wall, or in small burrow; 1 egg; 1 brood; April–July.
FEEDING Picks up tiny pieces of offal, fish oil, and marine invertebrates from surface of sea in flight.

HOMING IN ON FOOD
Petrels fly very low, scattered over vast areas of open sea. Their sharp sense of smell locates oily food and small flocks gather to feed.

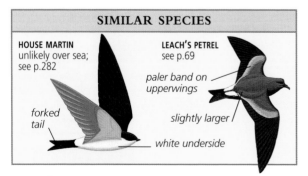

SIMILAR SPECIES

HOUSE MARTIN unlikely over sea; see p.282

forked tail

LEACH'S PETREL see p.69

paler band on upperwings

slightly larger

white underside

OCCURRENCE
Most breed in NW Europe but colonies also in Mediterranean; otherwise, lives out at sea. Difficult to see from most coasts but can be frequent in S Ireland just offshore; elsewhere, not so frequent as Leach's Petrel, even during storms.

Seen in the UK
J F M **A M J J A S O** N D

Length **14–17cm (5½–6½in)**	Wingspan **36–39cm (14–15½in)**	Weight **23–29g (¹³⁄₁₆–1¹⁄₁₆oz)**
Social **Small flocks**	Lifespan **Up to 20 years**	Status **Localized†**

| Order **Procellariiformes** | Family **Hydrobatidae** | Species ***Oceanodroma leucorhoa*** |

Leach's Petrel

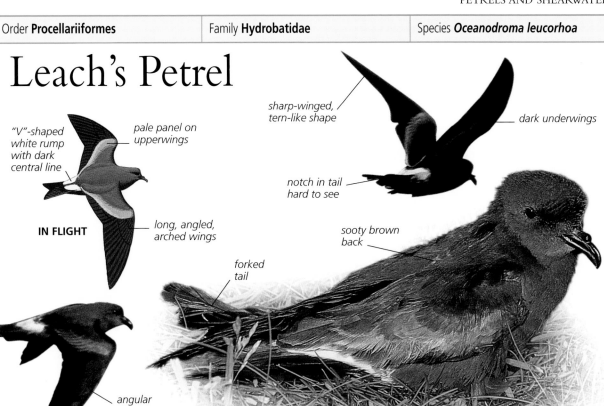

"V"-shaped white rump with dark central line

pale panel on upperwings

sharp-winged, tern-like shape

dark underwings

notch in tail hard to see

IN FLIGHT

long, angled, arched wings

sooty brown back

forked tail

angular shape

FLIGHT: quick, strong, tern-like, with strong beats, erratic twists, turns, leaps, and changes of speed.

Slightly larger than the Storm Petrel, Leach's Petrel is still a tiny bird to live out at sea all its life, buffeted by Atlantic gales. Like other petrels and shearwaters, it ventures to land only to breed and only at night (unless it is deep inside its burrow), but may be seen offshore from suitable headlands in autumn gales. It may then also be driven inland, appearing over reservoirs rather than being stranded in unlikely places like some other storm-driven birds.

VOICE Rattling, chattering coo at nest.
NESTING Burrow or cavity among rocks; one bird incubates, while other is at sea, returning only at night; 1 egg; 1 brood; April–July.
FEEDING Picks up tiny, floating pieces of offal, fish oil, jellyfish, and marine invertebrates, from surface in flight.

BLOWN ONTO BEACHES
Tired by their efforts to fly out of coastal bays against a gale, Leach's Petrels may briefly patter across the tideline or even over a beach.

SIMILAR SPECIES

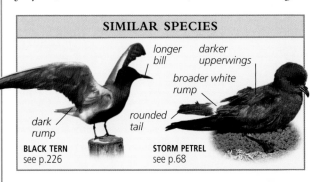

longer bill

darker upperwings

broader white rump

dark rump

rounded tail

BLACK TERN
see p.226

STORM PETREL
see p.68

OCCURRENCE
Breeds on few islands in NW Europe; more widespread in autumn in North Atlantic, but scarce in North Sea. Appears during gales off NW England and N Wales and is regular but rare inland in autumn gales.

| Seen in the UK |
| J F M A M J J A S O N D |

| Length **18–21cm (7–8½in)** | Wingspan **43–48cm (17–19in)** | Weight **40–50g (1⁷⁄₁₆–1¾oz)** |
| Social **Small flocks** | Lifespan **Up to 24 years** | Status **Localized†** |

Families **Sulidae, Phalacrocoracidae, Pelicanidae**

GANNETS, CORMORANTS, AND PELICANS

At first sight a mixed bunch, this group of water birds shares several characteristics, including a long inner wing with an obvious, backward-pointed "elbow" joint near the body, and broad webbing across all four toes (wildfowl have webs only between the front three). They all feed on fish, some being restricted to the sea, others coming inland too.

GANNETS

These are magnificent plunge-divers, seeing fish from high up and diving headlong, or fishing from a lower altitude if the fish are close to the surface, spearing into the water at an angle. They are often seen from the coast but spend winter well out at sea. They breed in a small number of large colonies, mostly on offshore islands. Gannets are among the most spectacular sights in European birdwatching.

CORMORANTS

The Cormorant is a generalist, able to feed in the open sea, in quiet estuaries, and in lakes or rivers. It nests in trees, as well as on cliffs. The Shag nests only on cliffs and feeds in saltwater. The Pygmy Cormorant is a freshwater bird in summer, nesting in marshes, but may move to the coast at other times.

CORMORANT
The big white thigh patch shows this Cormorant to be in breeding plumage.

PELICANS

Familiar, huge, ponderous birds on the water, known for the remarkable "pouch" beneath the bill, pelicans are brilliant fliers, often in beautifully coordinated lines, V-shaped flocks, or swirling packs. Among the world's biggest flying birds, they are always impressive.

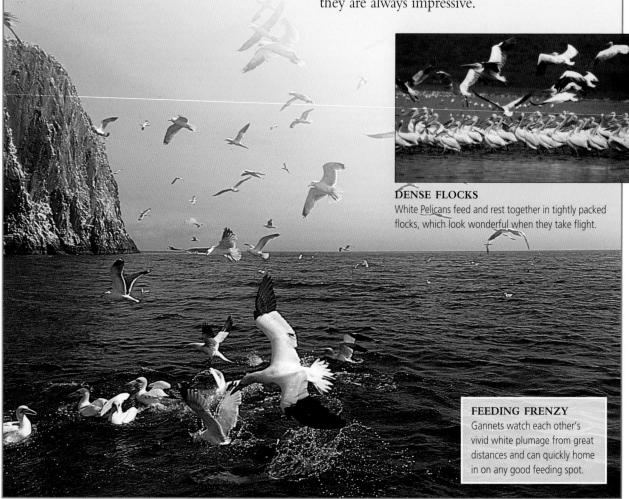

DENSE FLOCKS
White Pelicans feed and rest together in tightly packed flocks, which look wonderful when they take flight.

FEEDING FRENZY
Gannets watch each other's vivid white plumage from great distances and can quickly home in on any good feeding spot.

Order **Pelecaniformes**	Family **Sulidae**	Species ***Morus bassanus***

Gannet

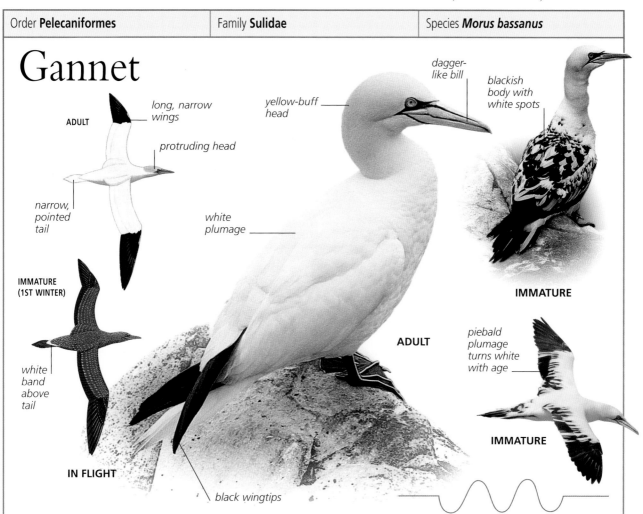

ADULT

long, narrow wings

protruding head

narrow, pointed tail

IMMATURE (1ST WINTER)

white band above tail

IN FLIGHT

black wingtips

yellow-buff head

dagger-like bill

blackish body with white spots

white plumage

ADULT

IMMATURE

piebald plumage turns white with age

IMMATURE

The biggest of the European seabirds, related to the even larger pelicans (see p.416), the Gannet is typically seen as a brilliant white bird offshore, circling and diving for fish, or flying singly or in groups. It is highly social at its nesting colonies and loosely so at sea. The Gannet's forward-facing eyes and cushioned head and neck equip it to pinpoint fast-moving fish and dive headlong to catch them.

VOICE Regular, rhythmic, throaty chorus at nest; silent at sea.

NESTING Pile of seaweed and debris on broad ledge high above sea; 1 egg; 1 brood; April–July.

FEEDING Catches fish such as mackerel and pollack underwater in shallow and sloping dive from air, or vertical dives from greater height.

FLIGHT: in strong winds, banks and veers like a giant shearwater; in light winds, steady, powerful flight with regular beats of straight wings.

DENSE COLONIES
Gannet colonies, usually along cliff ledges and steep slopes, are dense and often very large.

SIMILAR SPECIES

square tail

shorter bill

ARCTIC SKUA dark form, similar to juvenile in flight; see p.206

much smaller

GREAT BLACK-BACKED GULL immature, similar to immature in flight; see p.212

OCCURRENCE
Forms colonies on rocky islands north from NW France, occupying them from early spring until late autumn. Widespread in Atlantic and North Sea while feeding and migrating, some entering W Mediterranean; scarce in winter.

Seen in the UK
J F M A M J J A S O N D

Length **85–89cm (34–35in)**	Wingspan **1.65–1.8m (5½–6ft)**	Weight **2.8–3.2kg (6¼–7lb)**
Social **Flocks**	Lifespan **16–20 years**	Status **Localized**

Order **Pelecaniformes**	Family **Phalacrocoracidae**	Species ***Phalacrocorax carbo***

Cormorant

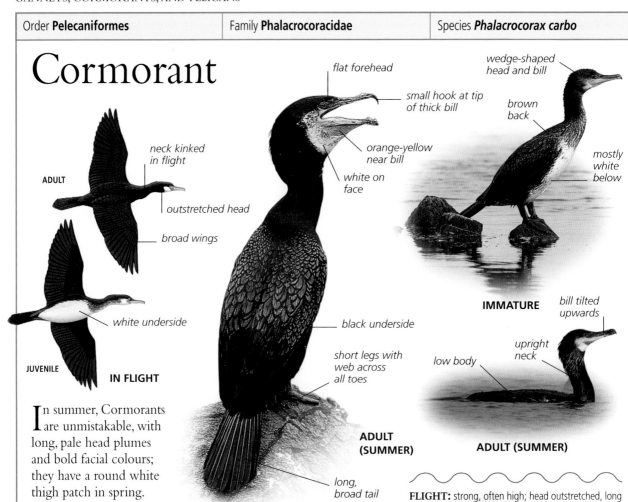

flat forehead

small hook at tip of thick bill

orange-yellow near bill

white on face

wedge-shaped head and bill

brown back

mostly white below

IMMATURE

ADULT

neck kinked in flight

outstretched head

broad wings

JUVENILE

white underside

IN FLIGHT

black underside

short legs with web across all toes

long, broad tail

ADULT (SUMMER)

bill tilted upwards

upright neck

low body

ADULT (SUMMER)

FLIGHT: strong, often high; head outstretched, long tail, rather broad wings with regular beats; long glides.

In summer, Cormorants are unmistakable, with long, pale head plumes and bold facial colours; they have a round white thigh patch in spring. They are duller in winter, but retain a distinct character, typified by their habit of perching with half-open wings, or swimming with back almost awash, neck upright, and bill angled upwards. Equally at home on salt- or fresh water, Cormorants are widespread and familiar in much of Europe.
VOICE Growling and cackling at nests and communal roosts, otherwise a quiet bird.
NESTING Bulky nest of sticks in tree and on cliff ledge, with white splashings beneath; 3 or 4 eggs; 1 brood; April–May.
FEEDING Catches fish in long underwater dive from surface; brings larger ones to surface before swallowing them.

SUBSPECIES

bold white head plumes in spring

P. c. sinensis
(mainland Europe, E England)

PERCHING
Cormorants have a distinctive perching stance, with half-open wings, upright neck, and bill angled upwards.

SIMILAR SPECIES

dagger-like bill

SHAG
see p.73

slim bill

shorter neck

slightly smaller

GREAT NORTHERN DIVER winter, similar to immature; see p.58

OCCURRENCE
Breeds widely but very locally through Europe. Prefers sheltered estuaries and bays at coast but breeds on cliffs; inland, on reservoirs, flooded pits, and even small pools. Often found in and around harbours and marinas.

Seen in the UK

J F M A M J J A S O N D

Length **80–100cm (32–39in)**	Wingspan **1.3–1.6m (4¼–5¼ft)**	Weight **2–2.5kg (4½–5½lb)**
Social **Flocks**	Lifespan **15–20 years**	Status **Secure**

Order **Pelecaniformes**	Family **Phalacrocoracidae**	Species *Phalacrocorax aristotelis*

Shag

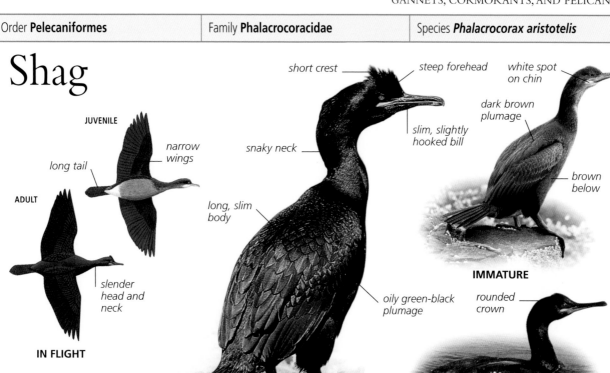

JUVENILE

narrow wings

long tail

ADULT

slender head and neck

IN FLIGHT

short crest — steep forehead — white spot on chin

snaky neck

dark brown plumage

slim, slightly hooked bill

long, slim body

brown below

oily green-black plumage

IMMATURE

rounded crown

ADULT (SUMMER)

ADULT (WINTER)

Although sometimes solitary, Shags tend to breed in sizeable groups and sometimes feed in tight flocks of hundreds where they are common. They prefer the fast tide races and rough water under rocks and cliffs, and swim in groups braving the most dangerous-looking conditions; they are rare inland. The Shag has an obvious close relationship with the Cormorant and the two birds can be difficult to tell apart, but a certain slim snakiness gives the Shag a different character.

VOICE Coarse, frenzied rattling at nests; silent at sea.
NESTING Heap of grass, sticks, and seaweed on broad cliff ledge or inside cave; 3 or 4 eggs; 1 brood; May.
FEEDING Catches fish underwater, after dive from surface, often with quick, arching forward leap.

FLIGHT: direct with quick beats of narrow wings; usually keeps very low over sea, even where Cormorants fly high.

SUBSPECIES

P. a. desmaresti juvenile (Mediterranean)

much whiter below

STANDING
The Shag stands with wings outstretched like the Cormorant, possibly an aid to digestion after a heavy meal of fish.

SIMILAR SPECIES

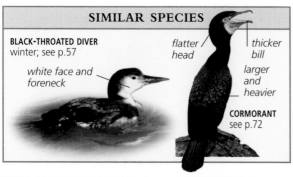

BLACK-THROATED DIVER winter; see p.57

white face and foreneck

flatter head

thicker bill

larger and heavier

CORMORANT see p.72

OCCURRENCE
Widespread on European coasts although scarcer in Mediterranean. Breeds on coastal cliffs and feeds off rocky coasts and islands. Rather scarce around harbours and estuaries and generally rare inland.

Seen in the UK
J F M A M J J A S O N D

Length **65–80cm (26–32in)**	Wingspan **90–105cm (35–41in)**	Weight **1.75–2.25kg (3¾–5lb)**
Social **Large flocks**	Lifespan **Up to 15 years**	Status **Secure**

Familiy **Ardeidae**

BITTERNS AND HERONS

EUROPEAN HERONS AND bitterns are waterside birds, apart from the Cattle Egret, but elsewhere in the world many feed in drier places. They share characteristics such as long legs, dagger-like bills, a kinked neck (thicker in bitterns) that gives them a sudden, fast lunge to grasp prey, and binocular vision that allows them to pinpoint prey with precision. They are mostly ground-living birds, but fly capably.

HERONS

The larger herons are long-necked and elegant, using skill and patience when searching for prey. Although primarily fish-eaters, they eat almost anything they can catch. Egrets are generally smaller (although the Great White Egret is very big) and mostly white. Some have long, elegant plumes in the breeding season. Herons and egrets develop bright bill and leg colours for short periods in spring and the facial skin may even "blush" brightly during courtship.

Most are social, breeding in colonies, but often fishing alone. The Cattle Egret feeds around live-stock and on rubbish tips, as well as on marshes, and flies to roost each evening in spectacular, flickering white flocks.

BITTERNS

Two groups are widespread worldwide, each represented by one species in Europe. The Bittern is large, heavy-bodied, and closely patterned with black on sandy buff. The Little Bittern is small, sexually dimorphic, with a large, pale, oval patch on each otherwise blackish wing. Both are shy and elusive.

REEDBED SKULKER
Bitterns need water within reeds so that they can ambush unsuspecting eels and other fish without coming out into the open.

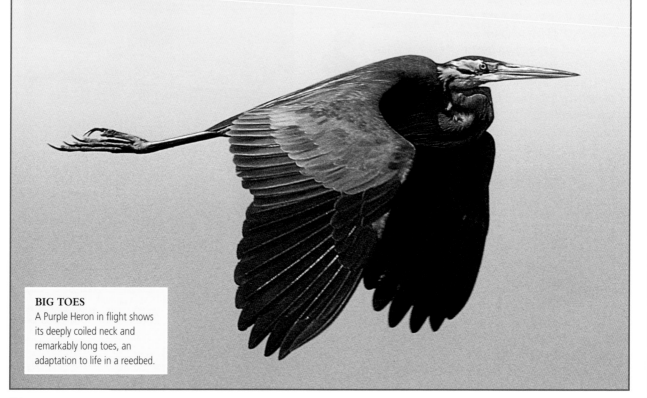

BIG TOES
A Purple Heron in flight shows its deeply coiled neck and remarkably long toes, an adaptation to life in a reedbed.

Order **Ciconiiformes**	Family **Ardeidae**	Species ***Botaurus stellaris***

Bittern 🔊 4

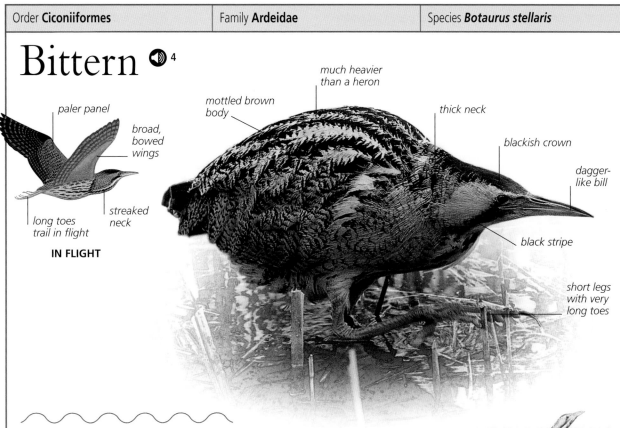

much heavier
than a heron

mottled brown
body

thick neck

blackish crown

dagger-like bill

black stripe

short legs
with very
long toes

paler panel

broad,
bowed
wings

long toes
trail in flight

streaked
neck

IN FLIGHT

FLIGHT: heavy, low, slow, somewhat unsteady;
on bowed, rounded wings, legs trailing.

Few birds are so restricted to a single
habitat as the Bittern is to wet
reedbeds. Even drier reedbeds are of no
use to it: it must have deeper water, so
that it can find fish in the shelter of the
reeds, at the edge of secret pools and
ditches. To maintain suitable conditions,
in a habitat that naturally dries out over
time, requires a great deal of expensive
management work: Bitterns have
gradually been lost from many past sites.
VOICE Deep, hollow, rhythmic boom,
ker-whooomp!
NESTING Broad, damp nest of reed stems well out of
sight in thick reedbed; 4–6 eggs; 1 brood; April–May.
FEEDING Catches fish, especially eels, in sudden grab
of outstretched bill.

FORAGING FOR FOOD
The Bittern mostly feeds at the edge of thick reeds,
moving slowly, with side-to-side shaking of the whole
body. It may be driven into more open areas by
freezing conditions.

STEALTHY FISHER
Bitterns rely on access to fish while
remaining inside thick cover,
typically in wet reedbeds.

OCCURRENCE
Rare bird of larger, wetter
reedbeds, very local and scattered
through Europe. In winter, more
widespread in W Europe, forced
out by frost into smaller patches
of reed or more open water where
it can reach small fish.

Seen in the UK
J F M A M J J A S O N D

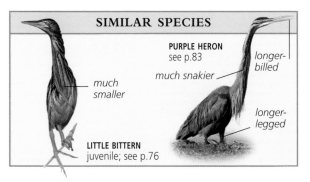

SIMILAR SPECIES

PURPLE HERON
see p.83

longer-billed

much snakier

much smaller

longer-legged

LITTLE BITTERN
juvenile; see p.76

"BITTERNING" STANCE
When alarmed, the Bittern adopts
a camouflage posture with an
upward-pointing bill.

Length **69–81cm (27–32in)**	Wingspan **1.25–1.35m (4–4½ft)**	Weight **0.9–1.1kg (2–2½lb)**
Social **Solitary**	Lifespan **10–12 years**	Status **Vulnerable†**

Order **Ciconiiformes**	Family **Ardeidae**	Species ***Ixobrychus minutus***

Little Bittern

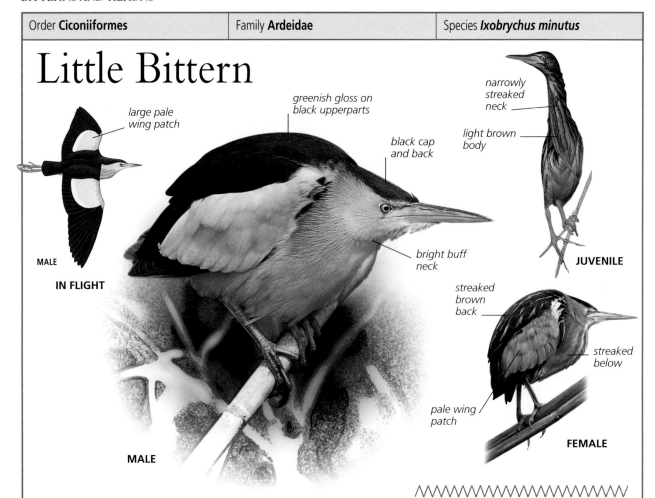

large pale wing patch

MALE

IN FLIGHT

greenish gloss on black upperparts

black cap and back

bright buff neck

MALE

narrowly streaked neck

light brown body

JUVENILE

streaked brown back

streaked below

pale wing patch

FEMALE

FLIGHT: quick, low, fast wingbeats, in sudden flurry; low over reedbed.

This tiny heron is secretive and usually difficult to see, except in brief, fast flights low over marshy areas when the large, oval, pale wing patches catch the eye. Occasionally, one will perch in view near the top of a stem or at the edge of an overhanging willow, and reveal its exquisite pattern. Males, especially, are beautifully and delicately coloured, with very subtle striping on the neck and a slight greenish gloss on the black upperparts.

VOICE Short, nasal call; nocturnal "song" is monotonously repeated single croak.

NESTING Small nest of stems in dense reeds or bush; 2–7 eggs; 1 brood; May–July.

FEEDING Hunts fish, frogs, shrimps, and big aquatic insects, using stealth and patience and sudden forward lunges to catch prey.

AQUATIC HUNTER
Shallow water with dense cover is ideal hunting territory for Little Bitterns, making them hard to see until they fly.

SIMILAR SPECIES

SQUACCO HERON juvenile, similar to juvenile; see p.79
• white wings
• pale head

NIGHT HERON juvenile, similar to juvenile; see p.77

larger, darker, and spotted

OCCURRENCE
Found from April to October in S and C Europe. Occupies reedbeds by rivers and marshes and also much smaller pools and flooded willow thickets. Rare spring migrant in UK.

Seen in the UK
J F M **A M** J J A S O N D

Length **33–38cm (13–15in)**	Wingspan **49–58cm (19½–23in)**	Weight **140–150g (5–5½oz)**
Social **Solitary**	Lifespan **Up to 10 years**	Status **Vulnerable†**

Order **Ciconiiformes**	Family **Ardeidae**	Species *Nycticorax nycticorax*

Night Heron

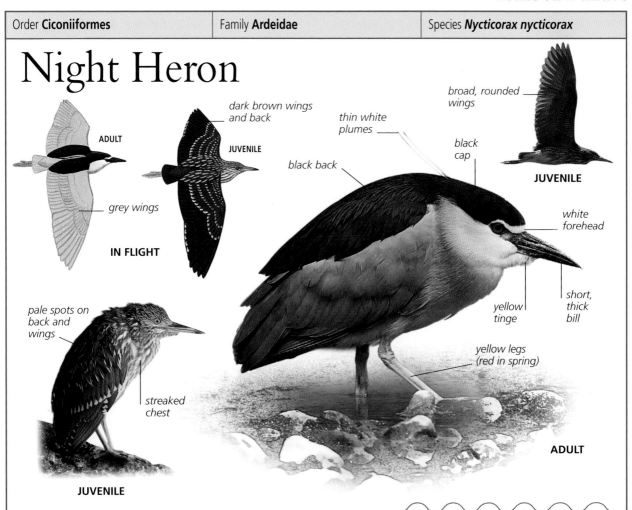

broad, rounded wings

dark brown wings and back

thin white plumes

black cap

ADULT

JUVENILE

black back

white forehead

JUVENILE

grey wings

IN FLIGHT

short, thick bill

yellow tinge

yellow legs (red in spring)

pale spots on back and wings

streaked chest

ADULT

JUVENILE

Night Herons are mostly active at dusk and dawn, but can be seen quite well by day if discovered at a roost. They stand on branches within trees and thickets near water, typically looking like motionless, pale spots from a distance. Once located, usually several are seen, but only when they choose to fly do the real numbers become apparent, as quite sizeable parties sometimes leave the trees. They feed in near-dark conditions, searching for fish, in typical heron style, at the water's edge.

VOICE Deep, low, short, crow-like croak.

NESTING Small stick nest in tree or bush; 3–5 eggs; 1 brood; April–July.

FEEDING Mostly nocturnal, taking small fish and large insects from water's edge.

FLIGHT: steady, direct; deep beats of slightly arched wings; sometimes in groups.

SHALLOW WADER
Night Herons fish at the edge of ponds and rivers, frequently being most active at dusk but fishing all day when they have young to feed.

SIMILAR SPECIES

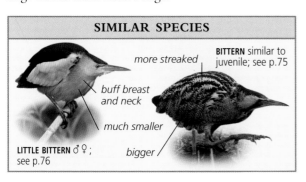

more streaked

BITTERN similar to juvenile; see p.75

buff breast and neck

much smaller

LITTLE BITTERN ♂♀; see p.76

bigger

OCCURRENCE
In waterside habitats, from reedbeds to tall trees by rivers and lakes, mostly from March to October in S and C Europe, but very localized in most areas. May appear farther north in spring; wintering birds may be escapees.

Seen in the UK
J F M A M J J A S O N D

Length **58–65cm (23–26in)**	Wingspan **90–100cm (35–39in)**	Weight **600–800g (21–29oz)**
Social **Roosts and breeds in flocks**	Lifespan **10–15 years**	Status **Declining**

| Order **Ciconiiformes** | Family **Ardeidae** | Species ***Bubulcus ibis*** |

Cattle Egret

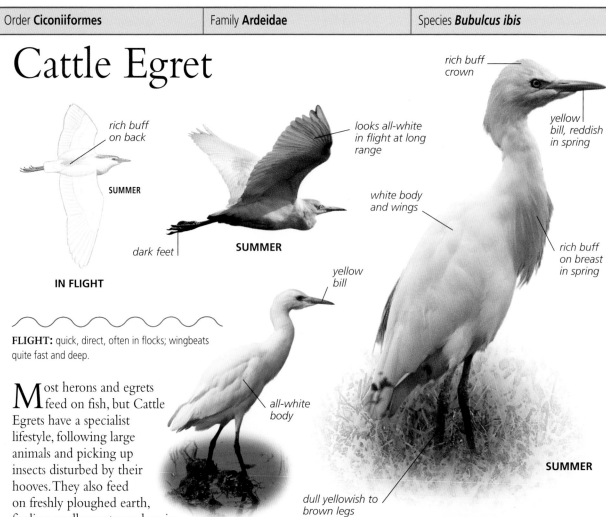

rich buff on back

SUMMER

IN FLIGHT

looks all-white in flight at long range

SUMMER

dark feet

rich buff crown

yellow bill, reddish in spring

white body and wings

rich buff on breast in spring

yellow bill

all-white body

dull yellowish to brown legs

WINTER

SUMMER

FLIGHT: quick, direct, often in flocks; wingbeats quite fast and deep.

Most herons and egrets feed on fish, but Cattle Egrets have a specialist lifestyle, following large animals and picking up insects disturbed by their hooves. They also feed on freshly ploughed earth, finding small prey turned up in the furrows, and forage on refuse tips as well. Towards evening, large flocks fly in distinctive, shapeless flurries of white, gathering to roost in trees (sometimes close to buildings), often in thousands.

VOICE Occasional short, croaking or creaking notes.

NESTING Shallow nest of sticks and reeds in tree; 4 or 5 eggs; 1 brood; April–June.

FEEDING Catches insects disturbed by cattle, sheep, and goats; also eats frogs, reptiles, and mice.

CATTLE FOLLOWER
Cattle Egrets typically follow cattle in Europe; in Africa, they gather around great herds of antelopes, buffaloes, and elephants.

SPARKLING WHITE
Flocks in flight present a flickering, tight-packed effect, often looking much whiter than they may appear on the ground.

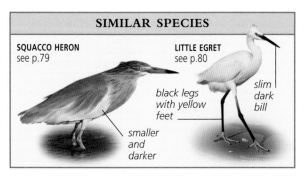

SIMILAR SPECIES

SQUACCO HERON
see p.79

LITTLE EGRET
see p.80

black legs with yellow feet

slim dark bill

smaller and darker

OCCURRENCE
Confined largely to S Spain and Portugal and extreme S France; rare vagrant farther north. Resident in coastal regions or centred on lakes with thickets in which it roosts. Feeds in fields and at refuse tips, often associated with livestock.

| Seen in the UK |
| J F M A M J J A S O N D |

| Length **45–50cm (18–20in)** | Wingspan **82–95cm (32–37in)** | Weight **300–400g (11–14oz)** |
| Social **Feeds and roosts in flocks** | Lifespan **Up to 10 years** | Status **Secure** |

| Order **Ciconiiformes** | Family **Ardeidae** | Species ***Ardeola ralloides*** |

Squacco Heron

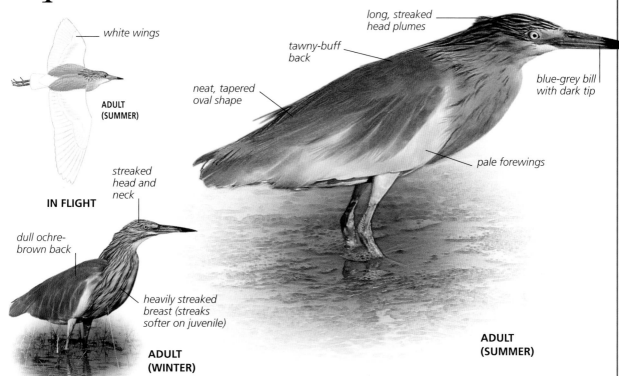

white wings

ADULT (SUMMER)

IN FLIGHT

long, streaked head plumes

tawny-buff back

neat, tapered oval shape

blue-grey bill with dark tip

pale forewings

streaked head and neck

dull ochre-brown back

heavily streaked breast (streaks softer on juvenile)

ADULT (WINTER)

ADULT (SUMMER)

In flight, the Squacco Heron is obvious because its pure white wings catch the eye at any angle. On the ground, however, it is an inconspicuous bird, the white all but hidden, the head withdrawn into squat, rounded shoulders. Typically found in overgrown ditches or streams, or on floating weeds in a larger river or marsh, it is easily overlooked unless disturbed. Very much a southern bird in Europe, it is found, very rarely, as a vagrant farther north.

VOICE Hoarse, nasal croaking call, but mostly silent.

NESTING Small nest of grass and reeds, low down in reeds; 4–6 eggs; 1 brood; April–June.

FEEDING Stands on floating weeds or in thick cover, hunting fish, frogs, and insects.

FLIGHT: low, quite quick, with fast beats of slightly arched wings; feet trail beyond tail.

WING STRETCH
This heron stands with an exaggerated forward neck stretch and open wings after preening.

WHITE IN FLIGHT
The bright white wings of the Squacco Heron are obvious only in flight, low over a marsh.

SIMILAR SPECIES

LITTLE BITTERN ♂♀; see p.76

darker back

black wingtips

CATTLE EGRET see p.78

larger and much whiter

OCCURRENCE
Mostly in Mediterranean region in summer, in all kinds of freshwater swamps, from weedy riversides to reedbeds and extensive floods and marshes. Only rare spring vagrant farther north.

Seen in the UK
| J | F | M | A | M | J | J | A | S | O | N | D |

| Length **40–49cm (16–19½in)** | Wingspan **71–86 cm (28–34in)** | Weight **230–350g (8–13oz)** |
| Social **Loose flocks** | Lifespan **5–10 years** | Status **Vulnerable** |

Order **Ciconiiformes**	Family **Ardeidae**	Species ***Egretta garzetta***

Little Egret

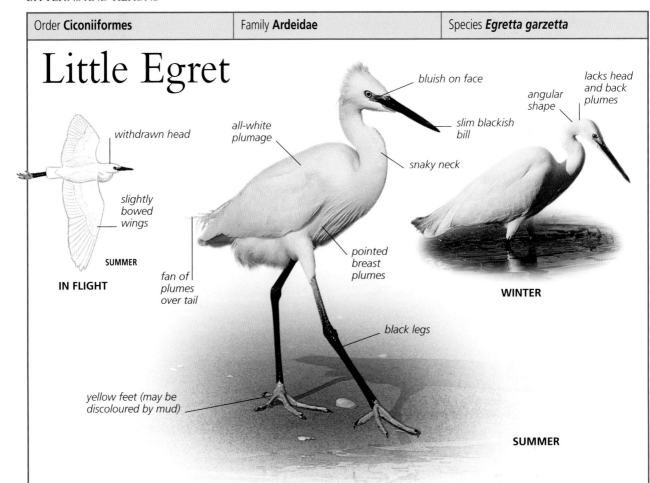

withdrawn head

slightly bowed wings

SUMMER

IN FLIGHT

bluish on face

slim blackish bill

all-white plumage

snaky neck

fan of plumes over tail

pointed breast plumes

black legs

yellow feet (may be discoloured by mud)

SUMMER

angular shape

lacks head and back plumes

WINTER

Steadily spreading northwards in western Europe, the Little Egret is a sparkling white heron of marshes, poolsides, and coasts. It is often lively, dashing about muddy creeks or even over seaweed-covered rocks in a frenzied fashion; however, like other herons, it spends much time standing still or wading in shallows, looking for prey. Little Egrets are often found in small, loose feeding flocks; they tend to form evening roosts in traditional spots, and these attract birds from far afield.

VOICE Generally silent.

NESTING Stick nest in tree, often mixed with those of other heron-like species; 3 or 4 eggs; 1 brood; April–July.

FEEDING Catches small fish, frogs, snails, and other wetland animals; may run around with flapping wings, or move more stealthily.

FLIGHT: direct, quick, with head withdrawn, legs trailing, wings only slightly bowed.

SOCIAL FEEDING
In areas where Little Egrets are common, small groups of these birds often feed together, or spread more loosely along a shore.

OCCURRENCE
Found in S Europe, north to S Great Britain, on watersides from rocky coasts to reedy lakes, but especially open, muddy or sandy shores. Breeds in treetop colonies, often with other herons and egrets.

Seen in the UK
J F M A M J J A S O N D

SIMILAR SPECIES

GREAT WHITE EGRET see p.81

much bigger

longer legs with dark feet

CATTLE EGRET see p.78

stockier

shorter, paler bill

Length **55–65cm (22–26in)**	Wingspan **88–106cm (35–42in)**	Weight **400–600g (14–21oz)**
Social **Small flocks**	Lifespan **Up to 10 years**	Status **Secure**

Order **Ciconiiformes**	Family **Ardeidae**	Species *Egretta alba*

Great White Egret

arched wings

all-white plumage (long back plumes in summer)

very long neck

yellow bill, often dark at tip

SUMMER

IN FLIGHT

yellowish or blackish legs with dark feet

WINTER

When it stands next to a Grey Heron, the actual size of the Great White Egret is apparent: it is truly a giant egret, as tall as the heron, if not standing a little higher. Slim, angular, but elegant, this stunningly white bird is easily seen at long range. It develops long back plumes in the breeding season, at which time the bill turns blackish. The Great White Egret often feeds in grassy, relatively dry, places, leaning forward, sometimes with a fast, shimmering tremor through the whole body as it homes in on its prey.

WINTER

FLIGHT: slow, direct, on arched wings; heavier, slower than Little Egret.

VOICE Mostly silent.
NESTING Shallow platform of sticks in tree; 2–5 eggs; 1 brood; April–July.
FEEDING Catches fish, amphibians, and small mammals in wet places.

NESTING ON TREES
Great White Egrets often perch on tall trees overlooking a marsh. They are sociable in summer, nesting in colonies in trees.

SIMILAR SPECIES

LITTLE EGRET
see p.80

much smaller

yellow feet

COURTSHIP DISPLAY
In spring, the Great White Egret spreads its long body plumes in a spectacular courtship display at the nest.

OCCURRENCE
Summer visitor, migrant, or winter visitor within SE Europe, rare at all times in W Europe. In reedbeds and extensive floods, or beside big, more open lakes, or on tall trees near marshes.

Seen in the UK
J F M A M J J A S O N D

Length **85–100cm (34–39in)**	Wingspan **1.45–1.7m (4¾–5½ft)**	Weight **1–1.5kg (2¼–3¼lb)**
Social **Small flocks**	Lifespan **10–15 years**	Status **Secure**

| Order **Ciconiiformes** | Family **Ardeidae** | Species *Ardea cinerea* |

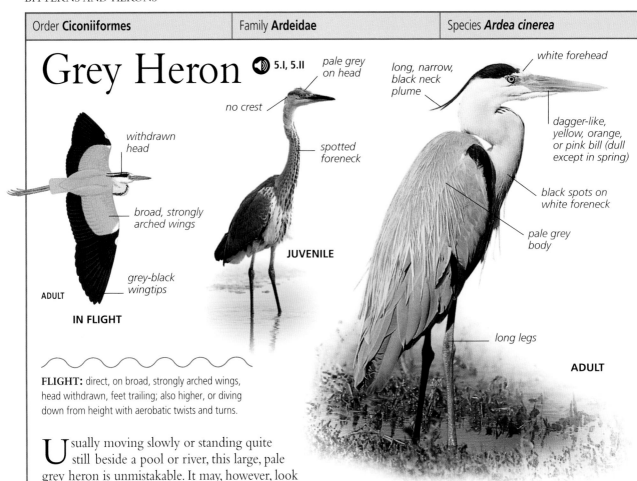

Grey Heron 🔊 5.I, 5.II

pale grey on head

no crest

spotted foreneck

JUVENILE

long, narrow, black neck plume

white forehead

dagger-like, yellow, orange, or pink bill (dull except in spring)

black spots on white foreneck

pale grey body

long legs

ADULT

withdrawn head

broad, strongly arched wings

grey-black wingtips

ADULT

IN FLIGHT

FLIGHT: direct, on broad, strongly arched wings, head withdrawn, feet trailing; also higher, or diving down from height with aerobatic twists and turns.

Usually moving slowly or standing quite still beside a pool or river, this large, pale grey heron is unmistakable. It may, however, look tall and slim with a long, erect neck, or round-shouldered and hunched with its head and neck withdrawn into the shoulders; it may also stand high in a treetop, or fly with surprising agility high overhead. It is typically shy, but in towns becomes remarkably bold and many now visit garden fish ponds on early-morning raids.
VOICE Short, harsh *fraink*; rattling and croaking sounds at nest.
NESTING Large nest of thick sticks in treetop (or bush where no tree is available); 4 or 5 eggs; 1 brood; January–May.
FEEDING Catches fish, frogs, rats, and other prey in its bill, usually after long, patient stalk before sudden strike.

PERCHING
The Grey Heron may sometimes be found perched on a treetop, usually in a hunched posture, with its head and neck drawn into the shoulders.

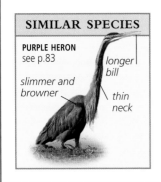

SIMILAR SPECIES

PURPLE HERON see p.83

slimmer and browner

longer bill

thin neck

SLOW, SILENT MOVER
This heron strides silently through shallows or long vegetation. It stands still for long spells.

OCCURRENCE
Frequents both freshwater and saltwater habitats, from salt marsh and rocky coasts to floods and fish ponds almost throughout Europe. Some regularly visit garden ponds or town lakes, especially in winter when much habitat is frozen.

Seen in the UK
J F M A M J J A S O N D

| Length **90–98cm (35–39in)** | Wingspan **1.75–1.95m (5¾–6½ft)** | Weight **1.6–2kg (3½–4½lb)** |
| Social **Solitary/Small flocks** | Lifespan **Up to 25 years** | Status **Secure** |

Order **Ciconiiformes**	Family **Ardeidae**	Species ***Ardea purpurea***

Purple Heron

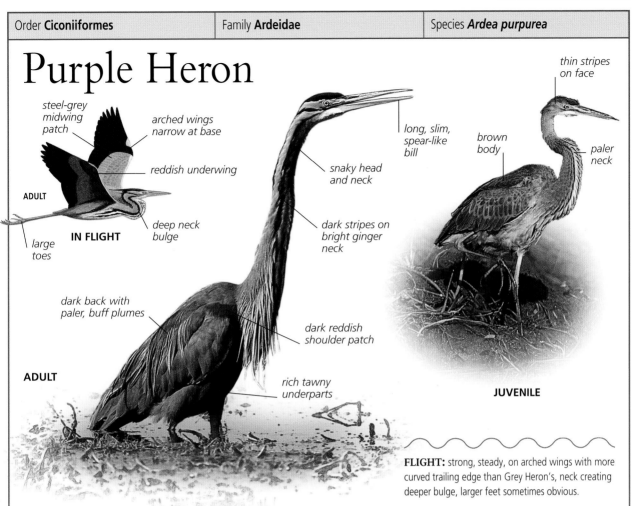

steel-grey midwing patch

arched wings narrow at base

reddish underwing

ADULT

IN FLIGHT

deep neck bulge

large toes

thin stripes on face

long, slim, spear-like bill

snaky head and neck

brown body

paler neck

dark stripes on bright ginger neck

dark back with paler, buff plumes

dark reddish shoulder patch

ADULT

rich tawny underparts

JUVENILE

FLIGHT: strong, steady, on arched wings with more curved trailing edge than Grey Heron's, neck creating deeper bulge, larger feet sometimes obvious.

Much more of a reedbed bird than the Grey Heron, the Purple Heron is consequently more difficult to see unless it flies over the reeds or chooses to feed at the edge of a reedy pool. It breeds in small groups, but is generally a less social bird than most herons. It has often been predicted that the Purple Heron will spread north and breed in the UK, but this has so far failed to develop: it remains a rather rare visitor north of its usual range.

VOICE Short, simple, harsh *krekk*.

NESTING Large pile of reed stems and other vegetation, often in reeds, sometimes in trees; 4 or 5 eggs; 1 brood; February–June.

FEEDING Catches small fish, frogs, and aquatic invertebrates in its long, slender bill.

FISHING

A secretive bird, the Purple Heron typically waits patiently at the water's edge or strides through reeds in search of prey.

SIMILAR SPECIES

thick neck

GREY HERON see p.82

BITTERN see p.75

stouter bill

stockier and paler

wider wings

much stockier

OCCURRENCE

Generally more southerly bird than Grey Heron, absent from N Europe. Typically in reedy marshes, tall sedge beds, and wet meadows. Migrants appear north of breeding range in reedbeds and overgrown flooded areas.

Seen in the UK
J F M A M J J A S O N D

Length **70–90cm (28–35in)**	Wingspan **1.1–1.45m (3½–4¾ft)**	Weight **1–1.5kg (2¼–3¼lb)**
Social **Solitary**	Lifespan **Up to 23 years**	Status **Vulnerable**

Families **Ciconiidae, Threskiornithidae**

STORKS

O F THE TWO SPECIES OF STORK in Europe, one species, the White Stork, is able to live close to people, exploiting buildings and electricity pylons as nesting places and feeding extensively on refuse tips. It is, however, under pressure from the destruction of freshwater habitats and the spread of intensive agriculture. The Black Stork is, in contrast, a forest bird and often nests on remote cliffs.

Both are migrants, spending the winter far south in Africa. White Storks migrate in huge flocks, creating exciting birdwatching as they cross the Mediterranean at the narrowest point, as they must glide and soar to save energy and can only gain the benefit of rising air over land. Black Storks may migrate alone or in smaller groups, but can be seen with other large migrants, such as eagles and kites, over the sea, or through mountain passes. They may be forced down temporarily by poor weather.

FROG FINDER
The Black Stork feeds on all kinds of small creatures, such as frogs, found in shallow water or on wet meadows.

Family **Phoenicopteridae**

FLAMINGOS

T HIS FAMILY OF EXTRAORDINARY birds includes very few species, scattered world-wide, and only one, the Greater Flamingo, is found in Europe. It breeds in just a few large colonies, including one at the Camargue in southern France and one in southern Spain, but is regularly seen in sizeable flocks at a number of other shallow, salty lagoons around the Mediterranean, its only habitat type.

Nesting colonies are on very low islands, each nest being built up from the mud: nests are vulnerable to flooding, or to falls in water level that allow predators to reach the colony. The flamingos may rear very few young for several years but periodically have a "boom" year that maintains their numbers. Young birds congregate in dense "crèches" and later tend to gather around the outer fringes of large flocks.

SPECTACULAR DISPLAY
Greater Flamingos gather together and raise their heads high in synchronized "marching" displays.

| Order **Ciconiiformes** | Family **Ciconiidae** | Species *Ciconia ciconia* |

White Stork

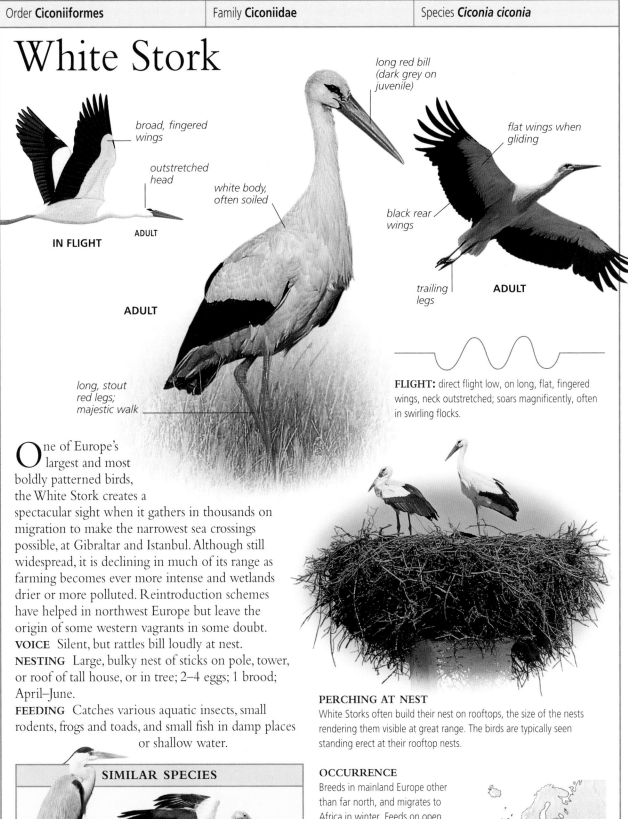

IN FLIGHT

broad, fingered wings

outstretched head

ADULT

long red bill (dark grey on juvenile)

white body, often soiled

ADULT

flat wings when gliding

black rear wings

trailing legs

ADULT

long, stout red legs; majestic walk

FLIGHT: direct flight low, on long, flat, fingered wings, neck outstretched; soars magnificently, often in swirling flocks.

One of Europe's largest and most boldly patterned birds, the White Stork creates a spectacular sight when it gathers in thousands on migration to make the narrowest sea crossings possible, at Gibraltar and Istanbul. Although still widespread, it is declining in much of its range as farming becomes ever more intense and wetlands drier or more polluted. Reintroduction schemes have helped in northwest Europe but leave the origin of some western vagrants in some doubt.

VOICE Silent, but rattles bill loudly at nest.

NESTING Large, bulky nest of sticks on pole, tower, or roof of tall house, or in tree; 2–4 eggs; 1 brood; April–June.

FEEDING Catches various aquatic insects, small rodents, frogs and toads, and small fish in damp places or shallow water.

PERCHING AT NEST
White Storks often build their nest on rooftops, the size of the nests rendering them visible at great range. The birds are typically seen standing erect at their rooftop nests.

SIMILAR SPECIES

grey (black and white in strong sun)

GREY HERON bowed wings in flight; see p.82

neck withdrawn in flight

WHITE PELICAN short legs; see p.416

OCCURRENCE
Breeds in mainland Europe other than far north, and migrates to Africa in winter. Feeds on open land near marshes, rivers, and lakes, including edges of towns and villages where it often nests on high perches.

| Seen in the UK |
| J F M A M J J A S O N D |

| Length **0.95–1.1m (3–3½ft)** | Wingspan **1.8–2.18m (6–7¼ft)** | Weight **2.5–4.5kg (5½–10lb)** |
| Social **Migrates in flocks** | Lifespan **Up to 25 years** | Status **Vulnerable** |

Order **Ciconiiformes**	Family **Ciconiidae**	Species **Ciconia nigra**

Black Stork

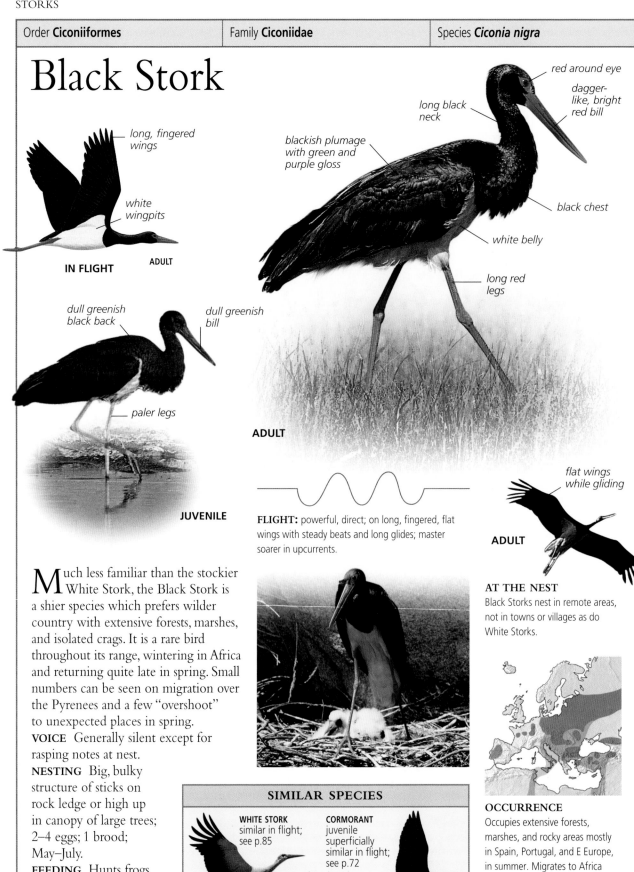

long, fingered wings

white wingpits

IN FLIGHT

ADULT

red around eye

dagger-like, bright red bill

long black neck

blackish plumage with green and purple gloss

black chest

white belly

long red legs

ADULT

dull greenish black back

dull greenish bill

paler legs

JUVENILE

FLIGHT: powerful, direct; on long, fingered, flat wings with steady beats and long glides; master soarer in upcurrents.

flat wings while gliding

ADULT

AT THE NEST
Black Storks nest in remote areas, not in towns or villages as do White Storks.

Much less familiar than the stockier White Stork, the Black Stork is a shier species which prefers wilder country with extensive forests, marshes, and isolated crags. It is a rare bird throughout its range, wintering in Africa and returning quite late in spring. Small numbers can be seen on migration over the Pyrenees and a few "overshoot" to unexpected places in spring.
VOICE Generally silent except for rasping notes at nest.
NESTING Big, bulky structure of sticks on rock ledge or high up in canopy of large trees; 2–4 eggs; 1 brood; May–July.
FEEDING Hunts frogs, newts, toads, and aquatic insects in wet places, and picks them up in its long, slim bill.

SIMILAR SPECIES

WHITE STORK similar in flight; see p.85

CORMORANT juvenile superficially similar in flight; see p.72

white head and breast

long tail

white chest

OCCURRENCE
Occupies extensive forests, marshes, and rocky areas mostly in Spain, Portugal, and E Europe, in summer. Migrates to Africa each autumn and very few are seen outside regular range.

Seen in the UK
J F M A M J J A S O N D

Length **90–105cm (35–41in)**	Wingspan **1.1–1.45m (3½–4¾ft)**	Weight **2.5–3kg (5½–6½lb)**
Social **Small flocks**	Lifespan **Up to 20 years**	Status **Rare**

| Order **Ciconiiformes** | Family **Threskiornithidae** | Species *Platalea leucorodia* |

Spoonbill

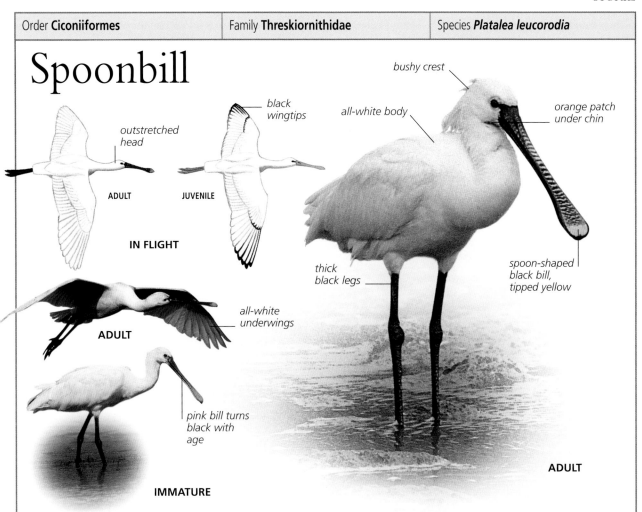

bushy crest

all-white body

orange patch under chin

outstretched head

black wingtips

ADULT **JUVENILE**

IN FLIGHT

spoon-shaped black bill, tipped yellow

thick black legs

all-white underwings

ADULT

pink bill turns black with age

IMMATURE

ADULT

Equipped with a flattened, broad-tipped bill, the Spoonbill is heron-like, but as white as an egret. It is a bird of marshes and lakes with extensive shallow water, but in winter it may also be found on coastal estuaries, striding through the shallows with its rather human-like walk. This, and its tall, upstanding presence, make it an unmistakable bird in Europe.

VOICE Silent.

NESTING Shallow platform of sticks and reed stems in reeds or tree; in colonies, rarely mixed with other species; 3 or 4 eggs; 1 brood; April–July.

FEEDING Holds bill slightly open, partially submerged, and sweeps it through water from side to side, to catch fish, molluscs, and crustaceans.

FLIGHT: strong, direct, swan-like, with head outstretched; regular wingbeats.

FLYING FLOCK
Lines and chevrons of Spoonbills tend to coordinate short glides between spells of steady wingbeats.

SIDEWAYS SWEEP
The Spoonbill wades slowly forwards in shallow water, sweeping its partly open bill sideways until it detects food; the bill is then snapped shut on the prey.

SIMILAR SPECIES

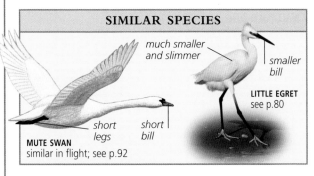

much smaller and slimmer

smaller bill

LITTLE EGRET
see p.80

short legs

short bill

MUTE SWAN
similar in flight; see p.92

OCCURRENCE
Mostly found in E Europe, locally in W, breeding around reedy lakes with surrounding bushes, but feeds on extensive salt pans, coastal marshes, and other areas of shallow water. Very few winter in W Europe.

| Seen in the UK |
| J F M **A M J J A S** O N D |

| Length **80–93cm (32–37in)** | Wingspan **1.2–1.35m (4–4½ft)** | Weight **1–1.5kg (2¼–3¼lb)** |
| Social **Small flocks** | Lifespan **25–30 years** | Status **Endangered** |

Order **Phoenicopteriformes**	Family **Phoenicopteridae**	Species *Phoenicopterus ruber*

Greater Flamingo

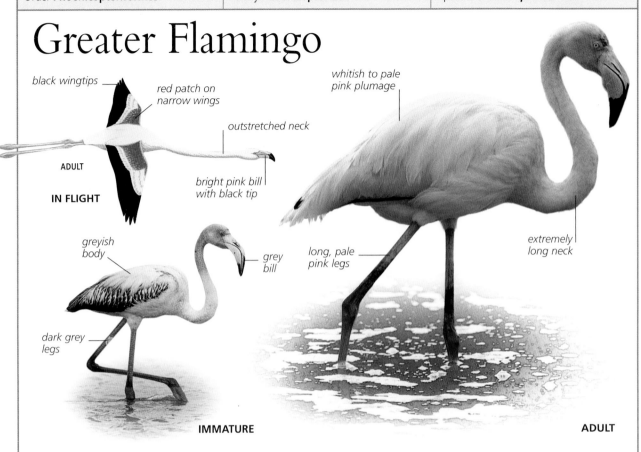

black wingtips

red patch on narrow wings

outstretched neck

ADULT

IN FLIGHT

bright pink bill with black tip

whitish to pale pink plumage

extremely long neck

greyish body

grey bill

long, pale pink legs

dark grey legs

IMMATURE

ADULT

Flamingos, of which there are a handful of species worldwide, are instantly recognizable. The downcurved bill, long neck, long legs, and red-splashed wings of the Greater Flamingo create a dramatic and easily identified bird, one of the more exotic in appearance in Europe. Although small groups occur, most live and nest in large flocks. Single birds found away from the main range are usually escapees.

VOICE Loud, deep honking; cackling notes give goose-like chorus.

NESTING Small pillar of mud in shallow water, safe from land-based predators; 1 egg; 1 brood; April–May.

FEEDING Sweeps its bill, upside down, through shallow water, picking up tiny crustaceans; often in very shallow water but also while the bird is belly-deep, or swimming like a swan.

FLIGHT: direct, quick, with neck outstretched and legs trailed giving spear shape, with narrow wings.

WADING FLOCK
Flocks of Greater Flamingos typically stand in the shallows, or wade more deeply into the water in long lines. Sometimes they swim like swans.

FLYING FLOCK
Flocks form irregular shapes or long, trailing lines while flying.

SIMILAR SPECIES

CHILEAN FLAMINGO
escapee
- grey legs with pink "knees"
- may be found on lakes of northwest Europe

OCCURRENCE
Breeds in a few places on large salty lakes in Spain, Portugal, S France, Sardinia, and Turkey; more widespread in Mediterranean as non-breeding bird, both on salt pans and natural lakes, usually in very open, exposed areas.

Seen in the UK
J F M A M J J A S O N D

Length **1.2–1.45m (4–4¾ft)**	Wingspan **1.4–1.7m (4½–5½ft)**	Weight **3–4kg (6½–8¾lb)**
Social **Large flocks**	Lifespan **Up to 20 years**	Status **Localized**

WILDFOWL

THIS LARGE GROUP OF water birds splits into clear groups, with a few "in between" species. They have webbed feet, rather short but specialized bills, and swim well, although many spend much of their time on dry land.

DUCKS

The two main groups are surface feeders (or dabbling ducks) and diving ducks. The former feed on land or from the water surface (sieving food through their bills, gleaning grain, plucking vegetation), sometimes tipping over ("upending") but rarely diving. The diving ducks feed beneath the surface, diving as they swim (not plunging from the air): some are animal feeders, others vegetarian; some species feed at night.

SHELDUCKS

A few large species fall between ducks and geese, with an easy walk and rather long legs and neck, but in other respects they are more like the true ducks.

GEESE

Geese are mostly large and terrestrial, feeding on dry land or marshes but returning to water (a lake or the sea) each night for a safe roost. They are social, flying in large flocks with loud, evocative calls – among the finest sights in Europe in winter.

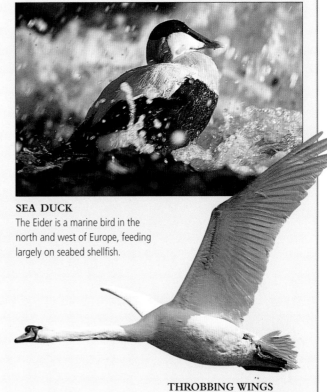

SEA DUCK
The Eider is a marine bird in the north and west of Europe, feeding largely on seabed shellfish.

THROBBING WINGS
The Mute Swan makes a unique humming noise with its wings while flying.

SWANS

European swans are all-white when adult (elsewhere there are black and white species). They are longer-necked than the geese, tending to be more aquatic, but also feed extensively on drier ground, often in mixed flocks.

LAND OR WATER
Ducks such as Wigeon feed on grassy areas and in shallow water, easily slipping between the two. They are highly gregarious.

Order **Anseriformes**	Family **Anatidae**	Species ***Cygnus columbianus***

Bewick's Swan 🔊 8

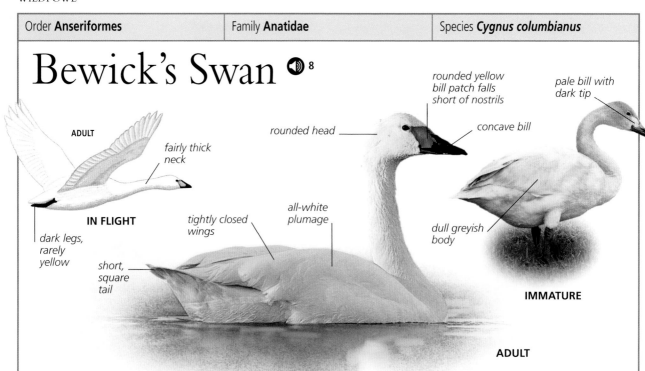

ADULT

fairly thick neck

IN FLIGHT

dark legs, rarely yellow

short, square tail

tightly closed wings

all-white plumage

rounded head

rounded yellow bill patch falls short of nostrils

concave bill

pale bill with dark tip

dull greyish body

IMMATURE

ADULT

FLIGHT: direct, strong; regular wingbeats, with simple quiet whistle from feathers at close range, no loud, throbbing sound.

The smallest of the swans, Bewick's Swan is typically rather stocky, although it can look surprisingly thin-necked at times. Unlike the Mute Swan, this is a thoroughly wild swan, although in certain places where it is fed in winter, it has become much more approachable. It is a very vocal bird, especially in flocks, its conversational chorus often penetrating the winter gloom over long distances.

VOICE Loud, bugling notes, less strident or trumpeting than Whooper Swan; often soft, conversational chorus from flocks.

NESTING Pile of grass stems and similar vegetation at edge of pool in tundra; 3–5 eggs; 1 brood; May–June.

FEEDING Often grazes on grass or cereal crops, or eats root crops in ploughed fields; feeds less often in water.

REMARK Subspecies *C. c. columbianus* (North America, very rare in Europe) has tiny yellow spot on black bill.

MIXED FLOCK
Bewick's Swans, mixed with other wildfowl, including Mute and Whooper Swans, can be watched closely from hides at several reserves. Elsewhere they are shy and wild.

YELLOW BILL
Any swan with yellow on the base of the bill will be a wild migrant to western Europe: a Bewick's or a Whooper Swan.

OCCURRENCE
Breeds in N Siberia. In winter, moves to lowlands of W Europe, mostly agricultural land, usually in traditional areas, occupied year after year. In some places, concentrates on reserves where it is fed.

Seen in the UK
J F M A M J J A S O N D

SIMILAR SPECIES

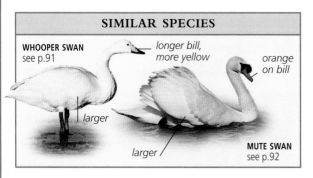

WHOOPER SWAN see p.91

longer bill, more yellow

larger

larger

orange on bill

MUTE SWAN see p.92

Length **1.15–1.27m (3¾–4¼ft)**	Wingspan **1.8–2.1m (6–7ft)**	Weight **5–6.5kg (11–14¼lb)**
Social **Flocks**	Lifespan **Up to 10 years**	Status **Localized**

Order **Anseriformes**	Family **Anatidae**	Species *Cygnus cygnus*

Whooper Swan 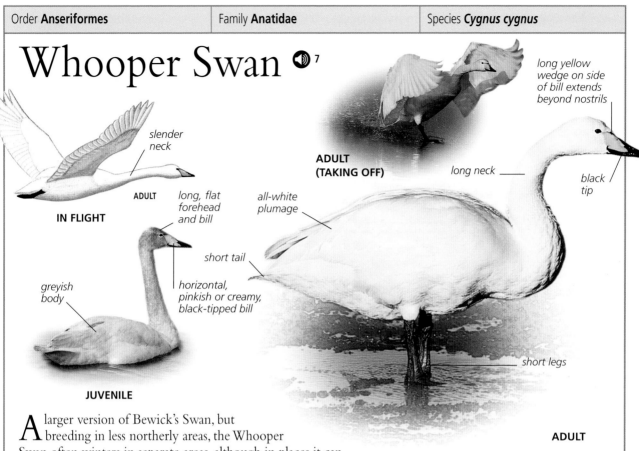 🔊 7

slender neck

IN FLIGHT

ADULT

long, flat forehead and bill

ADULT (TAKING OFF)

long yellow wedge on side of bill extends beyond nostrils

long neck

black tip

all-white plumage

greyish body

short tail

horizontal, pinkish or creamy, black-tipped bill

short legs

JUVENILE

ADULT

A larger version of Bewick's Swan, but breeding in less northerly areas, the Whooper Swan often winters in separate areas, although in places it can be found together with the Mute Swan and Bewick's Swan. The Whooper Swan is a wild, usually shy bird, far less approachable than the Mute Swan and, like Bewick's, usually more terrestrial. Although equally large, it is a more agile bird than the Mute Swan; however, the Whooper Swan lacks the arch-necked elegance (it holds its neck bolt upright and head horizontal) and rich bill colours of the latter.

VOICE Loud trumpeting call, slightly lower-pitched; simpler bugling than Bewick's Swan, often three or four syllables instead of two.

NESTING Big, domed structure of grass and reed stems at water's edge or built up from bottom of shallow lake; 5–8 eggs; 1 brood; April–June.

FEEDING Plucks leaves and stems from short vegetation on dry ground, or digs roots and waste crops from ploughed earth; feeds on aquatic plants mostly in summer.

FLIGHT: powerful and direct; regular wingbeats with little wing noise.

UPRIGHT NECKS
Whooper Swans have long, slim necks, held upright, with head horizontal, when alert.

DENSE FLOCKS
Whooper Swans are found in dense flocks on a few nature reserves where they are fed.

SIMILAR SPECIES

BEWICK'S SWAN
see p.90

rounder head

smaller

less yellow on bill

MUTE SWAN
see p.92

reddish orange bill

OCCURRENCE
Breeds in Scandinavia and Iceland on remote pools; in winter locally across NW and C to SE Europe on large lakes and marshes. Increasing numbers winter on reserves with Bewick's Swans, taking advantage of artificial feeding.

Seen in the UK
J F M A M J J A S O N D

Length **1.4–1.6m (4½–5¼ft)**	Wingspan **2.05–2.35m (6¾–7¾ft)**	Weight **9–11kg (20–24lb)**
Social **Flocks**	Lifespan **Up to 10 years**	Status **Secure**

Order **Anseriformes**	Family **Anatidae**	Species **Cygnus olor**

Mute Swan 🔊 6.I, 6.II

grey-brown plumage
becomes blotched
white

grey
bill

JUVENILE

black facial knob

reddish orange bill,
angled down

outstretched
neck

all-white
plumage

ADULT

IN FLIGHT

relatively long,
pointed tail

ADULT

long neck,
often curved
or upright

A large, familiar bird, strikingly white and obvious even at great range, the Mute Swan is generally quite tame, even semi-domesticated in its behaviour and choice of habitat. Territorial pairs are aggressive, even to people or their dogs, using impressive displays of arched wings and loud, hissing calls. In some floodplains, small groups regularly feed on dry land, a habit that is more consistent with the two "wild swans", Bewick's and Whooper.

VOICE Strangled trumpeting and hissing notes.

NESTING Huge pile of vegetation at water's edge; up to 8 eggs; 1 brood; March–June.

FEEDING Plucks vegetable matter from short grass in fields and salt marshes, pulls the same from shallow water, or upends in deeper water.

FLIGHT: heavy but powerful, direct, with neck outstretched; strong, regular wingbeats produce throbbing sound.

THREAT DISPLAY
When threatened, the Mute Swan raises its wings like sails, lowers its head, and makes a loud, rough hiss.

SHELTERED YOUNG
Small cygnets seek shelter and refuge between the wings of a parent swan.

NEST
The nest is a large mound of vegetation built at the water's edge. The female lays up to 8 eggs and incubates them.

OCCURRENCE
Many breed on park lakes and other small pools, others on natural lakes, reservoirs, and rivers, almost throughout Europe; in W Europe, commonly seen on sheltered sea coasts and marshes. May join other swans feeding on flat, open fields.

Seen in the UK
J F M A M J J A S O N D

SIMILAR SPECIES

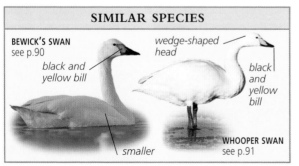

BEWICK'S SWAN
see p.90

black and
yellow bill

wedge-shaped
head

black
and
yellow
bill

WHOOPER SWAN
see p.91

smaller

Length **1.4–1.6m (4½–5¼ft)**	Wingspan **2.08–2.38m (6¾–7¾ft)**	Weight **10–12kg (22–26lb)**
Social **Small flocks**	Lifespan **15–20 years**	Status **Secure**

Order **Anseriformes**	Family **Anatidae**	Species *Anser albifrons*

White-fronted Goose

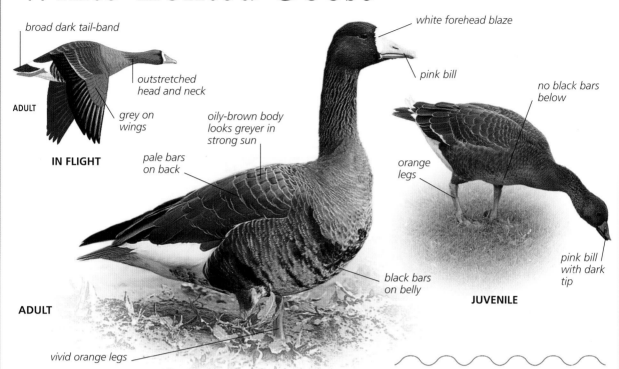

broad dark tail-band

outstretched head and neck

ADULT

grey on wings

IN FLIGHT

pale bars on back

oily-brown body looks greyer in strong sun

white forehead blaze

pink bill

no black bars below

orange legs

pink bill with dark tip

JUVENILE

black bars on belly

ADULT

vivid orange legs

One of the most colourful and lively of the grey geese, the White-fronted Goose returns each winter to regular locations. Its flocks often attract stragglers of other species, and hence are particularly significant for bird-watchers. Knowledge of this, more common, species and its variable appearance in different lighting conditions is valuable when trying to identify other geese.

VOICE High, yodelling, yelping notes, *kyu-yu, ku-yu-yu* or *lo-lyok.*

NESTING Down-filled nest on ground; 5 or 6 eggs; 1 brood; June.

FEEDING Grazes on firm ground during steady forward walk, taking grass, roots, some winter wheat, and grain.

SUBSPECIES

A. a. flavirostris (Greenland)

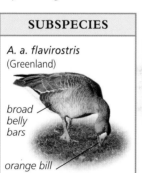

broad belly bars

orange bill

FLIGHT: flies in lines, "V"s, or irregular packs, head and neck outstretched.

WATERSIDE GOOSE
Water is essential for drinking and also as a safe refuge for night-time roosts. Floods, broad rivers, and estuaries are preferred.

SIMILAR SPECIES

GREYLAG GOOSE see p.96

larger

pink legs

LESSER WHITE-FRONTED GOOSE see p.418

yellow eye-ring

small, bright pink bill

OCCURRENCE
Breeds in Greenland and far N Russia. Winters on pastures and coastal marshes in Great Britain, Ireland, Low Countries, S France, and E Europe. Often with, or near, other geese in winter, sometimes in huge flocks.

Seen in the UK
J F M A M J J A S O N D

Length **65–78cm (26–31in)**	Wingspan **1.3–1.65m (4¼–5½ft)**	Weight **1.9–2.5kg (4¼–5½lb)**
Social **Flocks**	Lifespan **15–20 years**	Status **Secure**

Order **Anseriformes**	Family **Anatidae**	Species *Anser fabalis*

Bean Goose

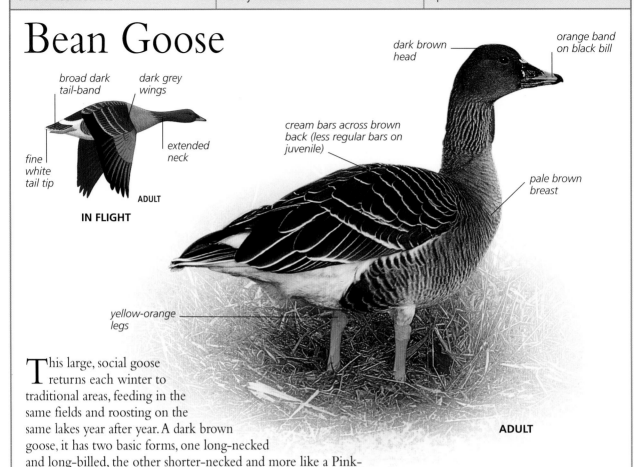

IN FLIGHT

broad dark tail-band

dark grey wings

fine white tail tip

extended neck

ADULT

dark brown head

orange band on black bill

cream bars across brown back (less regular bars on juvenile)

pale brown breast

yellow-orange legs

ADULT

This large, social goose returns each winter to traditional areas, feeding in the same fields and roosting on the same lakes year after year. A dark brown goose, it has two basic forms, one long-necked and long-billed, the other shorter-necked and more like a Pink-footed Goose in appearance. Except in the Low Countries it is a scarce bird, not usually seen in large numbers. Its long, dark head and neck and cleanly barred back help to identify it in flocks of White-fronted Geese, with which it sometimes mingles.

VOICE Deep, two- or three-syllable trumpeting, *ung-ung* or *unk-uk-uk*.

NESTING Down- and feather-lined hollow on ground near bog pools, in open tundra or in forest clearings; 4–6 eggs; 1 brood; June.

FEEDING Grazes on short grass; picks up grain and root crops from stubble or ploughed fields, often in traditional areas used for decades.

FLIGHT: strong and direct, long neck obvious; in lines of "V"s.

FLOCKS
Bean Geese feed in flocks, at times mixing with other geese, often on arable land.

OCCURRENCE
Breeds in N Scandinavia on bogs and tundra pools. In winter, mostly around S Baltic/North Sea and E Europe; one flock in England, one in Scotland. These are in traditional sites, threatened by disturbance and habitat change.

Seen in the UK
J F M A M J J A S O N D

SIMILAR SPECIES		SUBSPECIES

PINK-FOOTED GOOSE
see p.95
greyer and paler

pink legs

GREYLAG GOOSE
pale grey on wings in flight; see p.96

pale bill

pink on short bill

pink legs

A. f. rossicus
(NW Siberia)

orange patch on bill

shorter neck

Length **66–84cm (26–33in)**	Wingspan **1.47–1.75m (4¾–5¾ft)**	Weight **2.6–3.2kg (5¾–7lb)**
Social **Flocks**	Lifespan **Up to 10 years**	Status **Secure**

Order **Anseriformes**	Family **Anatidae**	Species *Anser brachyrhynchus*

Pink-footed Goose 🔊 9

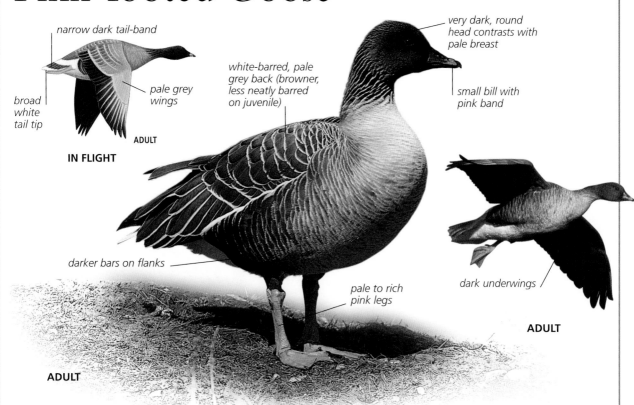

narrow dark tail-band

pale grey wings

broad white tail tip

IN FLIGHT

ADULT

white-barred, pale grey back (browner, less neatly barred on juvenile)

very dark, round head contrasts with pale breast

small bill with pink band

darker bars on flanks

pale to rich pink legs

dark underwings

ADULT

ADULT

With large population increases in recent decades, the Pink-footed Goose is found in tens of thousands in favoured places, with regular daily feeding and roosting regimes. Evening flights to the roosts, especially, are spectacular, unless the feeding geese are encouraged to stay away all night under the light of a full moon. By day, they feed in dense flocks on fields, and are sometimes surprisingly difficult to locate. They are usually wary and difficult to approach.

VOICE Like Bean Goose but less deep, resonant *ahng-unk* and frequent higher *wink-wink*.

NESTING Down-lined nest on ground in open tundra and exposed rocky slopes; 4–6 eggs; 1 brood; June–July.

FEEDING Large flocks eat grass, waste grain, sugar beet tops, carrots, and potatoes.

FLIGHT: direct, strong flight, head and neck short; forms long lines and "V" shapes.

FEEDING IN FLOCKS
Pink-footed Geese generally feed in dense groups with much noise and activity. They frequently mix with other geese species.

SIMILAR SPECIES

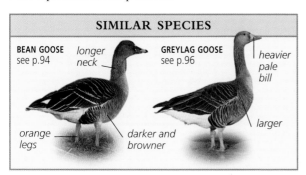

BEAN GOOSE see p.94

longer neck

orange legs

darker and browner

GREYLAG GOOSE see p.96

heavier pale bill

larger

OCCURRENCE
Breeds in Greenland, Iceland, and Svalbard. Moves to Great Britain and Low Countries in winter, roosting on large lakes, estuaries, and low-lying islands offshore; feeding on marshes, pasture, and arable land, close to coast.

Seen in the UK
J F M A M J J A S O N D

Length **64–76cm (25–30in)**	Wingspan **1.37–1.61m (4½–5¼ft)**	Weight **2.5–2.7kg (5½–6lb)**
Social **Large flocks**	Lifespan **10–20 years**	Status **Secure**

Order **Anseriformes**	Family **Anatidae**	Species *Anser anser*

Greylag Goose 10

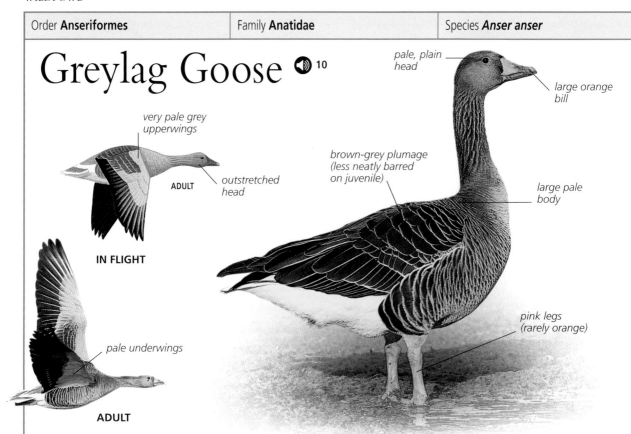

very pale grey
upperwings

ADULT

outstretched
head

IN FLIGHT

pale underwings

ADULT

pale, plain
head

large orange
bill

brown-grey plumage
(less neatly barred
on juvenile)

large pale
body

pink legs
(rarely orange)

ADULT

Of all grey geese, the Greylag (the direct ancestor of the domestic goose) most resembles the farmyard goose. It is also the most easily seen grey goose in the UK because it has been introduced in many lowland areas where sizeable flocks are now semi-tame and resident all year round. Winter visitors are still wild and shy. In much of eastern and central Europe, the Greylag is naturally resident in extensive marshes.
VOICE Loud, clattering, and honking notes like farmyard bird, *ahng-ahng-ahng, kang-ank*.
NESTING Sparsely lined ground nest, often on island; 4–6 eggs; 1 brood; May–June.
FEEDING Grazes; plucks grass and cereal shoots, digs for roots and waste grain.

FLIGHT: powerful, head outstretched; in "V"s and long lines.

SLOW FLIERS
Flocks of Greylag Geese in flight are rather slower and heavier than other grey geese but become agile when losing height before landing.

OCCURRENCE
Breeds widely in Europe. Large numbers from Iceland visit NW Europe in winter, coming to coastal marshes and pastures. Introduced (feral) birds common in some places, including S England and Scotland where they are resident and far less wild than most.

Seen in the UK
J F M A M J J A S O N D

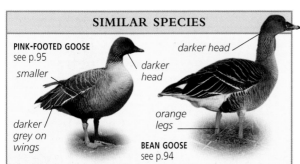

SIMILAR SPECIES

PINK-FOOTED GOOSE
see p.95

smaller

darker head

darker
head

darker
grey on
wings

orange
legs

BEAN GOOSE
see p.94

FEEDING
The Greylag Goose, like all grey geese, has a horizontal, head-down posture when feeding and shows a striking white rear.

Length **74–84cm (29–33in)**	Wingspan **1.49–1.68m (5–5½ft)**	Weight **2.9–3.7kg (6½–8¼lb)**
Social **Flocks**	Lifespan **15–20 years**	Status **Secure**

Order **Anseriformes**	Family **Anatidae**	Species ***Branta canadensis***

Canada Goose 11.I, 11.II

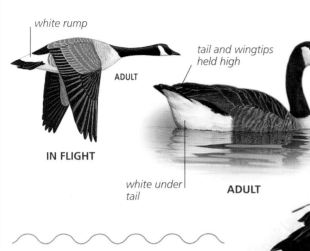

white rump

ADULT

IN FLIGHT

tail and wingtips held high

white under tail

ADULT

black bill

white chinstrap

black head and neck

swan-shaped, brown body (juvenile duller)

pale breast

black legs

ADULT

FLIGHT: strong, heavy but fast; with regular wingbeats; often in "V"s.

Originally imported from North America as an ornamental bird, the Canada Goose is now well established in many areas as a largely resident and rather tame bird, with little of the romance of "wild geese". Most have lost their migratory instinct. A remarkably successful and adaptable bird, it is sometimes considered a messy and aggressive pest in town parks. It often mingles with equally "artificial" groups of introduced Greylags. The Canada Goose is, nevertheless, a handsome bird.

VOICE Deep, loud, two-syllable, rising *ah-ronk!*
NESTING Down-lined scrape on ground, often on small island; loosely colonial; 5 or 6 eggs; 1 brood; April–June.
FEEDING Grazes on grass and cereals, takes some aquatic plants.

FLOCK ON WATER
Big flocks of Canada Geese are often seen on ornamental lakes in undisturbed estates.

HONKING PARTIES
Flocks of Canada Geese usually draw attention to themselves by their loud, honking calls.

FAMILY GROUP
The male and the female Canada Geese are alike and the goslings soon look like duller versions of their parents.

OCCURRENCE
Mostly in UK, Scandinavia, and Low Countries, on marshes, reservoirs, and flooded pits or surrounding grassland. Very few wild vagrants from North America are seen with other geese in W Europe in winter.

Seen in the UK
| J | F | M | A | M | J | J | A | S | O | N | D |

SIMILAR SPECIES

BARNACLE GOOSE see p.98

white face

black breast

smaller and greyer

GREYLAG GOOSE X CANADA GOOSE HYBRID
- duller head/face patterns
- orange bill
- often pinkish legs

Length **90–110cm (35–43in)**	Wingspan **1.5–1.8m (5–6ft)**	Weight **4.3–5kg (9½–11lb)**
Social **Flocks**	Lifespan **20–25 years**	Status **Localized**

Order **Anseriformes**	Family **Anatidae**	Species *Branta leucopsis*

Barnacle Goose

small, stubby black bill

black eye patch

cream-tinged white face (pure white on juvenile)

glossy black neck and chest

pale grey wings

ADULT

IN FLIGHT

ADULT

blue-grey back with black and white bars (irregular on juvenile)

strongly contrasted wings and underside

white underside

ADULT

ADULT

FLIGHT: strong, quick; flocks form irregular packs.

Few birds so numerous as this are restricted to such localized, traditional wintering sites. Barnacle Geese are predictably found, mostly on protected areas, from autumn until late spring, and are generally rather shy and unapproachable except when viewed from hides. They are not nearly so widespread as Canada Geese and, except for a handful of escapees and semi-tame groups, not so "suburbanized". Adult birds have strongly contrasted upper- and underparts, while the juveniles are duller and lack the cream tinge on the white face, which is so evident in the adults.

VOICE Harsh, short bark, creating chattering, yapping, unmusical chorus from flocks.

NESTING Feather-lined nest on ground or on cliff ledges in Arctic tundra; 4–6 eggs; 1 brood; May–June.

FEEDING Large flocks graze on grass, clover, and similar vegetation.

CONTRASTED COLOURS
Barnacle Geese, like other goose species, are especially prone to showing strong contrasts in low winter sun.

OCCURRENCE
Breeds in Greenland and Svalbard with populations remaining separate all year. Mostly in Iceland, W Scotland, Ireland, and Low Countries in winter, with migrants through Baltic, on grassy pastures and salt marshes.

IRREGULAR FLOCK
Flocks of Barnacle Geese form irregular packs in flight, not "V"s or chevrons.

SIMILAR SPECIES

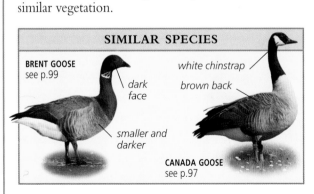

BRENT GOOSE
see p.99

dark face

smaller and darker

white chinstrap

brown back

CANADA GOOSE
see p.97

Seen in the UK
J F M A M J J A S O N D

Length **58–70cm (23–28in)**	Wingspan **1.32–1.45m (4¼–4¾ft)**	Weight **1.5–2kg (3¼–4½lb)**
Social **Flocks**	Lifespan **Up to 18 years**	Status **Localized**

Order **Anseriformes**	Family **Anatidae**	Species *Branta bernicla*

Brent Goose 12

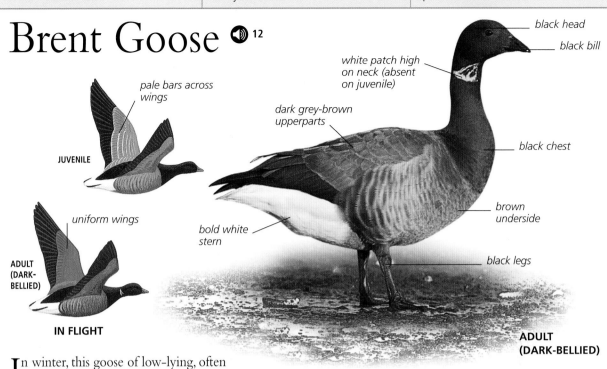

JUVENILE — pale bars across wings

ADULT (DARK-BELLIED) — uniform wings

IN FLIGHT

black head
black bill
white patch high on neck (absent on juvenile)
dark grey-brown upperparts
black chest
brown underside
bold white stern
black legs

ADULT (DARK-BELLIED)

In winter, this goose of low-lying, often muddy, coasts is common and increasingly tame in many areas, coming into estuaries and harbours and even feeding on roadside fields at high tide. Flocks are often on water, upending like ducks in order to feed. At low tide most are scattered over estuary mud or in the remaining narrow channels. Their pleasant, growling calls are far-carrying and typical of many estuaries from October to March. Although little longer than a Mallard, the Brent Goose usually looks much bigger.

VOICE Rhythmic, deep, throaty *rronk rronk*, creating loud, murmuring chorus from large flocks.

NESTING Feather-lined nest on ground near shallow pool; 4–6 eggs; 1 brood; May–June.

FEEDING Eats eelgrass and algae on mudflats, increasingly cereals and grass on fields.

FLIGHT: fast, strong; deep, quick wingbeats; in irregular masses or long lines.

LOOSE FLOCK
Loose flocks of Brent Geese rise from creeks and muddy channels.

ESTUARY BIRD
Brent Geese are commonly seen scattered over estuary mud and the adjacent arable land at low tide (pale-bellied birds pictured).

SUBSPECIES

B. b. hrota (Ireland, NE England)
whitish underparts

B. b. nigricans (vagrant from North America)
white flanks
white collar
blackish belly

SIMILAR SPECIES

BARNACLE GOOSE see p.98
white face
much paler

CANADA GOOSE see p.97
white chinstrap
much bigger

OCCURRENCE
Breeds on Arctic tundra. Mostly winters in Great Britain, Ireland, and Low Countries, with large migrations through Baltic. Pale-bellied birds from Greenland winter separately from dark-bellied Siberian breeders.

Seen in the UK
J F M A M J J A S O N D

Length **56–61cm (22–24in)**	Wingspan **1.1–1.21m (3½–4ft)**	Weight **1.3–1.6kg (2¾–3½lb)**
Social **Flocks**	Lifespan **12–15 years**	Status **Localized**

Order **Anseriformes**	Family **Anatidae**	Species *Tadorna tadorna*

Shelduck

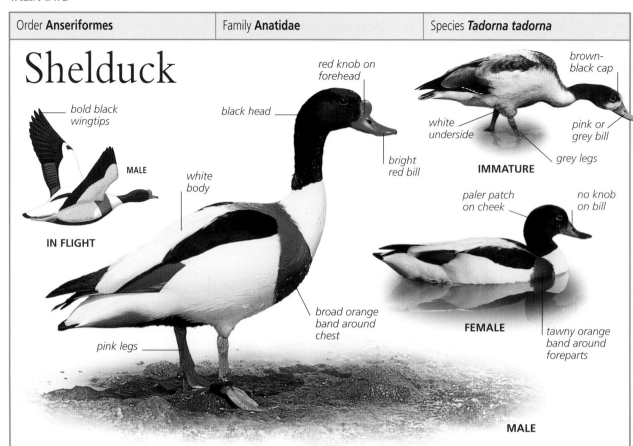

bold black wingtips

MALE

IN FLIGHT

white body

black head

red knob on forehead

bright red bill

brown-black cap

white underside

pink or grey bill

grey legs

IMMATURE

paler patch on cheek

no knob on bill

FEMALE

tawny orange band around foreparts

broad orange band around chest

pink legs

MALE

Mostly but not exclusively coastal, the Shelduck is widespread and easily identified. Family groups gather together in late summer when most adults fly to the Helgoland Bight (Germany) to moult; at other times, pairs or small, loose flocks are usual. The bright white plumage is easily visible at great range across dark estuary mud. With the ever-increasing number of gravel workings in lowland areas, Shelducks have been able to spread inland to take advantage of newly flooded, worked-out pits.

VOICE Goose-like *a-ank* and growled *grah grah*; various whistling notes from male and rhythmic *gagagagaga* from female in spring.

NESTING In holes on ground, between straw bales, in old buildings, under brambles, and also in trees; 8–10 eggs; 1 brood; February–August.

FEEDING Typically sweeps bill from side to side over wet mud to find algae, snails, and small crustaceans; also grazes and upends in shallow water.

GRAZING DUCKS
Pairs of Shelducks may sometimes be found feeding around the shores of lakes and reservoirs.

FLIGHT: strong, fast-flying, but rather heavy, goose-like action.

UPENDING
Shelducks often upend to feed on submerged plants and animals.

OCCURRENCE
Widespread as breeding and wintering bird on coasts but only locally in Mediterranean. Mostly found on sandy or muddy shores, especially sheltered estuaries, with some on freshwater lakes, reservoirs, or flooded pits well inland.

SIMILAR SPECIES

MALLARD ♂ similar to ♂♀; see p.101

greyer body

yellow bill

dark green head

Seen in the UK

| J | F | M | A | M | J | J | A | S | O | N | D |

Length **58–65cm (23–26in)**	Wingspan **1.1–1.33m (3½–4¼ft)**	Weight **0.85–1.4kg (1¾–3lb)**
Social **Flocks**	Lifespan **5–15 years**	Status **Secure**

Order **Anseriformes**	Family **Anatidae**	Species *Anas platyrhynchos*

Mallard 🔊 13.I, 13.II

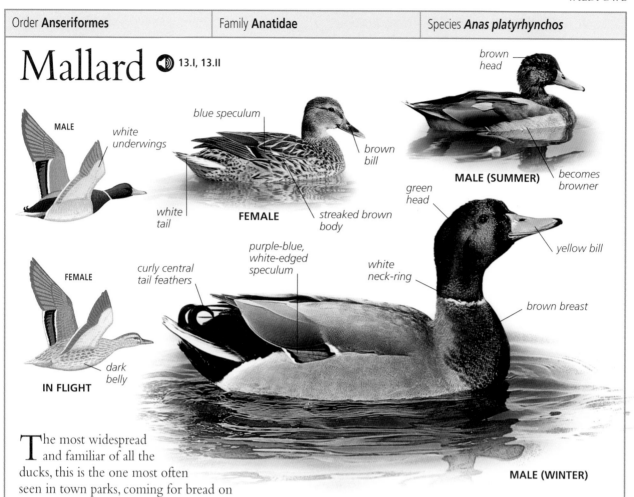

MALE
white underwings
white tail

FEMALE
blue speculum
brown bill
streaked brown body

brown head
MALE (SUMMER)
becomes browner

green head
yellow bill

curly central tail feathers
purple-blue, white-edged speculum
white neck-ring
brown breast

FEMALE
IN FLIGHT
dark belly

MALE (WINTER)

The most widespread and familiar of all the ducks, this is the one most often seen in town parks, coming for bread on lakes or on the riverside: but there are also many that are truly wild and shy. The different breeds of the farmyard duck are the domestic forms of the Mallard. They vary from very dark brown to all-white. The status of the wild form is obscured by the release of thousands bred for shooting.

VOICE Male whistles quietly; female has loud, raucous *quark quark*.
NESTING Down-lined nest on ground or in raised sites; 9–13 eggs; 1 brood; January–August.
FEEDING Takes small aquatic invertebrates, seeds, roots, shoots, and grain from shallows while upending or dabbling, or from dry ground.

FLIGHT: strong, fast; wingbeats mostly below body level; often in groups.

DUCKLINGS
Mallard ducklings follow the mother to water. They stay under her care until they are able to take care of themselves.

OCCURRENCE
Nests practically anywhere within reach of almost any kind of water, from towns to remote moorland pools and northern lakes, almost throughout Europe. In winter, more western, often on estuarine salt marshes but less so on open sea. Mostly feeds on arable fields and muddy margins of lakes.

Seen in the UK
J F M A M J J A S O N D

SIMILAR SPECIES

GADWALL ♀ similar to ♀; see p.102
bluish forewing
bigger bill
longer neck
grey bill
white wing patch
SHOVELER ♀ similar to ♀; see p.104
orange bill sides
PINTAIL ♀ similar to ♀; see p.103

Length **50–65cm (20–26in)**	Wingspan **81–95cm (32–37in)**	Weight **0.75–1.5kg (1¾–3¼lb)**
Social **Flocks**	Lifespan **15–25 years**	Status **Secure**

Order **Anseriformes**	Family **Anatidae**	Species *Anas strepera*

Gadwall

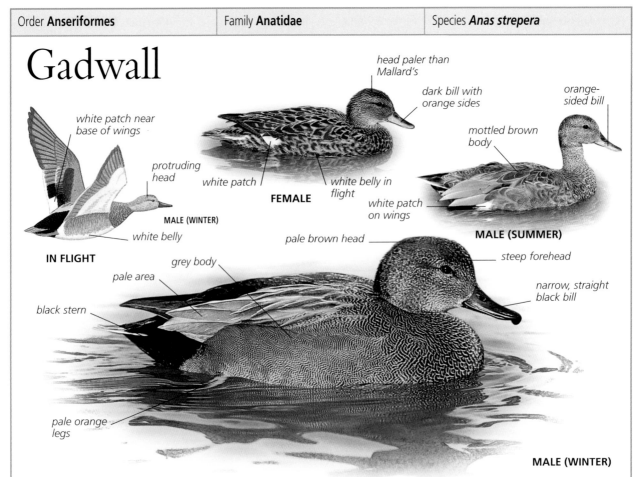

head paler than Mallard's

dark bill with orange sides

orange-sided bill

mottled brown body

white patch near base of wings

protruding head

white patch

FEMALE

white belly in flight

white patch on wings

MALE (SUMMER)

MALE (WINTER)

white belly

IN FLIGHT

pale brown head

steep forehead

grey body

pale area

black stern

narrow, straight black bill

pale orange legs

MALE (WINTER)

A large, elegant, surface-feeding duck, with a smaller, squarer head than the Mallard, the Gadwall is usually far less abundant. Dull colours at a distance reveal exquisite patterns at close range. Pairs are often seen flying over territories in spring, with characteristic calls attracting attention. In autumn and winter, Gadwalls often flock on reservoirs and pits, frequently scattered through flocks of Coots (see p.161), exploiting the food that the latter bring up from the bottom when they dive.

VOICE Male has high, nasal *pee* and croaked *ahrk*, female has loud quack.

NESTING Down-lined hollow on ground near water; 8–12 eggs; 1 brood; April–June.

FEEDING Mostly feeds in shallow water, dabbling and upending for seeds, insects, roots, and shoots of aquatic plants.

FLIGHT: strong, quick, direct, head protruding; frequently in pairs.

FEEDING GADWALL PAIR
The male (left) is "upending" to reach deeper food, a typical surface-feeding duck technique.

SIMILAR SPECIES

MALLARD ♀
similar to ♀; brown belly seen in flight; see p.101

browner head

short bill

blue speculum

WIGEON ♀
similar to ♀; see p.105

OCCURRENCE

Mostly breeds in mid- and W Europe, on lakes and rivers with reeds or wooded islands. In winter, more westerly, on open waters such as big reservoirs and flooded pits, but prefers some shelter. Scarce on salt marshes and quiet estuaries.

Seen in the UK
J F M A M J J A S O N D

Length **46–56cm (18–22in)**	Wingspan **84–95cm (33–37in)**	Weight **650–900g (23–32oz)**
Social **Flocks**	Lifespan **10–15 years**	Status **Vulnerable**

Order **Anseriformes**	Family **Anatidae**	Species *Anas acuta*

Pintail

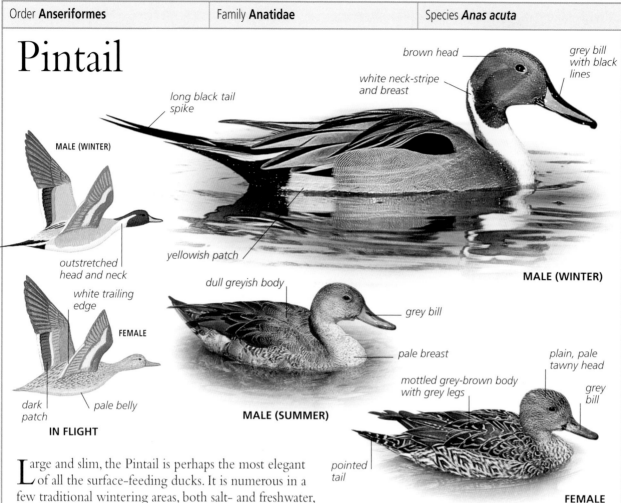

brown head

grey bill with black lines

white neck-stripe and breast

long black tail spike

MALE (WINTER)

outstretched head and neck

yellowish patch

MALE (WINTER)

white trailing edge

FEMALE

dull greyish body

grey bill

pale breast

plain, pale tawny head

grey bill

mottled grey-brown body with grey legs

dark patch

pale belly

IN FLIGHT

pointed tail

MALE (SUMMER)

FEMALE

Large and slim, the Pintail is perhaps the most elegant of all the surface-feeding ducks. It is numerous in a few traditional wintering areas, both salt- and freshwater, but otherwise rather scarce, usually in ones and twos among commoner waterfowl. Individuals in autumn flocks are always a bit of a challenge for the birdwatcher, before the striking winter plumage of the males has fully developed.

VOICE Male has low, short whistle; female's quack like Mallard's but quieter.
NESTING Leaf- and down-lined hollow on ground; 7–9 eggs; 1 brood; April–June.
FEEDING Mostly dabbles and upends in water but also grazes on grass and marsh and visits cereal fields for spilt grain.

FLIGHT: quick, straight, with head and neck outstretched, tail long.

UPENDING PINTAILS
Pintail drakes tip up to feed, revealing the long tail, black vent, and white belly.

SIMILAR SPECIES

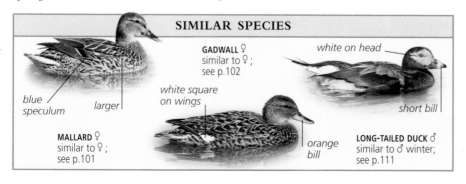

GADWALL ♀ similar to ♀; see p.102

white on head

blue speculum

larger

white square on wings

short bill

MALLARD ♀ similar to ♀; see p.101

orange bill

LONG-TAILED DUCK ♂ similar to ♂ winter; see p.111

OCCURRENCE
Breeds mostly in N and E Europe, sporadically in W, nesting on moorland and coastal marshes. In winter, flocks concentrate on traditional areas on estuaries and fresh marshes south to Mediterranean, with very small numbers turning up elsewhere.

Seen in the UK
J F M A M J J A S O N D

Length **53–70cm (21–28in)**	Wingspan **80–95cm (32–37in)**	Weight **550–1,200g (20–43oz)**
Social **Flocks**	Lifespan **15–25 years**	Status **Vulnerable**

Order **Anseriformes**	Family **Anatidae**	Species *Anas clypeata*

Shoveler

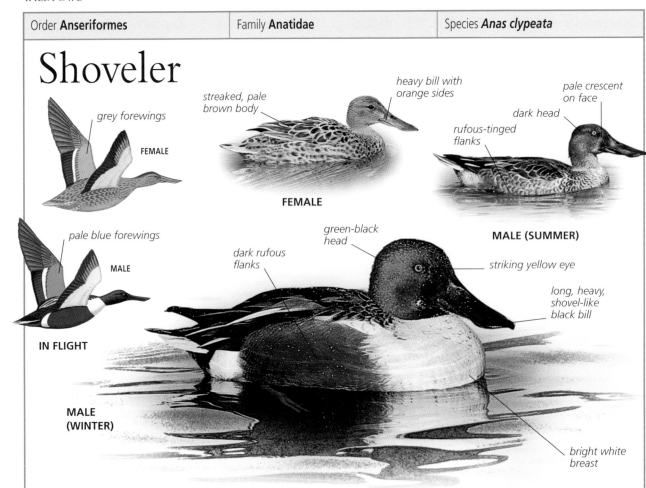

grey forewings

FEMALE

streaked, pale brown body

heavy bill with orange sides

FEMALE

pale crescent on face

dark head

rufous-tinged flanks

MALE (SUMMER)

pale blue forewings

MALE

IN FLIGHT

dark rufous flanks

green-black head

striking yellow eye

long, heavy, shovel-like black bill

MALE (WINTER)

bright white breast

Male Shovelers in breeding plumage are obvious and easily identified by their green heads, white breasts, and chestnut sides, while females are distinctive at close range but best identified by shape at a distance. They have the typical plumage of female dabbling ducks: streaked and pale brown overall. While taking flight, Shovelers make a characteristic "woofing" noise with their wings.

VOICE Male has deep *took took*; female has deep, quiet quack.

NESTING Down- or leaf-lined hollow near water; 8–12 eggs; 1 brood; March–June.

FEEDING Dabbles, often in tight, circular flocks, for seeds and invertebrates, with bill thrust forward on water surface or underwater and shoulders practically awash.

FLIGHT: quick, agile; strong, deep wingbeats, short-tailed effect.

FEEDING IN WATER
To reach slightly deeper food, Shovelers tip up on end, when the long, pointed wingtips become especially conspicuous.

SIMILAR SPECIES

browner forewing

smaller bill

GARGANEY ♂ summer, similar to ♂; see p.107

white line

MALLARD ♀ similar to ♀; see p.101

blue speculum on hindwing

OCCURRENCE
Breeds mostly in E Europe on reedy pools, generally in lowland areas. In winter, more widespread in W, on fresh water, marshes, and sheltered estuaries with grassy salt marshes crossed by creeks. Some reservoirs attract autumn flocks.

Seen in the UK
J F M A M J J A S O N D

Length **44–52cm (17½–20½in)**	Wingspan **70–84cm (28–33in)**	Weight **400–1,000g (14–36oz)**
Social **Flocks**	Lifespan **10–20 years**	Status **Secure**

Order **Anseriformes**	Family **Anatidae**	Species *Anas penelope*

Wigeon 🔊 14.I, 14.II

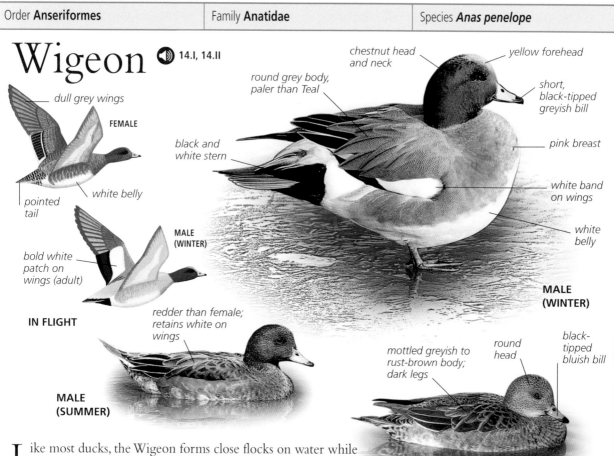

dull grey wings

FEMALE

white belly

pointed tail

bold white patch on wings (adult)

IN FLIGHT

MALE (WINTER)

black and white stern

round grey body, paler than Teal

chestnut head and neck

yellow forehead

short, black-tipped greyish bill

pink breast

white band on wings

white belly

MALE (WINTER)

redder than female; retains white on wings

MALE (SUMMER)

mottled greyish to rust-brown body; dark legs

round head

black-tipped bluish bill

FEMALE

L ike most ducks, the Wigeon forms close flocks on water while feeding, advancing across a salt marsh or meadow in a tight-packed mass. Such a flock looks richly colourful and adds to the effect with constant loud calls. Wigeon are generally shy and fly off when approached, large numbers forming wheeling flocks circling above a marsh or heading for the safety of a reservoir. They have good reason to be wary, being the prime target of many fowlers.

FLIGHT: fast, wader-like, head protruding, wings swept back and pointed, tail pointed.

VOICE Male has loud, explosive, musical whistle, *whee-oo*; female has deep, rough, abrupt growl.

NESTING In long vegetation on ground, near water; 8 or 9 eggs; 1 brood; April–July.

FEEDING Grazes on short grass, often in dense flocks; also feeds in shallow water, taking seeds, shoots, and roots.

GRAZING
Dense Wigeon flocks feed on short grass near water. The entire flock usually faces one way while feeding.

OCCURRENCE
Breeds in N Europe and N UK, on edges of moorland pools and lakes in forests. Much more widespread in winter on estuaries and freshwater marshes, and on grassy areas surrounding reservoirs and water-filled pits.

Seen in the UK
J F M A M J J A S O N D

SIMILAR SPECIES

smaller, darker body

yellow patch

TEAL ♂ similar to ♂ winter; see p.106

larger body; orange legs

white patch

MALLARD ♀ similar to ♀; see p.101

longer bill

orange legs

longer bill

GADWALL ♀ similar to ♀; see p.102

Length **45–51cm (18–20in)**	Wingspan **75–86cm (30–34in)**	Weight **500–900g (18–32oz)**
Social **Dense flocks**	Lifespan **Up to 15 years**	Status **Secure**

Order **Anseriformes**	Family **Anatidae**	Species **Anas crecca**

Teal

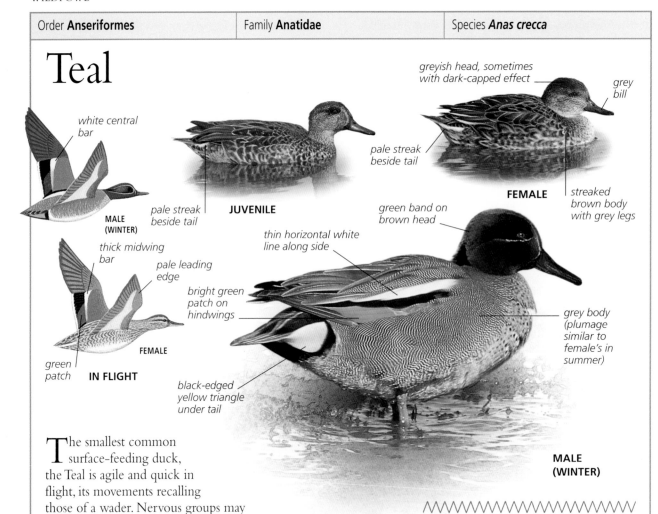

white central bar

MALE (WINTER)

pale streak beside tail

JUVENILE

greyish head, sometimes with dark-capped effect

grey bill

pale streak beside tail

FEMALE

streaked brown body with grey legs

green band on brown head

thin horizontal white line along side

bright green patch on hindwings

grey body (plumage similar to female's in summer)

thick midwing bar

pale leading edge

green patch

FEMALE

IN FLIGHT

black-edged yellow triangle under tail

MALE (WINTER)

The smallest common surface-feeding duck, the Teal is agile and quick in flight, its movements recalling those of a wader. Nervous groups may often swoop down to a sheltered bay, only to dart over the water surface and wheel up and away once more; sometimes several such approaches precede their eventual settling. In places, Teal occur in hundreds but 20–40 are more typical, scattered along well-vegetated or muddy shores, or in wet marshes.

VOICE Male has loud, ringing, high-pitched *crik crik* that can be easily heard at long range across marshes or estuaries; female has high quack.

NESTING Down-lined hollow near water; 8–11 eggs; 1 brood; April–June.

FEEDING Mostly in water or on muddy shores, taking plants and seeds.

FLIGHT: quick, active, twisting; swooping in to settle like waders.

DRAB DUCK
An absence of bright colours on the bill and legs helps to identify the female Teal.

OCCURRENCE
Breeds in N and E Europe on freshwater marshes and wet moors and heaths, including high moorland pools. Winters more widely in S and W Europe, mostly on fresh waters with muddy edges and around estuaries.

Seen in the UK
| J | F | M | A | M | J | J | A | S | O | N | D |

SIMILAR SPECIES

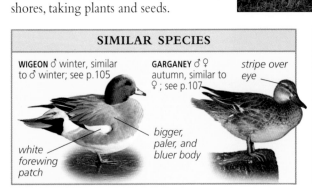

WIGEON ♂ winter, similar to ♂ winter; see p.105

GARGANEY ♂ ♀ autumn, similar to ♀; see p.107

stripe over eye

bigger, paler, and bluer body

white forewing patch

SUBSPECIES

vertical white line near chest

A. c. carolinensis ♂ (North America)

Length **34–38cm (13½–15in)**	Wingspan **58–64cm (23–25in)**	Weight **250–400g (9–14oz)**
Social **Small flocks**	Lifespan **10–15 years**	Status **Secure**

Order **Anseriformes**	Family **Anatidae**	Species *Anas querquedula*

Garganey

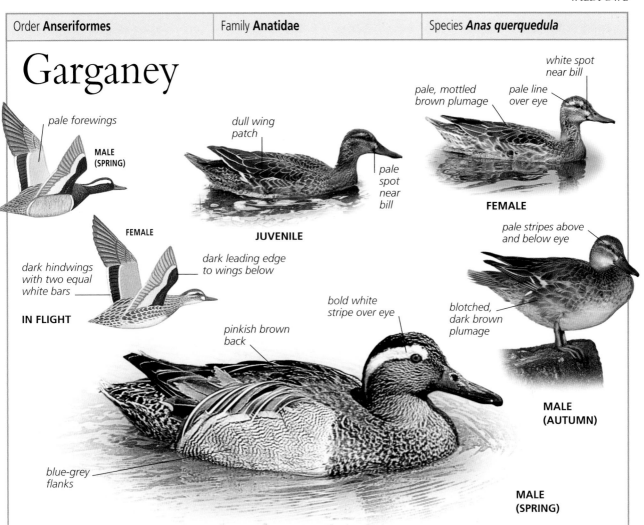

pale forewings

MALE (SPRING)

dull wing patch

pale spot near bill

JUVENILE

white spot near bill

pale, mottled brown plumage

pale line over eye

FEMALE

FEMALE

dark hindwings with two equal white bars

dark leading edge to wings below

IN FLIGHT

pale stripes above and below eye

bold white stripe over eye

blotched, dark brown plumage

pinkish brown back

MALE (AUTUMN)

blue-grey flanks

MALE (SPRING)

Small and colourful, the Garganey is unusual in Europe as a summer visiting duck that spends the winter in Africa. It is mostly scarce and thinly spread but spring flocks in the eastern Mediterranean can be substantial. In autumn, pairs or small groups can be found swimming with other wildfowl. They tend to associate with Teal and Shovelers and picking one or two autumn migrants out from a flock of mixed ducks is a challenge.

VOICE Male makes short, dry rattle; female rather silent but has short, high-pitched quack.

NESTING Down-lined hollow in vegetation near water; 8–11 eggs; 1 brood; May–June.

FEEDING Dabbles and upends in water, taking tiny invertebrates, roots, and seeds.

FLIGHT: quick, twisting and turning easily; flocks almost wader-like.

WATERSIDE DUCK
Garganeys like wet, grassy marshes and shallow floods with reeds and sedges in spring.

OCCURRENCE
Common in Mediterranean in spring, and scarce breeder in N and W Europe, mostly on wet, grassy, freshwater marshes. Small numbers of migrants join other ducks on lakes and reservoirs in autumn.

Seen in the UK
| J | F | M | A | M | J | J | A | S | O | N | D |

SIMILAR SPECIES

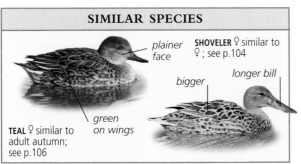

plainer face

SHOVELER ♀ similar to ♀; see p.104

longer bill

bigger

green on wings

TEAL ♀ similar to adult autumn; see p.106

Length **37–41cm (14½–16in)**	Wingspan **63–69cm (25–27in)**	Weight **250–500g (9–18oz)**
Social **Family groups**	Lifespan **Up to 10 years**	Status **Vulnerable**

Order **Anseriformes**	Family **Anatidae**	Species **Aythya fuligula**

Tufted Duck

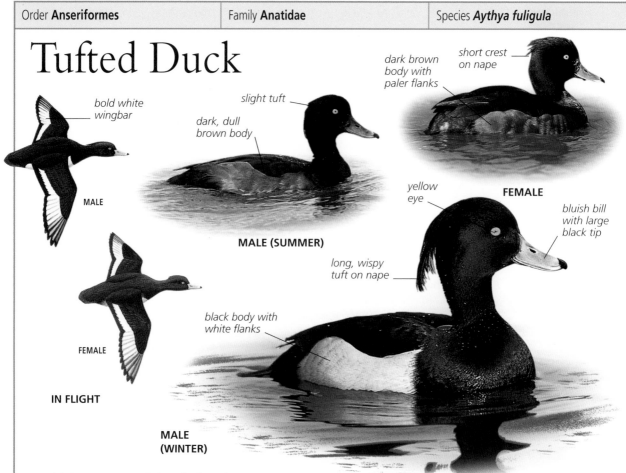

bold white wingbar

MALE

FEMALE

IN FLIGHT

slight tuft

dark, dull brown body

MALE (SUMMER)

dark brown body with paler flanks

short crest on nape

FEMALE

yellow eye

bluish bill with large black tip

long, wispy tuft on nape

black body with white flanks

MALE (WINTER)

This is a common diving duck, swimming and feeding in flocks, with individuals disappearing under in search of food. Males are strongly contrasted except in mid-summer, while females are dark and dull. Flocks are often mixed with Pochards and are worth scanning through for individuals of rarer species that are naturally attracted to their company. Tufted Ducks are sometimes semi-tame and come for food on ponds in town parks. Even flocks on lakes and reservoirs often tolerate a quite close approach, or simply swim away from disturbance.

VOICE Deep, grating growl; male calls with nasal whistles during courtship.

NESTING Down-lined hollow in long vegetation close to water; 8–11 eggs; 1 brood; May–June.

FEEDING Dives underwater from surface to find molluscs and insects.

/\

FLIGHT: fast but not manouevrable; flocks make tight, irregular packs.

WINTER FLOCK
Tufted Ducks, with Pochards, form quiet, sleepy flocks on inland waters; these flocks are sometimes quite large.

SIMILAR SPECIES

grey back on male

grey bill with tiny black tip

SCAUP ♂♀; ♀ has white face patch; see p.109

POCHARD ♀ similar to ♀; see p.110

white eye-ring

paler

OCCURRENCE
Widespread; breeds in long grass around fresh waters such as flooded pits. In winter, widespread and often abundant, with huge numbers on sheltered coastal waters, and small flocks on gravel pits, reservoirs, and sheltered coasts.

Seen in the UK
J F M A M J J A S O N D

Length **40–47cm (16–18½in)**	Wingspan **67–73cm (26–29in)**	Weight **450–1,000g (16–36oz)**
Social **Large flocks**	Lifespan **10–15 years**	Status **Secure**

Order **Anseriformes**	Family **Anatidae**	Species *Aythya marila*

Scaup

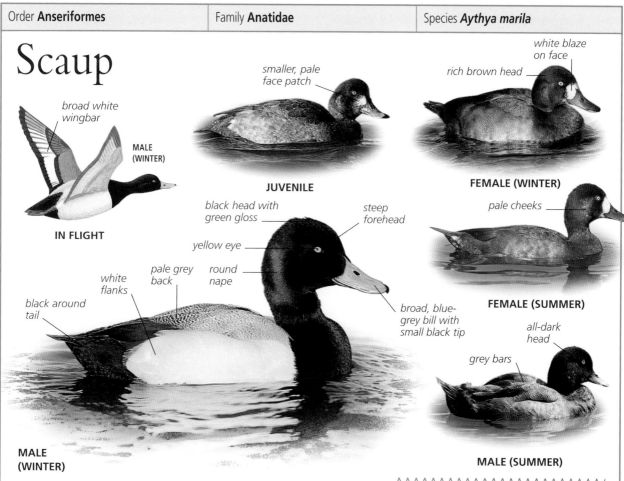

broad white wingbar

MALE (WINTER)

IN FLIGHT

smaller, pale face patch

JUVENILE

white blaze on face

rich brown head

FEMALE (WINTER)

pale cheeks

FEMALE (SUMMER)

black head with green gloss

yellow eye

steep forehead

round nape

pale grey back

white flanks

black around tail

broad, blue-grey bill with small black tip

all-dark head

grey bars

MALE (SUMMER)

MALE (WINTER)

FLIGHT: fast and direct; looks thickset and powerful; fast wingbeats.

Typically sea ducks, Scaup regularly appear inland in small numbers, usually associated with Tufted Ducks and Pochards, but similar-looking hybrids must be ruled out. Flocks of Scaup on the sea are attractive, if less lively than scoters or Long-tailed Ducks, tending to fly less and to seem much more settled and sedate on the water. They tend to prefer more sheltered parts of outer estuaries than the broad, open, windswept bays loved by the more energetic scoters. Flocks are generally quite approachable.

VOICE Male lets out low whistles in display, mostly silent otherwise; female has deep growl.

NESTING Nest lined with feathers and down, on ground, near water; 8–11 eggs; 1 brood; April–June.

FEEDING Dives from surface to find invertebrates, waste grain, and aquatic plants.

FLOCK ON SEA
Wintering Scaup are gregarious and swim in flocks of a few score on sheltered seas, with the white flanks of adult males showing up well.

SIMILAR SPECIES

TUFTED DUCK ♂♀; ♀ has less white on face; see p.108

black back

tuft

more black on tip of bill

red-brown head

POCHARD ♂ similar to ♂; see p.110

OCCURRENCE
Northern breeder, on wild moors and tundra in Scandinavia and Iceland. In winter, flocks found in regular, traditional places, mostly in S Baltic and North Sea, isolated groups and individuals turning up with Tufted Ducks inland.

Seen in the UK
J F M A M J J A S O N D

Length **42–51cm (16½–20in)**	Wingspan **67–73cm (26–29in)**	Weight **0.8–1.3kg (1¾–2¾lb)**
Social **Flocks**	Lifespan **10–12 years**	Status **Localized**

| Order **Anseriformes** | Family **Anatidae** | Species *Aythya ferina* |

Pochard

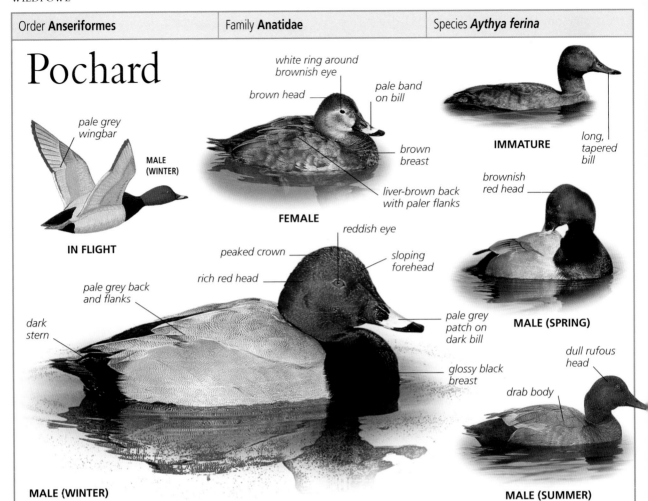

pale grey wingbar

MALE (WINTER)

IN FLIGHT

white ring around brownish eye

brown head

pale band on bill

brown breast

liver-brown back with paler flanks

FEMALE

long, tapered bill

IMMATURE

brownish red head

MALE (SPRING)

reddish eye

peaked crown

sloping forehead

rich red head

pale grey back and flanks

dark stern

pale grey patch on dark bill

glossy black breast

MALE (WINTER)

dull rufous head

drab body

MALE (SUMMER)

Together with the Tufted Duck, which often associates with it, the Pochard is one of the common inland diving ducks. Flocks are generally less active by day than Tufted Ducks, often sleeping for long periods. They are typically tightly packed and often made up largely of one sex, mostly males in the UK. In late autumn, hundreds of migrants may appear on a lake for a day or two and then move on at night. In summer, Pochards are dispersed and generally rare breeding birds in western Europe, including the UK.
VOICE Wheezing rise-and-fall call from displaying male; purring growl from female.
NESTING Large pad of leaves and down in reeds near water; 8–10 eggs; 1 brood; April–July.
FEEDING Dives from surface, taking seeds, shoots, and roots; often feeds by night.

FLIGHT: fast and direct, with fast, deep wingbeats; flies in loose flocks.

FLAPPING WINGS
Pochards rise up and flap their wings in a "comfort" movement used by many waterfowl species.

SIMILAR SPECIES

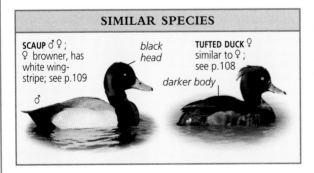

SCAUP ♂♀; ♀ browner, has white wing-stripe; see p.109

black head

TUFTED DUCK ♀ similar to ♀; see p.108

darker body

OCCURRENCE
Widespread breeder on reedy lakes in E Europe, rather scarce in W. Common non-breeder on fresh water in W Europe; big numbers on migration in late autumn and widespread smaller flocks on flooded pits and similar waters.

| Seen in the UK |
| J F M A M J J A S O N D |

| Length **42–49cm (16½–19½in)** | Wingspan **72–82cm (28–32in)** | Weight **700–1,000g (25–36oz)** |
| Social **Large flocks** | Lifespan **8–10 years** | Status **Secure** |

Order **Anseriformes**	Family **Anatidae**	Species *Clangula hyemalis*

Long-tailed Duck

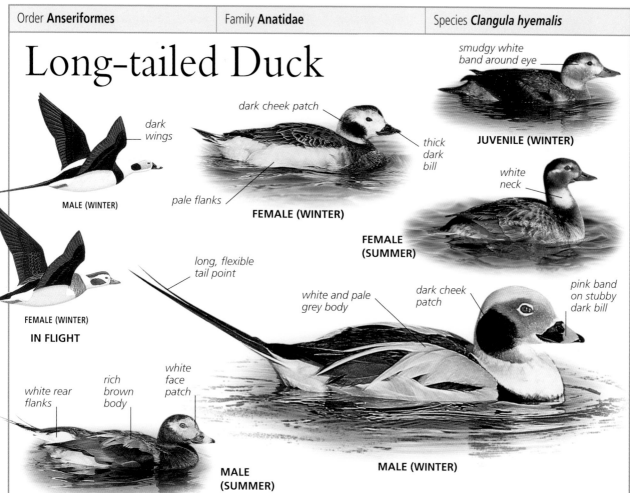

smudgy white band around eye

JUVENILE (WINTER)

dark wings

MALE (WINTER)

dark cheek patch

thick dark bill

pale flanks

FEMALE (WINTER)

white neck

FEMALE (SUMMER)

FEMALE (WINTER)

IN FLIGHT

long, flexible tail point

white and pale grey body

dark cheek patch

pink band on stubby dark bill

white rear flanks

rich brown body

white face patch

MALE (SUMMER)

MALE (WINTER)

While occasional individuals appear inland briefly, Long-tailed Ducks are essentially marine birds, living offshore in flocks, often mixed with scoters. They are generally lively and active, often flying low over the waves, splashing down, then flying again. When feeding, they spend long periods underwater. The irregular and complicated patterns, especially of males, may be somewhat confusing for novice birdwatchers, although in reality they are quite distinctive.

VOICE Male makes loud, rhythmic, yodelling calls, *a-ahulee*; female growls.

NESTING Down-lined hollow on ground near water; 4–6 eggs; 1 brood; May–June.

FEEDING Dives from surface to take molluscs and crustaceans.

FLIGHT: quick, rather heavy; small wings beat fast; splashes heavily onto water.

FAMILY GROUP
Breeding Long-tailed Ducks are restricted to the far north, but are often numerous on suitable lakes.

SIMILAR SPECIES

GOLDENEYE ♀ ; see p.116

plainer brown head

dark flanks

brown head with white stripe

longer bill

PINTAIL ♂ similar to ♂ ; see p.103

OCCURRENCE
Breeds in Iceland and Scandinavia on bleak moorland. Winters at sea off N Great Britain and in North Sea and Baltic, typically well offshore but drifting into bays and estuaries with tide, especially in early spring.

Seen in the UK
J F M A M J J A S O N D

Length **38–60cm (15–23½in)**	Wingspan **73–79cm (29–31in)**	Weight **520–950g (19–34oz)**
Social **Flocks**	Lifespan **Up to 10 years**	Status **Secure**

| Order **Anseriformes** | Family **Anatidae** | Species ***Melanitta nigra*** |

Common Scoter

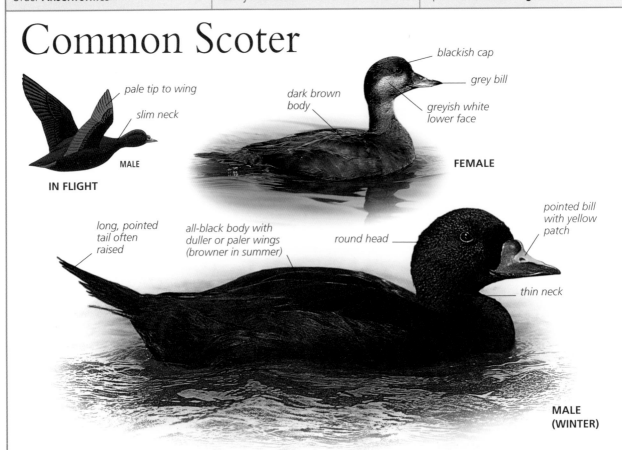

pale tip to wing

slim neck

MALE

IN FLIGHT

blackish cap

grey bill

dark brown body

greyish white lower face

FEMALE

long, pointed tail often raised

all-black body with duller or paler wings (browner in summer)

round head

pointed bill with yellow patch

thin neck

MALE (WINTER)

On a calm day, if Common Scoters are close inshore, their musical calls can be heard, but usually they are seen as distant dots appearing intermittently on the swell, or flying in long lines along the horizon. Migrants appear for very short stays inland in mid- and late summer. Common Scoters favour large, shallow, sheltered bays, although they are able to ride out storms with ease. Traditional sites may have thousands of birds, which are vulnerable to oil pollution. These sites may be inhabited throughout the year, with large numbers of moulting birds in bays with plentiful food in late summer and autumn.

VOICE Male has musical, piping whistle; female makes deep growls.

NESTING Down- and leaf-lined hollow near water, often on island; 6–8 eggs; 1 brood; March–June.

FEEDING Dives from surface to find shellfish, crustaceans, and worms.

FLIGHT: fast, low; in long, wavering lines and packs; rapid, deep wingbeats and sideways rolling action.

SOCIAL SEA DUCK
Large flocks of the very social Common Scoter often swim on heaving swell or fly low over the waves well offshore.

SIMILAR SPECIES

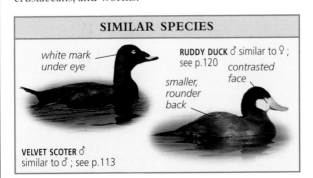

white mark under eye

VELVET SCOTER ♂
similar to ♂; see p.113

RUDDY DUCK ♂ similar to ♀; see p.120

contrasted face

smaller, rounder back

OCCURRENCE
Breeds on moorland pools in Iceland, Scandinavia, and N Great Britain. Winters on coasts around UK, North Sea, and Baltic, fewer south to Mediterranean. Flocks found in regular sites almost throughout year.

Seen in the UK
J F M A M J J A S O N D

| Length **45–54 cm (18–21½ in)** | Wingspan **79–90 cm (31–35 in)** | Weight **1.2–1.4 kg (2¾–3lb)** |
| Social **Large flocks** | Lifespan **10–15 years** | Status **Secure** |

| Order **Anseriformes** | Family **Anatidae** | Species ***Melanitta fusca*** |

Velvet Scoter

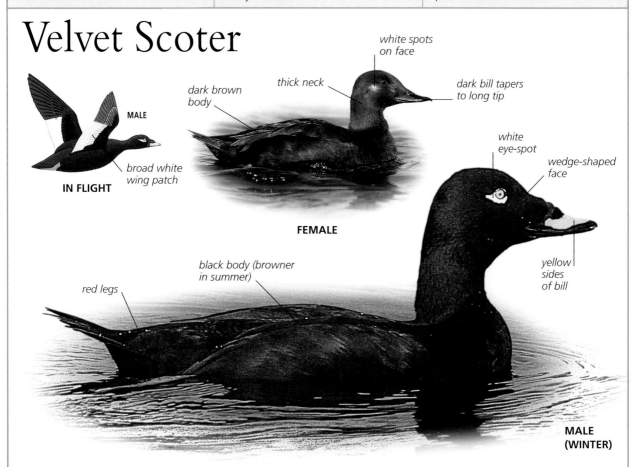

MALE

IN FLIGHT

broad white wing patch

white spots on face

thick neck

dark brown body

dark bill tapers to long tip

FEMALE

white eye-spot

wedge-shaped face

yellow sides of bill

black body (browner in summer)

red legs

MALE (WINTER)

A large, almost Eider-like diving duck, spending almost all of its time at sea, the Velvet Scoter is usually seen in small numbers in larger Common Scoter flocks. On the water, it is difficult to pick out from the smaller species, but the wing patches revealed in flight are immediately obvious. Females are dark-faced in fresh plumage but soon develop white face spots as the dark feather tips wear off. Individual variation adds to the identification problem. If a Velvet Scoter turns up inland, it may stay for a few days, giving a rare chance to get a good look at this surprisingly elegant duck.

VOICE Male whistles; female growls, but generally quiet, especially in winter.

NESTING Down-lined hollow near water; 6–8 eggs; 1 brood; May–July.

FEEDING Dives from surface, to find shellfish, shrimps, crabs, and marine worms.

FLIGHT: fast, low, heavy but strong; usually direct or in wide arc over sea.

WHITE WING PATCHES
Bold white wing patches distinguish the Velvet Scoter from the Common Scoter in flight or when it flaps its wings on the water.

SIMILAR SPECIES

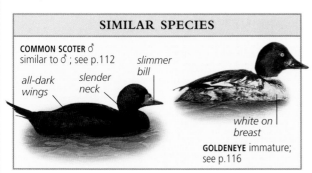

COMMON SCOTER ♂ similar to ♂; see p.112

all-dark wings

slender neck

slimmer bill

white on breast

GOLDENEYE immature; see p.116

OCCURRENCE
Breeds in Scandinavia, along coasts and on tundra pools. Winters in North Sea and Baltic on sheltered coasts. Small numbers join big Common Scoter flocks in summer and autumn.

| Seen in the UK |
| J F M A M J J A S O N D |

| Length **52–59 cm (20½–23 in)** | Wingspan **90–99 cm (35–39 in)** | Weight **1.1–2 kg (2½–4½ lb)** |
| Social **Flocks** | Lifespan **10–12 years** | Status **Localized** |

Order **Anseriformes**	Family **Anatidae**	Species **Somateria mollissima**

Eider

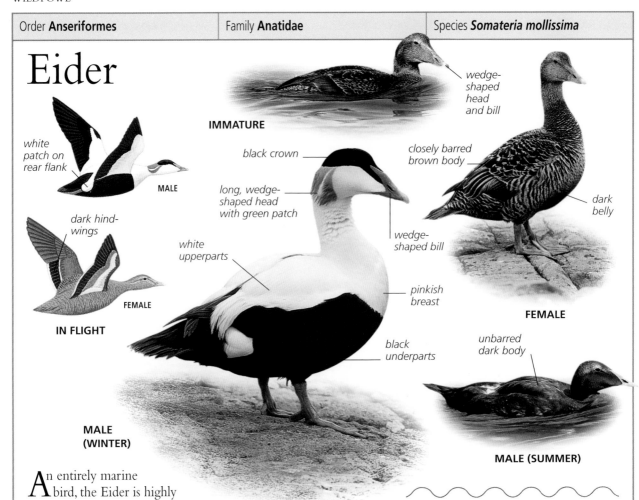

IMMATURE

wedge-shaped head and bill

white patch on rear flank

MALE

dark hind-wings

FEMALE

IN FLIGHT

black crown

long, wedge-shaped head with green patch

white upperparts

closely barred brown body

dark belly

FEMALE

wedge-shaped bill

pinkish breast

black underparts

unbarred dark body

MALE (WINTER)

MALE (SUMMER)

An entirely marine bird, the Eider is highly sociable and often seen in large rafts offshore. It is, however, equally familiar as a tame duck around coastal rocks and bays. Female Eiders with young in summer are easy to identify and so are spring males, calling and displaying, in northern harbours. In a few areas, flocks of Eiders remain all year but make no attempt to nest. These groups show remarkable fidelity to certain sites.

VOICE Male has sensuous, cooing *aa-ahooh*; female deep growls and *kok-kok-kok*.

NESTING Down-lined hollow on ground, exposed or well hidden; 4–6 eggs; 1 brood; April–June.

FEEDING Dives from surface to take crabs, shellfish, shrimps, and starfish.

FLIGHT: heavy, low, straight but fast, with deep, steady wingbeats.

MALE FLOCK
Large flocks of male Eiders gather offshore in estuaries and bays.

FEMALE AT NEST
The Eider makes a down-lined nest near water, often openly, on which the female sits tight to incubate.

SIMILAR SPECIES

VELVET SCOTER ♂ ♀
similar to ♂ winter in flight; see p.113

white patch on open wing

slimmer bill

MALLARD ♀ similar to ♀ ; see p.101

OCCURRENCE
Breeds in N Great Britain, Iceland, and Scandinavia, on low-lying coasts and islands with rocky shores and weedy bays. Winters on sea south to W France, with large flocks in sandy bays and over mussel beds. Very rare inland.

Seen in the UK
| J | F | M | A | M | J | J | A | S | O | N | D |

Length **50–71cm (20–28in)**	Wingspan **80–108cm (32–43in)**	Weight **1.2–2.8kg (2¾–6¼lb)**
Social **Large flocks**	Lifespan **10–15 years**	Status **Secure**

Order **Anseriformes**	Family **Anatidae**	Species ***Somateria spectabilis***

King Eider

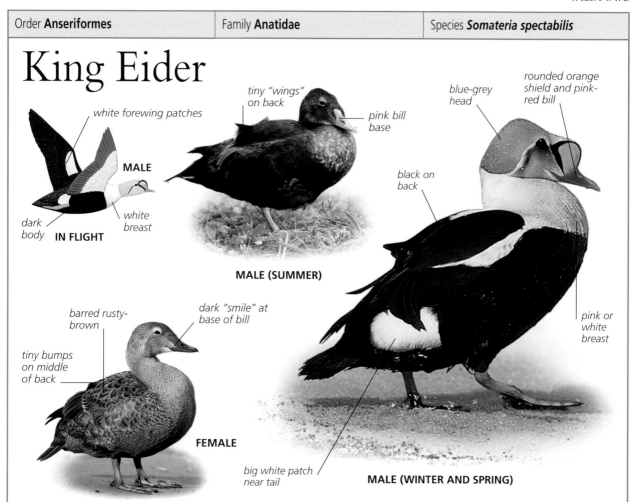

white forewing patches

MALE

dark body · **IN FLIGHT** · white breast

tiny "wings" on back

pink bill base

MALE (SUMMER)

blue-grey head

rounded orange shield and pink-red bill

black on back

pink or white breast

barred rusty-brown

dark "smile" at base of bill

tiny bumps on middle of back

FEMALE

big white patch near tail

MALE (WINTER AND SPRING)

This is a colourful eider, closely similar in many respects to the common Eider but a more northerly and rarer bird. It is usually seen as a rare stray in flocks of Eiders far to the south of its usual range, occasionally remaining for several weeks and sometimes returning in subsequent years. Males in full plumage are easy to tell from common Eiders, moulting males in summer less so, and females and young birds difficult, except with close scrutiny.

VOICE Male has cooing calls in spring; female has harsh, croaking note.

NESTING Nest lined with down from female's body, on ground near water, often on small island; 4–5 eggs; 1 brood; May–July.

FEEDING Dives for molluscs, crustaceans, and insect larvae from tundra pools in summer.

FLIGHT: direct, rather heavy but fast with steady wingbeats.

STRIKING APPEARANCE
The male is colourful and easy to tell in winter and spring, but females are much more like Eiders, requiring careful identification.

SIMILAR SPECIES

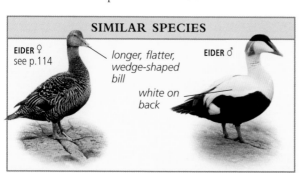

EIDER ♀ see p.114

longer, flatter, wedge-shaped bill

EIDER ♂

white on back

OCCURRENCE
Rare and local breeder in N Iceland and extreme N Scandinavia; otherwise rare, usually with Eiders, on shores of Scandinavia, Baltic, and northern North Sea, mostly autumn to spring.

Seen in the UK
J F M A M J J A S O N D

Length **60cm (24in)**	Wingspan **90–100cm (36–40in)**	Weight **1.5–2kg (3¼–4½lb)**
Social **Small flocks**	Lifespan **10–15 years**	Status **Secure**

115

Order **Anseriformes**	Family **Anatidae**	Species *Bucephala clangula*

Goldeneye

MALE (WINTER)
large white belly

FEMALE IN FLIGHT
extensive white on wing

JUVENILE (MALE)
body becomes white with age

black marks on sparkling white body

green-glossed black head with bold white spot

yellow eye

triangular dark bill

MALE (WINTER)

face develops white spot in winter

grey body

dark brown head

FEMALE
yellow patch on grey bill

There are usually more Goldeneyes in a group than is usually apparent until they fly off: typically, at least half of these expert divers are underwater at any one time. Usually shy, they are easily disturbed by people on the shore or by boats, flying off in tight-packed groups with a loud whistling from their wings. Flocks are typically predominantly females and immatures, although more adult males may appear in spring (summer males look like females).
VOICE Frequent nasal, mechanical *ze-zeee* in display; female has grating double note.
NESTING Down-lined tree hole and nest box; 8–11 eggs; 1 brood; April–June.
FEEDING Dives constantly from surface to find molluscs and crustaceans.

FLIGHT: very quick and strong, with rather short wings; fast, deep wingbeats create loud whistle.

FLYING
Goldeneyes are shy and quick to fly off. Their wings make a loud whistling sound.

RESTING FLOCK
After feeding well, Goldeneyes rest in flocks, head withdrawn and tails cocked.

SIMILAR SPECIES

SMEW ♂ winter, similar to ♂ winter; see p.117

grey flanks

white head

browner

dark neck

VELVET SCOTER ♀ similar to ♀; see p.113

OCCURRENCE
Breeds in N Europe (but only rarely in Scotland), in wooded areas beside cold freshwater lakes. Numbers often increased by provision of nest boxes. In winter, widespread on lakes, reservoirs, and estuaries.

Seen in the UK
J F M A M J J A S O N D

Length **42–50cm (16½–20in)**	Wingspan **65–80cm (26–32in)**	Weight **600–1,200g (21–43oz)**
Social **Small flocks**	Lifespan **Up to 8 years**	Status **Secure**

Order **Anseriformes**	Family **Anatidae**	Species ***Mergellus albellus***

Smew

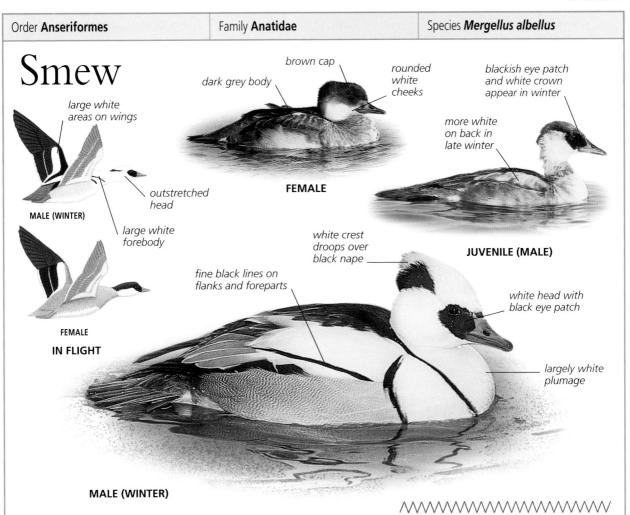

large white areas on wings

MALE (WINTER)

outstretched head

large white forebody

FEMALE
IN FLIGHT

dark grey body

brown cap

rounded white cheeks

FEMALE

blackish eye patch and white crown appear in winter

more white on back in late winter

JUVENILE (MALE)

white crest droops over black nape

fine black lines on flanks and foreparts

white head with black eye patch

largely white plumage

MALE (WINTER)

/\/\/\/\/\/\/\/\/\/\/\/\/\/\/\/\/\/\

FLIGHT: flies fast and low; broad white foreparts and outstretched neck very obvious.

In the UK, this is a scarce bird, found in small groups at most, but in the Low Countries and the Baltic, hundreds sometimes feed together in very active, busy flocks. The white males are usually much scarcer than females and immatures, collectively known as "redheads". Even where there are one or two males in a flock on a complex of gravel pits, they can be quite hard to spot as the birds tend to fly around a lot. They particularly associate with Goldeneyes and may also be found with Tufted Ducks.

VOICE Silent in winter.
NESTING Tree holes, often of Black Woodpecker, near water, or in nest boxes; 4–6 eggs; 1 brood; April–June.
FEEDING Dives often from surface, eating small fish and insect larvae.

STUNNING DRAKE
The winter male is one of the most attractive of European wildfowl. In summer, the male Smew looks like the female.

SIMILAR SPECIES

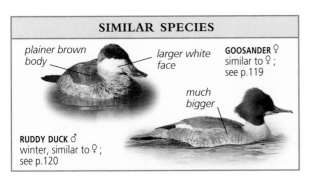

plainer brown body

larger white face

GOOSANDER ♀
similar to ♀;
see p.119

much bigger

RUDDY DUCK ♂
winter, similar to ♀;
see p.120

OCCURRENCE
Breeds in far NE Europe by lakes and rivers in forested areas. In winter, common in large, mobile flocks on Baltic and Low Country coasts, scarce on inland waters west to Great Britain, when a few turn up on pits and reservoirs.

Seen in the UK
J F M A M J J A S O N D

Length **36–44cm (14–17½in)**	Wingspan **55–69cm (22–27in)**	Weight **500–800g (18–29oz)**
Social **Flocks**	Lifespan **Up to 8 years**	Status **Vulnerable**

| Order **Anseriformes** | Family **Anatidae** | Species ***Mergus serrator*** |

Red-breasted Merganser

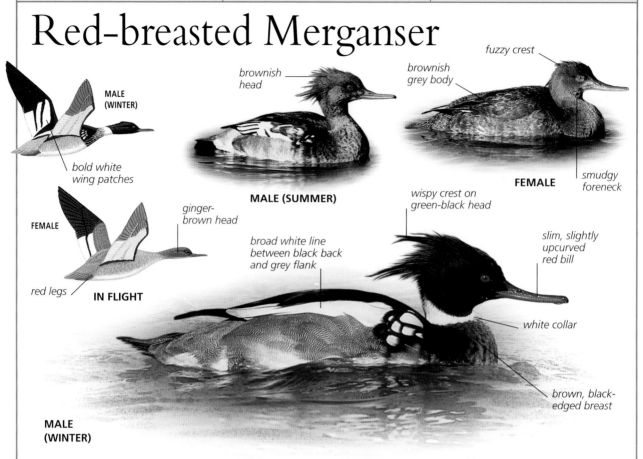

MALE (WINTER)

bold white wing patches

brownish head

fuzzy crest

brownish grey body

MALE (SUMMER)

FEMALE

smudgy foreneck

FEMALE

ginger-brown head

red legs

IN FLIGHT

wispy crest on green-black head

broad white line between black back and grey flank

slim, slightly upcurved red bill

white collar

MALE (WINTER)

brown, black-edged breast

A "sawbill" duck, the Red-breasted Merganser is found both on fast, clean rivers in hilly regions and at the coast in summer, and usually on the sea at other times. It often stands out on sandy shores or rocks. Males display to females in winter and spring with ritualized, jerky, curtseying movements, fanning their spiky crests and opening their bills. In winter, typically a male or two will be seen with a handful of "redheads" (females and immatures) but in places a few hundred might flock together.

VOICE Quiet, sometimes low, rolling croak or growl.

NESTING In long grass on ground or among rocks; 8–11 eggs; 1 brood; April–June.

FEEDING Dives from surface to find small fish and invertebrates.

FLIGHT: fast, direct, with long head and neck and tail giving marked cross-shape.

DISPLAYING MALES
Male Red-breasted Mergansers stretch forward and jerk their heads forward while raising the rear body, in energetic displays.

SIMILAR SPECIES

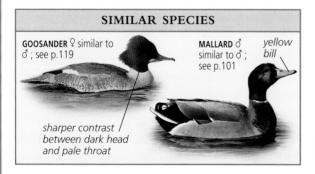

GOOSANDER ♀ similar to ♂; see p.119

sharper contrast between dark head and pale throat

MALLARD ♂ similar to ♂; see p.101

yellow bill

OCCURRENCE
Breeds by coasts or along fast rivers in N Great Britain, Iceland, Scandinavia, and Baltic region. Winters south to Greece and N France, mostly on coasts. Big moulting groups can be seen off sandy and rocky shores in late summer.

| Seen in the UK |
| J F M A M J J A S O N D |

| Length **51–62cm (20–24in)** | Wingspan **70–85cm (28–34in)** | Weight **0.85–1.25kg (1¾–2¾lb)** |
| Social **Family groups/Flocks** | Lifespan **Up to 8 years** | Status **Secure** |

| Order **Anseriformes** | Family **Anatidae** | Species **Mergus merganser** |

Goosander

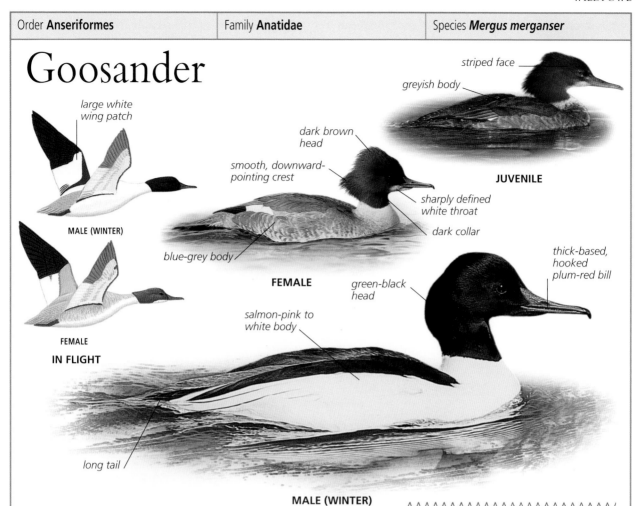

large white wing patch

MALE (WINTER)

FEMALE

IN FLIGHT

striped face

greyish body

JUVENILE

dark brown head

smooth, downward-pointing crest

sharply defined white throat

dark collar

blue-grey body

FEMALE

green-black head

thick-based, hooked plum-red bill

salmon-pink to white body

long tail

MALE (WINTER)

FLIGHT: often low, fast, and direct, with elongated but heavy shape.

The largest "sawbill", with a long, serrated bill for grasping fish, the Goosander is more of a freshwater bird than the Red-breasted Merganser, especially outside the breeding season. It is found in small groups in winter, often looking remarkably large on small inland lakes and pits on still, misty days. In summer, breeding pairs prefer upland reservoirs and shallower, fast-flowing, clear streams with plenty of boulders and stony shores. Usually a shy bird, the Goosander is easily scared off even at long range.

VOICE Harsh *karrr* and cackling notes.

NESTING Hole in trees near water; 8–11 eggs; 1 brood; April–July.

FEEDING Dives from surface, moving long distances underwater in larger lakes, to take fish.

LAZY MALES
In winter, male Goosanders swim about on open water, often drifting inactive for long periods. Males look like the females in summer.

SIMILAR SPECIES

RED-BREASTED MERGANSER ♂♀; ♂ has dark breast; see p.118

blurred face

dark breast

MALLARD ♂ similar to ♂♀; see p.101

♀

OCCURRENCE
Breeds beside rivers and lakes in Iceland, Scandinavia, and N Great Britain. Winters south to Balkans and France, mostly on fresh water. Bigger flocks mostly in regular sites on larger reservoirs, smaller numbers on pits or rivers.

| Seen in the UK |
| J F M A M J J A S O N D |

| Length **57–69cm (22½–27in)** | Wingspan **82–98cm (32–39in)** | Weight **1–1.6kg (2¼–3½lb)** |
| Social **Small flocks** | Lifespan **Up to 8 years** | Status **Secure** |

Order **Anseriformes**	Family **Anatidae**	Species *Oxyura jamaicensis*

Ruddy Duck

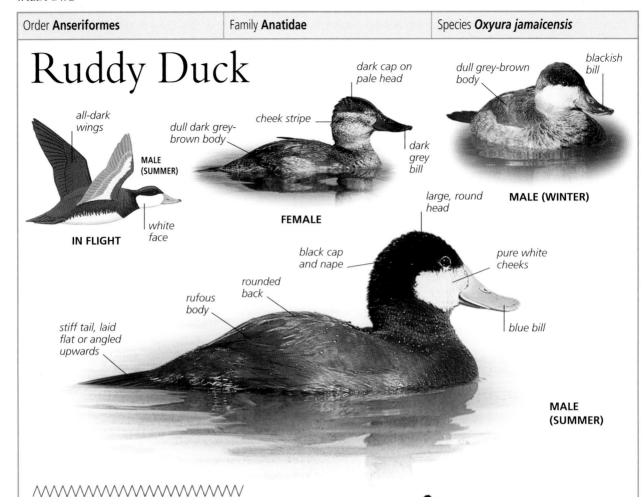

MALE (SUMMER)

all-dark wings

IN FLIGHT

white face

dark cap on pale head

cheek stripe

dull dark grey-brown body

FEMALE

dark grey bill

dull grey-brown body

blackish bill

MALE (WINTER)

large, round head

black cap and nape

pure white cheeks

rounded back

rufous body

blue bill

stiff tail, laid flat or angled upwards

MALE (SUMMER)

/\/\/\/\/\/\/\/\/\/\/\/\/\/\/\/\

FLIGHT: fast, low, weak, with whirring wingbeats; direct, with little agility.

An accidental introduction to Europe, the Ruddy Duck escaped from collections in the 1950s and has since become established in several countries. It is a freshwater bird, family parties pottering about reedy shores. It moves to larger lakes and reservoirs in winter, flocks numbering several hundreds in the most favoured places which have become traditional moulting and wintering areas.

VOICE Mostly silent; odd grunts, also slaps bill against chest in display.

NESTING Large, floating pile of vegetation in tall reeds, often "roofed" over by meshed stems; 6–10 eggs; 1 brood; April–June.

FEEDING Dives from surface, reappearing like a cork; takes insect larvae and seeds.

DISPLAYING MALE
The male Ruddy Duck vibrates his bill against the breast, pushing out air in a flurry of bubbles from the feathers.

OCCURRENCE
Breeds on reedy pools and flooded pits in Great Britain and less commonly, adjacent areas of continent. In larger reservoirs and more open waters in autumn, mostly in a few flocks at regular sites, ones and twos elsewhere.

Seen in the UK
J F M A M J J A S O N D

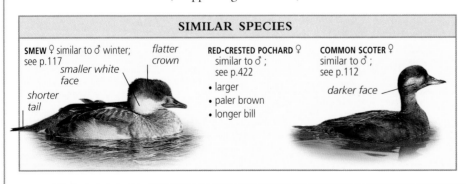

SIMILAR SPECIES

SMEW ♀ similar to ♂ winter; see p.117

smaller white face

shorter tail

flatter crown

RED-CRESTED POCHARD ♀ similar to ♂; see p.422
• larger
• paler brown
• longer bill

COMMON SCOTER ♀ similar to ♂; see p.112

darker face

Length **35 – 43cm (14 –17in)**	Wingspan **53 – 62cm (21– 24in)**	Weight **350 – 800g (13 – 29oz)**
Social **Winter flocks**	Lifespan **Up to 8 years**	Status **Secure†**

Families **Pandionidae, Accipitridae, Falconidae**

BIRDS OF PREY

THIS IS A MIXED GROUP, including birds that eat tiny insects, others that eat dead animals, and some that catch their own prey up to the size of small deer. Mostly splendid in flight, many are likely to remain perched for hours on end between feeding forays, while others are much more aerial, spending much of the day aloft.

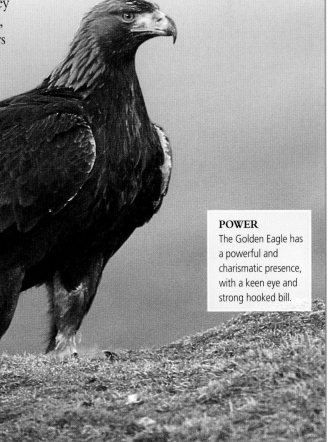

WIDE SPAN
Vultures, such as this Egyptian Vulture, have very long wings, soaring on warm air with little expenditure of energy.

VULTURES
Including some of Europe's biggest birds, the vultures soar high up, using superb eyesight to spot potential food on the ground: they eat meat, preferably freshly dead animals. They need warm, rising air or updraughts and live in southern Europe and mountainous areas.

EAGLES AND HAWKS
Eagles are powerful hunters with large eyes, powerful bills, and strong feet. Most have feathered legs. Buzzards are smaller, less strong, in particular smaller-billed, birds but also majestic fliers. Harriers are hunters over open ground, flying low as they try to surprise prey at close range. Bird-eating hawks such as the Sparrowhawk catch prey by surprise in a short, fast dash. Kites have long, notched tails that are swivelled, acting as rudders in their elegant flight.

The Osprey is a fish-eating specialist, diving onto its prey from the air, while the Short-toed Eagle is a "snake-eagle", one of a largely African group with large, yellow eyes, a big head, and unfeathered legs.

FALCONS
Big falcons catch large prey and eat infrequently, spending long periods perched, but look impressive in the air when they do fly; smaller falcons may be much more active. Some eat small mammals, others mostly insects or birds.

POWER
The Golden Eagle has a powerful and charismatic presence, with a keen eye and strong hooked bill.

Order **Accipitriformes**	Family **Accipitridae**	Species *Gyps fulvus*

Griffon Vulture

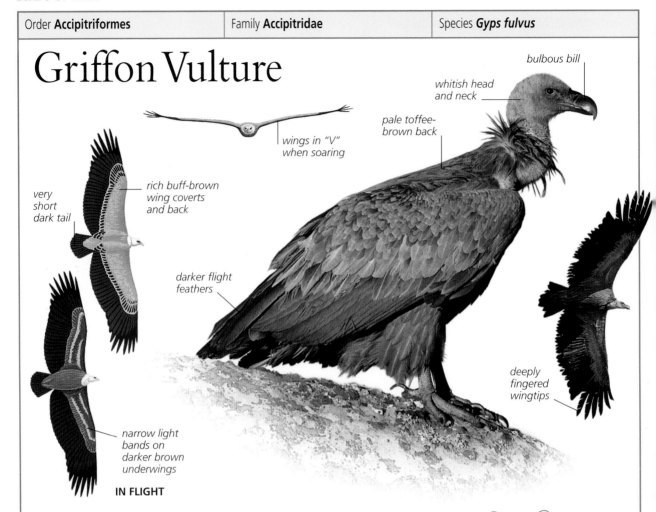

wings in "V" when soaring

bulbous bill

whitish head and neck

pale toffee-brown back

rich buff-brown wing coverts and back

very short dark tail

darker flight feathers

deeply fingered wingtips

narrow light bands on darker brown underwings

IN FLIGHT

A massive, long-winged, short-tailed bird, the Griffon Vulture spends much time sitting quietly on cliff ledges but flies off in search of food each day. It may be in the air early on cold, windy days, using the wind to help it soar, but on calm, hot days it waits until later in the day and uses rising currents of warm air that build up over bare ground or cliffs. It soars with its wings raised and twisted at the tips, the trailing edge bulging and also slightly arched, so that, as it slowly circles, its shape appears to change. From directly below it is broad- and square-winged but from many angles the wingtips appear more pointed.

VOICE Silent apart from coarse hissing when feeding.

NESTING On bare ledge in gorge or on high cliff, in loose colonies of ten or so to several scores of pairs; 1 egg; 1 brood; April–July.

FEEDING Finds carrion (dead sheep, goats, and smaller animals); often fed at special feeding stations.

FLIGHT: heavy, deep wingbeats; mostly magnificent soaring with wings in "V".

MASTER SOARER
The Griffon can travel great distances without flapping its wings at all, using warm upcurrents to gain height.

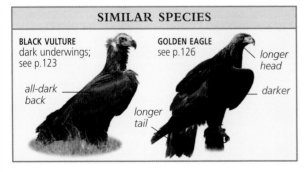

SIMILAR SPECIES

BLACK VULTURE dark underwings; see p.123

all-dark back

GOLDEN EAGLE see p.126

longer head

darker

longer tail

OCCURRENCE
Quite common in Portugal and Spain, rare in S France, Sardinia, Balkans, and Turkey. In all kinds of open areas, from lowlands to high, bleak mountain peaks, centred on a cliff or gorge where they roost and nest.

Seen in the UK
J F M A M J J A S O N D

Length **0.95–1.1m (3–3½ft)**	Wingspan **2.3–2.65m (7½–8¾ft)**	Weight **7–10kg (15–22lb)**
Social **Flocks**	Lifespan **Up to 25 years**	Status **Rare**

| Order **Accipitriformes** | Family **Accipitridae** | Species ***Aegypius monachus*** |

Black Vulture

pale head with black mask

pale brown ruff (darker on juvenile)

massive, dark brown body (juvenile paler)

fresh feathers very dark, fade paler

ADULT

very broad, square wings held flat

flat wings when soaring

very dark forewings

pale feet

ADULT

IN FLIGHT

FLIGHT: prolonged, expert soaring and gliding with very occasional deep, ponderous wingbeat; flaps heavily in cold, still air.

One of the world's largest flying birds, the Black Vulture's massive bulk and majestic soaring and gliding flight give it terrific impact whenever it is aloft. It exhibits great skill at utilizing every updraught or breath of wind to soar effortlessly without wingbeats. Its flat-winged flight gives the Black Vulture a very broad, rectangular shape, which is less elegant and shapely than a Griffon Vulture's. Unlike the Griffon Vulture, it nests and often perches in trees (rather than on cliffs), and also spends much time on the ground, especially near food such as a sheep or goat carcass.

VOICE Mostly silent.

NESTING Huge stick nest in flat-topped trees; 1 egg, 1 brood; April–June.

FEEDING Rarely catches live prey; mostly eats carrion; also feeds at special feeding stations.

GIANTS OF THE AIR
A very impressive bird, the Black Vulture has great presence in the sky, even among equally large Griffon Vultures; its pale head and feet may be obvious.

SIMILAR SPECIES

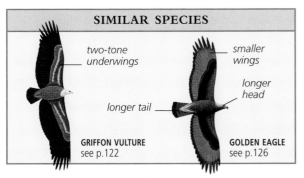

two-tone underwings

longer tail

GRIFFON VULTURE
see p.122

smaller wings

longer head

GOLDEN EAGLE
see p.126

OCCURRENCE
Restricted to C Spain, Majorca, and very rare in NE Greece. Resident all year in these small areas and only very rare vagrant elsewhere. Rare vulture of mountainous regions and rolling uplands with mixed forest and open ground.

| Seen in the UK |
| J F M A M J J A S O N D |

| Length **1–1.15m (3¼–3¾ft)** | Wingspan **2.5–2.85m (8¼–9¼ft)** | Weight **7–11.5kg (15–25lb)** |
| Social **Small flocks** | Lifespan **Up to 25 years** | Status **Vulnerable** |

123

| Order **Accipitriformes** | Family **Accipitridae** | Species **Neophron percnopterus** |

Egyptian Vulture

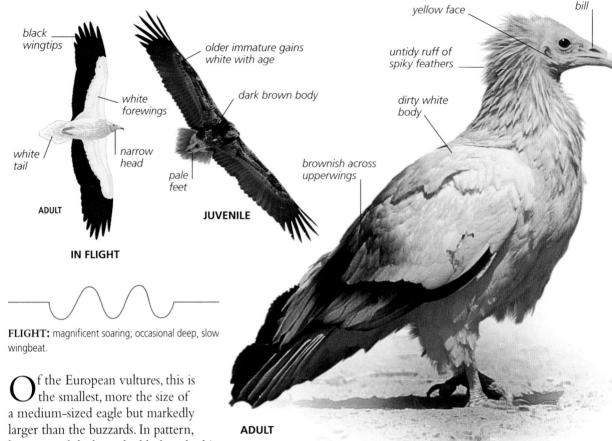

black wingtips

older immature gains white with age

dark brown body

white forewings

white tail

narrow head

pale feet

ADULT

JUVENILE

IN FLIGHT

brownish across upperwings

thin bill

yellow face

untidy ruff of spiky feathers

dirty white body

ADULT

FLIGHT: magnificent soaring; occasional deep, slow wingbeat.

Of the European vultures, this is the smallest, more the size of a medium-sized eagle but markedly larger than the buzzards. In pattern, however, adults have the black and white of White Storks (see p.85) or pelicans (see p.416), which are much bigger. Immatures are browner but spend their early years in Africa, and so are rather infrequently seen in Europe. On the ground, the plumage of an adult often looks dirty and drab, soiled by its foraging in filthy places, but against a blue sky, it is a splendid bird. Two or three Egyptian Vultures may often be seen associating with larger numbers of Griffon Vultures.

VOICE Silent.
NESTING Nest of sticks, bones, and rubbish, on cliff ledge or in small cave; 1–3 eggs; 1 brood; April–June.
FEEDING Finds all kinds of dead meat, offal, and scraps.

GLORIOUS FLIGHT
While often dirty-looking on the ground, the Egyptian Vulture against a deep blue sky in full sunlight looks stunning, almost translucent white and intense black.

SIMILAR SPECIES

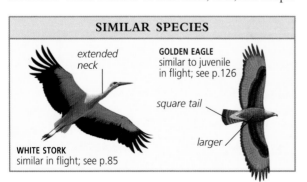

extended neck

GOLDEN EAGLE similar to juvenile in flight; see p.126

square tail

larger

WHITE STORK similar in flight; see p.85

OCCURRENCE
Summer visitor to Portugal and Spain, rare in S France, S Italy, and Balkans. In wooded mountainous areas, around gorges and cliffs, and also at refuse tips near small towns and villages, often with kites and larger vultures.

| Seen in the UK |
| J F M A M J J A S O N D |

| Length **55–65cm (22–26in)** | Wingspan **1.55–1.7m (5–5½ft)** | Weight **1.6–2.1kg (3½–4¾lb)** |
| Social **Small flocks** | Lifespan **10–15 years** | Status **Secure** |

Order **Accipitriformes**	Family **Accipitridae**	Species *Haliaeetus albicilla*

White-tailed Eagle

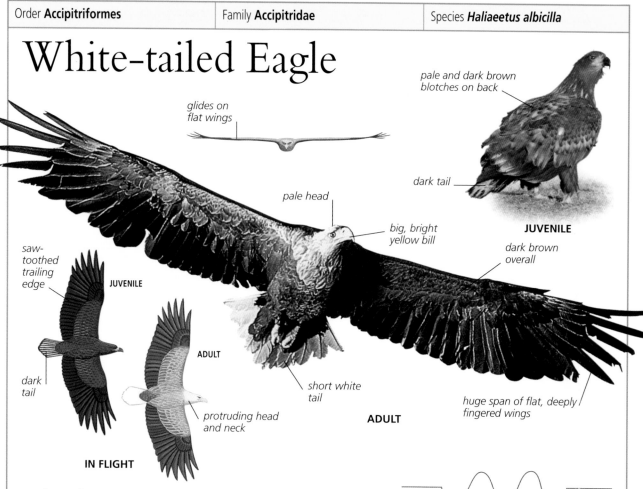

glides on flat wings

pale and dark brown blotches on back

dark tail

JUVENILE

pale head

big, bright yellow bill

dark brown overall

saw-toothed trailing edge

JUVENILE

ADULT

dark tail

protruding head and neck

short white tail

ADULT

huge span of flat, deeply fingered wings

IN FLIGHT

A huge, flat-winged bird, this eagle is now very rare over most of its former range. It survives in remote marshes and along rocky coasts and offshore islands, and appears on extensive damp coastal plains in winter. Its presence in Scotland is due to a recent reintroduction programme. Around small fishing harbours, it can become quite bold and relatively tame if unpersecuted. It typically sits upright on rocks or swoops into sheltered bays for fish.
VOICE Shrill yaps near nest in summer.
NESTING Huge pile of sticks on flat crowns of trees or cliff ledges; 2 eggs; 1 brood; March–July.
FEEDING Picks sick or dead fish and offal from water using its feet; eats dead animals and catches seabirds and hares.

FLIGHT: heavy and direct; wingbeats deep and elastic, or flexible; soars on flat wings.

SWOOPING ON PREY
This eagle dives for food with lumbering but expert agility, picking fish and offal from water with its feet.

OCCURRENCE
Most common in Scandinavia along rocky coasts, rare in central and E Europe, Balkans, Iceland, and W Scotland where reintroduced on offshore isles. Winters mostly in wide open lowlands, including farmland, with ones and twos appearing most years in some traditional areas.

Seen in the UK
J F M A M J J A S O N D

SIMILAR SPECIES

wings raised in "V"

shorter head

GRIFFON VULTURE see p.122

BLACK VULTURE see p.123

shorter head in flight

longer tail

shorter head

darker

wings raised in "V" when soaring

GOLDEN EAGLE see p.126

Length **70–92cm (28–36in)**	Wingspan **2–2.45m (6½–8ft)**	Weight **3.1–7kg (6¾–15lb)**
Social **Family groups**	Lifespan **Up to 20 years**	Status **Rare**

Order **Accipitriformes**	Family **Accipitridae**	Species *Aquila chrysaetos*

Golden Eagle

wings raised in slight "V"

white on tail and wings reduces with age

IMMATURE

pale tawny to yellowish head

dark brown plumage

blacker body than adult's

bulky body and wings

protruding head (less than White-tailed Eagle's)

IMMATURE

barred dark underwings

IN FLIGHT

ADULT

long tail with paler area at base

ADULT

While White-tailed Eagles and the large vultures have great bulk and a massive presence, the Golden Eagle combines size with elegance and even delicacy in the air. It is often seen far off over a high peak, literally a dot in the distance, but its wide, slow circling is frequently sufficient to identify it. Close views are harder to come by, a rare chance encounter on a high peak being really memorable.

VOICE Occasional shrill yelps and whistling *twee-oo*.

NESTING Massive pile of sticks, lined with wool and greenery, on broad cliff ledge or in old pine; 1–3 eggs; 1 brood; February–June.

FEEDING Eats much dead meat, mostly sheep and deer in winter; hunts grouse, Ptarmigan, crows, hares, and rabbits.

FLIGHT: direct flight steady; frequent glides; soars with wings raised; switchback display and occasional superfast stoop or plunge with wings curved back.

STANDING BIRD
A standing Golden Eagle looks majestic. The thick, heavily feathered legs are obvious on a perched bird.

OCCURRENCE
Widespread but sparse, most frequent in Scotland, Spain, parts of Scandinavia, Italy, Balkans, and also in Alps. Mostly over remote peaks or upland forests, more rarely on steep coasts, and stays high up, away from towns and villages, and roads and other developments (unlike Buzzards).

SIMILAR SPECIES

more patterned underwings

smaller

BUZZARD
less solidly stable in flight; see p.136

WHITE-TAILED EAGLE
see p.125

flat wings

bigger

shorter tail

GRIFFON VULTURE
see p.122

small head

broader wings

Seen in the UK
J F M A M J J A S O N D

Length **75–85cm (30–34in)**	Wingspan **1.9–2.2m (6¼–7¼ft)**	Weight **3–6.7kg (6½–15lb)**
Social **Family groups**	Lifespan **Up to 25 years**	Status **Rare**

| Order **Accipitriformes** | Family **Accipitridae** | Species *Circaetus gallicus* |

Short-toed Eagle

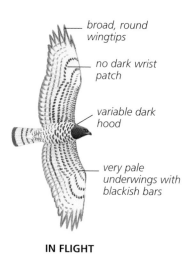

- broad, round wingtips
- no dark wrist patch
- variable dark hood
- very pale underwings with blackish bars

IN FLIGHT

- bulky, round head
- yellow eye
- pale brown upperside
- new feathers dark, old ones paler with ragged edges
- grey-white underside with fine bars
- bare legs
- long tail

FLIGHT: glides on bowed wings pushed forward; soars with wings very long and straight, head protruding in display; hovers with heavy, floppy action.

A large, impressive eagle, the Short-toed Eagle is sometimes seen perched at close range, on a high pylon or on top of a tall tree, when its crisply barred plumage and vivid yellow eyes give it a handsome and magnificent appearance. One of the "snake-eagles", this bird of prey has strong, bare legs, a thickly feathered, rounded head, and an owl-like face. While hunting it hovers before a long, fast plunge, with its head pulled back, wings almost closed, and chest thrust out, reaching out with its feet at the last moment.

VOICE Various short, abrupt calls, *kyo, meeok*.
NESTING Bulky stick nest in crown of large tree; 1 egg; 1 brood; April–June.
FEEDING Catches snakes and lizards, typically stooping onto them at speed after hover, sometimes from great height.

PERSISTENT HUNTER
Short-toed Eagles spend hours flying over open hillsides, hovering frequently, searching for prey.

SIMILAR SPECIES

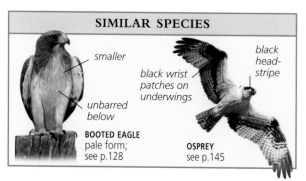

- smaller
- unbarred below
- **BOOTED EAGLE** pale form; see p.128
- black wrist patches on underwings
- black head-stripe
- **OSPREY** see p.145

OCCURRENCE
In summer, over high, open slopes, and rocky areas with short scrub, in Portugal, Spain, France, Italy, and Balkans. Prefers some woodland but mostly semi-natural vegetation such as aromatic, thorny scrub; absent from farmed areas.

| Seen in the UK |
| J F M A M J J A S O N D |

| Length **62–69cm (24–27in)** | Wingspan **1.62–1.78m (5¼–5¾ft)** | Weight **1.5–2.5kg (3¼–5½lb)** |
| Social **Family groups** | Lifespan **Up to 15 years** | Status **Rare** |

Order **Accipitriformes**	Family **Accipitridae**	Species ***Aquila pennata***

Booted Eagle

broad, round head

well-fingered wingtips

flat or bowed wings

diagonal pale bands on wings

white spots

whitish crescent on rump

BOTH FORMS FROM ABOVE

long tail with sharp corners

pale patch

round head

dull brown overall

PALE FORM

DARK FORM

IN FLIGHT

white underside

PALE FORM

FLIGHT: fast, with long glides and rather flappy wingbeats; frequent soaring.

Much more frequent than Bonelli's Eagle, the Booted Eagle is a small, buzzard-sized eagle, frequently mobbed by crows and other birds of prey. It occurs in pale and dark forms but its shape and proportions help identify it. It is typical of well-wooded, hot countryside in relatively lowland areas, avoiding the moister northwestern parts of Europe. Unlike the Buzzard, it is a summer visitor to Europe.
VOICE Buzzard-like *hi-yaaah* and loud, musical, wader-like whistle, *kli-kli-kli* in display.
NESTING Bulky stick nest deep inside canopy of tree, rarely on cliff ledge; 2 eggs; 1 brood; February–April.
FEEDING Catches reptiles, small birds, and small mammals on ground, often after very fast, near-vertical stoop from considerable height.

DISTINCTIVE PATTERN
In flight overhead, the Booted Eagle shows thin, translucent trailing edges to both wings and tail, and a pale inner primary patch; head-on it reveals bright white shoulder spots.

SIMILAR SPECIES

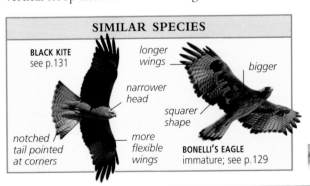

BLACK KITE see p.131

longer wings

narrower head

notched tail pointed at corners

more flexible wings

bigger

squarer shape

BONELLI'S EAGLE immature; see p.129

OCCURRENCE
In Spain, Portugal, France, and E Europe, in forests and warm, sunny, well-wooded, hilly country with mixed farmland and scrub, often close to villages. Thrives best in remote regions with little disturbance. From March to October.

Seen in the UK
J F M A M J J A S O N D

Length **42–51cm (16½–20in)**	Wingspan **1.1–1.35m (3½–4½ft)**	Weight **700–1,000g (25–36oz)**
Social **Family groups**	Lifespan **Up to 15 years**	Status **Rare**

| Order **Accipitriformes** | Family **Accipitridae** | Species *Aquila fasciata* |

Bonelli's Eagle

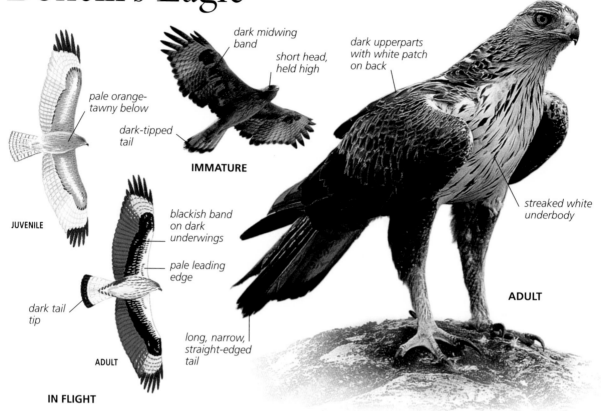

dark midwing band

short head, held high

dark upperparts with white patch on back

pale orange-tawny below

dark-tipped tail

IMMATURE

JUVENILE

blackish band on dark underwings

pale leading edge

dark tail tip

long, narrow, straight-edged tail

ADULT

IN FLIGHT

streaked white underbody

ADULT

A strong and potent predator, Bonelli's Eagle combines the power of a large eagle with the behaviour of a fast-flying, aggressive hawk. It spends much time perching on a ledge out of sight, but periodically soars over its territory or moves off to find food; it hunts rather low down and is usually inconspicuous. It is generally scarce and very localized, with isolated pairs here and there in traditional territories, mostly in areas with steep cliffs and crags between forested slopes. Only a few hundred pairs of Bonelli's Eagle remain in Europe.

VOICE Occasional bark or shrill yelp, but mostly silent.
NESTING Large stick nest in small cave, deep ledge, or sheer cliff, rarely in tree; 2 eggs; 1 brood; February–April.
FEEDING Elegant and powerful; hunts hares, rabbits, squirrels, partridges, crows, and pigeons.

FLIGHT: glides on flat wings with angled leading edge; wingbeats shallow; soars, sometimes stoops at great speed.

STRIKING APPEARANCE
In flight, Bonelli's Eagle looks big and square with quite a long tail, long flat wings, and a small head sweeping up from the deep chest; the white body catches the light.

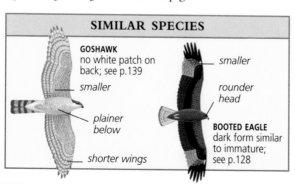

SIMILAR SPECIES

GOSHAWK no white patch on back; see p.139

smaller

smaller

plainer below

shorter wings

rounder head

BOOTED EAGLE dark form similar to immature; see p.128

OCCURRENCE
Occupies forested hills and crags in Spain, Portugal, S France, and Balkans; often nests and roosts in deep gorges, but not especially high up, and moves out into nearby hills and woodland to hunt. Resident.

Seen in the UK
J F M A M J J A S O N D

| Length **55–65cm (22–26in)** | Wingspan **1.45–1.65m (4¾–5½ft)** | Weight **1.5–2.5kg (3¼–5½lb)** |
| Social **Pairs/Families** | Lifespan **Up to 15 years** | Status **Endangered** |

Order **Accipitriformes**	Family **Accipitridae**	Species ***Milvus milvus***

Red Kite

bowed wings while soaring

whitish to pale red underside of tail

pale band on upperwings

ADULT

ADULT

forked tail

IN FLIGHT

paler than adult

IMMATURE

paler upperwings than adult's

pale rufous tail, deeply notched when closed

bold white patch contrasts with black wrist patch

ADULT

pale tawny to rust-red body

pale eye

whitish head

ADULT

A gility and mastery in the air are synonymous with the kites: the Red Kite adds the appeal of colour and pattern. It is easily separated from the heavier, less elegant Buzzard, having more of the lightness of a harrier, but even greater flexibility and elasticity in its movements. Where common, it gathers in groups of ten or even up to forty wherever food is concentrated.

VOICE High, long-drawn, wailing or squealing *weieie-ee-ow*, higher-pitched than Buzzard.

NESTING Large nest of sticks, rags, earth, and rubbish in tree, usually well-hidden; 2–4 eggs; 1 brood; March–June.

FEEDING Eats dead animals, such as rabbits or sheep; catches birds up to crow or gull size in surprise dash; also feeds on insects, earthworms, and voles.

FLIGHT: direct flight slow and steady with supple, deep wingbeats; often twists tail as rudder; soars well but not usually to any great height; very aerobatic.

FLEXIBLE FLIGHT
The kite flexes its wings and twists its long tail from side to side to exploit air currents to the full; it is capable of fast stoops and twisting dives.

SIMILAR SPECIES

BLACK KITE see p.131

BUZZARD see p.136

less contrasted below

duller body and tail

stiffer, shorter wings

short round tail

OCCURRENCE
Local in Great Britain, widespread in Spain, Portugal, France, parts of S Europe, and north to Baltic. In open countryside and wooded valleys, higher up in summer but in low valleys in winter, when it forages around towns and tips.

Seen in the UK
J F M A M J J A S O N D

Length **60–65cm (23½–26in)**	Wingspan **1.45–1.65m (4¾–5½ft)**	Weight **0.75–1.3kg (1¾–2¾lb)**
Social **Small flocks**	Lifespan **Up to 25 years**	Status **Secure**

Order **Accipitriformes**	Family **Accipitridae**	Species *Milvus migrans*

Black Kite

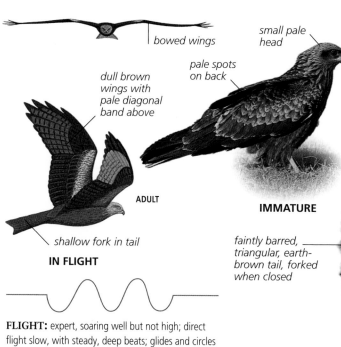

bowed wings

small pale head

dull brown wings with pale diagonal band above

pale spots on back

dull and dark overall

paler underside and head

ADULT

IMMATURE

shallow fork in tail

IN FLIGHT

faintly barred, triangular, earth-brown tail, forked when closed

FLIGHT: expert, soaring well but not high; direct flight slow, with steady, deep beats; glides and circles on depressed wings with tail often fanned.

ADULT

long wings

With all the elegance of the Red Kite, the Black Kite lacks the contrasted pattern and rich colours, although it is far from uniform and far from black. Even more than a Red Kite it is likely to snatch food from the surface of water in a fast, sweeping dive, using its feet to pick up the food and carry it as it feeds in mid-air. Generally it is more numerous in areas where both birds are found and more likely to form small groups.

VOICE High, whinnying *peeie-ee-i-ee-i-ee.*

NESTING Nest of sticks, earth, and scraps of all kinds in tree; 2–4 eggs; 1 brood; March–June.

FEEDING Takes a lot of dead or dying fish from water or along shoreline; much dead meat and offal or scraps of all kinds; dung, small birds, reptiles, and voles.

REMARK Groups fight and chase each other over rubbish tips.

SCAVENGER
Black Kites join other birds of prey and crows at carcasses and rubbish tips, and also snatch scraps with their feet in fast, accurate swoops.

OCCURRENCE
Widespread from Spain and Portugal to Finland and south to Balkans; rare visitor to UK. Feeds around rubbish tips and over open ground, wooded slopes, coasts, and rivers; more often associated with water than Red Kite and still around towns in some places.

Seen in the UK
J F M A M J J A S O N D

SIMILAR SPECIES

pale rump

flat wings

square tail

longer tail

BOOTED EAGLE dark form; see p.128

slimmer, rakish build

bolder wing pattern

no pale diagonal band on wing

RED KITE see p.130

MARSH HARRIER ♀ ; similar in flight; see p.134

Length **48–58cm (19–23in)**	Wingspan **1.3–1.55m (4¼–5ft)**	Weight **650–1,100g (23–39oz)**
Social **Small flocks**	Lifespan **Up to 20 years**	Status **Vulnerable**

Order **Accipitriformes**	Family **Accipitridae**	Species **Circus pygargus**

Montagu's Harrier

MALE

slender tapered wingtips

black bar across inner wings

red-brown bars on underwings

long, narrow black wingtips angled back

FEMALE

banded tail

white rump

pale below with bold streaks

IN FLIGHT

medium grey head

medium grey upperparts

streaked flanks

MALE

glides with wings raised

unmarked rufous below

JUVENILE

pale crescents above and below eye

dark brown above

FEMALE

Difficult to tell from the Hen Harrier in most circumstances, Montagu's Harrier is a slimmer, thin-winged bird more closely associated with arable farmland. It is also a summer visitor to Europe, and is absent in winter. This is the most delicate of all the elegant-looking birds of the family, the swept-back, tapered wingtips often enough to aid identification even at very long range.

VOICE High, clear *yek-yek-yek* from male, *chek-ek-ek-ek* from female.

NESTING Nest of stems and grasses on ground in corn or heather; 4 or 5 eggs; 1 brood; April–June.

FEEDING Catches small mammals, reptiles, and small birds on or near ground, diving from low, gliding flight.

FLIGHT: low, elegant, with wings raised in glides; wingbeats relaxed, supple.

IMMATURE MALE
Young males often look dark, with a mixture of brown feathers among the adult grey.

OCCURRENCE
Widespread in N to S Great Britain (very rare) and to Baltic, from April to September, over heaths, rough grassland, marshes, and rolling cereal fields, often nesting in tall crops. Migrants typically follow low-lying coasts but also use high mountain passes.

Seen in the UK
J F M A M J J A S O N D

SIMILAR SPECIES

HEN HARRIER ♂♀; ♂ has broader wings and white rump; see p.133

shorter and bulkier

blunter wingtips

♀

bigger and heavier

darker brown

MARSH HARRIER ♀ similar to ♀; see p.134

Length **40–45cm (16–18in)**	Wingspan **1–1.2m (3¼–4ft)**	Weight **225–450g (8–16oz)**
Social **Pairs/Small flocks**	Lifespan **Up to 15 years**	Status **Secure**

Order **Accipitriformes**	Family **Accipitridae**	Species **Circus cyaneus**

Hen Harrier

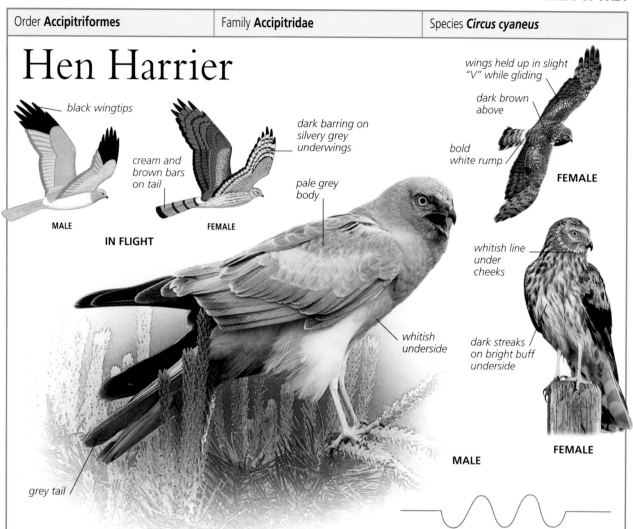

black wingtips

cream and brown bars on tail

dark barring on silvery grey underwings

pale grey body

MALE

FEMALE

IN FLIGHT

wings held up in slight "V" while gliding

dark brown above

bold white rump

FEMALE

whitish line under cheeks

whitish underside

dark streaks on bright buff underside

grey tail

MALE

FEMALE

FLIGHT: deceptively quick, sailing flight with wings raised or steady, deep wingbeats; soars well.

Hen Harriers frequent heather moors in summer but are often found over coastal marshes or low-lying, rough grassland in winter. Males and females are very different in appearance and echo the plumages of the closely related Montagu's Harrier. As with most birds of prey, females are larger and broader-winged than males.

VOICE Near nest, loud, irregular *week-eek-ik-ik-ik* from female; more even *chekekekekekek* from male.

NESTING Platform of stems on ground, in rushes or heather; 4–6 eggs; 1 brood; April–June.

FEEDING Hunts low over open ground, swooping down on small birds and voles.

NESTING
This female is carrying nesting material in its bill. Hen Harriers make a bulky pad of heather stems and grass on the ground.

SIMILAR SPECIES

MONTAGU'S HARRIER ♂♀; ♀ has longer, slimmer wing-tips; see p.132

grey rump

SHORT-EARED OWL similar to ♀; see p.245

shorter tail

black wingbar

big, round head

OCCURRENCE
Breeds in N and E Europe, mostly on moorland or heaths, locally in C and W Europe, on moors and sometimes open farmland. Widespread over open ground with short vegetation, including marshes, in W Europe in winter.

Seen in the UK

J F M A M J J A S O N D

Length **43–50cm (17–20in)**	Wingspan **1–1.2m (3¼–4ft)**	Weight **300–700g (11–25oz)**
Social **Roosts in groups**	Lifespan **Up to 15 years**	Status **Vulnerable**

Order **Accipitriformes**	Family **Accipitridae**	Species *Circus aeruginosus*

Marsh Harrier

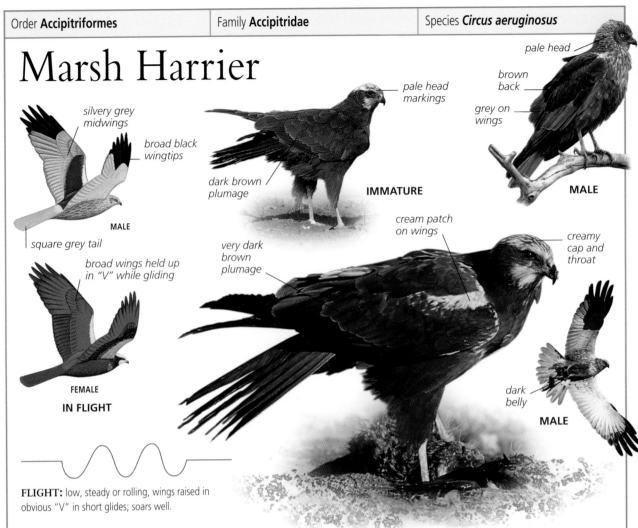

silvery grey midwings

broad black wingtips

MALE

square grey tail

dark brown plumage

pale head markings

IMMATURE

pale head

brown back

grey on wings

MALE

broad wings held up in "V" while gliding

very dark brown plumage

cream patch on wings

creamy cap and throat

FEMALE

IN FLIGHT

dark belly

MALE

FLIGHT: low, steady or rolling, wings raised in obvious "V" in short glides; soars well.

FEMALE

Long-winged and long-tailed, harriers fly low across open ground or marshland. The biggest and heaviest of them, the Marsh Harrier can be taken for a dark Buzzard or a Black Kite when soaring. It is closely associated with reedbeds, but may be seen over all kinds of open ground, especially flat pastures with ditches, when hunting or on migration. It often perches on bush tops or trees in the middle of a marsh for long spells. Males are generally smaller than females; they may breed in largely brown immature plumage.

VOICE Shrill *kee-yoo*, chattering *kyek-ek-ek-ek* or *kyi-yi-yi-yi*.

NESTING Large platform of reed stems among dense reeds over water; 4 or 5 eggs; 1 brood; April–July.

FEEDING Hunts low over marshes, diving to catch small birds, wildfowl, small mammals, and frogs.

FLIGHT PATTERN
Like all harriers, the Marsh Harrier has a slow flap and long glide flight, but with a heavier, less buoyant action.

OCCURRENCE
Widespread north to Great Britain (rare) and S Scandinavia, in reedy areas or long grass in marshes. N and E breeders move south in autumn; some W European birds remain all year, over marshes and flat, open countryside near coasts.

Seen in the UK
J F M A M J J A S O N D

SIMILAR SPECIES

pale band on forewings

streaked underside

twists tail in flight

HEN HARRIER ♀
similar to ♂♀;
see p.133

BLACK KITE
see p.131

Length **48–55cm (19–22in)**	Wingspan **1.1–1.25m (3½–4ft)**	Weight **400–800g (14–29oz)**
Social **Pairs/Family groups**	Lifespan **Up to 15 years**	Status **Secure**

Order **Acccipitriformes**	Family **Accipitridae**	Species ***Buteo lagopus***

Rough-legged Buzzard

white tail with dark bands near tip

whitish patches on primaries

IN FLIGHT

pale chest and blackish belly

ADULT

dark trailing edge (pale on juvenile) and wingtips

pale head

dark brown above

"frosty" pale feather edges

ADULT

FLIGHT: flight slightly more fluid and flexible than Buzzard; soars less, hovers frequently.

This northern buzzard sometimes appears in small numbers well to the south of its usual range in winter when food is short. It is clearly closely related to the Buzzard but usually sufficiently distinct to make identification straightforward. In wintering areas such as the Netherlands, there may be scores or hundreds of common Buzzards for every Rough-legged, but its regular hovering may draw attention to it. Its trademark feathered legs are often hard to see. Like some other northern species, its fortunes are closely linked to the fluctuating availability of its prey.

VOICE Loud, low, plaintive squeal, *pee-yow*.

NESTING Stick nest on cliff or in tree; 2–4 eggs; 1 brood; March–June.

FEEDING Drops onto small mammals, especially voles and small rabbits, from perch or after hover.

HEAD TO WIND
The pale head, dark belly, and pale vent show well as this individual hovers, head to wind, searching for prey on the ground.

SIMILAR SPECIES

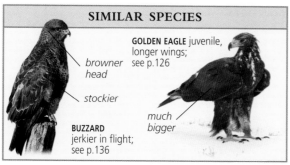

browner head

stockier

BUZZARD
jerkier in flight; see p.136

GOLDEN EAGLE juvenile, longer wings; see p.126

much bigger

OCCURRENCE
Breeds in Scandinavia in tundra and highland areas. Winters lower down in C Europe, few in Low Countries, very rare in UK except in years when small rodent food is scarce in north. Winter visitors often in low, expansive farmland.

Seen in the UK
J F M A M J J A S O N D

Length **50–60cm (20–23½in)**	Wingspan **1.2–1.5m (4–5ft)**	Weight **600–1,300g (21–46oz)**
Social **Family groups**	Lifespan **Up to 10 years**	Status **Secure**

| Order **Accipitriformes** | Family **Accipitridae** | Species ***Buteo buteo*** |

Buzzard

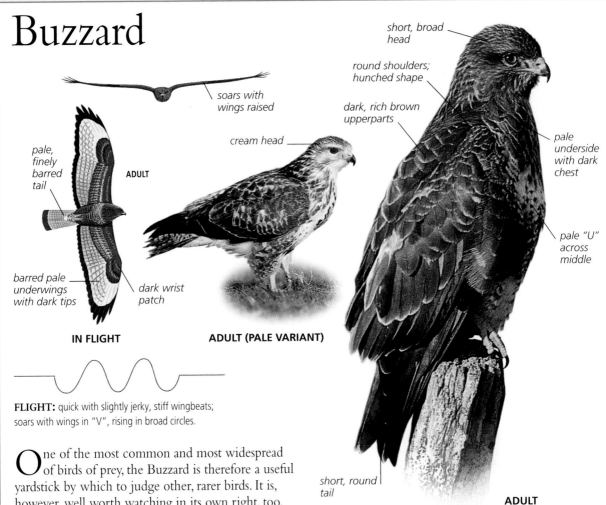

soars with wings raised

ADULT

pale, finely barred tail

barred pale underwings with dark tips

dark wrist patch

IN FLIGHT

cream head

ADULT (PALE VARIANT)

short, broad head

round shoulders; hunched shape

dark, rich brown upperparts

pale underside with dark chest

pale "U" across middle

short, round tail

ADULT

FLIGHT: quick with slightly jerky, stiff wingbeats; soars with wings in "V", rising in broad circles.

One of the most common and most widespread of birds of prey, the Buzzard is therefore a useful yardstick by which to judge other, rarer birds. It is, however, well worth watching in its own right, too, being an impressive and exciting raptor. It is very variable, albeit around a relatively constant basic pattern. It soars in wavering, rising circles over nesting woods and perches on telegraph poles and fence posts. In some areas, such as the wooded valleys of Wales, it may be the most common bird of prey.

VOICE Noisy; frequent ringing *pee-yaah* scream or weaker *mew*; calls often while flying.

NESTING Stick nest in tree, or at base of bush on cliff ledge; 2–4 eggs; 1 brood; March–June.

FEEDING Catches small mammals, rabbits, beetles, earthworms, and some birds; eats much dead meat, including road-kill rabbits.

HEAD TO WIND

A Buzzard is able to hang motionless in the wind while searching for food; it also hovers rather heavily with deep wingbeats in calmer air.

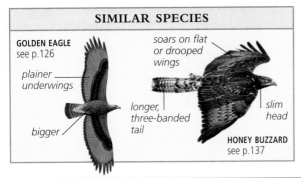

SIMILAR SPECIES

GOLDEN EAGLE see p.126

plainer underwings

bigger

soars on flat or drooped wings

longer, three-banded tail

slim head

HONEY BUZZARD see p.137

OCCURRENCE

Widespread except in far N Europe (summer visitor in NE Europe), in wooded farmland, hills, and moors near crags and forest. Many move to Low Countries and France in winter, occupying low, flat ground with scattered woodland.

Seen in the UK

| Length **50–57cm (20–22½in)** | Wingspan **1.13–1.28m (3¾–4¼ft)** | Weight **550–1,200g (20–43oz)** |
| Social **Family groups** | Lifespan **Up to 25 years** | Status **Secure** |

| Order **Accipitriformes** | Family **Accipitridae** | Species **Pernis apivorus** |

Honey Buzzard

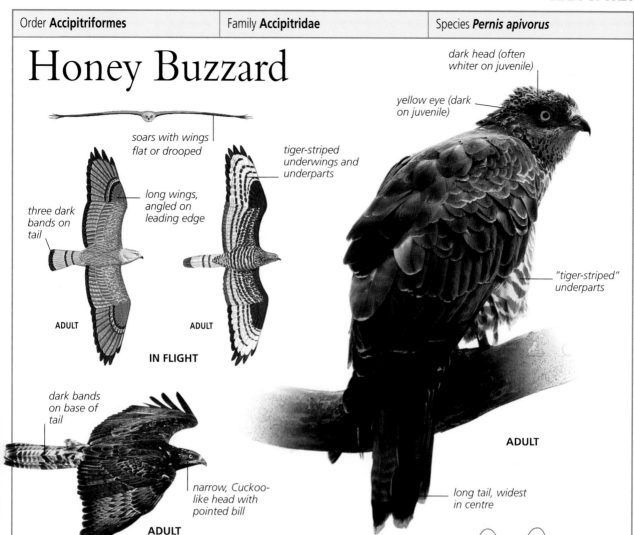

soars with wings flat or drooped

tiger-striped underwings and underparts

long wings, angled on leading edge

three dark bands on tail

ADULT

ADULT

IN FLIGHT

dark head (often whiter on juvenile)

yellow eye (dark on juvenile)

"tiger-striped" underparts

ADULT

dark bands on base of tail

narrow, Cuckoo-like head with pointed bill

long tail, widest in centre

ADULT

Not a true buzzard at all, this is a unique raider of wasp and bee nests, even walking about on the ground and digging out wax and grubs with its feet. It is secretive when breeding and more easily seen on migration, as it concentrates on short sea crossings over the Baltic and the Mediterranean on its way to and from tropical Africa. Exceptionally variable in colour and pattern, it requires careful observation for positive identification.

VOICE Infrequent whistling *peee-haa, pee-ee-aah*.
NESTING Small platform of sticks and greenery in tree, often on old crow's nest; 1–3 eggs; 1 brood; April–June.
FEEDING Eats wasp and bee grubs, wax, honey, adult insects, ant pupae, and small mammals and reptiles.

FLIGHT: direct flight easy with elastic, deep wing-beats; soars with wings bowed or flattish, tips drooped.

SIMILAR SPECIES

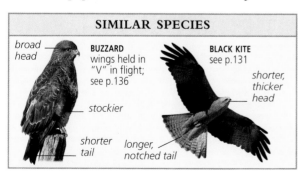

broad head

BUZZARD wings held in "V" in flight; see p.136

stockier

shorter tail

BLACK KITE see p.131

shorter, thicker head

longer, notched tail

BOLD PATTERN
The underside of most Honey Buzzards is heavily spotted and barred but the pattern varies reatly and some are much plainer.

OCCURRENCE
Widespread throughout Europe except in far N Scandinavia, and Iceland; rare breeder and migrant in UK. Occupies extensive forest or well-wooded hilly country, arriving in April, leaving in September. Migrants cross Mediterranean and mountain regions on regular routes.

| Seen in the UK |
| J F **M A M J J A S O** N D |

| Length **52–60cm (20½–23½in)** | Wingspan **1.35–1.5m (4½–5ft)** | Weight **600–1,100g (21–39oz)** |
| Social **Migrates in flocks** | Lifespan **Up to 25 years** | Status **Secure** |

137

| Order **Accipitriformes** | Family **Accipitridae** | Species *Accipiter nisus* |

Sparrowhawk

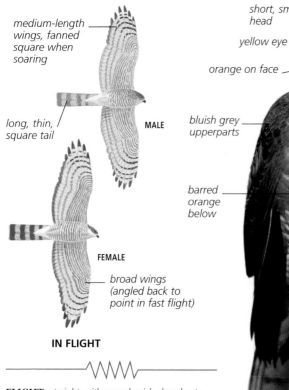

medium-length wings, fanned square when soaring

long, thin, square tail

MALE

FEMALE

broad wings (angled back to point in fast flight)

IN FLIGHT

FLIGHT: straight, with several quick, deep beats between short, flat glides; soars with wings forward, tail tight closed; deep, bouncing undulations in display.

short, small head

yellow eye

orange on face

bluish grey upperparts

barred orange below

MALE

browner above than adult

JUVENILE

brown bars below

pale line over eye

barred grey below

FEMALE

In many places still scarce after decades of accidental pesticide poisoning and centuries of persecution, the Sparrowhawk is common and familiar in other areas where its recovery has been complete. It typically soars over woods, perches inconspicuously, or dashes by, low, with a flap-flap-glide action. It is bold enough to hunt in gardens and parks but is essentially a forest-edge bird, extending its hunting range into more open country in winter. Males are much smaller than females.

VOICE Repetitive *kek-kek-kek-kek-kek*, thin, squealing *peee-ee*, but generally quiet away from nest.

NESTING Small, flat platform of thin twigs on flat branch close to trunk; 4 or 5 eggs; 1 brood; March–June.

FEEDING Hunts small birds, darting along hedges, woodland edges, or into gardens to take prey by surprise; males take tits and finches, females thrushes and pigeons.

AGILE HUNTER
Broad wings and a long tail give great manoeuvrability in tight spaces and accuracy when hunting.

OCCURRENCE
Throughout Europe, except in Iceland, in wooded farmland and hills and forest. In winter, in more open areas, including salt marshes with adjacent woodland. Hunts almost anywhere, including forays into gardens where small birds are fed.

Seen in the UK
J F M A M J J A S O N D

SIMILAR SPECIES

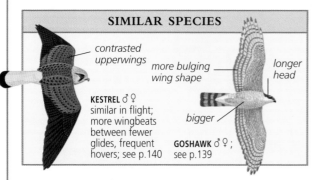

contrasted upperwings

more bulging wing shape

longer head

KESTREL ♂♀
similar in flight; more wingbeats between fewer glides, frequent hovers; see p.140

bigger

GOSHAWK ♂♀;
see p.139

| Length **28–40cm (11–16in)** | Wingspan **60–80cm (23½–32in)** | Weight **150–320g (5–12oz)** |
| Social **Family groups** | Lifespan **Up to 10 years** | Status **Secure** |

Order **Accipitriformes**	Family **Accipitridae**	Species ***Accipiter gentilis***

Goshawk

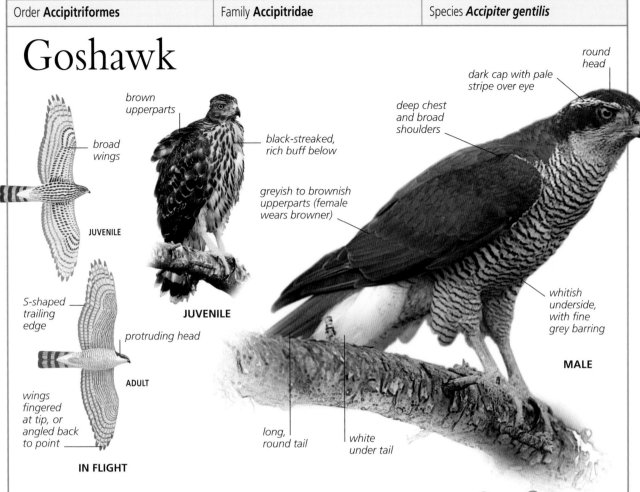

JUVENILE

broad wings

JUVENILE

brown upperparts

black-streaked, rich buff below

round head

dark cap with pale stripe over eye

deep chest and broad shoulders

greyish to brownish upperparts (female wears browner)

whitish underside, with fine grey barring

MALE

S-shaped trailing edge

protruding head

ADULT

wings fingered at tip, or angled back to point

IN FLIGHT

long, round tail

white under tail

A powerful, awesome predator, the Goshawk is a much more substantial hawk than the Sparrowhawk; females, especially, can look remarkably large. Goshawks are scarce, through persecution, in most areas, but making a comeback in others, including the UK where they have been illegally released or simply escaped to establish wild populations. They usually sit, well-hidden, in trees and occasionally soar over forest. Goshawks are best looked for over extensive woodland in early spring, soaring over their territories.
VOICE Woodpecker-like, nasal *gek-gek-gek* and *pi-aah*.
NESTING Remarkably large, flat-topped heap of sticks and greenery close to trunk of tall tree; 2–4 eggs; 1 brood; March–June.
FEEDING Hunts boldly in forest or clearings, catching birds from thrush size to crows, gamebirds, and other birds or prey; also eats rabbits and squirrels.

FLIGHT: direct flight fast, with deep, quick wingbeats between short glides; soars with wings at full stretch, tail rounded.

BOLD PREDATOR
Goshawks eat prey where they happen to catch it, or carry smaller items to regular perches.

OCCURRENCE
Widespread except in Iceland and Ireland, but mostly scarce. In well-wooded farmland and hills and forest, typically in mature wood-land with tall conifers but plenty of space beneath trees. Few in more open country in winter.

Seen in the UK
J F M A M J J A S O N D

SIMILAR SPECIES

small head

narrower tail

SPARROWHAWK ♂♀;
see p.138

BUZZARD
slower flight;
see p.136

shorter tail

Length **48–61cm (19–24in)**	Wingspan **0.95–1.25m (3–4ft)**	Weight **500–1,350g (18–48oz)**
Social **Family groups**	Lifespan **Up to 20 years**	Status **Secure**

| Order **Falconiformes** | Family **Falconidae** | Species *Falco tinnunculus* |

Kestrel

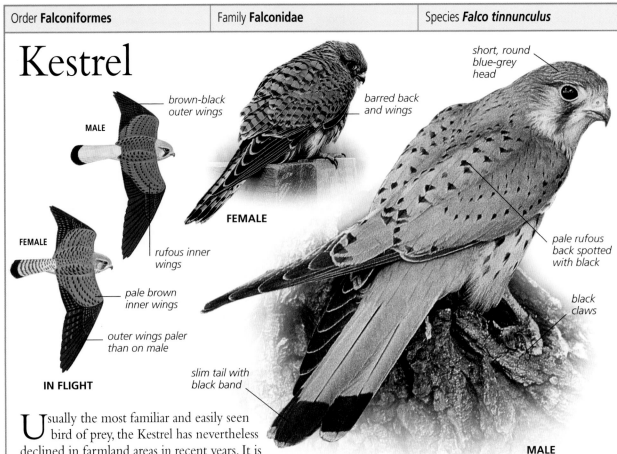

MALE
brown-black outer wings

barred back and wings

short, round blue-grey head

FEMALE

FEMALE
rufous inner wings

pale brown inner wings

outer wings paler than on male

IN FLIGHT

slim tail with black band

pale rufous back spotted with black

black claws

MALE

Usually the most familiar and easily seen bird of prey, the Kestrel has nevertheless declined in farmland areas in recent years. It is the pigeon-sized, long-winged, daytime hunter most often seen perched on telegraph poles or wires or hovering over roadsides, as if suspended on a string. Unlike Sparrowhawks, there is relatively little difference in size between the sexes, but much more in pattern: the male has a bluish grey head and red-brown upperparts while the female has a brown head and tail.

VOICE Nasal, complaining, whining *keee-eee-eeee* and variants.

NESTING On bare ledges on cliffs, in quarries, derelict buildings, high window-ledges, disused crows' nests or tree holes; 4–6 eggs; 1 brood; March–July.

FEEDING Catches small mammals, especially voles, and also beetles, lizards, earthworms, and small birds.

POISED FOR A DIVE
The Kestrel hovers frequently, its tail often spread like a fan. The fan-shaped tail acts as a brake when the bird is about to land.

FLIGHT: direct flight with deep wingbeats, few glides; hovers conspicuously; soars with wings and tail fanned; aerobatic around cliffs.

OCCURRENCE
Almost everywhere in Europe, from cities to remote mountains; common around woodland and heaths, until recently on farmland but declining as farming systems are modernized and food is restricted almost to roadside verges. Present all year but many move south in winter.

| Seen in the UK |
| J F M A M J J A S O N D |

SIMILAR SPECIES

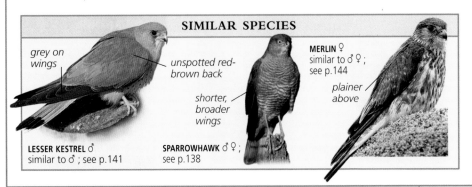

grey on wings

unspotted red-brown back

LESSER KESTREL ♂
similar to ♂; see p.141

shorter, broader wings

SPARROWHAWK ♂♀;
see p.138

MERLIN ♀
similar to ♂♀;
see p.144

plainer above

| Length **34–39cm (13½–15½in)** | Wingspan **65–80cm (26–32in)** | Weight **190–300g (7–11oz)** |
| Social **Family groups** | Lifespan **Up to 15 years** | Status **Declining** |

| Order **Falconiformes** | Family **Falconidae** | Species *Falco naumanni* |

Lesser Kestrel

blue-grey panel

MALE

dark outer wings

FEMALE

IN FLIGHT

pale cheek spot

black-barred back

FEMALE

blue-grey head

unspotted, rich red-brown back

MALE

finely spotted, deep pink-buff chest

white claws

blue tail with black band at tip

S haring the basic colours and patterns of the Kestrel, the male Lesser Kestrel can be distinguished by its unspotted back, but the female can be very difficult to tell apart. While the smaller size of the Lesser Kestrel is not normally obvious, its slightly stockier shape and shorter wings help in identifying it. It is also a more social bird, often breeding in tight colonies. Lesser Kestrel numbers have declined dramatically in Europe in recent decades. It is, however, not certain whether this is caused by problems in its wintering sites in Africa or in its summer range.

VOICE Fast, raucous, triple call, *chay-chay-chay*, and nasal, high, chattering notes.

NESTING On ledges or in cavities, in loose colonies; 3–6 eggs; 1 brood; April–July.

FEEDING Catches insects in air or from ground after hovering.

FLIGHT: light, quick, with shallow wingbeats; hovers like Kestrel.

bluish grey head

MALE

white underwings

brownish head

FEMALE

brown tail with black band at tip

HOVERING
The Lesser Kestrel looks much like the Kestrel while hovering; however, its chunkier body, shorter tail, and square-ended rear aid identification.

SIMILAR SPECIES

KESTREL ♂ ♀;
♀ very similar;
see p.140

spotted back

♂

OCCURRENCE
Breeds socially on buildings and cliffs and feeds over hot, open ground in Spain, Portugal, S France, S Italy, and Balkans. Summer visitor declining fast in most areas; very rare out of normal range.

Seen in the UK
J F M A M J J A S O N D

| Length **27–33cm (10½–13in)** | Wingspan **63–72cm (25–28in)** | Weight **90–200g (3¼–7oz)** |
| Social **Flocks** | Lifespan **5–7 years** | Status **Vulnerable†** |

141

Order **Falconiformes**	Family **Falconidae**	Species *Falco subbuteo*

Hobby

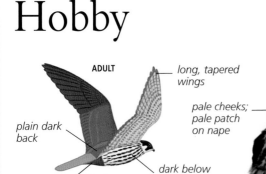

ADULT

long, tapered wings

plain dark back

reddish under tail

IN FLIGHT

dark below

black "moustache"

pale patch on cheeks and throat

pale cheeks; pale patch on nape

heavy streaks

slightly browner than adult

thick black streaks on pale underparts

no red under tail

JUVENILE

ADULT

rufous thighs

short, narrow, plain tail

FLIGHT: easy, relaxed with fluent wingbeats; hunts in gliding, swooping, patrolling flight with sudden twists and changes of height, direction, and pace.

No bird outdoes the Hobby for sheer elegance when it is hawking insects above a marsh, heath, or field on a summer evening. It floats over open space, speeding up to take prey: its seemingly effortless acceleration takes it into a dive, or a chase, or a smooth upward glide, before an extremely neat "take", using its feet to catch larger insects such as chafers and dragonflies. It is unusual among European falcons, being a summer visitor from Africa.

VOICE Clear, musical, whistled *kyu-kyu-kyu-kyu*.

NESTING No nest (like other falcons), lays eggs inside old nest of Rook or crow; 2 or 3 eggs; 1 brood; June–August.

FEEDING Catches small birds such as martins and swallows in flight and many insects such as dragonflies and large aerial beetles.

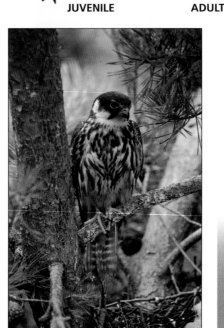

PINE TREE NURSERY
A crow's nest in a tall conifer makes an ideal place for the Hobby to nest.

DYNAMIC FLIGHT
Hobbies catch insects with deft turns, but make long, fast dives after small birds.

SIMILAR SPECIES

PEREGRINE see p.143
- stockier
- barred, not streaked, below
- broader across rump and shoulders in flight

plainer face

chunkier wings

MERLIN ♂♀; see p.144

OCCURRENCE
Most of Europe except far north, from April to October, breeding in clumps of trees. Hunts over open ground, heaths, farmland with trees, and marshy ground, especially around flooded pits with large flying insects.

Seen in the UK
J F **M A M J J A S O** N D

Length **28–35cm (11–14in)**	Wingspan **70–84cm (28–33in)**	Weight **130–340g (5–12oz)**
Social **Small feeding flocks**	Lifespan **Up to 10 years**	Status **Secure**

| Order **Falconiformes** | Family **Falconidae** | Species *Falco peregrinus* |

Peregrine 🔊 15.I, 15.II

ADULT

anchor-shaped wings

broad pale rump

bluish eye-ring and bill-base

short, square dark tail

IN FLIGHT

blue-grey upperparts

yellow eye-ring

yellow bill-base

white cheek patch

black lobes on each side of face and neck

white breast

large, solid body with broad shoulders

closely barred white underside

browner than adult above with buff edges

streaked below

ADULT

JUVENILE

buff tail tip

grey bars on flanks and belly

ADULT

yellow feet

FLIGHT: direct level flight fast with quick, regular, deep, whippy wingbeats; also soars on straight, flat wings; acrobatic, with long, fast, near-vertical stoops.

One of the larger falcons, the Peregrine is a symbol of survival against the odds, these being persecution and pesticide poisoning that threatened it with extinction. Now it has made a strong comeback; in the UK, it is more common than it has ever been, although parts of its former range remain unoccupied. As with most falcons and hawks, females are considerably larger than males. Pairs often remain together for long periods, soaring over nesting cliffs.

VOICE Loud, raucous calls at nest include throaty *haak-haak-haak-haak* and whining *kee-keee-eeeeee* and *wheeee-ip*.

NESTING On broad ledge or earthy scrape on cliff, in quarry, or more rarely on building or on flatter ground; 2–4 eggs; 1 brood; March–June.

FEEDING Kills birds of sizes ranging from thrush to pigeon or grouse, sometimes larger, often rising to take them from beneath, chasing in level flight, or stooping from great height.

STRIKING ADULT
Peregrines look dark against the sky, but a close view reveals black, white, and yellow adding sharp contrast to the overall grey.

SIMILAR SPECIES

smaller and darker; lighter build

KESTREL ♂♀; see p.140

lighter build

HOBBY found only in summer; see p.142

longer tail

OCCURRENCE
Widespread but scarce, breeding through Scandinavia, N and W Great Britain, Spain, Portugal, Alps, Italy, and Balkans, in hills and coasts with cliffs, increasingly in cities. Present all year, some wandering in winter.

| Seen in the UK |
| J F M A M J J A S O N D |

| Length **39–50cm (15½–20in)** | Wingspan **0.95–1.15m (3–3¾ft)** | Weight **600–1,300g (21–46oz)** |
| Social **Family groups** | Lifespan **Up to 15 years** | Status **Rare** |

| Order **Falconiformes** | Family **Falconidae** | Species *Falco columbarius* |

Merlin

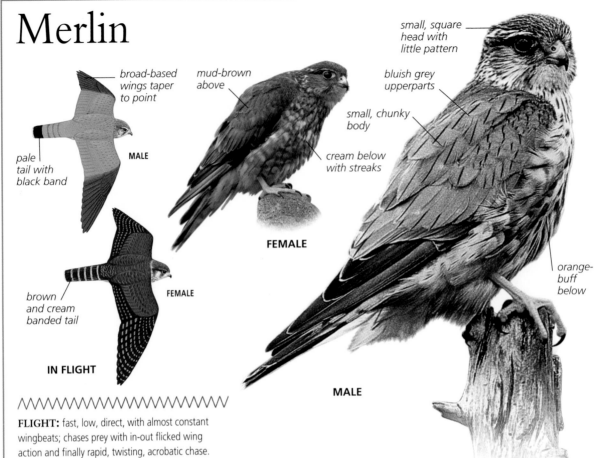

broad-based wings taper to point

mud-brown above

small, square head with little pattern

bluish grey upperparts

small, chunky body

cream below with streaks

pale tail with black band

MALE

FEMALE

orange-buff below

brown and cream banded tail

FEMALE

IN FLIGHT

MALE

FLIGHT: fast, low, direct, with almost constant wingbeats; chases prey with in-out flicked wing action and finally rapid, twisting, acrobatic chase.

A small, dynamic, chunky falcon of open ground, the Merlin usually keeps low, chasing down its prey in quick, agile flights. It spends much of its time perched on low posts, rocks, and even clods of earth, scanning the landscape. In summer, it is an elusive bird, especially if nesting on the ground, although tree-nesting pairs can be more demonstrative if approached, boldy diving at intruders.

VOICE Male has quick, sharp *kik-kik-ki-kik*; female has deeper, more nasal *kee-kee-kee-kee*; quiet away from nest and in winter.

NESTING Bare scrape on ground among heather or old crow's nest in tree; 3–6 eggs; 1 brood; April–June.

FEEDING Mostly eats small birds, caught in flight; also eats variety of large aerial insects.

LOW PERCH
A brown female Merlin perches on a low, mossy rock in a typical squat, upright pose, alert and ready to chase prey.

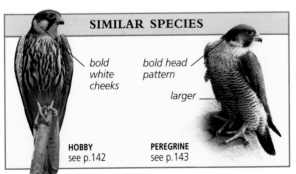

SIMILAR SPECIES

bold white cheeks

bold head pattern

larger

HOBBY
see p.142

PEREGRINE
see p.143

OCCURRENCE
Widespread but scarce breeder on moors in N Europe, sometimes using slopes with trees or edges of conifer plantations. In winter, over most of Europe in open country-side, especially pastureland and coastal marshes with open spaces.

Seen in the UK
J F M A M J J A S O N D

| Length **25–30cm (10–12in)** | Wingspan **60–65cm (23½–26in)** | Weight **140–230g (5–8oz)** |
| Social **Family groups** | Lifespan **Up to 10 years** | Status **Secure** |

Order **Accipitriformes**	Family **Pandionidae**	Species **Pandion haliaetus**

Osprey

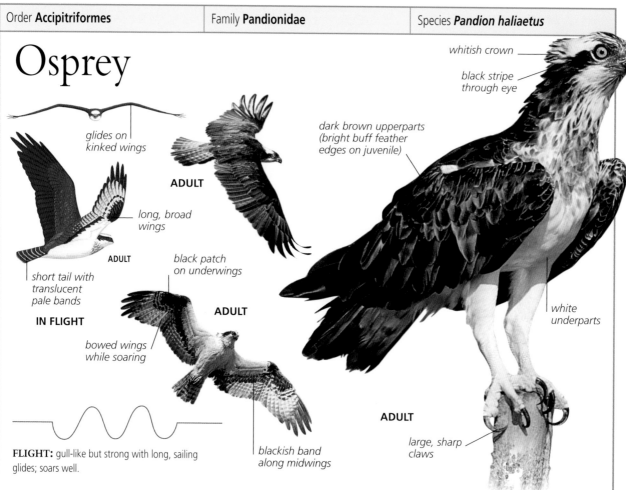

glides on kinked wings

ADULT

long, broad wings

ADULT

short tail with translucent pale bands

IN FLIGHT

black patch on underwings

ADULT

bowed wings while soaring

blackish band along midwings

FLIGHT: gull-like but strong with long, sailing glides; soars well.

whitish crown

black stripe through eye

dark brown upperparts (bright buff feather edges on juvenile)

ADULT

white underparts

large, sharp claws

B etween a Buzzard and a large eagle in size, the Osprey is impressive, and yet sometimes easily dismissed as a large immature gull at long range. Should it hover and then plunge for a fish, such uncertainty is quickly removed. Any reasonable view would reveal its unique combination of shape and pattern. The Osprey is rarely seen far from water, although it does nest and perch well away from the shore. It perches upright for hours at a time on a tree, buoy, or offshore rock.

VOICE Loud yelps and repeated, high, liquid *pyew pyew pyew* near nest.

NESTING Huge stick nest on trees or cliffs (in the past, on ruined buildings); 2 or 3 eggs; 1 brood; April–July.

FEEDING Catches fish in steep dive.

CARRYING FISH
The Osprey hovers well but heavily over water, and catches prey in a steep, headlong dive, swinging its feet forwards to grasp prey.

SIMILAR SPECIES

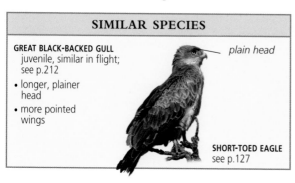

GREAT BLACK-BACKED GULL juvenile, similar in flight; see p.212
• longer, plainer head
• more pointed wings

plain head

SHORT-TOED EAGLE see p.127

OCCURRENCE
Breeds in wild and remote places in N Europe but much more adaptable in S. Appears in most of Europe except for Iceland, from March to October, along coasts and near large lakes and rivers.

Seen in the UK

J	F	M	A	M	J	J	A	S	O	N	D

Length **52–60cm (20½–23½in)**	Wingspan **1.45–1.7m (4¾–5½ft)**	Weight **1.2–2kg (2¾–4½lb)**
Social **Family groups**	Lifespan **Up to 30 years**	Status **Rare**

Families **Tetraonidae, Phasianidae**

GAMEBIRDS

A MIXED GROUP OF GROUND birds, these are all short-legged, short-billed species that feed on vegetable matter, some with a very restricted diet. Their chicks, however, require an abundance of energy-giving insects. Several have ritualized social behaviour, typified by the "lekking" of Black Grouse. Males display in order to get the best chance of being selected by a female, but take no part in incubating eggs or rearing the young.

GROUSE
Round-bodied species with feathered legs and feet, and typically cryptic plumages, grouse live in demanding conditions, including bleak heather moors and high mountain tops.

PHEASANTS
Long-tailed male pheasants are gorgeous birds, while females are generally smaller and duller. Some are secretive and hard to find.

PARTRIDGES
Small and rotund, partridges have far less difference between male and female than the grouse and pheasants, and the males take a greater part in caring for the family. They are social birds outside the breeding season. The Quail is a smaller species and a long-distance migrant, wintering in Africa.

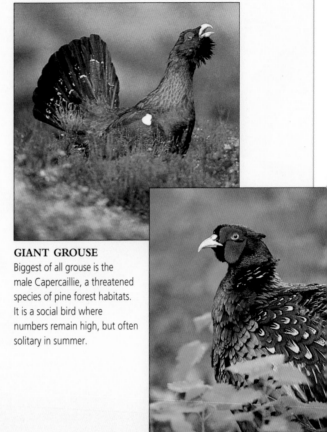

GIANT GROUSE
Biggest of all grouse is the male Capercaillie, a threatened species of pine forest habitats. It is a social bird where numbers remain high, but often solitary in summer.

FACIAL WATTLES
Several species of gamebirds, such as this Pheasant, have fleshy red appendages on the head. Pheasants have been introduced for shooting in many countries.

SHOW OFF
A male Black Grouse performs a courtship display at dawn; these ritualized displays are performed in groups in early spring.

146

| Order **Galliformes** | Family **Tetraonidae** | Species ***Bonasa bonasia*** |

Hazel Grouse

arched, pale grey-brown wings

whitish band on each side of back

IN FLIGHT

pale grey rump

black chin edged white

black throat

grey above, pale below with large dark spots

small, round head

boldly spotted flanks

dumpy body

white, black, and rufous mottles on flanks

MALE

broad grey tail with dark tip

FEMALE

A woodland grouse, this is a rare and elusive bird of northeast, central, and eastern Europe. It prefers deep, dark, coniferous forests, which makes it hard to see because it is shy, quiet, and inconspicuous. It often feeds on the ground in the shade of deep undergrowth and moves away out of sight as people approach.
VOICE Various liquid, slightly ticking notes and a curious song of fine, very high notes, falling in pitch, unexpected for such a large bird.
NESTING Shallow, lined depression well hidden on ground; 7–11 eggs; 1 brood; April–June.
FEEDING Eats various shoots, leaves, berries, and insects, mostly from the ground or in thick conifer sprays.

FLIGHT: fast, with quick wingbeats producing a distinctive whirring sound.

FOREST DWELLER
Hazel Grouse live secretive, quiet lives deep in forests and dense undergrowth; rare close views reveal beautifully marked and subtly coloured plumages.

SIMILAR SPECIES

BLACK GROUSE found in more open places; male blacker; see p.151

bigger and heavier

CAPERCAILLIE darker rump; see p.150

OCCURRENCE
Widespread in central European mountain forests, and farther north and east, but rare and local almost everywhere. Does not move outside normal breeding areas.

| Seen in the UK |
| J F M A M J J A S O N D |

| Length **34–39cm (12–15in)** | Wingspan **48–54cm (19–22in)** | Weight **350–490g (13–18oz)** |
| Social **Family groups** | Lifespan **Up to 7 years** | Status **Secure** |

147

| Order **Galliformes** | Family **Tetraonidae** | Species *Lagopus lagopus* |

Willow Grouse

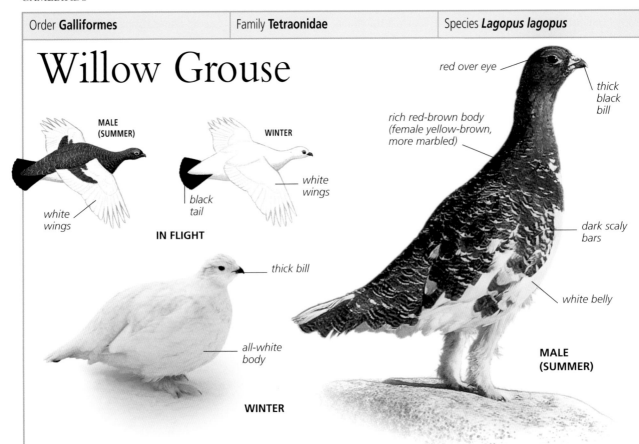

MALE
(SUMMER)

white
wings

WINTER

white
wings

black
tail

IN FLIGHT

thick bill

all-white
body

WINTER

red over eye

thick
black
bill

rich red-brown body
(female yellow-brown,
more marbled)

dark scaly
bars

white belly

MALE
(SUMMER)

A thickset, small-headed, round-bodied, chicken-like bird of moor and heath, the Willow Grouse is extensively shot for sport but, unlike the Pheasant, not reared and released. Small groups keep well out of sight until flushed at close range. The British and Irish race is distinctive, retaining an essentially unchanged plumage pattern all year round. Grouse have declined over many decades in most areas, struggling to maintain high numbers in a relatively artificial environment.

VOICE Remarkable, deep, staccato calls echo across moors, *kau-kau-kau-ka-ka-karrr-rrr-g'bak, g'bak, bak.*

NESTING Sparsely lined scrape on ground in heather; 6–9 eggs; 1 brood; April–May.

FEEDING Plucks shoots and seeds from heather while standing or walking slowly; also takes variety of berries and seeds.

FLIGHT: explosive escape, then long, fast, low flight with whirring beats and long glides on arched wings.

PATCHY TRANSITION
Moulting birds have a contrasted look; the dark head is the last to go white in autumn, and first to turn brown in spring.

SUBSPECIES

L. l. scoticus
(Great Britain, Ireland)
dark reddish
brown
dark wings

yellow-
brown

MALE

FEMALE

SIMILAR SPECIES

GREY PARTRIDGE
see p.153

PTARMIGAN ♂♀
winter; see p.149

slimmer
bill

barred
flanks

smaller

pale
brown

rusty sides of tail

OCCURRENCE
On heather moorland in Great Britain and Ireland, most on places managed for shooting, rarely moving from breeding areas even in hard winter weather. In northern forests and clearings in Scandinavia and extreme NE Europe.

Seen in the UK
| J | F | M | A | M | J | J | A | S | O | N | D |

| Length **37–42cm (14½–16½in)** | Wingspan **55–66cm (22–26in)** | Weight **650–750g (23–27oz)** |
| Social **Small flocks** | Lifespan **Up to 7 years** | Status **Secure** |

| Order **Galliformes** | Family **Tetraonidae** | Species *Lagopus muta* |

Ptarmigan

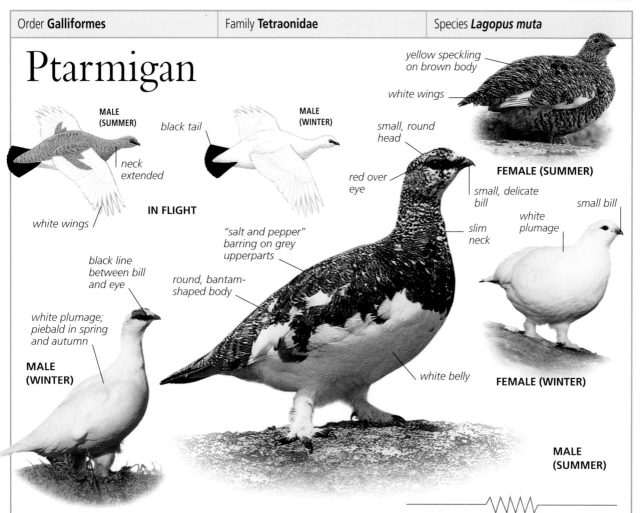

MALE (SUMMER)
black tail
neck extended
IN FLIGHT
white wings

MALE (WINTER)

yellow speckling on brown body
white wings
FEMALE (SUMMER)

small, round head
red over eye
small, delicate bill
slim neck

small bill
white plumage
FEMALE (WINTER)

"salt and pepper" barring on grey upperparts
round, bantam-shaped body
white belly

black line between bill and eye
white plumage; piebald in spring and autumn
MALE (WINTER)

MALE (SUMMER)

A high-altitude grouse in the south of its range, on lower, barren ground farther north (even within Scotland), the Ptarmigan is a smaller, more delicate version of the Willow Grouse. In the UK, it is found only on the highest Scottish peaks and extreme northern moors. It is difficult to separate from Willow Grouse in winter, and females require care to separate from Red Grouse in summer.

VOICE Low, dry, croaking notes, especially four-syllable *arr-kar-ka-karrrr*; also cackling "belch".

NESTING Scrape on ground, lightly lined with grass; 5–9 eggs; 1 brood; May–July.

FEEDING Shoots, leaves, buds, seeds, and berries of variety of low-growing shrubs; also takes insects, which are important food for chicks.

FLIGHT: flies up at close range with powerful, rising flight on stiff, fast-beating wings; long downhill glides.

SEASONAL CHANGE
Various parti-coloured plumage patterns can be seen on the Ptarmigan in spring and autumn.

SIMILAR SPECIES

WILLOW GROUSE summer, similar to ♂ summer; see p.148
redder brown

WILLOW GROUSE winter, similar to ♂ ♀ winter; see p.148
larger

thicker bill

OCCURRENCE
Breeds widely in Iceland, N and W Scandinavia, and very locally in Scotland, Pyrenees, and Alps, on open tundra or rocky shores, and boulder fields. In S Europe, only on highest stony peaks that mimic tundra environment.

| Seen in the UK |
| J F M A M J J A S O N D |

| Length **34–36cm (13½–14in)** | Wingspan **54–60cm (21½–23½in)** | Weight **400–600g (14–21oz)** |
| Social **Small flocks** | Lifespan **Up to 7 years** | Status **Secure** |

Order **Galliformes**	Family **Tetraonidae**	Species ***Tetrao urogallus***

Capercaillie

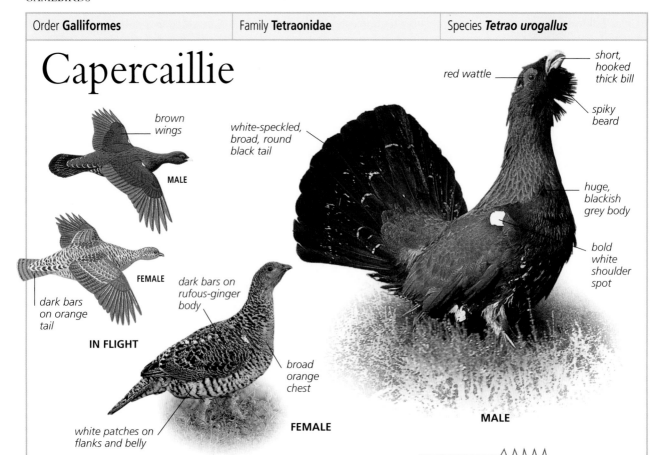

brown wings

MALE

white-speckled, broad, round black tail

red wattle

short, hooked thick bill

spiky beard

huge, blackish grey body

bold white shoulder spot

FEMALE

dark bars on orange tail

IN FLIGHT

dark bars on rufous-ginger body

broad orange chest

white patches on flanks and belly

FEMALE

MALE

The largest grouse and a bird of pine forest and boggy forest clearings with thick undergrowth, the Capercaillie is sensitive to disturbance and typically shy and secretive. It may burst almost from underfoot in a forest, but usually flies up at long range from an open clearing. It is nowhere common and in some areas, including Scotland, seriously threatened.

VOICE Pheasant-like crow; male in spring has prolonged, croaking "song" ending with cork-popping and gurgling notes.

NESTING Hollow on ground, often at bases of trees, lined with grass, pine needles, and twigs; 5–8 eggs; 1 brood; March–July.

FEEDING Pine needles, buds of several shrubs and trees, shoots and leaves, and berries of various herbs and shrubs, especially bilberry; feeds in trees in winter.

FLIGHT: often flies up far away and goes off in long, low, fast flight with heavy wingbeats; also bursts up at close range with great clatter.

SPRING DISPLAY
Where they are common, females may gather around displaying males in early spring.

OCCURRENCE
Breeds in Scotland and N Spain, widely in Scandinavia and from Alps eastwards, declining in many areas. Prefers ancient, natural pine forest; more sparsely found in pine plantations. Feeds in nearby boggy clearings with bilberry, juniper, and heather, and on treetops in winter, but remains within such areas all year.

Seen in the UK
J F M A M J J A S O N D

SIMILAR SPECIES

BLACK GROUSE ♀
similar to ♀;
see p.151

notched tail

greyer and smaller

PINE FOREST BIRD
The Capercaillie inhabits pine forest, feeding on the treetops in winter, and in marshy clearings nearby during the rest of the year.

Length **60–85cm (23½–34in)**	Wingspan **0.87–1.25m (2¾–4ft)**	Weight **1.5–4.4kg (3¼–9¾lb)**
Social **Family groups**	Lifespan **Up to 10 years**	Status **Secure†**

Order **Galliformes**	Family **Tetraonidae**	Species *Tetrao tetrix*

Black Grouse

broad white wingbar

elongated shape

undertail feathers raised in display

blue sheen on neck

bold white shoulder spot

curved, broad-tipped outer feathers on tail

fine pale bar on mid-brown wings

slightly notched tail

MALE

FEMALE

IN FLIGHT

white patch under tail

glossy black plumage

large, heavy, cockerel-like body

dark-barred, yellow-brown or grey plumage

FEMALE

MALE

A large grouse of moorland edges and forest clearings, the Black Grouse has declined over most of its European range. At the leks (the spring display sites), the males display with mock fights, to impress the reclusive females that watch from hidden vantage points nearby. They are subject to disturbance at leks, and the males usually fly off at long range if approached.

VOICE Female has gruff bark; displaying male has far-carrying, dove-like, rolling coo with regular rhythm and explosive "sneeze".

NESTING Hollow on ground beneath heather or bracken, with little or no lining; 6–10 eggs; 1 brood; April–July.

FEEDING Wide variety of seeds, berries, buds, shoots, leaves, and flowers of many shrubs, sedges, and trees; chicks eat insects.

FLIGHT: strong, often high, direct, over long distances with regular wingbeats; occasional glides.

DRAMATIC MALE
Males on open ground are easily visible at great distances.

COURTSHIP DISPLAY
In spring, males gather at dawn in open places to display with drooped wings and lyre-shaped tails.

SIMILAR SPECIES

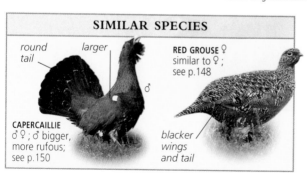

round tail

larger

RED GROUSE ♀ similar to ♀; see p.148

CAPERCAILLIE
♂♀; ♂ bigger, more rufous; see p.150

blacker wings and tail

OCCURRENCE

Widespread in N and W Britain, Scandinavia, Alps, and NE Europe, very local in Low Countries with long-term decline. Varied habitats including woodland, pastures, heaths, moors, or new plantations on heather moor.

Seen in the UK
J F M A M J J A S O N D

Length **40–55cm (16–22in)**	Wingspan **65–80cm (26–32in)**	Weight **0.75–1.4kg (1¾–3lb)**
Social **Flocks**	Lifespan **Up to 5 years**	Status **Vulnerable**

Order **Galliformes**	Family **Phasianidae**	Species *Alectoris rufa*

Red-legged Partridge

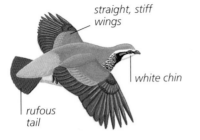

straight, stiff wings

white chin

rufous tail

IN FLIGHT

plain, pale brown upperparts

streaked foreneck

white stripe below cap

grey-brown cap

red bill

dark red-brown tail

black line around white face, speckled breast

FLIGHT: runs more than flies; wings straight, stiff, beating rapidly between flat-winged glides.

red legs

black, brown, and blue-grey barred flanks

This neat, colourful, and attractive partridge is seriously threatened by irresponsible introductions of other species within its range, producing a mixed hybrid population. Close views are required to rule out Red-legged Chukar hybrids which are widespread in England. In their native range, Red-legged Partridges are quite elusive birds of warm, open, stony slopes and fields; in the UK, they prefer light soils in arable areas. Red-legged Partridges can often be seen perched on haystacks, barns, and farm buildings.

VOICE Deep, gobbling and hissing or chuckling mechanical calls, *chuk-uk-ar, k'chuk-ar, k'chuk-ar.*

NESTING Grass-lined hollow scrape on ground beneath low vegetation; 7–20 eggs; 1 brood; April–June.

FEEDING Eats leaves, shoots, berries, acorns, and seeds, including beech-mast picked up from ground; chicks eat insects.

DRINKING PARTY
Temporary pools attract family groups to drink and bathe after rain in otherwise dry areas.

STAYING CLOSE
Family groups of Red-legged Partridges walk slowly over open ground or sit together inconspicuously in short stubble.

CAMOUFLAGE
Despite the bright patterns of this, the prettiest partridge, it is well camouflaged in most situations.

OCCURRENCE
Resident in Portugal, Spain, France, N Italy, and introduced in UK. Breeds on ground in places that have open slopes with scattered aromatic shrubs and much bare, stony, or sandy ground; in arable areas with dry, sandy fields; and less commonly on grassy heaths and coastal dunes.

Seen in the UK
J F M A M J J A S O N D

SIMILAR SPECIES

CHUKAR
see p.427

paler

plain breast

orange face

GREY PARTRIDGE
see p.153

Length **32–34cm (12½–13½in)**	Wingspan **45–50cm (18–20in)**	Weight **400–550g (14–20oz)**
Social **Family groups**	Lifespan **Up to 6 years**	Status **Vulnerable**

Order **Galliformes**	Family **Phasianidae**	Species **Perdix perdix**

Grey Partridge 🔊 16.I, 16.II

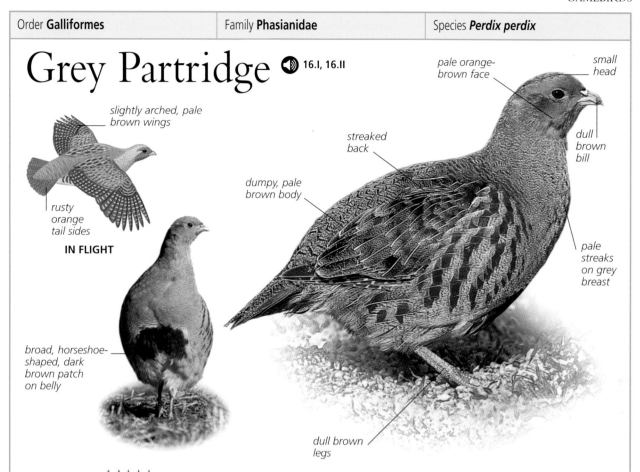

slightly arched, pale brown wings

rusty orange tail sides

IN FLIGHT

broad, horseshoe-shaped, dark brown patch on belly

pale orange-brown face

small head

streaked back

dumpy, pale brown body

dull brown bill

pale streaks on grey breast

dull brown legs

FLIGHT: low, fast, on bowed wings, with quick wingbeats and short glides.

This small, neat, grouse-like bird is typical of old-fashioned farmland with meadows, arable crops, and plenty of hedges; extensive cereal prairies suit it far less well. Its territorial call on summer evenings draws attention to it where it manages to survive in modern intensively farmed landscapes. It moves secretively through grassy habitats, often pausing to raise its head and look around. Family groups gather together in tight flocks, called "coveys" and sometimes fly off together in such groups if disturbed.
VOICE Distinctive, mechanical, creaky, low, rhythmic note, *kieeer-ik* or *ki-yik*.
NESTING Shallow scrape on ground, lined with some grass and leaves, well hidden under long grass; 10–20 eggs; 1 brood; April–June.
FEEDING Feeds as it walks over ground, taking seeds, leaves, and shoots; chicks feed on insects.

STUBBLE BIRD
Winter corn stubbles provide good habitat but are now rarely left for long. Intensive farming has led to large declines.

FAST FLIGHT
A covey dashes past low and fast on whirring wings, with frequent glides.

OCCURRENCE
Widespread from UK, France, extreme N Spain, east across Europe, and north to Finland. In farmland, heaths, dunes, and especially traditional grassy meadows with abundant insect food; in reduced numbers in modern farmland with grassy field margins and hedges.

Seen in the UK
J F M A M J J A S O N D

SIMILAR SPECIES

RED LEGGED PARTRIDGE
flies on flatter wings with fingered tips; see p.152

white face patch

larger and plainer

PHEASANT
juvenile; see p.155
• longer, cocked tail
• longer legs

Length **29–31cm (11½–12in)**	Wingspan **45–48cm (18–19in)**	Weight **350–450g (13–16oz)**
Social **Family groups**	Lifespan **Up to 5 years**	Status **Vulnerable**

153

| Order **Galliformes** | Family **Phasianidae** | Species *Coturnix coturnix* |

Quail 🔊 17

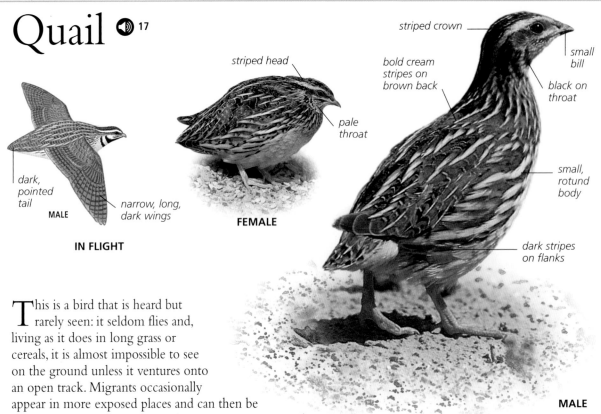

IN FLIGHT

MALE

dark, pointed tail

narrow, long, dark wings

FEMALE

striped head

pale throat

striped crown

bold cream stripes on brown back

small bill

black on throat

small, rotund body

dark stripes on flanks

MALE

This is a bird that is heard but rarely seen: it seldom flies and, living as it does in long grass or cereals, it is almost impossible to see on the ground unless it ventures onto an open track. Migrants occasionally appear in more exposed places and can then be watched more easily, although they remain secretive and skulking. When Quails do fly, they look unexpectedly long-winged, and may be confused with other species, such as young Partridges which can fly well before they are full grown. Quails usually fly in a short, fast, low arc before dropping down out of sight, and are unlikely to be flushed a second time. They are generally much more common and widespread in warmer, southern parts of Europe than farther north, but have declined in numbers in the face of modernized agriculture even there, and future prospects are not very bright.

VOICE Unique loud, far-carrying song, full, liquid, rhythmic *quick-we-wik*; also quiet mewing notes.

NESTING Slight hollow lined with vegetation and well hidden in crops or grass; up to 12 eggs; 1 brood; May–June.

FEEDING Walks slowly forwards, picking up seeds and shoots and snatching small insects from ground or foliage.

FLIGHT: low, quite quick; fast wingbeats and short glides, almost Snipe-like but drops quickly into cover.

EXPOSED MIGRANT
Migrants occasionally rest in fields with sparse crops and can sometimes be seen in the open.

SIMILAR SPECIES

GREY PARTRIDGE see p.153

rufous tail

rufous wings

longer legs

CORNCRAKE see p.157

OCCURRENCE
Widespread north to Baltic, but erratic at northern edge of its range. Breeds in extensive tracts of long grass or cereal fields, mostly in warm, dry areas. Increased numbers appear in some "Quail years".

| Seen in the UK |
| J **F** M **A M J J A S O** N D |

| Length **16–18cm (6½–7in)** | Wingspan **32–35cm (12½–14in)** | Weight **70–135g (2½–5oz)** |
| Social **Family groups** | Lifespan **Up to 8 years** | Status **Vulnerable** |

| Order **Galliformes** | Family **Phasianidae** | Species **Phasianus colchicus** |

Pheasant 🔊 18

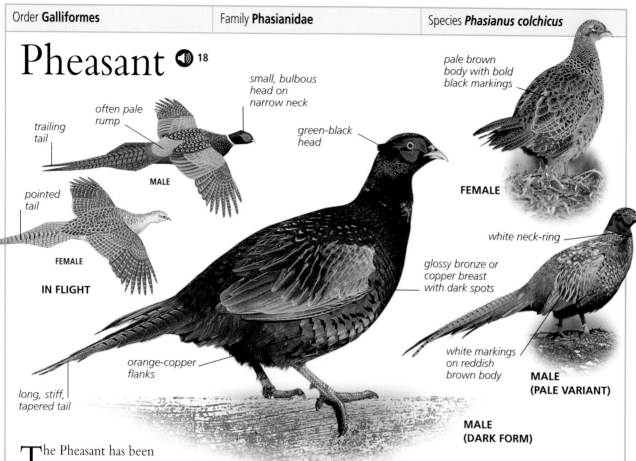

often pale rump

trailing tail

MALE

small, bulbous head on narrow neck

green-black head

pale brown body with bold black markings

FEMALE

pointed tail

FEMALE

IN FLIGHT

white neck-ring

glossy bronze or copper breast with dark spots

orange-copper flanks

white markings on reddish brown body

MALE (PALE VARIANT)

long, stiff, tapered tail

MALE (DARK FORM)

The Pheasant has been introduced into large parts of Europe, and the males' loud crowing calls at dusk are distinctive over much of the countryside. The status and behaviour of this species are difficult to specify because of the frequent presence of young birds reared and released, unprepared for life in the wild, to be shot. "Wild" birds frequently resort to marshy, reedy places, as well as woodland edges where they are most familiar and characteristic.

VOICE Loud, explosive *corr-kok!* with sudden whirr of wings; also loud clucking in flight.

NESTING Hollow on ground, under overhanging cover such as brambles, unlined or with thin scattering of grass stems; 8–15 eggs; 1 brood; April–July.

FEEDING Takes all kinds of food, from seeds and berries to insects and lizards, from ground in its powerful bill.

FLIGHT: low, short bursts with whirring wings, trailing tail; explosive escape from underfoot.

WHIRRING WINGS
The call of the richly patterned male Pheasant is followed by a sudden burst of wingbeats that create a very brief, loud whirring sound.

SIMILAR SPECIES

GREY PARTRIDGE
similar to ♀;
see p.153

BLACK GROUSE ♀
similar to ♀;
see p.151

smaller

shorter legs

round tail

shorter, notched tail

OCCURRENCE
Very local in Spain, Portugal, and S Scandinavia but widespread through mid- and W Europe. Found widely in varied habitats, chiefly in very mixed countryside, in arable fields, woods, reedbeds, heaths, and moorland edges.

Seen in the UK
J F M A M J J A S O N D

| Length **52–90cm (20½–35in)** | Wingspan **70–90cm (28–35in)** | Weight **0.9–1.4kg (2–3lb)** |
| Social **Small flocks** | Lifespan **Up to 7 years** | Status **Secure** |

Family **Rallidae**

RAILS, CRAKES, AND COOTS

RATHER SMALL, SLIM BIRDS, rails, crakes, and coots are narrow-bodied, allowing them to slip through dense vegetation; however, their deep bellies give a rounder appearance in a side view. Most live in wet places. Some are resident, others long-distance migrants.

The Moorhen is common and familiar, and easy to see; the Coot is more gregarious and also easy to watch in large numbers on almost any freshwater pool. Others, however, such as the smaller crakes and the Water Rail, live in such dense vegetation that they are difficult to see at all, or come only to the edge of the reeds or sedges occasionally to give a brief glimpse. They are, however, skulking rather than shy and can sometimes be watched very closely.

The Corncrake lives in dry fields of hay and clumps of irises or nettles, away from open water; it is hard to see but easy to hear its loud, repetitive "song". In most European countries it has declined severely with modernization of farming techniques.

RATCHET CALL
The repeated "crek crek" of the Corncrake is an evocative sound, which is sadly declining.

FAMILY TIES
Moorhens rear several broods and early young help feed later ones. In spring, however, females fight fiercely over males.

Families **Gruidae, Otididae**

CRANES AND BUSTARDS

CRANES ARE TALL, upstanding, long-striding birds, heron-like but with smaller bills and thicker necks that broaden into the shoulders. They have dramatic courtship displays, with elegant "dancing" and trumpeting calls. They migrate to southern Europe and Africa each autumn, flying majestically in long lines or V-shaped flocks, and use traditional wintering sites and intermediate resting and feeding areas.

Bustards are threatened birds of dry, open landscapes. The Great Bustard is huge, the Little Bustard pheasant-sized and quick, more duck-like, in flight. They are unable to survive in intensively farmed countryside and, already much reduced, face further declines.

MASSIVE MALES
Male Great Bustards are considerably bigger than the females but still can be difficult to locate in their remote habitats.

Order **Gruiformes**	Family **Rallidae**	Species **Crex crex**

Corncrake 🔊 19

strong, narrow but rounded, rufous wings

pink legs

ADULT

IN FLIGHT

less grey than male

white and brown bars on flanks

FEMALE

stout, short pink bill

soft grey and buff face

grey throat and breast

tawny back with bold black streaks

MALE

/\/\/\/\/\/\/\/\/\/\/\/\/\/\/\

FLIGHT: low, short flight with quick wingbeats and trailing feet; drops down to cover quickly.

Corncrakes skulk in hay (or iris and nettle beds early in spring) and are hard to see, but singing males are easy to hear especially at dusk. Migrants are generally rare and take people by surprise, suddenly rising underfoot and looking surprisingly rufous. The advent of advanced, intensive farming threatens the survival of Corncrakes in eastern Europe, where good numbers still remain; last-ditch conservation efforts have protected them in western Scotland. There they prefer hay in flowery meadows, with longer, rougher vegetation in field corners or overgrowing dry stone walls to give plenty of thick cover.

VOICE Loud, repeated double-note: at distance light, scratched or rasped *crik crik*; at close range hard, rattling, deep, vibrating *crrek crrek*.

NESTING Small, leaf- and grass-lined hollow on ground, with grass cover to conceal top; 8–12 eggs; 1 or 2 broods; May–August.

FEEDING Picks insects, seeds, leaves, and shoots from foliage and ground, in steady, springy walk.

PEERING FROM COVER
The Corncrake keeps well hidden in long grass and occasionally peers upwards into open view with its head raised.

SIMILAR SPECIES

greyer

green legs

dark wings

SPOTTED CRAKE
see p.159

speckled with white

QUAIL ♂♀; see p.154

smaller, rounder body

OCCURRENCE
Widespread but scarce or rare in France and C Europe; very rare in Ireland and W Scotland. Breeds in hayfields and wet grass with dense cover in spring and in late summer harvest (unable to survive in early-cut silage).

Seen in the UK
J F M **A M J J A S** O N D

Length **27–30cm (10½–12in)**	Wingspan **46–53cm (18–21in)**	Weight **135–200g (5–7oz)**
Social **Family groups**	Lifespan **5–7 years**	Status **Vulnerable**

Order **Gruiformes**	Family **Rallidae**	Species *Rallus aquaticus*

Water Rail

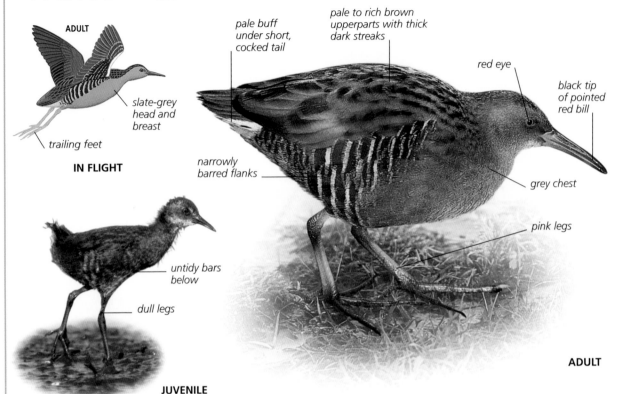

ADULT

slate-grey head and breast

trailing feet

IN FLIGHT

pale buff under short, cocked tail

pale to rich brown upperparts with thick dark streaks

red eye

black tip of pointed red bill

narrowly barred flanks

grey chest

pink legs

ADULT

untidy bars below

dull legs

JUVENILE

FLIGHT: quick, short, low flights with raised, whirring wings and dangling legs and toes.

This is often a difficult bird to see, not so much because it is shy but as a result of its habit of skulking in dense waterside vegetation; occasionally a Water Rail on open mud will show itself off remarkably well. Because of its habitat requirements, it is very patchily distributed and generally scarce, but large reedbeds can have big populations, best detected by listening at dawn and dusk for their loud, squealing calls.

VOICE Loud, hard, repetitive *kipkipkipkipkip*, frequent loud, squealing and grunting (generally pig-like) notes.

NESTING Shallow dish of broad leaves and grass stems, in vegetation raised a little above water level; 6–11 eggs; 2 broods; May–August.

FEEDING Mostly feeds on insects and molluscs but very opportunistic, taking even voles and small birds, dead animals, seeds, and berries.

REEDBED WADER
Water Rails typically wade through the shallows in and around reeds and swampy willow thickets, now and then appearing at the edges.

SIMILAR SPECIES

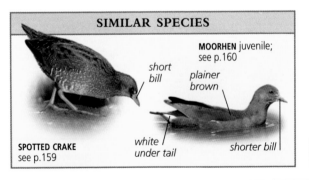

MOORHEN juvenile; see p.160

short bill

plainer brown

white under tail

shorter bill

SPOTTED CRAKE see p.159

OCCURRENCE
In most of Europe except N Scandinavia in wet reedbeds, sedges, and dense reedmace by pools; also in overgrown ditches, muddy ponds, sometimes flooded places under willows and alders, and overgrown riversides.

Seen in the UK
J F M A M J J A S O N D

Length **22–28cm (9–11in)**	Wingspan **38–45cm (15–18in)**	Weight **85–190g (3–7oz)**
Social **Family groups**	Lifespan **Up to 6 years**	Status **Secure†**

Order **Gruiformes**	Family **Rallidae**	Species *Porzana porzana*

Spotted Crake

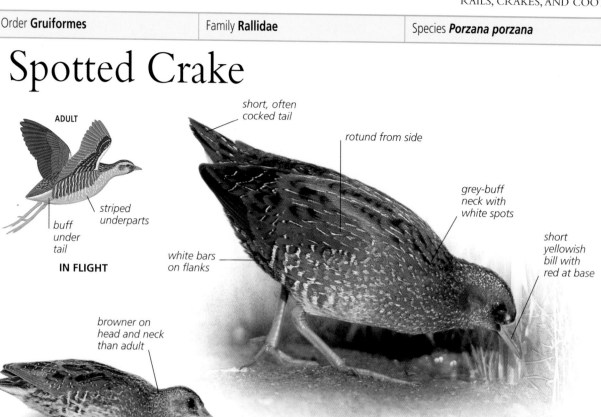

ADULT

IN FLIGHT

short, often cocked tail

rotund from side

grey-buff neck with white spots

short yellowish bill with red at base

striped underparts

buff under tail

white bars on flanks

browner on head and neck than adult

JUVENILE

ADULT

FLIGHT: short, quick flights if flushed from vegetation, dropping back into cover with dangling legs.

The Spotted Crake is another "shy" bird that hides itself in thick vegetation but, at times, allows remarkably close views: careful observation reveals a beautifully patterned and almost shiny-plumaged bird. Spotted Crakes in spring are elusive but can be detected by their nocturnal whiplash calls. Most in western Europe are seen on migration in autumn, where falling water levels have exposed bands of mud along the edges of reedbeds.

VOICE Repeated, rhythmic, whipped, or dripping *hwit, hwit, hwit*, at dusk or after dark.

NESTING Small saucer of leaves and stems, placed in upright stalks raised above water or in wet marsh; 8–12 eggs; 1 brood; May–July.

FEEDING Picks various small insects and aquatic invertebrates from mud, foliage, and water.

SLIM SHAPE
Like all crakes and rails, the Spotted Crake appears deep-bodied from the side but end-on, it is slim, easily able to slip between reeds and sedges.

SIMILAR SPECIES

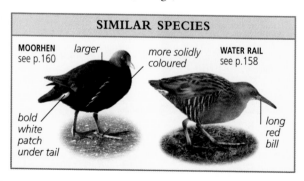

MOORHEN see p.160

larger

more solidly coloured

WATER RAIL see p.158

bold white patch under tail

long red bill

OCCURRENCE
Widespread except in far N Europe, but everywhere very patchy. Breeds in extensive flood-meadows; migrant in wet marsh in reedy places, often appearing at edge of muddy pools and generally elusive in dense cover rather than shy.

Seen in the UK
J F **M A M J J A S O N** D

Length **22–24cm (9–9½in)**	Wingspan **35cm (14in)**	Weight **70–80g (2½–2⅞oz)**
Social **Solitary**	Lifespan **Up to 5 years**	Status **Secure**

| Order **Gruiformes** | Family **Rallidae** | Species *Gallinula chloropus* |

Moorhen 🔊 20

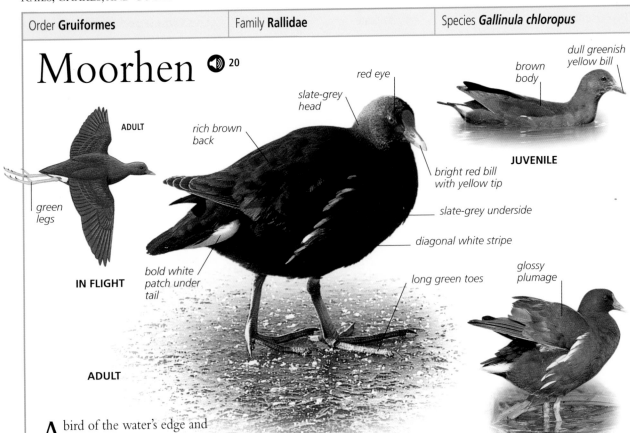

brown body

dull greenish yellow bill

JUVENILE

red eye

slate-grey head

rich brown back

ADULT

green legs

IN FLIGHT

bright red bill with yellow tip

slate-grey underside

diagonal white stripe

long green toes

bold white patch under tail

glossy plumage

ADULT

ADULT

A bird of the water's edge and nearby marshy ground, rather than open water, the Moorhen is widespread and surprisingly common in many areas as it can occupy anything from a wet ditch to a large lake. Small, loose groups move slowly, feeding on damp meadows, running to cover if disturbed, and even breaking into brief flight. Only rarely is a Moorhen seen way out on open water, looking a little uncomfortable (unlike the Coot) in such an exposed situation.
VOICE Loud, sudden, throaty or metallic notes from cover, *kurruk* or *kittik*, high *kik*, stuttering *kik-kikikikik-ik*.
NESTING Shallow bowl of leaves and stems, in vegetation from low reeds to high in trees but usually just above water, often in fallen or drooping branch; 5–11 eggs; 2 or 3 broods; April–August.
FEEDING Picks up seeds, fruit, shoots, roots, snails, insects, and occasionally eggs, from damp ground or shallows.

�win-winding line〉

FLIGHT: low, fluttery, with long legs trailing; often scutters over water to nearest cover.

FIGHTING FRENZY
Moorhens fight furiously in the breeding season, kicking with their feet; females fight over males.

OCCURRENCE
Widespread except in Iceland and N Scandinavia; in summer only in N and E Europe. Breeds on small ponds with overgrown margins or overhanging branches; found in ditches, rivers, ponds, lakes, and reservoirs of all kinds. Feeds in small groups, on open, wet, grassy ground, even in hedges, usually near water.

| Seen in the UK |
| J F M A M J J A S O N D |

SIMILAR SPECIES

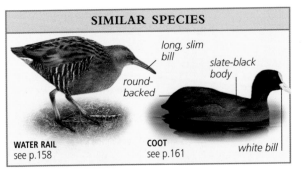

long, slim bill

slate-black body

round-backed

WATER RAIL
see p.158

COOT
see p.161

white bill

CLIMBER
Moorhens are surprisingly agile, climbing trees and dense hedgerow bushes.

| Length **32–35cm (12½–14in)** | Wingspan **50–55cm (20–22in)** | Weight **250–420g (9–15oz)** |
| Social **Small flocks** | Lifespan **Up to 15 years** | Status **Secure** |

Order **Gruiformes**	Family **Rallidae**	Species *Fulica atra*

Coot 🔊 21.I, 21.II

ADULT

blurred white face and throat

yellowish bill

JUVENILE

intensely black head

red eye

rounded rump

slate-black body

white facial shield and bill

pale rear edge

IN FLIGHT

ADULT

ADULT

large grey feet with lobed toes

FLIGHT: usually low, quite quick but heavy, lacking agility; big feet trailing.

These quarrelsome waterbirds are often found on wide open water on large reservoirs or flooded pits; they are rarely on the sea. They are also frequently seen feeding on nearby grassy banks. Feeding flocks are usually bigger and more coherent than the loose groups of Moorhens. Coots are also obviously bigger and more heavily built. Close views reveal their broadly lobed toes, more like a grebe's. While superficially duck-like, the Coot is really not very like any species of European duck.

VOICE Loud, explosive *kowk*, high, squeaky *teuwk*, *pik*, and similar notes; juvenile has loud whistling calls.

NESTING Large bowl of wet vegetation, in overhanging branches or reeds, or on mound of semi-floating debris at water's edge; 6–9 eggs; 1 or 2 broods; April–August.

FEEDING Dives easily to feed underwater, bouncing back up like a cork; eats grass, seeds, shoots, snails, tadpoles, and similar small aquatic creatures.

FAMILY GROUP
Coots often nest on town park lakes, where family groups are a familiar sight.

TERRITORIAL DISPLAY
Coots raise their wings and body feathers to impress and scare away rivals, and often resort to fights.

SIMILAR SPECIES

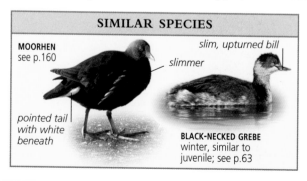

MOORHEN
see p.160

slimmer

pointed tail with white beneath

slim, upturned bill

BLACK-NECKED GREBE
winter, similar to juvenile; see p.63

OCCURRENCE
Widespread except in Iceland and N Scandinavia; in summer only in N and E Europe. Nests mostly on lakes and flooded pits, with marginal vegetation or overhanging branches. In winter, on bigger lakes and more open shores.

Seen in the UK
J F M A M J J A S O N D

Length **36–38cm (14–15in)**	Wingspan **70–80cm (28–32in)**	Weight **600–900g (21–32oz)**
Social **Large winter flocks**	Lifespan **Up to 15 years**	Status **Secure**

Order **Gruiformes**	Family **Gruidae**	Species *Grus grus*

Crane

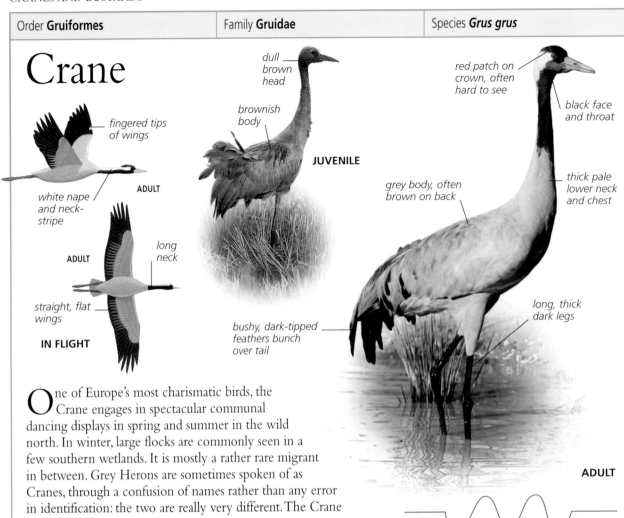

fingered tips of wings

ADULT

white nape and neck-stripe

ADULT

straight, flat wings

IN FLIGHT

long neck

dull brown head

brownish body

JUVENILE

bushy, dark-tipped feathers bunch over tail

red patch on crown, often hard to see

black face and throat

grey body, often brown on back

thick pale lower neck and chest

long, thick dark legs

ADULT

One of Europe's most charismatic birds, the Crane engages in spectacular communal dancing displays in spring and summer in the wild north. In winter, large flocks are commonly seen in a few southern wetlands. It is mostly a rather rare migrant in between. Grey Herons are sometimes spoken of as Cranes, through a confusion of names rather than any error in identification: the two are really very different. The Crane is considerably bigger and more dramatic than a heron.

VOICE Loud, deep, clanging *krro*; in spring, bugling notes as pairs display.

NESTING Big, rough mound of stalks and leaves on ground on which bird crouches, hard to see; 2 eggs; 1 brood; May–July.

FEEDING Strides majestically over ground, digging up roots, grain, and insect larvae; eats acorns in winter.

FLIGHT: strong, direct, with head and legs outstretched, wings held straight and flat; shallow beats between short glides.

FLYING IN A GROUP
Crane flocks fly in lines, "V"s, and irregular packs.

GROUP DISPLAYING
Large groups gather in spring to display, with graceful, rhythmic leaps and bows and loud trumpeting calls.

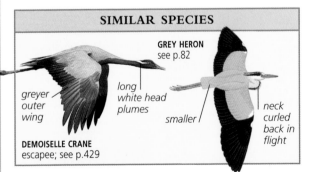

SIMILAR SPECIES

GREY HERON
see p.82

greyer outer wing

long white head plumes

smaller

neck curled back in flight

DEMOISELLE CRANE
escapee; see p.429

OCCURRENCE
Breeds in N Europe on remote bogs within forests or on wide, reedy marshes with little disturbance. Migrants on open ground near coasts. In winter, in rolling uplands, cork oak, and around large, boggy lakes in SW Europe.

Seen in the UK
J F M A M J J A S O N D

Length **0.96–1.19m (3–4ft)**	Wingspan **1.8–2.22m (6–7¼ft)**	Weight **4.5–6kg (10–13lb)**
Social **Large winter flocks**	Lifespan **Up to 20 years**	Status **Vulnerable**

Order **Gruiformes**	Family **Otididae**	Species **Otis tarda**

Great Bustard

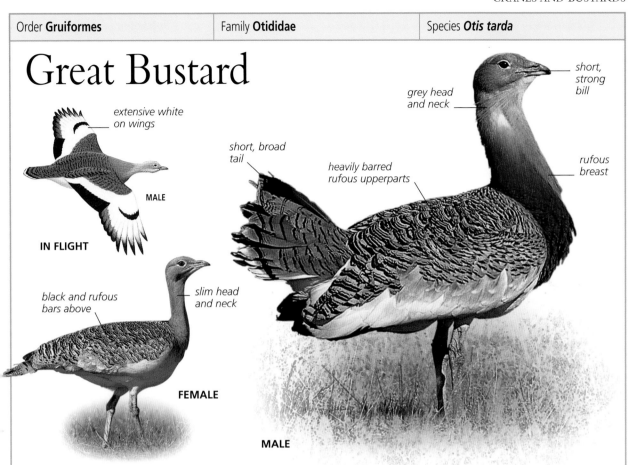

extensive white on wings

short, strong bill

grey head and neck

MALE

IN FLIGHT

short, broad tail

heavily barred rufous upperparts

rufous breast

black and rufous bars above

slim head and neck

FEMALE

MALE

This is one of the world's heaviest flying birds, the males being massive, heavy-bodied, thick-legged, strong-billed birds, and the females markedly smaller. They live in semi-natural steppe and remote areas of cereal cultivation, but agricultural intensification and irrigation threaten their future survival. Small groups are shy and easily disturbed, flying off powerfully with deep, slow wingbeats, revealing extensive areas of white. They are very rare outside their regular range, appearing at long intervals and quite erratically on open farmland in northwest Europe in winter or early spring.
VOICE Mostly silent.
NESTING Unlined scrape in soil; 2 or 3 eggs; 1 brood; April–June.
FEEDING Takes small rodents, reptiles, amphibians, and insects from ground.

FLIGHT: strong, low, direct, with continual powerful wingbeats.

DISPLAY
A displaying male Great Bustard is a remarkable sight, turning his wings over to reveal large areas of white.

OCCURRENCE
Very local in Spain, Portugal, and E Europe; resident on open plains with dry grass or cereals in undisturbed areas, typically in areas with extensive views all round. Very rare vagrant elsewhere.

SIMILAR SPECIES

LITTLE BUSTARD ♂♀; see p.164

very much smaller

TAKING OFF
The distinctive white underwings with black tips of the Great Bustard are clearly visible at take-off.

Seen in the UK
J F M A M J J A S O N D

Length **90–105cm (35–41in)**	Wingspan **2.1–2.4m (7–7¾ft)**	Weight **8–16kg (18–35lb)**
Social **Small flocks**	Lifespan **15–20 years**	Status **Declining**

163

Order **Gruiformes**	Family **Otitidae**	Species *Tetrax tetrax*

Little Bustard

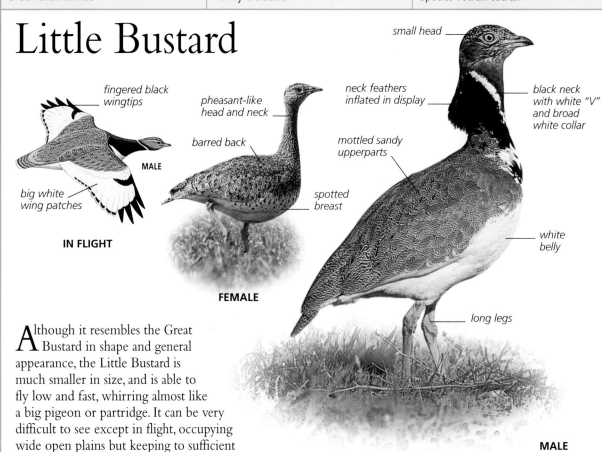

- small head
- fingered black wingtips
- pheasant-like head and neck
- neck feathers inflated in display
- black neck with white "V" and broad white collar
- barred back
- mottled sandy upperparts
- spotted breast
- white belly
- big white wing patches
- **MALE**
- **IN FLIGHT**
- long legs
- **FEMALE**
- **MALE**

Although it resembles the Great Bustard in shape and general appearance, the Little Bustard is much smaller in size, and is able to fly low and fast, whirring almost like a big pigeon or partridge. It can be very difficult to see except in flight, occupying wide open plains but keeping to sufficient cover in which to hide itself expertly. The Little Bustard has declined in many areas in the face of agricultural intensification and is further threatened by irrigation schemes.

VOICE Male has short gruff note repeated every 10 seconds or so, in spring; otherwise very quiet except for whistling noise from wings in flight. Female has low chuckling note.

NESTING Scrape on ground in thick cover; 3–5 eggs; 1 brood; April–June.

FEEDING Picks seeds, grain, shoots, buds, roots, and various insects from ground.

MALE DISPLAYING
In display, the male raises his head and neck feathers to show off the black and white pattern on the neck.

FLIGHT: fast, direct, partridge-like, with quick wingbeats and short glides with wings stiffly arched.

WINTER FLOCKS
Large groups gather outside the breeding season, flying fast over open, grassy plains.

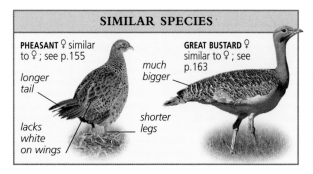

SIMILAR SPECIES

PHEASANT ♀ similar to ♀; see p.155
- longer tail
- lacks white on wings

GREAT BUSTARD ♀ similar to ♀; see p.163
- much bigger
- shorter legs

OCCURRENCE
Breeds in areas with open grass or cereals on rolling plains, often dry, stony places, in France (summer), Spain, Portugal, and Sardinia; local in Italy and Balkans. Rare vagrant outside usual breeding areas.

Seen in the UK	
J F M A M J J A S O N D	

Length **40–45cm (16–18in)**	Wingspan **83–91cm (33–36in)**	Weight **600–900g (21–32oz)**
Social **Winter flocks**	Lifespan **Up to 10 years**	Status **Vulnerable**

Families **Haematopodidae, Recurvirostridae, Burhinidae, Glareolidae, Charadriidae, Scolopacidae**

WADERS

CALLED SHOREBIRDS IN North America, and waders in Europe, some live far from any shore and several rarely wade. They are mostly long-legged but vary from short-billed to very long-billed, their beaks straight, curved down, or curved upwards. Some are among the world's longest-distance migrants. This large group includes the Oystercatcher, avocets, stilts, plovers, pratincoles, sandpipers, godwits, and curlews.

GROUPS

Plovers are short-billed birds: this group includes broad-winged lapwings and sharp-winged plovers, some "ringed" with black and white head and chest patterns. Pratincoles are plover-like but especially agile in flight. Long-legged, Avocets and stilts feed in shallow water. Small sandpipers can be abundant, flying in large flocks. Some feed on rocky shores, some on sand, others on mud or shallow water. Medium-sized sandpipers have longer legs and bills, are less gregarious, and have loud calls and striking patterns in flight. Larger godwits have bright summer plumages, while curlews are much bigger with no clear differences according to age, sex, or season.

JUVENILES
Many young waders, such as this Black-tailed Godwit, have colours that echo the breeding plumage of their parents.

STUNNING FLOCKS
High-tide roosts bring waders together in dense packs, which make a spectacular sight when they take flight.

RESTING TIME
Waders such as these Oystercatchers feed on exposed beaches, but take an hour or two to rest every high tide.

Order **Charadriiformes**	Family **Haematopodidae**	Species *Haematopus ostralegus*

Oystercatcher 🔊 22.I, 22.II

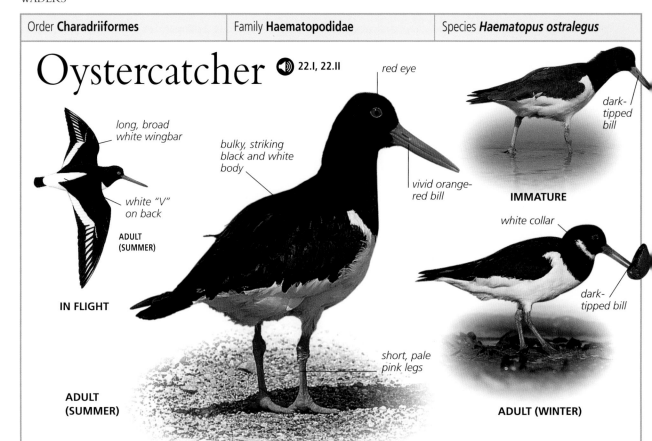

long, broad white wingbar

white "V" on back

ADULT (SUMMER)

IN FLIGHT

red eye

bulky, striking black and white body

vivid orange-red bill

dark-tipped bill

IMMATURE

white collar

dark-tipped bill

ADULT (WINTER)

short, pale pink legs

ADULT (SUMMER)

The dazzlingly patterned Oystercatcher is an extraordinarily distinctive bird in Europe, no other bird forming such tight-packed, often enormous, noisy flocks. Oystercatchers tend to "take over" and dominate whole estuaries with their clamorous presence. In some places, they have come into conflict with people for their supposed impact on commercial cockle fisheries. As cockles have declined on some estuaries, Oystercatchers have increasingly turned to farmland to feed.

VOICE Loud, strident *klip* or *kleep*, develops into penetrating *kleep-a-kleep, kleep-a-kleep*; shrill chorus from large flocks.

NESTING Shallow scrape in shingle or sand, often amongst rocks or grassy tussocks; 2 or 3 eggs; 1 brood; April–July.

FEEDING Probes for large marine worms and molluscs and prises shellfish from rocks and seaweed; also eats earthworms.

FLIGHT: fast, direct, on rapid wingbeats; flies into standing flocks, landing "on the run".

LARGE, NOISY FLOCKS
Oystercatchers feed in huge groups, and make the area ring with their ear-splitting chorus; they roost in tight flocks.

OCCURRENCE
Breeds on sandy, muddy, and rocky beaches, grassy islands, riverside grassland or shingle, and grassy fields along northern river valleys. Also found, at any time of year, on coasts. Rare migrant inland south of breeding areas.

Seen in the UK
J F M A M J J A S O N D

SIMILAR SPECIES

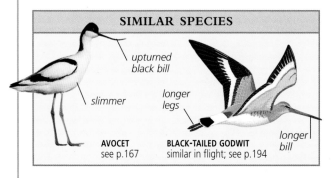

upturned black bill

slimmer

AVOCET
see p.167

longer legs

BLACK-TAILED GODWIT
similar in flight; see p.194

longer bill

Length **40–45cm (16–18in)**	Wingspan **80–85cm (32–34in)**	Weight **400–700g (14–25oz)**
Social **Large flocks**	Lifespan **Up to 15 years**	Status **Secure**

| Order **Charadriiformes** | Family **Recurvirostridae** | Species *Recurvirostra avosetta* |

Avocet

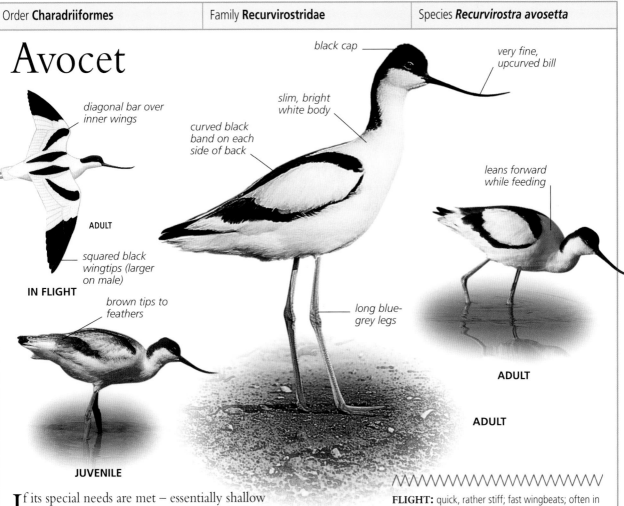

black cap

very fine, upcurved bill

slim, bright white body

curved black band on each side of back

leans forward while feeding

diagonal bar over inner wings

ADULT

squared black wingtips (larger on male)

IN FLIGHT

brown tips to feathers

JUVENILE

long blue-grey legs

ADULT

ADULT

If its special needs are met – essentially shallow slightly saline water and oozy mud, with drier islands – the Avocet may nest in quite large, loose, widely scattered colonies, not tight-packed like gulls or terns. However, it does form tightly packed flocks in winter. Flocks jostle shoulder-to-shoulder when feeding in a shallow tidal flow. With protection and management of habitats, Avocets have increased and spread in recent years.

VOICE Loud, fluty, somewhat Bee-eater-like (see p.257) *klute* or *kloop*.

NESTING Scrape on low islands or dry mud, bare or lined with grass and shell fragments; 3 or 4 eggs; 1 brood; April–July.

FEEDING Sweeps curved bill sideways through water to locate tiny shrimps and marine worms.

FLIGHT: quick, rather stiff; fast wingbeats; often in irregular packs.

TIGHT, ELEGANT FLOCKS
In winter, Avocets form tight-packed, synchronized flocks, flying and feeding together in elegant groups.

SIMILAR SPECIES

BLACK-WINGED STILT
see p.168

solid black back

short bill

straight bill

short legs

BLACK-HEADED GULL
winter; equally white at long range; see p.208

OCCURRENCE
Mostly found in S Baltic and North Sea coasts, Mediterranean area, and also SW Great Britain. Breeds on shallow, saline coastal lagoons and near muddy pools, at times on bare ground around ponds. In winter, on muddy estuaries.

Seen in the UK
| J | F | M | A | M | J | J | A | S | O | N | D |

| Length **42–46cm (16½–18in)** | Wingspan **67–77cm (26–30in)** | Weight **250–400g (9–14oz)** |
| Social **Winter flocks** | Lifespan **10–15 years** | Status **Localized** |

Order **Charadriiformes**	Family **Recurvirostridae**	Species **Himantopus himantopus**

Black-winged Stilt

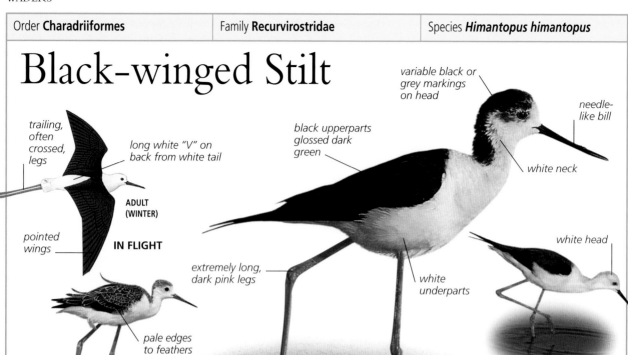

variable black or grey markings on head

needle-like bill

black upperparts glossed dark green

white neck

trailing, often crossed, legs

long white "V" on back from white tail

ADULT (WINTER)

pointed wings

IN FLIGHT

extremely long, dark pink legs

white underparts

white head

ADULT (WINTER)

ADULT (SUMMER)

pale edges to feathers on back

JUVENILE

In terms of leg length relative to size, the Black-winged Stilt represents the peak of development in the waders. The remarkably long legs enable the bird to wade out into deep waters; however, it picks its food from the water surface. This distinctive and elegant bird, one of Europe's most beautiful species, generally occurs in the Mediterranean region, with an extension northwards in France; it is typically associated with hot, open saltpans and coastal lagoons shimmering in the heat. It has some obvious similarities to its relative, the Avocet, but is essentially unique in Europe.

VOICE Noisy in summer, with strident, rasping *kyik kyik kyik* or *kreeek kreeek*; quiet in winter.

NESTING Shallow hollow in mud or sand, often on small islands in shallow water, lined with some grass or leaves; 3 or 4 eggs; 1 brood; April–June.

FEEDING Picks insects from wet mud, stems, and water surface, either tilting well forward or wading out into deeper water.

FLIGHT: strong, direct, quick, with long legs trailed (often crossed), pointed wings flicked in quite shallow beats; glides in wind.

MIGRANT FLOCKS
Before spreading out to pair and nest, flocks of Black-winged Stilts roost together in the shallows.

SIMILAR SPECIES

grey back

white back

upturned bill

BLACK-HEADED GULL winter; similar at long range; see p.208

blue-grey legs

AVOCET see p.167

OCCURRENCE
In Spain, Portugal, Mediterranean region, and W and N France; very rare vagrant farther north. Frequents shallow reedy pools, flooded fields and rice paddies, salt pans, and coastal lagoons, less commonly on sheltered estuaries.

Seen in the UK
J F M A M J J A S O N D

Length **33–36cm (13–14in)**	Wingspan **70cm (28in)**	Weight **250–300g (9–11oz)**
Social **Family groups**	Lifespan **Up to 10 years**	Status **Secure**

Order **Charadriiformes**	Family **Burhinidae**	Species ***Burhinus oedicnemus***

Stone-curlew

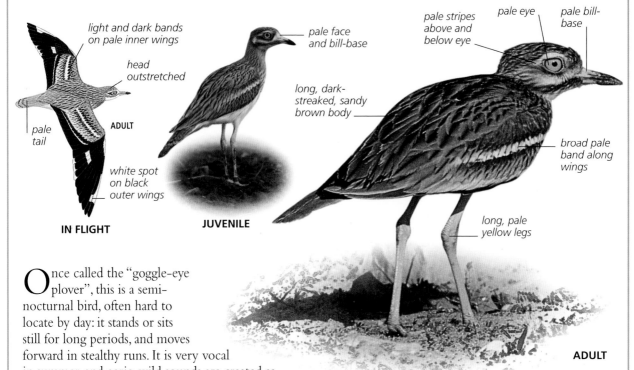

light and dark bands on pale inner wings

head outstretched

pale tail

ADULT

white spot on black outer wings

IN FLIGHT

pale face and bill-base

JUVENILE

pale stripes above and below eye

pale eye

pale bill-base

long, dark-streaked, sandy brown body

broad pale band along wings

long, pale yellow legs

ADULT

Once called the "goggle-eye plover", this is a semi-nocturnal bird, often hard to locate by day: it stands or sits still for long periods, and moves forward in stealthy runs. It is very vocal in summer, and eerie, wild sounds are created as birds communicate over long distances. This bird does not cope well with modern development. Coastal populations, especially, have largely gone, and it is only liaison between conservationists and sympathetic farmers that has helped it to survive in some regions; it struggles on in disturbed heathland and dunes elsewhere.

VOICE Loud notes recall Curlew and Oystercatcher, but with wild, wailing quality at times; *kur-li*, *klip*, piping *keeee*, *krr-leee*, and variations.

NESTING Shallow scrape on ground lined with shells, stones, and rabbit droppings; 2 eggs; 1 or 2 broods; April–August.

FEEDING Tilts forwards, plover-like, to pick up beetles, worms, snails, frogs, lizards, and mice.

FLIGHT: usually low, fast, strong, with steady wingbeats and long glides.

CAMOUFLAGED
Unless it moves, a sitting Stone-curlew is extremely difficult to see.

COURTING PAIR
The white patches on the wings and under the tail are revealed in courtship displays and confrontations.

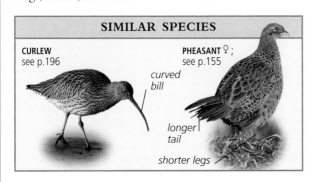

SIMILAR SPECIES	
CURLEW see p.196	**PHEASANT** ♀; see p.155

curved bill

longer tail

shorter legs

OCCURRENCE
Summer visitor to S Great Britain, France, Spain, Portugal, and Mediterranean area; breeds on heaths, shingle, cereal and arable fields with light, stony soil and sparse spring crops. Reduced numbers in SW Europe in winter.

Seen in the UK
J F **M A M J J A S O** N D

Length **40–45cm (16–18in)**	Wingspan **77–85cm (30–34in)**	Weight **370–450g (13–16oz)**
Social **Autumn flocks**	Lifespan **Up to 10 years**	Status **Vulnerable**

Order **Charadriiformes**	Family **Charadriidae**	Species *Charadrius hiaticula*

Ringed Plover 🔊 23

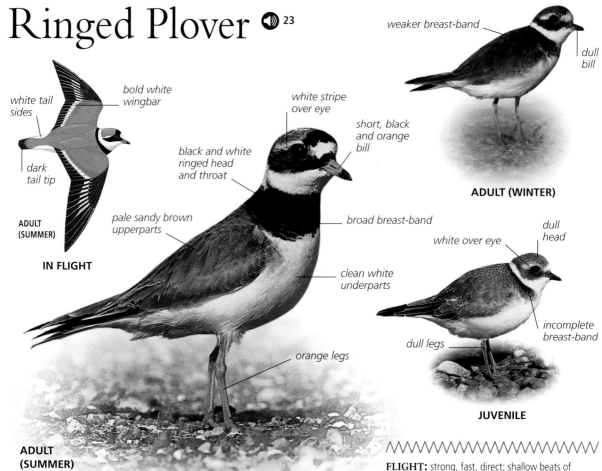

weaker breast-band

dull bill

ADULT (WINTER)

white tail sides

bold white wingbar

white stripe over eye

short, black and orange bill

black and white ringed head and throat

dark tail tip

broad breast-band

ADULT (SUMMER)

IN FLIGHT

pale sandy brown upperparts

clean white underparts

dull head

white over eye

incomplete breast-band

dull legs

orange legs

JUVENILE

ADULT (SUMMER)

FLIGHT: strong, fast, direct; shallow beats of angled wings; bat-like song-flight.

Along with the Dunlin, this species is one of the common "standards" by which other waders may be judged. There are several other "ringed" plovers with similarly patterned heads but none in Europe with such brightly coloured bill and legs. It is generally a coastal bird, although it does move inland, sometimes in places usually frequented by the Little Ringed Plover. In spring and autumn especially, substantial numbers may appear inland where conditions are right, sometimes pausing on migration for several days. It forms tightly packed flocks at high tide, often mixed with other waders. Usually, a large, tight flock will be more or less clearly separated, with each species bunched together within it.

VOICE Characteristic fluty whistle, a bright, mellow *too-li*; also sharp *queep*; repeated *too-wee-a too-wee-a* in song-flight.

NESTING Shallow scrape in sand or stones, lined with pebbles and grass stems; 4 eggs; 2 or 3 broods; April–August.

FEEDING Picks small insects and worms from ground.

"BROKEN WING LOOK"
If a predator threatens the nest or chicks, the parent plover feigns injury to lead it away.

SIMILAR SPECIES

LITTLE RINGED PLOVER
see p.171

duller bill

plain wing

duller legs

OCCURRENCE
Breeds on sand and shingle beaches, near gravel pits inland. Found at any time of year mostly on broad beaches, including estuaries, of all kinds, but fewest on rocky shores. Widespread migrant inland and on coasts.

Seen in the UK
J F M A M J J A S O N D

Length **17–19cm (6½–7½in)**	Wingspan **48–57cm (19–22½in)**	Weight **55–75g (2–2⅝oz)**
Social **Winter flocks**	Lifespan **5–10 years**	Status **Secure**

| Order **Charadriiformes** | Family **Charadriidae** | Species *Charadrius dubius* |

Little Ringed Plover

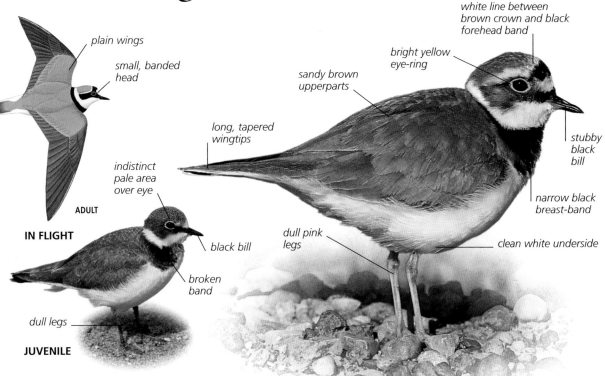

plain wings

small, banded head

ADULT

IN FLIGHT

indistinct pale area over eye

black bill

broken band

dull legs

JUVENILE

white line between brown crown and black forehead band

bright yellow eye-ring

sandy brown upperparts

long, tapered wingtips

dull pink legs

stubby black bill

narrow black breast-band

clean white underside

ADULT

Small and neat, precise in its movements as well as its appearance, this is a handsome little wader of freshwater shorelines and a variety of dry, rough, open spaces in the "waste ground" category. It is often at the waterside in spring and autumn, but as likely to breed on a patch of bulldozed rubble or coalmining waste. As such, it tends to be irregular in occurrence, breeding for a few years and then moving on.

VOICE Short, abrupt, whistled *piu* or *p'ew*; song rolling, harsh *crree-crree-crree-crree* in flight.

NESTING Hollow in bare ground, usually hard to spot; 4 eggs; 1 brood; April–June.

FEEDING Stands upright, then runs forwards and tilts to pick insects and small aquatic invertebrates from ground.

FLIGHT: quick, low, direct with angled, pointed wings; song-flight rolling, bat-like.

SPRING DISPLAY
Noisy males display on the ground with drooped wings, and also perform long, low song-flights over the territory.

OCCURRENCE
Widespread except in extreme north. Breeds in wide variety of natural, semi-natural, and derelict places, from sandy and shingly shores and gravel to flat, dry areas of waste ground, mining waste, and shingly riverbeds; scarce on sea coasts but occasional migrant on coastal lagoons.

| Seen in the UK |
| J F **M A M J J A S O** N D |

SIMILAR SPECIES

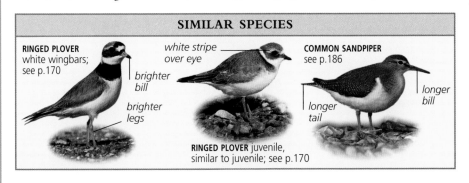

RINGED PLOVER
white wingbars; see p.170

brighter bill

brighter legs

white stripe over eye

longer tail

RINGED PLOVER juvenile, similar to juvenile; see p.170

COMMON SANDPIPER
see p.186

longer bill

| Length **14–15cm (5½–6in)** | Wingspan **42–48cm (16½–19in)** | Weight **30–50g (1¹⁄₁₆–1¾ oz)** |
| Social **Winter flocks** | Lifespan **5–10 years** | Status **Secure†** |

Order **Charadriiformes**	Family **Charadriidae**	Species *Charadrius alexandrinus*

Kentish Plover

swept-back,
pointed wings

long white
wingbar

**MALE
(SUMMER)**

IN FLIGHT

earth brown
upperparts

rufous-ginger cap
(dull in winter)

black bar on
forehead

JUVENILE

dark legs

white
forehead

short black bill

dusky eye
patch

brown chest
patch

black markings
on sides of breast
(browner in
winter)

clean white
underparts

dark legs

dark legs

FEMALE

**MALE
(SUMMER)**

Long gone from Kent
except as an occasional
visitor, the Kentish Plover is still quite
widespread just across the English Channel, but is commonest
around the Mediterranean. It prefers sandy places, such as the
embankments and waste areas around salt pans and
behind beaches, even around building sites near the
shore. Rare migrants farther north are generally found
within Ringed Plover flocks and their identification
requires careful observation, especially when juveniles
are about in late summer.

VOICE Short, sharp, whistled whip, whistled *bew-ip*;
rolled trilling notes.

NESTING Shallow hollow in sand, lined with pebbles
or shell fragments; 3 or 4 eggs; 2 broods; March–July.

FEEDING Takes small invertebrates such as flies and
sandhoppers, from ground, tilting forward after short
run in typical stop–start plover action.

FLIGHT: quick and dashing, on swept-back,
pointed wings; glides in to land.

PALE BEACH PLOVER
A spring male has almost entirely white underparts, with small chest
marks. Its short dashes on the beach give it a lively character.

SIMILAR SPECIES

RINGED PLOVER juvenile;
see p.170

pale
legs

LITTLE RINGED PLOVER
juvenile; see p.171

no wing-
stripe

pale legs

OCCURRENCE
Found mostly on sandy areas near
shores, also beside freshwater
lagoons and flooded areas of
waste ground, on S North Sea and
Channel coasts, W France, and
Mediterranean area. Migrants rare
on estuaries or inland waters.

Seen in the UK											
J	F	M	A	M	J	J	A	S	O	N	D

Length **15–17cm (6–6½in)**	Wingspan **50cm (20in)**	Weight **40–60g (1⁷⁄₁₆–2⅛oz)**
Social **Small flocks**	Lifespan **10 years**	Status **Declining**

Order **Charadriiformes**	Family **Charadriidae**	Species **Charadrius morinellus**

Dotterel

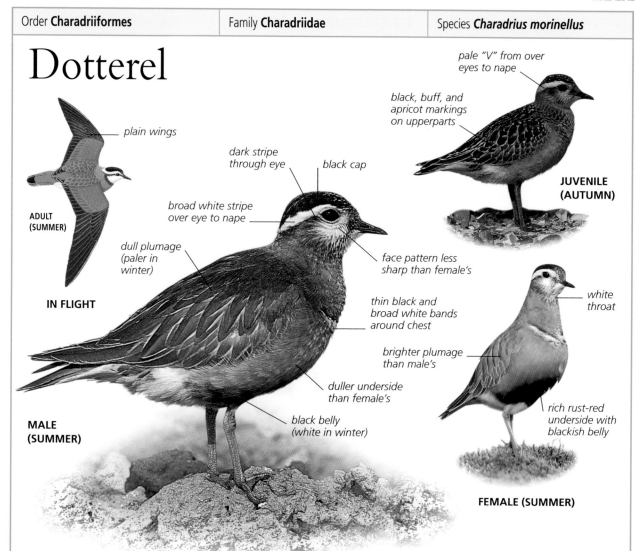

plain wings

ADULT (SUMMER)

IN FLIGHT

pale "V" from over eyes to nape

black, buff, and apricot markings on upperparts

JUVENILE (AUTUMN)

dark stripe through eye

black cap

broad white stripe over eye to nape

dull plumage (paler in winter)

face pattern less sharp than female's

thin black and broad white bands around chest

brighter plumage than male's

white throat

duller underside than female's

black belly (white in winter)

rich rust-red underside with blackish belly

MALE (SUMMER)

FEMALE (SUMMER)

One of the few European birds with reversed sexual roles, and females larger and brighter than males, the Dotterel is a mountain-top or tundra breeder that appears in small flocks at regular places in the lowlands, usually cereal fields, on migration. It is famously tame, almost recklessly so at times, and may be attracted to within a metre or two (3–7ft) by a whistled imitation of its call. Its future range may well diminish with the increasing effects of climate change.

VOICE Soft *pip pip* or sweet *wit-ee-wee*; rather silent outside breeding season.

NESTING Shallow scraped hollow on ground, usually under cover of low vegetation; 3 eggs; 1 brood; May–August.

FEEDING Eats flies, beetles, earthworms, spiders, and similar small terrestrial creatures, tilting forwards in typical plover fashion.

FLIGHT: quick, agile, with fast, deep wingbeats.

SIMILAR SPECIES

GOLDEN PLOVER
winter; see p.174

no white "V" over eye

no breast-band

BREEDING HABITAT
The Dotterel breeds in high, rolling, or flat-topped mountainous regions with low cover, or in tundra.

OCCURRENCE
Occupies wild northern tundra and mountainous areas with similar habitat south to Pyrenees, often with abundance of stones and scree. On migration, in lowland fields in traditional areas inland.

Seen in the UK
J F M **A M J J A S O** N D

Length **20–22cm (8–9in)**	Wingspan **57–64cm (22½–25in)**	Weight **90–145g (3¼–5oz)**
Social **Small flocks**	Lifespan **5–10 years**	Status **Secure†**

Order **Charadriiformes**	Family **Charadriidae**	Species *Pluvialis apricaria*

Golden Plover 🔊 25.I, 25.II

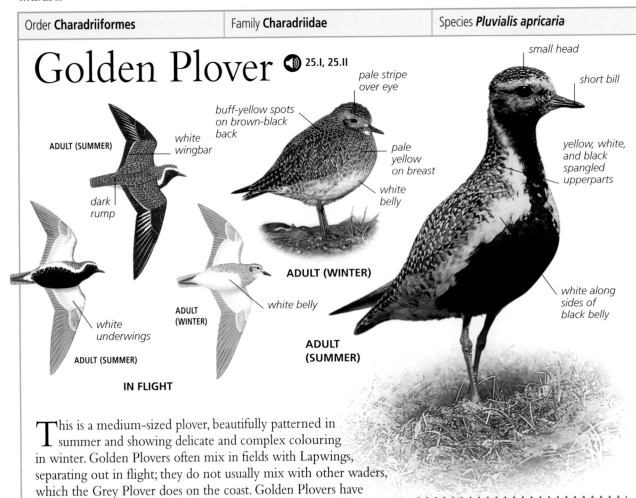

ADULT (SUMMER)

white wingbar

dark rump

pale stripe over eye

buff-yellow spots on brown-black back

pale yellow on breast

white belly

ADULT (WINTER)

white underwings

ADULT (SUMMER)

white belly

ADULT (WINTER)

ADULT (SUMMER)

IN FLIGHT

small head

short bill

yellow, white, and black spangled upperparts

white along sides of black belly

This is a medium-sized plover, beautifully patterned in summer and showing delicate and complex colouring in winter. Golden Plovers often mix in fields with Lapwings, separating out in flight; they do not usually mix with other waders, which the Grey Plover does on the coast. Golden Plovers have traditional migration and wintering areas that may be used for decades, so long as the habitat is not damaged.

FLIGHT: fast, straight, often high.

VOICE Plaintive, whistled *tleee*, higher *tlee*, *treeoleee*, and variants; *phee-oo*, *pheee-oo* in song-flight.
NESTING Shallow scrape, lined with scraps of lichen and heather, on ground in heather, grass, or bilberry, often in burned areas; 4 eggs; 1 brood; April–July.
FEEDING Takes variety of insects in summer, mostly earthworms in winter, often stolen by gulls.

SUBSPECIES

bolder black face and breast

white band

P. a. altifrons
(N Europe)

HIGH-FLYING FLOCK
Flocks of Golden Plovers often fly high, stringing out into long lines or in irregular packs.

OCCURRENCE
Breeds in N Europe, on high moorland or northern tundra, both on limestone grassland and acid heath with patches of burnt heather or bilberry. Widespread in winter on low-lying arable fields and pastures, coastal salt marsh, sometimes on estuary mud.

Seen in the UK
J F M A M J J A S O N D

RESTING FLOCK
When feeding, flocks spread evenly over fields, tightening into packs if alarmed or roosting.

SIMILAR SPECIES

silvery grey above

blacker below

GREY PLOVER
summer; similar to adult summer; see p.175

Length **26–29cm (10–11½in)**	Wingspan **67–76cm (26–30in)**	Weight **140–250g (5–9oz)**
Social **Winter flocks**	Lifespan **Up to 10 years**	Status **Secure**

Order **Charadriiformes**	Family **Charadriidae**	Species *Pluvialis squatarola*

Grey Plover 🔊 24

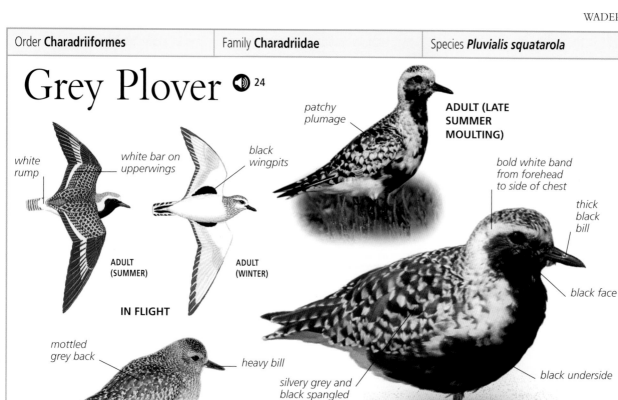

white rump

white bar on upperwings

black wingpits

ADULT (SUMMER)

ADULT (WINTER)

IN FLIGHT

patchy plumage

ADULT (LATE SUMMER MOULTING)

bold white band from forehead to side of chest

thick black bill

black face

black underside

mottled grey back

heavy bill

silvery grey and black spangled upperparts

pale underside

ADULT (WINTER)

ADULT (SUMMER)

This is primarily a coastal bird, scattered over mudflats when it is feeding and gathering in rather static flocks at high tide, unlike the large, mobile flocks of Golden Plovers. It usually mingles with godwits, Curlews, and Redshanks. Most Grey Plovers are easy to identify, but some are yellow and may be confused with Golden Plovers. At long range, they can be mistaken for other medium-sized waders; close up they look pale, but far out on the mud they can look remarkably dark in winter plumage.

VOICE High, plaintive *twee-oo-wee!*; also loud, melancholy, fluted song.

NESTING Scrape on ground in short vegetation, usually on dry rises; 4 eggs; 1 brood; May–July.

FEEDING Pulls worms, molluscs, and crustaceans from mud, in winter; eats mainly insects in summer in Arctic tundra.

FLIGHT: quick, with deep wingbeats; sometimes quite active, twisting descent to roost.

HIGH-TIDE ROOST
High tide forces dispersed feeding Grey Plovers to gather together in more compact flocks.

SIMILAR SPECIES

spangled yellow and black above

KNOT
winter; see p.181

smaller

longer bill

GOLDEN PLOVER
summer; see p.174

OCCURRENCE
Breeds on northern tundra. Mostly found on large muddy estuaries, but sometimes on sandy or rocky shores, from autumn to spring. Flocks may roost on adjacent pasture, or shallow coastal lagoons. Rare bird inland.

Seen in the UK
J F M A M J J A S O N D

Length **27–30cm (10½–12in)**	Wingspan **71–83cm (28–33in)**	Weight **200–250g (7–9oz)**
Social **Winter flocks**	Lifespan **Up to 10 years**	Status **Secure†**

Order **Charadriiformes**	Family **Charadriidae**	Species ***Vanellus vanellus***

Lapwing 🔊 26.I, 26.II

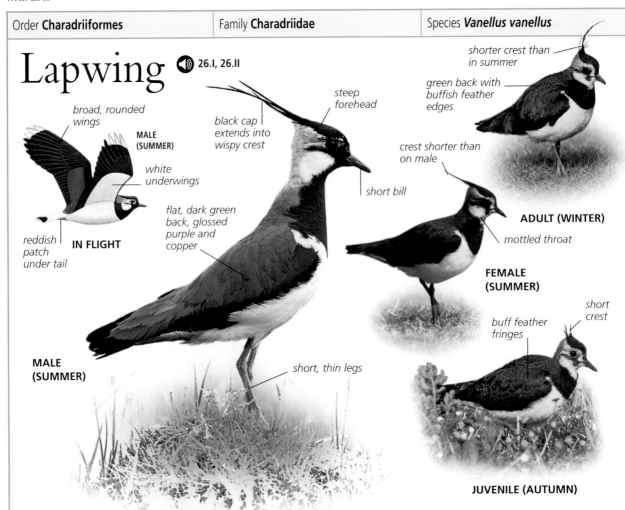

broad, rounded wings

MALE (SUMMER)

white underwings

reddish patch under tail

IN FLIGHT

flat, dark green back, glossed purple and copper

black cap extends into wispy crest

steep forehead

short bill

MALE (SUMMER)

short, thin legs

shorter crest than in summer

green back with buffish feather edges

ADULT (WINTER)

crest shorter than on male

mottled throat

FEMALE (SUMMER)

short crest

buff feather fringes

JUVENILE (AUTUMN)

A familiar and much-loved part of the farmed countryside in Europe, the distinctive-looking Lapwing is sadly declining in most areas as farming systems change. It breeds in loose colonies scattered over suitable fields or moors, but gathers into flocks for the rest of the year, often mixed with Golden Plovers and Black-headed Gulls (see p.208).

VOICE Nasal, strained *weet* or *ee-wit*; wheezy variations on this theme; passionate song in spring, *whee-er-ee, a wheep-wheep!* accompanied by loud throbbing from wings.

NESTING Grass-lined shallow hollow on ground; 3 or 4 eggs; 1 brood; April–June.

FEEDING Often taps foot on ground to attract or reveal prey; tilts forwards to pick insects and spiders from ground, or pull earthworms from soil.

FLIGHT: unique flappy flight with steady beats of broad, round wings.

ROOSTING FLOCK
Flocks rest in tight groups; otherwise, they tend to be loosely scattered.

FLYING FLOCK
Flocks of Lapwings fly in lines, "V"s, or irregular masses, rising steadily as a group, often circling and returning.

OCCURRENCE
Breeds on wet moors, riverside pastures, upland fields, and farmland (decreasing), almost throughout Europe. In winter, moves south and west, feeds on arable fields, meadows, salt marsh and muddy reservoir edges; in estuaries in hard weather.

Seen in the UK
J F M A M J J A S O N D

Length **28–31cm (11–12in)**	Wingspan **70–76cm (28–30in)**	Weight **150–300g (5–11oz)**
Social **Winter flocks**	Lifespan **Up to 10 years**	Status **Secure†**

Order **Charadriiformes**	Family **Glareolidae**	Species *Glareola pratincola*

Collared Pratincole

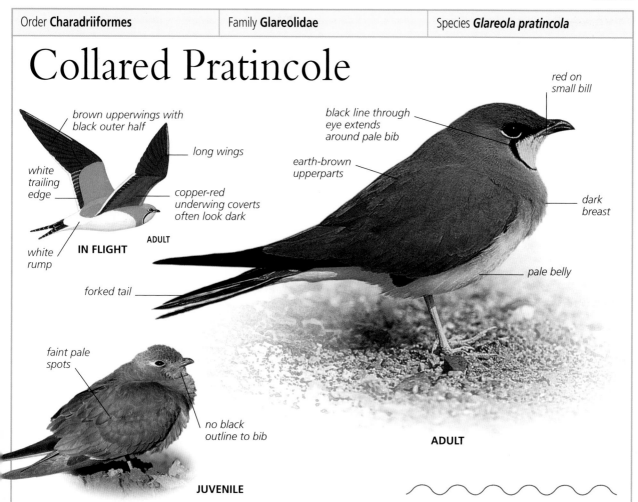

brown upperwings with black outer half

long wings

white trailing edge

copper-red underwing coverts often look dark

white rump

IN FLIGHT

ADULT

forked tail

red on small bill

black line through eye extends around pale bib

earth-brown upperparts

dark breast

pale belly

ADULT

faint pale spots

no black outline to bib

JUVENILE

FLIGHT: elegant, swooping action, changing pace and direction, with erratic twists and turns.

A lovely, specialized wader with an aerial feeding technique that has helped it to evolve a swallow-like form, the Collared Pratincole is basically a Mediterranean bird which occasionally strays farther north. It is a long, tapered bird, but when standing hunched up with its feathers fluffed out, it can look dumpy, almost round except for its protruding wingtips and tail. In the air, however, it has the skill and manoeuvrability of a Black Tern (see p.226). The Collared Pratincole often feeds in small parties.

VOICE Sharp, far-carrying, tern-like *kit*, *kitik*, rhythmic *kirri-tik-kit-ik*.

NESTING Shallow scrape in dry mud on ground; loose colonies; 2 or 3 eggs; 1 brood; April–July.

FEEDING Catches insects in bill while flying.

RESTING BETWEEN MEALS
The Collared Pratincole typically sits or stands on the ground for long spells between bouts of feeding.

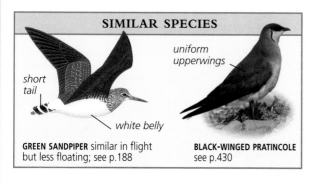

SIMILAR SPECIES

uniform upperwings

short tail

white belly

GREEN SANDPIPER similar in flight but less floating; see p.188

BLACK-WINGED PRATINCOLE see p.430

OCCURRENCE
In summer, in S Spain, Portugal, France, Italy, and Balkans, rare vagrant elsewhere. In extensive areas of flat, dry mud and damp pasture, bare ground, marshes and deltas drained for farmland, and salt pans.

Seen in the UK
J F M A M J J A S O N D

Length **24–28cm (9½–11in)**	Wingspan **60–70cm (23½–28in)**	Weight **50–80g (1¾–2⅞oz)**
Social **Flocks**	Lifespan **Up to 5 years**	Status **Endangered**

Order **Charadriiformes**	Family **Scolopacidae**	Species *Calidris alpina*

Dunlin 🔊 27.I, 27.II

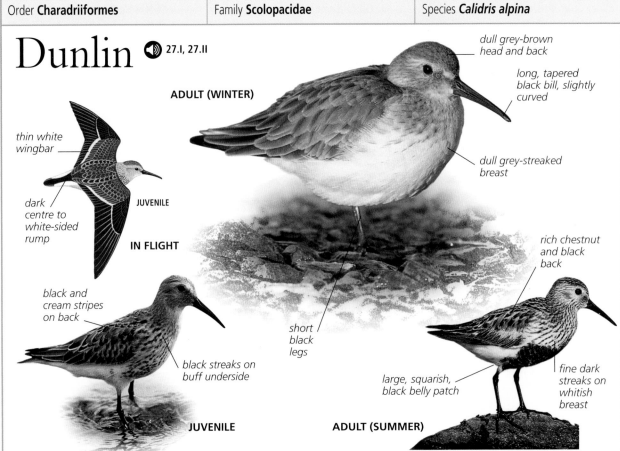

ADULT (WINTER)

dull grey-brown head and back

long, tapered black bill, slightly curved

dull grey-streaked breast

thin white wingbar

JUVENILE

dark centre to white-sided rump

IN FLIGHT

black and cream stripes on back

black streaks on buff underside

short black legs

rich chestnut and black back

large, squarish, black belly patch

fine dark streaks on whitish breast

JUVENILE

ADULT (SUMMER)

Widespread and covering a variety of wetland habitats, the Dunlin is the typical small wader of Europe, and is often used as the yardstick to assess other species. In spring, the streaked adults look rather sleek, while autumn juveniles have a certain brightness of colour and complexity of pattern. The Dunlin also has a distinctive call that allows it to be identified easily.

VOICE Thin, reedy, vibrant *shrree* or rasping *treerrr*; song-flight develops this into longer, trilled or pulsating "pea whistle".

NESTING Small, grass-lined, shallow scoop on ground or in grassy tussock; 4 eggs; 1 brood; May–July.

FEEDING Plods rather lethargically, on mud or drier shores, sometimes wading quite deeply, probing and picking up worms, insects, and molluscs.

REMARK Subspecies *C. a. alpina* (N Scandinavia) has long, curved bill and bright chestnut back in summer; *C. a. arctica* (Greenland) has short bill and dull body; *C. a. schinzii* (S Scandinavia and UK) has dull body.

FLIGHT: fast, dashing; flocks tight and well coordinated, often sweeping way out over sea and back again in spectacular manoeuvres.

WINTER ROOST
This group of Dunlins at high tide has been forced onto a small, exposed piece of rocky shore; when the tide recedes, they will disperse.

SIMILAR SPECIES

larger

paler back

greyer

white on belly

KNOT
see p.181

SANDERLING
see p.179

OCCURRENCE
In summer, breeds on wet moors, wet places on heaths, and northern isles, right up to the tundra, in far N and NW Europe. In all kinds of wet places from floods to wet fields but mostly on large estuaries.

Seen in the UK
J F M A M J J A S O N D

Length **16–20cm (6½–8in)**	Wingspan **35–40cm (14–16in)**	Weight **40–50g (1⁷⁄₁₆–1¾oz)**
Social **Flocks**	Lifespan **Up to 10 years**	Status **Common**

| Order **Charadriiformes** | Family **Scolopacidae** | Species *Calidris alba* |

Sanderling

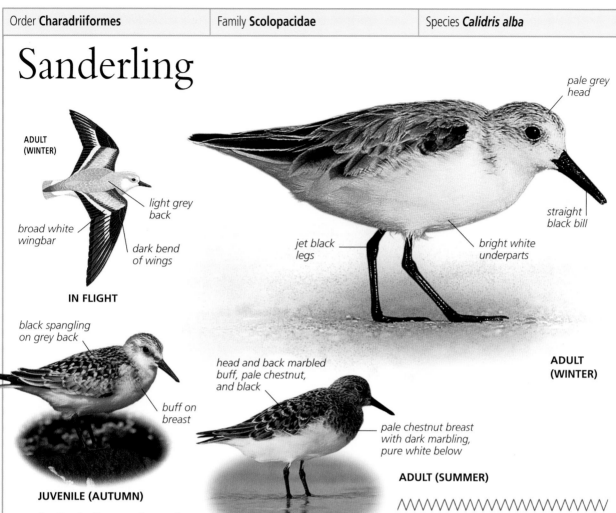

ADULT (WINTER)

light grey back

broad white wingbar

dark bend of wings

IN FLIGHT

pale grey head

straight black bill

bright white underparts

jet black legs

ADULT (WINTER)

black spangling on grey back

buff on breast

JUVENILE (AUTUMN)

head and back marbled buff, pale chestnut, and black

pale chestnut breast with dark marbling, pure white below

ADULT (SUMMER)

FLIGHT: fast, low, often swirling round and back again; groups well coordinated.

The Sanderling stands out from the other birds belonging to the sandpiper family in appearance and general behaviour. In winter, it is by far the whitest, and it is particularly quick and nimble, darting along the waves as they move in and out, to snatch up tiny items rolled up by the surf. At high tide, Sanderlings and Dunlins often mix, the Sanderlings making a paler splash against the Dunlins in the packed roosting flock.
VOICE Sharp, hard, short *plit* or *twik twik*.
NESTING Scrape on ground part-filled with willow leaves by chance; 4 eggs; 1 brood; May–July.
FEEDING Snatches marine worms, crustaceans, molluscs, sandhoppers, and similar animal matter from beach.

FEEDING ALONG WAVES
Small groups of Sanderlings dash in and out along the edge of the waves on a sandy beach.

SIMILAR SPECIES

DUNLIN winter, slower in actions; see p.178

longer bill

browner and duller

smaller

LITTLE STINT summer, pale "V" on back; see p.183

OCCURRENCE
Breeds in northern tundra; otherwise, migrants in Europe from late summer to late spring. Wintering flocks typically on broad sandy beaches, but also found on shorelines of all kinds, sometimes inland in May.

Seen in the UK
| J | F | M | A | M | J | J | A | S | O | N | D |

| Length **20–21cm (8–8½in)** | Wingspan **36–39cm (14–15½in)** | Weight **50–60g (1¾–2⅛oz)** |
| Social **Winter flocks** | Lifespan **Up to 10 years** | Status **Secure** |

Order **Charadriiformes**	Family **Scolopacidae**	Species *Calidris ferruginea*

Curlew Sandpiper

pale eye-ring and chin

ADULT (SUMMER)

long, slim, slightly downcurved bill

pale stripe over eye

dark back with even, pale buff scales

pale peachy buff breast

white belly

long black legs

JUVENILE (AUTUMN)

white rump

broad white wingbar

dark cap

JUVENILE (AUTUMN)

IN FLIGHT

long wings

no streaks below

JUVENILE (AUTUMN)

Very much linked with the Little Stint in birdwatchers' minds, as they are often found together, the Curlew Sandpiper tends to be scarcer in early spring in the Mediterranean and rather more erratic in western Europe in autumn. It follows the same early adult, later juvenile migration pattern as the Little Stint. It is noticeable in a group of Dunlins, being just a little more elegant and elongated in its proportions.
VOICE Distinctive soft, trilling, rolled *chirr-up*.
NESTING Simple shallow scrape on ground; 4 eggs; 1 brood; May–July.
FEEDING Typically exploits longer legs and bill to wade more deeply and probe into softer mud than Dunlin, in search of small worms.

FLIGHT: quick and direct with occasional erratic twists and tumbles.

WHITE RUMP
Only this bird and some much rarer sandpiper species have an unmarked white rump.

SPRING GEMS
Curlew Sandpiper migrants in spring, in coppery red breeding colour, are superbly colourful birds. They tend to wade more often and more deeply than Dunlins.

SIMILAR SPECIES

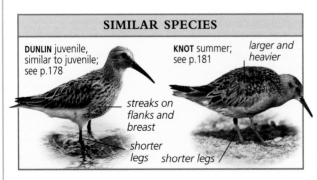

DUNLIN juvenile, similar to juvenile; see p.178

KNOT summer; see p.181

larger and heavier

streaks on flanks and breast

shorter legs

shorter legs

OCCURRENCE
Breeds in high Arctic region. Mostly in shallow fresh water and on muddy edges of coastal or inland lagoons. Chiefly adults in SE Europe in spring and in W Europe in late summer; followed by autumn juveniles.

Seen in the UK
J F M A M J J A S O N D

Length **18–23cm (7–9in)**	Wingspan **38–41cm (15–16in)**	Weight **45–90g (1⅝–3¼oz)**
Social **Small groups**	Lifespan **Up to 10 years**	Status **Localized**

Order **Charadriiformes**	Family **Scolopacidae**	Species *Calidris canutus*

Knot

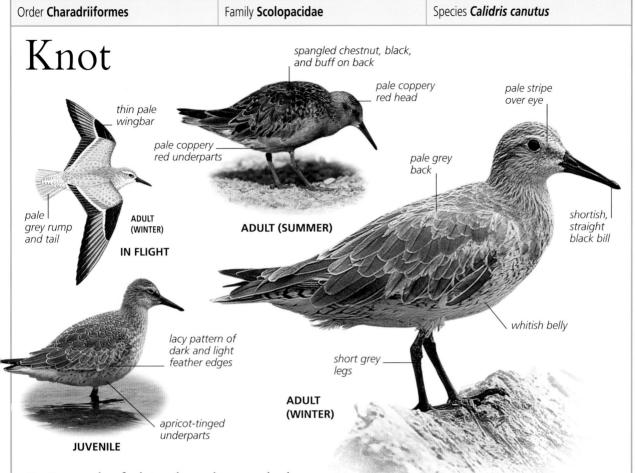

spangled chestnut, black, and buff on back

pale coppery red head

pale stripe over eye

thin pale wingbar

pale coppery red underparts

pale grey back

shortish, straight black bill

pale grey rump and tail

ADULT (WINTER)

IN FLIGHT

ADULT (SUMMER)

whitish belly

lacy pattern of dark and light feather edges

short grey legs

ADULT (WINTER)

apricot-tinged underparts

JUVENILE

Many waders flock together and some make dense packs when they roost at high tide, but few are as social at all times as the Knot. It forms enormous flocks, sometimes totalling hundreds of thousands. Such flocks flying over estuaries, moving to new feeding areas, or perhaps disturbed from a roost, are among the most dramatic of all bird spectacles. The rare solitary Knot is likely to be one of the occasional migrants that turn up near pools and reservoirs inland. In autumn, these may be juveniles and can be exceptionally tame, probably never having seen a human before in their short life. Knot flocks typically swarm over mudflats in slow, steady progression, heads down, feeding avidly.

VOICE Rather quiet; dull, short *nut*, occasionally bright, whistled note; no obvious flight note.

NESTING Shallow hollow on ground in cold tundra, usually near water; 3 or 4 eggs; 1 brood; May–July.

FEEDING Takes insects and plant material in summer, and molluscs and marine worms in winter.

FLIGHT: quick, strong; quite shallow wingbeats; flocks make coordinated movements.

ROOSTING
Knots and Dunlins stand shoulder to shoulder as they wait for the tide to recede.

SIMILAR SPECIES

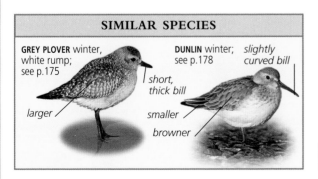

GREY PLOVER winter, white rump; see p.175

larger

DUNLIN winter; see p.178

slightly curved bill

short, thick bill

smaller

browner

OCCURRENCE
Breeds in Arctic tundra. Found in W Europe from late summer to late spring; biggest numbers in winter in dense flocks on large muddy estuaries and in small numbers on wide variety of shorelines.

Seen in the UK
J F M A M J J A S O N D

Length **23–27cm (9–10½in)**	Wingspan **47–54cm (18½–21½in)**	Weight **125–215g (4–8oz)**
Social **Large flocks**	Lifespan **Up to 10 years**	Status **Localized**

181

Order **Charadriiformes**	Family **Scolopacidae**	Species *Calidris temminckii*

Temminck's Stint

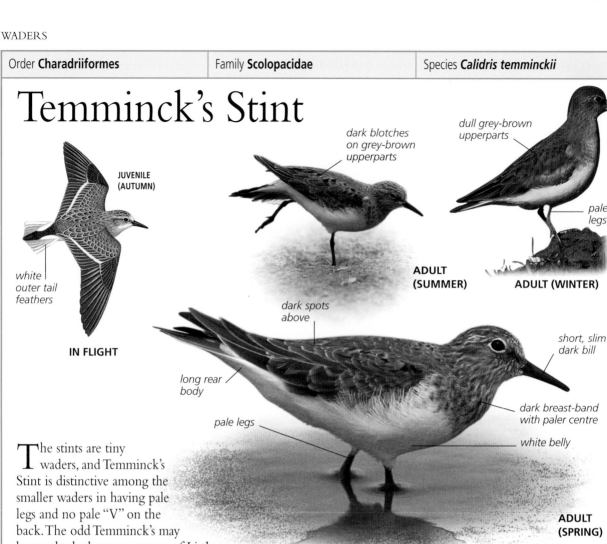

JUVENILE
(AUTUMN)

white
outer tail
feathers

IN FLIGHT

dark blotches
on grey-brown
upperparts

**ADULT
(SUMMER)**

dull grey-brown
upperparts

pale
legs

ADULT (WINTER)

dark spots
above

long rear
body

pale legs

short, slim
dark bill

dark breast-band
with paler centre

white belly

**ADULT
(SPRING)**

The stints are tiny waders, and Temminck's Stint is distinctive among the smaller waders in having pale legs and no pale "V" on the back. The odd Temminck's may be overlooked among groups of Little Stints that appear in spring around southern European lakes. It does not actually flock with Little Stints, but mingles more incidentally: unlike its commoner relative, it feeds in overgrown, swampy places rather than on open shores. Small groups appear in northwest Europe in spring; in autumn, usually single juveniles are seen on migration, when they may be exceptionally tame. They have a distinctive lacy pattern above each feather with thin brown and buff fringes.

VOICE Quick, spluttering, dry trill, *tirr-r-r tirr-r-r.*
NESTING Shallow, unlined hollow in vegetation; 4 eggs; 1 brood; May–June.
FEEDING Picks and probes for tiny invertebrates among short vegetation or on sticky, wet mud.

FLIGHT: fast, direct; often rises high and fast if flushed.

SINGING MALE
Males settle on stumps and trees, overlooking the breeding territory, after their high display flights with trilling songs.

OCCURRENCE
Rare breeder in N Scandinavia, but widespread as migrant. Quite frequent in E Europe, rare in NW Europe, often in twos or threes in late spring or single juveniles in autumn, turning up beside fresh water on muddy or weedy shores.

Seen in the UK
J F M **A M J J A S** O N D

SIMILAR SPECIES

pale "V"
on back

black
legs

LITTLE STINT
see p.183

COMMON SANDPIPER
see p.186

bobs
tail

larger

Length **13–15cm (5–6in)**	Wingspan **34–37cm (13½–14½in)**	Weight **20–40g (11/16–17/16oz)**
Social **Solitary/Small flocks**	Lifespan **Up to 5 years**	Status **Secure†**

| Order **Charadriiformes** | Family **Scolopacidae** | Species *Calidris minuta* |

Little Stint

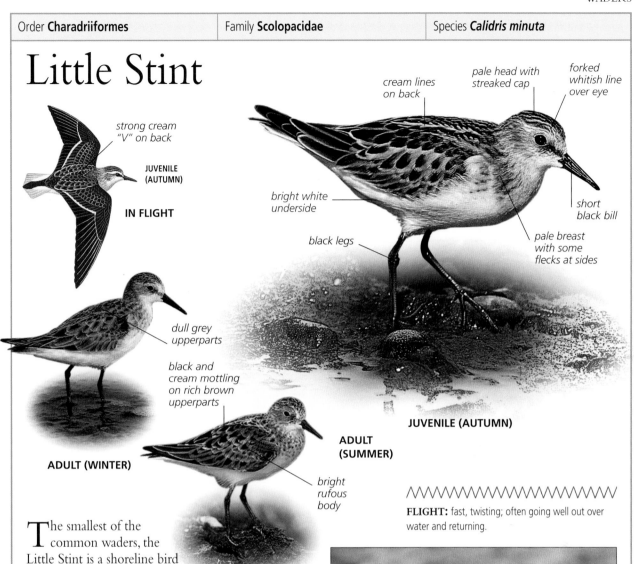

strong cream "V" on back

JUVENILE (AUTUMN)

IN FLIGHT

cream lines on back

pale head with streaked cap

forked whitish line over eye

bright white underside

black legs

short black bill

pale breast with some flecks at sides

JUVENILE (AUTUMN)

dull grey upperparts

black and cream mottling on rich brown upperparts

ADULT (WINTER)

ADULT (SUMMER)

bright rufous body

FLIGHT: fast, twisting; often going well out over water and returning.

The smallest of the common waders, the Little Stint is a shoreline bird around the Mediterranean in spring, moving far to the north in summer. In autumn, adults move south early, to be followed by a larger wave of juveniles in western Europe, a pattern followed by several wader species. Little Stints are often mixed up with larger numbers of Dunlins and, sometimes, Curlew Sandpipers.

VOICE Hard, dry, sharp *tip* or *trip*, sometimes *ti-ti-trip*.
NESTING Small, shallow scrape on ground, close to water; 4 eggs; 1 brood; May–July.
FEEDING Scampers about at water's edge, finding tiny animal matter; does not often wade deeply.

MIGRANT JUVENILE
Most autumn migrants are clean, bright, well-marked juveniles. They are often remarkably tame.

SIMILAR SPECIES

DUNLIN juvenile; see p.178

larger

longer bill

duller on flanks and belly

no "V" on back

SANDERLING summer; see p.179

larger

OCCURRENCE
Breeds on tundra. On migration, appears beside all kinds of muddy pools and lagoons, less so on sea coast. Adults found mostly in SE Europe in spring; majority in W Europe being small parties of juveniles in autumn.

| Seen in the UK |
| J F M **A M J J A S O N** D |

| Length **12–14cm (4¾–5½in)** | Wingspan **34–37cm (13½–14½in)** | Weight **20–40g (¹¹⁄₁₆–1⁷⁄₁₆oz)** |
| Social **Small flocks** | Lifespan **Up to 10 years** | Status **Secure†** |

Order **Charadriiformes**	Family **Scolopacidae**	Species *Calidris maritima*

Purple Sandpiper

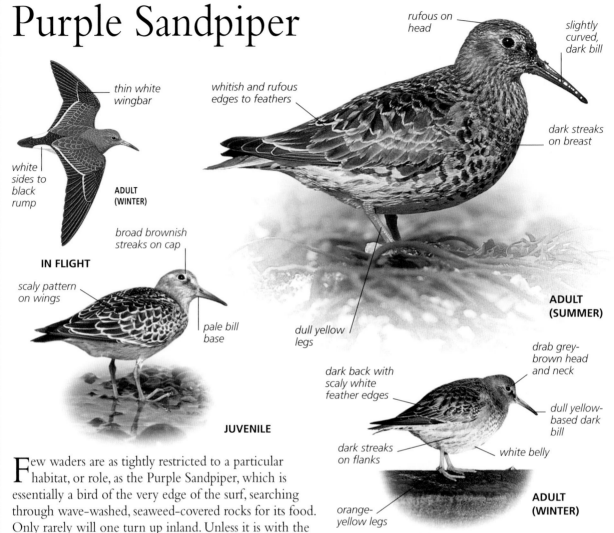

thin white wingbar

white sides to black rump

ADULT (WINTER)

IN FLIGHT

broad brownish streaks on cap

scaly pattern on wings

pale bill base

JUVENILE

rufous on head

slightly curved, dark bill

whitish and rufous edges to feathers

dark streaks on breast

dull yellow legs

ADULT (SUMMER)

dark back with scaly white feather edges

dark streaks on flanks

orange-yellow legs

drab grey-brown head and neck

dull yellow-based dark bill

white belly

ADULT (WINTER)

Few waders are as tightly restricted to a particular habitat, or role, as the Purple Sandpiper, which is essentially a bird of the very edge of the surf, searching through wave-washed, seaweed-covered rocks for its food. Only rarely will one turn up inland. Unless it is with the more nervous Turnstones, it may well be absurdly tame. Like most waders, the Purple Sandpiper will not leave for its breeding grounds until mid-May and can return in July; hence it is present for most months of the year in western Europe, despite being a non-breeding visitor.

VOICE Simple, low, liquid *weet* or *weet-wit*.

NESTING Slight scrape on ground, on wide open tundra; 4 eggs; 1 brood; May–July.

FEEDING Variety of insects, spiders, and other invertebrates, chiefly periwinkles and similar molluscs in winter.

FLIGHT: low, fast, darting flights from rock to rock.

SIMILAR SPECIES

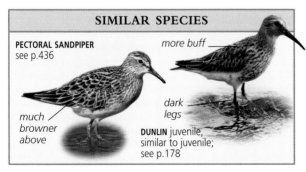

PECTORAL SANDPIPER see p.436

more buff

much browner above

dark legs

DUNLIN juvenile, similar to juvenile; see p.178

INCONSPICUOUS
A dark wader on dark, weedy rocks, the Purple Sandpiper is easily overlooked.

OCCURRENCE
Breeds in Iceland and Scandinavia, on tundra and mountains. Widespread in winter, preferring rocky shores, usually with plentiful seaweed, at times on bare rock and stony beaches, also piers, harbour walls, and other artificial sites.

Seen in the UK
J F M A M J J A S O N D

Length **20–22cm (8–9in)**	Wingspan **40–44cm (16–17½in)**	Weight **60–75g (2⅛–2⅝oz)**
Social **Small flocks**	Lifespan **Up to 10 years**	Status **Secure†**

Order **Charadriiformes**	Family **Scolopacidae**	Species *Arenaria interpres*

Turnstone

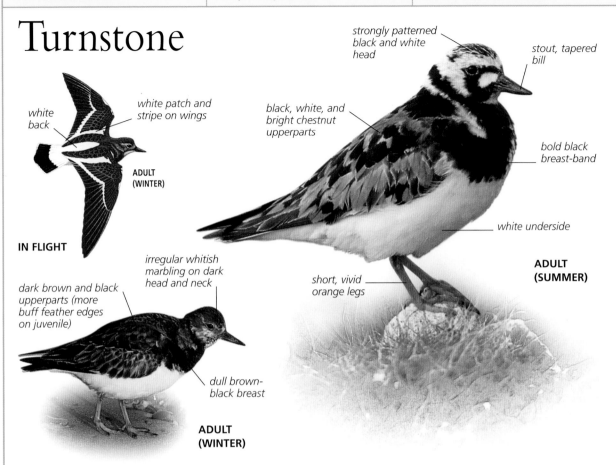

strongly patterned black and white head

stout, tapered bill

white back

white patch and stripe on wings

black, white, and bright chestnut upperparts

bold black breast-band

ADULT (WINTER)

IN FLIGHT

white underside

ADULT (SUMMER)

irregular whitish marbling on dark head and neck

short, vivid orange legs

dark brown and black upperparts (more buff feather edges on juvenile)

dull brown-black breast

ADULT (WINTER)

While most waders like soft ground, chiefly mud or sand, the Turnstone is equally at home on rocks, although sandy beaches with a tangle of seaweed, shells, and small stones at the high-tide mark are ideal for it. It makes a good living searching through such debris, which is very rich in small invertebrates and regularly refreshed by high tides. Turnstones are typically noisy, active, and often quite tame.

FLIGHT: fast, low, flickering.

VOICE Fast, hard, staccato calls, *tukatukatuk, teuk, tchik*.

NESTING Scantily lined scrape on ground close to shore in islands and on rocky coasts; 4 eggs; 1 brood; May–July.

FEEDING Stirs up and turns over weed, stones, shells, and beach debris to find invertebrates.

TIGHT ROOST
High tide sees scores of Turnstones packed close together for an hour or two.

QUARRELSOME FEEDERS
Small groups of Turnstones bicker as they feed along the shore.

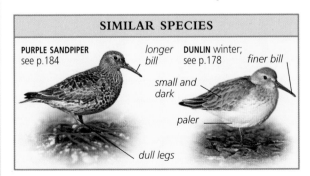

SIMILAR SPECIES

PURPLE SANDPIPER see p.184

longer bill

DUNLIN winter; see p.178

finer bill

small and dark

paler

dull legs

OCCURRENCE
Breeds on rocky coasts around Scandinavia. At other times, on sea coasts of all kinds, from open mud to rocks, but especially hard coasts and gravelly tidelines. Occasional migrants turn up inland but soon move on.

Seen in the UK
J F M A M J J A S O N D

Length **21–24cm (8½–9½in)**	Wingspan **44–49cm (17½–19½in)**	Weight **80–110g (2⅞–3⅝oz)**
Social **Flocks**	Lifespan **Up to 10 years**	Status **Secure**

| Order **Charadriiformes** | Family **Scolopacidae** | Species **Actitis hypoleucos** |

Common Sandpiper 🔊 28

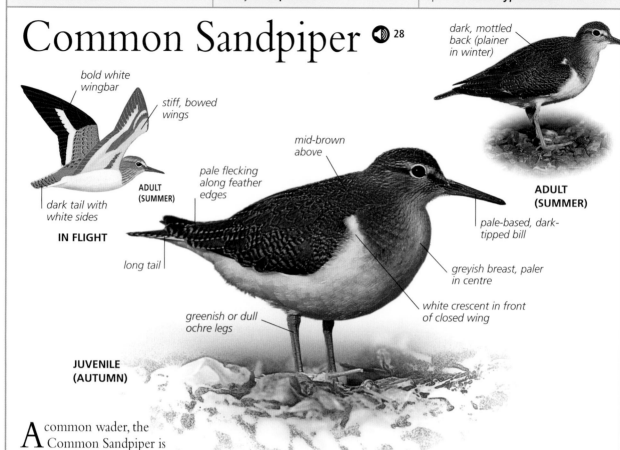

bold white wingbar

stiff, bowed wings

ADULT (SUMMER)

dark tail with white sides

IN FLIGHT

long tail

greenish or dull ochre legs

pale flecking along feather edges

mid-brown above

dark, mottled back (plainer in winter)

ADULT (SUMMER)

pale-based, dark-tipped bill

greyish breast, paler in centre

white crescent in front of closed wing

JUVENILE (AUTUMN)

A common wader, the Common Sandpiper is much more widespread than its northern counterparts, the Green and Wood Sandpipers. A few may even be seen in winter, although the great majority go to Africa for the winter months. Typically a freshwater bird, it may also sometimes be seen on rocky sea shores. It is usually found in small numbers, of rarely more than ten or so together, strung out along a shore rather than in tight groups; they usually hold their heads low and swing their tails up and down in a constant swaying bob.

VOICE Loud, ringing, sharp *tew-tew-tew* or *tyew-yu-yu*; many summer calls include fast, trilling *teu-i teu-i teu-i, chip, tidledi tidledi tidledi.*

NESTING Small, grass-lined hollow on ground, often on grassy banks; 4 eggs; 1 brood; April–July.

FEEDING Skips and saunters along waterside, snatching insects and also some worms and molluscs.

FLIGHT: highly characteristic, low over water, with stiff, flickering beats of bowed wings.

BATHING
All waders bathe regularly, even in cold weather, to help keep their plumage in tiptop condition.

SIMILAR SPECIES

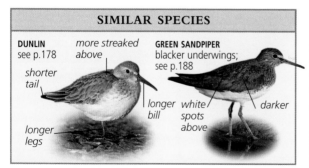

DUNLIN see p.178

more streaked above

shorter tail

longer legs

GREEN SANDPIPER blacker underwings; see p.188

longer bill

white spots above

darker

OCCURRENCE
Breeds on rocky streams and lake sides with shingle and grassy banks locally throughout Europe. On migration, in all kinds of waterside habitats, from reservoirs and streams to muddy estuaries and even rocky foreshores.

Seen in the UK
| J | F | | | | | | | | | N | D |

| Length **19–21cm (7½–8½in)** | Wingspan **32–35cm (12½–14in)** | Weight **40–60g (1⁷⁄₁₆–2⅛oz)** |
| Social **Small flocks** | Lifespan **Up to 10 years** | Status **Secure** |

Order **Charadriiformes**	Family **Scolopacidae**	Species **Philomachus pugnax**

Ruff

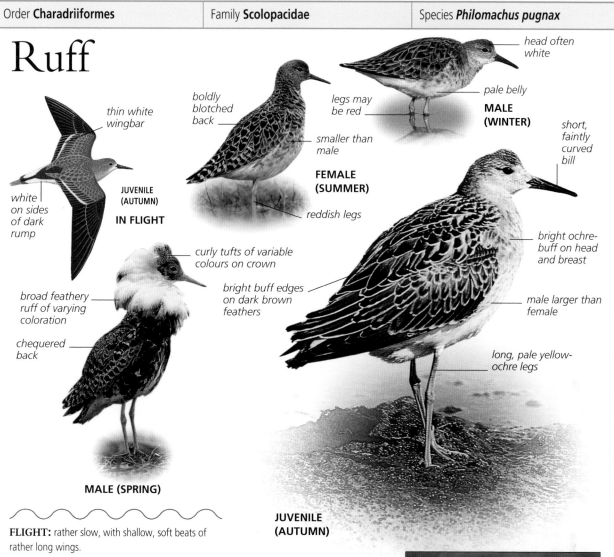

thin white wingbar

boldly blotched back

legs may be red

head often white

pale belly

MALE (WINTER)

white on sides of dark rump

JUVENILE (AUTUMN)

IN FLIGHT

smaller than male

FEMALE (SUMMER)

reddish legs

short, faintly curved bill

curly tufts of variable colours on crown

bright buff edges on dark brown feathers

bright ochre-buff on head and breast

broad feathery ruff of varying coloration

male larger than female

chequered back

long, pale yellow-ochre legs

MALE (SPRING)

JUVENILE (AUTUMN)

FLIGHT: rather slow, with shallow, soft beats of rather long wings.

Male Ruffs in spring look extraordinary, and the females in summer are boldly blotched; in winter, they retain little individuality. Juveniles in autumn, which are most often seen in Europe, are much more consistent in appearance. They appear in mid-autumn on wet, muddy edges of lakes and reservoirs, looking quite sedate compared with smaller waders or even Redshanks, with a steady, plodding action that rarely gets close to a run.

VOICE Very quiet; occasionally low, gruff *wek*.

NESTING Grass-lined scrape, well hidden in deep vegetation at edge of marsh; 4 eggs; 1 brood; April–July.

FEEDING Probes in soft mud for worms, insects, insect larvae, and seeds.

DISPLAYING
Male Ruffs display in groups to females, with mock battles, their unusual breeding plumage creating a striking spectacle.

SIMILAR SPECIES

more spotted above

less scaly back

white eye-stripe

browner

WOOD SANDPIPER autumn juvenile, similar to autumn juvenile; see p.189

REDSHANK similar to adult winter; see p.190

OCCURRENCE
Breeds on wet meadowland; declining and local in NW Europe, more widespread in NE. At other times, on wet fields and marshes, muddy freshwater margins, most commonly autumn juveniles, some winter on western estuaries.

Seen in the UK
J F M A M J J A S O N D

Length **20–32cm (8–12½in)**	Wingspan **46–58cm (18–23in)**	Weight **70–230g (2½–8oz)**
Social **Small flocks**	Lifespan **10–15 years**	Status **Secure†**

Order **Charadriiformes**	Family **Scolopacidae**	Species *Tringa ochropus*

Green Sandpiper 🔊 29.I, 29.II

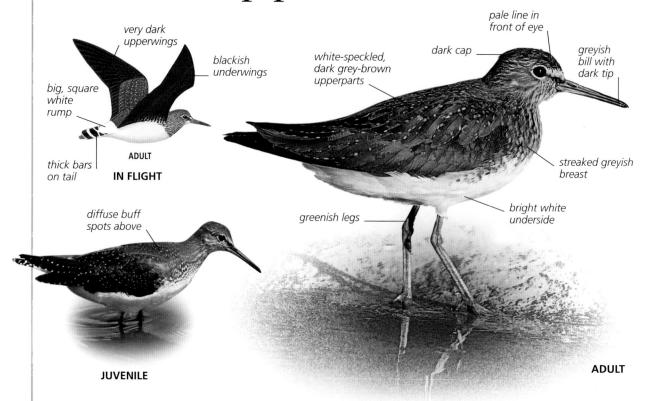

very dark upperwings

blackish underwings

big, square white rump

thick bars on tail

ADULT
IN FLIGHT

white-speckled, dark grey-brown upperparts

pale line in front of eye

dark cap

greyish bill with dark tip

streaked greyish breast

bright white underside

greenish legs

diffuse buff spots above

JUVENILE

ADULT

Like other *Tringa* sandpipers, this bird is often seen in twos, threes, or fours; it does not gather close together in tight flocks or in larger numbers. Often one or two fly up from a muddy pool and shoot around the sky, sometimes returning, sometimes moving quite far. They are often seen in or near coastal marshes but not on open mudflats. Getting close to Green Sandpipers, without a hide, is usually rather difficult as they tend to be very alert and quick to fly off, looking black and white as they take to the air.
VOICE Loud, full-throated, liquid, almost yodelling *tllu-eet, weet-weet!*
NESTING Old nest of thrush or similar bird in tree near forest bog; 4 eggs; 1 brood; May–July.
FEEDING Often up to belly in water, probing and picking insects, crustaceans, and worms.

∧∧∧∧∧∧∧∧∧∧∧∧∧∧∧∧∧∧∧∧∧

FLIGHT: flies fast, rising steeply when flushed, with quick, flicked beats of angled wings.

MUD WADER
This sandpiper usually wades on muddy shores, close to cover, often bobbing its tail; it is typically less active than the Common Sandpiper.

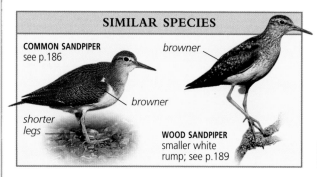

SIMILAR SPECIES

COMMON SANDPIPER see p.186

browner

browner

shorter legs

WOOD SANDPIPER smaller white rump; see p.189

OCCURRENCE
Breeds in N and NE Europe. Local in winter; widespread migrant. Mostly on small pools, streams, wet ditches, salt-marsh creeks, muddy edges of reservoirs, and in more overgrown areas than other sandpipers.

Seen in the UK
J F M A M J J A S O N D

Length **21–24cm (8½–9½in)**	Wingspan **41–46cm (16–18in)**	Weight **70–90g (2½–3¼oz)**
Social **Small flocks**	Lifespan **Up to 10 years**	Status **Secure†**

Order **Charadriiformes**	Family **Scolopacidae**	Species *Tringa glareola*

Wood Sandpiper

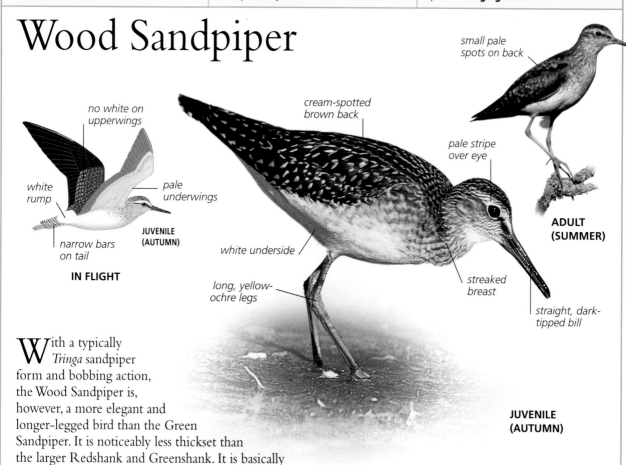

small pale
spots on back

cream-spotted
brown back

pale stripe
over eye

**ADULT
(SUMMER)**

no white on
upperwings

white
rump

pale
underwings

streaked
breast

straight, dark-
tipped bill

white underside

narrow bars
on tail

**JUVENILE
(AUTUMN)**

IN FLIGHT

long, yellow-
ochre legs

**JUVENILE
(AUTUMN)**

With a typically *Tringa* sandpiper form and bobbing action, the Wood Sandpiper is, however, a more elegant and longer-legged bird than the Green Sandpiper. It is noticeably less thickset than the larger Redshank and Greenshank. It is basically a freshwater bird, not seen on open sea shores, often found in weedy pools or paddling about on floating vegetation. Many Wood Sandpipers pass through eastern and southern Europe in spring, when they are scarce migrants in western Europe. In autumn, they are still relatively uncommon but more regular and predictable in western Europe, especially in August. Ones and twos then appear on sheltered muddy shores of reservoirs or on lagoons near the coast, feeding in a rather nervous, jumpy manner, easily disturbed and ready to fly off at some height.

VOICE Distinctive quick, sharp *chiff-iff-iff-iff*.

NESTING Small, leaf-lined scrape on ground, occasionally old nest in tree; 4 eggs; 1 brood; May–July.

FEEDING Steps delicately over vegetation, picking up insects and small aquatic invertebrates.

FLIGHT: strong, quick, light, with flicking wingbeats; often rises high if disturbed.

SHALLOW WATER WADER
The Wood Sandpiper feeds beside muddy pools or on shallow floods, flying off quickly and noisily if disturbed.

SIMILAR SPECIES

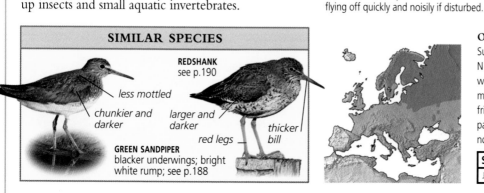

REDSHANK
see p.190

less mottled

chunkier and
darker

larger and
darker

red legs

thicker
bill

GREEN SANDPIPER
blacker underwings; bright
white rump; see p.188

OCCURRENCE
Summer visitor, breeding in N and NE Europe. Migrants widespread in south and west, most on muddy pools, weedy fringes of shallow lagoons, salt pans, and often near coast, but not on estuarine mud.

Seen in the UK											
J	F	M	A	M	J	J	A	S	O	N	D

Length **19–21cm (7½–8½in)**	Wingspan **36–40cm (14–16in)**	Weight **50–90g (1¾–3¼oz)**
Social **Small flocks**	Lifespan **Up to 10 years**	Status **Declining**

Order **Charadriiformes**	Family **Scolopacidae**	Species *Tringa totanus*

Redshank 🔊 30

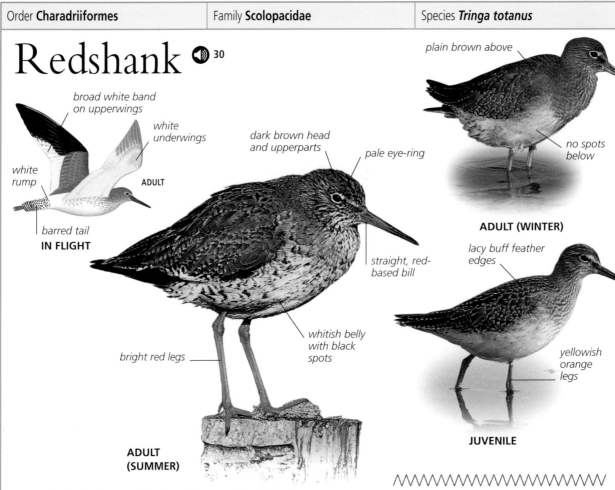

broad white band on upperwings

white underwings

ADULT

white rump

barred tail

IN FLIGHT

dark brown head and upperparts

pale eye-ring

straight, red-based bill

whitish belly with black spots

bright red legs

ADULT (SUMMER)

plain brown above

no spots below

ADULT (WINTER)

lacy buff feather edges

yellowish orange legs

JUVENILE

Its noisy behaviour makes the widespread Redshank one of the most obvious shoreline birds. It roosts in tight flocks at high tide, looking noticeably dark brown compared with paler godwits and Knots. It is declining fast in areas where farmland is drained or agriculture intensified, and has also been affected by the loss of salt-marsh habitats. Nevertheless, it remains frequent on many coasts.

VOICE Loud, ringing calls, "bouncing" *tyew-yu-yu, teu, teu-hu*, sharp annoyed *tewk, tewk*; song *tu-yoo tu-yoo tu-yoo*.

NESTING Simple, sparsely lined hollow on ground, often with grass intertwined above it, forming canopy; 4 eggs; 1 brood; April–July.

FEEDING Probes and picks from mud, taking insects, earthworms, marine worms, crustaceans, and molluscs.

FLIGHT: fast, direct, gliding to ground; raises wings as it settles.

DENSE ROOSTS
Flocks of Redshanks are pushed tightly together by the rising tide. They tend to remain separate from other waders.

SIMILAR SPECIES

KNOT winter; see p.181

smaller

shorter legs

larger

paler

longer bill

BAR-TAILED GODWIT winter; see p.195

OCCURRENCE
Breeds on salt marshes, wet pastures, near freshwater pools, and on wet upland moors in N and E Europe. Otherwise, in wet places, on fresh water and salt coasts; mostly on estuaries but likely in almost any small creek or marsh.

Seen in the UK
J F M A M J J A S O N D

Length **27–29cm (10½–11½in)**	Wingspan **45–52cm (18–20½in)**	Weight **85–155g (3–5oz)**
Social **Winter flocks**	Lifespan **Up to 10 years**	Status **Declining**

| Order **Charadriiformes** | Family **Scolopacidae** | Species *Tringa erythropus* |

Spotted Redshank

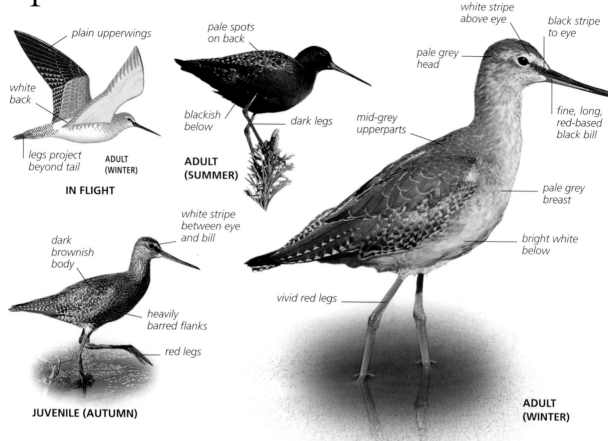

plain upperwings

white back

legs project beyond tail

ADULT (WINTER)

IN FLIGHT

pale spots on back

blackish below

dark legs

ADULT (SUMMER)

white stripe above eye

black stripe to eye

pale grey head

white stripe between eye and bill

mid-grey upperparts

fine, long, red-based black bill

pale grey breast

bright white below

dark brownish body

heavily barred flanks

red legs

vivid red legs

JUVENILE (AUTUMN)

ADULT (WINTER)

Of the larger waders, the Spotted Redshank is one of the more dynamic and energetic in its feeding actions: small groups are often found leaping, running, upending, and diving for tiny fish in shallow water. Individual migrants are generally located by their highly distinctive flight calls. They are scarce in winter, and are mostly seen in late summer or autumn, as they are restricted to the far northern parts of Europe as breeding birds.

VOICE Loud, sharp, clearly enunciated *tchew-it!*
NESTING Hollow on open ground; 4 eggs; 1 brood; May–July.
FEEDING Often in water, dashing after prey, not probing; takes fish fry, worms, and molluscs.

FLIGHT: fast and direct; legs trail (occasionally tucked forwards).

FEEDING
Small groups of Spotted Redshanks feed in creeks and pools, darting after prey and even upending like ducks.

SIMILAR SPECIES

REDSHANK similar to adult winter; see p.190

GREENSHANK see p.192

browner

shorter bill

shorter legs

dull green legs

slightly upturned bill

OCCURRENCE
Breeds in forest bogs and on open tundra in far N Europe. At other times, in freshwater and brackish lagoons, salt-marsh creeks, edges of lakes and reservoirs inland, with small numbers wintering in estuaries.

| Seen in the UK |
| J F M A M J J A S O N D |

| Length **29–32cm (11½–12½in)** | Wingspan **48–52cm (19–20½in)** | Weight **135–250g (5–9oz)** |
| Social **Small flocks** | Lifespan **Up to 10 years** | Status **Secure** |

Order **Charadriiformes**	Family **Scolopacidae**	Species *Tringa nebularia*

Greenshank 🔊 31

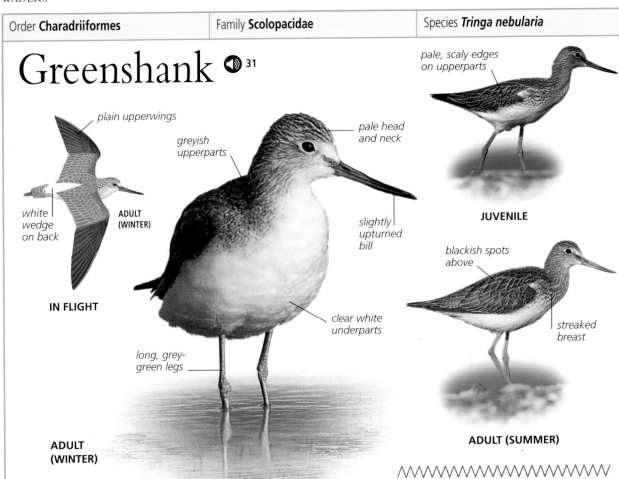

plain upperwings

greyish upperparts

pale head and neck

white wedge on back

ADULT (WINTER)

slightly upturned bill

IN FLIGHT

clear white underparts

long, grey-green legs

ADULT (WINTER)

pale, scaly edges on upperparts

JUVENILE

blackish spots above

streaked breast

ADULT (SUMMER)

∧∧∧∧∧∧∧∧∧∧∧∧∧∧∧∧∧∧∧∧∧

FLIGHT: fast, strong, with regular wingbeats; looks long and tapered.

One of the most beautiful of waders, despite a lack of strong colour or pattern, the Greenshank is an elegant, delicate-looking bird. It is, nevertheless, noticeably bigger than a Redshank, being part way to a godwit in size. It is easily located by its loud, ringing calls that echo around estuaries and inland pools. In summer, this is a bird of wild and remote places, shy and difficult to observe.

VOICE Main call loud, ringing, even-pitch *tew-tew-tew*, without accelerating "bounce" or hysterical quality of Redshank.

NESTING Scrape on ground, often near logs, stones, or posts, in grass or heather; 4 eggs; 1 brood; May–July.

FEEDING Probes while wading in shallow water, often very active, running and chasing fish; eats worms, insects, and crustaceans.

ELEGANT STANCE
Its long bill and long legs help to give the Greenshank a particularly delicate, elegant appearance.

SIMILAR SPECIES

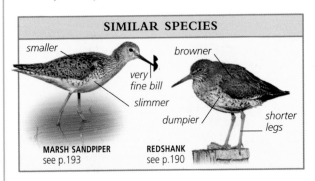

smaller

very fine bill

slimmer

MARSH SANDPIPER
see p.193

browner

dumpier

shorter legs

REDSHANK
see p.190

OCCURRENCE
Breeds on moorland near northern pools in NW Europe. On migration near water, including reservoirs well inland, but not often on exposed mudflats of larger estuaries. Winters in more sheltered salt-marsh creeks.

Seen in the UK
J F M A M J J A S O N D

Length **30–35cm (12–14in)**	Wingspan **53–60cm (21–23½in)**	Weight **140–270g (5–10oz)**
Social **Small flocks**	Lifespan **Up to 10 years**	Status **Secure**

Order **Charadriiformes**	Family **Scolopacidae**	Species *Tringa stagnatilis*

Marsh Sandpiper

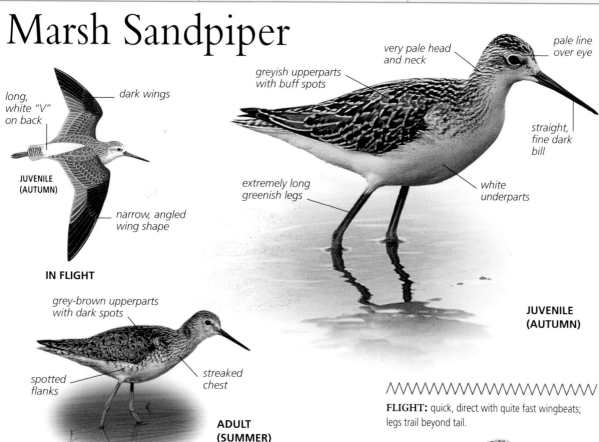

long, white "V" on back

dark wings

JUVENILE (AUTUMN)

narrow, angled wing shape

IN FLIGHT

very pale head and neck

greyish upperparts with buff spots

pale line over eye

straight, fine dark bill

extremely long greenish legs

white underparts

JUVENILE (AUTUMN)

grey-brown upperparts with dark spots

spotted flanks

streaked chest

ADULT (SUMMER)

FLIGHT: quick, direct with quite fast wingbeats; legs trail beyond tail.

I ts long legs and very fine, straight bill make this a particularly delicate and elegant wader, almost a stilt among the sandpipers. It is markedly smaller than a Redshank but needs to be carefully distinguished, when seen on its own, from a Greenshank, also a rather refined-looking bird. It typically stalks daintily around the edge of freshwater muddy pools. Marsh Sandpipers are generally rare in western Europe, although they may be seen regularly in a few areas of southeast Europe.

VOICE Quick, sharp *kyew* or high *kyu kyu kyu*.

NESTING Scantily lined scrape in grassy bog and marsh, or on open boggy clearing in northern forest; 4 eggs; 1 brood; May–July.

FEEDING Picks small insects and crustaceans from mud or water surface.

PALE LOOKS
A browner bird in summer, with black spots above, the Marsh Sandpiper ususally looks pale and rather colourless.

SIMILAR SPECIES

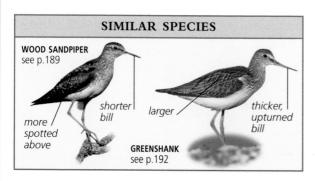

WOOD SANDPIPER see p.189

shorter bill

more spotted above

larger

thicker, upturned bill

GREENSHANK see p.192

OCCURRENCE
Breeds in N and extreme E Europe, in forest clearings. Migrates through eastern Mediterranean, rare farther west in late spring or autumn. Mostly in freshwater marshes and lagoons.

Seen in the UK
J F M A M J J A S O N D

Length **22–25cm (9–10in)**	Wingspan **50cm (20in)**	Weight **80–90g (2⅞–3¼oz)**
Social **Small flocks**	Lifespan **Up to 10 years**	Status **Secure†**

Order **Charadriiformes**	Family **Scolopacidae**	Species *Limosa limosa*

Black-tailed Godwit

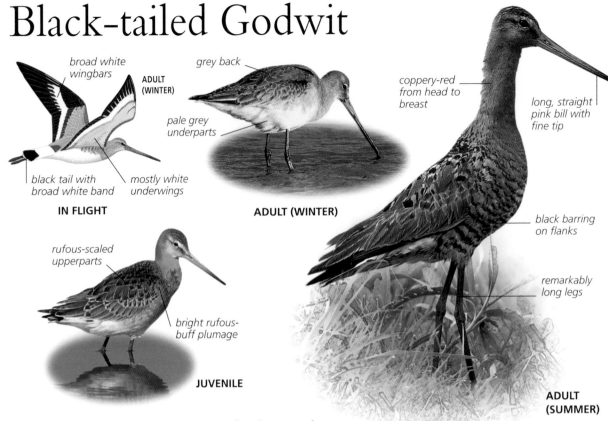

broad white wingbars

ADULT (WINTER)

grey back

coppery-red from head to breast

long, straight pink bill with fine tip

pale grey underparts

black tail with broad white band

mostly white underwings

IN FLIGHT

ADULT (WINTER)

black barring on flanks

rufous-scaled upperparts

remarkably long legs

bright rufous-buff plumage

JUVENILE

ADULT (SUMMER)

This is one of Europe's larger and more handsome waders, boldly patterned in flight (when it is unmistakable) and characterized by especially long legs. It usually stands with its body well forward, bill probing almost at its toes. The Black-tailed Godwit breeds in wet meadowland, where it is susceptible both to drainage and sudden spring floods. In winter, it resorts to relatively few estuaries, often rather narrow and enclosed with long, narrow areas of rich mud; these are occupied year after year. It is generally much less widespread than the Bar-tailed Godwit but may gather in hundreds in traditional wintering places. Spring flocks before migration look stunning in red plumage.
VOICE Noisy in spring with nasal *weeka-weeka-weeka*; quick *vi-vi-vi* in flight.
NESTING Shallow scrapes on ground in rich vegetation; 3 or 4 eggs; 1 brood; May–July.
FEEDING Probes deeply, often in water up to its belly, for worms, molluscs, and seeds.

FLIGHT: quick, direct flight with shallow, stiff wingbeats; head well outstretched, legs trail far beyond tail.

WINTER FLOCKS
From autumn to late winter, Black-tailed Godwits are found in flocks in quite small, sheltered, muddy estuaries.

SIMILAR SPECIES

OYSTERCATCHER similar in flight; see p.166

shorter bill

more pied

plain wings

shorter legs above joint

BAR-TAILED GODWIT see p.195

OCCURRENCE
Breeds in N and W Europe, in wet meadowland and flooded pasture; otherwise, mostly coastal. Widely spread except in far N Scandinavia but everywhere localized, even in winter, when most are on traditional, muddy, narrow estuaries.

Seen in the UK
J F M A M J J A S O N D

Length **36–44cm (14–17½in)**	Wingspan **62–70cm (24–28in)**	Weight **280–500g (10–18oz)**
Social **Winter flocks**	Lifespan **10–15 years**	Status **Vulnerable**

| Order **Charadriiformes** | Family **Scolopacidae** | Species *Limosa lapponica* |

Bar-tailed Godwit

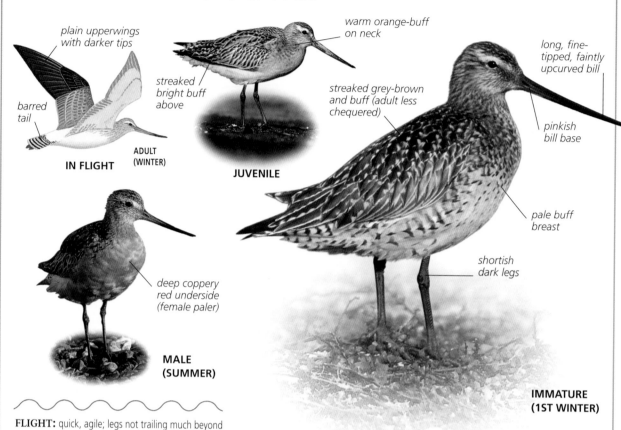

plain upperwings with darker tips

barred tail

IN FLIGHT

ADULT (WINTER)

streaked bright buff above

warm orange-buff on neck

JUVENILE

streaked grey-brown and buff (adult less chequered)

long, fine-tipped, faintly upcurved bill

pinkish bill base

pale buff breast

shortish dark legs

IMMATURE (1ST WINTER)

deep coppery red underside (female paler)

MALE (SUMMER)

FLIGHT: quick, agile; legs not trailing much beyond tail; often acrobatic.

While Black-tailed Godwits breed in Europe, Bar-tailed Godwits breed in the far northern tundra, but they are otherwise much more widespread on shores of all kinds. They prefer extensive mudflats, groups scattering over them to probe for food, and are driven at high tide to large, mixed roosts where they tend to keep a little separate from the Curlews, Redshanks, and other species close by. Flocks flying to roost may arrive quite high up and dive down with much acrobatic twisting and rolling.

VOICE In flight, quick, yelping *kirruk kirruk*.
NESTING Small scrape on ground on drier patch in cold tundra; 4 eggs; 1 brood; May–July.
FEEDING Probes for large marine worms and molluscs.

HIGH-TIDE FLURRY
A rising tide pushes a group of godwits off a mud bank, to seek a safe roost on a nearby marsh.

SIMILAR SPECIES

straighter bill

longer legs

CURLEW see p.196

downcurved bill

larger

BLACK-TAILED GODWIT bold wing pattern in flight; see p.194

OCCURRENCE
Arctic breeder on tundra; in Europe, mostly in scattered flocks on broad estuaries, but also seen in small numbers on smaller beaches and rocky shores, lingering until May and returning from July onwards.

Seen in the UK
J F M A M J J A S O N D

| Length **33–42cm (13–16½in)** | Wingspan **61–68cm (24–27in)** | Weight **280–450g (10–16oz)** |
| Social **Winter flocks** | Lifespan **10–15 years** | Status **Vulnerable** |

Order **Charadriiformes**	Family **Scolopacidae**	Species **Numenius arquata**

Curlew 🔊 32.I, 32.II

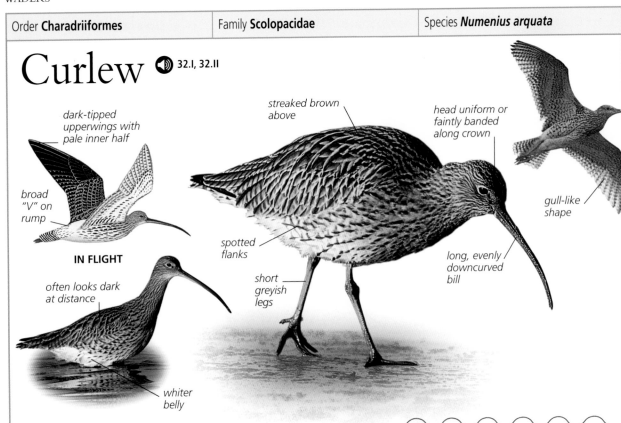

dark-tipped
upperwings with
pale inner half

broad
"V" on
rump

IN FLIGHT

streaked brown
above

head uniform or
faintly banded
along crown

gull-like
shape

spotted
flanks

long, evenly
downcurved
bill

short
greyish
legs

often looks dark
at distance

whiter
belly

A breeding bird in much of Europe, the Curlew is also widespread and common on shorelines of all kinds and around many inland waters. It is easily recognized both by its shape and its voice; in spring, it has one of the most beautiful of all European bird songs. Curlews at long range on mudflats or roosting on a sand spit tend to look large and in most circumstances rather dark, although close views, or bright sun, reveal a quite pale, sandy-brown colour.

VOICE Typical calls loud, full *whoy, haup, cur-li*, hoarse, throaty *cu-cu-cew*, longer, slow, repeated *cur-lew*; song begins slowly, accelerates into ecstatic, rich, bubbling trill.

NESTING Shallow hollow, lined with grass, on ground; 4 eggs; 1 brood; April–July.

FEEDING Probes and picks up worms, insects, crabs, starfish, and molluscs.

FLIGHT: strong, direct, gull-like, quite slow beats; often in lines or "V"s.

MIXED ROOST
Curlews stand tall beside godwits and other waders at high-tide roosts.

OPPORTUNIST
Curlews are able to use their long bills to feed on wave-washed rocks, as well as on mud.

OCCURRENCE
Breeds widely in N and W Europe, on riverside meadows, bogs in heaths, wet moors, and northern shores and islands. Winters on estuaries, especially larger, muddy ones, but also small creeks, salt marshes, and wet grassland.

SIMILAR SPECIES

BAR-TAILED GODWIT
immature, winter
adult;
see p.195

upcurved
bill

WHIMBREL
see p.197

more
angled
bill

smaller and
darker

Seen in the UK
J F M A M J J A S O N D

Length **50–60cm (20–23½in)**	Wingspan **80–100cm (32–39in)**	Weight **575–950g (21–34oz)**
Social **Winter flocks**	Lifespan **10–20 years**	Status **Declining**

Order **Charadriiformes**	Family **Scolopacidae**	Species **Numenius phaeopus**

Whimbrel

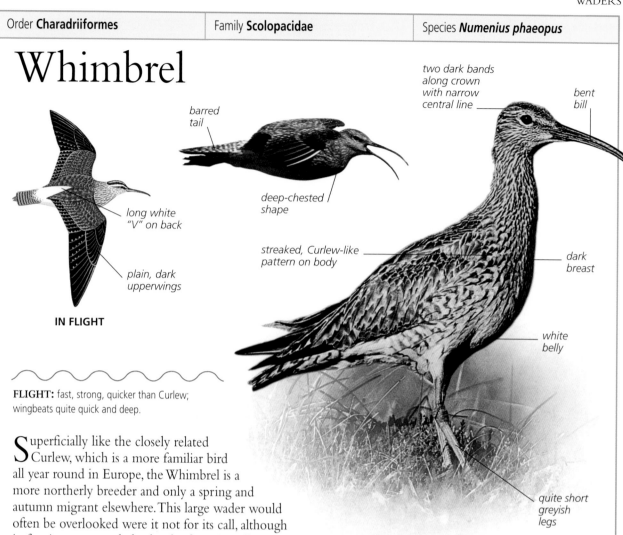

two dark bands
along crown
with narrow
central line

bent
bill

barred
tail

deep-chested
shape

streaked, Curlew-like
pattern on body

dark
breast

white
belly

long white
"V" on back

plain, dark
upperwings

IN FLIGHT

quite short
greyish
legs

FLIGHT: fast, strong, quicker than Curlew;
wingbeats quite quick and deep.

Superficially like the closely related
Curlew, which is a more familiar bird
all year round in Europe, the Whimbrel is a
more northerly breeder and only a spring and
autumn migrant elsewhere. This large wader would
often be overlooked were it not for its call, although
in fact its compact, dark, chunky form is really quite
distinct from the lankier, paler Curlew. It is rather
more squat and a little larger than the straight-billed
godwits. As with most "streaky brown birds", a close
view reveals an exquisite pattern of fine streaks, bars,
and spots. In Europe, it is very much a ground or
waterside bird, but in winter in Africa it often perches
up on trees or even overhead cables.
VOICE Song loud, rich, rippling trill; in flight, loud,
even, fast *pipipipipipipip* on one pitch.
NESTING Simple, shallow scrape on ground; 4 eggs;
1 brood; May–July.
FEEDING Takes insects, snails, earthworms, crabs, and
marine worms.

MIGRANT WADER
For much of the summer, Whimbrels are on dry ground, but migrants
may be seen wading at the edges of pools or along the sea shore.

SIMILAR SPECIES

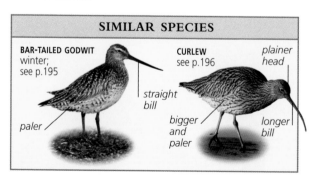

BAR-TAILED GODWIT
winter;
see p.195

CURLEW
see p.196

plainer
head

straight
bill

paler

bigger
and
paler

longer
bill

OCCURRENCE
Breeds on open heaths and moors
in far N and NW Europe; on
migration, on many coasts. Flies
over almost any open landscapes,
especially moving north in spring,
but prefers undisturbed estuaries
and rarely lingers inland.

Seen in the UK
J F M **A M J J A S O** N D

Length **40–46cm (16–18in)**	Wingspan **71–81cm (28–32in)**	Weight **270–450g (10–16oz)**
Social **Spring flocks**	Lifespan **10–15 years**	Status **Secure†**

Order **Charadriiformes**	Family **Scolopacidae**	Species *Phalaropus fulicarius*

Grey Phalarope

broad white wingbar

FEMALE (SUMMER)

IN FLIGHT

black face

thick, dark-tipped yellow bill

orange-red underside

FEMALE (SUMMER)

MALE (SUMMER)

black eye patch

yellow-based dark bill

pearly grey back

white cheeks

ADULT (WINTER)

white underparts

Like other phalaropes, this species has "reversed roles": females are brighter than males, and the males incubate eggs and rear the chicks. A more northerly breeding bird than other phalaropes, it is, however, the most common along European coasts in autumn, sometimes turning up inland after autumn gales. Its frequent swimming is distinctive but inland it is often found on muddy shorelines like other waders. At sea, it is easily overlooked but sometimes gathers in small, swimming groups which fly off low and fast if disturbed by a ship.

VOICE High *prip* or *whit*.

NESTING Small, grassy hollow in northern tundra; 4 eggs; 1 brood; June–July.

FEEDING Picks invertebrates from mud and surface of water, often while swimming.

FLIGHT: slightly fluttery, erratic, low flight over waves with shallow wingbeats.

SWIMMING JUVENILE
The Grey Phalarope swims on the open sea and may be brought close inshore by autumn gales, but is usually able to cope with rough seas.

SIMILAR SPECIES

RED-NECKED PHALAROPE winter, similar to adult winter; see p.199

more striped above

SANDERLING winter, similar to adult winter; see p.179

very fine bill

pale head

OCCURRENCE
Rare breeder in Iceland. Otherwise lives at sea, sometimes off headlands on migration in storms; a few may be blown onto all kinds of shores and inland pools by gales in autumn, but always rare, especially in breeding plumage.

Seen in the UK

Length **20–22cm (8–9in)**	Wingspan **37–40cm (14½–16in)**	Weight **50–75g (1¾–2⅝oz)**
Social **Small flocks**	Lifespan **Up to 10 years**	Status **Secure†**

| Order **Charadriiformes** | Family **Scolopacidae** | Species *Phalaropus lobatus* |

Red-necked Phalarope

blackish wings with strong white stripe

FEMALE (SUMMER)

looks very dark

IN FLIGHT

dark face

white throat

bright red neck (less red on male)

long buff stripes on dark grey back

fine black bill

FEMALE (SUMMER)

black cap

black mask

striped blackish back

all-black bill

JUVENILE

black eye patch

grey above

needle-fine bill

ADULT (WINTER)

A tiny, delicate wader, the Red-necked Phalarope spends much of its time at sea, swimming with foreparts held up, and tail and wingtips upswept. This is a common breeder in the far north and winters in large numbers in the Middle East, but is a rare bird in most of Europe. In much of western Europe, it is an occasional autumn migrant, usually in juvenile plumage, and is much less frequent inland than the Grey Phalarope. Careful observation is required to be certain of identification in non-breeding plumages.
VOICE Sharp *twik* and quick, twittering notes.
NESTING Small, round hollow in grass tussocks in wet marshes; 4 eggs; 1 brood; April–July.
FEEDING Feeds at water's edge on insects, or picks insects from water surface, often spinning like a top.

FLIGHT: fast, low, darting flight, with fluttering effect, on broad-based wings.

SIMILAR SPECIES

GREY PHALAROPE winter, similar to adult winter; see p.198

thicker bill

paler back

MARSHLAND NESTER
In summer, the shallows of reedy lakes or stony pools on northern islands are the best places to look for the Red-necked Phalarope (male pictured).

OCCURRENCE
Breeds on northern pools and wet marshes in extreme N and NW Europe. Winters at sea. Rare migrants in spring and autumn, mostly juveniles, on coastal lagoons; much less often storm-blown inland than Grey Phalarope.

Seen in the UK
J F M **A M J J A S O** N D

| Length **17–19cm (6½–7½in)** | Wingspan **30–34cm (12–13½in)** | Weight **25–50g (⅞–1¾oz)** |
| Social **Winter flocks** | Lifespan **Up to 10 years** | Status **Secure†** |

Order **Charadriiformes**	Family **Scolopacidae**	Species *Gallinago gallinago*

Snipe 🔊 33.I, 33.II

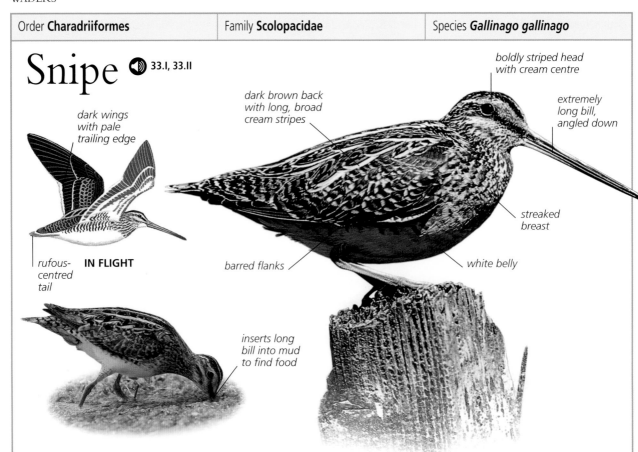

dark wings with pale trailing edge

dark brown back with long, broad cream stripes

boldly striped head with cream centre

extremely long bill, angled down

streaked breast

rufous-centred tail

IN FLIGHT

barred flanks

white belly

inserts long bill into mud to find food

The Snipe needs floods and oozy, watery mud, which allow its extraordinarily long, thin bill to be inserted into the ground so that it can detect and grasp worms; it cannot survive for very long without soft ground. With the increasing drying out or tidying up of the modern landscape, with water constrained into firm channels, the Snipe and its remarkable spring displays have disappeared from vast areas of its former range. It is still seen at the edge of marshes, or occasionally flushed from almost underfoot amongst wet rushes. While displaying, it has a high, steeply undulating flight and dives with its tail fanned out.
VOICE Sharp, short, rasping *scaap!*; in spring, bright, rhythmic, musical *chip-per, chip-per, chip-per* from perch; also short, wavering, throbbing "bleat" from tail feathers in switchback display flight.
NESTING Grass-lined shallow scrape in dense vegetation; 4 eggs; 1 or 2 broods; April–July.
FEEDING Probes deeply in soft mud for worms.

/\/\/\/\/\/\/\/\/\/\/\/\/\/\/\/\

FLIGHT: quick, rolling from side to side with flicked beats of angled-back wings; sudden, fast escape flight; settles with sudden flurry of wings.

RESTING
This medium-sized wader may sit quietly for long spells beside a tussock of rushes or grass and is less active than most other waders.

SIMILAR SPECIES

JACK SNIPE reluctant to fly; see p.201

smaller

shorter bill

WOODCOCK see p.202

barred head

bigger

OCCURRENCE
Prefers wet marshes and boggy heaths at all times, breeding through NW and N Europe. Outside breeding season, in all kinds of freshwater marshes with shallow water and soft mud, moving to coasts in freezing conditions.

Seen in the UK
J F M A M J J A S O N D

Length **25–28cm (10–11in)**	Wingspan **37–43cm (14½–17in)**	Weight **80–120g (2⅞–4oz)**
Social **Small flocks**	Lifespan **5–10 years**	Status **Secure†**

Order **Charadriiformes**	Family **Scolopacidae**	Species *Lymnocryptes minimus*

Jack Snipe

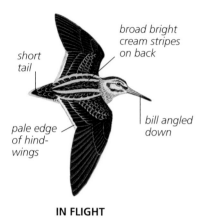

looks very dark
on upperside

striped crown
with black centre

bill shorter
than
Snipe's

striped, green-
glossed back

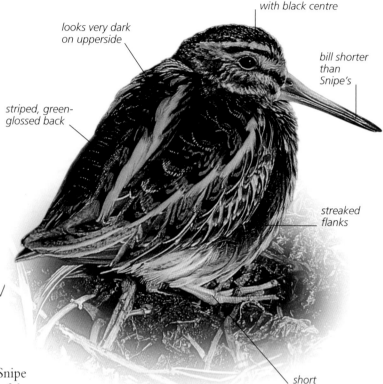

short
tail

broad bright
cream stripes
on back

bill angled
down

pale edge
of hind-
wings

IN FLIGHT

streaked
flanks

short
greenish legs

FLIGHT: quite slow, almost flitting compared with
Snipe's; wings angled back.

While Snipe are generally skulking but often feed in the open, Jack Snipe almost never do, keeping to the depths of deep vegetation in very wet places. These handsome little birds are generally seen as they fly up, practically only when they are almost trodden on, and even then they go just a short distance before dropping down again. Close views on the ground are mostly restricted to spells of very cold weather when they are forced into unexpected places or stand out on ice. Wintering birds regularly appear at traditional places year after year, even in very small, marshy spots near pools or at the upper edge of estuarine salt marshes. In favoured spots, groups of ten or twenty Jack Snipe may feed in loose flocks, flying up singly.

VOICE Usually quiet; muffled "galloping" *og-ogok og-ogok* sound in display flight.

NESTING Hollow in dry hummock of grass or moss in bog; 4 eggs; 1 brood; May–July.

FEEDING Walks forward with bouncy action, probing for insect larvae, worms, and seeds.

WELL HIDDEN
The Jack Snipe feeds in dense vegetation in wet places and is
very difficult to see on the ground.

SIMILAR SPECIES

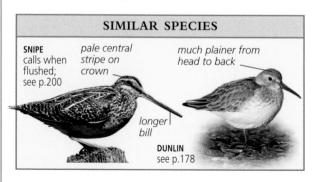

SNIPE
calls when
flushed;
see p.200

pale central
stripe on
crown

much plainer from
head to back

longer
bill

DUNLIN
see p.178

OCCURRENCE
Breeds in northern bogs; more
southerly in winter. Outside the
breeding season, in very wet
grass, rushy places with standing
water and mud, edges of
reedbeds, and upper edges of
weedy salt marshes, in deep cover.

Seen in the UK
J F **M** A M J J A S O N **D**

Length **17–19cm (6½–7½in)**	Wingspan **30–36cm (12–14in)**	Weight **35–70g (1¼–2½oz)**
Social **Small flocks**	Lifespan **5–10 years**	Status **Vulnerable†**

Order **Charadriiformes**	Family **Scolopacidae**	Species ***Scolopax rusticola***

Woodcock

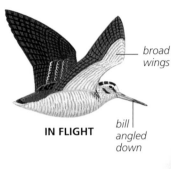

IN FLIGHT

broad wings

bill angled down

dead-leaf pattern on upperparts

eyes set far back on head

bold black bars on back of head

angular head

long, straight, thick-based bill

evenly barred pale underside

An extremely difficult bird to see because of its cryptic coloration, the Woodcock can usually be observed only at woodland edges at dusk in spring or summer while "roding". This is a mysterious territorial or courtship display at just over treetop height, involving fast quivering of bowed wings with regular grunts and whistles. At other times, it remains determinedly out of sight in thick vegetation on the woodland floor, or feeding in wet ditches or bogs at night. Only rarely, usually in severe weather, is it seen on the ground. If disturbed, it gets up with a clatter and flies off quite low and fast, sometimes turning back in a wide arc.

VOICE In display, diagnostic sharp, high whistle and deep throaty grunt, *tsi-wip grr grrr, tsi-wip grr grrr.*

NESTING Slight hollow in dead leaves, under brambles, or other cover in woods; 4 eggs; 1 brood; March–August.

FEEDING Probes for worms, beetles, and seeds in rich leaf mould, muddy ditches, and streamsides.

FLIGHT: quite quick and direct; flies up with loud wing noise and dashes away in zigzag.

EVENING FLIGHT
In summer, Woodcocks fly over regular circuits above woodland areas at dusk.

DIFFICULT TO SPOT
A Woodcock on its nest, or resting on the ground, is exceedingly difficult to see even at very close range.

SIMILAR SPECIES

smaller

striped, not barred, head

much longer bill

SNIPE
see p.200

striped head

GREAT SNIPE
see p.438

OCCURRENCE
Widespread except in Iceland and most of Spain and Portugal; many move west and south in winter. Breeds in woodland of all kinds with soft, damp earth, bogs, and ditches nearby; frequents similar areas in winter in small numbers.

Seen in the UK
| J | F | M | A | M | J | J | A | S | O | N | D |

Length **33–38cm (13–15 in)**	Wingspan **55–65cm (22–26in)**	Weight **250–420g (9–15oz)**
Social **Family groups**	Lifespan **Up to 10 years**	Status **Vulnerable**

Families **Stercorariidae, Laridae, Sternidae**

SKUAS, GULLS, AND TERNS

MOST OF THESE WATER birds live at sea but others are freshwater species for part or all of the year. They swim well and fly expertly: terns hover and dive, while larger gulls are able to soar in upcurrents or a good breeze. Gulls walk easily but skuas, and especially the short-legged terns, are not nearly so agile on the ground. All defend their nests boldly, some terns and all the skuas quite likely to strike human intruders on the head if they approach too closely.

SKUAS

Piratical seabirds, skuas kill their own prey but get most of their food by chasing other seabirds and forcing them to drop or disgorge it. Some species have several plumage forms and their immatures are rather different from adults.

GULLS

While the Kittiwake is a maritime gull, others breed inland or move inland in winter to some extent,

but many remain on the coast. They forage in flocks, and the larger species are fiercely predatory. Sexes are alike but immature plumages are quite different from the adults: the larger species take four years to gain adult colours.

TERNS

Mostly smaller than gulls, and longer-tailed, terns are long-distance migrants. Some have black caps in summer and these dive from the air for fish; the "marsh terns" are darker in summer and dip to pick up food from the surface as they fly.

FISHER
A Common Tern looks into the water for fish: it will dive headlong to grasp one in its bill.

MASSIVE GULL
The Great Black-backed Gull is the world's biggest gull. Capable of killing rabbits and birds, it feeds mostly on dead fish and scraps.

Family **Alcidae**

AUKS

PENGUIN-LIKE
Auks look like northern equivalents of the southern hemisphere penguins.

EXCLUSIVELY SEABIRDS, AUKS come to land only to breed on cliff ledges or in burrows, in noisy colonies, and spend the winter at sea. They swim and dive expertly, using their wings underwater, but in flight their small wings whirr rapidly to keep them airborne. They are vulnerable to pollution, often forming the bulk of the victims of oil spills around Atlantic coasts. Some Puffin colonies have disappeared as tunnelling birds have eroded all the available soil; others have suffered from declining fish stocks.

| Order **Charadriiformes** | Family **Stercorariidae** | Species ***Stercorarius skua*** |

Great Skua

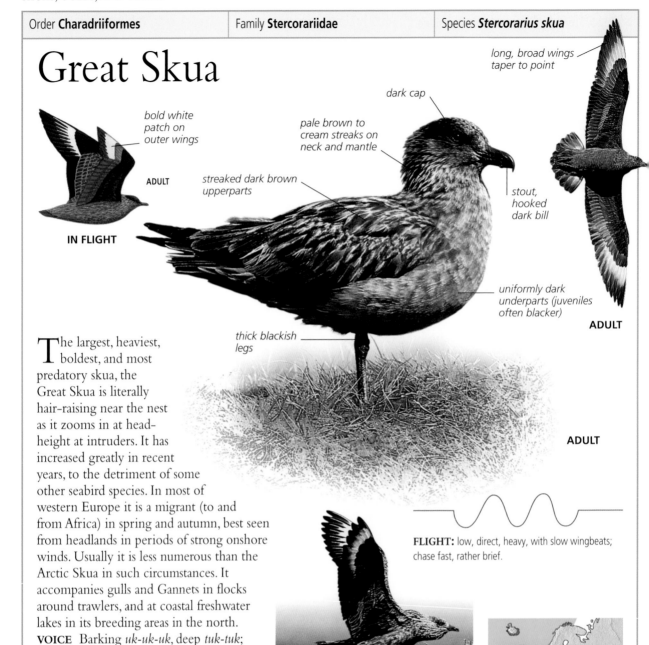

long, broad wings taper to point

dark cap

pale brown to cream streaks on neck and mantle

bold white patch on outer wings

ADULT

streaked dark brown upperparts

IN FLIGHT

stout, hooked dark bill

uniformly dark underparts (juveniles often blacker)

ADULT

thick blackish legs

ADULT

The largest, heaviest, boldest, and most predatory skua, the Great Skua is literally hair-raising near the nest as it zooms in at head-height at intruders. It has increased greatly in recent years, to the detriment of some other seabird species. In most of western Europe it is a migrant (to and from Africa) in spring and autumn, best seen from headlands in periods of strong onshore winds. Usually it is less numerous than the Arctic Skua in such circumstances. It accompanies gulls and Gannets in flocks around trawlers, and at coastal freshwater lakes in its breeding areas in the north.
VOICE Barking *uk-uk-uk*, deep *tuk-tuk*; silent at sea.
NESTING Simple hollow on ground on moorland; 2 eggs; 1 brood, May–June.
FEEDING Steals fish from other seabirds up to size of Gannet; kills many birds up to size of Kittiwake; eats much offal, carrion, and eggs.

FLIGHT: low, direct, heavy, with slow wingbeats; chase fast, rather brief.

FLASHING WING PATCHES
Great Skuas display on their breeding grounds, showing off their bold white wing patches.

OCCURRENCE
Breeds from Scotland northwards, on islands and remote moors and hills. Widespread off W European coasts and out at sea in spring and autumn; sometimes brought closer inland by gales and often passing longer headlands in any weather. Rare in winter.

Seen in the UK
J F **M A M J J A S O N** D

SIMILAR SPECIES

less uniform coloration

HERRING GULL immature; see p.211

slimmer

less white on wing

long tail

ARCTIC SKUA see p.206

smaller

long tail

POMARINE SKUA see p.205

| Length **50–58cm (20–23in)** | Wingspan **1.25–1.4m (4–4½ft)** | Weight **1.2–2kg (2¾–4½lb)** |
| Social **Small flocks** | Lifespan **10–20 years** | Status **Secure** |

Order **Charadriiformes**	Family **Stercorariidae**	Species *Stercorarius pomarinus*

Pomarine Skua

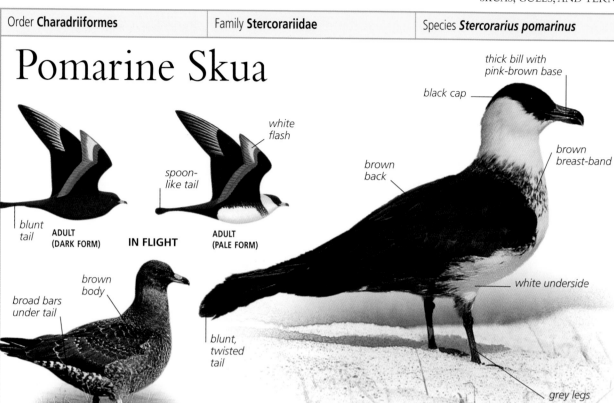

thick bill with pink-brown base

black cap

brown back

brown breast-band

white underside

grey legs

white flash

spoon-like tail

blunt tail

ADULT (DARK FORM)

IN FLIGHT

ADULT (PALE FORM)

ADULT (SUMMER; PALE FORM)

brown body

broad bars under tail

blunt, twisted tail

JUVENILE (AUTUMN; DARK FORM)

Pomarine Skuas breed in the far north and so are seldom seen in Europe in summer, but in spring small groups of adults pass by southern and western headlands in a short, concentrated migration; in autumn, larger numbers can be seen around west European coasts over a period of many weeks. These migrants, however, tend to be widely scattered and often far offshore, and it usually needs a good onshore wind to bring some within easy range of a birdwatcher ashore.

VOICE Usually silent away from breeding sites.

NESTING Shallow scrape on open ground in Arctic tundra; 2 eggs; 1 brood; June.

FEEDING Eats lemmings and seabirds in summer; otherwise fish, stolen from other birds, and offal.

FLIGHT: direct flight steady, strong, straight; wingbeats smooth and powerful; piracy involves fast, active chase.

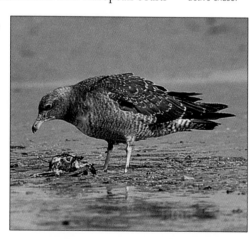

AUTUMN MIGRANT
Tired migrants after gales may rest on beaches and forage for food like gulls.

OCCURRENCE
Breeds in extreme NE Europe. On passage mostly found in North Sea and Atlantic. Occurs in variable numbers: usually scarce; at times concentrated movements in spring; occasional larger, more prolonged influxes in late autumn to North Sea; very few in winter.

Seen in the UK
J F M A M J J A S O N D

SIMILAR SPECIES

smaller and slimmer

ARCTIC SKUA see p.206

GREAT SKUA see p.204

bigger, broader-winged

pale upperwings with dark tip

HERRING GULL immature; see p.211

Length **46–51cm (18–20in)**	Wingspan **1.13–1.25m (3¾–4ft)**	Weight **550–900g (20–32oz)**
Social **Small flocks**	Lifespan **10–15 years**	Status **Secure†**

205

Order **Charadriiformes**	Family **Stercorariidae**	Species *Stercorarius parasiticus*

Arctic Skua

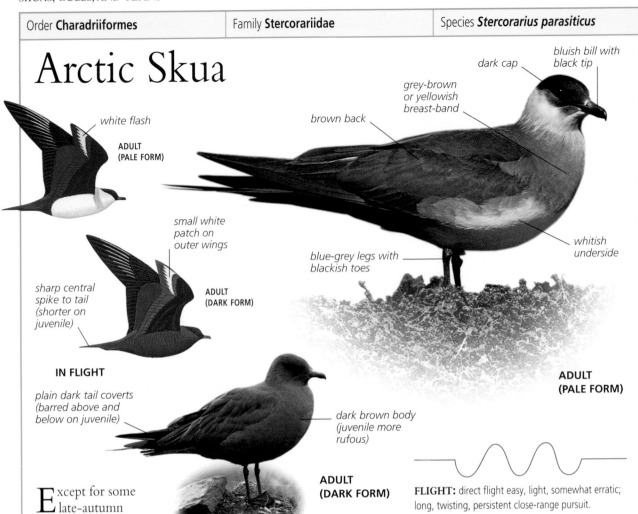

ADULT (PALE FORM)
white flash

small white patch on outer wings

sharp central spike to tail (shorter on juvenile)

ADULT (DARK FORM)

IN FLIGHT

plain dark tail coverts (barred above and below on juvenile)

dark cap

bluish bill with black tip

grey-brown or yellowish breast-band

brown back

blue-grey legs with blackish toes

whitish underside

ADULT (PALE FORM)

dark brown body (juvenile more rufous)

ADULT (DARK FORM)

FLIGHT: direct flight easy, light, somewhat erratic; long, twisting, persistent close-range pursuit.

Except for some late-autumn influxes of Pomarines, this is generally the most common skua in Europe. Learning the variety in this species will help identification of the rarer skuas. On its breeding grounds, it is a magnificent, dynamic bird, with fast, swooping, high display flights; it also attacks human intruders with great courage. At sea, it is a pirate, chasing other seabirds in order to make them disgorge fish. Its swift, dogged, and acrobatic pursuit of terns and small gulls, often in pairs, is always exciting to watch.

VOICE In summer, loud, nasal, wailing *ahh-yeow, eee-air, ka-wow* etc; silent at sea.
NESTING Hollow on ground in moss or heather; 2 eggs; 1 brood; May–June.
FEEDING Robs terns and gulls of fish; also catches fish, small birds, and voles, and eats some berries and insects.

ELEGANCE IN THE AIR
The long-winged, slender Arctic Skua, with its central tail spike, is one of the most beautifully shaped seabirds in flight.

OCCURRENCE
Breeds on northern moors and islands from Scotland north into Arctic. Spring and autumn migrants appear off most European coasts, especially North Sea and Atlantic; usually most common skua in early autumn. Rare inland after storms.

Seen in the UK
J F **M A M J J A S O N** D

SIMILAR SPECIES

POMARINE SKUA see p.205
blunt tail

COMMON GULL immature, similar to pale form; white rump; see p.214

dark tail-band

more upperwing contrast

dark tail-band

more upperwing contrast

HERRING GULL immature, similar to dark form; white rump; see p.211

Length **37–44cm (14½–17½in)**	Wingspan **0.97–1.15m (3¼–3¾ft)**	Weight **380–600g (13–21oz)**
Social **Small flocks**	Lifespan **10–15 years**	Status **Secure†**

Order **Charadriiformes**	Family **Stercorariidae**	Species *Stercorarius longicaudus*

Long-tailed Skua

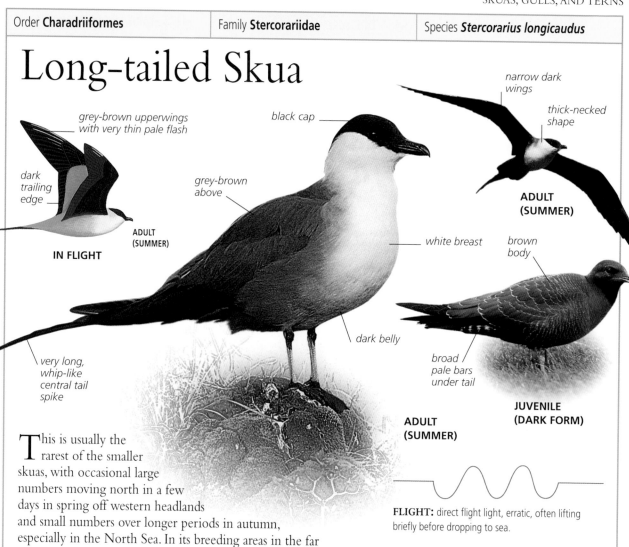

narrow dark wings

thick-necked shape

ADULT (SUMMER)

grey-brown upperwings with very thin pale flash

black cap

dark trailing edge

grey-brown above

ADULT (SUMMER)

IN FLIGHT

white breast

brown body

dark belly

very long, whip-like central tail spike

broad pale bars under tail

ADULT (SUMMER)

JUVENILE (DARK FORM)

This is usually the rarest of the smaller skuas, with occasional large numbers moving north in a few days in spring off western headlands and small numbers over longer periods in autumn, especially in the North Sea. In its breeding areas in the far north, it is very bold and may even perch on people's heads. It flies low and easily, rather tern-like, and rarely chases other seabirds. Like some other birds that feed mostly on lemmings in summer, its numbers (and hence its breeding success) vary from year to year according to the lemming population. Unlike the Arctic Skua, it does not have a dark form when adult, but juveniles are very variable.

VOICE Wailing gull-like squeal and high alarm notes in summer; silent at sea.

NESTING Hollow on ground in tundra or on high mountains; 2 eggs; 1 brood; June.

FEEDING Eats mostly lemmings, voles, and small birds in summer; at sea, feeds on offal and fish, mostly self-caught.

FLIGHT: direct flight light, erratic, often lifting briefly before dropping to sea.

AGRESSIVE ADULT
Breeding birds fly around intruders, calling loudly, their flexible tail spikes very obvious.

SIMILAR SPECIES

breast-band

POMARINE SKUA
broader wings;
see p.205

thick tail

paler belly

ARCTIC SKUA
see p.206

larger

OCCURRENCE
Breeds in N and W Norway and extreme N Sweden. Migrates through North Sea, around Western Isles of Scotland and off W Spain and Portugal in brief spring movement of adults in flocks and more prolonged autumn passage.

Seen in the UK
J F **M A M** J J **A S O** N D

Length **35–41cm (14–16in)**	Wingspan **1.05–1.12m (3½–3¾ft)**	Weight **250–450g (9–16oz)**
Social **Small flocks**	Lifespan **Up to 10 years**	Status **Secure†**

| Order **Charadriiformes** | Family **Laridae** | Species *Larus ridibundus* |

Black-headed Gull 🔊 34.I, 34.II

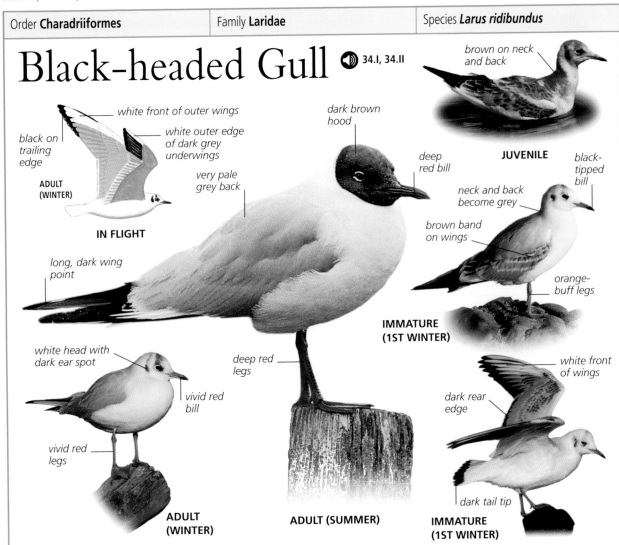

brown on neck and back

JUVENILE

white front of outer wings

black on trailing edge

white outer edge of dark grey underwings

very pale grey back

dark brown hood

deep red bill

black-tipped bill

ADULT (WINTER)

IN FLIGHT

long, dark wing point

neck and back become grey

brown band on wings

orange-buff legs

IMMATURE (1ST WINTER)

white head with dark ear spot

vivid red bill

deep red legs

vivid red legs

ADULT (WINTER)

ADULT (SUMMER)

white front of wings

dark rear edge

dark tail tip

IMMATURE (1ST WINTER)

Common and familiar, this is a small, agile, very white-looking gull and is never truly black-headed: it is one of the "hooded" gulls with a dark brown head when breeding but a pale head with a dark ear spot in other plumages. Its dark underwing gives a flickering effect in flight. It has always been a frequent bird inland, by no means confined to the sea or the coast. Numbers have increased somewhat with extra reservoirs and flooded pits providing safe roosts and refuse tips offering an abundance of food.

VOICE Loud, squealing, laughing, and chattering calls, *kwarrr, kee-arr, kwuk, kuk-kuk*.
NESTING Pile of stems on ground in vegetation, on marsh; 2 or 3 eggs; 1 brood; May–June.
FEEDING Takes worms, seeds, fish, and insects, from ground and water; catches insects in flight.

FLIGHT: light, buoyant, very agile; glides a lot; steady beats of pointed wings.

OCCURRENCE
Breeds from coastal marshes to upland pools, widespread but local. Often numerous and widespread at other times, from coasts to farm-land, reservoirs, refuse tips, and along rivers through towns and cities; in summer, even high on hills.

| Seen in the UK |
| J F M A M J J A S O N D |

| SIMILAR SPECIES | | |

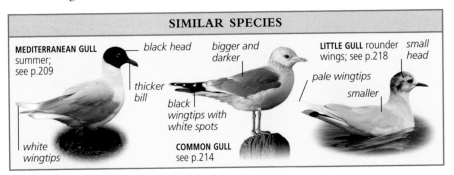

MEDITERRANEAN GULL summer; see p.209

black head

thicker bill

white wingtips

bigger and darker

black wingtips with white spots

COMMON GULL see p.214

LITTLE GULL rounder wings; see p.218

small head

pale wingtips

smaller

| Length **34–37cm (13½–14½in)** | Wingspan **1–1.1m (3¼–3½ft)** | Weight **225–350g (8–13oz)** |
| Social **Large flocks** | Lifespan **10–15 years** | Status **Secure** |

Order **Charadriiformes**	Family **Laridae**	Species *Larus melanocephalus*

Mediterranean Gull

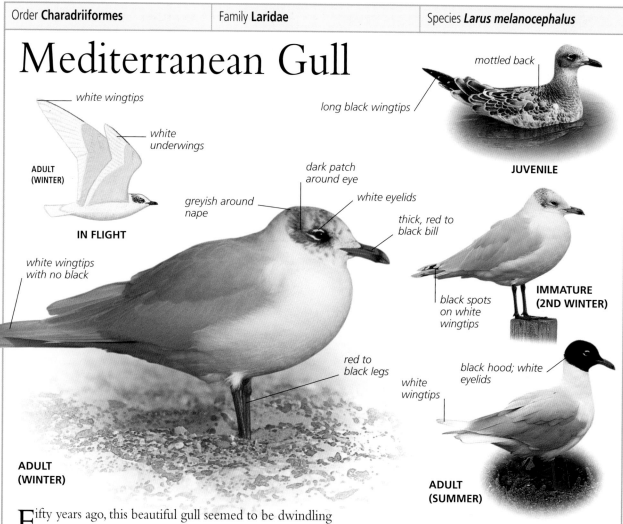

mottled back

long black wingtips

JUVENILE

white wingtips

white underwings

ADULT (WINTER)

IN FLIGHT

dark patch around eye

greyish around nape

white eyelids

thick, red to black bill

white wingtips with no black

red to black legs

black spots on white wingtips

IMMATURE (2ND WINTER)

white wingtips

black hood; white eyelids

ADULT (WINTER)

ADULT (SUMMER)

Fifty years ago, this beautiful gull seemed to be dwindling towards eventual oblivion, but recently its numbers have staged a remarkable recovery; it has spread, albeit patchily, to areas of western Europe far beyond its previous range. Along the North Sea and English Channel coasts, it has become a regular non-breeding visitor, and now nests in a number of Black-headed Gull colonies. It is a tricky bird to find among large numbers of more common gulls in some plumages, but breeding plumage adults are highly distinctive.

VOICE Nasal, rising and falling *eeu-err eeu-err*.

NESTING Grass-lined nest on sand, shingle, or in marsh; 3 eggs; 1 brood; May–June.

FEEDING Forages for fish, aquatic invertebrates, worms, and offal on beaches, and in tips, fields, and sewage outflows.

FLIGHT: easy, graceful but quite stiff beats of straight wings; not much gliding or soaring.

OCCURRENCE
Breeds on shallow lagoons and coastal marshes, scattered and rare in W Europe, more common in SE. In winter, on estuaries, beaches, lakes, harbours, and at times at tips but rare far inland, mostly in E Europe, increasing in NW Europe, especially English Channel region.

Seen in the UK
J F M A M J J A S O N D

SIMILAR SPECIES

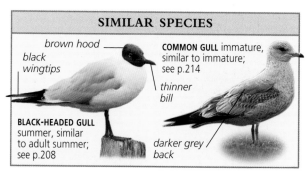

brown hood

black wingtips

COMMON GULL immature, similar to immature; see p.214

thinner bill

BLACK-HEADED GULL summer, similar to adult summer; see p.208

darker grey back

IMMATURE
The immature (1st winter) has a dark mask, a pale grey panel on the upperwing, and black wingtips and tail tip. Common Gull immatures are darker on the back.

Length **36–38cm (14–15in)**	Wingspan **0.98–1.05m (3¼–3½ft)**	Weight **200–350g (7–13oz)**
Social **Flocks**	Lifespan **10–15 years**	Status **Secure**

Order **Charadriiformes**	Family **Laridae**	Species *Larus (cachinnans) michahellis*

Yellow-legged Gull

vivid yellow bill
with large red spot

white head

mid-grey
back

sharply defined
wingtips with
extensive black
and white

long black wingtips,
white spots wear
off in summer

blackish
bill

pale to deep
yellow legs

rust-brown
body

**IMMATURE
(1ST WINTER)**

ADULT

IN FLIGHT

ADULT

Until recently, this was considered a race of the Herring Gull, and its exact status is still controversial. It is essentially the Mediterranean replacement of the more northerly Herring Gull, with darker races on the Atlantic islands (Canaries, Azores, and Madeira) and different birds, perhaps of a different species again, to the east. In Asia, the situation is even more complex. Mediterranean Yellow-legged Gulls are big, handsome birds, with an obvious close relationship to the typical seaside Herring Gull of northwest Europe. They now breed side-by-side in a few places, without hybridizing.

VOICE Deeper than Herring Gull's, more like Lesser Black-backed Gull's.
NESTING Pile of grass on ground, cliff ledge, or building; 2 or 3 eggs; 1 brood; May.
FEEDING Takes aquatic invertebrates, molluscs, fish, and offal, from water or ground.

FLIGHT: strong, easy, elegant, with powerful, shallow wingbeats.

SUBSPECIES

L. cachinnans cachinnans
(rare N Europe) winter

paler back

longer, paler
yellow legs

BOLD PATTERN
The adult Yellow-legged Gull has a striking contrast between the extensive black wingtip and the rest of the underwing.

OCCURRENCE
In summer, breeds in S Europe, chiefly on rocky islands and off-shore stacks but often scavenges around docks and towns. In late summer/autumn, moves north; frequent in Low Countries and SE England, on tips and beaches.

Seen in the UK
J F M A M J J A S O N D

SIMILAR SPECIES

HERRING GULL
see p.211

pink legs

HERRING GULL immature,
similar to immature;
see p.211

less crisp
markings
on wings
and tail

LESSER BLACK-BACKED GULL
less sharply defined
wingtips; see p.213

darker
back

Length **55–65cm (22–26in)**	Wingspan **1.3–1.5m (4¼–5ft)**	Weight **750–1200g (27–43oz)**
Social **Flocks**	Lifespan **Up to 10 years**	Status **Secure†**

Order **Charadriiformes**	Family **Laridae**	Species *Larus argentatus*

Herring Gull 🔊 35

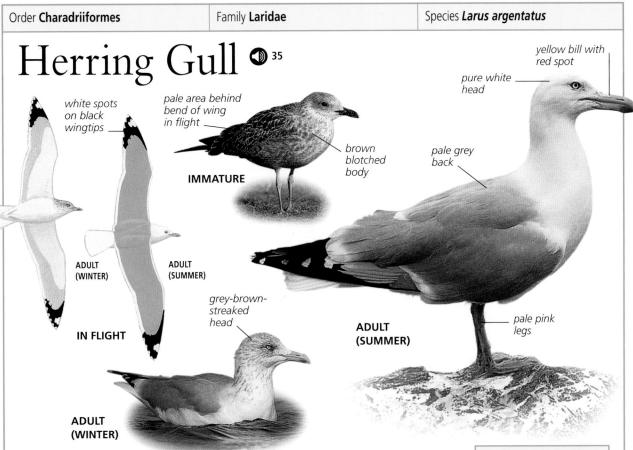

white spots on black wingtips

pale area behind bend of wing in flight

IMMATURE

brown blotched body

yellow bill with red spot

pure white head

pale grey back

ADULT (WINTER)

ADULT (SUMMER)

IN FLIGHT

grey-brown-streaked head

ADULT (SUMMER)

pale pink legs

ADULT (WINTER)

Often considered a nuisance in towns, where it breeds on rooftops and begins calling very loudly, early on summer mornings, the Herring Gull has actually declined over much of Europe. It is mainly a bird of sea cliffs in summer, but roams over all kinds of shorelines and far inland, feeding on tips and roosting on large reservoirs. Flocks returning to evening roosts in long lines or "V"s look dramatic. In winter, groups typically forage around outflows from pipes and sewers, around small harbours, or out on the mudflats at low tide.

VOICE Loud, squealing notes, yelps, barks, *kyow, kee-yow-yow-yow, ga-ga-ga, kuk-kuk*.

NESTING Grass-lined nest on ground, cliff ledge, or building; 2 or 3 eggs; 1 brood; May.

FEEDING Takes fish, molluscs, insects, offal, and scraps of all kinds from ground or water.

FLIGHT: steady, powerful, with continual easy wingbeats; masterly soaring, gliding.

IMMATURE
It takes about four years for the clear grey back and whiter underside to gradually appear.

SUBSPECIES

L. a. argentatus (Scandinavia) winter

larger, darker grey

less black on wingtips

OCCURRENCE
Breeds widely in NW Europe on cliffs, islands, and rooftops. Widespread in winter on beaches, reservoirs, often abundant at refuse tips, frequent on adjacent farmland, and likely to fly over almost anywhere from time to time.

Seen in the UK
J F M A M J J A S O N D

SIMILAR SPECIES

dark eye

smaller

small bill with no red spot

darker grey

no pale area on upperwings

greenish legs

rich yellow legs

COMMON GULL see p.214

YELLOW-LEGGED GULL see p.210

LESSER BLACK-BACKED GULL immature, similar to immature; see p.213

Length **55–67cm (22–26in)**	Wingspan **1.3–1.6m (4¼–5¼ft)**	Weight **750–1,250g (27–45oz)**
Social **Flocks**	Lifespan **10–20 years**	Status **Secure**

Order **Charadriiformes**	Family **Laridae**	Species *Larus marinus*

Great Black-backed Gull

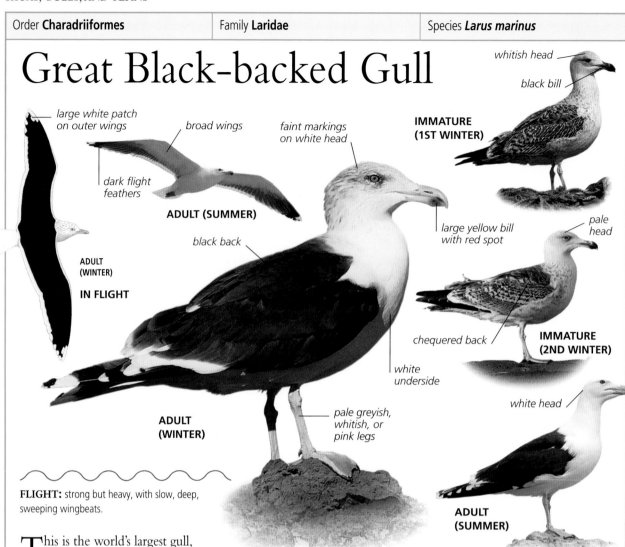

whitish head

black bill

IMMATURE (1ST WINTER)

large white patch on outer wings

broad wings

faint markings on white head

dark flight feathers

ADULT (SUMMER)

black back

large yellow bill with red spot

pale head

ADULT (WINTER)

IN FLIGHT

chequered back

IMMATURE (2ND WINTER)

white underside

white head

ADULT (WINTER)

pale greyish, whitish, or pink legs

ADULT (SUMMER)

FLIGHT: strong but heavy, with slow, deep, sweeping wingbeats.

This is the world's largest gull, heavily built, big-billed, and fiercely predatory. The size of the bill is a good guide to its identity even in immature plumages. It is generally less abundant than the Herring Gull, although it does form flocks of hundreds in areas where it is common, even in summer when such gatherings follow trawlers off northern Scotland. In winter, it usually forms only a small proportion of the gull flocks on reservoirs inland but is widespread on many coasts.

VOICE Deep, barking notes, hoarse *yowk*, gruff *ow-ow-ow*.
NESTING Shallow grass- or weed-lined scrape on cliff ledge or pinnacle; 3 eggs; 1 brood; May–June.
FEEDING Bold and predatory in summer, eating seabirds and voles; eats fish, crustaceans, offal, and rubbish from sea, beaches, and tips.

POWERFUL PRESENCE
Very big and strongly contrasted in pattern, Great Black-backed Gulls always dominate other gulls.

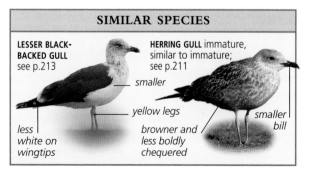

SIMILAR SPECIES

LESSER BLACK-BACKED GULL
see p.213

smaller

HERRING GULL immature, similar to immature; see p.211

yellow legs

smaller bill

less white on wingtips

browner and less boldly chequered

OCCURRENCE
Widespread in NW Europe, on rocky coasts, breeding sparsely on rock pinnacles and offshore stacks, often in flocks around coastal pools. In winter, on beaches, harbours, tips, and reservoirs, increasingly inland in W Europe.

Seen in the UK
J F M A M J J A S O N D

Length **64–78cm (25–31in)**	Wingspan **1.5–1.7m (5–5½ft)**	Weight **1–2.1kg (2¼–4¾lb)**
Social **Flocks**	Lifespan **10–20 years**	Status **Secure**

Order **Charadriiformes**	Family **Laridae**	Species ***Larus fuscus***

Lesser Black-backed Gull

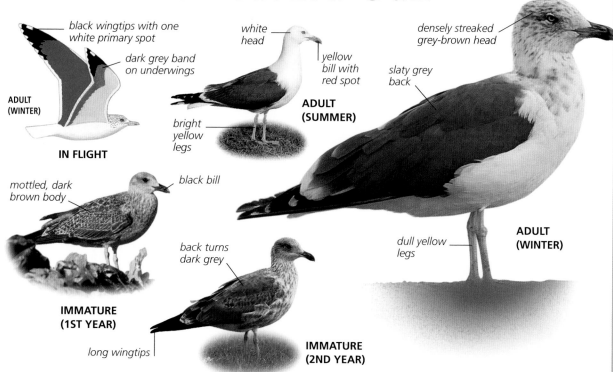

black wingtips with one white primary spot

dark grey band on underwings

ADULT (WINTER)

IN FLIGHT

white head

yellow bill with red spot

bright yellow legs

ADULT (SUMMER)

densely streaked grey-brown head

slaty grey back

dull yellow legs

ADULT (WINTER)

mottled, dark brown body

black bill

IMMATURE (1ST YEAR)

long wingtips

back turns dark grey

IMMATURE (2ND YEAR)

In summer, this is a remarkably handsome gull, immaculate in slate-grey and pure white with vivid yellow legs and bill. It has the same basic pattern as other "white-headed" gulls, with black and white wingtips. The black areas have extra pigment that strengthens them, while the white spots are weak and disappear as the feathers become old and worn. The Lesser Black-backed Gull used to be a summer visitor to west Europe, but has established large wintering populations inland. Nevertheless, it remains a strong migrant and can often be seen in spring and autumn, high overhead, flying over land.

VOICE Deep, throaty, wailing calls, various barks, yelps, *kyow, kyow-yow-yow, ga-ga-ga*.

NESTING Pile of grass on ground; 2 or 3 eggs; 1 brood; May.

FEEDING Takes fish, worms, molluscs, and edible refuse; feeds on seabirds in summer.

REMARK Subspecies *L. f. graellsii* (NW Europe) is palest above; *L. f. fuscus* (Scandinavia) is smaller, blacker, white-headed all year, long-winged, and more marine.

FLIGHT: majestic, gliding, soaring; direct flight powerful with regular beats.

SUBSPECIES

L. f. intermedius (Netherlands)

darker grey back

HANDSOME ADULT
In spring, this is one of the most immaculate of European gulls, with a vivid bill and leg colours.

OCCURRENCE
Breeds on cliffs, islands, moorland, and rooftops in N and NW Europe. In winter, at tips and reservoirs, on beaches, and often on farmland; most migrate south to Africa but many remain in W Europe. Parties often fly high over land in spring.

Seen in the UK
J F M A M J J A S O N D

SIMILAR SPECIES

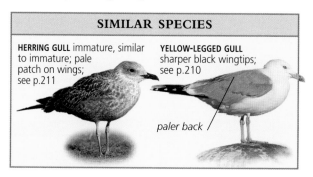

HERRING GULL immature, similar to immature; pale patch on wings; see p.211

YELLOW-LEGGED GULL sharper black wingtips; see p.210

paler back

Length **52–67cm (20½–26in)**	Wingspan **1.28–1.48m (4¼–4¾ft)**	Weight **650–1,000g (23–36oz)**
Social **Large flocks**	Lifespan **10–15 years**	Status **Secure**

| Order **Charadriiformes** | Family **Laridae** | Species *Larus canus* |

Common Gull

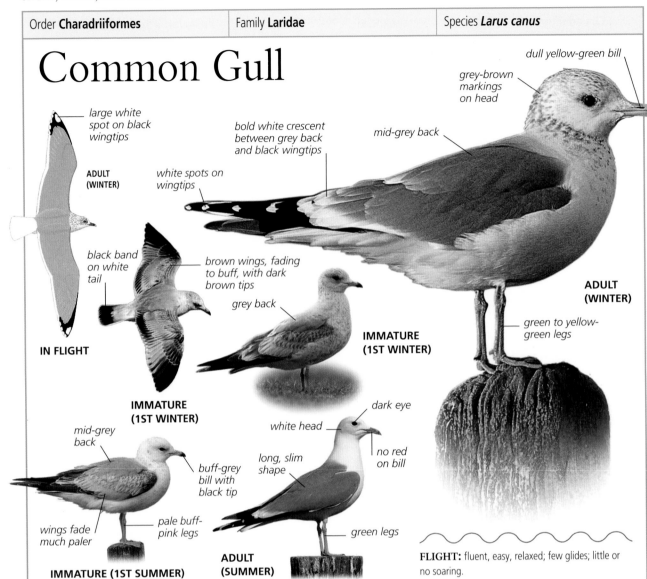

dull yellow-green bill

grey-brown markings on head

mid-grey back

large white spot on black wingtips

ADULT (WINTER)

bold white crescent between grey back and black wingtips

white spots on wingtips

ADULT (WINTER)

green to yellow-green legs

black band on white tail

brown wings, fading to buff, with dark brown tips

grey back

IN FLIGHT

IMMATURE (1ST WINTER)

IMMATURE (1ST WINTER)

dark eye

white head

mid-grey back

buff-grey bill with black tip

long, slim shape

no red on bill

wings fade much paler

pale buff-pink legs

green legs

IMMATURE (1ST SUMMER)

ADULT (SUMMER)

FLIGHT: fluent, easy, relaxed; few glides; little or no soaring.

Rather like the Herring Gull in its general pattern, the Common Gull is not as common in many areas and even in winter, when it is more widespread, it has a curiously local distribution. In England, for example, it is abundant on fields in some counties but quite scarce in others nearby. It becomes adult in three years, taking longer than the smaller gulls but a year or two less than the larger species. The plumage changes that occur with age and season are easily seen but, as with other gulls, male and female are alike.

VOICE Loud, high, nasal, squealing *kee-ee-ya*, *kee-ar-ar-ar-ar*, short *gagagaga*.
NESTING Pad of grass on ground or low stump; 2 or 3 eggs; 1 brood; May–June.
FEEDING Takes worms, insects, fish, and molluscs from ground or water.

OCCURRENCE
Widespread but local, breeding on coasts and moors in N and NW Europe. In winter, on farmland, especially grassy pastures, all kinds of coasts, reservoirs, some on tips, but generally more unevenly distributed than Black-headed Gull and less universally common.

| Seen in the UK |
| J F M A M J J A S O N D |

SIMILAR SPECIES

HERRING GULL see p.211

paler

yellow bill with red spot

red spot on bill

bigger and paler

pink legs

BLACK-HEADED GULL winter; white triangle on outer wings; see p.208

bigger

YELLOW-LEGGED GULL see p.210

| Length **38–44cm (15–17½in)** | Wingspan **1.05–1.25m (3½–4ft)** | Weight **300–500g (11–18oz)** |
| Social **Flocks** | Lifespan **Up to 10 years** | Status **Declining** |

Order **Charadriiformes**	Family **Laridae**	Species *Larus tridactyla*

Kittiwake 🔊 36

black triangle on wingtips

pale outer wings

black collar

ADULT

JUVENILE

black zigzag on wings

IN FLIGHT

dark eye

white head and breast

blue-grey back

ADULT (SUMMER)

short blackish legs

collar turns grey

pale green-yellow bill

black zigzag across upperwings

IMMATURE (1ST WINTER)

dull and dingy by summer

IMMATURE (1ST SUMMER)

dark ear-spot

grey back of head

all-black wingtips

ADULT (WINTER)

~~~~~~~~~~

FLIGHT: easy, elegant; in wind, bounds in series of steep, arcing banks over waves on angled wings.

One of the most maritime of the gulls, the Kittiwake mostly comes to land only to breed, but some also visit freshwater pools near the coast to drink and bathe. Flocks of non-breeding immatures may loaf about on beaches or flat rocky platforms during the summer and a few, in winter, stay around harbours. Most feed well out at sea and, in winter, lead a tough life, enduring the gales and rain of mid-ocean for months. In summer, they nest on sheer cliffs with the tiniest of ledges and make the coast ring to their distinctive calls. They are often in large colonies close to Guillemots, Razorbills, and Puffins (see pp.229–232).
VOICE Ringing, nasal, rhythmic *kiti-a-wake!* often repeated in summer, also high, thin mewing note.
NESTING Nest of weed on tiny ledge on sheer cliff or seaside building; 2 or 3 eggs; 1 brood, May–June.
FEEDING Takes mostly fish from surface or in shallow dive; eats offal from trawlers.

EYE-CATCHING CHICK
The sharp black collar and wing markings are obvious on juveniles.

OCCURRENCE
Breeds on sheer northern and western coastal cliffs often in mixed seabird colonies. Widespread at sea in winter but scarcer on coasts; common off headlands and rare but regularly inland on migration.

Seen in the UK
| J | F | M | A | M | J | J | A | S | O | N | D |

SIMILAR SPECIES

white spots on wingtips

LITTLE GULL
juvenile, similar to immature; see p.218

much smaller

green legs

COMMON GULL
see p.214

darker back

HERRING GULL
see p.211

much larger

white spots on wingtips

pink legs

Length **38–40cm (15–16in)**	Wingspan **0.95–1.1m (3–3½ft)**	Weight **300–500g (11–18oz)**
Social **Large flocks**	Lifespan **Up to 10 years**	Status **Secure**

Order **Charadriiformes**	Family **Laridae**	Species *Larus hyperboreus*

Glaucous Gull

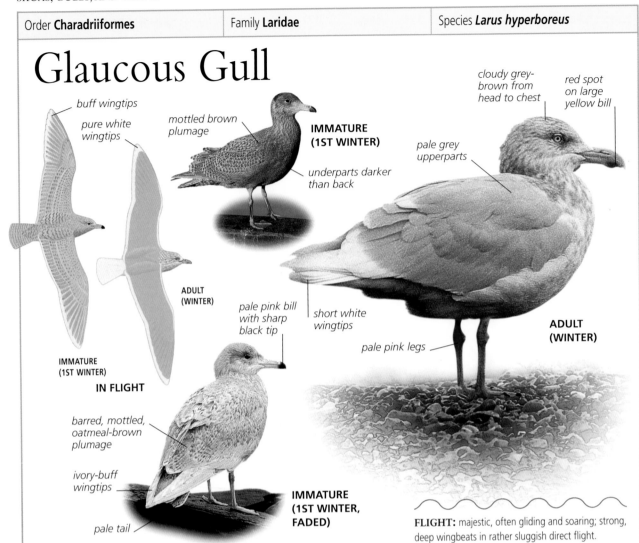

buff wingtips

pure white wingtips

mottled brown plumage

IMMATURE (1ST WINTER)

underparts darker than back

cloudy grey-brown from head to chest

red spot on large yellow bill

pale grey upperparts

short white wingtips

pale pink legs

ADULT (WINTER)

ADULT (WINTER)

IMMATURE (1ST WINTER)

IN FLIGHT

pale pink bill with sharp black tip

barred, mottled, oatmeal-brown plumage

ivory-buff wingtips

pale tail

IMMATURE (1ST WINTER, FADED)

FLIGHT: majestic, often gliding and soaring; strong, deep wingbeats in rather sluggish direct flight.

This is essentially a winter bird in Europe (although it does breed in Iceland and Spitsbergen), hanging on into early spring in northwest Europe while the snow lingers farther north. This fiercely predatory gull follows fishing fleets and is found around northern harbours, but also joins inland gull flocks, feeding on refuse tips and roosting on reservoirs. Finding "white-winged" gulls (Glaucous and Iceland) in winter flocks is an interesting challenge: distinguishing between the two can be difficult.

VOICE Much like Herring Gull, wailing and yapping notes.
NESTING Pad of grass and stems on cliff ledges or ground; 2 or 3 eggs; 1 brood; May–June.
FEEDING Takes fish, invertebrates, and all kinds of offal and rubbish; more predatory in summer.

ELEGANT SUMMER PLUMAGE
In its immaculate grey and white summer plumage, the Glaucous Gull is a handsome bird.

SIMILAR SPECIES

ICELAND GULL see p.217

browner

smaller bill

dark wingtips and tail-band

slightly smaller

HERRING GULL immature, similar to immature; see p.211

OCCURRENCE
Breeds locally in Iceland. Scarce in winter on beaches, around harbours, tips, and reservoirs in NW Europe, usually among flocks of more common gulls, and often in groups of gulls around trawlers far out at sea.

Seen in the UK
J F M A M J J A S O N D

Length **62–70cm (24–28in)**	Wingspan **1.42–1.62m (4¾–5¼ft)**	Weight **1–2kg (2¼–4½lb)**
Social **Flocks**	Lifespan **10–20 years**	Status **Secure**

Order **Charadriiformes**	Family **Laridae**	Species *Larus glaucoides*

Iceland Gull

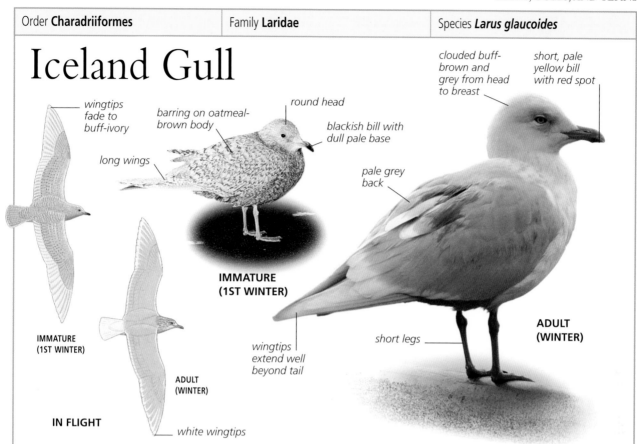

wingtips fade to buff-ivory

barring on oatmeal-brown body

round head

clouded buff-brown and grey from head to breast

short, pale yellow bill with red spot

blackish bill with dull pale base

long wings

pale grey back

IMMATURE (1ST WINTER)

IMMATURE (1ST WINTER)

ADULT (WINTER)

IN FLIGHT

white wingtips

wingtips extend well beyond tail

short legs

ADULT (WINTER)

It is unusual to find two species so closely matched in plumage colour and pattern as Iceland and Glaucous Gulls. The Iceland Gull is nearly always the scarcer of the two, but appears inland as well as around coastal harbours (and well out at sea) in ones and twos – visitors from Arctic Greenland. It is a handsome bird, especially in summer plumage; like Glaucous Gulls, the oatmeal-coloured immatures with ivory wingtips are striking. To separate the two species, details of shape and structure are more important than plumage.

VOICE Shrill squealing notes and barking calls like Herring Gull.

NESTING Small grassy nest on cliff ledges or ground; 2 or 3 eggs; 1 brood; June.

FEEDING Fish, molluscs, crustaceans, rubbish, and offal, from water, fields, and rubbish tips.

FLIGHT: steady, easy, heavy-bellied; wings rather straight-out, taper to point.

IMMATURE
In their first and second years, Iceland Gulls fade almost to white by summer, and are difficult to age with certainty.

OCCURRENCE
Breeds in Greenland. In winter, common in Iceland, much scarcer in Great Britain and Ireland, often following fishing vessels and seen around harbours; generally rare in mainland Europe. Usually in flocks of more common gulls at tips, reservoirs, and beaches.

Seen in the UK
J F M A M J J A S O N D

SIMILAR SPECIES

GLAUCOUS GULL see p.216

shorter wings

larger

GLAUCOUS GULL immature, similar to immature; see p.216

thicker bill

dark-tipped pink bill

dark wingtips

HERRING GULL immature, similar to immature; see p.211

darker

Length **52–60cm (20½–23½in)**	Wingspan **1.3–1.45m (4¼–4¾ft)**	Weight **750–1000g (27–36oz)**
Social **Flocks**	Lifespan **Up to 10 years**	Status **Secure†**

217

Order **Charadriiformes**	Family **Laridae**	Species *Larus minutus*

Little Gull

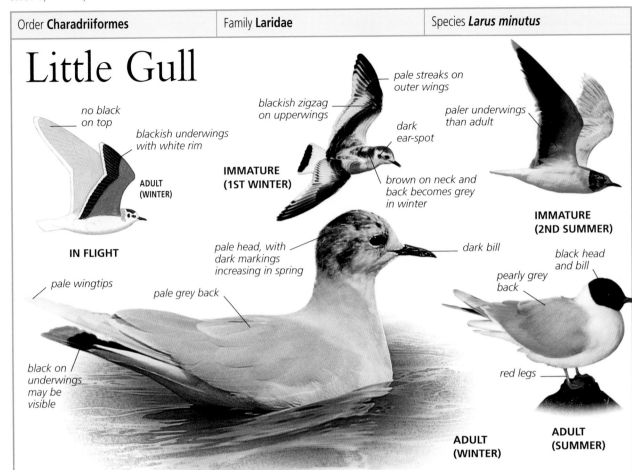

no black on top

blackish underwings with white rim

ADULT (WINTER)

pale streaks on outer wings

blackish zigzag on upperwings

dark ear-spot

brown on neck and back becomes grey in winter

IMMATURE (1ST WINTER)

paler underwings than adult

IMMATURE (2ND SUMMER)

IN FLIGHT

pale wingtips

black on underwings may be visible

pale head, with dark markings increasing in spring

pale grey back

dark bill

black head and bill

pearly grey back

red legs

ADULT (WINTER)

ADULT (SUMMER)

Short-legged, small-billed, delicate and elegant, this gull is reminiscent of the marsh terns, feeding like a Black Tern over open water. It tends to appear over lakes and reservoirs in small groups in spring and autumn, also like the terns, but immatures may linger for weeks in the summer. It combines the typical "hooded" gull sequence of plumages with a strongly contrasted immature pattern rather like that of the Kittiwake. In most of Europe, it is much less abundant than other gulls, with which it often associates.

VOICE Low, rapid tern-like calls, *kek-kek-kek, akar akar akar.*

NESTING Grassy nest on ground or in dense marsh vegetation; 3 eggs; 1 brood; May–June.

FEEDING Mostly picks up insects, aquatic invertebrates, and fish from surface of water in dipping flight.

FLIGHT: light, buoyant, erratic; shallow, quick flicks of wings, frequent turns.

PALE UPPERWINGS
Adults have no trace of black on the upperside of the wings.

OCCURRENCE
Mostly breeds in E Europe, on wet grassy marshes and floods; at other times, on coastal lagoons (around coasts and over reservoirs on migration). Winters west to Ireland and frequent migrant on W. European coasts, but mostly scarce and somewhat erratic inland.

Seen in the UK

| J | F | M | A | M | J | J | A | S | O | N | D |

SIMILAR SPECIES

brown hood

larger

MEDITERRANEAN GULL white underwings; see p.209

BLACK-HEADED GULL white triangle on outer wings; see p.208

thick bill

KITTIWAKE immature, similar to immature; see p.215

greyer back

thin black collar

larger

Length **25–27cm (10–10½in)**	Wingspan **70–77cm (28–30in)**	Weight **90–150g (3¼–5oz)**
Social **Small flocks**	Lifespan **5–10 years**	Status **Declining**

Order **Charadriiformes**	Family **Sternidae**	Species *Sterna albifrons*

Little Tern

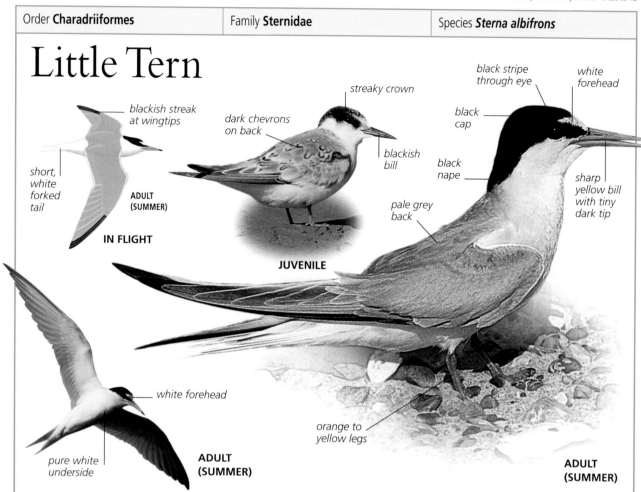

blackish streak at wingtips

short, white forked tail

ADULT (SUMMER)

IN FLIGHT

dark chevrons on back

streaky crown

blackish bill

JUVENILE

black stripe through eye

white forehead

black cap

black nape

sharp yellow bill with tiny dark tip

pale grey back

white forehead

pure white underside

ADULT (SUMMER)

orange to yellow legs

ADULT (SUMMER)

Small, quick, nervous, and now rare, the Little Tern is a lively coastal bird; it is rare inland but seen along most coasts. Its pale colours and small size are usually obvious at first glance, especially in flight. At its nesting colonies, it is noisy and aggressive to intruders but easily disturbed – most colonies are on popular beaches and now succeed only if specially protected. Climate change, causing a rise in the sea level, also threatens this bird, which often nests right at the edge of the sea and risks losing eggs and chicks to high tides.

VOICE Sharp, high, rapid chattering *kirri-kirri-kirri* and *kititit*.
NESTING Shallow scoop on sand or shingle beach; 2 or 3 eggs; 1 brood; May–June.
FEEDING Plunges for fish after a brief, whirring hover, fast but light with quick "smack" into water, often near beach.

FLIGHT: quick, flickering wingbeats; hovers briefly with very quick whirring beats.

TINY TERNS
Little Terns are smaller and whiter than Common Terns which do not have white foreheads all year round.

OCCURRENCE
Breeds on narrow sand and shingle beaches, very locally south from Baltic, thriving only where protected; also inland in S Spain and Portugal and E Europe. Mostly coastal migrant in spring and autumn, rare inland.

Seen in the UK
J F M **A M J J A S O** N D

SIMILAR SPECIES

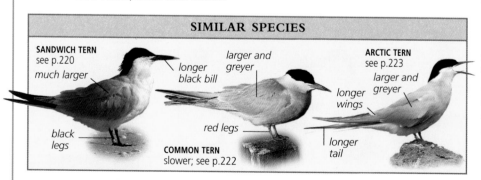

SANDWICH TERN
see p.220
much larger

longer black bill

black legs

larger and greyer

red legs

COMMON TERN
slower; see p.222

ARCTIC TERN
see p.223

larger and greyer

longer wings

longer tail

Length **22–24cm (9–9½in)**	Wingspan **48–55cm (19–22in)**	Weight **50–65g (1¾–2⅜oz)**
Social **Small flocks**	Lifespan **Up to 10 years**	Status **Declining**

| Order **Charadriiformes** | Family **Sternidae** | Species *Sterna sandvicensis* |

Sandwich Tern

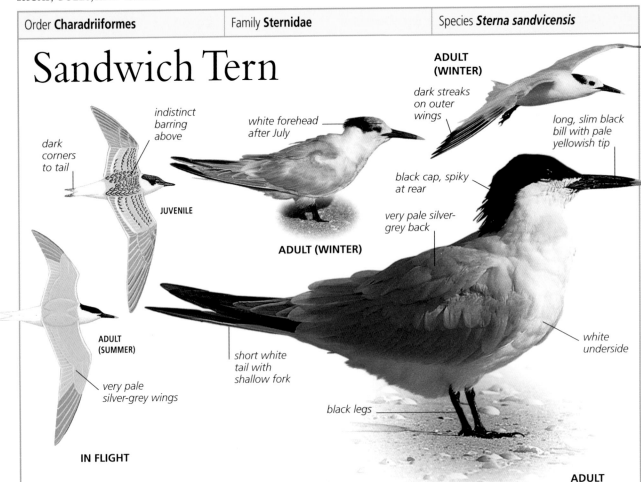

ADULT (WINTER)

dark streaks on outer wings

long, slim black bill with pale yellowish tip

indistinct barring above

dark corners to tail

white forehead after July

JUVENILE

black cap, spiky at rear

very pale silver-grey back

ADULT (WINTER)

white underside

ADULT (SUMMER)

very pale silver-grey wings

short white tail with shallow fork

black legs

IN FLIGHT

ADULT (SUMMER)

A large, active, noisy bird, the Sandwich Tern has a spiky crest, a long, sharp bill, and long, angular wings which are often held away from the body and slightly drooped. It seems almost to swagger, much more so than the smaller Common and Arctic Terns. It is equally distinctive in flight, looking very white, which helps to emphasize its size. The Sandwich Tern plunges for fish from a good height, with a loud "smack" as it enters the water. It is easily disturbed at the nesting colony and prone to desert, even after several good breeding seasons.

VOICE Loud, harsh, rhythmic *kerr-ink* or *kear-ik!*

NESTING Shallow scoop in sand or shingle; 1 or 2 eggs; 1 brood; May–June.

FEEDING Catches fish, especially sandeels, in dive from air.

FLIGHT: strong, direct; wings long and angular, tail short; regular shallow wingbeats.

BUSY COLONY
Sandwich Tern colonies on sand dunes are large, containing hundreds of nests.

OCCURRENCE
Widespread but local breeding bird north to Baltic. Prefers sandy coasts, shallow coastal lagoons, and offshore islands. Rare migrant inland but quite widely seen on all kinds of coasts.

Seen in the UK

SIMILAR SPECIES

smaller and greyer

short red legs

COMMON TERN
see p.222

rounder cap

thicker, shorter, all-black bill

GULL-BILLED TERN
see p.221

bulkier

white forewing wedge

BLACK-HEADED GULL
see p.208

| Length **36–41cm (14–16in)** | Wingspan **95–105cm (37–43in)** | Weight **210–260g (7–9oz)** |
| Social **Flocks** | Lifespan **Up to 10 years** | Status **Declining** |

| Order **Charadriiformes** | Family **Sternidae** | Species *Sterna nilotica* |

Gull-billed Tern

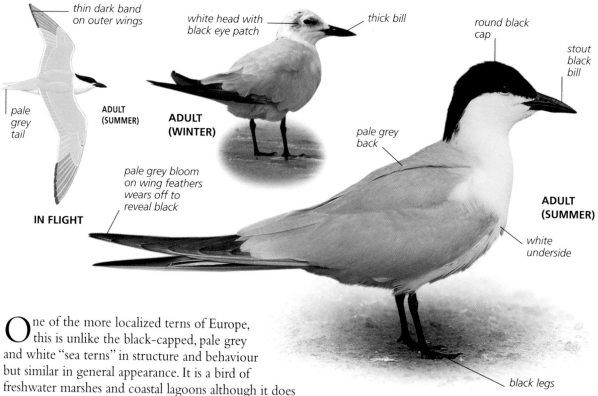

thin dark band on outer wings

pale grey tail

ADULT (SUMMER)

IN FLIGHT

white head with black eye patch

thick bill

ADULT (WINTER)

pale grey bloom on wing feathers wears off to reveal black

round black cap

stout black bill

pale grey back

ADULT (SUMMER)

white underside

black legs

One of the more localized terns of Europe, this is unlike the black-capped, pale grey and white "sea terns" in structure and behaviour but similar in general appearance. It is a bird of freshwater marshes and coastal lagoons although it does migrate over the sea. In winter, in Africa, Gull-billed Terns feed over the open plains with huge numbers of animals; in Europe, they also feed over fields where livestock disturb insects, which they snatch in the air like giant swallows. They require careful separation from Sandwich Terns outside their usual range, but in reality are generally relatively easy to identify. Despite having a characteristically grey tail, they usually look very pale, especially in winter.

VOICE Nasal, deep *gur-wik*, laughing notes and rattling call.

NESTING Grass-lined small hollow on sand or mud near water; 3 eggs; 1 brood, May–June.

FEEDING Takes most food while flying, dipping to snatch insects from ground or in air; eats some small birds, rodents, and frogs.

FLIGHT: direct flight easy, languid, slightly more gull-like than smaller terns.

FLIGHT PATTERN
In flight, the Gull-billed Tern shows long, tapered wings with dusky trailing edges towards sharp tips.

OCCURRENCE
Breeds and feeds around lagoons, rice paddies, marshes, wet fields, and high grassland, mostly in S and E Europe, very locally in North Sea area. Generally only very rare migrant outside S Europe, usually on or near coast.

| Seen in the UK |
| J F M A M J J A S O N D |

SIMILAR SPECIES

SANDWICH TERN
see p.220

spikier black cap

longer, slimmer bill with pale tip

greyer

red legs

COMMON TERN
see p.222

red on bill

WHISKERED TERN
winter;
see p.227

smaller and darker

| Length **35–42cm (14–16½in)** | Wingspan **76–86cm (30–34in)** | Weight **200–250g (7–9oz)** |
| Social **Flocks** | Lifespan **Up to 10 years** | Status **Endangered†** |

Order **Charadriiformes**	Family **Sternidae**	Species **Sterna hirundo**

Common Tern 🔊 37.I, 37.II

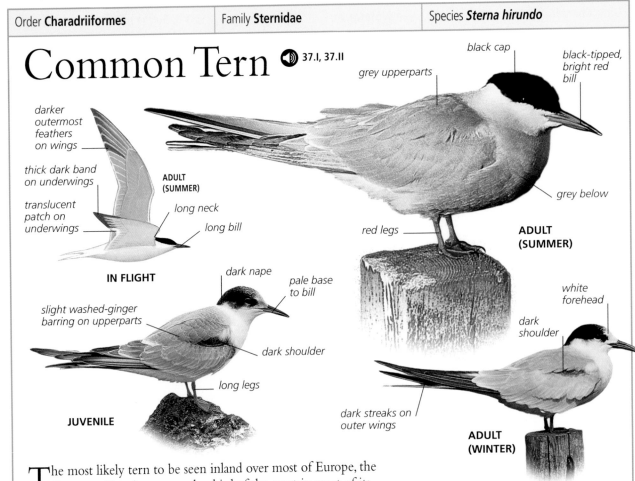

darker outermost feathers on wings

thick dark band on underwings

translucent patch on underwings

ADULT (SUMMER)

long neck

long bill

IN FLIGHT

black cap

grey upperparts

black-tipped, bright red bill

grey below

red legs

ADULT (SUMMER)

dark nape

pale base to bill

slight washed-ginger barring on upperparts

dark shoulder

long legs

JUVENILE

white forehead

dark shoulder

dark streaks on outer wings

ADULT (WINTER)

The most likely tern to be seen inland over most of Europe, the Common Tern is very much a bird of the coast in most of its range. It is a typical black-capped, pale-bodied tern, rather grey, with a red bill and legs. It usually plunge-dives for prey, which it may quickly swallow or carry off in its bill for either its mate or chicks back at the nest. The Common Tern often mixes with Arctic and Sandwich Terns.

VOICE Grating, thin, falling *kreee-yair*, sharp *kik kik*, ringing *keeer*, rapid *kirrikirrikirrik*.

NESTING Scrape in sand or dry earth on ground; 2–4 eggs; 1 brood; May–June.

FEEDING Plunges from air for fish and aquatic invertebrates; picks some insects and fish from water surface in flight.

FLIGHT: steady, relaxed, shallow, spring-like wingbeats; soars high above colony.

DIVING FOR FISH
The Common Tern is a classic plunge-diver, hovering before diving headlong for fish.

OCCURRENCE
Widespread, breeding inland in C and E Europe, mostly in coasts in W Europe, but also locally on gravel pits and shingly rivers. Migrant almost everywhere on coasts; moderately common inland on freshwater areas.

Seen in the UK
J **F** **M** **A** **M** **J** **J** **A** **S** **O** N D

SIMILAR SPECIES

ARCTIC TERN no dark streaks on more transparent outer wings in flight; see p.223

whiter below

ROSEATE TERN no dusky band under wingtips in flight; see p.224

larger and whiter

shorter bill

black bill

black legs

SANDWICH TERN see p.220

Length **31–35cm (12–14in)**	Wingspan **82–95cm (32–37in)**	Weight **90–150g (3¼–5oz)**
Social **Flocks**	Lifespan **Up to 10 years**	Status **Secure**

| Order **Charadriiformes** | Family **Sternidae** | Species *Sterna paradisaea* |

Arctic Tern

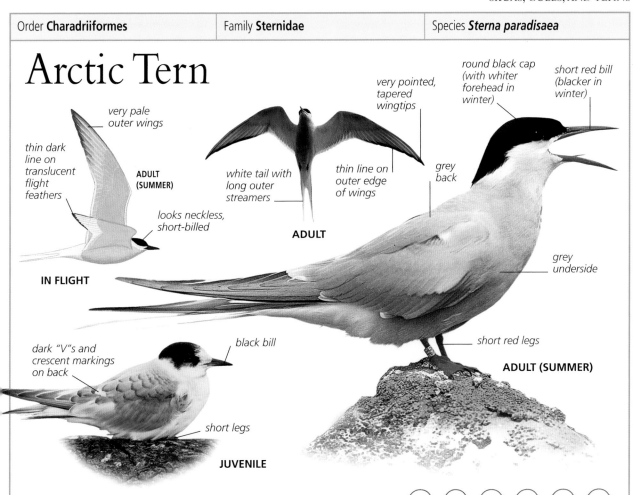

very pale outer wings

thin dark line on translucent flight feathers

ADULT (SUMMER)

looks neckless, short-billed

IN FLIGHT

very pointed, tapered wingtips

white tail with long outer streamers

thin line on outer edge of wings

ADULT

round black cap (with whiter forehead in winter)

short red bill (blacker in winter)

grey back

grey underside

short red legs

ADULT (SUMMER)

dark "V"s and crescent markings on back

black bill

short legs

JUVENILE

A more northerly bird and more strictly maritime than the Common Tern, the Arctic Tern forms the slightly more elegant half of one of the really difficult species pairings in Europe. Good views are usually needed to separate it from the Common Tern. Arctic Terns breed as far north as any bird, and also winter as far south as almost any other: they are often credited with enjoying more hours of daylight than any other bird on earth.

VOICE Grating, sharp *kee-yaah*, rising *pee-pee-pee*, *kik*, *kreerr*.
NESTING Scrape in sand or shingle, or hollow in rock; 2 eggs; 1 brood; May–June.
FEEDING Plunges for fish, often pausing at intervals before final dive; takes some insects from water surface.

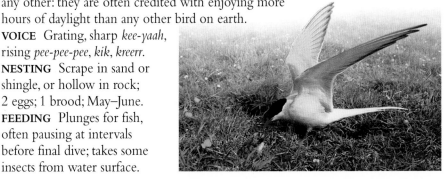

FLIGHT: relaxed, very buoyant; shorter inner, longer outer wing than Common Tern, shorter head, neckless effect, longer tail.

SILVER WINGS
The uniformly pale silver-grey upperwing of the adult shows well here as it feeds its chick.

OCCURRENCE
Breeds in far north, south to Great Britain, mostly on offshore islands, also on sandy or gravelly beaches. Migrant around North Sea and Atlantic coasts, usually scarce inland, occasional flocks appearing briefly in spring.

| Seen in the UK |
| J F **M A M J J A S O** N D |

SIMILAR SPECIES

COMMON TERN
see p.222

dark wedge on outer wings

dusky band under wingtips

ROSEATE TERN
see p.224

blacker bill

longer head, neck, and bill

whiter

WHISKERED TERN
juvenile, similar to juvenile; see p.227

stockier and greyer

| Length **32–35cm (12½–14in)** | Wingspan **80–95cm (32–37in)** | Weight **80–110g (2⅞–4oz)** |
| Social **Flocks** | Lifespan **Up to 10 years** | Status **Secure** |

Order **Charadriiformes**	Family **Sternidae**	Species *Sterna dougallii*

Roseate Tern

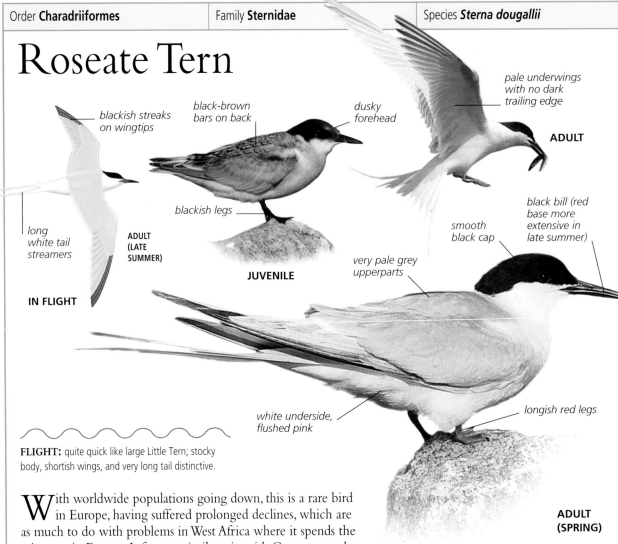

blackish streaks on wingtips

black-brown bars on back

dusky forehead

pale underwings with no dark trailing edge

ADULT

long white tail streamers

ADULT (LATE SUMMER)

blackish legs

JUVENILE

smooth black cap

very pale grey upperparts

black bill (red base more extensive in late summer)

IN FLIGHT

white underside, flushed pink

longish red legs

ADULT (SPRING)

〰️〰️〰️〰️〰️

FLIGHT: quite quick like large Little Tern; stocky body, shortish wings, and very long tail distinctive.

With worldwide populations going down, this is a rare bird in Europe, having suffered prolonged declines, which are as much to do with problems in West Africa where it spends the winter as in Europe. It forms a similar trio with Common and Arctic Terns but is rather easier to tell from them, with some features more reminiscent of the whiter, larger Sandwich Tern. Like the Arctic Tern, but unlike the Common Tern, it is unlikely to be seen in northwest Europe in full winter plumage.

VOICE Harsh croaking note and musical, quick *chu-vik*, unlike other terns.

NESTING Grassy nest often in tall vegetation or under shelter of tussock; 1 or 2 eggs; 1 brood; May–June.

FEEDING Plunges for fish, especially sandeels and sprats after fast, winnowing hover.

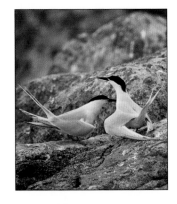

ELEGANT DISPLAY
Roseate Terns are at their most graceful when they are displaying during their spring courtship.

OCCURRENCE
Scattered very locally in Great Britain, Ireland, and NW France, breeding in small numbers on vegetated islands. Scarce or rare migrant off headlands or at mouth of estuaries; extremely rare inland.

Seen in the UK
J F M **A M J J A S O** N D

SIMILAR SPECIES

COMMON TERN dark band on tip of underwings in flight; see p.222

greyer

SANDWICH TERN see p.220

spiky crest

pale-tipped black bill

ARCTIC TERN see p.223

greyer

shorter legs

Length **33–38cm (13–15in)**	Wingspan **75–80cm (30–32in)**	Weight **95–130g (3³⁄₈–5oz)**
Social **Small flocks**	Lifespan **Up to 10 years**	Status **Endangered**

Order **Charadriiformes**	Family **Sternidae**	Species *Sterna caspia*

Caspian Tern

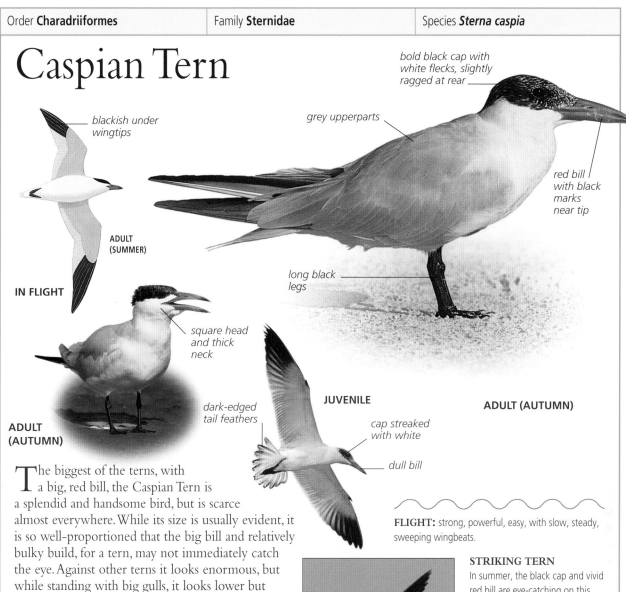

bold black cap with white flecks, slightly ragged at rear

grey upperparts

red bill with black marks near tip

blackish under wingtips

long black legs

ADULT (SUMMER)

IN FLIGHT

square head and thick neck

dark-edged tail feathers

ADULT (AUTUMN)

JUVENILE

cap streaked with white

dull bill

ADULT (AUTUMN)

FLIGHT: strong, powerful, easy, with slow, steady, sweeping wingbeats.

The biggest of the terns, with a big, red bill, the Caspian Tern is a splendid and handsome bird, but is scarce almost everywhere. While its size is usually evident, it is so well-proportioned that the big bill and relatively bulky build, for a tern, may not immediately catch the eye. Against other terns it looks enormous, but while standing with big gulls, it looks lower but longer. In flight, the angular wings and large dark area under the wingtips can even create a miniature Gannet-like effect at times. It typically flies steadily over water, head angled down, looking for fish.

VOICE Deep, explosive *kree-ahk*; very noisy at breeding colony.

NESTING Shallow scrape on ground in sand or shingle; 2 or 3 eggs; 1 brood; May–June.

FEEDING Plunges for fish; may fly long distances from colony to feed.

STRIKING TERN
In summer, the black cap and vivid red bill are eye-catching on this giant tern.

OCCURRENCE
Most breed in Baltic Sea on low islands and coasts. Rare migrant in E Europe and Mediterranean, rarer still in Atlantic and North Sea. Usually coastal, very rare on lakes and reservoirs inland.

Seen in the UK
J F M A M J J A S O N D

SIMILAR SPECIES

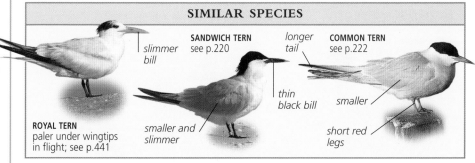

slimmer bill

SANDWICH TERN see p.220

longer tail

COMMON TERN see p.222

thin black bill

smaller

ROYAL TERN paler under wingtips in flight; see p.441

smaller and slimmer

short red legs

Length **48–55cm (19–22in)**	Wingspan **0.96–1.11m (3–3¾ft)**	Weight **200–250g (7–9oz)**
Social **Flocks**	Lifespan **Up to 10 years**	Status **Endangered†**

225

| Order **Charadriiformes** | Family **Sternidae** | Species *Chlidonias niger* |

Black Tern

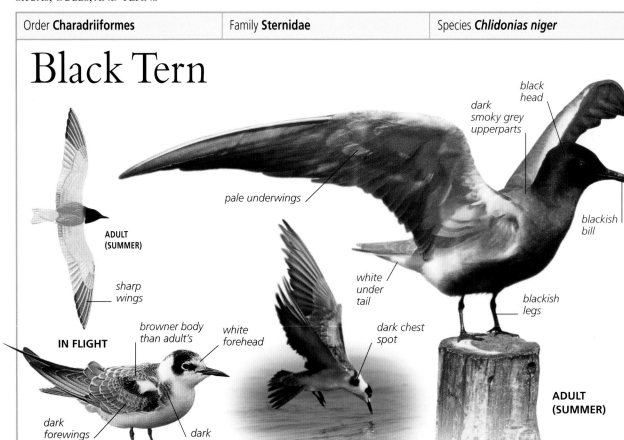

black head

dark smoky grey upperparts

pale underwings

blackish bill

ADULT (SUMMER)

sharp wings

IN FLIGHT

white under tail

dark chest spot

blackish legs

ADULT (SUMMER)

browner body than adult's

white forehead

dark forewings

dark chest spot

JUVENILE

ADULT (WINTER)

Marsh terns (*Chlidonias* spp.) are small and delicate, dipping to the surface of water to feed rather than plunging like the sea terns (*Sterna* spp.). Of the three species, the Black Tern is the most widespread and the most uniformly dark-coloured in summer. In much of west Europe, migrating Black Terns move through in large groups, unexpectedly and quickly in spring, but small numbers are much more predictable over longer periods in autumn. Larger flocks in autumn may contain the rarer White-winged Black Tern, and so are always worth close scrutiny.

VOICE Short, low, squeaky calls, *kik, kik-keek*.
NESTING Nest of stems and waterweed in marsh; 3 eggs; 1 brood; May–June.
FEEDING Dips to take insects, small fish, crustaceans, and amphibians from water.

FLIGHT: light, buoyant, easy turns and dips to water; direct flight quite straight, rhythmic.

TYPICAL PERCH
Black Terns often settle on posts and buoys in lakes and reservoirs between bouts of feeding.

OCCURRENCE
Mostly breeds in E Europe. Widespread migrant through Europe, especially common in autumn in W, over marshes, lagoons, salt pans, and reservoirs; local in W and S Europe in summer. Occasional big flocks inland, but erratic.

SIMILAR SPECIES

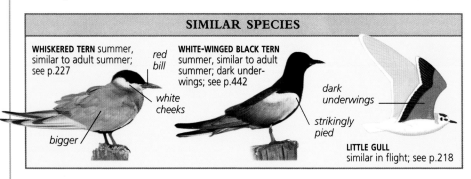

WHISKERED TERN summer, similar to adult summer; see p.227

red bill

white cheeks

bigger

WHITE-WINGED BLACK TERN summer, similar to adult summer; dark underwings; see p.442

dark underwings

strikingly pied

LITTLE GULL similar in flight; see p.218

see p.227 ... see p.442 ... see p.218

Seen in the UK
J F M A M J J A S O N D

| Length **22–24cm (9–9½in)** | Wingspan **63–68cm (25–27in)** | Weight **50–75g (1¾–2⅝oz)** |
| Social **Flocks** | Lifespan **Up to 10 years** | Status **Declining** |

Order **Charadriiformes**	Family **Sternidae**	Species *Chlidonias hybrida*

Whiskered Tern

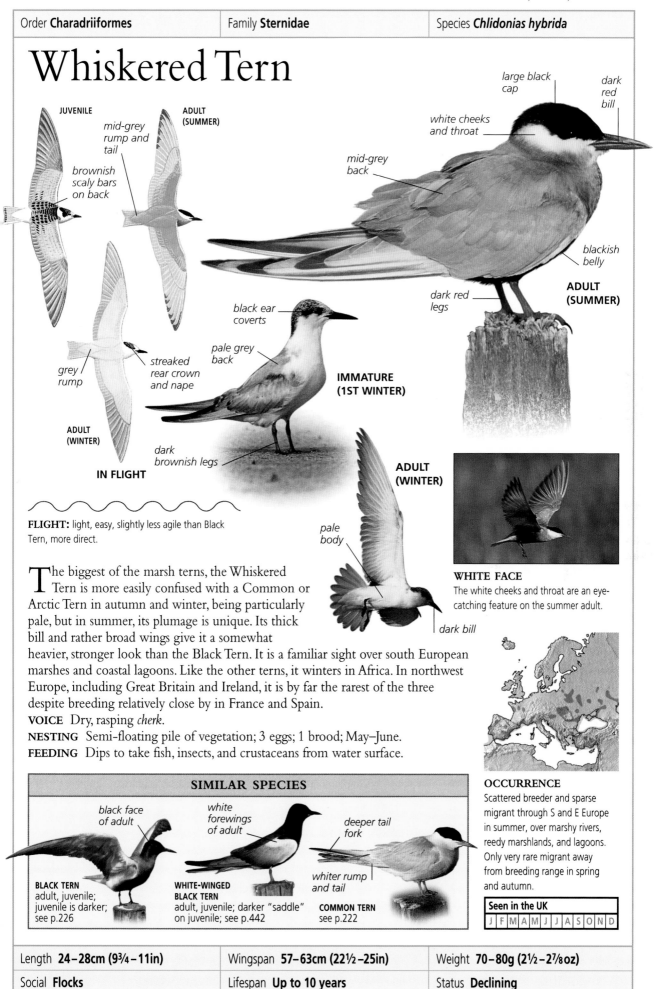

large black cap

dark red bill

white cheeks and throat

mid-grey back

JUVENILE

mid-grey rump and tail

ADULT (SUMMER)

brownish scaly bars on back

blackish belly

ADULT (SUMMER)

dark red legs

black ear coverts

pale grey back

IMMATURE (1ST WINTER)

grey rump

streaked rear crown and nape

ADULT (WINTER)

dark brownish legs

IN FLIGHT

ADULT (WINTER)

pale body

dark bill

WHITE FACE
The white cheeks and throat are an eye-catching feature on the summer adult.

FLIGHT: light, easy, slightly less agile than Black Tern, more direct.

The biggest of the marsh terns, the Whiskered Tern is more easily confused with a Common or Arctic Tern in autumn and winter, being particularly pale, but in summer, its plumage is unique. Its thick bill and rather broad wings give it a somewhat heavier, stronger look than the Black Tern. It is a familiar sight over south European marshes and coastal lagoons. Like the other terns, it winters in Africa. In northwest Europe, including Great Britain and Ireland, it is by far the rarest of the three despite breeding relatively close by in France and Spain.

VOICE Dry, rasping *cherk*.
NESTING Semi-floating pile of vegetation; 3 eggs; 1 brood; May–June.
FEEDING Dips to take fish, insects, and crustaceans from water surface.

OCCURRENCE
Scattered breeder and sparse migrant through S and E Europe in summer, over marshy rivers, reedy marshlands, and lagoons. Only very rare migrant away from breeding range in spring and autumn.

Seen in the UK
J F M A M J J A S O N D

SIMILAR SPECIES

black face of adult

white forewings of adult

deeper tail fork

BLACK TERN
adult, juvenile; juvenile is darker; see p.226

WHITE-WINGED BLACK TERN
adult, juvenile; darker "saddle" on juvenile; see p.442

whiter rump and tail

COMMON TERN
see p.222

Length **24–28cm (9¾–11in)**	Wingspan **57–63cm (22½–25in)**	Weight **70–80g (2½–2⅞oz)**
Social **Flocks**	Lifespan **Up to 10 years**	Status **Declining**

| Order **Charadriiformes** | Family **Alcidae** | Species ***Alle alle*** |

Little Auk

slender wings

WINTER

white trailing edge

IN FLIGHT

white sides of neck curve up behind cheeks

black face and cap

short, stumpy black bill

white streaks on shoulders

WINTER

black of back extends as point on to sides of chest

/\

FLIGHT: fast, low; wings longish, slightly swept back, wader-like but blur of fast, whirring beats.

all-black head and breast

SUMMER

The smallest auk, and the most northerly, the Little Auk is rare in most of Europe and best known as a late autumn visitor to the North Sea. In some years, large numbers appear; in others it is scarce. In "good" years, autumn gales may sweep a few score well inland. Breeding colonies are often huge, with vast numbers of birds flying around overhead, often very high up beside towering cliffs. Fit, alert birds swim with head raised and tail cocked, while tired or sick birds are hunched, with drooped wings. They are vulnerable to predators such as gulls and skuas, or even crows, when they are exhausted and driven inland. The Little Auk opens its wings slightly as it dives for food, and returns to the surface like a cork, swimming buoyantly on the roughest seas, but tired birds on inland waters are often inactive.

VOICE Shrill, twittering, or chattering notes and trills; silent at sea.

NESTING Burrow high above shore; 1 egg; 1 brood; June.

FEEDING Dives for fish, plankton, and crustaceans.

STORM-BLOWN MIGRANTS
In late autumn, some Little Auks are driven close inshore by gales. They may be seen unexpectedly over rocky shores or wide, sandy beaches.

SIMILAR SPECIES

larger

RAZORBILL
see p.232

large, triangular bill

thick bill

PUFFIN
see p.229

OCCURRENCE
Breeds in Arctic on islands. Mostly rare late autumn or winter visitor to NW Europe, sometimes briefly numerous in North Sea after northerly gales. Rare storm-blown birds appear inland.

| Seen in the UK |
| J F M A M J J A S O N D |

| Length **17–19cm (6½–7½in)** | Wingspan **40–48cm (16–19in)** | Weight **140–170g (5–6oz)** |
| Social **Small flocks** | Lifespan **Up to 10 years** | Status **Secure†** |

Order **Charadriiformes**	Family **Alcidae**	Species *Fratercula arctica*

Puffin

plain black wings

disc-like, grey-white sides of face

dark eye

deep, triangular bill, patterned blue-grey, orange, yellow, and red

black upperparts and neck

ADULT (SUMMER)

ADULT (SUMMER)

IN FLIGHT

white underside

FLIGHT: fast, direct, low; wingbeats quick, whirring; may fly higher over sea or when circling colony in flocks.

grooves on bill increase with age

vivid orange legs

ADULT (SUMMER)

smaller, duller bill (loses colourful sheath)

dusky grey face (as on juvenile)

ADULT (WINTER)

Puffins are more localized than Guillemots, requiring more earth in which to burrow or cavities in rocks in summer. In winter, they are far out in the Atlantic. Summer birds are often seen flying by from headlands in the north and west. However, winter ones, which lack the distinctive bill ornamentation seen in the breeding season, are generally rare close inshore. Occasionally, Puffins are blown far inland during autumn gales, and turn up in unexpected places.

VOICE At nest, loud, cooing growl, *aaarr, karr-oo-arr.*

NESTING Occupies ready-made burrow, digs burrow into soft earth, or finds cavity between boulders; 1 egg; 1 brood; May–June.

FEEDING Dives from water surface to catch fish and squid.

RUNNING THE GAUNTLET
Adults bringing fish back to their chicks are often harried by gulls.

OCCURRENCE
Breeds on coasts and islands from Iceland south to NW France, in cliff cavities, scree, or on grassy slopes. Widespread migrant offshore, but scarce in winter when most are far out in Atlantic. Very rare inland after storms.

Seen in the UK
J F **M A M J J A S O N** D

SIMILAR SPECIES

LITTLE AUK faster wingbeats in flight; see p.228

smaller

small bill

RAZORBILL see p.232

larger and heavier

thick black bill

dagger-shaped bill

larger

GUILLEMOT see p.231

Length **26–29cm (10–11½in)**	Wingspan **47–63cm (18½–25in)**	Weight **310–500g (11–18oz)**
Social **Small flocks**	Lifespan **10–20 years**	Status **Vulnerable**

Order **Charadriiformes**	Family **Alcidae**	Species **Cepphus grylle**

Black Guillemot

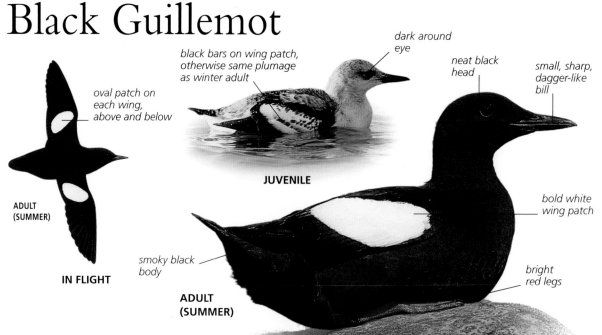

black bars on wing patch, otherwise same plumage as winter adult

dark around eye

neat black head

small, sharp, dagger-like bill

oval patch on each wing, above and below

JUVENILE

bold white wing patch

smoky black body

bright red legs

ADULT (SUMMER)

IN FLIGHT

ADULT (SUMMER)

Not nearly so social as other auks, the Black Guillemot prefers small islets and rocky headlands around northern coasts and archipelagos where pairs swim about close to the shore all year round. These expert swimmers and divers often penetrate far into deep inlets in quiet, calm waters. In summer, their unique plumage makes them easily identifiable. They are distinctive in winter as well, when they retain the clean white wing patches, but have a mottled white back and a dusky cap and eye patch. The winter bird may be confused with similar-looking species when encountered unexpectedly but the pale head and pointed bill help to separate it from ducks and grebes.

VOICE Shrill, high whistle extends into fast trill; quick, thin *sip-sip-sip* notes occasionally heard.

NESTING Crevice or cavity between boulders, or hole in harbour wall; 1 egg; 1 brood; May–June.

FEEDING Dives underwater to catch small fish and crustaceans.

FLIGHT: low, quick, direct, with fast, whirring wingbeats.

AWKWARD ON LAND
Black Guillemots usually sit horizontally, less upright than Guillemots, and are not as agile on land as Puffins.

OCCURRENCE
Breeds on coasts in N Europe, usually around rocky islets with boulders and cavities in rocks. Usually resident, only rare elsewhere in winter. Strictly marine, extremely rare inland.

Seen in the UK
J F M A M J J A S O N D

SIMILAR SPECIES

no white wing patches

PUFFIN see p.229

stumpy tail

blacker above

thick bill

GUILLEMOT winter; see p.231

black wings

SLAVONIAN GREBE winter; see p.62

Length **30–32cm (12–12½in)**	Wingspan **52–58cm (20½–23in)**	Weight **340–450g (12–16oz)**
Social **Family groups**	Lifespan **Up to 10 years**	Status **Declining**

| Order **Charadriiformes** | Family **Alcidae** | Species *Uria aalge* |

Guillemot

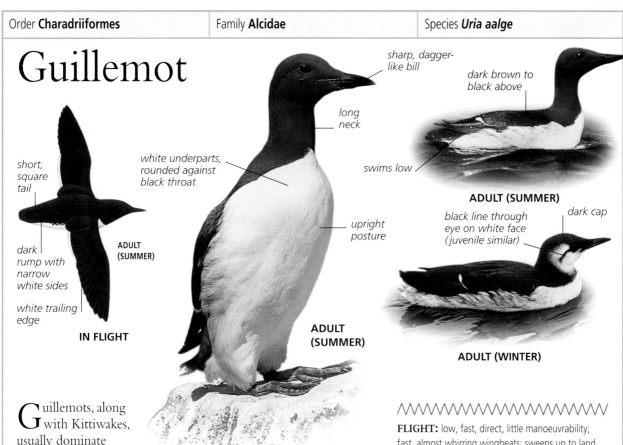

sharp, dagger-like bill

long neck

white underparts, rounded against black throat

upright posture

short, square tail

dark rump with narrow white sides

white trailing edge

IN FLIGHT

ADULT (SUMMER)

ADULT (SUMMER)

dark brown to black above

swims low

ADULT (SUMMER)

black line through eye on white face (juvenile similar)

dark cap

ADULT (WINTER)

Guillemots, along with Kittiwakes, usually dominate seabird colonies which densely pack ledges of sea cliffs in summer. Guillemots swim offshore in large "rafts" under the cliffs. Off headlands, they are often seen flying by, low and fast. In winter, however, they are seen inshore only during or after gales. In the south of their range, they are quite brown and easily distinguished from Razorbills; northern birds are blacker and more difficult to identify.

VOICE At colony, loud, whirring, growling chorus, *arrrr-rr-rr*; juveniles make surprisingly loud, musical whistle at sea.
NESTING On bare ledge on sheer cliff; 1 egg; 1 brood; May–June.
FEEDING Dives from surface to catch fish deep underwater.

/\/\/\/\/\/\/\/\/\/\/\/\/\/\/\/\/\/\

FLIGHT: low, fast, direct, little manoeuvrability; fast, almost whirring wingbeats; sweeps up to land on ledge.

LARGE FLOCKS
Large flocks of Guillemots swim on the sea under the breeding colonies.

LARGE COLONIES
Guillemots crowd steep coastal cliffs in the breeding season; colonies are often mixed with Razorbills.

OCCURRENCE
Breeds on rocky coasts of Iceland, Scandinavia, Great Britain, Ireland, NW France, Spain, and Portugal, chiefly on sheer cliffs, also on flat-topped stacks. Scarce inshore in winter, even after gales.

| Seen in the UK |
| J F M A M J J A S O N D |

SIMILAR SPECIES

RAZORBILL
see p.232
flatter head
pointed tail

BRUNNICH'S GUILLEMOT
see p.442
thicker, blunter bill

thicker bill with white streak

longer wings

smaller

MANX SHEARWATER
see p.67

| Length **38–54cm (15–21½in)** | Wingspan **64–73cm (25–29in)** | Weight **850–1,130g (30–40oz)** |
| Social **Small flocks** | Lifespan **10–20 years** | Status **Secure** |

Order **Charadriiformes**	Family **Alcidae**	Species *Alca torda*

Razorbill

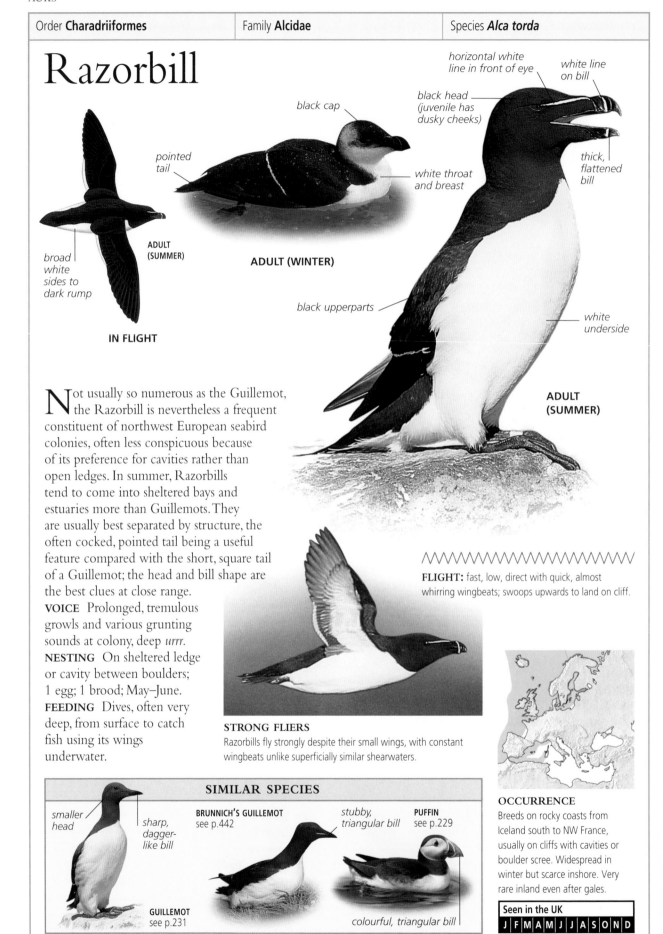

IN FLIGHT

broad white sides to dark rump

pointed tail

ADULT (SUMMER)

black cap

ADULT (WINTER)

white throat and breast

horizontal white line in front of eye

white line on bill

black head (juvenile has dusky cheeks)

thick, flattened bill

black upperparts

white underside

ADULT (SUMMER)

Not usually so numerous as the Guillemot, the Razorbill is nevertheless a frequent constituent of northwest European seabird colonies, often less conspicuous because of its preference for cavities rather than open ledges. In summer, Razorbills tend to come into sheltered bays and estuaries more than Guillemots. They are usually best separated by structure, the often cocked, pointed tail being a useful feature compared with the short, square tail of a Guillemot; the head and bill shape are the best clues at close range.
VOICE Prolonged, tremulous growls and various grunting sounds at colony, deep *urrr*.
NESTING On sheltered ledge or cavity between boulders; 1 egg; 1 brood; May–June.
FEEDING Dives, often very deep, from surface to catch fish using its wings underwater.

FLIGHT: fast, low, direct with quick, almost whirring wingbeats; swoops upwards to land on cliff.

STRONG FLIERS
Razorbills fly strongly despite their small wings, with constant wingbeats unlike superficially similar shearwaters.

SIMILAR SPECIES

smaller head

sharp, dagger-like bill

GUILLEMOT see p.231

BRUNNICH'S GUILLEMOT see p.442

stubby, triangular bill

PUFFIN see p.229

colourful, triangular bill

OCCURRENCE
Breeds on rocky coasts from Iceland south to NW France, usually on cliffs with cavities or boulder scree. Widespread in winter but scarce inshore. Very rare inland even after gales.

Seen in the UK
J F M A M J J A S O N D

Length **37–39cm (14½–15½in)**	Wingspan **63–67cm (25–26in)**	Weight **590–730g (21–26oz)**
Social **Small flocks**	Lifespan **10–20 years**	Status **Secure**

Family **Columbidae**

PIGEONS AND DOVES

THIS IS A RATHER ARTIFICIAL distinction in a large family found worldwide. In Europe, some species commonly called "doves" (Stock Dove and Rock Dove) are more like the "pigeons", being rather larger and heavier, and shorter-tailed, than the more delicate species that are usually called doves.

They are all round-bodied, soft-plumaged birds whose plumage seems to come away easily in an "explosion" of feathers in any collision, perhaps helping them to escape predators. They have short, usually red, legs and small bills with the nostrils in a fleshy bump at the base (the "cere"). Bill and leg colours can be bright and obvious but are of limited value in identification, which more often rests on differences in wing and tail patterns. There is little variation in appearance between sexes and seasons, and juveniles look much like their parents, generally being a little duller or marked with paler feather edges.

Pigeons and doves drink by sucking water up in a continuous draught, unlike other birds that have to raise their heads to tip water back into their throats. They have loud, simple vocalizations with little obvious differentiation between calls and songs, which are good identification clues, but, with the exception of the Collared Dove, do not call in flight. Their wings make loud clapping sounds, either in display or in a sudden take-off when disturbed, serving the purpose of alarm calls.

Nests are flimsy affairs and eggs are always pure, unmarked white. Shells may be found on the ground where they are dropped, far from the nest, by the parent birds after hatching. Breeding seasons are long and nesting is timed to coincide with a local abundance of food.

COLOURFUL
Far from being a dull, grey bird, a Woodpigeon seen close-up is a handsome bird.

Family **Cuculidae**

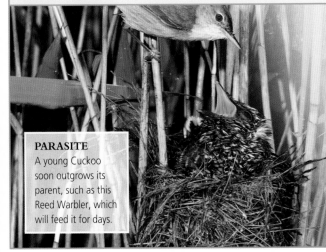

PARASITE
A young Cuckoo soon outgrows its parent, such as this Reed Warbler, which will feed it for days.

CUCKOOS

EUROPE HAS TWO SPECIES but there are many cuckoos elsewhere; they are brood parasites, laying their eggs in the nests of other species which then unwittingly rear their young. Hence cuckoos are not found in family groups.

Cuckoos have short, curved bills, small heads, rather long, broad tails, and wide-based, tapered wings that give a curious appearance in flight, beating below body level.

Order **Columbiformes**	Family **Columbidae**	Species *Columba livia*

Rock Dove

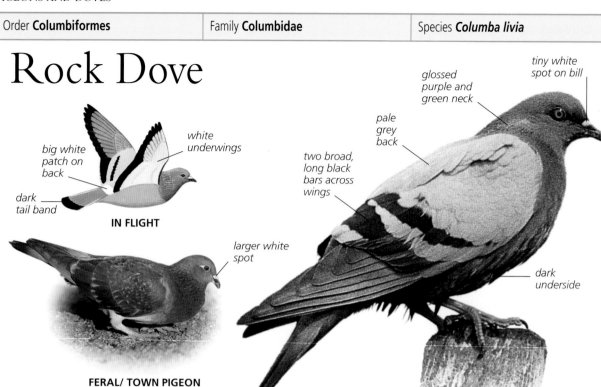

big white patch on back

white underwings

dark tail band

IN FLIGHT

larger white spot

FERAL/ TOWN PIGEON

glossed purple and green neck

tiny white spot on bill

pale grey back

two broad, long black bars across wings

dark underside

⋀⋀⋀⋀⋀⋀⋀⋀⋀⋀⋀⋀⋀⋀⋀⋀⋀⋀

FLIGHT: fast, swooping; direct flight striking, wings swept back, quick, deep beats; swoops and glides around cliffs with wings in steep "V".

Ancestor of the domestic pigeon, the Rock Dove as a truly wild bird has long been "diluted" in most areas by domestic pigeons reverting to the wild state: the "feral" or town pigeons. Only in parts of northwest Europe do "pure" Rock Doves with immaculate plumage patterns persist: in most areas, different plumage patterns and colours are found even in groups living entirely wild. The true Rock Dove is a bird of cliffs, inland or – more particularly in Europe – by the sea, from which it moves to fields to feed each day.

VOICE Deep, rolling, moaning coo, *oo-ooh-oorr, oo-roo-coo.*

NESTING Loose, untidy, sparse nest on ledge, in cavity; 2 eggs; 3 broods; all year.

FEEDING Forages on fields and rough grassland, picking up seeds, buds, berries, and small invertebrates.

DASHING FLIGHT
Rock Dove flocks fly with dash and agility, their white underwings flashing conspicuously.

CLIFF-EDGE BREEDER
Ledges and cavities form ideal sheltered nest sites for wild Rock Doves; this nesting bird has a "pure" plumage pattern with an unspotted back.

OCCURRENCE
Breeds on coasts of Great Britain and Ireland all year round; also on cliffs in S Europe. Feral birds widespread, from coastal cliffs to city centres, often feeding on arable land.

Seen in the UK
J F M A M J J A S O N D

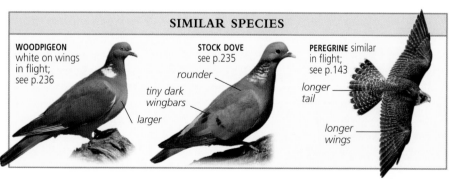

SIMILAR SPECIES

WOODPIGEON
white on wings in flight;
see p.236

larger

STOCK DOVE
see p.235

rounder

tiny dark wingbars

PEREGRINE similar in flight;
see p.143

longer tail

longer wings

Length **31–35cm (12–14in)**	Wingspan **63–70cm (25–28in)**	Weight **250–350g (9–13oz)**
Social **Flocks**	Lifespan **Up to 10 years**	Status **Secure**

Order **Columbiformes**	Family **Columbidae**	Species ***Columba oenas***

Stock Dove 38

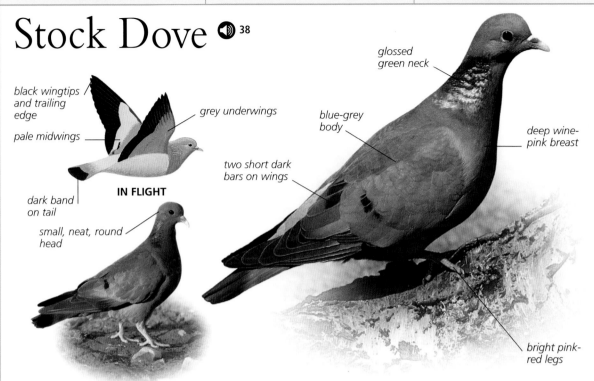

black wingtips and trailing edge

pale midwings

grey underwings

IN FLIGHT

dark band on tail

small, neat, round head

two short dark bars on wings

glossed green neck

blue-grey body

deep wine-pink breast

bright pink-red legs

A handsome bird of farms and parkland, the Stock Dove also finds suitable nesting habitat in quarries and crags in remote upland areas. It is slightly smaller than a Woodpigeon, rounder and blunter-winged than a "racing pigeon" or the town pigeon of city streets. It is easily overlooked, but its song is distinctive and display flights frequently draw attention to it. It regularly mixes with more numerous Woodpigeons, Jackdaws (see p.375), and Rooks (see p.376) when feeding in fields, and roosts with them in woodland.

VOICE Deep, rhythmic, booming coo, repeated several times with increased emphasis, *ooo-woo ooo-woo.*

NESTING Tree hole, ledge, or cavity in building, quarry, or cliff; 2 eggs; 2 or 3 broods; all year.

FEEDING Forages widely on ground looking for seeds, grain, buds, shoots, roots, leaves, and berries; does not visit gardens.

FLIGHT: fast, powerful; deep wingbeats; display flight gliding on steeply raised wings, rocking from side to side.

SOCIAL BIRD
Evening gatherings can be large, but are often out-numbered by Woodpigeons in woodland roosts.

GROUND FEEDER
Seeds are washed up at the edges of freshwater floods, and Stock Doves often gather to exploit such abun-dance of food.

OCCURRENCE
Widespread except in far N Europe: mostly summer visitor in E Europe, resident in W. In wide variety of places from lowland farms and parkland with many old trees to higher moors with cliffs and quarries.

Seen in the UK
J F M A M J J A S O N D

SIMILAR SPECIES

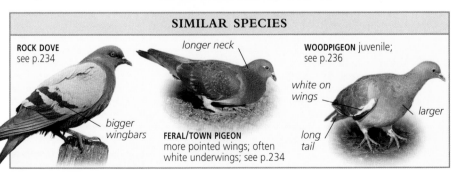

ROCK DOVE see p.234

bigger wingbars

longer neck

FERAL/TOWN PIGEON more pointed wings; often white underwings; see p.234

WOODPIGEON juvenile; see p.236

white on wings

long tail

larger

Length **32–34cm (12½–13½in)**	Wingspan **63–69cm (25–27in)**	Weight **290–330g (11–12oz)**
Social **Flocks**	Lifespan **Up to 10 years**	Status **Secure**

Order **Columbiformes**	Family **Columbidae**	Species **Columba palumbus**

Woodpigeon 🔊 39

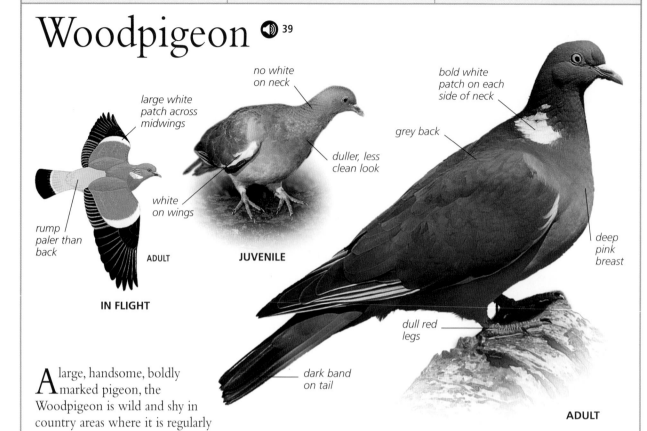

large white
patch across
midwings

white
on wings

rump
paler than
back

ADULT

IN FLIGHT

no white
on neck

duller, less
clean look

JUVENILE

bold white
patch on each
side of neck

grey back

deep
pink
breast

dull red
legs

dark band
on tail

ADULT

A large, handsome, boldly marked pigeon, the Woodpigeon is wild and shy in country areas where it is regularly shot, but visits gardens and becomes surprisingly tame in town parks where it is left undisturbed. It sometimes forms huge flocks, becoming a dramatic part of the country scene in winter. In summer, its dreamy, cooing song is one of the typical sounds of woodland areas. Single birds in flight can easily be mistaken for birds of prey, but any reasonable view should remove such confusion.

VOICE Husky, muffled cooing, oft-repeated, *coo-coo-cu, cu-coo, cook*; loud wing clatter.

NESTING Thin platform of twigs in tree or bush; 2 eggs; 1 or 2 broods; April–September (often autumn).

FEEDING Eats buds, leaves, berries, and fruit in trees; also takes food from ground; feeds at bird-tables where undisturbed.

FLIGHT: quick, direct, with even, strong, deep wingbeats; takes off with powerful clatter when surprised; flies in large flocks.

FORAGING ON GROUND
The Woodpigeon often forages for food on the ground, sometimes in flocks. It takes seeds, grain, and shoots.

OCCURRENCE
Widespread except in Iceland and N Scandinavia; summer visitor only in N and E Europe. Breeds in variety of woodland and farmland with trees, town parks, and big gardens. In winter, flocks feed on open ground but farmland remains most important.

Seen in the UK
J F M A M J J A S O N D

SIMILAR SPECIES

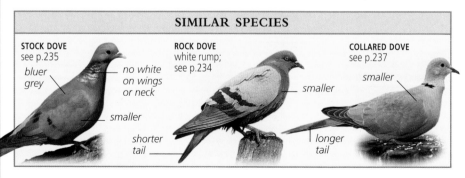

STOCK DOVE
see p.235

bluer
grey

no white
on wings
or neck

smaller

ROCK DOVE
white rump;
see p.234

smaller

COLLARED DOVE
see p.237

smaller

shorter
tail

longer
tail

Length **40–42cm (16–16½in)**	Wingspan **75–80cm (30–32in)**	Weight **480–550g (17–20oz)**
Social **Large flocks**	Lifespan **Up to 10 years**	Status **Secure**

| Order **Columbiformes** | Family **Columbidae** | Species *Streptopelia decaocto* |

Collared Dove 🔊 40

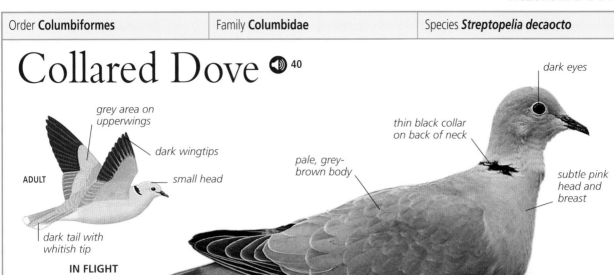

grey area on upperwings

dark wingtips

ADULT

small head

dark tail with whitish tip

IN FLIGHT

dark eyes

thin black collar on back of neck

pale, grey-brown body

subtle pink head and breast

red legs

no collar

sandy buff body

JUVENILE

ADULT

A remarkable natural phenomena of the 20th century is the spread of the Collared Dove from extreme southeast Europe to the whole of the continent. It is now a common sight in farms and suburbs in Europe, its rather monotonous triple coo a familar sound on summer mornings. It relies heavily on food provided incidentally by people, and increasingly on food put out specifically for smaller birds. Its display flights are easily seen over any built-up area with scattered trees in gardens or parks.

VOICE Loud, frequently-repeated triple coo, *cu-cooo-cuk*, or *cooo-coo-coo*; unusually for a pigeon also a flight call, a nasal *gwurrrr*.

NESTING Small platform of twigs and rubbish; 2 eggs; 2 or 3 broods, sometimes more; all year.

FEEDING Picks up grain, seeds, buds, and shoots from ground in parks, fields, paddocks, and gardens; often at bird-tables for seeds.

FLIGHT: quick, direct, often long, straight flight, or rising to glide down in wide arcs on flat wings; wings typically angled back, bowed.

CONIFERS PREFERRED
Collared Doves typically roost and nest in tall, dense coniferous trees, often in parks or gardens.

OCCURRENCE
In most of Europe except S Spain, Portugal, and N Scandinavia. Breeds in pines and warm wooded areas in S Europe. Widespread in gardens, parks, and around farm buildings in W Europe after massive expansion of range.

| Seen in the UK |
| J F M A M J J A S O N D |

SIMILAR SPECIES

TURTLE DOVE see p.238

chequered back

thin white tail rim

shorter tail

FERAL/TOWN PIGEON see p.234

stockier

patchy colours

more upright when perched

KESTREL ♀; see p.140

narrow wings

narrow tail

| Length **31–33cm (12–13in)** | Wingspan **47–55cm (18½–22in)** | Weight **150–220g (5–8oz)** |
| Social **Small flocks** | Lifespan **Up to 10 years** | Status **Secure†** |

237

Order **Columbiformes**	Family **Columbidae**	Species *Streptopelia turtur*

Turtle Dove 🔊 41

pale grey head

barred black-and-white neck patch

blue-grey midwings

ADULT

blue-grey rump

dark spots on bright brown back

pink breast

white belly

IN FLIGHT

blackish tail with white tip

pale brownish head and neck

dull neck patch

less regular pattern

dull brown body

ADULT

JUVENILE

/\/\/\/\/\/\/\/\/\/\/\/\/\/\/\/\/\

FLIGHT: light, buoyant, springy, often rolling sideways; wings angled back, flicking downward beats; also glides on flat wings in display flight.

Unlike the Collared Dove, the Turtle Dove remains a country bird, inhabiting well-wooded areas and farmland with large hedges. Flocks form on stubble fields in late summer, eager for spilled grain. The Turtle Dove is also seen along coasts in spring, migrating in small groups as it returns north from Africa. It is in serious decline as agricultural intensification takes hold over most of Europe, and its purring song, which used to be a frequent feature of high summer, is now heard less often.

VOICE Deep, purring, pleasant crooning *rooorrrr rooorrrr*.

NESTING Small platform of thin twigs in hedge or tree; 2 eggs; 2 or 3 broods; May–July.

FEEDING On ground, takes seeds and shoots of arable weeds.

HEDGEROW SPECIALIST
The loss of tall, dense hedgerows has caused a widespread decline in Turtle Doves.

SIMILAR SPECIES

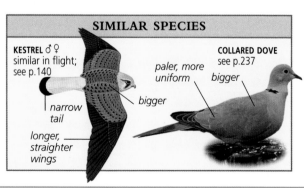

KESTREL ♂ ♀ similar in flight; see p.140

paler, more uniform

COLLARED DOVE see p.237

bigger

bigger

narrow tail

longer, straighter wings

OCCURRENCE
Summer visitor to most of Europe except Iceland, Ireland, and Scandinavia, declining in numbers. In wooded farmland, broadleaved woods with sunny clearings, and thick, old hedgerows.

Seen in the UK
J F **M A M J J A S** O N D

Length **26–28cm (10–11in)**	Wingspan **47–53cm (18½–21in)**	Weight **130–180g (4–6oz)**
Social **Small flocks**	Lifespan **Up to 10 years**	Status **Declining**

| Order **Cuculiformes** | Family **Cuculidae** | Species **Cuculus canorus** |

Cuckoo

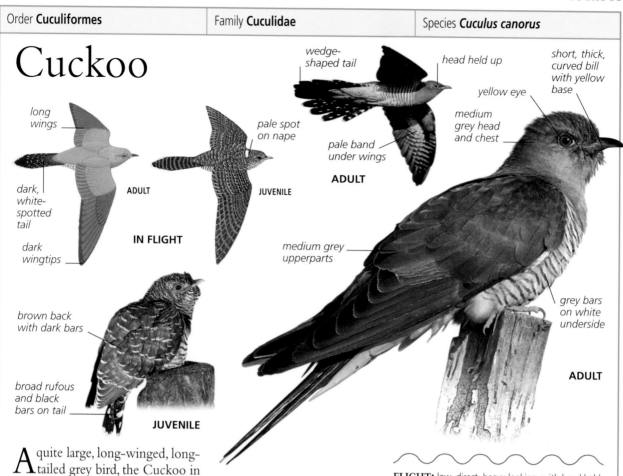

wedge-shaped tail

head held up

short, thick, curved bill with yellow base

yellow eye

medium grey head and chest

pale spot on nape

long wings

pale band under wings

ADULT

dark, white-spotted tail

ADULT

JUVENILE

dark wingtips

IN FLIGHT

medium grey upperparts

grey bars on white underside

brown back with dark bars

broad rufous and black bars on tail

JUVENILE

ADULT

A quite large, long-winged, long-tailed grey bird, the Cuckoo in spring is familiar to everyone by its call, but not its appearance. In late summer, it is the barred, brown young cuckoo that is more often seen, calling loudly to be fed by almost any bird that passes by: its call and huge, orange gape prove irresistible. Cuckoos typically perch low down in or on the edge of trees, but are often easier to see singing or calling from telephone wires; they also fly about from tree to tree, giving frequent short flight views.

VOICE Familiar loud, bright *cuc-coo*, sometimes *cuc-cuc-coo*, much more staccato than Collared Dove song, also rough, laughing *wha-wha-wha*; loud, rich, throaty bubble from female and loud, thin, hissing *ssee-ssee-ssee* from juvenile begging food.

NESTING Lays eggs in other birds' nests; 1–25 (usually 9) eggs per female, 1 per nest; May–June.

FEEDING Drops to ground to pick up large, hairy caterpillars; also eats small insects.

FLIGHT: low, direct, heavy-looking, with head held up, wings below horizontal; quick, deep downward beats; often swoops up to perch.

GIANT CHICK
Cuckoo chicks are often reared by small foster parents such as Reed Warblers.

OCCURRENCE
Summer visitor to all Europe except Iceland, migrating back south early in autumn. On bushy moorland and heaths, in woods and well-wooded farmland, around reedbeds, and wherever small birds nest.

| Seen in the UK |
| J F M **A M J J A S** O N D |

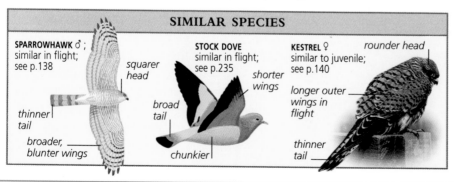

SIMILAR SPECIES

SPARROWHAWK ♂; similar in flight; see p.138

squarer head

thinner tail

broader, blunter wings

STOCK DOVE similar in flight; see p.235

broad tail

shorter wings

chunkier

KESTREL ♀ similar to juvenile; see p.140

rounder head

longer outer wings in flight

thinner tail

| Length **32–34cm (12½–13½in)** | Wingspan **55–65cm (22–26in)** | Weight **105–130g (4–5oz)** |
| Social **Solitary** | Lifespan **Up to 10 years** | Status **Secure** |

Families **Strigidae, Tytonidae**

OWLS

OWLS ARE highly specialized birds with exellent eyesight and hearing. They see well in low light levels, although not in complete darkness, and many can pinpoint prey accurately by sound alone. Their ears are slightly asymmetrical in size, shape, or position. As an owl twists and bobs its head it is using this adaptation to get a "fix" on its prey. Owls often attract the attention of smaller birds (and also sometimes Jays and Magpies) if discovered by day, and mixed parties "mob" the roosting owl with loud calls, sometimes diving at its head.

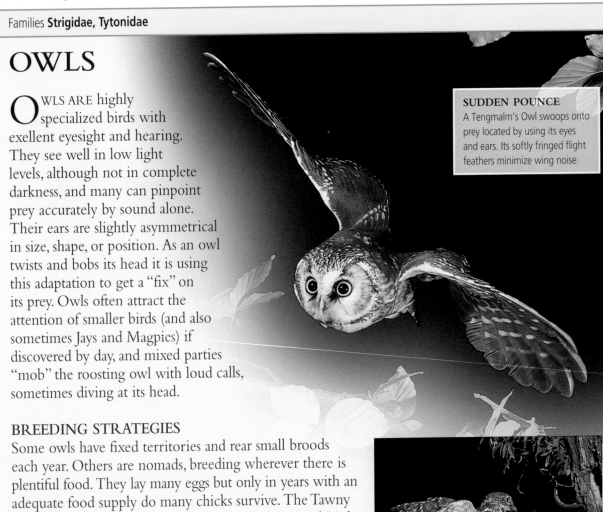

SUDDEN POUNCE
A Tengmalm's Owl swoops onto prey located by using its eyes and ears. Its softly fringed flight feathers minimize wing noise.

BREEDING STRATEGIES

Some owls have fixed territories and rear small broods each year. Others are nomads, breeding wherever there is plentiful food. They lay many eggs but only in years with an adequate food supply do many chicks survive. The Tawny and Tengmalm's are typical woodland owls; Scops and Little Owls live in more open surroundings. The Eagle Owl is a massive and powerful predator, as is the Snowy Owl of far northern tundras. The two "eared" owls are very alike in plumage pattern and overall shape, and both hunt over open ground. The Short-eared Owl lives on heaths and marshes and hunts even in full daylight, while the Long-eared inhabits woods and thickets and hunts only after dark.

FORWARD SWING
Owls can swing their whole body forward, to grip with their feet, whether while landing or striking prey.

Family **Caprimulgidae**

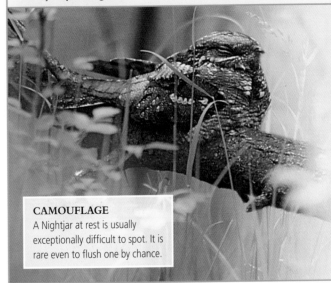

CAMOUFLAGE
A Nightjar at rest is usually exceptionally difficult to spot. It is rare even to flush one by chance.

NIGHTJARS

SUMMER MIGRANTS to Europe, taking advantage of an abundance of moths, the nightjars spend the day motionless and emerge at dusk to feed. These remarkably agile, light-weight fliers have large wings and tail. Their strange songs help to identify them. Nightjars occupy open heathland or lightly wooded places with wide clearings, often flying around bush tops and trees to catch moths in flight. They may approach people at dusk, as if curious about intruders in their territory.

Order **Strigiformes**	Family **Strigidae**	Species ***Strix aluco***

Tawny Owl 🔊 42.I, 42.II

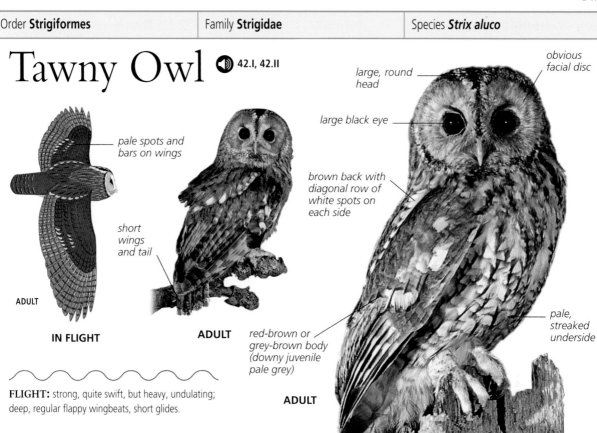

pale spots and bars on wings

short wings and tail

ADULT

IN FLIGHT

ADULT

red-brown or grey-brown body (downy juvenile pale grey)

large, round head

obvious facial disc

large black eye

brown back with diagonal row of white spots on each side

pale, streaked underside

ADULT

FLIGHT: strong, quite swift, but heavy, undulating; deep, regular flappy wingbeats, short glides.

This is the owl that hoots after dark, but its vocal repertoire is quite wide and a loud, yapping *ke-wik* is heard more regularly through the year than the beautiful, wavering hoot. It is often seen merely as a large, big-headed silhouette, or a vague shape flying from a roadside pole at night. Sometimes small birds mob it by day, giving away its presence, or it can be found in trees or ivy above splashes of white droppings. It can then be watched quite closely with care and proves to be an impressive and extremely beautiful bird.

VOICE Loud, excited yapping notes, variations on nasal *ke-wick!* or *keeyip*; long, musical, breathy, quavering hoot, *hoo hoo-hoooo hoo-ho-ho*.

NESTING Hole in tree or building or in old stick nest of crow or Magpie; 2–5 eggs; 1 brood; April–June.

FEEDING Drops down to take voles, mice, rats, frogs, beetles, and earthworms from ground; catches many small birds as they are roosting or incubating eggs at night.

NIGHT HUNTER
Tawny Owls begin to call at dusk but only start to hunt when it is quite dark.

OCCURRENCE
Resident almost throughout Europe except Iceland, Ireland, and N Scandinavia. In all kinds of woodland and wooded areas such as farmland with tall hedges and trees, and large gardens with conifers or evergreen broadleaves.

Seen in the UK
J F M A M J J A S O N D

SIMILAR SPECIES

ear tufts

orange eye

LONG-EARED OWL
see p.244

URAL OWL
see p.444

larger and greyer

yellow eye

whiter face

smaller

TENGMALM'S OWL
see p.243

Length **37–39cm (14½–15½in)**	Wingspan **94–104cm (37–41in)**	Weight **330–590g (12–21oz)**
Social **Family groups**	Lifespan **Up to 10 years**	Status **Secure**

Order **Strigiformes**	Family **Strigidae**	Species **Bubo bubo**

Eagle Owl

dark brown wings with pale patch

IN FLIGHT

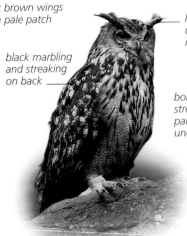

black marbling and streaking on back

large ear tufts, usually angled in shallow "V"

boldly streaked, pale underside

pale "V" on upper face

large, deep orange eye, circled with black

pale area around bill

A massive bird and one of Europe's most powerful predators, the Eagle Owl even kills other owls and birds of prey quite frequently in order to claim exclusive use of territory. Mostly a bird of cliffs and crags, it may be found relatively close to villages and farms, although many prefer wilder places remote from human habitation. It calls early in the year and is not at all easy to track down in summer: careful scrutiny of likely ledges, cavities, and trees on occupied cliffs is often to no avail. Its huge eyes give it really exceptional vision in poor light and hunting is almost entirely nocturnal.

VOICE Song deep, booming hoot, *oo-hu*, carries 2–4km (1–2½ miles); also loud barking alarm notes, *kvek, kwa*, or *kwa-kwa-kwa*.

NESTING Unlined cavity in tree or deep, sheltered cliff ledge; 2 or 3 eggs; 1 brood; April–May.

FEEDING Eats wide range of food from small rodents to much bigger prey, including birds such as crows, pigeons, and thrushes, and small mammals such as rats, hares, and squirrels.

REMARK Subspecies *B. b. ascalaphus* (Middle East) is paler, buff below, and has yellower eyes.

FLIGHT: direct, heavy but strong; wings slightly arched in frequent glides; head looks very big.

ELUSIVE OWL
Good camouflage colours render immobile Eagle Owls extremely difficult to spot.

OCCURRENCE
Widespread in mainland Europe but everywhere sparse, mostly in forested mountain areas with gorges, cliffs, and deep ravines with deep caves or large ledges, and on big, old trees. Not found outside usual breeding areas.

Seen in the UK
J F M A M J J A S O N D

SIMILAR SPECIES

smaller and slimmer

LONG-EARED OWL
see p.244

no ear tufts

much smaller

TAWNY OWL
see p.241

no ear tufts

dark eye

smaller

BUZZARD
see p.136

Length **59–73cm (23–29in)**	Wingspan **1.38–1.7m (4½–5½ft)**	Weight **1.5–3kg (3¼–6½lb)**
Social **Solitary**	Lifespan **10–20 years**	Status **Vulnerable**

Order **Strigiformes**	Family **Strigidae**	Species **Aegolius funureus**

Tengmalm's Owl

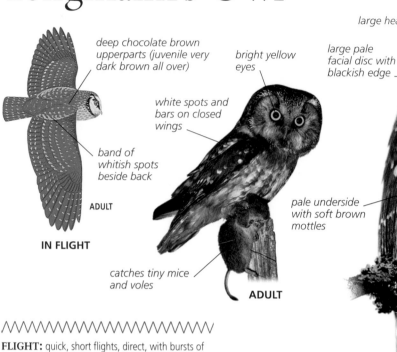

deep chocolate brown
upperparts (juvenile very
dark brown all over)

bright yellow
eyes

high brow

large head

large pale
facial disc with
blackish edge

white spots and
bars on closed
wings

band of
whitish spots
beside back

ADULT

IN FLIGHT

pale underside
with soft brown
mottles

catches tiny mice
and voles

ADULT

ADULT

FLIGHT: quick, short flights, direct, with bursts of quick beats between short glides.

A small to medium-sized owl, Tengmalm's Owl is a difficult bird to see, preferring dense forests and being active only at night. It is best located by looking for signs of owls (droppings and pellets) in the vicinity of likely nest holes (such as Black Woodpecker holes), or by listening for its calls, which are fortunately frequent and carry as much as 3km (2 miles) on calm nights. The combination of its call and the size and shape of the likely silhouette view, helps identification; Little or Scops Owls are not found in dense forested habitats and other species are mostly noticeably larger.

VOICE Hoarse, unmusical *chiak*; song 5–8 whistles, rising and accelerating, *pu-pu-po-po-po-po-po-po*.

NESTING Unlined tree cavity or old woodpecker hole; 3–6 eggs; 1 brood; May–June.

FEEDING Watches and listens for voles from tree perch within canopy, rarely more exposed.

CURIOUS EXPRESSION
The high brows give a permanently alert or alarmed expression to a Tengmalm's Owl.

OCCURRENCE
Mostly breeds in NE Europe, sparsely and very locally in C European uplands, rare in Pyrenees. Resident in dense forest with small clearings, not moving much from breeding places at any time of year.

Seen in the UK
J F M A M J J A S O N D

SIMILAR SPECIES

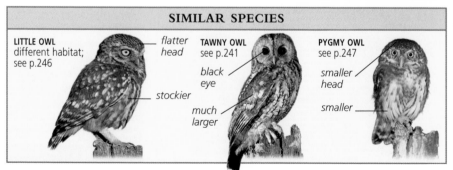

LITTLE OWL
different habitat;
see p.246

flatter
head

stockier

TAWNY OWL
see p.241

black
eye

much
larger

PYGMY OWL
see p.247

smaller
head

smaller

Length **22–27cm (9–10½in)**	Wingspan **50–62cm (20–24in)**	Weight **150–200g (5–7oz)**
Social **Solitary**	Lifespan **Up to 10 years**	Status **Secure†**

Order **Strigiformes**	Family **Strigidae**	Species *Asio otus*

Long-eared Owl

pale patch on outer wings

ear tufts, folded back

dark surround to bright orange-red eye

long ear tufts, raised

mottled upperwings

dark wrist patch

grey tips

IN FLIGHT

closely streaked underside

FLIGHT: looks like Short-eared Owl but less often seen by day; slightly shorter-winged, less buoyant.

A large, handsome bird, the Long-eared Owl can be found in winter in communal roosts of a handful to twenty or more birds. These are often found in tall pines, but also resort to dense thickets of willow and hawthorn, where they can be extremely hard to see; they are sometimes given away by splashes of droppings and regurgitated pellets on the ground. Unless disturbed, they rarely move before it is almost dark: only occasionally may one be found hunting in better light, inviting confusion with the Short-eared Owl.

VOICE Song deep, moaning, short hoot, *oo oo oo* or *uh uh*; juvenile begs for food with high, sharp, "squeaky-hinge" *eee-ip*.

NESTING Old nest of crow, squirrel drey, or under thick growth of bracken or brambles; 3–5 eggs; 1 brood; March–June.

FEEDING Hunts from perch or in flight, catching small rodents and roosting birds.

WINTER ROOST
A typical winter roost is in a thorn or willow thicket, or a pine tree, where several owls may sit close together, relaxed, or stretched tall when alarmed.

OCCURRENCE
Widespread except in Iceland and N Scandinavia; summer only in NE Europe. Mostly breeds in coniferous woodland and shelter belts near moors, heaths, and marshes; roosts in thickets, old, tall hedgerows, belts of willows near marshes, and similar low, thick cover near open ground.

Seen in the UK
J F M A M J J A S O N D

SIMILAR SPECIES

yellow eye

EAGLE OWL
see p.242

much larger

black eye

rounder and darker

white trailing edge

SHORT-EARED OWL
very similar in flight;
see p.245

TAWNY OWL
see p.241

Length **35–37cm (14–14½in)**	Wingspan **84–95cm (33–37in)**	Weight **210–330g (7–12oz)**
Social **Roosts in small flocks**	Lifespan **10–15 years**	Status **Secure**

Order **Strigiformes**	Family **Strigidae**	Species ***Asio flammeus***

Short-eared Owl

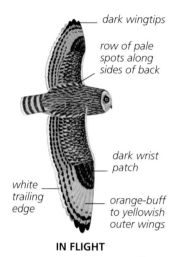

dark wingtips

row of pale spots along sides of back

white trailing edge

dark wrist patch

orange-buff to yellowish outer wings

whitish underwings with narrow dark bar at angle

white belly

complex buff marbling on upperparts

large, round head with tiny tufts usually hidden

blackish ring around large, cold yellow eye

buff-white underside with fine dark streaks

IN FLIGHT

FLIGHT: low, wavering, quite quick, with slow beats of stiff wings, quite high upstroke; floating, banking glides.

One of the owls most likely to be seen by day, the Short-eared Owl hunts like a harrier, flying low over open ground, often in good light well before dusk. Its numbers and distribution reflect the fluctuating numbers of voles. It may appear for a year or two in suburban areas where fields are neglected in advance of development, but is more frequent on coastal marshes and, in summer, over upland moors and young conifer plantations. It is easily confused with the Long-eared Owl in flight but Long-eareds are more strictly nocturnal.

FLOATING HUNTER
Its long wings and light weight make the Short-eared Owl remarkably buoyant when hunting.

VOICE Nasal bark, *kee-aw*, or hoarse, whip-like *ke-ow*; song deep, soft, quick booming hoot, *boo-boo-boo-boo* in display flight.
NESTING Unlined scrape on ground; 4–8 eggs; 1 or 2 broods; April–July.
FEEDING Hunts by flying slowly over ground or watching from perch; eats small rodents and some birds.

OCCURRENCE
Widespread through Europe, mostly in N but erratically in S, largely linked with variations in prey populations. In all kinds of rough grassland, marshes, heaths, upland moors, and plantations; many temporary habitats occupied opportunistically when large numbers of voles present.

Seen in the UK
| J | F | M | A | M | J | J | A | S | O | N | D |

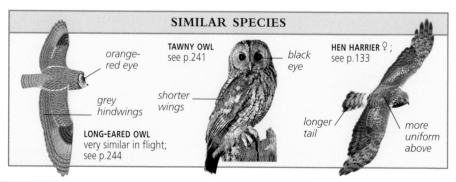

SIMILAR SPECIES

orange-red eye

grey hindwings

LONG-EARED OWL
very similar in flight;
see p.244

TAWNY OWL
see p.241

black eye

shorter wings

HEN HARRIER ♀;
see p.133

longer tail

more uniform above

Length **34–42cm (13½–16½in)**	Wingspan **90–105cm (35–41in)**	Weight **260–350g (9–13oz)**
Social **Small flocks**	Lifespan **10–15 years**	Status **Vulnerable†**

Order **Strigiformes**	Family **Strigidae**	Species ***Athene noctua***

Little Owl

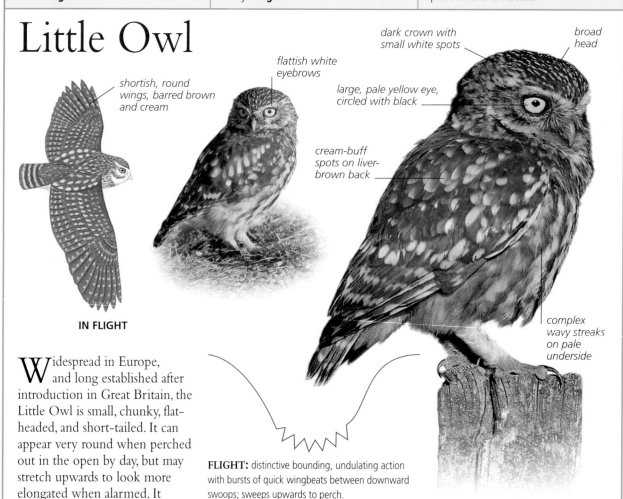

shortish, round wings, barred brown and cream

IN FLIGHT

flattish white eyebrows

dark crown with small white spots

broad head

large, pale yellow eye, circled with black

cream-buff spots on liver-brown back

complex wavy streaks on pale underside

Widespread in Europe, and long established after introduction in Great Britain, the Little Owl is small, chunky, flat-headed, and short-tailed. It can appear very round when perched out in the open by day, but may stretch upwards to look more elongated when alarmed. It hunts at dusk but sometimes perches quite openly in daylight, often attracting the noisy attention of small birds. Its undulating flight may briefly recall a woodpecker or large thrush. In much of Europe, it lives in ruins and old barns with tiled roofs, or on hillsides with boulders and stones scattered over the slopes.

FLIGHT: distinctive bounding, undulating action with bursts of quick wingbeats between downward swoops; sweeps upwards to perch.

VOICE Loud, musical, plaintive calls, rising *keeeooo*, sharper *werro!*, short *kip kip kip*.

NESTING In long, narrow hole in tree, bank, or building; 2–5 eggs; 1 brood; May–July.

FEEDING Mostly takes small rodents and large insects from ground; also picks small birds and earthworms from ground.

SQUAT SILHOUETTE
A rounded, short-tailed, thin-legged shape on a post or branch at dusk is likely to be a Little Owl.

OCCURRENCE
Widespread resident through Europe north to Great Britain and Baltic. In great variety of terrain, on open rocky slopes and islands, farmland and parkland with old trees and outbuildings, and even semi-desert areas with tumbled rocks and cliffs.

Seen in the UK

| J | F | M | A | M | J | J | A | S | O | N | D |

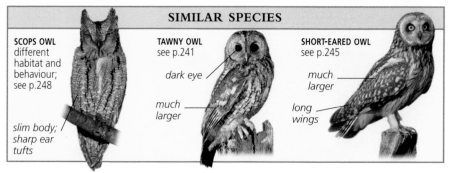

SIMILAR SPECIES

SCOPS OWL different habitat and behaviour; see p.248

slim body; sharp ear tufts

TAWNY OWL see p.241

dark eye

much larger

SHORT-EARED OWL see p.245

much larger

long wings

Length **21–23cm (8½–9in)**	Wingspan **50–56cm (20–22in)**	Weight **140–200g (5–7oz)**
Social **Family groups**	Lifespan **Up to 10 years**	Status **Declining**

| Order **Strigiformes** | Family **Strigidae** | Species *Glaucidium passerinum* |

Pygmy Owl

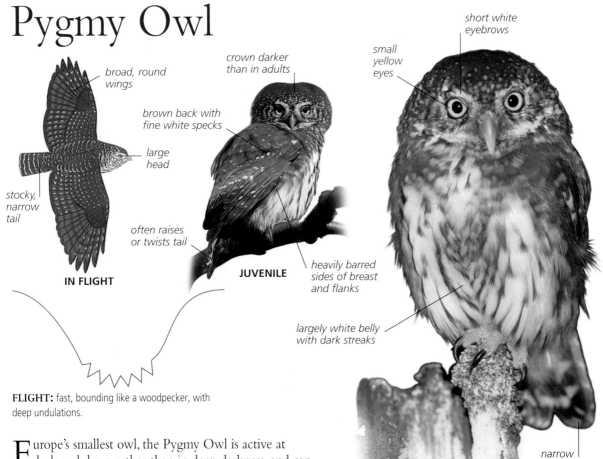

broad, round wings

large head

stocky, narrow tail

IN FLIGHT

crown darker than in adults

brown back with fine white specks

often raises or twists tail

JUVENILE

heavily barred sides of breast and flanks

largely white belly with dark streaks

short white eyebrows

small yellow eyes

narrow barred tail

ADULT

FLIGHT: fast, bounding like a woodpecker, with deep undulations.

Europe's smallest owl, the Pygmy Owl is active at dusk and dawn rather than in deep darkness, and can sometimes be seen perched on top of a tall, prominent coniferous tree. It may also be attracted to imitations of its call. It hunts small and medium-sized birds, taking some that are larger than itself in a bold, fearless chase.

VOICE A thin, thrush-like *seeee*; in autumn, a series of thin, forced, squeaky whistles, usually 5–10, rising in pitch; in spring, repetition of a simple piping note, similar to Bullfinch's call, 7–8 notes per 10 seconds.

NESTING Uses a natural or an old woodpecker hole in a tree; 4–7 eggs; 1 brood; April–June.

FEEDING Hunts small mammals (mostly mice and voles) and woodland birds, taking them by surprise on perch or on the ground.

JAUNTY TAIL
A typically rounded owl, the Pygmy Owl nevertheless has a medium-length tail that is often slightly raised at an angle to its back, giving it an alert, perky look.

SIMILAR SPECIES

wider, whiter facial disc

TENGMALM'S OWL
white spots along shoulder, larger eyes; see p.243

OCCURRENCE
Prefers coniferous (especially spruce) or mixed forest in Alpine areas and far north of Europe; rarely moves out of breeding areas.

| Seen in the UK |
| J F M A M J J A S O N D |

| Length **15–19cm (6–7½in)** | Wingspan **32–39cm (12½–15½in)** | Weight **50–65g (1¾–2⅜oz)** |
| Social **Family groups** | Lifespan **5–10 years** | Status **Secure** |

Order **Strigiformes**	Family **Strigidae**	Species *Otus scops*

Scops Owl

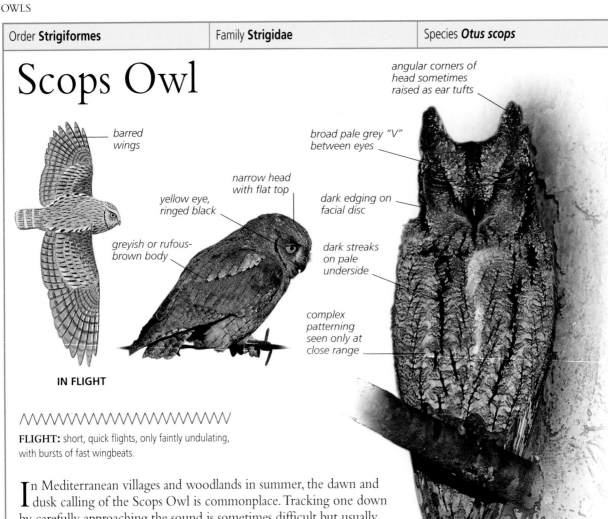

barred wings

angular corners of head sometimes raised as ear tufts

broad pale grey "V" between eyes

narrow head with flat top

yellow eye, ringed black

dark edging on facial disc

greyish or rufous-brown body

dark streaks on pale underside

complex patterning seen only at close range

IN FLIGHT

FLIGHT: short, quick flights, only faintly undulating, with bursts of fast wingbeats.

In Mediterranean villages and woodlands in summer, the dawn and dusk calling of the Scops Owl is commonplace. Tracking one down by carefully approaching the sound is sometimes difficult but usually just a matter of time; with patience it may be possible to see one really well if it perches close to a streetlight. Daytime views are much more difficult to get: it is practically impossible to track one down to a visible roost. Little Owls are often found in nearby areas, so identification requires some care: Little Owls are resident but in most areas Scops Owls are found in summer; Scops Owls are more often seen on roofs and church towers in the middle of villages, while Little Owls tend to be on the edges of villages or around farm outbuildings and isolated barns; Little Owls look more rounded or squat, with a broad, flatter head, while a Scops Owl is more tapered towards the wingtips and tail. They are only very rare vagrants (usually in spring) north of their regular breeding range.

VOICE Distinctive at dusk: single, fluty, indrawn musical whistle, *pew* or *tyuh* repeated unvaryingly every 2–3 seconds.

NESTING Cavity in tree, wall, or building; 4 or 5 eggs; 1 brood; April–June.

FEEDING Mostly drops down from perch to take large insects.

OCCURRENCE
In summer, found widely in S Europe and north to C France and Alps. In small towns, parks, and wooded areas, often around older buildings and churchyards, but also in mixed woodland. Most migrate in winter, only some staying in S Europe.

Seen in the UK
J F M A M J J A S O N D

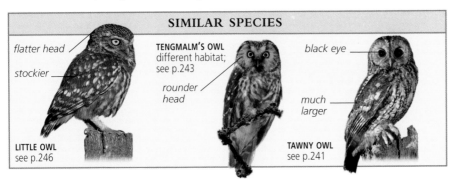

SIMILAR SPECIES

flatter head

stockier

LITTLE OWL
see p.246

TENGMALM'S OWL
different habitat; see p.243

rounder head

black eye

much larger

TAWNY OWL
see p.241

Length **19–21cm (7½–8½in)**	Wingspan **47–54cm (18½–21½in)**	Weight **150g (5oz)**
Social **Family groups**	Lifespan **Up to 10 years**	Status **Declining†**

| Order **Strigiformes** | Family **Tytonidae** | Species *Tyto alba* |

Barn Owl 43

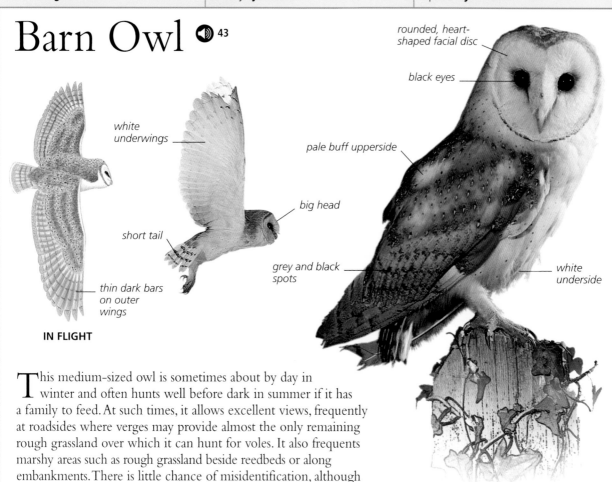

rounded, heart-shaped facial disc

black eyes

pale buff upperside

grey and black spots

white underside

white underwings

short tail

big head

thin dark bars on outer wings

IN FLIGHT

This medium-sized owl is sometimes about by day in winter and often hunts well before dark in summer if it has a family to feed. At such times, it allows excellent views, frequently at roadsides where verges may provide almost the only remaining rough grassland over which it can hunt for voles. It also frequents marshy areas such as rough grassland beside reedbeds or along embankments. There is little chance of misidentification, although other owls appearing "white" in car headlights at night can be taken for it.

VOICE Hissing, snoring calls from nest, nasal *hi-wit*, rolling, shrill shriek and high squeal of alarm.
NESTING Big hole in tree, stack of hay bales, or building; 4–7 eggs; 1 brood; May–June.
FEEDING Hunts from perch or in low flight; catches voles, mice, rats, and occasionally birds.

FLIGHT: light, agile, spring-like action with quite quick, deep wingbeats; hovers and plunges head-first into long grass with wings pulled back.

NIGHT HUNTER
Barn Owls are usually nocturnal but they may be seen before sunset if they have young to feed.

SUBSPECIES

T. a. guttata (C and E Europe)

deep orange-buff underside

SIMILAR SPECIES

SHORT-EARED OWL see p.245

yellow eyes

dark wing patches

much larger

whiter above

SNOWY OWL see p.444

TAWNY OWL see p.241

browner

streaked below

OCCURRENCE
Widespread but sparse in SE, C, and W Europe; absent from Iceland, Scandinavia, and NE Europe. Breeds and hunts in open areas, from farmland to marshes with reedbeds and moors, and young plantations.

Seen in the UK
| J | F | M | A | M | J | J | A | S | O | N | D |

| Length **33–39cm (13–15½in)** | Wingspan **85–93cm (34–37in)** | Weight **290–460g (10–16oz)** |
| Social **Family groups** | Lifespan **5–10 years** | Status **Declining** |

Order **Caprimulgiformes**	Family **Caprimulgidae**	Species **Caprimulgus europaeus**

Nightjar 🔊 44

bright white spots near wingtips

MALE

long, narrow wings

long tail

FEMALE

white corners to tail

barred, mottled, and spotted grey-brown body

white marks on cheek

flat head

tiny bill

MALE

elongated body and tail

FEMALE

IN FLIGHT

One of Europe's most charismatic small birds, the Nightjar sings at dusk with a remarkable prolonged, purring trill. It hawks quite low over heathland and around clumps of trees or isolated bushes and quite frequently flies over to quiet, still observers to fly around them in the same way, seeking moths. It is difficult to find by day and sadly the full effect of its beautiful, cryptic plumage cannot often be appreciated.

VOICE Deep, nasal, mechanical *gooik*; song fantastic prolonged *churr*, varying abruptly in pitch; a soft purr at long range, harder, more wooden rattle close-up, *prrrrrrrooorrrrrrrprrrrrrrrooorrrrrrrrr*.

NESTING Unlined scrape on ground; 2 eggs; 1 or 2 broods; May–July.

FEEDING Catches insects, mainly moths, in flight, using broad wide-open gape, mostly at dusk and dawn.

FLIGHT: light, buoyant, erratic, floating and drifting or bounding with quick, deep wingbeats; sometimes twists and turns like dead leaf.

ADULT BY NEST
The "dead leaf" or bark-like camouflage makes a nesting Nightjar exceptionally difficult to find.

SIMILAR SPECIES

GRASSHOPPER WARBLER
higher song with sharper trill; see p.334

rufous collar

RED-NECKED NIGHTJAR
different song; see p.445

OCCURRENCE
Very local and erratic throughout Europe except N Britain, Iceland, and N Scandinavia, on heaths and open ground with low undergrowth or clearings in forested regions. Migrates to Africa in winter.

Seen in the UK
J F **M A M J J A S** O N D

Length **26–28cm (10–11in)**	Wingspan **54–60cm (21½–23½in)**	Weight **75–100g (2⅝–3⅝oz)**
Social **Solitary**	Lifespan **Up to 10 years**	Status **Declining†**

Family **Apodidae**

SWIFTS

No BIRDS ARE MORE specialized than the swifts. They have tiny bills but large, broad mouths, in which they catch flying insects. Their tapered bodies and long, stiff, scythe-shaped wings are aerodynamically ideal for sustained flight. They have a good turn of speed when displaying, but generally feed at a much slower pace, gliding efficiently and turning dextrously to catch their small prey.

Their feet are minute, with all four toes pointing forwards, just enough to cling to a rough surface but making it impossible for them to perch on a wire or twig: indeed, they are almost never seen settled, as they dive into the cavities where they nest with no discernible pause.

Swifts have become extremely reliant on buildings for nesting and few now nest in holes in cliffs or trees. However, modern buildings are useless to swifts, which concentrate on old housing and structures such as church towers. They must face an uncertain future.

JUVENILE MARKINGS
Young swifts look very like their parents, but can be told at very close range by the fine whitish fringes to their feathers. Once they fly from the nest they may not settle again for three years.

Identification can be difficult, but good views reveal differences in shape and pattern between most species. All are social birds, often flying in fast-moving, closely packed groups during the breeding season. They arrive late in spring and leave in late summer for Africa. There, they feed in company with several similar species of African-nesting swifts.

SCREAMING PARTY
A group of Swifts dashes by at rooftop height, with a chorus of loud, piercing calls. This seems to have a strong social significance within the birds of a breeding colony.

Order **Apodiformes**	Family **Apodidae**	Species **Apus pallidus**

Pallid Swift

darker brown wingtips

whitish chin and throat

pale mud-brown under wings (pale-edged feathers)

ADULT

pale brown diagonal band on upperwings

ADULT

more mottled than adult with obvious pale feather edges

wingtips darker than midwings

IN FLIGHT

JUVENILE

Very like a common Swift, the Pallid Swift is perceptibly paler and more mud- or clay-brown when seen well; it is also broader-winged, shorter-tailed, and broader-headed. As it is so often seen flying against the sky, a good view may not be easy to achieve, but if it flies low against a darker background, plumage differences should be visible. In many southern European towns, both species are common, allowing opportunities both for comparison and confusion. Pallid Swifts have sometimes been seen well north of their usual range very late in the summer or autumn when swifts have normally long since migrated to Africa, but this alone is not sufficient to identify late swifts such as Pallid: very occasionally, a common Swift will linger as well. Such isolated wanderers outside the normal range need careful observation for positive identification.

VOICE Scream like common Swift's but usually falls in pitch, more disyllabic, lower in pitch, but hard to separate with certainty.

NESTING Unlined cavity in roof space, old building, or wall; 2 or 3 eggs; 1 brood; May–June.

FEEDING Like Swift, takes food entirely in air, catching flying insects and drifting spiders in its mouth.

FLIGHT: fast, typical swift-type flight on stiff, scythe-like wings, with slightly slower wingbeats; longer glides than Swift on average.

OCCURRENCE
Breeds in S Europe, mostly near coasts; more inland in S Spain and Italy, in older areas of towns and villages. Migrates to Africa in winter, but only very rare vagrant north of breeding range. Feeds over all kinds of open countryside.

Seen in the UK
J F M A M J J A S O N D

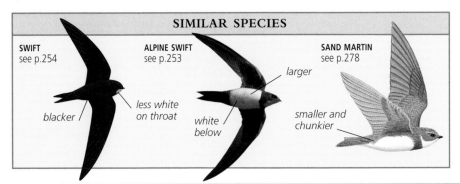

SIMILAR SPECIES

SWIFT
see p.254

blacker

ALPINE SWIFT
see p.253

less white on throat

white below

SAND MARTIN
see p.278

larger

smaller and chunkier

Length **16–18cm (6½–7in)**	Wingspan **39–46cm (15½–18in)**	Weight **50g (1¾oz)**
Social **Flocks**	Lifespan **10–15 years**	Status **Secure†**

Order **Apodiformes**	Family **Apodidae**	Species **Apus melba**

Alpine Swift

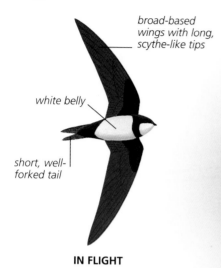

broad-based wings with long, scythe-like tips

white belly

short, well-forked tail

IN FLIGHT

FLIGHT: strong, powerful, sweeping flight; easy, graceful beats of stiff, scythe-like wings.

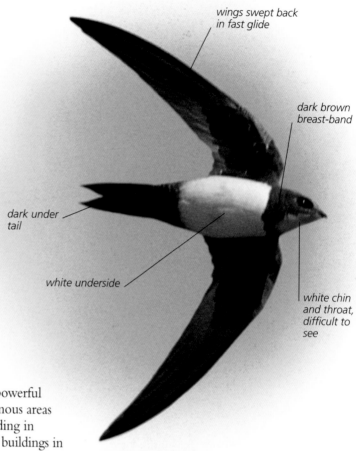

wings swept back in fast glide

dark brown breast-band

dark under tail

white underside

white chin and throat, difficult to see

The Alpine Swift is a uniquely large and powerful swift in Europe. It likes cliffs in mountainous areas but is not always found at high altitude, breeding in many lower, deeply incised ravines and in tall buildings in towns and old villages. It often mixes with other swift species and Crag Martins and is frequently seen in the air with choughs (see pp.373–4). It is not always easy to judge size, so silhouette views are not necessarily adequate to identify possible Alpine Swifts out of their usual range: the possibility of partly white Swifts should also be borne in mind.

VOICE Loud chorus of Greenfinch-like trills, rising and falling and changing in speed and pitch, *titititititi-ti-ti-ti-ti-ti ti ti.*

NESTING Shallow cup of grass and stems in cavity in building or cliff; 2 or 3 eggs; 1 brood; April–June.

FEEDING Exclusively aerial, catching insects in air in open mouth.

STRONG FLIER
In silhouette, an Alpine Swift may momentarily recall a Hobby.

OCCURRENCE
Summer visitor and breeder in S Europe north to Alps. Over all kinds of open country, especially hill towns, cliffs, and gorges, from sea level to high hills, between April and September. Rarely strays north in spring.

Seen in the UK
J F M A M J J A S O N D

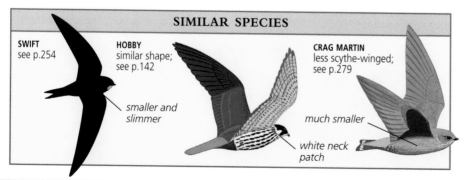

SIMILAR SPECIES

SWIFT
see p.254

HOBBY
similar shape;
see p.142

smaller and slimmer

CRAG MARTIN
less scythe-winged;
see p.279

much smaller

white neck patch

Length **20–23cm (8–9in)**	Wingspan **51–58cm (20–23in)**	Weight **75–100g (2⅝–3⅝oz)**
Social **Flocks**	Lifespan **10–15 years**	Status **Secure†**

Order **Apodiformes**	Family **Apodidae**	Species *Apus apus*

Swift 🔊 45

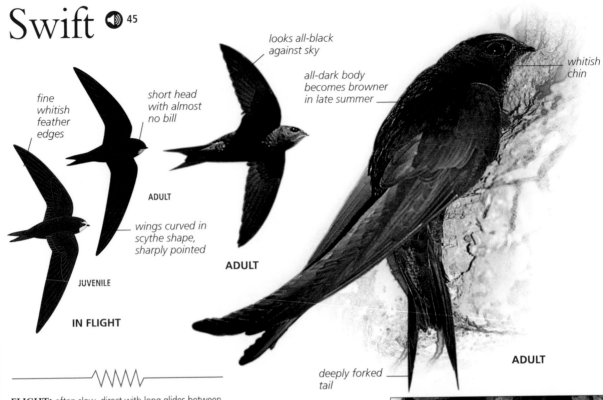

looks all-black against sky

all-dark body becomes browner in late summer

whitish chin

fine whitish feather edges

short head with almost no bill

ADULT

wings curved in scythe shape, sharply pointed

ADULT

JUVENILE

IN FLIGHT

ADULT

deeply forked tail

FLIGHT: often slow, direct with long glides between flurries of deep wingbeats, wings very rigid; also faster dashing flights in groups with flickering wingbeats.

No other bird is more aerial than the Swift. Immature Swifts may spend three years aloft before returning to breed: like seabirds, they come to land only to breed. Swifts appear in Europe late in spring and depart for Africa early in autumn. Flocks fly very high or at rooftop level; they are seldom seen perching on wires or clinging to walls or roofs like martins or swallows. Their scythe-like wings and loud, screaming calls make identification simple, but Pallid Swifts in southern Europe complicate the matter.

VOICE Loud, screeching, shrill screams from flocks, *shrreeee, sirrr*.

NESTING Feather-lined cavity in building, more rarely in cliff; 2 or 3 eggs; 1 brood; May–June.

FEEDING Entirely aerial, taking flying insects in bill.

HIDDEN NESTER
Swifts nest deep inside holes, mostly in older buildings, rarely now in cliffs.

SCREAMING PARTIES
Feeding Swifts fly much more slowly than may be thought, but noisy, chasing groups are genuinely fast.

OCCURRENCE
Widespread in summer except in Iceland; arrives late and leaves early. Feeds over any kind of open area, including towns, villages, and some larger S European cities, but needs old civic buildings and housing for nesting, usually excluded from new developments.

Seen in the UK
J F M **A M J J A S** O N D

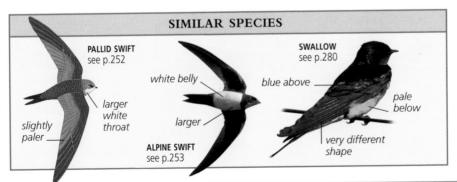

SIMILAR SPECIES

PALLID SWIFT see p.252

slightly paler

larger white throat

white belly

larger

ALPINE SWIFT see p.253

SWALLOW see p.280

blue above

pale below

very different shape

Length **16–17cm (6½in)**	Wingspan **42–48cm (16½–19in)**	Weight **36–50g (1¼–1¾oz)**
Social **Flocks**	Lifespan **Up to 10 years**	Status **Secure**

Families **Alcedinidae, Meropidae, Coraciidae, Upupidae**

KINGFISHERS, BEE-EATERS, ROLLERS, AND HOOPOE

THESE SPECIES AND THE woodpeckers fall between the swifts and nightjars and the Passerines (perching or song birds) and are often termed "near passerines". They are grouped here for convenience rather than for any more meaningful relationship.

KINGFISHERS

The "original" kingfisher from which the family takes its name, the European species is a fish-eater (others are dry land birds that catch insects). It is often first detected by its piercing call or a splash as it dives for a fish.

BEE-EATERS

True to their name, bee-eaters do eat bees and wasps, wiping away their stings against a perch, but they also catch many other insects in their acrobatic, swooping and gliding flight. They breed socially, nesting in burrows in earth banks.

ROLLERS

Rather crow-like in character, Rollers are much more colourful, especially in mid-summer when paler feather edges have worn away to reveal the rich colours beneath.

ALERT
A Roller perches upright on the edge of a tree, looking for prey.

HOOPOE

Striking and boldly patterned in a photograph, the Hoopoe is often surprisingly inconspicuous as it shuffles on the ground in the dappled light and shade beneath a hedge or in a sunny orchard. Only when it flies does it suddenly catch the eye.

JEWEL-LIKE
The Bee-eater is a beautifully patterned bird, its mixture of colours appealing rather than gaudy.

BOLDLY BARRED
The Hoopoe has broad black and white bands over its back and wings.

FISHING
The European Kingfisher plunge-dives into water to catch fish. A transparent membrane protects the eye during the dive.

Order **Coraciiformes**	Family **Alcedinidae**	Species *Alcedo atthis*

Kingfisher

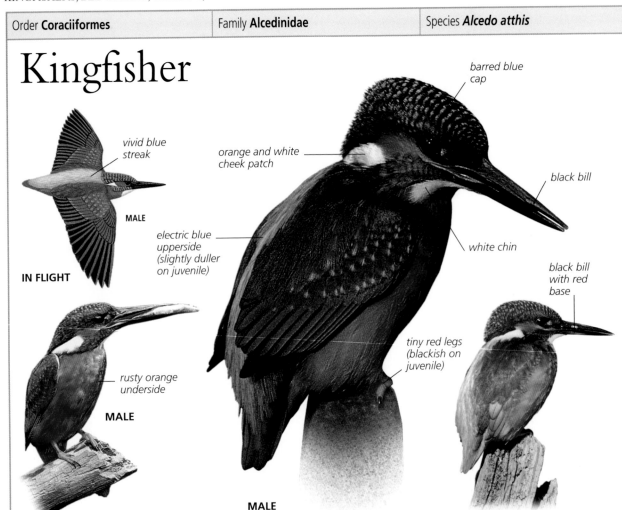

vivid blue streak

MALE

IN FLIGHT

orange and white cheek patch

barred blue cap

black bill

electric blue upperside (slightly duller on juvenile)

white chin

black bill with red base

rusty orange underside

MALE

tiny red legs (blackish on juvenile)

MALE

FEMALE

Most people seeing one for the first time think the Kingfisher is surprisingly small: about Starling-sized or a little less. It is also, despite its bright colours, much more unobtrusive than may be expected: in the dappled shade of flickering foliage above rippling water, it can be extremely hard to see. Often it is the sharp call that gives it away, followed by a glimpse of a bright blue back flying off over water, but sometimes it allows really close, clear views. It is particularly vulnerable to hard winter weather and populations consequently fluctuate greatly from year to year. Occasionally a Kingfisher will take advantage of a garden pond full of goldfish, but visits are usually brief as Kingfishers are shy birds and quick to fly off if disturbed.

VOICE Quite loud, sharp, high *kit-cheeee* or *cheee*; also high, fast trill in spring.

NESTING Deep tubular tunnel, lined with fish bones, in soft earth cliff over water; 5–7 eggs; 2 broods; May–July.

FEEDING Catches fish, small aquatic invertebrates, and amphibians in dive from perch or mid-air hover.

FLIGHT: low, direct, fast; poor manoeuvrability; quick, almost whirring wingbeats.

OCCURRENCE
In most of Europe, N to S Scotland, Baltic, and extreme S Scandinavia. Summer visitor only in north and east of range, from which birds move southwest in winter. Along rivers and canals, on marshes, flooded pits, and coastal areas including salt-marsh creeks, especially in winter.

Seen in the UK
J F M A M J J A S O N D

DRAMATIC DIVER
The Kingfisher makes a dramatic dive usually from a low perch, but sometimes also from a brief hover.

Length **16–17cm (6½in)**	Wingspan **24–26cm (9½–10in)**	Weight **35–40g (1¼–1⁷⁄₁₆oz)**
Social **Pairs**	Lifespan **5–10 years**	Status **Declining**

| Order **Coraciiformes** | Family **Meropidae** | Species **Merops apiaster** |

Bee-eater

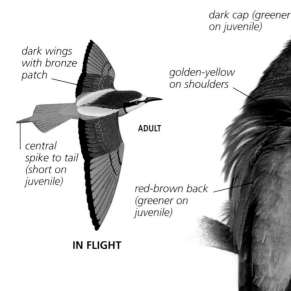

dark cap (greener on juvenile)

long, pointed bill

dark wings with bronze patch

golden-yellow on shoulders

large yellow throat

ADULT

central spike to tail (short on juvenile)

red-brown back (greener on juvenile)

clear green-blue underside

ADULT (AT NEST)

IN FLIGHT

translucent silver and copper underwings

ADULT

FLIGHT: rises on stiff, fast-beating wings; stalls, circles, and glides down, or chases prey with further beats of wings and flat-winged glides.

ADULT

long tail

tail spike may break off

black edge

One of the more colourful of Europe's birds, the Bee-eater is unique also in its shape, actions, and calls: these combine to make it easy to identify even without its colour. There are, however, several similar species in Africa and the Middle East. Bee-eaters often perch on wires, and so are easy to see from moving vehicles beside roads; they also fly around calling, drawing attention to themselves, and breed in colonies. They do indeed eat bees and seem to be somewhat immune to bee and wasp stings, although they do wipe away the stings of their prey before swallowing them. With care, Bee-eaters can be watched closely around breeding colonies and take little notice of people while feeding in elegant, swooping flight.

VOICE Distinctive, far-carrying, deep, quite liquid notes, *prroop prroop*.
NESTING Burrows in sandy banks or even flatter ground; 4–7 eggs; 1 brood; May–June.
FEEDING Catches insects in flight, in prolonged, fast swoops and slow, gliding flights or sallies from perch.

SOCIAL BIRDS
Bee-eaters are found in flocks all year round and frequently perch almost shoulder to shoulder.

OCCURRENCE
Breeds in S and E Europe, north to C France and Alps in summer. Rare migrant farther north in spring or autumn. Usually in warm, often sandy areas with orchards, bushy areas, open grassland, and low earth cliffs.

| Seen in the UK |
| J F M A M J J A S O N D |

SIMILAR SPECIES

STARLING
♂♀; similar basic shape; see p.380

shorter wings

| Length **27–29cm (10½–11½in)** | Wingspan **36–40cm (14–16in)** | Weight **50–70g (1¾–2½oz)** |
| Social **Flocks** | Lifespan **5–10 years** | Status **Declining** |

257

Order **Coraciiformes**	Family **Coraciidae**	Species **Coracias garrulus**

Roller

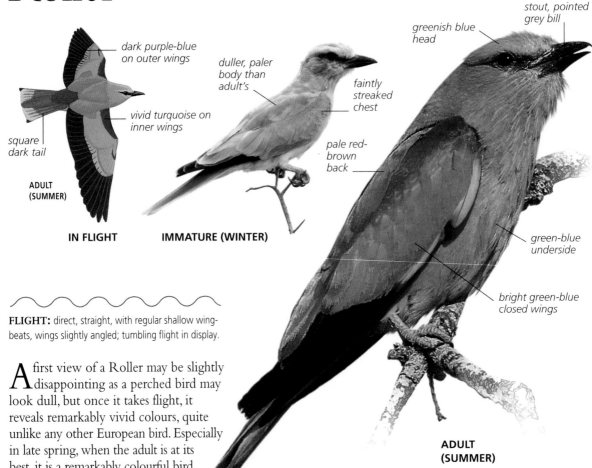

dark purple-blue on outer wings

duller, paler body than adult's

greenish blue head

stout, pointed grey bill

faintly streaked chest

vivid turquoise on inner wings

square dark tail

pale red-brown back

ADULT (SUMMER)

IN FLIGHT

IMMATURE (WINTER)

green-blue underside

bright green-blue closed wings

ADULT (SUMMER)

FLIGHT: direct, straight, with regular shallow wing-beats, wings slightly angled; tumbling flight in display.

A first view of a Roller may be slightly disappointing as a perched bird may look dull, but once it takes flight, it reveals remarkably vivid colours, quite unlike any other European bird. Especially in late spring, when the adult is at its best, it is a remarkably colourful bird, as the dull, pale feather edges of winter wear away. Rollers are most characteristic of southeast Europe, less common in southwest Europe, and rare vagrants north of the breeding range. They often perch on wires or telephone poles, and so are usually quite easy to detect; they may also perch on the sides of trees, tucked in the shade under the canopy. In Africa, Rollers concentrate more around herds of animals or at fires, where insects are forced to fly and reveal themselves. They are very rare in summer in Europe north of their usual range.

VOICE Hard, crow-like *rak, rak-aaak,* or *rack-ak-ak.*

NESTING Hole in tree, wall, or building, or old crow nest in tree; 4–7 eggs; 1 brood; May–June.

FEEDING Eats large insects and small rodents, usually caught on ground after flurried drop from perch.

HOLE NESTER
A big, rotten cavity in an old tree is a typical nest site for this bold, strong bird.

OCCURRENCE
Breeds in S Europe, north to Baltic States in E Europe; present from May to August. In variety of open countryside with orchards, woods, bushes, and rough grassland, often perched on overhead wires or tops of isolated bushes.

Seen in the UK
J F M A M J J A S O N D

Length **30cm (12in)**	Wingspan **52–57cm (20½–22½in)**	Weight **120–190g (4–7oz)**
Social **Small flocks**	Lifespan **Up to 10 years**	Status **Declining†**

Order **Coraciiformes**	Family **Upupidae**	Species **Upupa epops**

Hoopoe 🔊 46

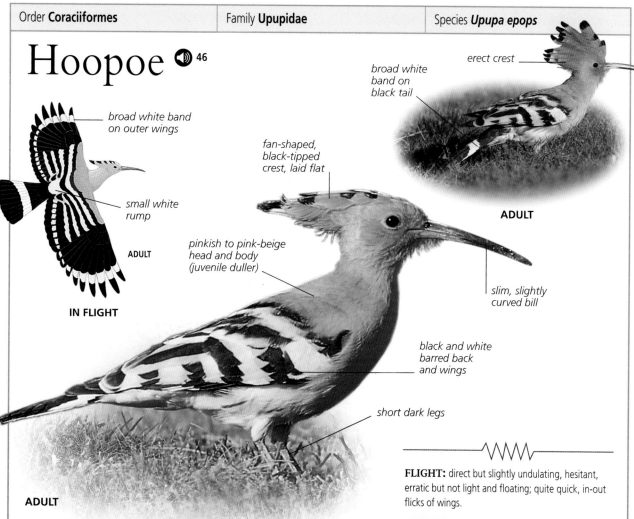

broad white band on outer wings

small white rump

ADULT

IN FLIGHT

fan-shaped, black-tipped crest, laid flat

pinkish to pink-beige head and body (juvenile duller)

erect crest

broad white band on black tail

ADULT

slim, slightly curved bill

black and white barred back and wings

short dark legs

ADULT

FLIGHT: direct but slightly undulating, hesitant, erratic but not light and floating; quite quick, in-out flicks of wings.

Unobtrusive in the dappled shade of a tree in a sunny Mediterranean grove, the Hoopoe bursts to vivid life as it takes flight, revealing a dazzling pattern of black and white. When it settles, it may raise its unique fan-shaped crest, which may also be fanned in flight. It calls from a rooftop or tree, with crest raised, but otherwise remains quiet and quite hard to spot. Its colours are quite subdued, not vivid, but the pattern is remarkable and quite unlike any other European bird: identification is simple.

VOICE Soft, low, quite quick, hollow *poop-poop-poop*, often repeated; hoarse *scheer*.

NESTING Hole in tree or wall; 5–8 eggs; 1 brood; April–July.

FEEDING Walks on ground, probing and picking with bill, taking grubs, insects, and worms.

BLUR OF WHITE
As it alights at the nest, the Hoopoe spreads its wings in a blur of black and white.

SIMILAR SPECIES

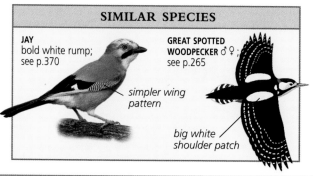

JAY
bold white rump; see p.370

simpler wing pattern

GREAT SPOTTED WOODPECKER ♂ ♀; see p.265

big white shoulder patch

OCCURRENCE
Widespread breeder and scarce migrant outside breeding areas north to Baltic; seen in summer only, except in S Spain, S Portugal, and Balearics. In open woodland, parks, gardens, old villages and farmsteads, and orchards.

Seen in the UK
J F M A M J J A S O N D

Length **26–28cm (10–11in)**	Wingspan **44–48cm (17½–19in)**	Weight **60–75g (2⅛–2⅝oz)**
Social **Family groups**	Lifespan **5–10 years**	Status **Secure**

Family **Picidae**

WOODPECKERS AND WRYNECK

MOST WOODPECKERS are tied to tree habitats but accept a wide variety of species, age, and size of tree: the Great Spotted Woodpecker may feed in willow thickets in winter, but needs bigger branches in which to nest. Others feed on the ground: the Green Woodpecker, an ant-eater, feeds on grassland much more than in trees. Others, however, are more exacting and require large amounts of dead wood, and struggle to survive in modern forests with intensive management.

There are two main groups in Europe: the green woodpeckers and the pied, or spotted, woodpeckers. Green and Grey-headed Woodpeckers are large, rather plainly patterned, with loud, laughing calls. Spotted woodpeckers are boldly barred and spotted with black and white and have varying amounts of red. They have short, sharp calls but also frequently "drum" in spring, hammering their bills hard against a resonant branch in a short, rapid drum-roll.

WRYNECK

The Wryneck is brown, barred, and streaked, and unlike other woodpeckers in its posture (it does not so often use its tail as a prop), although its calls and general behaviour indicate a close relationship. An ant-eating specialist, it often feeds on the ground. It is a migrant.

CAMOUFLAGE
Cryptic coloration makes the Wryneck difficult to see amongst branches, but it is a beautiful bird if seen well.

NUT-FEEDER
Great Spotted Woodpeckers wedge large nuts and seeds into bark for easier feeding, hammering them open with their bills.

FADED GREEN
The Green Woodpecker in worn, faded late-summer plumage, looks more brown than green.

| Order **Piciformes** | Family **Picidae** | Species **_Dryocopus martius_** |

Black Woodpecker

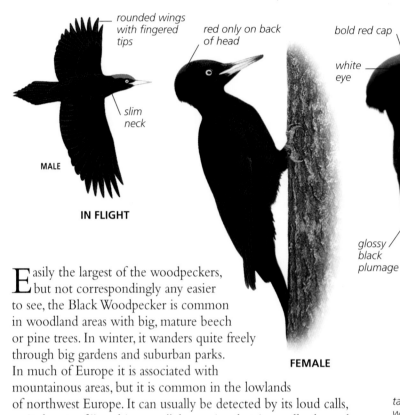

rounded wings with fingered tips

slim neck

MALE

IN FLIGHT

red only on back of head

FEMALE

dagger-like pale bill with dark tip

bold red cap

white eye

glossy black plumage

tail used as prop while perching upright

MALE

Easily the largest of the woodpeckers, but not correspondingly any easier to see, the Black Woodpecker is common in woodland areas with big, mature beech or pine trees. In winter, it wanders quite freely through big gardens and suburban parks. In much of Europe it is associated with mountainous areas, but it is common in the lowlands of northwest Europe. It can usually be detected by its loud calls, or its bursts of "machine-gun" drumming, but is usually shy and not easy to approach.

VOICE Loud, high, plaintive, long _pyuuu_; loud, rolling, far-carrying _krri-krri-krri-krri-krri_; loud Green Woodpecker-like laugh, louder, more irregular. Long, loud drumming.

NESTING Large oval hole, 9 x 12cm (3½ x 5in) in diameter, in big tree; 4–6 eggs; 1 brood; April–June.

FEEDING Digs insect larvae from tree branches and trunks and fallen timber; eats ants on ground.

FLIGHT: direct, strong, not undulating; head up, wings beat mostly below body level; swoops up to perch with quick flurry.

HEAVY FLIGHT
Although large and heavy, the shape is typical thin-necked, square-winged woodpecker in flight.

SIMILAR SPECIES

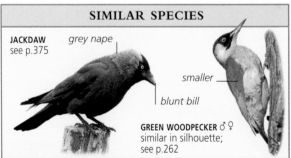

JACKDAW see p.375

grey nape

blunt bill

smaller

GREEN WOODPECKER ♂♀ similar in silhouette; see p.262

JACKDAW see p.375
GREEN WOODPECKER ♂♀ similar in silhouette; see p.262

OCCURRENCE
Breeds widely from N Spain east through France, north to Scandinavia; absent from most of Italy, UK, and Iceland. Associated with big trees in mature woods or clumps within patchy forest. Wanders more widely in winter.

| Seen in the UK |
| J F M A M J J A S O N D |

| Length **40–46cm (16–18in)** | Wingspan **67–73cm (26–29in)** | Weight **250–370g (9–13oz)** |
| Social **Solitary** | Lifespan **Up to 10 years** | Status **Secure** |

Order **Piciformes**	Family **Picidae**	Species **Picus viridis**

Green Woodpecker 🔊 47

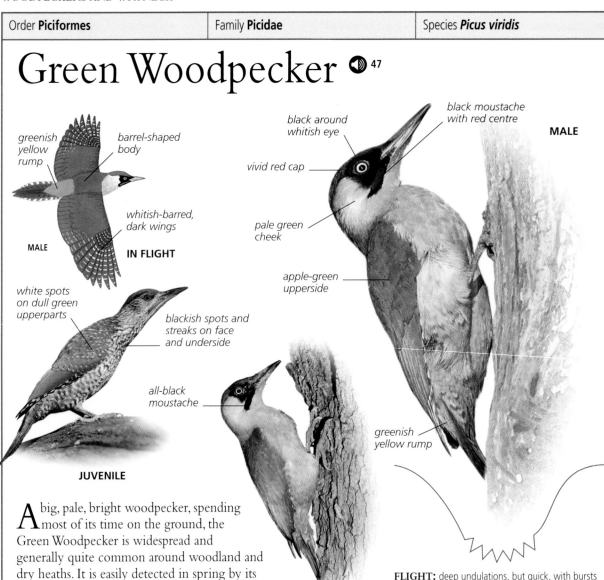

greenish yellow rump

barrel-shaped body

whitish-barred, dark wings

MALE

IN FLIGHT

black around whitish eye

black moustache with red centre

MALE

vivid red cap

pale green cheek

apple-green upperside

white spots on dull green upperparts

blackish spots and streaks on face and underside

all-black moustache

greenish yellow rump

JUVENILE

FEMALE

A big, pale, bright woodpecker, spending most of its time on the ground, the Green Woodpecker is widespread and generally quite common around woodland and dry heaths. It is easily detected in spring by its loud calls; its typical flight call is also far-carrying and distinctive. It excavates its own nest hole but has a less powerful bill than the pied woodpeckers, feeding far less on insect larvae in timber or under bark, and it rarely drums. It is a typical woodpecker in flight, having a deeply undulating action and a final upward swoop to a perch.

VOICE Loud, shrill, bouncing *keu-keu-keuk*; song ringing, slightly descending, laughing *kleu-kleu-kleu-keu-keu*.

NESTING Large hole in tree, 6.5cm (2½in) in diameter; 5–7 eggs; 1 brood; May–July.

FEEDING Eats ants and ant eggs and larvae, using long, sticky tongue to probe nests.

FLIGHT: deep undulations, but quick, with bursts of fast wingbeats between closed-winged glides.

SUBSPECIES
greyer head
black around eye
P. v. sharpei ♂ (Spain, Portugal)

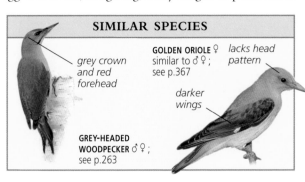

SIMILAR SPECIES

grey crown and red forehead

GOLDEN ORIOLE ♀ similar to ♂♀; see p.367

lacks head pattern

darker wings

GREY-HEADED WOODPECKER ♂♀; see p.263

OCCURRENCE
Widespread resident except in Iceland, Ireland, and most of N Scandinavia. In or around broadleaved and mixed woodland and heath-like places with bushes and clumps of trees. Regularly feeds on large lawns and other open grassy areas with ants.

Seen in the UK
J F M A M J J A S O N D

Length **30–33cm (12–13in)**	Wingspan **40–42cm (16–16½in)**	Weight **180–220g (6–8oz)**
Social **Solitary**	Lifespan **5–10 years**	Status **Declining**

Order **Piciformes**	Family **Picidae**	Species *Picus canus*

Grey-headed Woodpecker

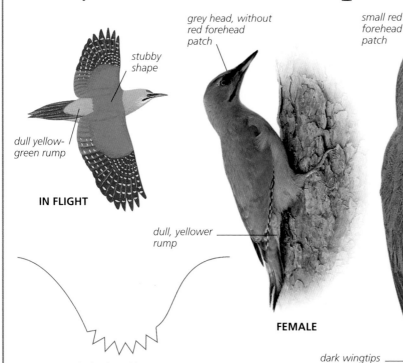

stubby shape

grey head, without red forehead patch

small red forehead patch

slender black moustache

pale grey-green back

IN FLIGHT

dull yellow-green rump

dull, yellower rump

FEMALE

dark wingtips and tail frame

FLIGHT: quick, deeply undulating, swoops up to perch.

MALE

Very like a Green Woodpecker at first glance, the Grey-headed is smaller-billed and a greyer-looking bird overall, a little stockier in flight with a less obvious narrow neck. It can be lured closer by imitating its distinctive call, which is by far the easiest way to locate it.

VOICE Series of loud notes, less ringing than the Green Woodpecker, becoming both slower and lower in pitch, characteristically 'fading out'.

NESTING Excavates hole in tree, such as aspen, beech, or oak, about 5.5cm (2¼in) across; 7–9 eggs; 1 brood; April–July.

FEEDING Eats insects, especially ants taken from ground, but more varied diet than the Green Woodpecker, including sap from holes in bark.

SIMILAR SPECIES

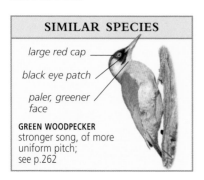

large red cap

black eye patch

paler, greener face

GREEN WOODPECKER stronger song, of more uniform pitch; see p.262

TYPICAL WOODPECKER
Like other woodpeckers, the Grey-headed uses its stiff, spread tail as a support when perching upright on a branch or stump, but it can hang beneath a branch, clinging on with its strong feet and claws.

OCCURRENCE
Widespread resident in forests, parks, and riverside trees, also in higher upland mixed forest, in central and eastern Europe.

Seen in the UK											
J	F	M	A	M	J	J	A	S	O	N	D

Length **27–30cm (11–12in)**	Wingspan **38–40cm (15–16in)**	Weight **125–165g (4–6oz)**
Social **Family groups**	Lifespan **5–10 years**	Status **Declining**

| Order **Piciformes** | Family **Picidae** | Species *Picoides tridactylus* |

Three-toed Woodpecker

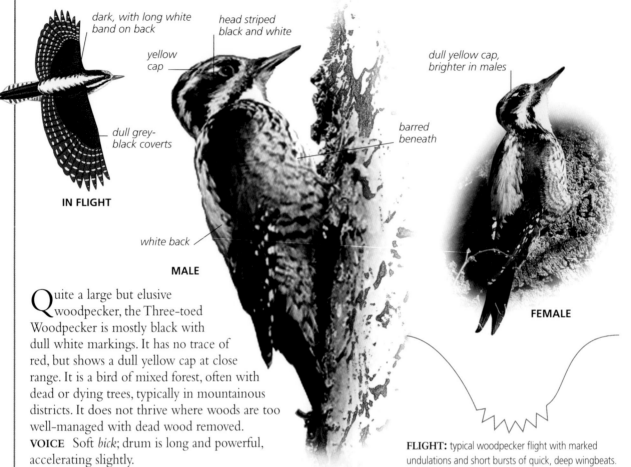

dark, with long white band on back

yellow cap

head striped black and white

dull grey-black coverts

IN FLIGHT

white back

MALE

barred beneath

dull yellow cap, brighter in males

FEMALE

Quite a large but elusive woodpecker, the Three-toed Woodpecker is mostly black with dull white markings. It has no trace of red, but shows a dull yellow cap at close range. It is a bird of mixed forest, often with dead or dying trees, typically in mountainous districts. It does not thrive where woods are too well-managed with dead wood removed.

VOICE Soft *bick*; drum is long and powerful, accelerating slightly.

NESTING Excavates a cavity about 5cm (2in) wide in trunk or larger branch of dead or dying tree; 3–5 eggs; 1 brood; April–June.

FEEDING Drills holes to take sap from bark and strips bark from dead trees to reach insect larvae beneath, especially of wood-boring beetles.

FLIGHT: typical woodpecker flight with marked undulations and short bursts of quick, deep wingbeats.

NEST CAVITY
In typical woodpecker style, Three toed Woodpecker excavates a nest hole in a pine tree and can most easily be located there in summer as it returns to feed its young.

SIMILAR SPECIES

red cap

pink or red under tail

WHITE BACKED WOODPECKER; see p.446

OCCURRENCE
Scarce resident woodpecker of mixed or coniferous forest, especially mature spruce, with dead trees intermixed, in north and, very locally, central Europe.

| Seen in the UK |
| J F M A M J J A S O N D |

| Length **22–24cm (9–9½in)** | Wingspan **34–38cm (13½–15in)** | Weight **65–75g (2⅜–2⅝oz)** |
| Social **Family groups** | Lifespan **5–10 years** | Status **Secure** |

Order **Piciformes**	Family **Picidae**	Species ***Dendrocopos major***

Great Spotted Woodpecker 🔊 48.I, 48.II

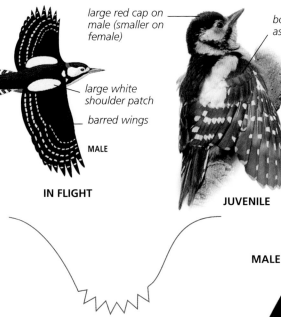

large red cap on male (smaller on female)

large white shoulder patch

barred wings

MALE

IN FLIGHT

body and wings as adult but duller

JUVENILE

red patch on back of head

bold black and white upperparts

bright buff underside

MALE

large vivid red patch under tail

no red on nape

FLIGHT: fast, springy bounds, deeply undulating, with short bursts of whirring wingbeats.

FEMALE

The common woodpecker in most areas, the Great Spotted announces itself in spring by a loud drumming: a rapid, abrupt "drum roll" made by hammering the bill against a resonant branch. It uses its stiff tail as a prop, so that it can grip a branch while resting upright against it. Its grip is secure enough to enable it to hang beneath a branch without the help of its tail for a time. Careful observation is required to be sure of woodpecker identification where several woodpecker species overlap.

VOICE Loud, hard, explosive *tchik!*, less often fast, chattering rattle of alarm; loud, fast, very short drum.

NESTING Digs hole, diameter 5–6cm (2–2¼in), in trunk or branch of tree; 4–7 eggs; 1 brood; April–June.

FEEDING Finds insects and larvae beneath bark, digging them out with strong bill; also takes seeds and berries; visits gardens for nuts, seeds, cheese, and fat.

NUT FEEDER
The woodpecker uses its stiff tail to help secure a good grip on a basket of peanuts.

OCCURRENCE
Inhabits mature woods and even scrub, locally visiting gardens, all over Europe except for Iceland, Ireland, and extreme N Scandinavia. Some migrants from N Europe move south and west in winter, turning up on open islands at times.

Seen in the UK
| J | F | M | A | M | J | J | A | S | O | N | D |

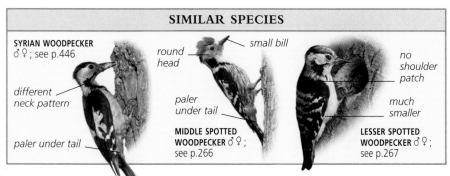

SIMILAR SPECIES

SYRIAN WOODPECKER ♂♀; see p.446

different neck pattern

paler under tail

round head

small bill

paler under tail

MIDDLE SPOTTED WOODPECKER ♂♀; see p.266

no shoulder patch

much smaller

LESSER SPOTTED WOODPECKER ♂♀; see p.267

Length **22–23cm (9in)**	Wingspan **34–39cm (13½–15½in)**	Weight **70–90g (2½–3¼oz)**
Social **Solitary**	Lifespan **5–10 years**	Status **Secure**

| Order **Piciformes** | Family **Picidae** | Species ***Dendrocopos medius*** |

Middle Spotted Woodpecker

white barring on wings

MALE

IN FLIGHT

flame-red cap on small white head

unmarked white cheeks

duller cap than male's

FEMALE

weak, short bill

black neck patch extends onto side of chest

white shoulder patch

finely streaked yellow-buff underside

pinkish under tail

MALE

A Central European bird, the Middle Spotted Woodpecker is indeed medium-sized among the pied woodpeckers. Much less accommodating than other woodpeckers in its choice of habitat, it requires tall, old woodland with some old and dying trees and some small clearings, with a selection of decaying branches in which it can nest. In many regions with intensively managed woodland and young plantations, it is unable to survive. It is relatively quiet and fond of staying high in trees, so it is easy to overlook. It calls more often in spring in preference to drumming.

VOICE Song quite slow repetition of nasal *kvek-kvek-kvek-kvek*, infrequent weak *kik*, quick, rhythmic *kuk-uk kuk-uk- kuk-uk*; does not drum.

NESTING Excavates hole in rotten branch, 4cm (1½in) diameter; 4–7 eggs; 1 brood; May–June.

FEEDING Finds insects, larvae, and sap in high branches, often in dead or dying wood.

FLIGHT: typical quick, bounding undulations with bursts of fast wingbeats.

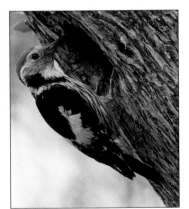

SECRETIVE NESTER
Until the young begin to call, this woodpecker, like other wood-peckers, is quiet around the nest.

OCCURRENCE
Breeds locally in N Spain, France, and east to E Europe and Balkans. Mostly in older woodland with some dead and decaying trees and usually not able to survive in over-managed woods and young or uniform plantations.

| Seen in the UK |
| J F M A M J J A S O N D |

SIMILAR SPECIES

GREAT SPOTTED WOODPECKER ♂♀; see p.265
slightly different head pattern
bolder red under tail
bigger bill
barred above
LESSER SPOTTED WOODPECKER ♂♀; see p.267
different head pattern
lacks white shoulder patch
SYRIAN WOODPECKER ♂♀; see p.446

| Length **19–22cm (7½–9in)** | Wingspan **35cm (14in)** | Weight **60–75g (2⅛–2⅝oz)** |
| Social **Solitary** | Lifespan **5–10 years** | Status **Secure** |

Order **Piciformes**	Family **Picidae**	Species ***Dendrocopos minor***

Lesser Spotted Woodpecker

broad, rounded wings

red cap

black cap

black cheek patch

short tail

MALE

IN FLIGHT

some red on crown (more on male)

black back with broad white bars

barred back

JUVENILE

FEMALE

buff-white underside, finely streaked

MALE

FLIGHT: quite weak and uncertain; bursts of wingbeats between swoops with closed wings in deep, bouncy undulations.

Certainly the smallest of the woodpeckers, this is also the least strikingly patterned, its barring somewhat blurred and diffuse. It is, however, clearly a pied woodpecker although it spends much of its time in the higher, more slender branches of trees, unlike the others. It prefers limes, elms, and other trees with very upright twigs, and uses its tail as a prop like most other woodpeckers, clinging more or less upright to its perch. Because of its size and generally quiet demeanour, it is easy to overlook, but in most areas is genuinely rather scarce.

VOICE Sharp, weak *tchik*, nasal, peevish *pee-pee-pee-pee-pee-pee* especially in spring; weak drum.

NESTING Hole in tree, 3cm (1¼in) in diameter; 4–6 eggs; 1 brood; May–June.

FEEDING Chips out insects and their larvae from beneath loose or rotten bark; also takes insects from thick, woody plant stems close to ground.

OCCURRENCE
In most of Europe except Iceland, Ireland, N UK, and much of Spain and Portugal. Widespread in woodland, copses, orchards, and tall hedges with old or diseased trees. Resident, except for local movements which take it into gardens and parks.

Seen in the UK
J F M A M J J A S O N D

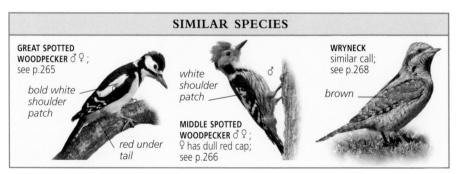

SIMILAR SPECIES

GREAT SPOTTED WOODPECKER ♂♀; see p.265

bold white shoulder patch

red under tail

white shoulder patch

♂

MIDDLE SPOTTED WOODPECKER ♂♀; ♀ has dull red cap; see p.266

WRYNECK similar call; see p.268

brown

Length **14–15cm (5½–6in)**	Wingspan **25–27cm (10–10½in)**	Weight **18–22g (⅝–¹³⁄₁₆oz)**
Social **Solitary**	Lifespan **5–10 years**	Status **Secure**

Order **Piciformes**	Family **Picidae**	Species *Jynx torquilla*

Wryneck

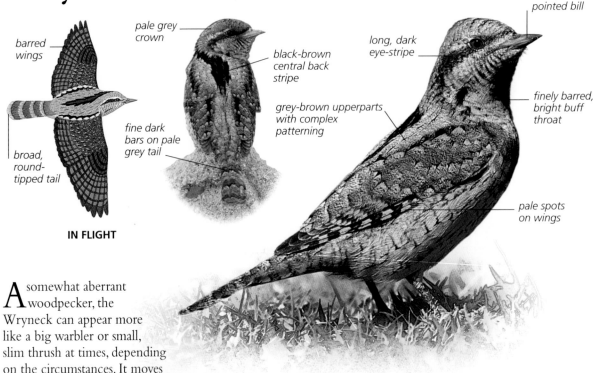

barred wings

pale grey crown

black-brown central back stripe

grey-brown upperparts with complex patterning

short, slim, pointed bill

long, dark eye-stripe

finely barred, bright buff throat

fine dark bars on pale grey tail

broad, round-tipped tail

IN FLIGHT

pale spots on wings

A somewhat aberrant woodpecker, the Wryneck can appear more like a big warbler or small, slim thrush at times, depending on the circumstances. It moves about on the ground, flits up into trees or bushes, or slips through foliage, but also clambers around on thick branches and trunks of trees, although it usually perches across branches rather than upright like the more common woodpeckers. At moderate range it is rather dull and inconspicuous, but close views reveal both an intricate pattern and clean, bright golden-buff colours. Once located, the Wryneck may often be watched really closely for long periods, especially on migration. Occasionally it may then turn up in unexpected places such as parks and gardens.

VOICE Quick, repeated, nasal notes, *kwee-kee-kee-kee-kee-kee-kee*, lower than Kestrel's or Lesser Spotted Woodpecker's.

NESTING Existing hole in tree or wall; 7–10 eggs; 1, occasionally 2, broods; May–June.

FEEDING Often on ground, eating ants and ant larvae; various other insects, spiders, woodlice, and some berries.

FLIGHT: usually short flights, slightly undulating, with flurries of quick beats.

CRYPTIC COLOURS
The mottled pattern of a Wryneck gives excellent camouflage against the bark of a tree and it can be very difficult to spot.

OCCURRENCE
Widespread but scarce in summer, except in Iceland, Ireland, UK, and N Scandinavia. Breeds in farmed countryside with trees, copses, and more extensive pine or mixed forest; migrants often near coast. Scarce migrant in UK, chiefly in autumn.

Seen in the UK
J F M **A M J** J **A S** O N D

SIMILAR SPECIES

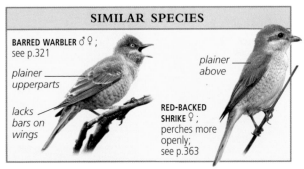

BARRED WARBLER ♂♀;
see p.321

plainer upperparts

lacks bars on wings

RED-BACKED SHRIKE ♀;
perches more openly;
see p.363

plainer above

Length **16–17cm (6½in)**	Wingspan **25–27cm (10–10½in)**	Weight **30–45g (1¹⁄₁₆–1⅝oz)**
Social **Solitary**	Lifespan **5–10 years**	Status **Declining**

Family **Alaudidae**

LARKS

Almost exclusively ground birds, except when singing, larks are quite stocky but long-bodied birds, bulkier than pipits or wagtails, but less chunky than most finches. They have thick, triangular bills – between the insect-eating bill of a pipit and the seed-eating bill of a finch, reflecting their varied diet. They fly strongly, with quite long, often rather angular wings.

Larks have faintly short legs but long toes and claws, especially the claws on their hind toes, which seem to be an adaptation for walking through grassy vegetation. They move easily on the ground in a quick walk or run, and feed on open ground: the Skylark, for example, will rarely feed in the shadow of a hedge, preferring to keep well out in the open where it has a good all-round view and from where it can fly in any direction.

Being birds of open spaces, larks have no perches from which to sing: they do sing from the ground or a post, but are at their best when singing in a special high song-flight. The Skylark sings for minutes on end in a simple rising hover, while the Woodlark flies in wide circles as it sings.

Plumages of males and females, winter and summer, are usually much alike, although some juveniles are sufficiently different to look unusual. Some species are very difficult to identify: calls

STRONG FLIER
Skylarks have large wings: these give them a slightly thrush-like look in flight but their more angular wings have a straighter rear edge.

and songs are helpful but awkward plumage points such as underwing colour (on Crested and Thekla Larks) can be hard to see and structural differences (such as wingtip length on Short-toed and Lesser Short-toed Larks) can be frustratingly difficult to be sure of.

UPSTANDING CREST
Several larks have a vestigial crest, but two, the very similar Crested and Thekla larks, have obvious, triangular crests that can be held erect. This Crested Lark shows the sharp point well.

Order **Passeriformes**	Family **Alaudidae**	Species *Alauda arvensis*

Skylark 49.I, 49.II

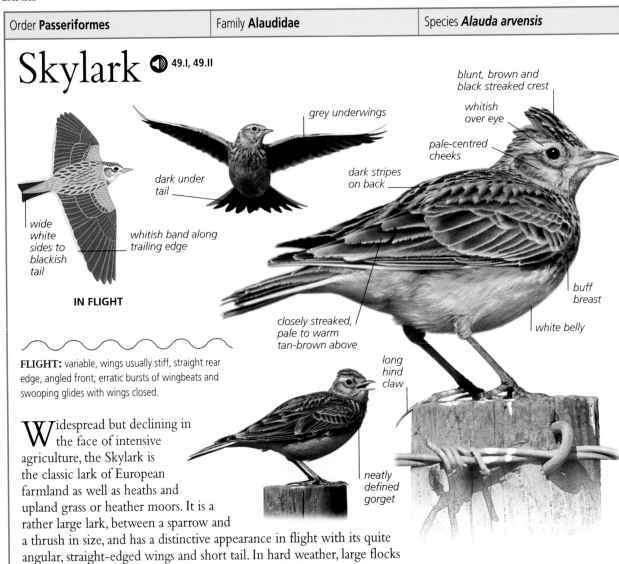

blunt, brown and black streaked crest

whitish over eye

pale-centred cheeks

grey underwings

dark under tail

dark stripes on back

dark stripes on back

buff breast

white belly

wide white sides to blackish tail

whitish band along trailing edge

closely streaked, pale to warm tan-brown above

long hind claw

IN FLIGHT

neatly defined gorget

FLIGHT: variable, wings usually stiff, straight rear edge, angled front; erratic bursts of wingbeats and swooping glides with wings closed.

Widespread but declining in the face of intensive agriculture, the Skylark is the classic lark of European farmland as well as heaths and upland grass or heather moors. It is a rather large lark, between a sparrow and a thrush in size, and has a distinctive appearance in flight with its quite angular, straight-edged wings and short tail. In hard weather, large flocks may pass over by day heading for milder refuges, looking very like flocks of Redwings (see p.314). When feeding, flocks tend to move more loosely, looking uncoordinated in comparison with most finch and bunting flocks.

VOICE Calls chirruping *shrrup*, *trrup*, higher *seee*; song from perch or in high, soaring flight, fast, rich, continuous outpouring, at distance sounding thinner and high-pitched.

NESTING Grassy cup on ground, in crop or grass; 3–5 eggs; 2 or 3 broods; April–July.

FEEDING Forages on ground in grass or on bare earth, eating seeds, shoots, grain, and insects.

SONG-FLIGHT
The Skylark rises vertically in song-flight with constant flickering; it has a rising hover and final steep plunge.

OCCURRENCE
Widespread except in Iceland, breeding on open moorland, heaths, cultivated areas in lowlands, especially cereals, and extensive pastures. In winter, widespread on arable land, with birds from N and E Europe moving south and west in sizeable flocks.

Seen in the UK
J F M A M J J A S O N D

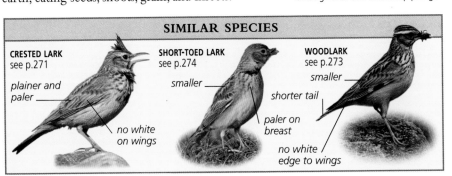

SIMILAR SPECIES

CRESTED LARK
see p.271

plainer and paler

no white on wings

SHORT-TOED LARK
see p.274

smaller

paler on breast

no white edge to wings

WOODLARK
see p.273

smaller

shorter tail

Length **18–19cm (7–7½in)**	Wingspan **30–36cm (12–14in)**	Weight **33–45g (1³⁄₁₆–1⅝oz)**
Social **Flocks**	Lifespan **Up to 5 years**	Status **Vulnerable**

Order **Passeriformes**	Family **Alaudidae**	Species *Galerida cristata*

Crested Lark 🔊 50

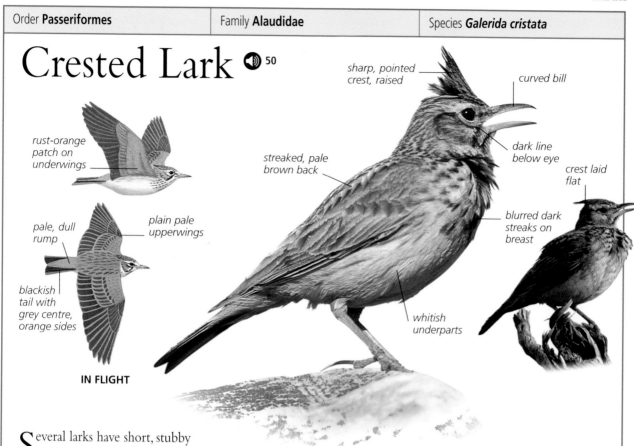

sharp, pointed crest, raised

curved bill

dark line below eye

crest laid flat

streaked, pale brown back

blurred dark streaks on breast

rust-orange patch on underwings

pale, dull rump

plain pale upperwings

blackish tail with grey centre, orange sides

whitish underparts

IN FLIGHT

S everal larks have short, stubby crests, which may be raised but still look blunt: only the Crested and Thekla Larks have really obvious pointed crests in Europe. The two are difficult to tell apart, but it is the Crested that is by far the more widespread and common, both in range and habitat selection. It is typically, however, a bird of farmed land, often seen at the side of roads, flying up in front of passing traffic to reveal its broad, round wings and short tail. It seldom perches on bushes, as the Thekla Lark sometimes does.

VOICE Rich, fluty, liquid call, *tree-loo-ee or vee-vee-teu*; song from perch or in high, circling flight similar in quality with fluty, melancholy notes.

NESTING Small hollow on ground, in grass, lined with fine stems; 3–6 eggs; 2 or 3 broods; April–June.

FEEDING Forages on ground, often on bare patches, for insects, seeds, and shoots.

FLIGHT: floppy, heavy, bounding, with bursts of slowish wingbeats and swooping glides; song-flight high, circling.

SLIM AND ALERT
A Crested Lark in mild alarm raises its crest and stretches tall and slim; when relaxed, it will look rounder.

OCCURRENCE
Widespread but patchily distributed breeding bird north to Denmark and Baltic States; rare vagrant farther north. Typically in cultivated areas or semi-natural vegetation with few trees, sometimes in semi-derelict places or disturbed ground with light, sandy soils, and on airport grassland.

Seen in the UK
J F M A M J J A S O N D

SIMILAR SPECIES

much shorter crest

white edge to wings

shorter crest

THEKLA LARK
greyer underwings; stronger streaks on breast; see p.272

LESSER SHORT-TOED LARK
see p.446

SKYLARK
see p.270

Length **17–19cm (6½–7½in)**	Wingspan **30–35cm (12–14in)**	Weight **30–35g (1¹/₁₆–1¼oz)**
Social **Small flocks**	Lifespan **Up to 5 years**	Status **Declining†**

Order **Passeriformes**	Family **Alaudidae**	Species *Galeridae theklae*

Thekla Lark

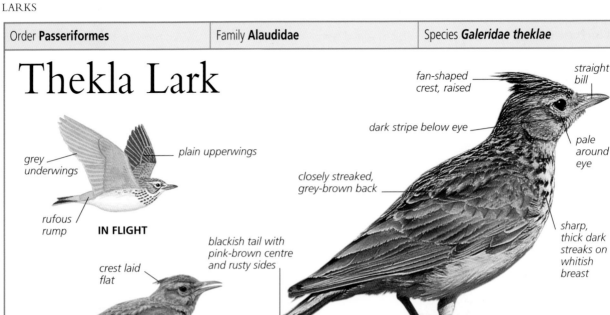

grey underwings

plain upperwings

rufous rump **IN FLIGHT**

fan-shaped crest, raised

straight bill

dark stripe below eye

pale around eye

closely streaked, grey-brown back

sharp, thick dark streaks on whitish breast

blackish tail with pink-brown centre and rusty sides

crest laid flat

white belly

Like the Crested Lark, the Thekla Lark has a quite obvious pointed crest, although somewhat blunter and more fan-shaped than the Crested's sharp spike. Theklas are found less in cereal fields than Cresteds, although they do occupy stony slopes with small corn fields separated by bushes and hedges. More usually, they occupy orchards and clearings in open woodland, or rough, open areas of stony grassland and barren rocky slopes. Plumage and call differences from other larks (especially the Crested Lark) are very subtle, and its identification is often based on a combination of factors.

FLIGHT: series of quick flaps between short glides; high, soaring song-flight.

VOICE Full-throated, musical call, *tu-tewi, tew-tewi-loo*, variable number of notes; song varied, liquid, rich warble in flight, much like Crested Lark's.

NESTING Shallow hollow on ground, in grass or other vegetation; 3–5 eggs; 2 broods; April–June.

FEEDING Picks shoots, seeds, and insects from ground.

CAMOUFLAGE
Thekla and Crested Larks vary only slightly in colour, both often matching the general colour of the local rocks and soil.

OCCURRENCE
Breeds in Spain, Portugal, and very locally in S France. In dry, cultivated areas with trees, rocky, grassy hillsides, and mountain slopes, either open and treeless, or bushy slopes with scattered boulders and taller trees. Strictly resident.

Seen in the UK
J F M A M J J A S O N D

SIMILAR SPECIES

CRESTED LARK more orange underwings; see p.271

longer bill

white tail sides

SKYLARK white trailing edge to wings; see p.270

WOODLARK blackish edge of wings; see p.273

smaller

Length **15–17cm (6–6½in)**	Wingspan **30–35cm (12–14in)**	Weight **30g (1¹⁄₁₆oz)**
Social **Small flocks**	Lifespan **Up to 5 years**	Status **Vulnerable**

Order **Passeriformes**	Family **Alaudidae**	Species *Lullula arborea*

Woodlark 51

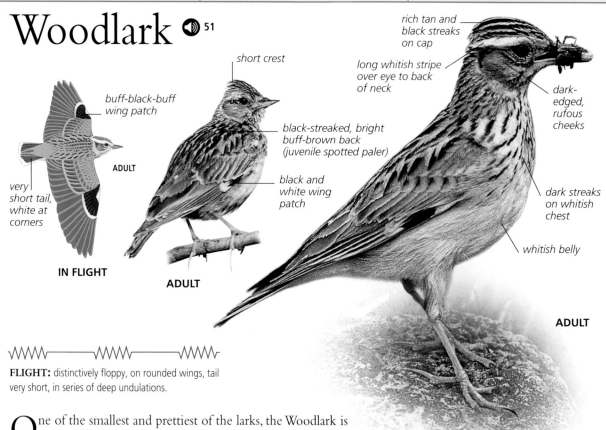

short crest

buff-black-buff wing patch

ADULT

very short tail, white at corners

IN FLIGHT

ADULT

black-streaked, bright buff-brown back (juvenile spotted paler)

black and white wing patch

rich tan and black streaks on cap

long whitish stripe over eye to back of neck

dark-edged, rufous cheeks

dark streaks on whitish chest

whitish belly

ADULT

WWWW ——— WWWW ——— WWWW

FLIGHT: distinctively floppy, on rounded wings, tail very short, in series of deep undulations.

One of the smallest and prettiest of the larks, the Woodlark is principally a bird of open woodland, woodland clearings, sandy heaths, and felled or replanted conifer plantations on sandy soils. In early spring, males sing from trees or in a wandering, circling song-flight, producing a highly distinctive song. In winter, small flocks wander widely over cultivated ground and under thinly scattered trees. When feeding Woodlarks are approached, they may fly off at some distance, or crouch and rely on camouflage to avoid detection, not flying up until the last moment.

VOICE Call varies on three-syllable pattern, first low and quiet *t'loo-i* or *ti-loooi*; song rich, slow, fluty diminuendos, *tlootlootloo*, *twee twee twee twee*, *dyoo dyoo dyoo dyoo*, *dlui dlui dlui*, in high, circling flight.

NESTING Hair- and grass-lined nest on ground near bush; 3 or 4 eggs; 2 broods; April–June.

FEEDING Picks up insects and small seeds from ground, often on bare, sandy patches.

GROUND FEEDER
The Woodlark spends most of its time feeding or standing on the ground, or on low logs and stumps.

OCCURRENCE
Widespread up to S Great Britain and S Scandinavia; in summer, only in north and east of range, breeding in open woodland, on bushy heaths, and especially in felled woodland such as extensive conifer plantations with areas of bare, sandy ground and short grass. On fields in winter.

Seen in the UK
J F M A M J J A S O N D

SIMILAR SPECIES

SKYLARK
see p.270

longer tail

larger

CRESTED LARK
see p.271

upstanding crest

smaller and rustier

paler and plainer

thicker bill

LINNET ♀;
see p.390

Length **15cm (6in)**	Wingspan **27–30cm (10½–12in)**	Weight **24–36g (⅞–1⁵⁄₁₆oz)**
Social **Winter flocks**	Lifespan **Up to 5 years**	Status **Vulnerable**

Order **Passeriformes**	Family **Alaudidae**	Species *Calandrella brachydactyla*

Short-toed Lark

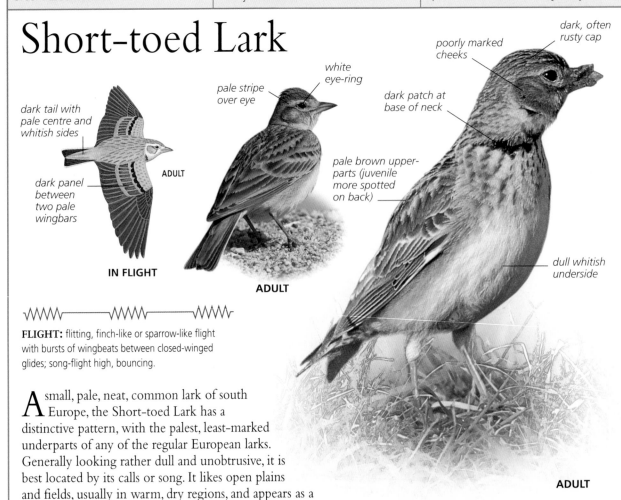

dark tail with pale centre and whitish sides

ADULT

dark panel between two pale wingbars

IN FLIGHT

pale stripe over eye

white eye-ring

ADULT

pale brown upper-parts (juvenile more spotted on back)

poorly marked cheeks

dark, often rusty cap

dark patch at base of neck

dull whitish underside

ADULT

FLIGHT: flitting, finch-like or sparrow-like flight with bursts of wingbeats between closed-winged glides; song-flight high, bouncing.

A small, pale, neat, common lark of south Europe, the Short-toed Lark has a distinctive pattern, with the palest, least-marked underparts of any of the regular European larks. Generally looking rather dull and unobtrusive, it is best located by its calls or song. It likes open plains and fields, usually in warm, dry regions, and appears as a rare migrant outside the normal breeding range regularly in very small numbers. As a migrant, it is often found in coastal areas, particularly sandy fields and grasslands.

VOICE Chirruping, sparrowy *chrrit* or *trilp*, sometimes buzzy like Lesser Short-toed Lark's; song of short, spitting, unmusical bursts or longer, more varied, fast warbling with calls intermixed.

NESTING Shallow nest on ground in grass, lined with finer material; 3–5 eggs; 2 broods; May–July.

FEEDING Searches ground for seeds and insects.

SLENDER LARK
The Short-toed is a rather long and slim lark, with the long wings and tail giving it a tapered shape.

OCCURRENCE
Widespread in Spain, Portugal, Italy, Balkans, and local in France, breeding in dry open places from cultivated land or rough grassland to semi-desert. Migrates to Africa in winter. Some wander farther north as rare migrants in spring and autumn.

Seen in the UK
J F M A M J J A S O N D

SIMILAR SPECIES

SKYLARK
white edge to wings in flight;
see p.270

streaked breast

longer wingtips

LESSER SHORT-TOED LARK
see p.446

more streaked breast

CORN BUNTING
see p.413

bigger bill

much bigger

Length **14–16cm (5½–6½in)**	Wingspan **30cm (12in)**	Weight **25g (⅞oz)**
Social **Small flocks**	Lifespan **Up to 5 years**	Status **Vulnerable**

| Order **Passeriformes** | Family **Alaudidae** | Species *Melanocorypha calandra* |

Calandra Lark

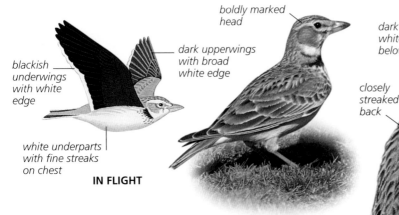

boldly marked head

dark upperwings with broad white edge

blackish underwings with white edge

white underparts with fine streaks on chest

IN FLIGHT

streaked cap

large, triangular, pale bill with dark ridge

dark cheeks, white-edged below

closely streaked back

large black neck patch

FLIGHT: low, heavy, shallow but sometimes quick wingbeats; song-flight high, drifting, with unusually slow wingbeats.

This large, hefty lark of Mediterranean regions is characteristic of open plains: either dry steppe grassland or cultivated areas with vast expanses of corn. Calandra Larks may also congregate in marshy areas, especially in salty areas in depressions or near the sea; non-breeding flocks sometimes number scores or hundreds. Like most larks, they sing in flight, drifting around high up with slow, stiff wingbeats. Resident in southwest Europe, more migratory in southeast Europe, Calandras are extremely rare vagrants farther north outside their breeding range.

VOICE Dry, sizzly or trilling *schrreeup*; song in high flight prolonged, rich, varied like Skylark's but slower.

NESTING Grass cup on ground, in vegetation; 4–7 eggs; 2 broods; April–June.

FEEDING Searches ground for seeds, shoots, and insects.

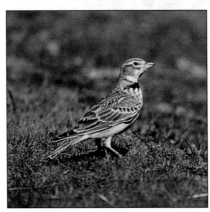

VARIABLE PATCH
The black neck patch is obvious when the lark raises its head, but is hidden when it is hunched down.

OCCURRENCE
Resident in Spain, Portugal, S France, Italy, and locally in Balkans; extremely rare outside its usual breeding range. In farmland and open, dry, stony grassland in lowlands, sometimes in flocks in saline depressions with shrubby growth.

Seen in the UK
J F M A M J J A S O N D

SIMILAR SPECIES

no dark neck patch

smaller

SHORT-TOED LARK
see p.274

much smaller neck patch

CORN BUNTING
see p.413

plainer

pale wings

paler wings

smaller and paler

SKYLARK
see p.270

| Length **17–20cm (6½–8in)** | Wingspan **35–40cm (14–16in)** | Weight **45–50g (1⅝–1¾oz)** |
| Social **Flocks** | Lifespan **Up to 5 years** | Status **Declining†** |

Order **Passeriformes**	Family **Alaudidae**	Species ***Eremophila alpestris***

Shorelark

pale centre to dark tail

plain wings

tiny "horns"

primrose-yellow face

ADULT (WINTER)

IN FLIGHT

ADULT (SUMMER)

pale yellow face and throat (juvenile lacks yellow)

black pattern on head duller than in summer

mid-brown upperparts

broad black upper chest-band

variable brown lower chest-band

white underparts

ADULT (WINTER)

An odd distribution sees the Shorelark as a breeding bird in upland Scandinavia and mountains of southeast Europe and North Africa; in between, principally around the North and Baltic Seas, it is a winter bird. As such, it prefers sandy shores and beaches with strandlines and quiet little wet and marshy spots where the receding tide leaves little pools and patches of shrubby vegetation. It may mix with Snow Buntings in such places. Before leaving in spring, groups of Shorelarks may develop full summer colours as the dull feather edges of winter wear away, creating a pattern quite unlike other European larks. Breeding birds in the Balkans are greyer, less brown, on the back than northern birds.

VOICE Pipit-like, thin *tseeeep* or louder *seep-seep*; prolonged repetition of quiet warbling song from perch or in flight.

NESTING Hair-lined grass cup, on ground; 4 eggs; 1 or 2 broods; May–July.

FEEDING Creeps about unobtrusively on ground, taking seeds, insects, crustaceans, and tiny molluscs.

FLIGHT: swift, swooping, undulating, with frequent wing closures; often circles around low over ground before landing.

HANDSOME LARK
Inconspicuous as it feeds on the ground, the Shorelark is nevertheless an attractive bird close up.

SIMILAR SPECIES

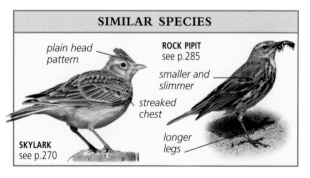

plain head pattern

ROCK PIPIT see p.285

smaller and slimmer

streaked chest

longer legs

SKYLARK see p.270

OCCURRENCE
Breeds in mountainous areas of Scandinavia. In winter, quite scarce and local around Baltic and North Seas. Mostly coastal, on beaches and marshes especially just around high-tide mark, less often on nearby open arable land.

Seen in the UK
J F M A M J J A S O N D

Length **14–17cm (5½–6½in)**	Wingspan **30–35cm (12–14in)**	Weight **35–45g (1¼–1⅝oz)**
Social **Small flocks**	Lifespan **Up to 5 years**	Status **Secure†**

Family **Hirundinidae**

MARTINS AND SWALLOWS

COLLECTIVELY KNOWN AS "hirundines", these are highly aerial birds, feeding almost entirely by catching flying insects while on the wing. They have tiny bills but wide mouths. Their feet are very small, but strong enough to give a good grasp on a wire or twig: they perch frequently, unlike swifts.

MARTINS
Martins are stockier than most swallows and lack the very long outer tail feathers that are so prominent on their close relatives. They have rather broad-based wings that taper to a point and deeply forked tails on a barrel-shaped body. House Martins make obvious mud-pellet nests on buildings while Sand Martins tunnel into sand cliffs in sizeable colonies.

SWALLOWS
The most elegant of the group, the swallows tend to feed lower down than the martins, and on

SUN-BATHING
House Martins take advantage of a rooftop in warm autumn sunlight. Their white rumps are fluffed out and obvious.

larger prey, with a more fluent, swooping flight. All have elongated outer tail feathers, which are longest on the oldest and fittest males. Red-rumped Swallows make mud-pellet nests like House Martins, but with an entrance "porch", while Swallows nest inside small buildings in a more concealed position.

In late summer and autumn, flocks of swallows and martins gather together, often using reed-beds as roosts, before migrating to Africa. House Martins seem to remain at great heights while in Africa and are little observed. Swallows from Europe occupy different parts of southern Africa during their stay there.

WIRE BIRDS
An important social trait of swallows is their habit of gathering on wires before migrating south.

| Order **Passeriformes** | Family **Hirundinidae** | Species *Riparia riparia* |

Sand Martin

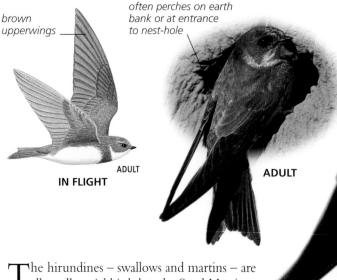

brown upperwings

often perches on earth bank or at entrance to nest-hole

IN FLIGHT

ADULT

ADULT

all-brown upperparts

brown breast-band

upright posture while perching on twigs or wires

white underparts

brown wings (juvenile has pale feather edges on wings)

ADULT

The hirundines – swallows and martins – are all small, aerial birds but the Sand Martin is the smallest, with the weakest, most fluttering flight. This is belied by the fact that it is the earliest to arrive in Europe each spring, often reaching the UK in early March. Conditions at this time are still very taxing for a bird that relies on flying insects for food. It is then that Sand Martins are restricted almost entirely to lakes and reservoirs where early insects are most reliable. They soon concentrate on their traditional colonies, but are also quick to exploit new possibilities, even small roadside cuttings and sand quarries which may only be suitable for a year or two. Artificial embankments specially made for them are successful.

VOICE Low, dry, slightly rasping or chattering *chrrrrp*; song rambling, chattering, weak twitter.

NESTING Bores long hole into earth or soft sandstone; 4 or 5 eggs; 2 broods; April–July.

FEEDING Aerial; catches insects in flight, often over water; sometimes feeds on bare ground.

FLIGHT: weak, fluttery, with fast in-out wing flicks, wings angled well back; faster when flocks going to roost in reedbeds, or if predator nearby.

COLONIES
Sand Martin colonies are easy to see in earth banks and sand quarries, but restricted to a few localities.

OCCURRENCE
Breeds in earth cliffs, sandy river banks, and gravel pits throughout Europe except Iceland. Widespread in river valleys, typically near water, and most often over water in early spring, but also in moorland areas with eroded earth cliffs.

| Seen in the UK |
| J F M **A M J J A S O** N D |

SIMILAR SPECIES

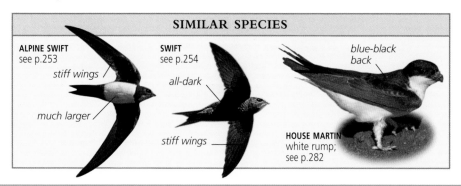

ALPINE SWIFT
see p.253

stiff wings

much larger

SWIFT
see p.254

all-dark

stiff wings

blue-black back

HOUSE MARTIN
white rump;
see p.282

| Length **12cm (4¾in)** | Wingspan **26–29cm (10–11½in)** | Weight **13–14g (⁷⁄₁₆–½oz)** |
| Social **Small flocks** | Lifespan **Up to 5 years** | Status **Declining** |

| Order **Passeriformes** | Family **Hirundinidae** | Species *Ptynoprogne rupestris* |

Crag Martin

whitish collar
below dark
cheek

dull brown back
and rump with
grey tinge

finely
streaked,
brownish
grey chin

brown tail
with oblong
white spots
near tip

blackish wedge
on underwings

very pale
brownish
grey
underside

dusky rear
underbody

IN FLIGHT

Of the European
martins, this is the largest
and the most uniform in colour, and the
finest flier. It soars and floats confidently near cliffs, using
the upcurrents expertly, often sweeping backwards and forwards
across the cliff face like the end of a pendulum, neatly tilting over
and turning at the end of each traverse. It is often accompanied by
smaller, less accomplished House Martins during these flights.
VOICE Short, high, metallic clicking notes, dry *tshirr*;
fast, twittering song.
NESTING Mud nest under overhang of cliff or building
or in cave; 4 or 5 eggs; 1 or 2 broods; April–June.
FEEDING Aerial, catching flying insects and drifting
spiders in air.

FLIGHT: smooth, elegant, to and fro across face of
cliff, around high peaks, or over water; agile, gliding
with few quick wingbeats, fast turns.

TAIL SPOTS
The white spots on the tail of the
Crag Martin are diagnostic but
sometimes difficult to see.

MUD GATHERER
Close views are often possible as
Crag Martins almost ignore people
as they gather at a puddle to
collect mud for their nests.

OCCURRENCE
All year in S Europe, breeding in
Spain, Portugal, Alps, Italy, and
Balkans. Typically in mountainous
areas or lowlands with gorges and
broad, stony riverbeds; also in
older parts of towns around
Mediterranean, using buildings
as cliffs; often at great altitude
around peaks.

| Seen in the UK |
| J F M A M J J A S O N D |

SIMILAR SPECIES

SAND MARTIN
see p.278

stiff wings

much smaller

whiter below

HOUSE MARTIN
white rump;
see p.282

much
bigger

whiter below

ALPINE SWIFT
see p.253

| Length **14–15cm (5½–6in)** | Wingspan **32cm (12½in)** | Weight **20–25g (11/16–7/8oz)** |
| Social **Small flocks** | Lifespan **Up to 5 years** | Status **Secure** |

| Order **Passeriformes** | Family **Hirundinidae** | Species *Hirundo rustica* |

Swallow 🔊 52

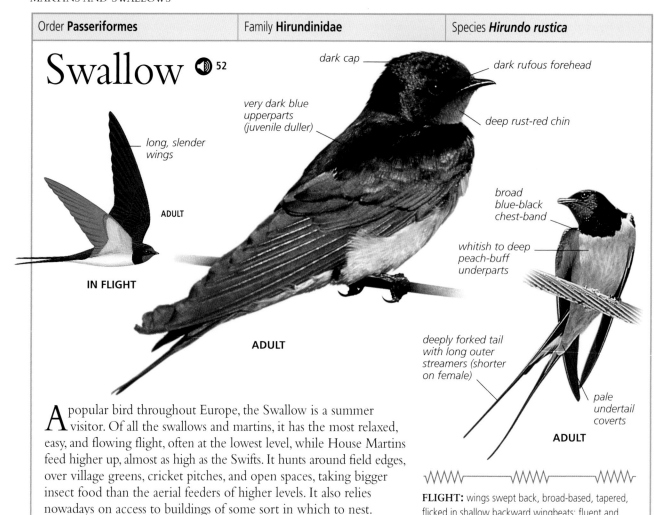

dark cap

dark rufous forehead

very dark blue
upperparts
(juvenile duller)

deep rust-red chin

long, slender
wings

ADULT

IN FLIGHT

ADULT

broad
blue-black
chest-band

whitish to deep
peach-buff
underparts

deeply forked tail
with long outer
streamers (shorter
on female)

pale
undertail
coverts

ADULT

A popular bird throughout Europe, the Swallow is a summer
visitor. Of all the swallows and martins, it has the most relaxed,
easy, and flowing flight, often at the lowest level, while House Martins
feed higher up, almost as high as the Swifts. It hunts around field edges,
over village greens, cricket pitches, and open spaces, taking bigger
insect food than the aerial feeders of higher levels. It also relies
nowadays on access to buildings of some sort in which to nest.
VOICE Calls distinctively liquid *swit-swit-swit*, nasal *vit-vit-vit*,
tsee-tsee; song quick,
chirruping, twittering
warble with characteristic
trills.
NESTING Open-topped
cup of mud and straw,
on beam or ledge in
outbuilding, shed, or barn;
4–6 eggs; 2 or 3 broods;
April–August.
FEEDING Flies low,
swerving to catch flying
insects in its mouth,
mostly large flies.

FLIGHT: wings swept back, broad-based, tapered,
flicked in shallow backward wingbeats; fluent and
graceful with much swerving, rolling from side to side.

AGILE FLIGHT
Swallows dive from the nest to
dash out through an open door
or window.

AUTUMN FLOCKS
Before migrating in autumn,
Swallows and House Martins
gather in substantial, twittering
flocks on overhead wires.

OCCURRENCE
In summer, throughout Europe
except Iceland. Often near water,
especially in spring and autumn,
feeding over grassy or cultivated
river valleys, open space, or rich
farmland with hedgerows; nests in
and around farms and villages but
not often in suburbia.

Seen in the UK
| J | F | M | A | M | J | J | A | S | O | N | D |

SIMILAR SPECIES

RED-RUMPED SWALLOW
pale rump; see p.281

all-dark

black
under tail

pale
chin

HOUSE MARTIN
white rump; see p.282

much smaller

SWIFT
never on
open perch;
see p.254

thin
wings

| Length **17–19cm (6½–7½in)** | Wingspan **32–35cm (12½–14in)** | Weight **16–25g (⁹⁄₁₆–⅞oz)** |
| Social **Migrant flocks** | Lifespan **Up to 5 years** | Status **Declining** |

| Order **Passeriformes** | Family **Hirundinidae** | Species *Hirundo daurica* |

Red-rumped Swallow

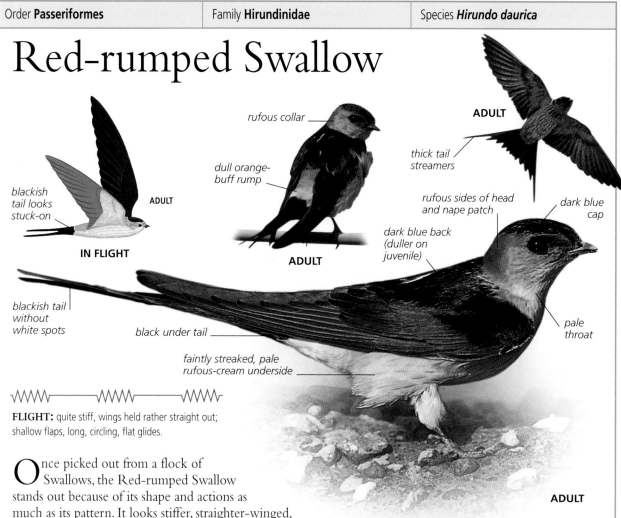

ADULT

rufous collar

dull orange-buff rump

ADULT

ADULT

thick tail streamers

rufous sides of head and nape patch

dark blue cap

dark blue back (duller on juvenile)

rufous collar

pale throat

blackish tail looks stuck-on

ADULT

IN FLIGHT

blackish tail without white spots

black under tail

faintly streaked, pale rufous-cream underside

ADULT

FLIGHT: quite stiff, wings held rather straight out; shallow flaps, long, circling, flat glides.

Once picked out from a flock of Swallows, the Red-rumped Swallow stands out because of its shape and actions as much as its pattern. It looks stiffer, straighter-winged, and slightly less fluent and relaxed in flight, enough to make it distinct to a practised eye. It is a bird of south Europe but appears with increasing frequency (if still unpredictably) farther north in spring and late autumn. In summer, it prefers areas with cliffs and gorges, inland or on the coast, nesting in caves or beneath natural overhangs as much as on buildings.

VOICE Quite distinct thin *queek* or *tsek*, sharper *keeer*; song lower, harsher than Swallow's.

NESTING Semi-spherical mud nest with entrance tube, under overhang, in cave or under eaves; 3–5 eggs; 2 or 3 broods; April–June.

FEEDING Takes insects in air, catching them in its mouth like other members of its family.

RUFOUS COLLAR
The rufous patch between the dark cap and back is easy to see on a perched bird, less so in flight.

SIMILAR SPECIES

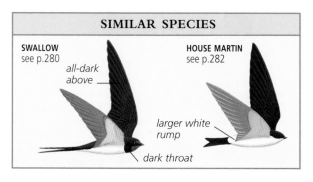

SWALLOW
see p.280

all-dark above

HOUSE MARTIN
see p.282

larger white rump

dark throat

OCCURRENCE
Bird of S Europe, especially Spain, Portugal, and Balkans; rare migrant farther north in late spring or autumn. Often in mountain areas with cliffs, also around coastal cliffs, gorges, and older towns and villages in summer.

| Seen in the UK |
| J F M A M J J A S O N D |

| Length **14–19cm (5½–7½in)** | Wingspan **30–35cm (12–14in)** | Weight **20g (¹¹⁄₁₆oz)** |
| Social **Small flocks** | Lifespan **Up to 5 years** | Status **Secure** |

Order **Passeriformes**	Family **Hirundinidae**	Species **Delichon urbicum**

House Martin

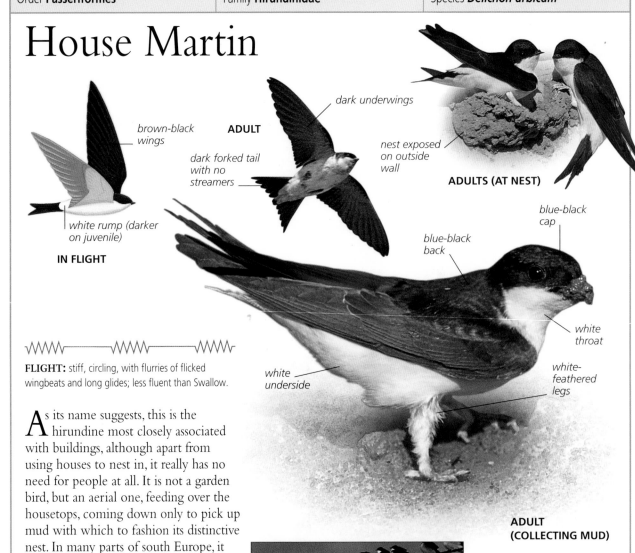

ADULT

dark underwings

brown-black wings

dark forked tail with no streamers

nest exposed on outside wall

ADULTS (AT NEST)

blue-black cap

blue-black back

white rump (darker on juvenile)

IN FLIGHT

white throat

white underside

white-feathered legs

ADULT (COLLECTING MUD)

vvvvv vvvvv vvvvv

FLIGHT: stiff, circling, with flurries of flicked wingbeats and long glides; less fluent than Swallow.

As its name suggests, this is the hirundine most closely associated with buildings, although apart from using houses to nest in, it really has no need for people at all. It is not a garden bird, but an aerial one, feeding over the housetops, coming down only to pick up mud with which to fashion its distinctive nest. In many parts of south Europe, it still breeds in remote places, nesting on cliffs high in the mountains.

VOICE Hard, quick, chirping *prrit* or *chrrit, tchirrip*; song twittering improvisation of similar notes.

NESTING Enclosed mud nest with entrance at top, fixed under eaves or overhang; 4 or 5 eggs; 2 or 3 broods; April–September.

FEEDING Catches flying insects and drifting spiders, high in air, in its mouth.

AUTUMN FLOCK
House Martin flocks gather on wires in autumn before migrating south to Africa.

OCCURRENCE
In summer, in all of Europe except Iceland, typically abundant in south over towns, villages, open areas, mountain gorges, reservoirs, and reed beds. In N and W Europe, typical breeding bird of modern suburbs as well as older farmsteads and villages, but now rare on natural cliffs.

Seen in the UK
| J | F | M | A | M | J | J | A | S | O | N | D |

SIMILAR SPECIES

SWALLOW
see p.280

all-dark above

SAND MARTIN
dark rump;
see p.278

brown above

SWIFT
does not perch;
see p.254

larger

all-dark plumage

Length **12cm (4¾in)**	Wingspan **26–29cm (10–11½in)**	Weight **15–21g (⁹⁄₁₆–¾oz)**
Social **Flocks**	Lifespan **Up to 5 years**	Status **Secure**

Family **Motacillidae**

PIPITS AND WAGTAILS

WHILE SIMILAR TO LARKS, these are smaller, slimmer birds with longer tails and a more steeply undulating flight. They lack the larks' prolonged song-flights but the pipits have more ritualized song-flight patterns and less varied songs.

PIPITS
Streaky brown is the typical description of a pipit: species can be hard to tell apart. Calls help, as does the time of year, habitat, and location. Similar species pairs may have different lifestyles, such as Meadow Pipits (moorland in summer, lowlands in winter) and Tree Pipits (woodland edge in summer, Africa in winter). There is little plumage variation between sexes and seasons.

WAGTAILS
More boldly patterned or more colourful than pipits, the wagtails are often associated with water or wet meadowland. Pied and White Wagtails, however, are more likely than almost any other bird to be seen on tarmac or concrete in urban areas and even the Grey Wagtail,

GREY OR YELLOW?
Although called the Grey Wagtail, this bird confuses many people with its yellow coloration.

which breeds beside fast-flowing streams, is a regular bird on urban rooftops in winter.

Male and female plumages are often different and winter plumages are duller than summer ones; juveniles are also recognizably different. Some species are resident in Europe, others migrate to Africa for the winter.

LONG CLAW
Meadow and Tree Pipits are closely similar, but the Meadow Pipit has a long hind claw, at least as long as the toe, as seen here: on a Tree Pipit it is shorter.

| Order **Passeriformes** | Family **Motacillidae** | Species **Anthus spinoletta** |

Water Pipit

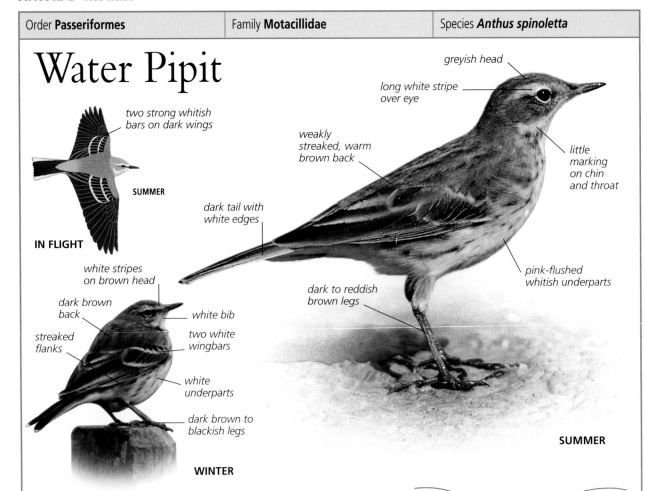

two strong whitish bars on dark wings

SUMMER

IN FLIGHT

greyish head

long white stripe over eye

weakly streaked, warm brown back

little marking on chin and throat

dark tail with white edges

pink-flushed whitish underparts

dark to reddish brown legs

white stripes on brown head

dark brown back

streaked flanks

white bib

two white wingbars

white underparts

dark brown to blackish legs

WINTER

SUMMER

Unusual in Europe, Water Pipits breed in high mountain areas and move down in winter, which takes many of them north-wards rather than south. These winter birds visit muddy edges of reservoirs, muddy places around reedbeds, and salt-marsh pools, very unlike their summer territories – alpine pastures and boulder-strewn slopes around the snow line. Migrants are generally shy and not easy to watch closely; care must be taken to separate them from migrant Rock Pipits of Scandinavian origin.

VOICE Call between squeaky Meadow Pipit and fuller Rock Pipit, quite strong, thin *fist*; song strong series of trills in high song-flight like Rock Pipit's.

NESTING Grass-lined cup on ground among grass; 4 or 5 eggs; 2 broods; May–July.

FEEDING Takes small insects and other invertebrates from ground.

FLIGHT: strong, with bursts of wingbeats; often flies off to considerable height and distance; drops to ground in long, fast dive.

SHY BIRD
Water Pipits are large, wary birds, and are not very easy to spot and identify.

OCCURRENCE
Breeds locally at high altitude in Pyrenees, Alps, Italy, and Balkans, most often on high pastures with scattered boulders. In winter, spreads widely across W and S Europe, in marshy areas, coastal marshes, and lagoons with muddy edges.

| Seen in the UK |
| J F M A M J J A S O N D |

SIMILAR SPECIES

ROCK PIPIT see p.285

duller

less white below

more buff

WHEATEAR ♀; white rump; see p.306

streaked breast

short tail

SKYLARK see p.270

| Length **17cm (6½in)** | Wingspan **23–28cm (9–11in)** | Weight **20–36g (¹¹⁄₁₆–1⁵⁄₁₆oz)** |
| Social **Small flocks** | Lifespan **Up to 5 years** | Status **Vulnerable** |

Order **Passeriformes**	Family **Motacillidae**	Species *Anthus petrosus*

Rock Pipit

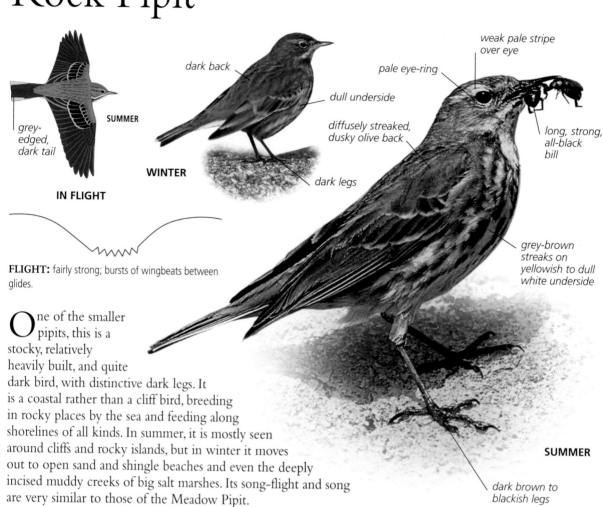

grey-edged, dark tail

SUMMER

IN FLIGHT

dark back

WINTER

dull underside

diffusely streaked, dusky olive back

dark legs

weak pale stripe over eye

pale eye-ring

long, strong, all-black bill

grey-brown streaks on yellowish to dull white underside

SUMMER

dark brown to blackish legs

FLIGHT: fairly strong; bursts of wingbeats between glides.

One of the smaller pipits, this is a stocky, relatively heavily built, and quite dark bird, with distinctive dark legs. It is a coastal rather than a cliff bird, breeding in rocky places by the sea and feeding along shorelines of all kinds. In summer, it is mostly seen around cliffs and rocky islands, but in winter it moves out to open sand and shingle beaches and even the deeply incised muddy creeks of big salt marshes. Its song-flight and song are very similar to those of the Meadow Pipit.

VOICE Call rather full, more slurred than Meadow, *feest* or *pseeep*, usually singly; song richer, stronger trill in similar song-flight.

NESTING Hair-lined nest on ground, in cavity in rocks; 4 or 5 eggs; 1 or 2 broods; April–July.

FEEDING Forages on grass and rocks above cliffs in summer, more often on weedy and stony beaches in winter; picks up insects, sandhoppers, small periwinkles, and similar creatures.

IDENTICAL IN WINTER
The Scandinavian subspecies looks exactly like the Rock Pipit in winter but turns up inland more often.

OCCURRENCE
Breeds on all rocky coasts of Scandinavia, Shetlands, N and W Great Britain, Ireland, and NW France. Winters widely on softer coasts and is common around salt-marsh creeks and muddy inlets, in S to W Spain, with Scandinavian birds moving south.

Seen in the UK
J F M A M J J A S O N D

SIMILAR SPECIES

WATER PIPIT summer; see p.284

plainer below

MEADOW PIPIT see p.286

paler, more buff

stronger whitish wingbars

pale legs

SUBSPECIES

L. a.littoralis (Scandinavia) spring

greyer back

less streaked

Length **16.5cm (6½in)**	Wingspan **23–28cm (9–11in)**	Weight **20–30g ($^{11}/_{16}$–1$^1/_{16}$oz)**
Social **Small flocks**	Lifespan **Up to 5 years**	Status **Secure**

| Order **Passeriformes** | Family **Motacillidae** | Species *Anthus pratensis* |

Meadow Pipit 🔊 53

pale stripe over eye

slim, weak, all-dark bill

dark streak or patch on sides of neck

soft blackish streaks on greyish, olive-, or yellowish brown back (darker on juvenile)

ADULT

dark tail with broad white sides

IN FLIGHT

evenly streaked chest and flanks

olive-buff or creamy underside (yellower on juvenile)

pale orange-brown legs

ADULT

very long hind claw

A small, streaky brown bird, the Meadow Pipit is worth looking at closely for the subtleties and beautiful patterns of its plumage. It gives the impression of constant nervous energy and worry; its calls may have a slightly hysterical quality. Winter flocks make shorter calls, more like the "pip-it" of their name. In summer, Meadow Pipits prefer heaths and wide open moors, often quite boggy places up on the hills. Their tinkling songs are characteristic of summer days in the open hills. In winter, many move to open farmland. These common, widespread birds often fall prey to Merlins and are parasitized by Cuckoos.

VOICE Sharp, weak, squeaked *pseeep* or *tsee*, frenetic repetition in alarm; winter flocks have short, quiet *pip*, *pi-pip* calls, short *tit*; song long series of simple repeated notes and trills, in parachuting song-flight starting and ending on ground.

NESTING Nest lined with fine stems in grass on ground; 4 or 5 eggs; 2 broods; May–July.

FEEDING Shuffles about on ground, picking up insects and other tiny invertebrates; eats some seeds.

FLIGHT: quite slow, erratic bounds and slight undulations with bursts of wingbeats; flies up weakly, jerkily.

DELICATE PATTERN
A close view of this streaky brown bird reveals a beautiful, intricate pattern.

OCCURRENCE
Breeds widely in NW, N, and E Europe; in winter, in W, SW, and S Europe. Nests on heaths, moorland, coasts, dunes, and bogs from sea level to high hills; in winter, mostly on lowland farmland and marshy places near coasts.

Seen in the UK
J F M A M J J A S O N D

SIMILAR SPECIES

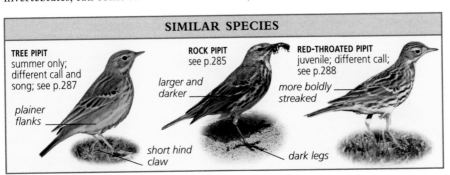

TREE PIPIT
summer only; different call and song; see p.287

plainer flanks

short hind claw

ROCK PIPIT
see p.285

larger and darker

dark legs

RED-THROATED PIPIT
juvenile; different call; see p.288

more boldly streaked

| Length **14.5cm (5¾in)** | Wingspan **22–25cm (9–10in)** | Weight **16–25g (⁹⁄₁₆–⅞oz)** |
| Social **Flocks** | Lifespan **Up to 5 years** | Status **Secure** |

| Order **Passeriformes** | Family **Motacillidae** | Species *Anthus trivialis* |

Tree Pipit 🔊 54

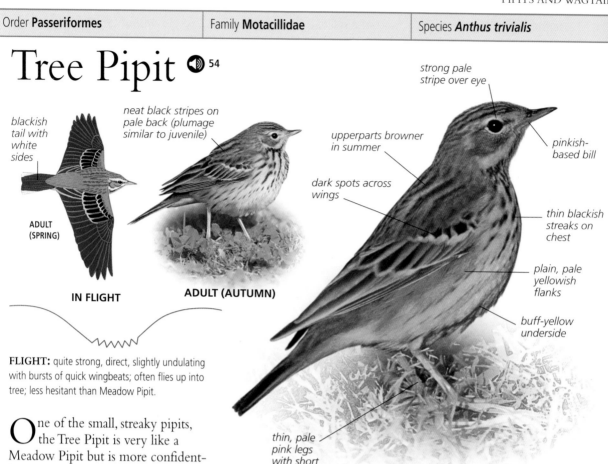

blackish tail with white sides

neat black stripes on pale back (plumage similar to juvenile)

strong pale stripe over eye

upperparts browner in summer

pinkish-based bill

dark spots across wings

thin blackish streaks on chest

plain, pale yellowish flanks

buff-yellow underside

ADULT (SPRING)

IN FLIGHT

ADULT (AUTUMN)

thin, pale pink legs with short claws

ADULT (SPRING)

FLIGHT: quite strong, direct, slightly undulating with bursts of quick wingbeats; often flies up into tree; less hesitant than Meadow Pipit.

One of the small, streaky pipits, the Tree Pipit is very like a Meadow Pipit but is more confident-looking and sleeker, although thickset: small points of character rather than plumage features separate these little brown birds. It also has a superb song, rich and musical, in a distinctive song-flight, so summer males are not so difficult to identify. For autumn migrants, a call-note may be necessary for positive identification. While they do often occur within sight of each other, Tree and Meadow Pipits have different habitats, Tree Pipits occurring mostly on woodland edges and Meadow Pipits on heaths or moorlands.

VOICE Distinctive calls, including low, hissy buzz, *teeess* or *teaze*, thin, sharp *tzit*; loud, sweet song, with long series of notes and fast trills ending in loud, slow *sweee-sweee-sweee*, from perch or in flight ending on tree or bush.

NESTING Grassy cup on ground in thick grass; 4–6 eggs; 1 or 2 broods; April–July.

FEEDING Takes small insects from ground.

STRIKING SONG
Whether from a tree or in flight, the Tree Pipit's song is rich and musical with Canary-like trills.

OCCURRENCE
Breeds in most of Europe except in Ireland and Iceland. Occurs from spring to autumn only, usually in open woodland, woodland glades, or around edges of plantations, on bushy heaths and moors with scattered trees; migrants in more open areas at coasts.

| Seen in the UK |
| J F **M A M J J A S O** N D |

SIMILAR SPECIES

MEADOW PIPIT
sharper call;
see p.286

longer hind claw

ROCK PIPIT
see p.285

darker

dark legs

crest

bigger and heavier

SKYLARK
see p.270

| Length **15cm (6in)** | Wingspan **25–27cm (10–10½in)** | Weight **20–25g (11/16–⅞oz)** |
| Social **Solitary** | Lifespan **Up to 5 years** | Status **Secure** |

Order **Passeriformes**	Family **Motacillidae**	Species *Anthus cervinus*

Red-throated Pipit

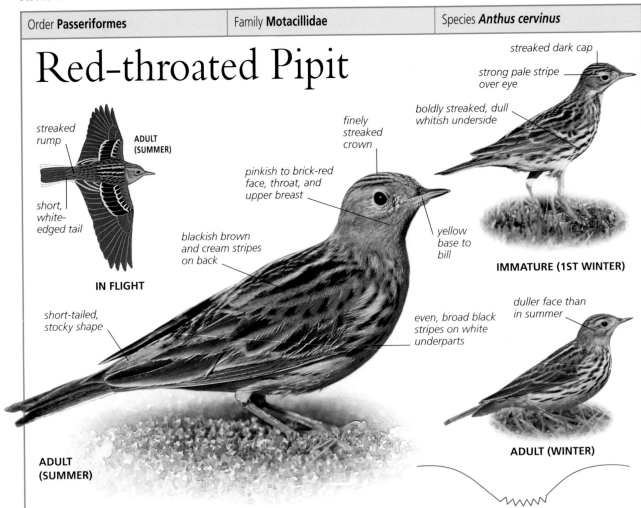

IN FLIGHT

streaked rump

ADULT (SUMMER)

short, white-edged tail

pinkish to brick-red face, throat, and upper breast

finely streaked crown

blackish brown and cream stripes on back

short-tailed, stocky shape

yellow base to bill

even, broad black stripes on white underparts

streaked dark cap

strong pale stripe over eye

boldly streaked, dull whitish underside

IMMATURE (1ST WINTER)

duller face than in summer

ADULT (WINTER)

ADULT (SUMMER)

In summer, this is a pipit of the far north; in spring it may be found in damp, grassy places and around pools and salt pans in southeast Europe. It is a regular but rare autumn migrant in west Europe. Although it is just another "streaky pipit", it does have a call note that, once heard, is remarkably distinctive, instantly revealing the presence of a calling bird flying over or flushed from the grass.

VOICE Call distinctive: high, slightly explosive, penetrating, fading out *psseeeeee*, also harder *chup*; song rhythmic repetition of sharp, fine, ringing notes and buzzy trills.

NESTING Grassy cup on ground in vegetation; 4 or 5 eggs; 1 brood; May–June.

FEEDING Takes insects and other invertebrates from ground; eats some small seeds.

FLIGHT: stronger than Meadow Pipit, less hesitant, more direct like Tree Pipit.

VARIABLE RED
This adult Red-throated Pipit is at the reddest-faced, least-streaked extreme of summer.

SIMILAR SPECIES

MEADOW PIPIT different call; see p.286

duller

less streaked

TREE PIPIT different call; see p.287

plainer flanks

OCCURRENCE
Breeds in extreme N Scandinavia on tundra, mountains, and in willow swamp. Widespread migrant in damp places in C and E Europe, but rare in W; likely on open ground, swampy areas, coastal dunes, and islands.

Seen in the UK
J F M A M J J A S O N D

Length **14–15cm (5½–6in)**	Wingspan **22–25cm (9–10in)**	Weight **16–25g (⁹⁄₁₆–⁷⁄₈oz)**
Social **Small flocks**	Lifespan **Up to 5 years**	Status **Secure†**

| Order **Passeriformes** | Family **Motacillidae** | Species **Anthus campestris** |

Tawny Pipit

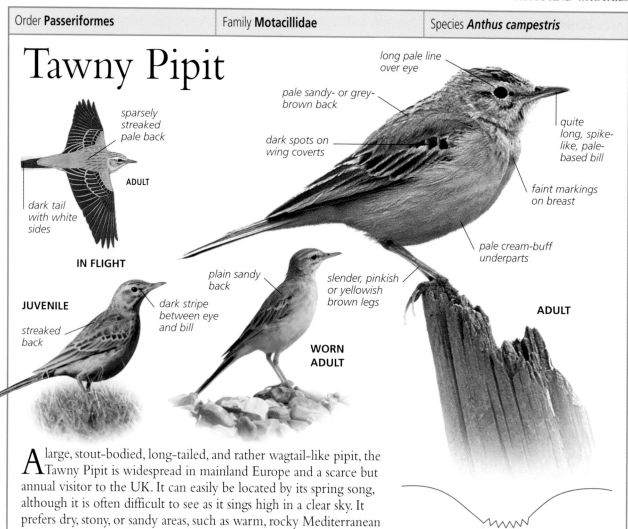

long pale line over eye

pale sandy- or grey-brown back

dark spots on wing coverts

quite long, spike-like, pale-based bill

faint markings on breast

pale cream-buff underparts

sparsely streaked pale back

ADULT

dark tail with white sides

IN FLIGHT

JUVENILE

streaked back

plain sandy back

dark stripe between eye and bill

slender, pinkish or yellowish brown legs

WORN ADULT

ADULT

A large, stout-bodied, long-tailed, and rather wagtail-like pipit, the Tawny Pipit is widespread in mainland Europe and a scarce but annual visitor to the UK. It can easily be located by its spring song, although it is often difficult to see as it sings high in a clear sky. It prefers dry, stony, or sandy areas, such as warm, rocky Mediterranean slopes with scattered bushes and aromatic shrubs, or sand dunes by the sea. Pipits are often difficult to identify, especially out of their usual range, but a summer Tawny in a typical situation is usually quite easy to pick out with confidence.

VOICE Sparrow-like *schilp*, more grating, emphatic *tsee-i*, short *chup*; song in high undulating flight loud repetition of ringing, low-high double note *tchu-veee tchu-veee*.

NESTING Grass-lined cup in short vegetation on ground; 4 or 5 eggs; 1 or 2 broods; April–June.

FEEDING Catches and eats mostly insects on ground.

FLIGHT: fast, direct; undulating with bursts of quick wingbeats; flies off long distance, going quite high.

DARK SPOTS AND STREAKS
A row of dark spots and feather centres relieve an otherwise nearly uniform pale buff appearance.

OCCURRENCE
Breeds on bushy, stony slopes, in dry cultivated land with much stony soil, in grassland, and in dunes. Widespread in Europe north to Baltic but most typical of warmer areas in S Europe. Rare migrants farther north likely near coast.

| Seen in the UK |
| J F M A M J J A S O N D |

SIMILAR SPECIES

RICHARD'S PIPIT
similar to juvenile;
explosive call;
see p.447

pale between eye and bill

more heavily streaked

larger

YELLOW WAGTAIL
juvenile; see p.291

less buff

WATER PIPIT
different call;
see p.284

darker

dark legs

| Length **15–18cm (6–7in)** | Wingspan **28–30cm (11–12in)** | Weight **35g (1¼oz)** |
| Social **Solitary** | Lifespan **Up to 5 years** | Status **Vulnerable** |

Order **Passeriformes**	Family **Motacillidae**	Species **Motacilla alba**

Pied Wagtail 🔊 55

blackish rump

white streaks on wings

MALE (SUMMER)

IN FLIGHT

greyer back than male's

FEMALE (PIED)

greyer head and upperparts than adult male's

JUVENILE

buffish below

black cap, chin, and throat (white chin and throat outside breeding season)

whitish face

black breast

black back

sooty flanks

white belly

MALE (SUMMER; PIED)

long, white-edged black tail

FLIGHT: quick, direct, with long undulating bounds and bursts of wingbeats.

Widespread and familiar, the Pied (or White) Wagtail is frequently seen in and around towns, often feeding on areas of tarmac, concrete, or stone slabs. It is also frequently seen on roofs, from which it typically calls before moving off: its call is a useful indicator of its presence. In summer, it can be found anywhere from builder's yards and woodsheds to remote quarries and natural cliffs and along stony river or lake sides. Although creating few identification problems, its non-breeding plumages are quite complex.

VOICE Calls loud, musical *chrip*, *chuwee*, *chrruwee*, and variants, merging into harder, unmusical *tissik* or *chiswit*; song mixes similar calls and trills.

NESTING Grassy cup in cavity in bank, cliff, or woodpile, in outbuilding or under bridge; 5 or 6 eggs; 2 or 3 broods; April–August.

FEEDING Feeds very actively on ground, roofs, or waterside mud or rocks, walking, running, leaping up or sideways, or flying in pursuit of flies; takes insects, molluscs, and some seeds.

M. a. alba

White Wagtail
The form found on mainland Europe; it is greyer and whiter than the Pied (*M. a. yarrellii*).

greyer cap

JUVENILE

browner wings with white bars

pale grey back

MALE

SIMILAR SPECIES

GREY WAGTAIL ♂♀; yellow rump; see p.292

yellow under tail

YELLOW WAGTAIL juvenile, similar to juvenile; different call; see p.291

browner

OCCURRENCE
Breeds throughout Europe; found only in summer in N and E Europe but widespread in winter. Very varied habitat, often near water and in built-up areas, feeding on car parks, pavements, and roof-tops, but not usually in gardens.

Seen in the UK
| J | F | M | A | M | J | J | A | S | O | N | D |

Length **18cm (7in)**	Wingspan **25–30cm (10–12in)**	Weight **19–27g (11/16–7/8oz)**
Social **Winter flocks**	Lifespan **Up to 5 years**	Status **Secure**

Order **Passeriformes**	Family **Motacillidae**	Species **Motacilla flava**

Yellow Wagtail 🔊 56

two white bars on blackish wings

MALE (SPRING)

IN FLIGHT

green crown

bright yellow stripe over eye

green back

MALE (SPRING)

bright yellow underparts

white sides to black tail

long, spindly black legs

pale stripe over eye

white lines on wings

buff underside

JUVENILE (AUTUMN)

pale line over eye

grey-green back

FEMALE (SPRING)

Elegant and colourful, the Yellow Wagtail, particularly the summer male, is a highly distinctive bird. However, autumn birds, especially juveniles, cause confusion with rarer species and also juvenile Pied Wagtails, which can appear strongly yellowish. The call always helps to identify it. In summer, it lives around pools and reservoirs and damp, grassy fields where horses and cattle disturb the insects it eats. In winter, it is found near big mammal herds on African plains.

VOICE Call distinctive, loud, full, flat, or rising *tsli*, or *tsweep* or *tswi-eep*; song repetition of brief, chirping phrases.

NESTING Grassy cup in vegetation on ground; 5 or 6 eggs; 2 broods; May–July.

FEEDING Forages on ground, skipping and leaping after flies in short flycatching sallies; eats insects and other invertebrates.

FLIGHT: strong but undulating, with long, sweeping bounds; flurries of quick wingbeats.

FEEDING
The Yellow Wagtail is usually found around livestock in damp fields and pastures: it eats insects dislodged from the grass by the grazing cattle and horses.

SUBSPECIES

M. f. flava (C Europe)

long white stripe over eye

blue-grey crown and cheeks

glossy black crown and cheeks

M. f. feldegg (SE Europe)

OCCURRENCE
Widespread in summer, breeding throughout Europe except for Ireland and Iceland. Often near water, in wet fields and pastures with livestock. Migrant flocks often on muddy reservoir edges or adjacent grass.

Seen in the UK
J F M **A M J J A S O** N D

SIMILAR SPECIES

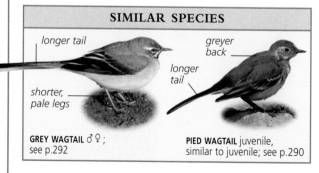

longer tail

shorter, pale legs

GREY WAGTAIL ♂♀; see p.292

greyer back

longer tail

PIED WAGTAIL juvenile, similar to juvenile; see p.290

Length **17cm (6½in)**	Wingspan **23–27cm (9–10½in)**	Weight **16–22g (⁹⁄₁₆–¹³⁄₁₆oz)**
Social **Small flocks**	Lifespan **Up to 5 years**	Status **Secure**

Order **Passeriformes**	Family **Motacillidae**	Species *Motacilla cinerea*

Grey Wagtail 🔊 57

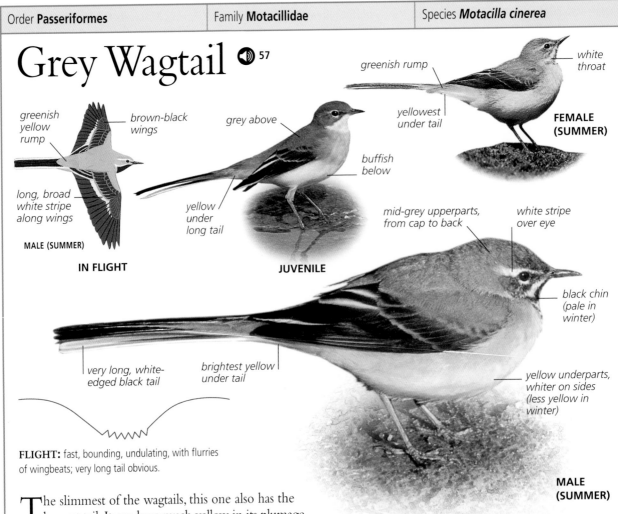

greenish rump

white throat

FEMALE (SUMMER)

yellowest under tail

greenish yellow rump

brown-black wings

grey above

long, broad white stripe along wings

MALE (SUMMER)

IN FLIGHT

yellow under long tail

JUVENILE

buffish below

mid-grey upperparts, from cap to back

white stripe over eye

black chin (pale in winter)

very long, white-edged black tail

brightest yellow under tail

yellow underparts, whiter on sides (less yellow in winter)

MALE (SUMMER)

FLIGHT: fast, bounding, undulating, with flurries of wingbeats; very long tail obvious.

The slimmest of the wagtails, this one also has the longest tail. It can have much yellow in its plumage and can be confused with the Yellow Wagtail; it may also be mistaken for the Pied Wagtail which often inhabits the same areas of clear, fast-flowing, rocky streams in summer and shallow pools in winter, and has a similar call. In winter, the Grey Wagtail may feed on almost any puddle, even on a flat rooftop in a city centre or at a garden pond. Visits to such places by this shy bird are invariably short but revealed by its calls.

VOICE Sharp, explosive, metallic *tchik* or *zi*, or *zi-zi*; song penetrating, metallic, sharp trills and warbles.

NESTING Grassy cup in hole in bank, wall, tree roots, or under bridge; 4–6 eggs; 2 broods; April–August.

FEEDING Catches flies and small invertebrates on ground or in air; quite active, bouncy feeder.

SUBTLE BEAUTY
Even a female or young Grey Wagtail has a lovely combination of smoky grey, buff, yellow, white, and black.

SIMILAR SPECIES

YELLOW WAGTAIL ♂♀ summer; see p.291

shorter tail

PIED WAGTAIL ♂♀: see p.290

black legs

no yellow under tail

OCCURRENCE
Widespread breeder north to Great Britain, Ireland, and S Scandinavia, along clean, often tree-lined rivers or more open upland streams. Very widespread near water in winter, briefly at puddles in towns and cities.

Seen in the UK
J F M A M J J A S O N D

Length **18–19cm (7–7½in)**	Wingspan **25–27cm (10–10½in)**	Weight **15–23g (9/16 – 13/16 oz)**
Social **Family groups**	Lifespan **Up to 5 years**	Status **Secure†**

Families **Troglodytidae, Cinclidae, Bombycillidae, Prunellidae**

WRENS, DIPPERS, WAXWINGS, AND ACCENTORS

THIS GROUP – ANOTHER convenient grouping rather than a collection of near relatives – includes families that are widespread in the northern hemisphere and one family (accentors) that is absent from the New World.

WRENS

Primarily an American family, with just one species in Europe, the wrens are small, brown, barred birds with loud voices and an "irritable" character. The Wren, whose scientific name means "cave dweller", is likely to be found in dark, damp, cobweb-filled places under hedges and around sheds, searching for insects.

DIPPERS

Superficially wren-like but larger, the Dipper swims, wades, and walks underwater. It is always at the water's edge, even flying along a twisting water course rather than across dry land.

WINTER FLOCK
Waxwings take a breather after drinking, before returning to gorge themselves once more on a crop of berries.

WAXWINGS

Upright, crested, short-legged, eye-catching birds, Waxwings are sociable and often very tame. Their numbers in western Europe vary greatly from year to year.

ACCENTORS

Small, slim-billed, shuffling ground birds, accentors are often overlooked. The Dunnock, however, is common in many habitats and a frequent garden songster that deserves to be a more popular favourite.

ROCK HOPPER
A Dipper stands beside a rushing torrent, into which it is likely to plunge.

ABUNDANT
Dunnocks are among north-west Europe's most common birds, with a wide choice of habitat types.

VIBRANT SONG
A Wren shakes with the effort as it pours out a remarkable song, part of the woodland chorus.

293

Order **Passeriformes**	Family **Troglodytidae**	Species ***Troglodytes troglodytes***

Wren 🔊 58

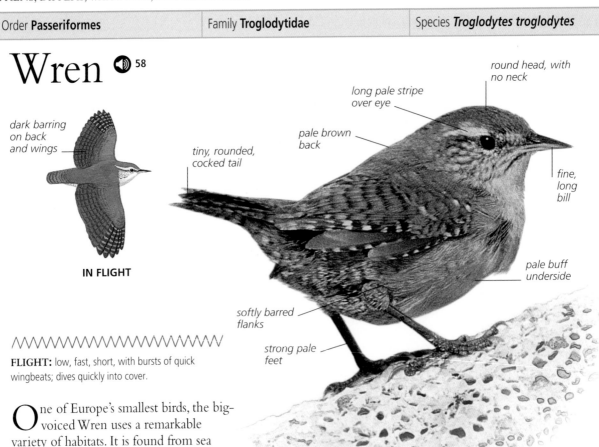

dark barring on back and wings

IN FLIGHT

round head, with no neck

long pale stripe over eye

pale brown back

tiny, rounded, cocked tail

fine, long bill

pale buff underside

softly barred flanks

strong pale feet

/\

FLIGHT: low, fast, short, with bursts of quick wingbeats; dives quickly into cover.

One of Europe's smallest birds, the big-voiced Wren uses a remarkable variety of habitats. It is found from sea level to high up in mountain areas, from forest to almost open spaces; subspecies exist in remote island groups. It spends most of the time low down, on or near the ground, often in deep thickets of bramble or bracken or in ornamental shrubberies. Cold winters cause dramatic declines but Wren populations can recover quite quickly.

VOICE Dry, hard calls with irritable, rattling quality, *chit*, *chiti*, *tzerrr*; song loud, full-throated, warbling outburst with characteristic low, hard trill and fast, ringing notes.

NESTING Small, loose ball of leaves and grass, tucked in bank, under overhang; 5 or 6 eggs; 2 broods; April–July.

FEEDING Forages in dark, damp places under hedges, around buildings, shrubberies, in ditches, and in patches of dead bracken and similar low, thick cover; finds insects and spiders and feeds on scraps scattered under bushes.

DETERMINED SINGER
With tail raised and bill wide open, a singing Wren puts all its effort into a loud, vibrant song.

SIMILAR SPECIES

DUNNOCK see p.297

longer tail

ROBIN juvenile, similar to adult; see p.300

larger and greyer

larger and spotted

longer tail

SUBSPECIES

T. t. zetlandicus (Shetland)

coarsely barred flanks

greyer brown

OCCURRENCE
Breeds in practically all of Europe except far north; in N and E Europe only in summer. Lives anywhere from open clifftops and heaths to broadleaved and coniferous woodland, parks, gardens, and hedges.

Seen in the UK
| J | F | M | A | M | J | J | A | S | O | N | D |

Length **9–10cm (3½–4in)**	Wingspan **13–17cm (5–6½in)**	Weight **8–13g (⁵⁄₁₆–⁷⁄₁₆ oz)**
Social **Roosts in flocks**	Lifespan **2–5 years**	Status **Secure**

| Order **Passeriformes** | Family **Cinclidae** | Species *Cinclus cinclus* |

Dipper

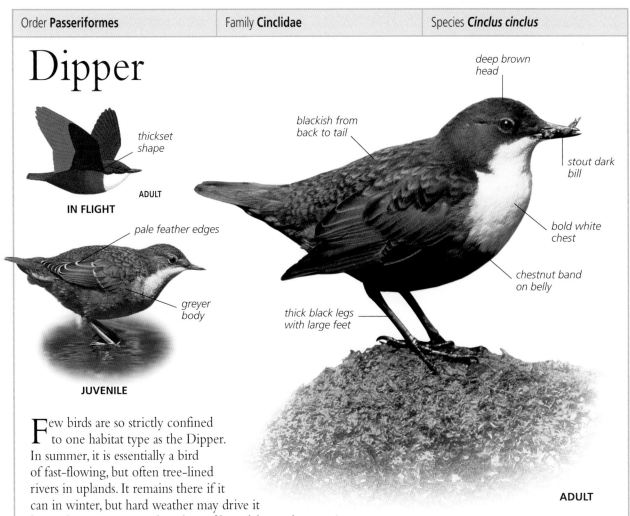

thickset shape

ADULT

IN FLIGHT

pale feather edges

greyer body

JUVENILE

deep brown head

blackish from back to tail

stout dark bill

bold white chest

chestnut band on belly

thick black legs with large feet

ADULT

F ew birds are so strictly confined to one habitat type as the Dipper. In summer, it is essentially a bird of fast-flowing, but often tree-lined rivers in uplands. It remains there if it can in winter, but hard weather may drive it lower down or even to the edges of large lakes and reservoirs or the sea coast. It is quite at home swimming and diving, or simply walking into the water and disappearing underneath as it searches for food. Its springy, bouncing movements and call are also distinctive.
VOICE Sharp, hard, abrupt, and penetrating *dzit* or *djink*; song loud, rich warbling mixed with explosive, grating notes.
NESTING Ball-shaped nest of moss and grass in hole in bank, under overhang or bridge, and behind waterfall; 4–6 eggs; 2 broods; April–July.
FEEDING Unique, walking into water, swimming and diving from surface, or wading into shallows, foraging for caddis-fly and other larvae, small fish, crustaceans, and molluscs.
REMARK Subspecies *C. c. hibernicus* (Scotland and Ireland) has narrow, darker chestnut belly band.

FLIGHT: low, fast, along stream line; fast bursts of wingbeats.

OCCURRENCE
Local in upland areas, absent from Iceland, W France, and NE Europe, but breeding widely elsewhere in suitable habitat: clean, fresh rivers, in moorland areas or tree-lined valleys, or deep in shady gorges. In winter, some move out to larger areas of water, rarely coasts.

Seen in the UK
J F M A M J J A S O N D

SUBSPECIES

C. c. cinclus (N Europe, N France)

blacker

all-dark belly

CAMOUFLAGE PATTERN
The bright white chest surprisingly serves to render the Dipper less conspicuous in the ripples and reflections of a stony river.

| Length **18cm (7in)** | Wingspan **25–30cm (10–12in)** | Weight **55–75g (2–2⅝oz)** |
| Social **Solitary** | Lifespan **Up to 5 years** | Status **Secure†** |

| Order **Passeriformes** | Family **Bombycillidae** | Species **Bombycilla garrulus** |

Waxwing

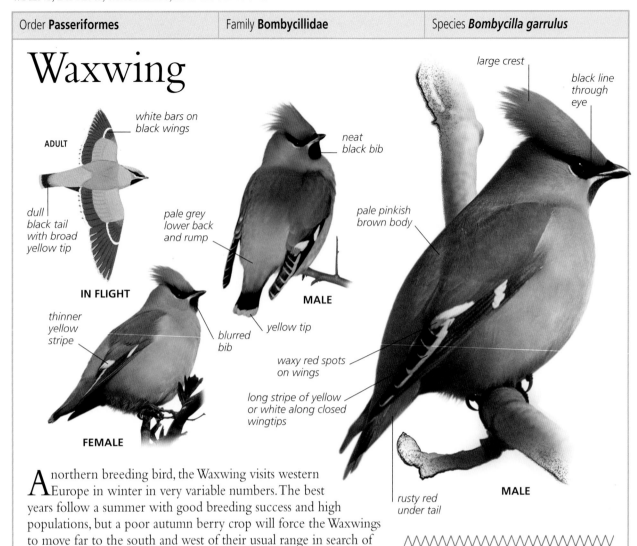

ADULT

white bars on black wings

dull black tail with broad yellow tip

IN FLIGHT

large crest

black line through eye

neat black bib

pale grey lower back and rump

pale pinkish brown body

MALE

thinner yellow stripe

blurred bib

yellow tip

waxy red spots on wings

long stripe of yellow or white along closed wingtips

FEMALE

rusty red under tail

MALE

A northern breeding bird, the Waxwing visits western Europe in winter in very variable numbers. The best years follow a summer with good breeding success and high populations, but a poor autumn berry crop will force the Waxwings to move far to the south and west of their usual range in search of food. Although flocks in flight might superficially suggest Starlings, identification is very easy; the birds' tameness helps as they feed in urban areas or gardens.

VOICE Silvery, high, metallic trill on even pitch, *trrreee* or *siirrrrr*.
NESTING Moss-lined nest of twigs in birch or conifer; 4–6 eggs; 1 brood; May–June.
FEEDING Eats insects in summer; in winter some insects, often caught in flight, but mostly large berries such as rowan, hawthorn, and cotoneaster; also eats apples and other fruit.

FLIGHT: direct, swooping or swerving, with long, shallow undulations, quick wingbeats; flocks keep formation like waders.

OCCURRENCE
Breeds in conifer forest in extreme NE Europe. In winter, frequent in N Scandinavia, irregular in S Scandinavia and E Europe. Numbers are erratic, sometimes large, in W Europe, big flocks coinciding with high population and lack of food in N Europe.

Seen in the UK
| J | F | M | A | M | J | J | A | S | O | N | D |

SIMILAR SPECIES

sharper bill

dark rump

STARLING ♂♀; similar in flight; see p.380

RESTING FLOCK
Waxwings feed greedily, stripping shrub of berries, and drink a great deal. Between bouts of feeding, flocks rest in undisturbed trees nearby.

| Length **18cm (7in)** | Wingspan **32–35cm (12½–14in)** | Weight **45–70g (1⅝–2½oz)** |
| Social **Flocks** | Lifespan **Up to 5 years** | Status **Secure†** |

Order **Passeriformes**	Family **Prunellidae**	Species *Prunella modularis*

Dunnock 🔊 59

black streaks on rich brown back and wings

IN FLIGHT

mid-grey breast

black and brown streaks on back

brown cheeks

soft, warm brown streaks on flanks

ADULT

streaked brown cap

brown eye

fine dark bill

grey throat

line of pale spots across wings

uneven, grey and brown streaking below

JUVENILE

orange-brown legs

ADULT

The generally quite dull and unobtrusive looks of the Dunnock bely its unusual mating habits: it forms one-male-two-female or even one-female-two-male trios when breeding. Easily overlooked, it is widely distributed in a great variety of places, like the Wren. Its sharp calls and fast, high-pitched but slightly "flat" song call attention to it. If disturbed, it generally flies at near ground-level into the nearest thick bush, and is sometimes taken for some rare, vagrant warbler.

VOICE Loud, high, penetrating *pseeep*, thin, vibrant *teeee*; song quick, slightly flat, high-pitched, fast warble with little contrast or variation in pitch.

NESTING Small grassy cup, lined with hair and moss, in bush or hedge; 4 or 5 eggs; 2 or 3 broods; April–July.

FEEDING Forages on ground, shuffling, crouched, often in or around bushes, close to cover; picks up small insects and seeds; feeds on scraps beneath bird-tables and grated cheese under shrubberies.

FLIGHT: short, flitting, whirring; wings round, tail quite long.

SHUFFLING FEEDER
Dunnocks creep forward, flicking their tails, picking food from the ground, without the bouncy hop of House Sparrows.

OCCURRENCE
Breeds throughout Europe except in Iceland. Present only in summer in N and E Europe; in some parts of S Europe in winter. Widespread, on heaths and moors with low, dense scrub and exposed coastal areas as well as in higher forest, bushy gardens, ornamental flowerbeds, and parks.

Seen in the UK
J F M A M J J A S O N D

SIMILAR SPECIES

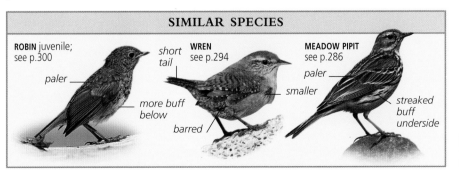

ROBIN juvenile; see p.300

paler

more buff below

short tail

WREN see p.294

barred

smaller

MEADOW PIPIT see p.286

paler

streaked buff underside

Length **14cm (5½in)**	Wingspan **19–21cm (7½–8½in)**	Weight **19–24g (¹¹⁄₁₆–⁷⁄₈oz)**
Social **Family groups**	Lifespan **Up to 5 years**	Status **Secure**

Order **Passeriformes**	Family **Prunellidae**	Species *Prunella collaris*

Alpine Accentor

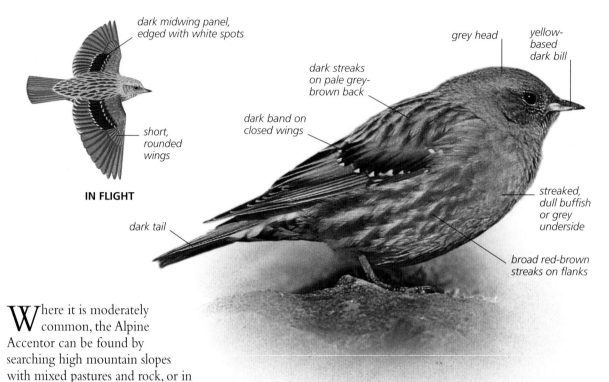

dark midwing panel, edged with white spots

grey head

yellow-based dark bill

dark streaks on pale grey-brown back

dark band on closed wings

short, rounded wings

IN FLIGHT

dark tail

streaked, dull buffish or grey underside

broad red-brown streaks on flanks

Where it is moderately common, the Alpine Accentor can be found by searching high mountain slopes with mixed pastures and rock, or in almost entirely rocky places at high altitude. In areas where it is more thinly spread, locating it can be quite difficult. In winter, accentors move to lower levels and turn up quite regularly at traditional sites outside the breeding range, usually hilltops, but also centred on old buildings such as castle complexes on rocky outcrops. They can be quite tame in winter, but are often shy and elusive in summer in the mountains. In shape and behaviour, they resemble large Dunnocks.

VOICE Short, trilling or rolling calls, *trru, tschirr, drrp*; song erratic, uneven series of trills and squeaky notes, sometimes in flight.

NESTING Grassy nest in rock crevice or under rocks; 3–5 eggs; 2 broods; May–August.

FEEDING Forages on ground, finding insects, spiders, and seeds.

FLIGHT: quite strong, lark- or thrush-like with flurries of wingbeats, quick swoops.

OCCURRENCE
Breeds at high altitude mostly in Pyrenees and Alps, and locally in Italy and Balkans, usually on wide open slopes with short grass and plenty of boulders, or almost wholly rocky places. Sparse at lower altitude in winter, a few moving outside breeding range to Mediterranean islands.

Seen in the UK
J F M A M J J A S O N D

SIMILAR SPECIES

DUNNOCK greyer on breast; see p.297

plainer wings

less reddish flanks

CHARACTERISTIC MARKING
This Alpine Accentor on rocky ground reveals the obvious dark wing panel that is usually the most distinctive feature at a distance.

Length **15–17cm (6–6½in)**	Wingspan **22cm (9in)**	Weight **25g (⅞oz)**
Social **Family groups**	Lifespan **Up to 5 years**	Status **Secure**

Family **Turdidae**

CHATS AND THRUSHES

B IRDS IN THIS GROUP are characterized by
rather short but strong bills, stout legs, quite
large heads, big eyes, and an all-round solid build.
Some are common, others very rare; some are
resident, others migrate. They occupy a wide
range of habitats from gardens to forest, mountain,
and moor, and include some of the finest of
European bird songsters.

CHATS
Smaller than the thrushes and less stoutly built,
the chats are varied: most have different seasonal
plumages, with male and female looking different
in summer and juveniles looking much like
winter adults.

The wheatears occupy open places from high,
bleak moors to hot Mediterranean heaths. The
nightingales live in dense shrubbery in woods or
beside heaths. Stonechats are year-round residents
on open heath, while Whinchats are summer
migrants. The chats demonstrate that
there is usually more than one way
to exploit a habitat or food supply.

THRUSHES
The spotted thrushes look the same all year and
male and female are alike, while the Blackbird
and rock thrushes have sexual (and sometimes
seasonal) differences in plumage. Superb singers,
they make up the bulk
of the spring dawn
chorus in much of
northern Europe. Many
are migrants, although
in some cases, such as
the Blackbird, winter
immigrants to western
Europe join others of
the same species.

INTERMEDIATE
The Nightingale fits neatly between
larger thrushes and smaller chats
in size and shape.

SONG THRUSH
Several of the thrushes are excellent songsters,
none more so than the Song Thrush whose
repetitive phrases include many strong, clear,
musical notes.

WINTER FEATHERS
The whitish edges on the feathers of this
Rock Thrush will wear off by summer, to
give a clear blue and orange appearance,
quite unlike any other European species.

| Order **Passeriformes** | Family **Turdidae** | Species *Erithacus rubecula* |

Robin 🔊 60.I, 60.II

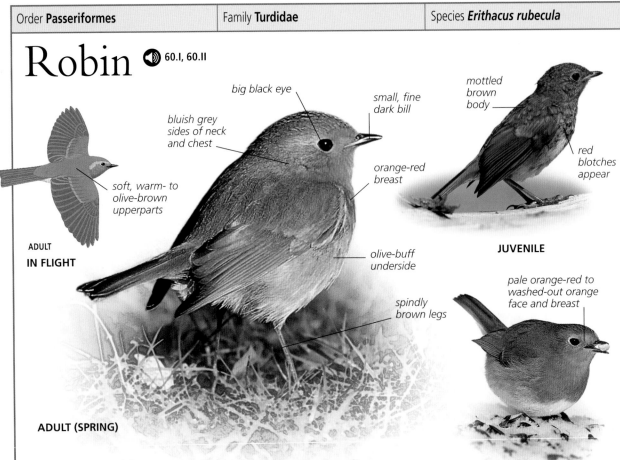

big black eye

small, fine
dark bill

bluish grey
sides of neck
and chest

orange-red
breast

soft, warm- to
olive-brown
upperparts

**ADULT
IN FLIGHT**

olive-buff
underside

spindly
brown legs

ADULT (SPRING)

mottled
brown
body

red
blotches
appear

JUVENILE

pale orange-red to
washed-out orange
face and breast

ADULT (WINTER)

This is a typical forest or woodland-edge species in most of its range, adapted to follow foraging animals such as wild boar: it picks up food from the earth overturned by the animals. In the UK, it follows gardeners turning the soil, and has become remarkably tame. In most of continental Europe, Robins are much shyer birds. Robins are easily identified (although juveniles have no red at first) and have a distinctive song.

VOICE Sharp, short, abrupt *tik*, series of quick *tik-ik-ik-ik-ik*, high, thin *seeep*; song rich, full, varied warbling in long, musical series, some phrases like Garden Warbler's (see p.320); in autumn/winter more mellow, melancholy.

NESTING Domed nest of leaves and grass in bank, dense bush or hedge, or thick ivy; 4–6 eggs; 2 broods; April–August.

FEEDING Mostly on ground, hopping and flitting in search of spiders, insects, worms, berries, and seeds; comes to feeders and bird-tables for seed mixtures.

FLIGHT: short, flitting darts into cover; longer flights weak, flitting, with bursts of wingbeats.

IN A DIFFERENT LIGHT
In some lights, the white breast spot below the red bib may be very obvious.

SIMILAR SPECIES

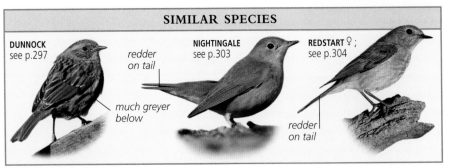

DUNNOCK
see p.297

much greyer
below

redder
on tail

NIGHTINGALE
see p.303

REDSTART ♀;
see p.304

redder
on tail

OCCURRENCE
Widespread, but absent from Iceland; summer visitor in N and E Europe. In all kinds of forest, especially more open woodland, as well as on bushy heaths, in gardens with hedges and shrubberies, and in town parks.

Seen in the UK
J F M A M J J A S O N D

| Length **14cm (5½in)** | Wingspan **20–22cm (8–9in)** | Weight **16–22g (⁹⁄₁₆–¹³⁄₁₆oz)** |
| Social **Family groups** | Lifespan **3–5 years** | Status **Secure** |

Order **Passeriformes**	Family **Turdidae**	Species *Luscinia svecica*

Bluethroat

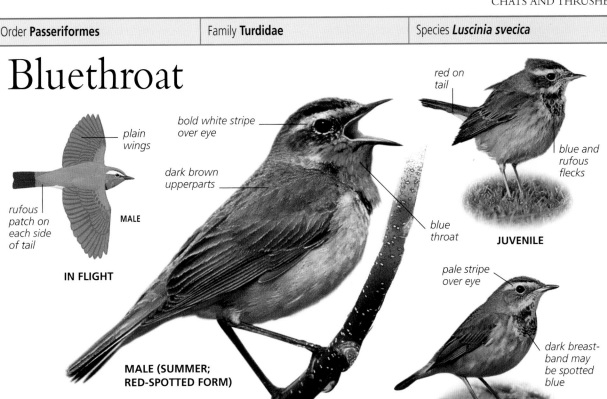

plain wings

MALE

rufous patch on each side of tail

IN FLIGHT

bold white stripe over eye

dark brown upperparts

blue throat

MALE (SUMMER; RED-SPOTTED FORM)

red on tail

blue and rufous flecks

JUVENILE

pale stripe over eye

dark breast-band may be spotted blue

FEMALE

This is chiefly a bird of wet places, such as thickets at the edge of reedbeds and swampy ground within northern forests. In the UK, it is a scarce migrant, often in similar places and usually on the coast, so it is frequently difficult to watch. Not being a regular garden bird it is often overlooked, despite its unusual looks. It also sounds remarkable, its rich song including excellent mimicry. Its general form and actions recall the Robin.

VOICE Sharp, hard *tak*, softer *wheet*, often with hard note as *wheet-turrc*; song powerful, bright, musical, accelerating into melodious outburst with much mimicry.

NESTING Small grassy cup in low bush; 5–7 eggs; 1 brood; May–June.

FEEDING Forages on ground close to cover, picking up seeds, insects, and berries.

REMARK Subspecies *L. s. svecica* (North Europe) has rufous central breast spot; *L. s. magna* (Eastern Europe) has no spot.

FLIGHT: low, quite quick, flitting, usually short distance into nearby cover.

MUSICAL SONG
Males vigorously sing from concealed perches in dense waterside thickets and low bushes.

OCCURRENCE
Breeds locally in France, Low Countries, Scandinavia, and NE and C Europe. Prefers wet thickets, moist woods, heaths, and bushes on tundra. On migration, a few appear west of usual range, in coastal thickets and reeds during March to October.

Seen in the UK
J F **M A M J J A** S **O** N D

SIMILAR SPECIES

plainer head without stripe

no stripe over eye

more uniform tail

ROBIN
see p.300

NIGHTINGALE
see p.303

SUBSPECIES

L. s. cyanecula
(S and C Europe)

white central breast spot

Length **14cm (5½in)**	Wingspan **20–22cm (8–9in)**	Weight **15–23g ($^9/_{16}$–$^{13}/_{16}$oz)**
Social **Solitary**	Lifespan **Up to 5 years**	Status **Secure**

Order **Passeriformes**	Family **Turdidae**	Species **Luscinia luscinia**

Thrush Nightingale

greyish back

dull tail

IN FLIGHT

pale eye-ring

softly mottled breast

ADULT (FRONT VIEW)

soft, pale, buff-brown and greyish olive

plain head

pale chest, mottled with olive-grey

ADULT

dull rusty-brown tail

Ʌ/Ʌ/Ʌ/Ʌ/Ʌ/Ʌ/Ʌ/Ʌ/Ʌ/Ʌ/Ʌ/Ʌ/Ʌ/Ʌ/Ʌ/Ʌ

FLIGHT: low, short, flitting flights between bushes.

Very like the Nightingale, the Thrush Nightingale replaces the more familiar bird in the north and east of Europe. It is variably mottled beneath and generally duller, without such a rusty-red tail as its southwestern counterpart. Equally difficult to see in dense undergrowth, it has a riveting song, full of loud, fast, rich phrases, which draws attention to it.

VOICE Song rich, throbbing, varied warble of varying pace; lacks the typical crescendo of Nightingale, with more clicking and throaty gurgling notes, less pure, beautiful quality as a whole.

NESTING Nest of grass and stems in dense bush close to ground; 4 or 5 eggs; 1 brood, May–June.

FEEDING Mostly under deep cover on the ground, eating insects, grubs, berries, and a few seeds.

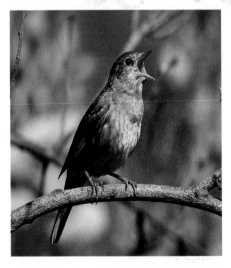

HIDDEN SONGSTER
Males sing from deep within thickets and dense woodland, they bear a strong resemblance to a Nightingale but have a slightly less varied song, with fewer high, pure notes.

OCCURRENCE
Summer visitor to E Europe north to S Scandinavia, Finland, south to Black Sea; in dense, often damp woods and copses, waterside bushes, rarely gardens; vagrant in the UK and W Europe.

SIMILAR SPECIES

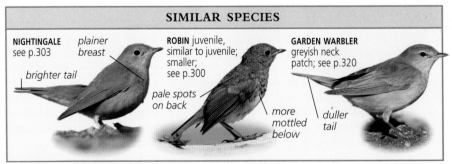

NIGHTINGALE see p.303

plainer breast

brighter tail

ROBIN juvenile, similar to juvenile; smaller; see p.300

pale spots on back

more mottled below

GARDEN WARBLER greyish neck patch; see p.320

duller tail

Seen in the UK

J	F	M	A	M	J	J	A	S	O	N	D
			A	M	J	J	A				

Length **15–17cm (6–7in)**	Wingspan **23–26cm (9–10in)**	Weight **18–27g (⅝–1oz)**
Social **Solitary/Family groups**	Lifespan **Up to 5 years**	Status **Secure**

Order **Passeriformes**	Family **Turdidae**	Species *Luscinia megarhynchos*

Nightingale 🔊 61

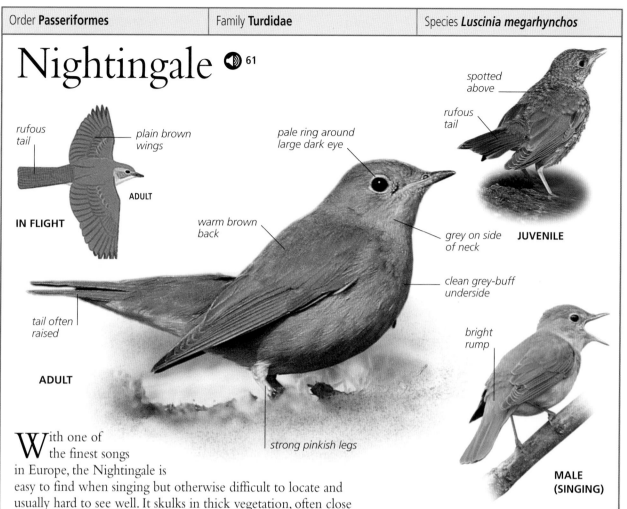

rufous tail

plain brown wings

pale ring around large dark eye

spotted above

rufous tail

IN FLIGHT

ADULT

warm brown back

grey on side of neck

JUVENILE

clean grey-buff underside

tail often raised

bright rump

ADULT

strong pinkish legs

MALE (SINGING)

With one of the finest songs in Europe, the Nightingale is easy to find when singing but otherwise difficult to locate and usually hard to see well. It skulks in thick vegetation, often close to the ground, although with a little patience a clear view can sometimes be obtained. In places, it sings much more openly, but is likely to drop out of sight immediately if approached too closely. Although quite plain in appearance, its identification is usually straightforward.

VOICE Calls include low, mechanical, grating *kerrr*, loud, bright *hweet*; song brilliant but unstructured, very varied, some phrases extremely fast with sudden change from high to low pitch; long, slow, plaintive notes build to sudden throaty trill.

NESTING Cup of grass and leaves in dense bushy cover close to ground; 4 or 5 eggs; 1 brood; May–June.

FEEDING Forages in clear spaces under dense, dark cover, in ditches, and under thickets for worms, larvae, beetles, and berries.

FLIGHT: low, short, flitting, with wings and tail fanned briefly as it dives into cover.

POWERFUL SONG
Males sing more consistently at dawn and dusk, and bursts of song are often intermittent by day.

OCCURRENCE
In Europe from April to August; common in S Europe, scarce in NW as far as England and Germany. Breeds in many kinds of thickets that are dense to ground level, from bushy gullies and overgrown gardens to woodland with bushy (especially coppiced) undergrowth and clumps of dense bushes on heaths.

Seen in the UK
J F **M A M J J A** S O N D

SIMILAR SPECIES

THRUSH NIGHTINGALE see p.302

mottled on chest

duller

ROBIN juvenile, similar to juvenile; see p.300

smaller

GARDEN WARBLER see p.320

duller

smaller

Length **16–17cm (6½in)**	Wingspan **23–26cm (9–10in)**	Weight **18–27g (⅝–¹⁵⁄₁₆oz)**
Social **Solitary**	Lifespan **Up to 5 years**	Status **Secure†**

Order **Passeriformes**	Family **Turdidae**	Species *Phoenicurus phoenicurus*

Redstart

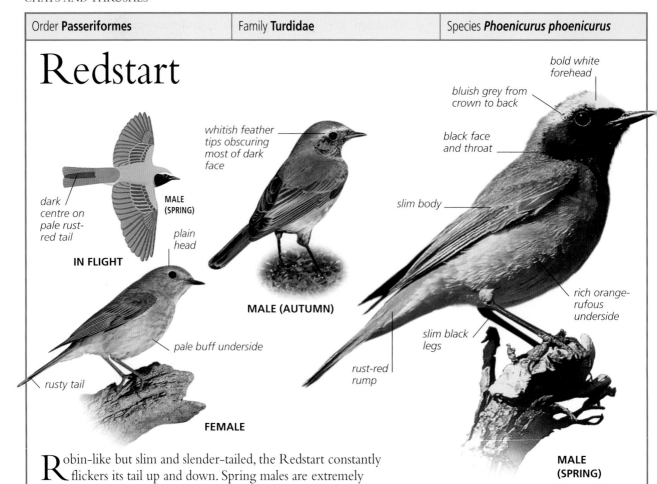

bold white forehead

bluish grey from crown to back

black face and throat

slim body

whitish feather tips obscuring most of dark face

dark centre on pale rust-red tail

MALE (SPRING)

plain head

IN FLIGHT

MALE (AUTUMN)

rich orange-rufous underside

slim black legs

rust-red rump

pale buff underside

rusty tail

FEMALE

MALE (SPRING)

Robin-like but slim and slender-tailed, the Redstart constantly flickers its tail up and down. Spring males are extremely handsome birds, best located by following up their short, sweet song. A woodland bird, the Redstart prefers to nest in old woods with plenty of space beneath the canopy in which it can feed. As a migrant, it often appears in thickets and bushes, both inland (often in willow thickets beside lakes and reservoirs) and more commonly along the coast.

VOICE Clear, rising *wheet* or *hueeee*; *huee-tic*; sharp *tac*; song brief, bright, musical warble, often beginning with several low, rolling notes, finishing in weak trill.

NESTING Grassy nest lined with feathers and hair, in hole or nest box; 5–7 eggs; 1 brood; May–June.

FEEDING In foliage or drops to ground, finding insects, spiders, caterpillars, small worms, and some berries.

FLIGHT: quite quick and agile, flitting from tree to tree; often drops briefly to ground.

AUTUMN PLUMAGE
Autumn females and juveniles have pale wingbars and a bright buffy appearance overall.

OCCURRENCE
Breeds in most of Europe (except Iceland and Ireland), in open woodland or old woods with little undergrowth, some in scattered trees on rocky slopes. Present from April to October, moving to Africa in winter. Migrants are often near the coast or in willow thickets beside reservoirs inland.

Seen in the UK
| J | F | M | A | M | J | J | A | S | O | N | D |

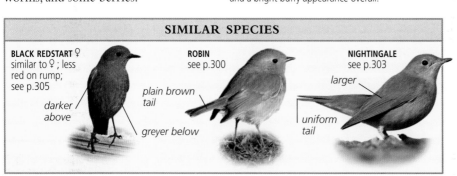

SIMILAR SPECIES

BLACK REDSTART ♀
similar to ♀; less red on rump; see p.305

darker above

ROBIN
see p.300

plain brown tail

greyer below

NIGHTINGALE
see p.303

larger

uniform tail

Length **14cm (5½in)**	Wingspan **20–24cm (8–9½in)**	Weight **12–20g ($^7/_{16}$–$^{11}/_{16}$oz)**
Social **Solitary**	Lifespan **Up to 5 years**	Status **Vulnerable**

Order **Passeriformes**	Family **Turdidae**	Species *Phoenicurus ochruros*

Black Redstart 🔊 62

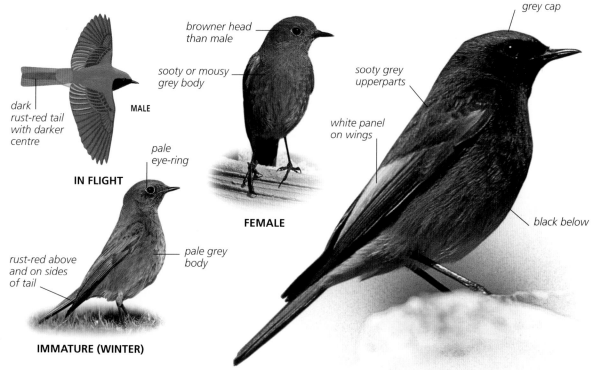

dark rust-red tail with darker centre

MALE

IN FLIGHT

browner head than male

sooty or mousy grey body

FEMALE

grey cap

sooty grey upperparts

white panel on wings

black below

pale eye-ring

rust-red above and on sides of tail

pale grey body

IMMATURE (WINTER)

MALE (SPRING)

A bird of rocky slopes with scree and crags, or deep gorges, the Black Redstart also readily occupies towns and villages with older buildings that offer holes in which to nest and rough or waste ground where it can feed. It may move into industrial sites and run-down areas of larger cities. In winter, a few use quarries and rocky coves along the coast, but most prefer rough ground, from new building sites to derelict land with brick and concrete rubble.

VOICE Call hard, rattling or creaky notes, short *tsip, tucc-tucc, titititic*; song hesitant warble with strange stone-shaking trills and rattles, carries far in town or on cliff where elusive.

NESTING Grassy nest in hole in building, on ledge, in cavity in cliff or fallen rocks; 4–6 eggs; 2 broods; May–July.

FEEDING Leaps and flies after insects, drops to ground from high perch or boulder to pick up beetles, grubs, worms, some berries, and seeds.

FLIGHT: quick, agile, darting through small spaces, dashing across roofs, with bursts of flicking wingbeats.

IMMATURE MALE
Males often sing and sometimes breed while still in immature grey plumage.

OCCURRENCE
Breeds in most of Europe except Iceland, N Great Britain (very rare in S), and N Scandinavia, in towns and villages with old buildings, cities and derelict industrial areas, cliffs, gorges, mountain areas, and often in old quarries along coast. In winter, often in quarries or along rocky coast.

SIMILAR SPECIES

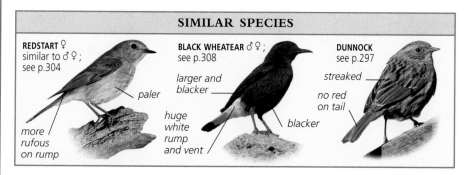

REDSTART ♀ similar to ♂♀; see p.304

more rufous on rump

paler

BLACK WHEATEAR ♂♀; see p.308

larger and blacker

huge white rump and vent

blacker

DUNNOCK see p.297

streaked

no red on tail

Seen in the UK
J F M A M J J A S O N D

Length **14.5cm (5¾in)**	Wingspan **23–26cm (9–10in)**	Weight **14–20g (½–¹¹⁄₁₆oz)**
Social **Family groups**	Lifespan **Up to 5 years**	Status **Secure**

| Order **Passeriformes** | Family **Turdidae** | Species *Oenanthe oenanthe* |

Wheatear

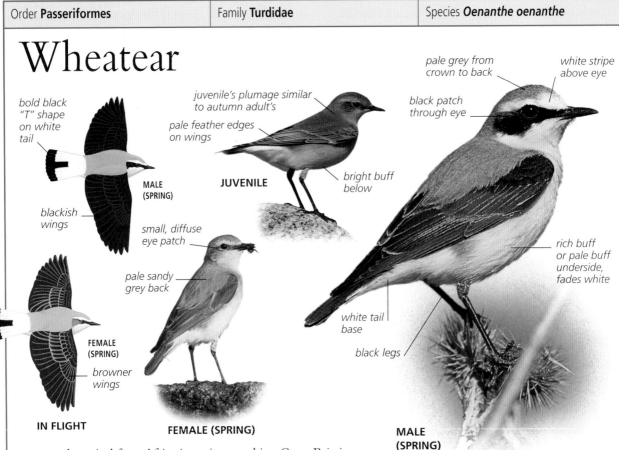

bold black "T" shape on white tail

MALE (SPRING)

blackish wings

juvenile's plumage similar to autumn adult's

pale feather edges on wings

JUVENILE

bright buff below

pale grey from crown to back

white stripe above eye

black patch through eye

rich buff or pale buff underside, fades white

small, diffuse eye patch

pale sandy grey back

white tail base

black legs

MALE (SPRING)

FEMALE (SPRING)

browner wings

IN FLIGHT

FEMALE (SPRING)

An early arrival from Africa in spring, reaching Great Britain in early March, the Wheatear breeds in open areas with grassy places on which it feeds adjacent to scree, stone walls, crags, or, more rarely, holes in sandy ground in which to nest. It is a frequent migrant outside its breeding areas, turning up along coasts, on farmland, and on grass beside reservoirs. Very much a terrestrial bird, it usually avoids trees and bushes. It frequently flies ahead of people, not going far, and revealing its distinctive white rump each time it moves.

VOICE Hard *chak-chak*, bright *wheet-chak-chak*; song long, rambling, quick warble with rolling, scratchy notes, often in song-flight.

NESTING Grassy cup, in hole in ground, rabbit burrow, or under fallen rocks, in stone wall; 5 or 6 eggs; 1 or 2 broods; April–July.

FEEDING Bouncy hops, short runs, on open ground, picking up insects and spiders; sometimes catches flies in flight or with sudden short, fluttery leap.

FLIGHT: low, flitting, quite strong, undulating; sometimes swoops up to perch.

ROCK HOPPER
The Wheatear has strong legs and feet, ideal for the rocky habitat in which it is often found.

SUBSPECIES

O. o. leucorhoa (Greenland; W Europe in spring)

richer colours

larger

SIMILAR SPECIES

BLACK-EARED WHEATEAR ♂♀; buff back; see p.307

more white on tail

WHINCHAT ♂♀; streaky brown rump; see p.309

smaller

OCCURRENCE
Breeds almost throughout Europe but very local, where open grassy or heathy ground is mixed with scree, boulders, and cliffs, typically at rather high altitude or in hilly areas. Migrants encountered on fields, grassy areas, dunes, and golf courses, from March to October.

Seen in the UK
| J | F | M | A | M | J | J | A | S | O | N | D |

| Length **14.5–15.5cm (5¾–6in)** | Wingspan **26–32cm (10–12½in)** | Weight **17–30g (⅝–1¹⁄₁₆oz)** |
| Social **Small flocks** | Lifespan **Up to 5 years** | Status **Secure** |

306

Order **Passeriformes**	Family **Turdidae**	Species *Oenanthe hispanica*

Black-eared Wheatear

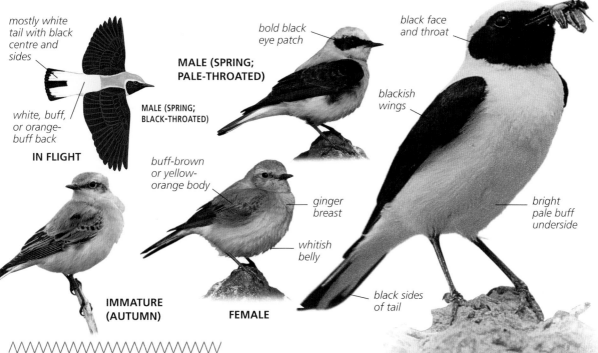

mostly white tail with black centre and sides

white, buff, or orange-buff back

IN FLIGHT

MALE (SPRING; PALE-THROATED)

bold black eye patch

black face and throat

blackish wings

MALE (SPRING; BLACK-THROATED)

buff-brown or yellow-orange body

ginger breast

whitish belly

bright pale buff underside

IMMATURE (AUTUMN)

FEMALE

black sides of tail

MALE (SPRING; BLACK-THROATED)

FLIGHT: quick, light, direct, long tail allows good manoeuvrability; often swoops up to raised perch.

Slimmer, lighter, and less solid than a Wheatear, the Black-eared Wheatear occurs in two forms – black-throated and pale-throated – and requires careful identification in plumages other than the spring male's, which is bold and striking. It combines some of the actions of the smaller chats with the typical behaviour of ground-feeding wheatears. This southern European wheatear is common on warm, stony Mediterranean slopes, readily perching on low bushes and tall stems.

VOICE Wheezy *tssch*, hard *tack*; song fast, rattling warble, quite bright and explosive, sometimes with mimicry.

NESTING Grassy cup in hole, under boulders or stones, or at base of bush; 4 or 5 eggs; 1 or 2 broods; April–June.

FEEDING Watches from bush top or stone, drops to ground, or chases after insects; eats some small seeds.

REMARK Subspecies *O. h. hispanica* (SW Europe) has less black on face and throat and yellower back; *O. h. melanoleuca* (S Italy, Balkans) has more black on face, whiter back, and longer wingtips. Both have black- and pale-throated forms.

SLENDER FORM
This is a slim, elegant wheatear, often perching on bushes, using its tail to maintain its balance.

OCCURRENCE
Very locally in Spain, Portugal, and Mediterranean countries, in variety of open, often barren places with scattered bushes, rocks, and high stony pastures, from March to October. Only rare vagrant farther north in spring or autumn.

Seen in the UK
J F M A M J J A S O N D

SIMILAR SPECIES

broader black tail band

smaller and much stockier

white only on rump

WHEATEAR ♂♀;
see p.306

STONECHAT ♂♀;
see p.310

Length **13.5–15cm (5¼–6in)**	Wingspan **25–30cm (10–12in)**	Weight **15–25g (⁹⁄₁₆–⁷⁄₈oz)**
Social **Family groups**	Lifespan **Up to 5 years**	Status **Vulnerable**

307

Order **Passeriformes**	Family **Turdidae**	Species **Oenanthe leucura**

Black Wheatear

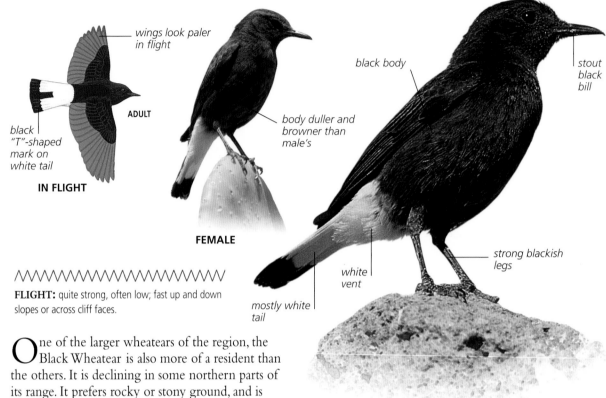

wings look paler in flight

ADULT

black "T"-shaped mark on white tail

IN FLIGHT

black body

stout black bill

body duller and browner than male's

FEMALE

strong blackish legs

white vent

mostly white tail

FLIGHT: quite strong, often low; fast up and down slopes or across cliff faces.

MALE (SPRING)

One of the larger wheatears of the region, the Black Wheatear is also more of a resident than the others. It is declining in some northern parts of its range. It prefers rocky or stony ground, and is often on or around the base of sheer cliffs, being surprisingly inconspicuous in the strong light and shade of scree slopes or boulders. If it flies, however, its very large and striking white rump and tail become immediately obvious.

VOICE Bright, whistled *pewp*, hard *tet-tet*; song low, rich or lighter, harsh twittering, sometimes in song-flight.

NESTING Grassy cup in hole in ground, rabbit burrow, under fallen rocks, or in stone wall; 5 or 6 eggs; 1 or 2 broods; April–July.

FEEDING Forages on ground, moving up and down slopes in short flights; swoops from perches on insects and spiders.

UPRIGHT STANCE
Like all wheatears and chats, the Black Wheatear has a bold, upright posture on strong legs, and moves with quick, leaping hops.

OCCURRENCE
Breeds on slopes with rocks and scree from Pyrenees southwards through Spain and Portugal. Resident there but does not move outside this restricted range. Often seen perched on cliffs, crags, and boulders or feeding on patches of short grass.

Seen in the UK
J F M A M J J A S O N D

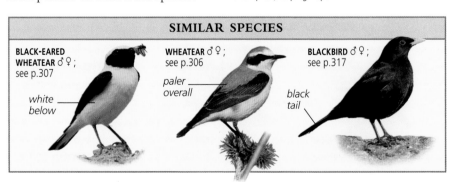

SIMILAR SPECIES

BLACK-EARED WHEATEAR ♂♀; see p.307

white below

WHEATEAR ♂♀; see p.306

paler overall

BLACKBIRD ♂♀; see p.317

black tail

Length **16–18cm (6½–7in)**	Wingspan **30–35cm (12–14in)**	Weight **25–35g (⅞–1¼oz)**
Social **Family groups**	Lifespan **Up to 5 years**	Status **Endangered**

| Order **Passeriformes** | Family **Turdidae** | Species **Saxicola rubetra** |

Whinchat

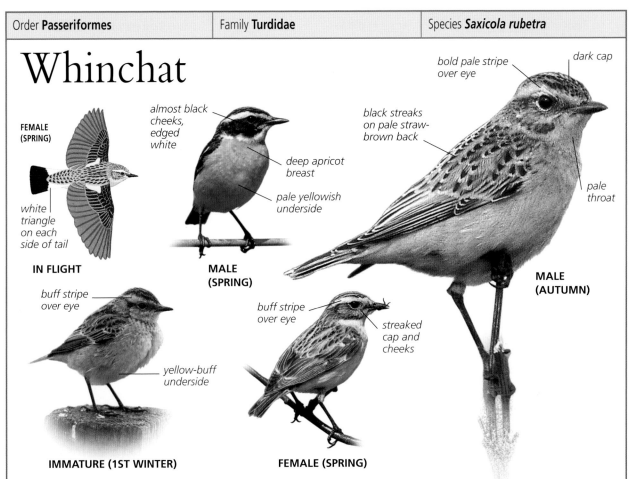

FEMALE (SPRING)

white triangle on each side of tail

IN FLIGHT

almost black cheeks, edged white

deep apricot breast

pale yellowish underside

MALE (SPRING)

bold pale stripe over eye

dark cap

black streaks on pale straw-brown back

pale throat

MALE (AUTUMN)

buff stripe over eye

yellow-buff underside

IMMATURE (1ST WINTER)

buff stripe over eye

streaked cap and cheeks

FEMALE (SPRING)

Declining in much of its range as its preferred habitats are altered, the Whinchat is a bird of grassland with tall, woody stems or small bushes which give it an open perch quite close to the ground. Young conifer plantations serve it well for a few years but "rough", uncultivated ground is often not tolerated in agricultural or suburban areas and so the Whinchat is squeezed out. It is a summer visitor to Europe, unlike the similar but resident Stonechat.

VOICE Loud, short, *tictic* or *tuc-tuc-tuc*, *wheet* or *wheet-tuk*; song varied, at best Robin-like but with clicks, rattles, and grating notes mixed in.

NESTING Grassy nest low in tussock, bush, or ground; 5 or 6 eggs; 1 or 2 broods; May–July.

FEEDING Watches from perch and drops to ground to pick up insects and worms; also feeds on some seeds and berries.

FLIGHT: short, low, flitting, quite quick, usually on to isolated, slender upright stem or fence.

SPRING PERFECTION
A male in spring is a superbly patterned, crisply coloured bird.

OCCURRENCE
Present from April to September in open places with heather, grass, scattered taller stems, or young trees. Widespread but increasingly scarce and localized; absent from Iceland. Migrants typically rest near coasts in open grassy or marshy places.

| Seen in the UK |
| J F M **A M J J A S O** N D |

SIMILAR SPECIES

WHEATEAR ♂♀;
see p.306

larger

more white on tail

SEDGE WARBLER ♂♀
similar to ♀;
see p.328

plain tail

no pale stripe over eye

dark throat

STONECHAT ♂♀;
see p.310

| Length **12.5cm (5in)** | Wingspan **21–24cm (8½–9½in)** | Weight **16–24g (⁹⁄₁₆–⁷⁄₈oz)** |
| Social **Family groups** | Lifespan **Up to 5 years** | Status **Secure** |

Order **Passeriformes**	Family **Turdidae**	Species *Saxicola torquatus*

Stonechat 🔊 63

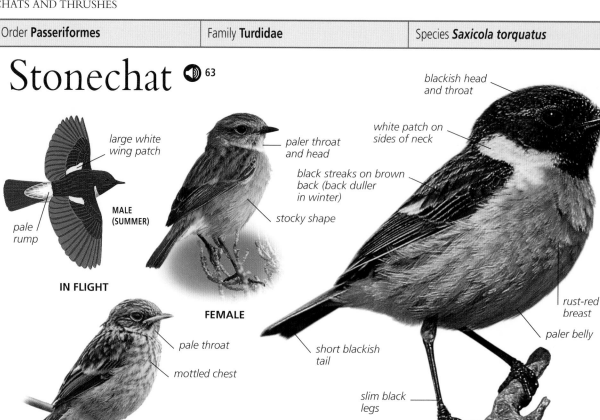

large white wing patch

pale rump

MALE (SUMMER)

IN FLIGHT

paler throat and head

black streaks on brown back (back duller in winter)

stocky shape

FEMALE

blackish head and throat

white patch on sides of neck

rust-red breast

paler belly

short blackish tail

slim black legs

MALE (SUMMER)

pale throat

mottled chest

JUVENILE

Small, chunky, and upright, the Stonechat often perches on the tops of bushes or on overhead wires in otherwise rather open places. Heaths, upland moors, and stretches of grassland with gorse thickets above coastal cliffs are perfect for it; in winter, it may move to the coast to escape hard weather, and inland breeding populations may temporarily disappear after bad winters. Migrant Siberian Stonechats are more like pale Whinchats in some respects but resident Stonechats are usually easily identified.

VOICE Hard, scolding *tsak* or *tsak-tsak*, sharp *wheet*, often *wheet-tak-tak*; song sometimes in flight, rapid, chattery warble with some chattering and grating notes, less musical than Whinchat's.

NESTING Grassy cup, lined with hair and feathers, often in dense grass with entrance tunnel; 5 or 6 eggs; 2 broods; May–July.

FEEDING Drops to ground to pick up insects, spiders, worms, and some seeds; catches some insects in flight, returning to eat them on a perch.

FLIGHT: low, quick, direct, whirring, onto prominent perch.

SUBSPECIES

S. t. maura (Siberia); clear rufous rump

pale line over eye

white feather fringes

OCCURRENCE
Breeds in most of Europe except Iceland, Scandinavia, and NE Europe; rather scarce inland in NW Europe. Likes open places with gorse, heather, and bushes, on heaths or above coastal cliffs, and dunes.

Seen in the UK
J F M A M J J A S O N D

SIMILAR SPECIES

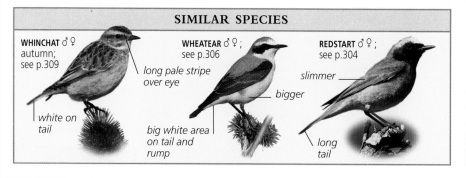

WHINCHAT ♂♀ autumn; see p.309

long pale stripe over eye

white on tail

WHEATEAR ♂♀; see p.306

bigger

big white area on tail and rump

REDSTART ♂♀; see p.304

slimmer

long tail

Length **12.5cm (5in)**	Wingspan **18–21cm (7–8½in)**	Weight **14–17g (½–⅝oz)**
Social **Family groups**	Lifespan **Up to 5 years**	Status **Declining†**

Order **Passeriformes**	Family **Turdidae**	Species *Monticola solitarius*

Blue Rock Thrush

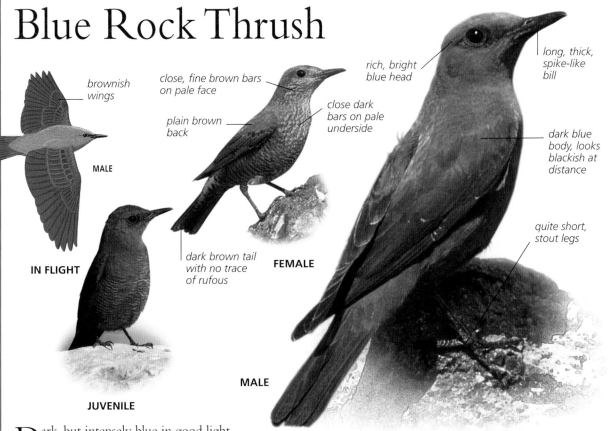

brownish wings

MALE

IN FLIGHT

JUVENILE

close, fine brown bars on pale face

plain brown back

dark brown tail with no trace of rufous

FEMALE

rich, bright blue head

close dark bars on pale underside

long, thick, spike-like bill

dark blue body, looks blackish at distance

quite short, stout legs

MALE

Dark, but intensely blue in good light and at close range, the Blue Rock Thrush is mostly found around cliffs and deep mountain gorges; it also occurs around coastal villages and developments, perching freely on roofs and wires. In more remote places, it is often best located by its loud song. Females are more problematical than males but equally distinctive if seen well. The thrush-like silhouette, with a particularly long, thick, spike-like bill, is a useful feature.

VOICE Deep, thrush-like *chook*, higher squeaky notes; song rich, musical warbling, melancholy, Blackbird-like, carrying far across gorges and cliffs.

NESTING Grassy cup in hole in wall or cliff or under rocks; 4 or 5 eggs; 1 or 2 broods; May–July.

FEEDING Picks insects, spiders, worms, lizards, berries, and seeds from ground.

FLIGHT: swift, direct; flappy over long distance, recalling Blackbird.

ELUSIVE ON CLIFFS
The blue male is handsome when seen well but is surprisingly difficult to spot against rocks.

OCCURRENCE
Breeds in Spain, Portugal, and Mediterranean area, where mostly resident. In gorges, rocky areas with crags and boulders in mountains, and also around buildings and quarries, often near coasts.

Seen in the UK											
J	F	M	A	M	J	J	A	S	O	N	D

SIMILAR SPECIES

BLACKBIRD ♂♀; ♀ more uniform; see p.317

blacker

♂

ROCK THRUSH juvenile, similar to juvenile, ♀; see p.312

smaller and brighter

shorter rufous tail

SPOTLESS STARLING ♂♀; see p.381

stockier

dark and glossy

shorter tail

Length **21–23cm (8½–9in)**	Wingspan **35–40cm (14–16in)**	Weight **60–80g (2⅛–2⅞oz)**
Social **Family groups**	Lifespan **5–10 years**	Status **Vulnerable†**

| Order **Passeriformes** | Family **Turdidae** | Species *Monticola saxatilis* |

Rock Thrush

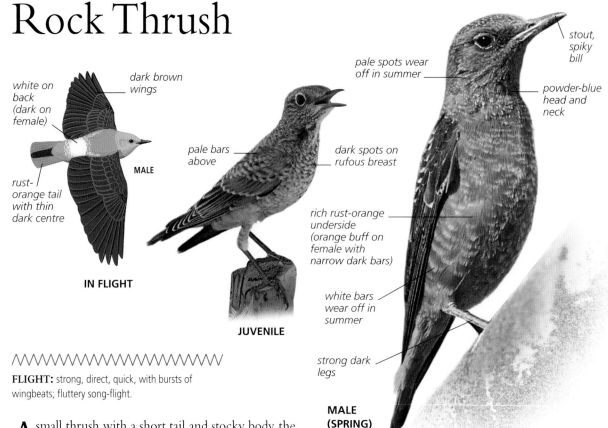

white on back (dark on female)

dark brown wings

MALE

rust-orange tail with thin dark centre

IN FLIGHT

pale bars above

dark spots on rufous breast

JUVENILE

pale spots wear off in summer

stout, spiky bill

powder-blue head and neck

rich rust-orange underside (orange buff on female with narrow dark bars)

white bars wear off in summer

strong dark legs

MALE (SPRING)

FLIGHT: strong, direct, quick, with bursts of wingbeats; fluttery song-flight.

A small thrush with a short tail and stocky body, the Rock Thrush is characteristic of high alpine pastures, rocky slopes, and small upland fields with stone walls. It perches on boulders, poles, overhead wires, and other prominent places and so may be relatively easy to see. Its song-flight also catches the eye, although finding a small bird in a habitat that is generally so open and expansive can be difficult. Identifying it is usually simple enough: males especially are quite striking.

VOICE Squeaky *whit* and hard *chak*; song fluty, soft, Blackbird-like rich, musical warble, descending, often in song-flight.

NESTING Grassy cup in hole in wall or cavity among rocks or scree; 4 or 5 eggs; 1 brood; May–June.

FEEDING Looks for food from high perch, dropping down onto insects, small reptiles, and worms; also eats berries and seeds.

SUMMER COLOURS
Fresh feathers have whitish tips, but by mid-summer, these wear off to create a more uniform appearance.

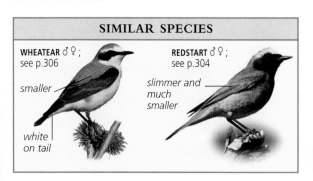

SIMILAR SPECIES

WHEATEAR ♂♀; see p.306

smaller

white on tail

REDSTART ♂♀; see p.304

slimmer and much smaller

OCCURRENCE
Found from March to September in S Europe north to Alps and Pyrenees, very rare outside this range. Breeds in high alpine meadows and on grassy slopes with boulders and crags; also on cliffs and in deep gorges.

Seen in the UK
J F M A M J J A S O N D

| Length **17–20cm (6½–8in)** | Wingspan **30–35cm (12–14in)** | Weight **50–70g (1¾–2½oz)** |
| Social **Family groups** | Lifespan **Up to 5 years** | Status **Declining†** |

Order **Passeriformes**	Family **Turdidae**	Species *Turdus philomelos*

Song Thrush 🔊 64

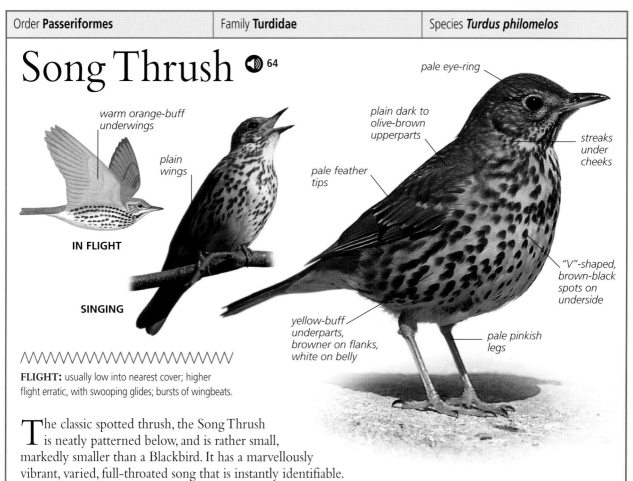

warm orange-buff underwings

plain wings

IN FLIGHT

SINGING

pale eye-ring

plain dark to olive-brown upperparts

pale feather tips

streaks under cheeks

"V"-shaped, brown-black spots on underside

yellow-buff underparts, browner on flanks, white on belly

pale pinkish legs

/\/\/\/\/\/\/\/\/\/\/\/\/\/\/\/\

FLIGHT: usually low into nearest cover; higher flight erratic, with swooping glides; bursts of wingbeats.

The classic spotted thrush, the Song Thrush is neatly patterned below, and is rather small, markedly smaller than a Blackbird. It has a marvellously vibrant, varied, full-throated song that is instantly identifiable. A declining bird in many areas, it relies on some woodland or tree cover, or at least big, bushy hedges in farmland. It is equally at home in mixed or deciduous woodland with some clearings and well-wooded gardens or town parks.

VOICE Short, thin, high *stip*; loud alarm rattle; song loud, exuberant, shouted, each separated phrase of 2–4 notes repeated 2–4 times, some musical, some whistled, others harsh or rattled.

NESTING Grassy cup lined with mud and dung, low in bush, hedge, or tree; 3–5 eggs; 2 or 3 broods; March–July.

FEEDING Hops and runs across open ground, stopping to detect and extract earthworms; eats many snails, slugs, other invertebrates, berries, and fruit; shy visitor to bird-tables, but eats scattered scraps and apples.

ELDERBERRY TREAT
Autumn berries provide welcome food for the Song Thrush, in addition to the usual diet of worms and snails.

OCCURRENCE
Breeds in almost all of Europe except Iceland; in summer, only in N and E Europe, resident and winter visitor in S and W. In broadleaved woodland, parkland, farmland with trees and hedges, gardens, parks with lawns, and shrubberies.

Seen in the UK
J F M A M J J A S O N D

SIMILAR SPECIES

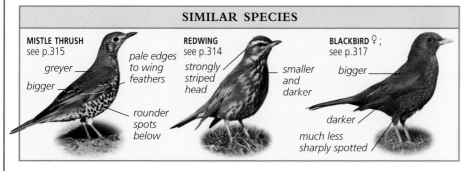

MISTLE THRUSH see p.315

greyer

bigger

pale edges to wing feathers

rounder spots below

REDWING see p.314

strongly striped head

smaller and darker

BLACKBIRD ♀; see p.317

bigger

darker

much less sharply spotted

Length **23cm (9in)**	Wingspan **33–36cm (13–14in)**	Weight **70–90g (2½–3¼oz)**
Social **Family groups**	Lifespan **Up to 5 years**	Status **Secure**

Order **Passeriformes**	Family **Turdidae**	Species *Turdus iliacus*

Redwing

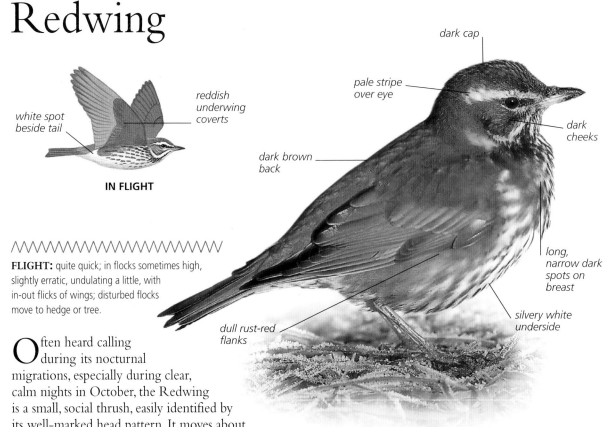

IN FLIGHT

white spot
beside tail

reddish
underwing
coverts

dark cap

pale stripe
over eye

dark
cheeks

dark brown
back

long,
narrow dark
spots on
breast

silvery white
underside

dull rust-red
flanks

FLIGHT: quite quick; in flocks sometimes high, slightly erratic, undulating a little, with in-out flicks of wings; disturbed flocks move to hedge or tree.

Often heard calling during its nocturnal migrations, especially during clear, calm nights in October, the Redwing is a small, social thrush, easily identified by its well-marked head pattern. It moves about in flocks, often mixed with Fieldfares, and, in winter, feeds in loose congregations in fields or in closer groups, feeding on berries in hedgerows. It is not generally a garden bird but will come to larger gardens for food during hard weather, to which it is particularly susceptible. Breeding pairs form small, scattered groups.

VOICE Flight call, often at night, high, thin, simple *seeeeh*, also *chuk*, *chittuk*; song variable, monotonous repetition of short phrases and chuckling notes with rising or falling pattern.

NESTING Cup of grass and twigs, in low bush or shrub; 4–6 eggs; 2 broods; April–July.

FEEDING Often on ground, in winter in loose flocks advancing across field, finding worms, insects, and seeds; also in hedges, feeding on berries; in hard weather, visits gardens for apples and berries.

BERRY EATERS
Hedgerow berry crops are quickly exhausted by mixed flocks of Redwings and Fieldfares descending on them.

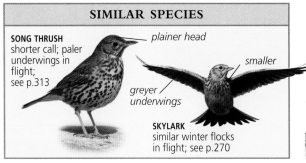

SIMILAR SPECIES

SONG THRUSH
shorter call; paler underwings in flight; see p.313

plainer head

greyer underwings

SKYLARK
similar winter flocks in flight; see p.270

smaller

OCCURRENCE
Breeds in N and E Europe; winters in N and S Europe. Nests in birch woods and conifer forest; in winter, on bushy heaths, in farmland with hedges and old pastures, in larger, undisturbed parks, and in gardens, especially in hard weather.

Seen in the UK
J F M A M J J A S O N D

Length **21cm (8½in)**	Wingspan **33–35cm (13–14in)**	Weight **55–75g (2–2⅝oz)**
Social **Winter flocks**	Lifespan **Up to 5 years**	Status **Secure**

| Order **Passeriformes** | Family **Turdidae** | Species *Turdus viscivorus* |

Mistle Thrush 🔊 65

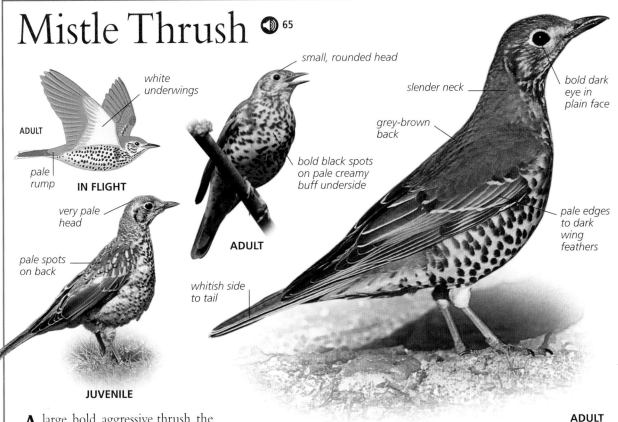

ADULT

white underwings

pale rump

IN FLIGHT

small, rounded head

bold black spots on pale creamy buff underside

ADULT

very pale head

pale spots on back

whitish side to tail

slender neck

grey-brown back

bold dark eye in plain face

pale edges to dark wing feathers

JUVENILE

ADULT

A large, bold, aggressive thrush, the Mistle Thrush is by far the largest of the "spotted" thrushes and also Europe's biggest true songbird. It is usually found in pairs, but families join up in larger groups during autumn when berries are abundant. In winter, single Mistle Thrushes often defend berry-laden trees against other birds, maintaining a food supply through the colder months. While Song Thrushes often slip away at low level if disturbed, Mistle Thrushes tend to go up to a much greater height and fly off over greater distances.

VOICE Loud, slurred, harsh, rattling chatter *tsairrrk-sairr-sairr-sairrk*; song loud, wild, fluty, not very varied, series of short, repetitive phrases.

NESTING Big, loose cup of roots, leaves, twigs, and grass, often quite exposed high on tree branch; 3–5 eggs; 2 broods; March–June.

FEEDING Bounding hops on ground, searching for worms, seeds, and invertebrates; eats many berries, sometimes coming to larger gardens for fruit.

〰〰〰〰〰〰〰〰〰〰〰〰〰〰

FLIGHT: strong, direct, sometimes undulating with long swoops between bursts of wingbeats; often high and far-ranging.

PALE THRUSH
Against the dark foliage of a conifer, this bird may look very pale.

OCCURRENCE
Breeds in most of Europe except extreme N; summer visitor in N and E Europe. In parkland, farmland with tall trees, orchards, on edges of moorland near mature forest, woodland clearings, and lower scrub, often feeding on open grassland and large lawns.

| Seen in the UK |
| J F M A M J J A S O N D |

SIMILAR SPECIES

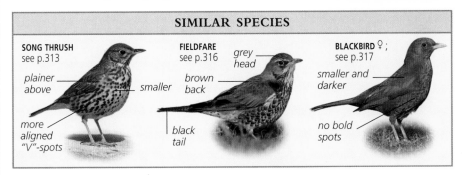

SONG THRUSH
see p.313

plainer above

smaller

more aligned "V"-spots

FIELDFARE
see p.316

grey head

brown back

black tail

BLACKBIRD ♀;
see p.317

smaller and darker

no bold spots

| Length **27cm (10½in)** | Wingspan **42–48cm (16½–19in)** | Weight **110–140g (4–5oz)** |
| Social **Winter flocks** | Lifespan **5–10 years** | Status **Secure** |

Order **Passeriformes**	Family **Turdidae**	Species *Turdus pilaris*

Fieldfare

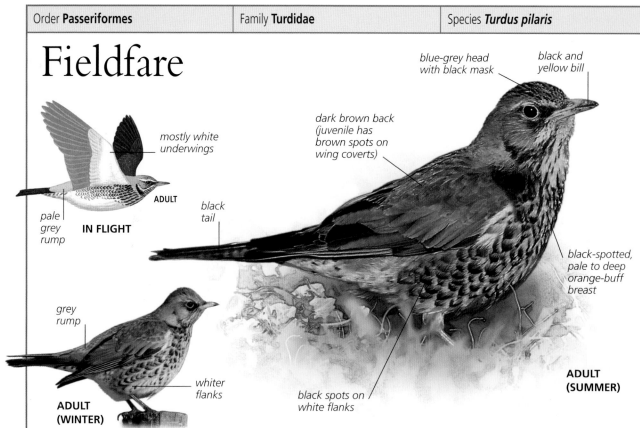

blue-grey head with black mask

black and yellow bill

dark brown back (juvenile has brown spots on wing coverts)

mostly white underwings

ADULT

black tail

pale grey rump

IN FLIGHT

black-spotted, pale to deep orange-buff breast

grey rump

whiter flanks

black spots on white flanks

ADULT (WINTER)

ADULT (SUMMER)

A large, striking, and handsome thrush, the Fieldfare has a distinctive call and a unique combination of colours. The white underwing is a useful feature for identification, as is the tendency to move around in flocks and to nest colonially. Flocks in flight keep more or less together but drift along in irregular lines and shapeless packs, less coordinated than, for example, some of the smaller finches.

VOICE Distinctive loud, soft or harder, chuckling *chak-chak-chak* or *tsak-tsak-tsak*, low, nasal Lapwing-like *weeip*; song rather poor, unmusical mixture of squeaks, warbles, and whistles.

NESTING Cup of grass and twigs, in bush or tree, often in loose colonies; 5 or 6 eggs; 1 or 2 broods; May–June.

FEEDING Mostly eats worms and insects on ground; also takes apples, berries, and other fruit from trees, hedges, and bushes.

FLIGHT: quite strong, somewhat undulating, with bursts of wingbeat; irregular glides, quite slow and erratic; often in flocks.

NOMADIC FLOCKS
Fieldfares flock in winter, moving about and feeding together. They often mix with Redwings and interact with thrushes such as Blackbirds and Mistle Thrushes.

OCCURRENCE
Breeds across N and E Europe in wooded regions. Widespread, social winter visitor through all of W and S Europe, in wooded areas, bushy heaths, and farmland (especially old pastures and orchards) with hedges and scattered trees. Visits gardens in severe weather.

Seen in the UK
J	F	M	A	M	J	J	A	S	O	N	D

SIMILAR SPECIES

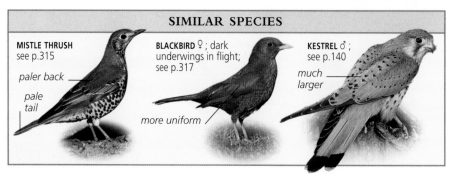

MISTLE THRUSH see p.315

paler back

pale tail

BLACKBIRD ♀; dark underwings in flight; see p.317

more uniform

KESTREL ♂; see p.140

much larger

Length **25cm (10in)**	Wingspan **39–42cm (15½–16½in)**	Weight **80–130g (2⅞–5oz)**
Social **Winter flocks**	Lifespan **5–10 years**	Status **Secure**

| Order **Passeriformes** | Family **Turdidae** | Species ***Turdus merula*** |

Blackbird 🔊 66

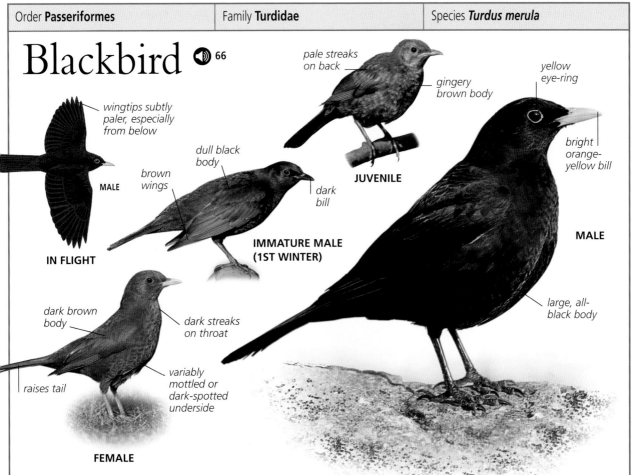

wingtips subtly paler, especially from below

MALE

IN FLIGHT

brown wings

dull black body

dark bill

IMMATURE MALE (1ST WINTER)

pale streaks on back

gingery brown body

JUVENILE

yellow eye-ring

bright orange-yellow bill

MALE

large, all-black body

dark brown body

dark streaks on throat

variably mottled or dark-spotted underside

raises tail

FEMALE

One of Europe's most familiar birds, the Blackbird is also a common example of a species with very obvious male and female differences. Black adult males are unique while females are always darker than other thrushes, although with a variable tendency to be spotted on the underparts. They range from remote mountain forests to gardens and parks, and are among the most regular garden birds and bird-table visitors in many areas. Blackbirds create most of the spring dawn chorus in suburban and woodland areas.

VOICE Low, soft *chook*, frequent loud, sharp *pink pink pink*; alarm rattle fast, hysterical outburst of sharp rattling notes, high, thin, slightly rough *srreee*; song superb, musical, full-throated, mellow warbling with many variations, phrases often ending in weak, scratchy sounds.

NESTING Grass and mud cup, lined with grass, in shrub, bush, low in tree or hedge; 3–5 eggs; 2–4 broods; March–August.

FEEDING Finds worms, insects, and invertebrates of all kinds on ground, often noisily exploring leaf litter; feeds on fruit and berries in bushes; often visits bird-tables, and eats scattered apples and bread.

FLIGHT: usually quite low, quick, swooping into cover; more undulating over longer range with flurries of wingbeats; raises tail on landing.

OCCURRENCE
Breeds over almost whole of Europe but rare in Iceland. In woods, gardens, parks, and farmland with tall hedges all year, in some areas garden lawn and shrubbery specialist, but essentially bird of woodland with rotting leaf litter on ground.

| Seen in the UK |
| J F M A M J J A S O N D |

SIMILAR SPECIES

SONG THRUSH similar to ♀; see p.313

paler

more clearly spotted below

short tail

STARLING ♂♀; see p.380

stockier

paler legs

paler wings

white breast-band

RING OUZEL ♂♀; see p.318

| Length **24–25cm (9½–10in)** | Wingspan **34–38cm (13½–15in)** | Weight **80–110g (2⅞–4oz)** |
| Social **Family groups** | Lifespan **Up to 5 years** | Status **Secure** |

Order **Passeriformes**	Family **Turdidae**	Species *Turdus torquatus*

Ring Ouzel

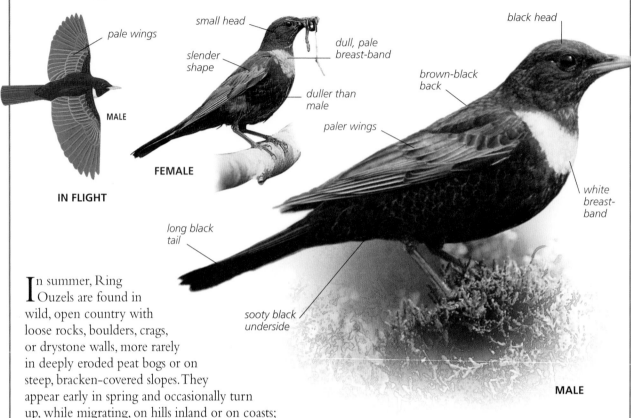

pale wings

MALE

IN FLIGHT

small head

slender shape

dull, pale breast-band

duller than male

FEMALE

paler wings

long black tail

sooty black underside

black head

brown-black back

white breast-band

MALE

In summer, Ring Ouzels are found in wild, open country with loose rocks, boulders, crags, or drystone walls, more rarely in deeply eroded peat bogs or on steep, bracken-covered slopes. They appear early in spring and occasionally turn up, while migrating, on hills inland or on coasts; in autumn, they are more often found by the sea, particularly on dunes overgrown with berry bushes. They tend to be rather shy and wild, quick to fly off out of sight. They are usually seen with head up, tail cocked, and wings drooped, or a head and bill may just be visible above a skyline rock. Ring Ouzels are declining in areas subject to increased human disturbance on summer weekends.

VOICE Loud, hard, rhythmic *tak-tak-tak*; various chattering and chuckling calls; song loud, wild, simple repetition of short phrases with musical, fluty quality.

NESTING Big, loose cup of grass, twigs, soil, and leaves, in steep bank, rock cavity, or fallen stone wall; 5 or 6 eggs; 2 broods; April–June.

FEEDING Feeds on insects, worms, seeds, and berries; eats berries in bushes on migration.

FLIGHT: fast, direct; often over long distance, recalling Mistle Thrush but lower; frequently flies off over ridge out of sight.

SUBSPECIES

T. t. alpestris
(S Europe)

pale wing panel

white "scales"

SIMILAR SPECIES

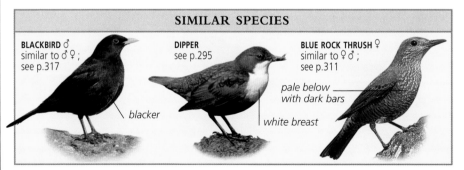

BLACKBIRD ♂
similar to ♂♀;
see p.317

blacker

DIPPER
see p.295

white breast

BLUE ROCK THRUSH ♀
similar to ♀♂;
see p.311

pale below with dark bars

OCCURRENCE
Breeds locally through Europe, except in Iceland and NE, mostly on high ground, on open moors with rocky places, gullies, exposed tors, and eroded peat bogs. Migrants in early spring and late autumn seen on hills and coasts.

Seen in the UK

J F M A M J J A S O N D

Length **23–24cm (9–9½in)**	Wingspan **38–42cm (15–16½in)**	Weight **95–130g (3⅜–5oz)**
Social **Family groups**	Lifespan **5–10 years**	Status **Secure**

Family **Sylviidae**

WARBLERS AND ALLIES

MOSTLY SMALLER THAN the thrushes and chats, most warblers fall into several neat groups, best recognized by their generic names.

Locustella warblers have grasshopper- or cricket-like songs; they are hard to see and identify, and have narrow heads, wings with curved outer edges, and long undertail coverts beneath a rounded tail.

Acrocephalus warblers are mostly reedbed birds, with spiky bills, flattish heads, rather long tails, and strong feet that give a grip on upright stems. Their songs are rich and hurried, often with repetitive patterns; calls are churring.

Hippolais warblers are green or pale brown, with spike-like bills. Wing length is a vital clue to their identity. They have short undertail coverts and square tails, and hurried, rambling songs.

Sylvia warblers are small, lively, perky birds with short bills, often peaked heads, and slim, sometimes cocked tails; some have brightly coloured eye-rings. Their calls are short and hard ("tak") but their songs are often beautifully rich.

Phylloscopus warblers are mostly green and yellowish; they are delicate, slipping easily through foliage, have sweet "hooeet" calls, and distinctive songs.

DIMORPHISM
A few species, such as the Blackcap (male pictured), have different male and female plumages.

PERSISTENT SINGERS
Male warblers sing a lot, especially if they are unable to find a mate, when they sing for weeks on end.

Family **Muscicapidae**

BRIGHT CHARACTER
Although dull in plumage, the Spotted Flycatcher's bright eyes and alertness make it a distinctive bird.

FLYCATCHERS

THERE ARE TWO GROUPS OF flycatchers: one includes basically brown ones (Spotted, Red-breasted), the other, birds in which the summer male is black and white (the "pied" group). They are short-billed, upright, long-winged, short-tailed birds. Male and female Spotted Flycatchers are alike, but in the others summer males are very different from female and winter plumages.

All are migrants, the Spotted Flycatcher being one of the last to arrive in spring. They mainly catch flies on the wing, although the pied group also drop to the ground; Spotted Flycatchers characteristically fly out and return to the same perch.

Order **Passeriformes**	Family **Sylviidae**	Species *Sylvia borin*

Garden Warbler 🔊 67

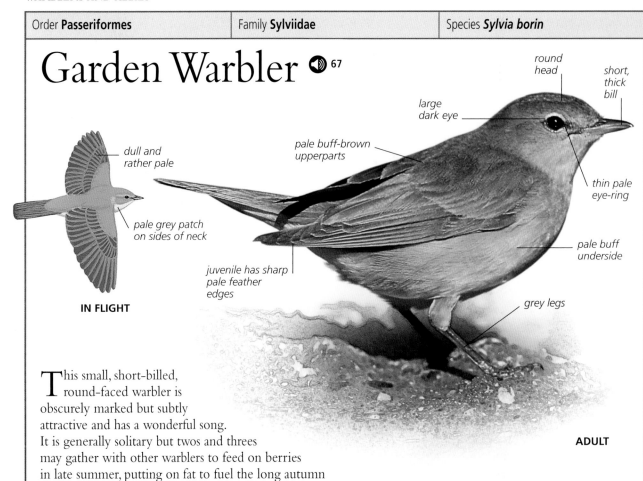

dull and rather pale

pale grey patch on sides of neck

IN FLIGHT

large dark eye

round head

short, thick bill

pale buff-brown upperparts

thin pale eye-ring

pale buff underside

juvenile has sharp pale feather edges

grey legs

ADULT

This small, short-billed, round-faced warbler is obscurely marked but subtly attractive and has a wonderful song. It is generally solitary but twos and threes may gather with other warblers to feed on berries in late summer, putting on fat to fuel the long autumn migration. It appears in gardens and thickets, often near the coast or beside lakes and reservoirs, in autumn, pausing while on migration in areas where it does not nest. The Garden Warbler's movements are a little slower and heavier than a Willow Warbler or a Chiffchaff.

VOICE Call thick, soft *tchak*, low *chek-chek*, *churrr*; song brilliant outpouring of fast, rather even but varied warbling, very rich, throaty, musical, usually without acceleration and emphasis of Blackcap's.

NESTING Shallow, skimpy cup of grass and moss in bush; 4 or 5 eggs; 1 brood; May–July.

FEEDING Takes insects and spiders from foliage, slipping through with ease; eats many berries and seeds, in autumn, coming to honeysuckle and elder in gardens.

FLIGHT: slightly hesitant; heavy, short flights through trees.

LACK OF PATTERN
The soft grey neck patch shows well here, but there is very little pattern on a Garden Warbler.

OCCURRENCE
Breeds in most of Europe, but absent from Iceland and most of Ireland. Present from April to September in open woodland, tall thickets, shrubs, and trees, and wooded parks, often alongside Blackcaps with little obvious habitat difference.

Seen in the UK
J F M **A M J J A S O** N D

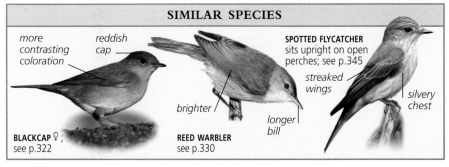

SIMILAR SPECIES

more contrasting coloration

reddish cap

BLACKCAP ♀; see p.322

brighter

REED WARBLER see p.330

longer bill

SPOTTED FLYCATCHER sits upright on open perches; see p.345

streaked wings

silvery chest

Length **14 cm (5½ in)**	Wingspan **20–24cm (8–9½in)**	Weight **16–23g (⁹⁄₁₆–⁷⁄₈oz)**
Social **Solitary**	Lifespan **Up to 5 years**	Status **Secure**

Order **Passeriformes**	Family **Sylviidae**	Species *Sylvia nisoria*

Barred Warbler

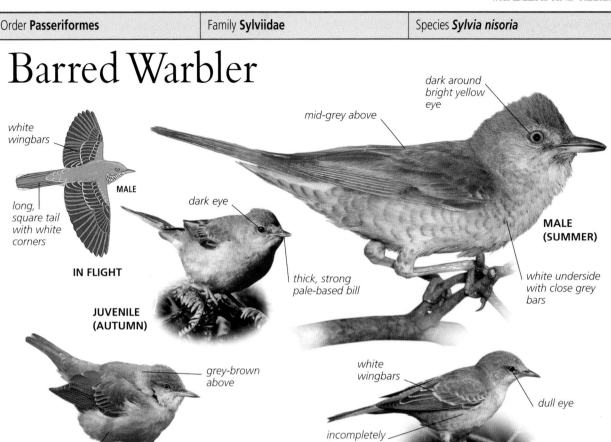

dark around bright yellow eye

mid-grey above

white wingbars

MALE

long, square tail with white corners

IN FLIGHT

dark eye

JUVENILE (AUTUMN)

thick, strong pale-based bill

MALE (SUMMER)

white underside with close grey bars

grey-brown above

IMMATURE (1ST WINTER)

dull whitish underside

white wingbars

dull eye

incompletely barred underside

FEMALE

One of the larger warblers of Europe, the Barred Warbler is almost Wryneck-like at times, heavily barred beneath and pale-eyed, with a rather severe expression. In autumn, when it is most likely to be seen on migration in northwest Europe, most are pale, almost unbarred juveniles, but they still have a heavy, clumsy, rather aggressive character, and may crash about in low bushes. They are typically skulking birds, not easy to watch, but eventually emerge on the bush tops if conditions are calm and dry.

VOICE Loud, dry, hard rattle, *trrr-r-r-rt*; song long, bright, musical warble, like high-pitched Garden Warbler's.

NESTING Substantial nest in thorny bush or scrub; 4 or 5 eggs; 1 brood; May–July.

FEEDING Takes insects and spiders from foliage; tugs at berries.

FLIGHT: low, heavy, long-winged, tail flaunted or spread; high, fluttery song-flight.

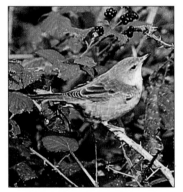

AUTUMN MIGRANT
The autumn bird is pale and stocky with dark eyes and pale wingbars.

OCCURRENCE
Breeds in E Europe west to N Italy, in bushy places and woodland clearings; present from April to October. Rare migrant, chiefly in autumn, in NW Europe, on coasts, usually in thickets on dunes or low coastal hills.

Seen in the UK
J F M A M J J **A S O** N D

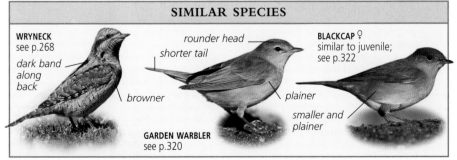

SIMILAR SPECIES

WRYNECK see p.268

dark band along back

browner

GARDEN WARBLER see p.320

rounder head

shorter tail

plainer

BLACKCAP ♀ similar to juvenile; see p.322

smaller and plainer

Length **15–17cm (6–6½in)**	Wingspan **15–20cm (6–8in)**	Weight **12–15g (⁷⁄₁₆–⁹⁄₁₆oz)**
Social **Solitary**	Lifespan **Up to 5 years**	Status **Secure†**

| Order **Passeriformes** | Family **Sylviidae** | Species *Sylvia atricapilla* |

Blackcap 🔊 68

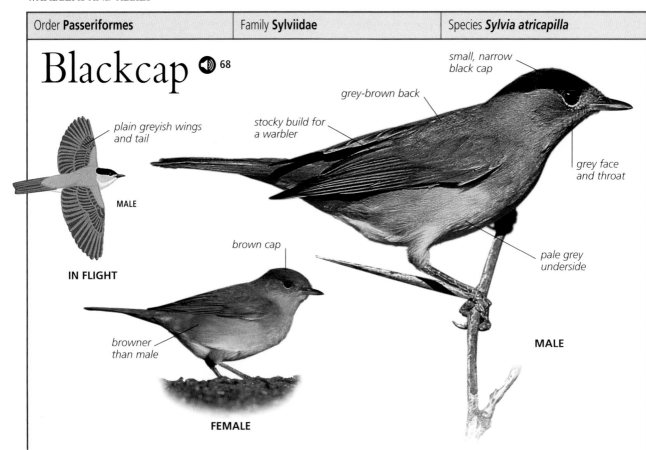

small, narrow black cap

grey-brown back

stocky build for a warbler

plain greyish wings and tail

MALE

IN FLIGHT

grey face and throat

pale grey underside

MALE

brown cap

browner than male

FEMALE

One of the more common *Sylvia* warblers, mostly found in thick undergrowth or bushy woodland, the Blackcap has a brilliant song and typically hard, unmusical calls. A few stay in northwest Europe for the winter, and many more in south Europe, especially in orchards, vineyards, and olive groves. Blackcaps may visit gardens in autumn to feed on honeysuckle or other berries, and again in winter when some rely on food put out on bird-tables. Like other *Sylvia* warblers, they are not particularly social, but several may feed close together in a tree such as an elder with an abundance of berries.
VOICE Distinct short, hard *tak*; song brilliant, usually short but sometimes prolonged, fast, varied warbling with bright, clear notes, often accelerating and growing in volume soon after start.
NESTING Small cup of grass and stems in bush; 4 or 5 eggs; 2 broods; April–July.
FEEDING Takes insects from foliage; also feeds on many soft, fleshy berries, especially elder.

/\/\/\/\/\/\/\/\/\/\/\/\/\/\/\/\

FLIGHT: short, quite heavy, flitting, with flurries of quick, flicking wingbeats.

RICH SONG
A male's fast warbling is usually distinct from a Garden Warbler's longer song, but the Blackcap can imitate its close relative.

OCCURRENCE
Breeds in most of Europe except Iceland and N Scandinavia. In summer in N Europe; increasing in UK in winter, more in Spain, Portugal, Italy, and Balkans. In woods, parks, and large bushy gardens, with plenty of thick undergrowth.

| Seen in the UK |
| J F M A M J J A S O N D |

SIMILAR SPECIES

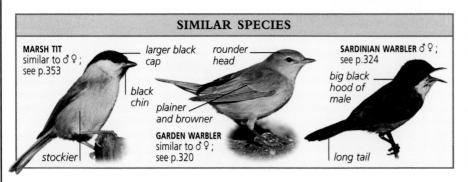

MARSH TIT
similar to ♂♀;
see p.353

larger black cap

black chin

stockier

rounder head

plainer and browner

GARDEN WARBLER
similar to ♂♀;
see p.320

SARDINIAN WARBLER ♂♀;
see p.324

big black hood of male

long tail

| Length **13cm (5in)** | Wingspan **20–23cm (8–9in)** | Weight **14–20g (½–¹¹⁄₁₆oz)** |
| Social **Solitary** | Lifespan **Up to 5 years** | Status **Secure** |

Order **Passeriformes**	Family **Sylviidae**	Species *Sylvia curruca*

Lesser Whitethroat

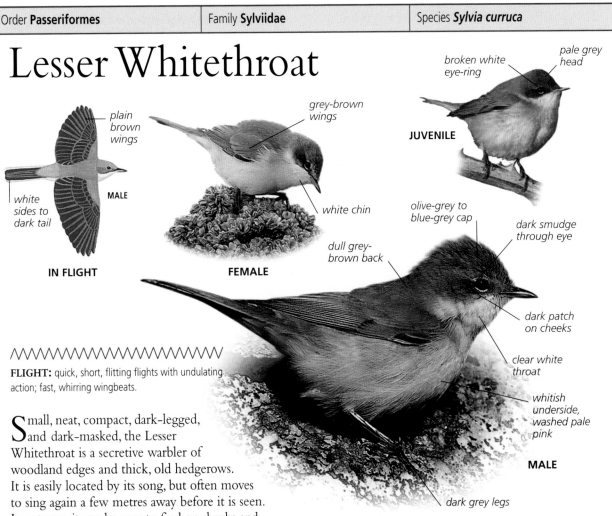

plain brown wings

white sides to dark tail

MALE

IN FLIGHT

grey-brown wings

white chin

FEMALE

broken white eye-ring

pale grey head

JUVENILE

olive-grey to blue-grey cap

dark smudge through eye

dull grey-brown back

dark patch on cheeks

clear white throat

whitish underside, washed pale pink

MALE

dark grey legs

/\/\/\/\/\/\/\/\/\/\/\/\/\/\

FLIGHT: quick, short, flitting flights with undulating action; fast, whirring wingbeats.

Small, neat, compact, dark-legged, and dark-masked, the Lesser Whitethroat is a secretive warbler of woodland edges and thick, old hedgerows. It is easily located by its song, but often moves to sing again a few metres away before it is seen. In autumn, it can be easy to find on shrubs and trees with berries, sometimes with other warblers but not forming properly coordinated flocks. Young birds at this time are particularly bright and smart.

VOICE Sharp, short, metallic *tak*, very thin *chi*; song in two parts, beginning with low, quiet, muffled warble, becoming short, loud, wooden rattle *chikachikachikachikachikachika*.

NESTING Cup of twigs or grass, lined with hair and roots, in shrub; 4–6 eggs; 1 brood; May–June.

FEEDING Picks insects from foliage; eats many berries in late summer.

WOODEN RATTLE
The male sits upright as he sings, usually moving to a new perch before the next loud rattled phrase.

OCCURRENCE
Summer visitor and breeding bird from April to October in most of Europe west to mid-France and UK; not in Italy, Spain, Portugal, N Scandinavia, and Iceland. In quite tall, dense thickets often at woodland edge, or as part of tall, dense hedges.

Seen in the UK
J F M A M J J A S O N D

SIMILAR SPECIES

WHITETHROAT ♂
similar to ♂♀;
see p.325

rusty wings

pale legs

red eye-ring

pinker below

SUBALPINE WARBLER
♂♀; see p.326

BLACKCAP ♂♀;
see p.322

dark cap

grey throat

Length **13cm (5in)**	Wingspan **17–19cm (6½–7½in)**	Weight **10–16g (³/₈–⁹/₁₆oz)**
Social **Solitary**	Lifespan **Up to 5 years**	Status **Secure**

| Order **Passeriformes** | Family **Sylviidae** | Species *Sylvia melanocephala* |

Sardinian Warbler

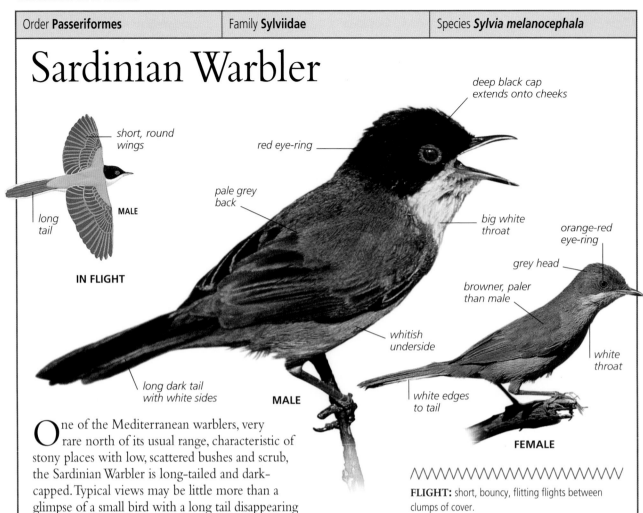

short, round wings

MALE

long tail

IN FLIGHT

deep black cap extends onto cheeks

red eye-ring

pale grey back

big white throat

orange-red eye-ring

grey head

browner, paler than male

whitish underside

white throat

long dark tail with white sides

MALE

white edges to tail

FEMALE

ne of the Mediterranean warblers, very rare north of its usual range, characteristic of stony places with low, scattered bushes and scrub, the Sardinian Warbler is long-tailed and dark-capped. Typical views may be little more than a glimpse of a small bird with a long tail disappearing into a bush, perhaps not to be seen again. In some places, it frequents taller trees in gardens and orchards. This warbler has a distinctive rapid, rattling call that gives away its presence at frequent intervals, however, and patience is usually rewarded by a better view. It is often seen in pairs or small family groups, but does not form larger flocks.

VOICE Loud, hard, short call and frequent fast, hard rattle, *krr-rr-rr-rr-rr-rr-rr-rr-rr-t*; song fast, unmusical, rattling chatter with calls interspersed.

NESTING Small, neat cup in low bush; 3–5 eggs; 2 broods; April–July.

FEEDING Takes small insects and spiders, mostly low in vegetation or on ground beneath.

/\/\/\/\/\/\/\/\/\/\/\/\/\/\/\/\/\

FLIGHT: short, bouncy, flitting flights between clumps of cover.

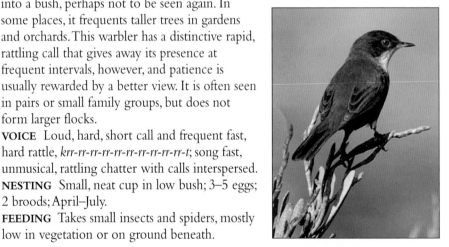

BRIGHT EYE-RING
Even on the browner female Sardinian Warbler, the red eye-ring is a distinct feature.

OCCURRENCE
Resident in most of Spain, Portugal, S France, Mediterranean region, and very rare farther north. In bushy areas, sometimes in open woodland with scrub, more often thickets around buildings, thorny growth over stone walls, and similar areas.

| Seen in the UK |
| J F M A M J J A S O N D |

SIMILAR SPECIES

RUPPELL'S WARBLER ♂ similar to ♂; see p.451

black throat

stockier

SUBALPINE WARBLER ♂ similar to ♂; see p.326

bluer back

reddish breast

smaller black cap on male

BLACKCAP ♂ ♀; see p.322

grey throat

| Length **13–14cm (5–5½in)** | Wingspan **15–18cm (6–7in)** | Weight **10–14g (⅜–½oz)** |
| Social **Family groups** | Lifespan **Up to 5 years** | Status **Secure** |

Order **Passeriformes**	Family **Sylviidae**	Species *Sylvia communis*

Whitethroat

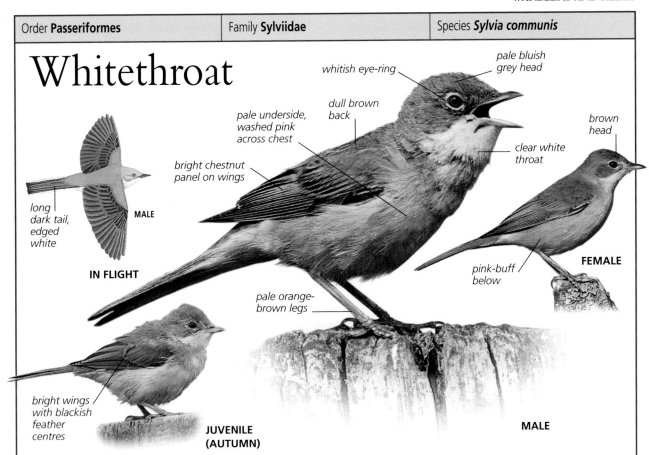

whitish eye-ring

pale bluish grey head

dull brown back

pale underside, washed pink across chest

brown head

bright chestnut panel on wings

clear white throat

long dark tail, edged white

MALE

IN FLIGHT

pink-buff below

FEMALE

pale orange-brown legs

bright wings with blackish feather centres

JUVENILE (AUTUMN)

MALE

Typically a bird of open spaces with low bushes and scrub, the Whitethroat likes overgrown tracksides, railway embankments, hedgerows and fence-lines with brambles, or thorny thickets around heaths. It sings often, sometimes from a low perch, sometimes from a high wire, but frequently in short, jerky, bouncy song-flights. It is often quite secretive, keeping low down in thick vegetation, but gives itself away by its irritable calls and eventually succumbs to its insatiable curiosity and appears out in the open.

VOICE Harsh, grating *tcharr*, scolding, softer *churr*, sweet, musical *wheet-a-wheet-a-whit*; song often in fluttery song-flight, quick, chattery, rambling warble with dry, scratchy quality.

NESTING Small, neat cup of grass and stems low in thorny shrub; 4 or 5 eggs; 2 broods; April–July.

FEEDING Picks insects from foliage; takes lots of berries and some seeds in late summer and autumn, sometimes visiting gardens.

FLIGHT: low, bouncy or jerky, flitting, undulating, with flicked, untidy tail.

LIVELY SINGER
The male sings with much more vigour than melody, from a bush top or overhead wire.

OCCURRENCE
Breeds almost throughout Europe except for Iceland and much of Scandinavia. In bushy, dry, and heathy places with low, thorny scrub, dense herbs such as nettles, hedges, and thickets; seen from April to October.

Seen in the UK
J F M **A M J J A S O** N D

SIMILAR SPECIES

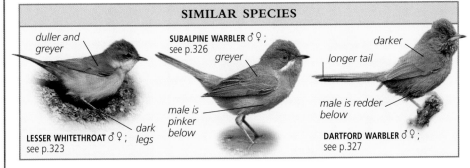

duller and greyer

SUBALPINE WARBLER ♂♀; see p.326

greyer

darker

longer tail

male is pinker below

male is redder below

LESSER WHITETHROAT ♂♀; see p.323

dark legs

DARTFORD WARBLER ♂♀; see p.327

Length **14cm (5½in)**	Wingspan **19–23cm (7½–9in)**	Weight **12–18g (7/16–5/8oz)**
Social **Solitary**	Lifespan **Up to 5 years**	Status **Secure**

| Order **Passeriformes** | Family **Sylviidae** | Species ***Sylvia cantillans*** |

Subalpine Warbler

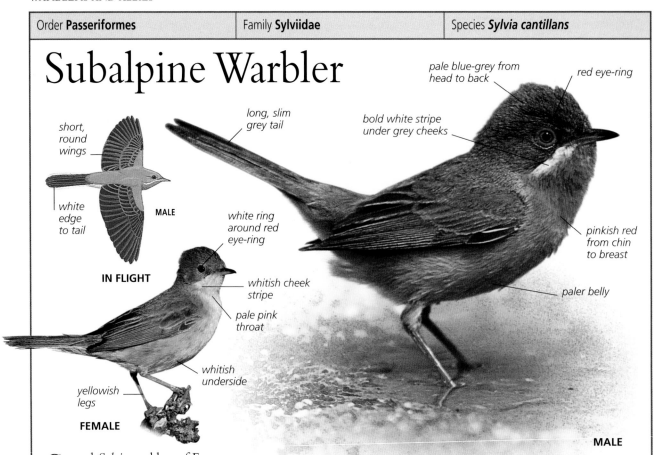

pale blue-grey from head to back

red eye-ring

bold white stripe under grey cheeks

short, round wings

long, slim grey tail

white edge to tail

MALE

IN FLIGHT

white ring around red eye-ring

whitish cheek stripe

pale pink throat

whitish underside

yellowish legs

FEMALE

pinkish red from chin to breast

paler belly

MALE

Several *Sylvia* warblers of Europe occupy the southern regions, mostly around the Mediterranean; the Subalpine Warbler is typical, inhabiting warm, sun-bathed slopes and fields with rough, tangled hedges and thickets of aromatic shrubs and spiny bushes. It dives out of sight into the spikiest of these and can be frustratingly elusive at times, although it often appears on top and launches into a brief, bouncy song-flight in full view. Females are paler than adult males, which are easy to identify. Females and immatures, which are even paler, are more difficult, especially if they turn up as vagrants farther north in autumn.

VOICE Call sharp, ticking or clicking *tet*, sometimes quickly repeated; song high-pitched, Linnet-like, musical warbling, fast, with quick variation in pitch.

NESTING Small, neat cup nest in low vegetation; 3 or 4 eggs; 2 broods; April–June.

FEEDING Forages in low scrub and herbs, or higher in leafy trees, searching for insects and spiders.

FLIGHT: short flights weak, quick, undulating, with bursts of wingbeats.

WHITE "MOUSTACHE"
Males, and sometimes females, have an obvious white stripe from the bill to the side of the throat.

OCCURRENCE
Breeds on bushy slopes, in low, tangled hedges and thorny thickets, and in open, evergreen oak woods in Spain, Portugal, and Mediterranean Europe, from April to September. Migrants at times appear farther north in low, dense undergrowth near coasts.

| Seen in the UK |
| J F M A M J J A S O N D |

SIMILAR SPECIES

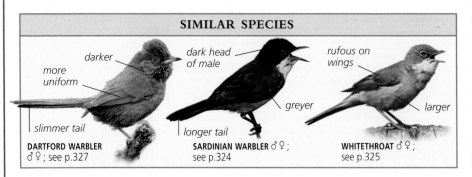

more uniform

darker

slimmer tail

DARTFORD WARBLER
♂♀; see p.327

dark head of male

longer tail

greyer

SARDINIAN WARBLER ♂♀;
see p.324

rufous on wings

larger

WHITETHROAT ♂♀;
see p.325

| Length **12–13cm (4¾–5in)** | Wingspan **13–18cm (5–7in)** | Weight **9–12g (¹¹⁄₃₂–⁷⁄₁₆oz)** |
| Social **Solitary** | Lifespan **Up to 5 years** | Status **Secure** |

Order **Passeriformes**	Family **Sylviidae**	Species *Sylvia undata*

Dartford Warbler

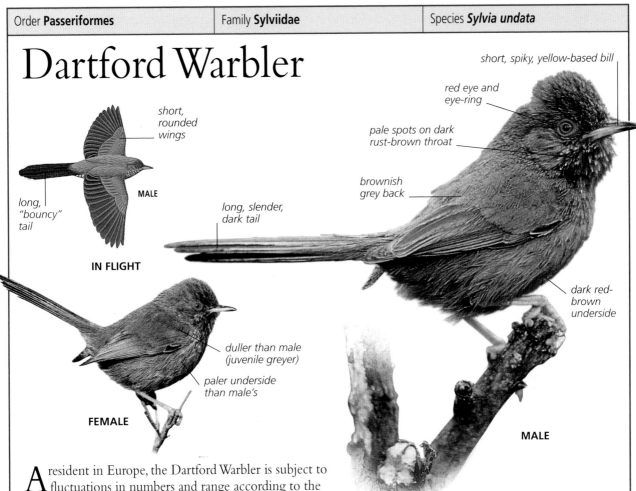

short, spiky, yellow-based bill

red eye and eye-ring

pale spots on dark rust-brown throat

brownish grey back

dark red-brown underside

short, rounded wings

MALE

long, "bouncy" tail

IN FLIGHT

long, slender, dark tail

duller than male (juvenile greyer)

paler underside than male's

FEMALE

MALE

A resident in Europe, the Dartford Warbler is subject to fluctuations in numbers and range according to the severity of winter weather. It prefers warm, flat heaths and slopes with short herbaceous and shrubby growth, including thick heather and clumps of gorse, where it often skulks and is hard to see. It may flick from one bush to another but disappears from sight frustratingly quickly. In warm, still weather, however, it will come to the top and reveal its distinctive colours and shape.

VOICE Very distinctive buzzy call, low *chrrrr* or *djarrr*; song quick, rattling warble with some brighter notes, quite low pitch, little variety, sometimes given in flight.

NESTING Grassy cup lined with finer stems, low down in gorse or heather; 3–5 eggs; 2 or 3 broods; April–July.

FEEDING Finds insects and many spiders in low vegetation.

FLIGHT: quick, undulating with tail flirting; bursts of wingbeats over short distances.

BRIGHT MALE
Only a good view reveals the rich colours of the male.

OCCURRENCE
Breeds very locally in suitable habitat in S Britain, NW, W, and S France, Spain, Portugal, Italy, and on many Mediterranean islands. Found on heaths with heather and gorse and some small bushes, and on warm bushy slopes with few trees but plenty of aromatic and thorny shrubs, all year round.

Seen in the UK
J F M A M J J A S O N D

SIMILAR SPECIES

MARMORA'S WARBLER
♂♀; very local;
see p.451

grey

shorter tail

greyer above

SUBALPINE WARBLER
♂♀; see p.326

dark cap of male

greyer

white throat

SARDINIAN WARBLER ♂♀;
see p.324

Length **12–13cm (4¾–5in)**	Wingspan **13–18cm (5–7in)**	Weight **9–12g (¹¹⁄₃₂–⁷⁄₁₆oz)**
Social **Solitary**	Lifespan **Up to 5 years**	Status **Vulnerable**

| Order **Passeriformes** | Family **Sylviidae** | Species **Acrocephalus schoenobaenus** |

Sedge Warbler 69

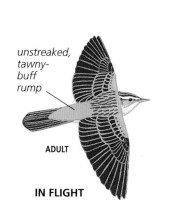

unstreaked, tawny-buff rump

ADULT

IN FLIGHT

blackish and cream streaks on cap

wide silver-white stripe over eye

dark line from bill through eye

ADULT

soft greyish streaks on tawny back

buff across chest (finely streaked on juvenile) and flanks

whitish underside

ADULT

This is one of the *Acrocephalus* warblers, birds of wetlands, especially reedbeds, that fall into two groups, streaked and unstreaked. A small, well-marked, active bird with a loud, fast, varied song, the Sedge Warbler is quite common and widespread but restricted largely to waterside or boggy habitats. It is not exclusively a reedbed warbler, preferring more variety, such as various sedges, nettles, willow, hawthorn scrub, willowherb, and umbellifers intermixed, so sometimes it may be found in hedges beside wet ditches or even drier places with thick, vertical stem growth. It appears as a migrant mostly in similar habitats.

VOICE Call dry, rasping *tchrrrr*, sharper *tek*; song loud, fast, varied, excitable mix of whistles, warbles, clicks, and trills with much mimicry.

NESTING Deep nest of grass mixed with moss, cobwebs, and plant down; 5 or 6 eggs; 1 or 2 broods; April–July.

FEEDING Forages in reeds, sedges, nettles, and bushes, for small insects, spiders, and some seeds.

/\/\/\/\/\/\/\/\/\/\/\/\/\/\

FLIGHT: short, flitting flights, quite jerky; tail sometimes fanned.

VIGOROUS SONGSTER
A singing bird frequently climbs to the top of a bush or reed stem.

OCCURRENCE
Widespread as breeder except in Iceland. In reeds, from narrow ditches to extensive reedbeds, and associated wetland vegetation such as sedges and reedmace; more rarely in nettles, willowherb, and other rank growth, often with thorn bushes, from April to October.

Seen in the UK
J F M A M J J A S O N D

SIMILAR SPECIES

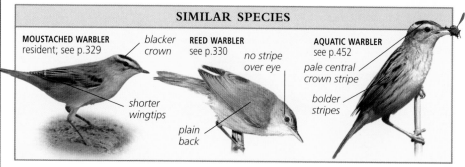

MOUSTACHED WARBLER resident; see p.329

blacker crown

shorter wingtips

REED WARBLER see p.330

no stripe over eye

plain back

AQUATIC WARBLER see p.452

pale central crown stripe

bolder stripes

| Length **13cm (5in)** | Wingspan **17–21cm (6½–8½in)** | Weight **10–13g (⅜–⁷⁄₁₆oz)** |
| Social **Solitary** | Lifespan **Up to 5 years** | Status **Secure†** |

| Order **Passeriformes** | Family **Sylviidae** | Species **Acrocephalus melanopogon** |

Moustached Warbler

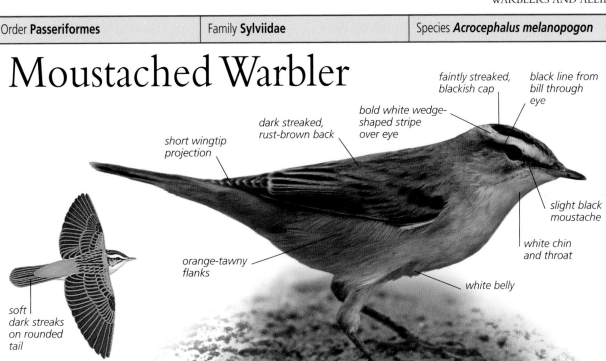

- short wingtip projection
- dark streaked, rust-brown back
- bold white wedge-shaped stripe over eye
- faintly streaked, blackish cap
- black line from bill through eye
- slight black moustache
- white chin and throat
- white belly
- orange-tawny flanks
- soft dark streaks on rounded tail

IN FLIGHT

FLIGHT: short, low, flitting flights across reeds.

A streaked *Acrocephalus* warbler, the Moustached Warbler is unusual in that it is a resident in its restricted range in Europe. It is only a very rare vagrant outside its usual range. It is quite distinctive when seen with the Sedge Warbler, its most similar relative, but care is required when identifying potential out-of-range vagrants. Its song is a useful clue in the usual breeding areas. It often tilts over and cocks its tail which the Sedge Warbler does not. Its shorter wingtip is sometimes discernible in a close view, helping to confirm identification.

VOICE Call like Sedge Warbler's but more throaty, *trek* or clicking *trk-tk-tk-tk*; song fast and varied, with frequent Nightingale-like rising whistles.

NESTING Deep grassy nest lined with plant down, in reeds; 5 or 6 eggs; 1 brood; April–June.

FEEDING Eats insects and other small invertebrates, from mud and dense wetland vegetation.

STRIKING HEAD PATTERN
A wedge of white over the eye and a silky white chin are obvious features of the Moustached Warbler in a good view.

SIMILAR SPECIES

- paler breast
- paler
- longer wingtips

SEDGE WARBLER see p.328

WHINCHAT ♂♀; different habitat and posture; see p.309

- different shape

OCCURRENCE
Very local in S Europe, breeding in S and E Spain, S France, Balearics, Italy, and Balkans. In reedbeds and dense waterside sedge or rushes. Resident and very rarely noted outside its breeding range.

| Seen in the UK |
| J F M A M J J A S O N D |

| Length **12–13cm (4¾–5in)** | Wingspan **17–21cm (6½–8½in)** | Weight **10–15g (³⁄₈–⁹⁄₁₆oz)** |
| Social **Solitary** | Lifespan **Up to 5 years** | Status **Secure†** |

Order **Passeriformes**	Family **Sylviidae**	Species *Acrocephalus scirpaceus*

Reed Warbler 🔊 70

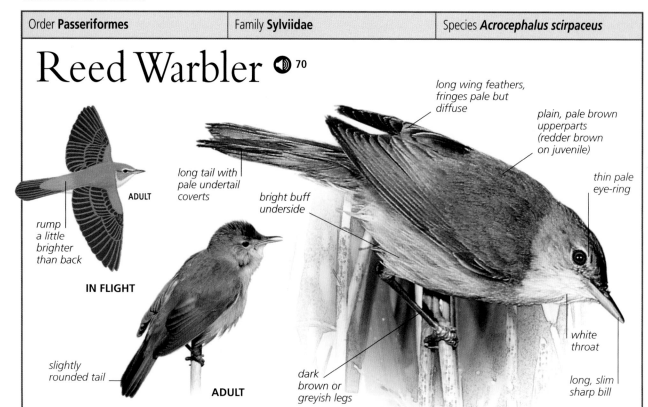

long wing feathers, fringes pale but diffuse

plain, pale brown upperparts (redder brown on juvenile)

thin pale eye-ring

ADULT

rump a little brighter than back

IN FLIGHT

long tail with pale undertail coverts

bright buff underside

white throat

long, slim sharp bill

slightly rounded tail

dark brown or greyish legs

ADULT

Basically a reedbed bird, the Reed Warbler may sometimes breed away from reeds, in drier spots or in willows growing over shallow water, for example. Its plain colours make it very like some other, rarer, warblers, but unlike the common Sedge Warbler. Its repetitive song is also distinctive as a rule, although subject to some variation. On migration, Reed Warblers may be found in unexpected places, such as thickets and hedgerows, posing identification problems with less closely related species such as Melodious Warblers.

VOICE Call simple, low *churr* or *chk*; song rhythmic, repetitive, low, with occasional high, musical variations, *trrik trrik trrik, chrr chrr chrr chrr, chewe chewe trrrt trrrt trrrt tiri tiri*.

NESTING Deep nest of grass, reedheads, and moss, woven around several upright stems in reedbed; 3–5 eggs; 2 broods; May–July.

FEEDING Forages for insects and spiders on mud and in thick, wet vegetation and foliage of willows; also eats some seeds.

ADULT

/\

FLIGHT: short, low, jerky flitting flights between reeds or willows, tail low, sometimes spread as it tilts over and dives into cover.

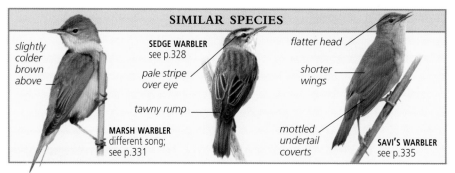

GRASPING REEDS
The Reed Warbler is adept at grasping vertical stems and shuffling through dense reedbeds.

OCCURRENCE
Widespread as breeding bird and summer visitor north to Great Britain and S Scandinavia. In reedbeds, especially extensive, wet ones, but also in reedy ditches and willows beside lakes and rivers. Migrants on coasts between April and October.

Seen in the UK

SIMILAR SPECIES

slightly colder brown above

SEDGE WARBLER
see p.328

flatter head

pale stripe over eye

shorter wings

tawny rump

MARSH WARBLER
different song;
see p.331

mottled undertail coverts

SAVI'S WARBLER
see p.335

Length **13–15cm (5–6in)**	Wingspan **18–21cm (7–8½in)**	Weight **11–15g (³⁄₈–⁹⁄₁₆oz)**
Social **Solitary**	Lifespan **Up to 5 years**	Status **Secure**

Order **Passeriformes**	Family **Sylviidae**	Species ***Acrocephalus palustris***

Marsh Warbler

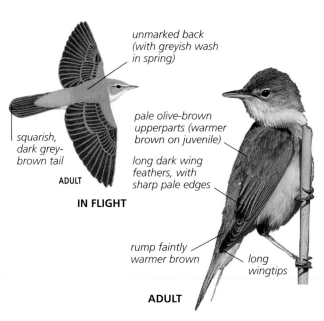

IN FLIGHT

unmarked back
(with greyish wash
in spring)

squarish,
dark grey-
brown tail

ADULT

pale olive-brown
upperparts (warmer
brown on juvenile)

long dark wing
feathers, with
sharp pale edges

rump faintly
warmer brown

long
wingtips

ADULT

pale bill with
dark ridge

thin whitish
eye-ring

yellowish white
underside

pale legs

ADULT

An unstreaked *Acrocephalus* warbler, the Marsh Warbler is a bird of wet riversides and boggy places with an abundance of rich, thick vegetation; it is not usually a reedbed species. Migrants occur rarely, near the coast, and require patience and close observation for positive identification. Unless the full song is heard, this is a tricky species. Its habitat is always restricted and often rather temporary in nature, so it remains a rare and somewhat erratic breeding bird – one of the last of the summer migrants to arrive in summer.

VOICE Call short, hard *chek* or *chk*; song full of remarkable mimicry (of African as well as European birds), fluent, fast, with twangy, nasal, whistling notes, trills and slower, lower intervals or pauses.
NESTING Quite shallow cup of grass, suspended from tall stems in thick vegetation by "basket handles"; 4 or 5 eggs; 1 brood; June–July.
FEEDING Forages in and under thick plant cover for insects and spiders; also takes some berries.

FLIGHT: low, short, flitting flights with whirring wingbeats; jerky, bounding action.

SUPERB SONGSTER
Marsh Warblers usually sing from bushes, nettles, and other tall, rank vegetation.

OCCURRENCE
Local summer bird, from extreme SE England (where it is rare) across C, SE, and E Europe, and extreme S Scandinavia. Prefers thick wetland vegetation, with or without a mixture of reeds among sedges, willowherb, nettles, and umbellifers. Rare migrant on coasts and islands from May to September.

Seen in the UK
J F M **A M J J A S** O N D

SIMILAR SPECIES

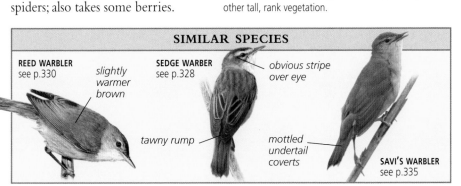

REED WARBLER
see p.330

slightly
warmer
brown

SEDGE WARBLER
see p.328

obvious stripe
over eye

tawny rump

mottled
undertail
coverts

SAVI'S WARBLER
see p.335

Length **13–15cm (5–6in)**	Wingspan **18–21cm (7–8½in)**	Weight **11–15g (³⁄₈–⁹⁄₁₆oz)**
Social **Solitary**	Lifespan **Up to 5 years**	Status **Secure**

Order **Passeriformes**	Family **Sylviidae**	Species *Acrocephalus arundinaceus*

Great Reed Warbler 🔊 71

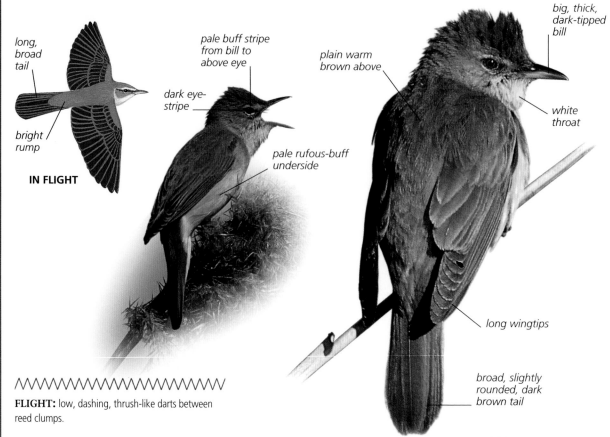

long, broad tail

bright rump

IN FLIGHT

pale buff stripe from bill to above eye

dark eye-stripe

pale rufous-buff underside

plain warm brown above

big, thick, dark-tipped bill

white throat

long wingtips

broad, slightly rounded, dark brown tail

∧∧∧∧∧∧∧∧∧∧∧∧∧∧∧∧∧∧∧

FLIGHT: low, dashing, thrush-like darts between reed clumps.

Indeed a massive reed warbler, this large, almost thrush-sized warbler typically inhabits reedbeds, but can be found in remarkably small wet spots near rivers or even along ditches and irrigation channels, with just small strips or patches of reed and tall grass. It appears regularly, in very small numbers, north of its usual range, individuals sometimes remaining for a week or two, singing strongly. The song is immediately distinctive: loud and raucous, with a hesitant, frog-like quality.

VOICE Call rolling, harsh *krrrrr* or shorter *tshak*; song remarkably loud, hesitant or full-flowing but repetitive, separate phrases alternately croaking, whistling, warbling, *grik grik grik, jeek jeek chik grrr grrr grrr girik girik girik*.

NESTING Large, deep nest slung in vertical reed stems above water; 3–6 eggs; 1 or 2 broods; May–August.

FEEDING Takes insects and varied invertebrates from foliage and reeds, crashing through stems in search of food.

BOLD SONGSTER
From the top of giant reeds, Giant Reed Warblers create a loud and unmistakable chorus of raucous song.

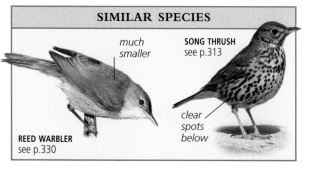
SIMILAR SPECIES

much smaller

SONG THRUSH see p.313

clear spots below

REED WARBLER see p.330

OCCURRENCE
Breeds in mainland Europe north to S Scandinavia; local summer visitor. In reedbeds and reedy ditches or strips of reed beside rivers or floods. Present from May to August, when migrants sometimes appear north of usual range.

Seen in the UK
J F M A M J J A S O N D

Length **16–20cm (6½–8in)**	Wingspan **25–26cm (10in)**	Weight **30–40g (1¹/₁₆–1⁷/₁₆oz)**
Social **Solitary**	Lifespan **Up to 5 years**	Status **Secure†**

Order **Passeriformes**	Family **Sylviidae**	Species *Cisticola juncidis*

Fan-tailed Warbler

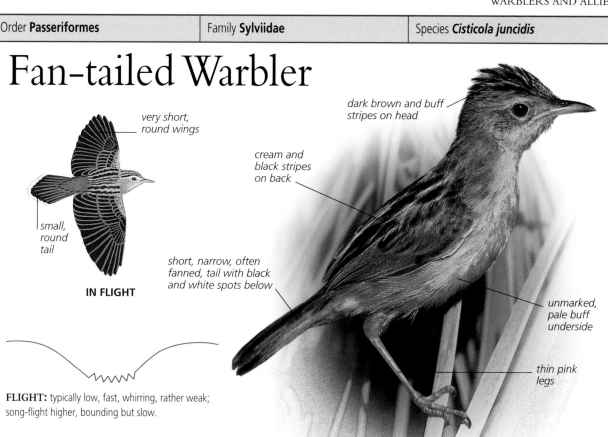

IN FLIGHT

very short, round wings

small, round tail

dark brown and buff stripes on head

cream and black stripes on back

short, narrow, often fanned, tail with black and white spots below

unmarked, pale buff underside

thin pink legs

FLIGHT: typically low, fast, whirring, rather weak; song-flight higher, bounding but slow.

Small and insignificant, the Fan-tailed Warbler or Zitting Cisticola is the one European representative of a widespread African and south Asian genus of small, confusingly similar warblers. It is usually revealed by its song, a repetition of a single, sharp, penetrating note given with each bound of a deeply undulating song-flight. Visually, it looks unlike any other European bird despite its basic small, streaky impression, but that itself may make it puzzling if it is silent and skulking in low vegetaion. Females may have two or more broods, paired with different males.

VOICE Loud chip call; song usually in deeply undulating song-flight, single short, sharp, penetrating note with each bound, *zeet...zeet...zeet...zeet.*
NESTING Deep, flexible, pear- or flask-shaped nest of grass, feathers, and cobwebs in tall grass; 4–6 eggs; 2 or 3 broods; April–June.
FEEDING Takes insects, spiders, and seeds from rough grass.

DEAD GRASS PATTERN
The pale and dark streaks on the back camouflage this warbler in brown grass and reed stems.

OCCURRENCE
Local breeder around Mediterranean, in Spain, Portugal, and on Atlantic coast of France. In usual range all year but subject to reductions in range in hard winters. In grassy places, marshes, dunes, and sometimes cereal fields with grassy edges.

Seen in the UK
J F M A M J J A S O N D

SIMILAR SPECIES

SEDGE WARBLER see p.328

bolder stripe over eye

bigger

bold stripe over eye

bigger

WINCHAT ♂♀; perches more openly; see p.309

GRASSHOPPER WARBLER see p.334

bigger and longer

long, slim tail

Length **10–11cm (4–4½in)**	Wingspan **12–15cm (4¾–6in)**	Weight **10g (⅜oz)**
Social **Solitary**	Lifespan **Up to 5 years**	Status **Secure†**

333

Order **Passeriformes**	Family **Sylviidae**	Species *Locustella naevia*

Grasshopper Warbler

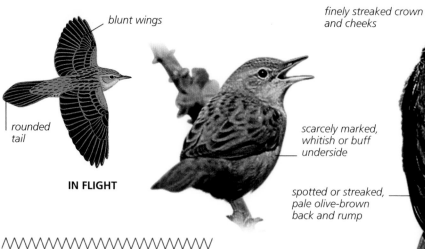

blunt wings

rounded tail

IN FLIGHT

finely streaked crown and cheeks

scarcely marked, whitish or buff underside

spotted or streaked, pale olive-brown back and rump

long, broad rounded tail

FLIGHT: low, brief, flitting flights; raises slightly fanned tail as it dives out of sight.

Warblers are split into several different families: this is the most common of the *Locustella* warblers, which are small, streaked, round-tailed, and highly skulking birds, usually hard to see. They have long, trilled, chirping, or rattling songs often likened to the sound of some insects such as crickets; these are usually heard most often at dusk or on warm, still, sultry summer days. These warblers are not to be expected in tall bushes or trees, or openly flitting about in hedgerows.

VOICE Loud call, piercing *psit*; song remarkable, prolonged, unvarying mechanical "reel", fast, hard ticking at close range on one high, sharp note, waxes and wanes as head is turned: *sirrrrrrrrrrrrrrrrrrrrrrrrrrrrrrrrrrrr.*

NESTING Small nest of grass and leaves in dense, low vegetation; 5 or 6 eggs; 2 broods; May–July.

FEEDING Forages in very low, thick vegetation, creeping mouse-like on or near ground, finding mostly small insects and spiders.

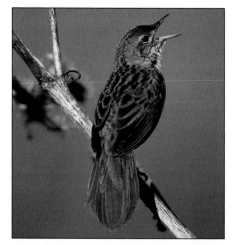

HIGH-PITCHED SONG
Many people are unable to hear such high-pitched sounds as the Grasshopper Warbler's song.

OCCURRENCE
Widespread from Ireland, east to Finland and Russia, south to C France, N Spain, and Alps in summer. In marshy areas with grass, low thickets, heathy places, and grassy meadows with thorny bushes where grass grows up through thickets.

Seen in the UK
J F M A M J J A S O N D

SIMILAR SPECIES

SEDGE WARBLER see p.328

more obvious stripe over eye

plain back and tail

REED WARBLER see p.330

DUNNOCK see p.297

bigger and stouter

greyer

Length **12.5cm (5in)**	Wingspan **15–19cm (6–7½in)**	Weight **11–15g (3⁄8–9⁄16oz)**
Social **Solitary**	Lifespan **Up to 5 years**	Status **Secure**

| Order **Passeriformes** | Family **Sylviidae** | Species *Locustella luscinioides* |

Savi's Warbler

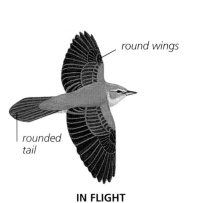

round wings

rounded tail

IN FLIGHT

long, flat head slopes into long, slender bill

pale throat

brown-buff underside with paler belly

plain brown above

curved outer edge to closed wings

/\

FLIGHT: short, flitting flight between reed clumps. Longer migration flights at night.

long, thick brown undertail coverts

dark under tail

long tail, rounded at tip

An exception to the *Locustella* rule, being plain rather than streaked, Savi's Warbler is more like the plain-backed Reed and Marsh Warblers. It is also, like the Reed Warbler, a bird of dense reedbeds, much less adaptable to various grassy habitats than the more widespread Grasshopper Warbler. It is easily detected by its song (although many may not realize that it is a bird singing at all), especially around dawn and dusk, and patience may reveal its small, dark form, singing from a reed stem. Savi's Warbler is usually rather scarce even in its breeding areas and is rarely seen as a migrant outside its breeding range. It needs to be separated with care from the similarly coloured reed warbler group but the family characteristics, including the round-edged wings, long, thick undertail coverts and rounded tail help in identification, if the bird is seen closely. Savi's Warblers spend the winter in Africa.

VOICE Short, sharp, metallic call; song like Grasshopper Warbler but more slurred, less ticking, faster, lower buzz, *zurrrrrrrrrrrrrrrr*.

NESTING Large, untidy, loose nest of grass in reeds or sedges; 4 eggs; 2 broods; April–June.

FEEDING Forages for insects and spiders in dense vegetation.

OCCURRENCE
Very local; breeding range scattered across Europe from Spain and Portugal to extreme SE England and east into Asia. Appears from April to September in extensive wet reedbeds. Very rare migrant away from this habitat on coast.

| Seen in the UK |
| J F M A M J J A S O N D |

SIMILAR SPECIES

straight-edged wings

shorter

REED WARBLER different song; see p.330

subtly streaked back and crown

shorter-tailed

GRASSHOPPER WARBLER see p.334

darker

CETTI'S WARBLER see p.336

| Length **14–15cm (5½–6in)** | Wingspan **15–20cm (6–8in)** | Weight **12–15g (7/16–9/16oz)** |
| Social **Solitary** | Lifespan **Up to 5 years** | Status **Secure†** |

Order **Passeriformes**	Family **Sylviidae**	Species *Cettia cetti*

Cetti's Warbler 🔊 72

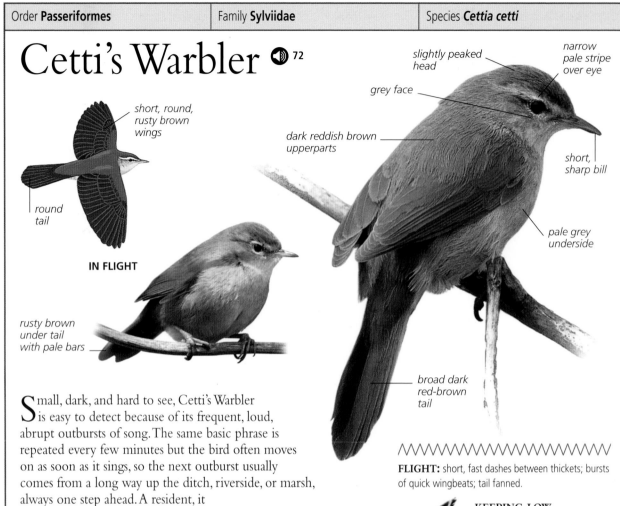

slightly peaked head

narrow pale stripe over eye

grey face

dark reddish brown upperparts

short, sharp bill

pale grey underside

broad dark red-brown tail

short, round, rusty brown wings

round tail

IN FLIGHT

rusty brown under tail with pale bars

Small, dark, and hard to see, Cetti's Warbler is easy to detect because of its frequent, loud, abrupt outbursts of song. The same basic phrase is repeated every few minutes but the bird often moves on as soon as it sings, so the next outburst usually comes from a long way up the ditch, riverside, or marsh, always one step ahead. A resident, it has spread north, subject to the vagaries of winter weather, hard weather causing occasional widespread setbacks for several years.

VOICE Explosive, metallic *chich* or *plit*; song highly distinctive, sudden loud outburst of full-throated, shouted notes: *chee! chewee! chewechewechwewewe!*

NESTING Deep cup of grass and leaves in dense vegetation; 3–5 eggs; 1 or 2 broods; April–June.

FEEDING Forages in dense cover, on or near ground, for insects, spiders, snails, and some seeds.

FLIGHT: short, fast dashes between thickets; bursts of quick wingbeats; tail fanned.

KEEPING LOW
This warbler is usually seen low down in dense thickets: it rarely moves high into a bush or tree.

OCCURRENCE
Breeds in S Europe in Mediterranean area, Spain, Portugal, France, north to Low Countries, and sparsely in S Great Britain where hard weather causes periodic reductions. In damp areas, beside rivers, ditches, reedbeds, wet thickets, and often, but by no means always, near extensive marshes.

Seen in the UK
J F M A M J J A S O N D

SIMILAR SPECIES

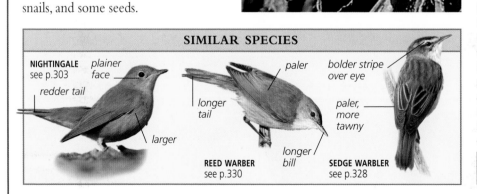

NIGHTINGALE see p.303

plainer face

redder tail

larger

paler

longer tail

longer bill

REED WARBLER see p.330

bolder stripe over eye

paler, more tawny

SEDGE WARBLER see p.328

Length **14cm (5½in)**	Wingspan **15–19cm (6–7½in)**	Weight **12–18g (7/16–⅝oz)**
Social **Solitary**	Lifespan **Up to 5 years**	Status **Secure**

Order **Passeriformes**	Family **Sylviidae**	Species *Hippolais icterina*

Icterine Warbler

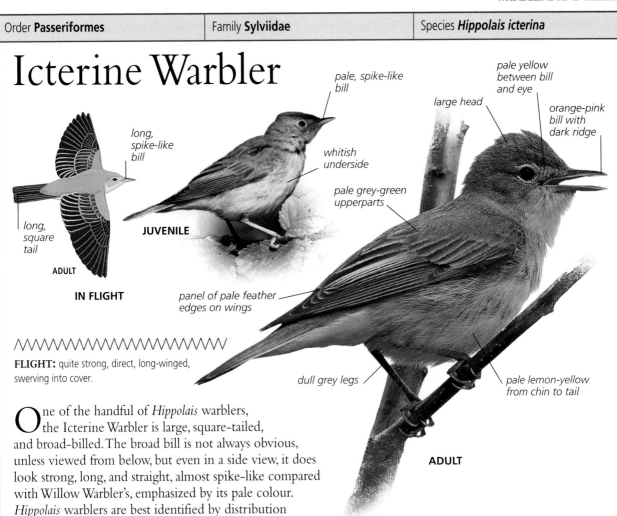

IN FLIGHT

long, spike-like bill

long, square tail

ADULT

pale, spike-like bill

JUVENILE

whitish underside

pale grey-green upperparts

panel of pale feather edges on wings

pale yellow between bill and eye

large head

orange-pink bill with dark ridge

ADULT

dull grey legs

pale lemon-yellow from chin to tail

FLIGHT: quite strong, direct, long-winged, swerving into cover.

One of the handful of *Hippolais* warblers, the Icterine Warbler is large, square-tailed, and broad-billed. The broad bill is not always obvious, unless viewed from below, but even in a side view, it does look strong, long, and straight, almost spike-like compared with Willow Warbler's, emphasized by its pale colour. *Hippolais* warblers are best identified by distribution and structure, especially the proportions of the various elements of wing, tail, and undertail coverts, which help to separate them from each other and from confusingly similar *Acrocephalus* species.

VOICE Call melodious *ti-ti-looi* or *di-deroi*, hard *tik*; song loud, fast, prolonged, varied warbling with many imitations, short, shrill, nasal notes and *dideroi* call intermixed.

NESTING Deep cup nest suspended from forked branch in tree; 4 or 5 eggs; 1 brood; May–August.

FEEDING Takes insects from foliage; pulls berries from twigs with tug of bill.

GENERIC CHARACTER
Hippolais warblers are heavy, with plain faces and dagger-like bills.

OCCURRENCE
Widespread as summer visitor and breeding bird from E France eastwards and northwards except in N Scandinavia. In open mixed, deciduous, or coniferous woodland between April and September. Spring and especially autumn migrants on NW European coasts including E Great Britain.

Seen in the UK
J F M A M J J A S O N D

SIMILAR SPECIES

MELODIOUS WARBLER see p.338

rounder head

shorter wings with pale panel

dark eye-stripe

smaller

notched tail

WILLOW WARBER see p.339

smaller head and bill

browner; no green or yellow

REED WARBLER see p.330

Length **13.5cm (5–6in)**	Wingspan **20–24cm (8–9½in)**	Weight **10–14g (⅜–½oz)**
Social **Solitary**	Lifespan **Up to 5 years**	Status **Secure**

| Order **Passeriformes** | Family **Sylviidae** | Species *Hippolais polyglotta* |

Melodious Warbler

rather long, round wings

ADULT

IN FLIGHT

trace of paler panel on wings

thick, spiky pale bill

JUVENILE

big dark eye in pale face

grey-green upperparts

pale yellow between eye and bill (no dark line)

yellow throat and breast

dull brown legs

ADULT

FLIGHT: rather weak, fluttering flight, usually over short distances.

A replacement of the more easterly Icterine Warbler in southwest Europe, the Melodious Warbler is confusingly similar. Both appear on west European coasts as migrants and require care for reliable separation, especially in autumn when juvenile plumages further confuse the issue. The Melodious and Icterine Warblers are basically green and yellow birds while other *Hippolais* warblers are duller, more pale brown and buff. The Melodious has a plainer wing with a shorter wingtip (primary feather) projection when perched than the Icterine.

VOICE Short clicks and sparrow-like chattering; song fast, rambling, not very accomplished warble, including rattling notes and shrill whistles but generally not much contrast in tone.

NESTING Deep cup in small branches of tree or large bush; 4 or 5 eggs; 1 brood; May–July.

FEEDING Takes insects from foliage; pulls berries from twigs in autumn.

SPRING SONG
The Melodious Warbler's song is a disappointment for a bird with this name: it is a quick, rather uninspired, rambling warble.

OCCURRENCE
Breeds in S and W Europe, France, Spain, Portugal, and Italy. Present from April to October, in light woodland, scrub, hedges, and orchards, with spring (and less often autumn) migrants on W European coasts including S Great Britain.

| Seen in the UK |
| J F **M A M J J A S** O N D |

SIMILAR SPECIES

ICTERINE WARBLER
see p.337

longer wings with more obvious panel

dark eye-stripe

no trace of yellow

shorter bill

WILLOW WARBLER
see p.339

GARDEN WARBLER
see p.320

| Length **12–13cm (4¾–5in)** | Wingspan **18–20cm (7–8in)** | Weight **11–14g (⅜–½oz)** |
| Social **Solitary** | Lifespan **Up to 5 years** | Status **Secure†** |

Order **Passeriformes**	Family **Sylviidae**	Species *Phylloscopus trochilus*

Willow Warbler 🔊 73

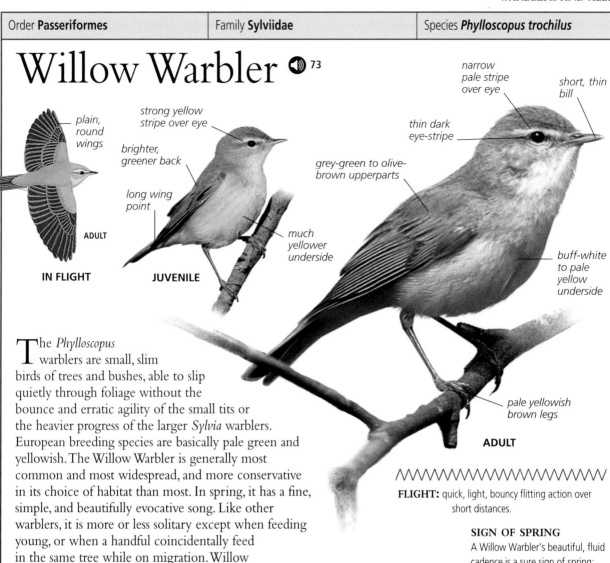

plain, round wings

ADULT

IN FLIGHT

strong yellow stripe over eye

brighter, greener back

long wing point

much yellower underside

JUVENILE

narrow pale stripe over eye

short, thin bill

thin dark eye-stripe

grey-green to olive-brown upperparts

buff-white to pale yellow underside

pale yellowish brown legs

ADULT

The *Phylloscopus* warblers are small, slim birds of trees and bushes, able to slip quietly through foliage without the bounce and erratic agility of the small tits or the heavier progress of the larger *Sylvia* warblers. European breeding species are basically pale green and yellowish. The Willow Warbler is generally most common and most widespread, and more conservative in its choice of habitat than most. In spring, it has a fine, simple, and beautifully evocative song. Like other warblers, it is more or less solitary except when feeding young, or when a handful coincidentally feed in the same tree while on migration. Willow Warblers are more grey-brown above and dull white below, less green and yellow, in the far north and northeast of Europe.

VOICE Sweet, simple, double call *hoo-eet*; song lovely, cascading, trilling warble, rising, full notes then falling thinner and fading away with slight flourish.

NESTING Small, domed nest of grass on or near ground in thick cover; 6 or 7 eggs; 1 brood; April–May.

FEEDING Picks insects and spiders from foliage, slipping gently and easily through leaves; catches some flies in air.

FLIGHT: quick, light, bouncy flitting action over short distances.

SIGN OF SPRING
A Willow Warbler's beautiful, fluid cadence is a sure sign of spring: in April, dozens may appear overnight and start singing.

OCCURRENCE
Breeds everywhere north from mid-France and C Europe except for Iceland. Present from April to October; common migrant in S Europe. Prefers light woodland, scrub, and bushes of all kinds, especially birch and willow, but not often gardens.

Seen in the UK
J F M A M J J A S O N D

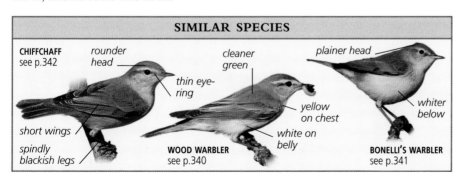

SIMILAR SPECIES

CHIFFCHAFF see p.342
rounder head
thin eye-ring
short wings
spindly blackish legs

cleaner green
yellow on chest
white on belly
WOOD WARBLER see p.340

plainer head
whiter below
BONELLI'S WARBLER see p.341

Length **11cm (4¼in)**	Wingspan **17–22cm (6½–9in)**	Weight **6–10g (7/32–3/8oz)**
Social **Solitary**	Lifespan **Up to 5 years**	Status **Secure**

| Order **Passeriformes** | Family **Sylviidae** | Species *Phylloscopus sibilatrix* |

Wood Warbler

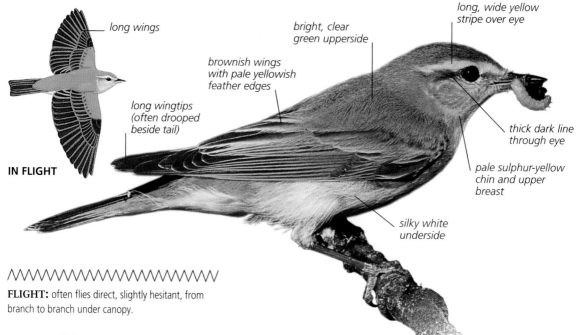

long wings

long wingtips (often drooped beside tail)

IN FLIGHT

bright, clear green upperside

brownish wings with pale yellowish feather edges

long, wide yellow stripe over eye

thick dark line through eye

pale sulphur-yellow chin and upper breast

silky white underside

MMMMMMMMMMMM

FLIGHT: often flies direct, slightly hesitant, from branch to branch under canopy.

One of the larger *Phylloscopus* warblers, the Wood Warbler is also the brightest, with areas of pure lemon yellow and clear green. It is restricted to high woodland with open space beneath the trees and far less generally distributed than the Willow Warbler or the Chiffchaff. It is also curiously rare away from its nesting woods, not usually seen near the coast during migration. It is best located by its characteristic song in early summer, becoming elusive later.

VOICE Call sweet, loud *sweet*; two song types: less frequent plaintive, low, sweet *sioo sioo sioo*, more often quick, sharp, ticking accelerating into fast, silvery, vibrant trill, *ti-ti-ti-ti-ti-tik-ik-ik-ikirrrrrrrrrrrrrrrr.*

NESTING Domed grassy nest in dead leaves on ground; 6 or 7 eggs; 1 brood; May–June.

FEEDING Moves through foliage easily, gently, and unobtrusively, picking insects and spiders.

ECSTATIC SONG
The fast, metallic trill seems to take over the whole body of a singing Wood Warbler as it vibrates to its own song.

OCCURRENCE
Local summer visitor breeding in UK, France, and east across Europe except N Scandinavia. In old woods with open space beneath canopy and leaf litter on ground, from April to August. Rare outside breeding areas.

| Seen in the UK |
| J F M **A M J J A S** O N D |

SIMILAR SPECIES

WILLOW WARBLER
see p.339

duller above

less yellow below

smaller and duller

short wings

CHIFFCHAFF
see p.342

plainer head

greyer

BONELLI'S WARBLER
see p.341

| Length **13cm (5in)** | Wingspan **19–24cm (7½–9½in)** | Weight **7–12g (¼–⁷⁄₁₆oz)** |
| Social **Solitary** | Lifespan **Up to 5 years** | Status **Secure†** |

| Order **Passeriformes** | Family **Sylviidae** | Species *Phylloscopus bonelli* |

Bonelli's Warbler

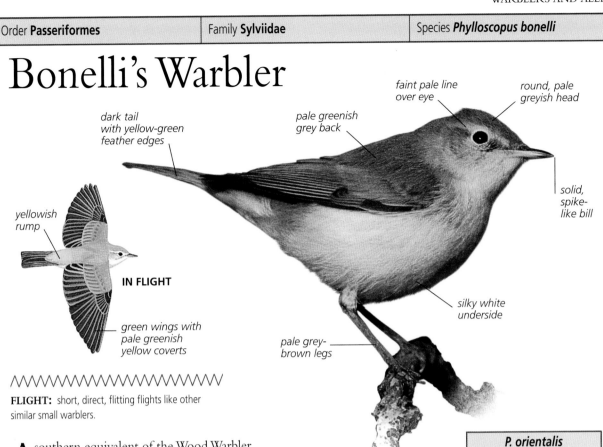

faint pale line over eye

round, pale greyish head

pale greenish grey back

dark tail with yellow-green feather edges

solid, spike-like bill

yellowish rump

IN FLIGHT

green wings with pale greenish yellow coverts

silky white underside

pale grey-brown legs

/\

FLIGHT: short, direct, flitting flights like other similar small warblers.

A southern equivalent of the Wood Warbler, Bonelli's Warbler is much less bright. It has an obviously similar but simpler, slightly bubbling song, often given from the top of a clump of dense oaks on a valley side slope, or from a dense conifer. In either case, Bonelli's Warbler can be hard to spot. Patience is usually rewarded but views are often brief as the bird is constantly moving, threading its way quietly through the foliage.

VOICE Call bright, finch-like *hoo-eet* or *chew-eee*; song loose, dribbling, bubbly trill on one note, less metallic than Cirl Bunting's, less ticking than Wood Warbler's, *s'r'r'r'r'r'rrrrrrrrrrrrrrr*.

NESTING Domed grassy nest on ground, under tussock or in cavity in bank; 5 or 6 eggs; 1 brood; May–July.

FEEDING Picks insects from foliage.

SUBTLE FEATURES
Bonelli's Warbler lacks striking features: it takes a few minutes of patient watching to identify it.

P. orientalis

Eastern Bonelli's Warbler
Formerly considered a subspecies of *P. bonelli*, now a species in its own right; SE Europe, Middle East; call a hard chipp.

greyer above

OCCURRENCE
Breeds in Spain, Portugal, S France, Italy, and Balkans between April and August. In deciduous and coniferous woodland, in clumps of oak on bushy slopes and quite small bushy pines; very rare migrant outside this range.

| Seen in the UK |
| J F M A M J J A S O N D |

SIMILAR SPECIES

striped head

brighter

yellow below

WOOD WARBLER
see p.340

stripe over eye

duller below

WILLOW WARBLER
see p.339

stripe over eye

short wings

smaller

CHIFFCHAFF
see p.342

| Length **11–12cm (4¼–4¾in)** | Wingspan **19–23cm (7½–9in)** | Weight **7–11g (¼–⅜oz)** |
| Social **Solitary** | Lifespan **Up to 5 years** | Status **Secure** |

| Order **Passeriformes** | Family **Sylviidae** | Species **Phylloscopus collybita** |

Chiffchaff 🔊 74

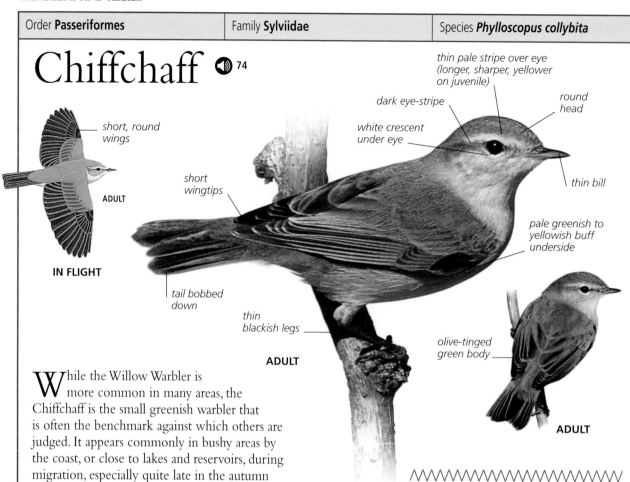

short, round wings

IN FLIGHT

ADULT

thin pale stripe over eye (longer, sharper, yellower on juvenile)

dark eye-stripe

round head

white crescent under eye

thin bill

short wingtips

pale greenish to yellowish buff underside

tail bobbed down

thin blackish legs

olive-tinged green body

ADULT

ADULT

While the Willow Warbler is more common in many areas, the Chiffchaff is the small greenish warbler that is often the benchmark against which others are judged. It appears commonly in bushy areas by the coast, or close to lakes and reservoirs, during migration, especially quite late in the autumn (when it may sing quite frequently). Sometimes a migrant will appear for a day or so, singing, in a large garden, but in summer it is a bird of taller trees in well-wooded parks or woodland. Distinguishing a Chiffchaff from a Willow Warbler can be a real problem but it is worth persisting and learning their different characters. A frequent downward bob of the tail is a good clue to a Chiffchaff.

VOICE Call slurred, almost single syllable, sweet *hweet*; song easy, loud, bright, even-paced repetition of simple notes, *chip-chap-chip-chap-chap-chup-chap-chap-chip*.
NESTING Domed grass nest very low in bush or herbs; 5 or 6 eggs; 1 or 2 broods; April–July.
FEEDING Takes insects and spiders from foliage, slipping easily through without jerky leaps of tits.

FLIGHT: short, low, slow, weak, undulating action.

PERSISTENT SINGER
Early arrivals sing almost constantly before the leaves are on the trees. Chiffchaffs sing again on migration in autumn.

SUBSPECIES
P. c. tristis (Siberia, very rare vagrant in W Europe)
curved pale wing-bar
greyer

SIMILAR SPECIES

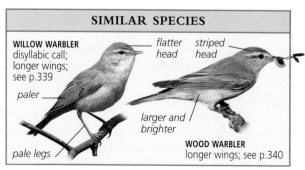

WILLOW WARBLER disyllabic call; longer wings; see p.339
paler
pale legs
flatter head
striped head
larger and brighter
WOOD WARBLER longer wings; see p.340

OCCURRENCE
Breeds in most of Europe except for Iceland; many winter in S Europe, fewer in W Europe. In woods, wooded parks, large gardens, and lower thickets especially on migration (willows near water especially in March).

Seen in the UK
J F M A M J J A S O N D

| Length **10–11cm (4–4¼ in)** | Wingspan **15–21cm (6–8½ in)** | Weight **6–9g (⁷⁄₃₂–¹¹⁄₃₂ oz)** |
| Social **Solitary** | Lifespan **Up to 5 years** | Status **Secure†** |

Order **Passeriformes**	Family **Sylviidae**	Species **Regulus regulus**

Goldcrest 🔊 75

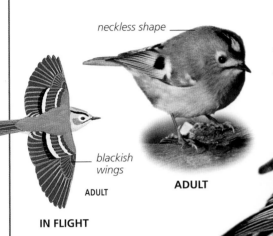

neckless shape

ADULT

blackish wings

ADULT

IN FLIGHT

broad white "V"-shaped bar on wings

dull to bright olive-green plumage

black stripe with yellow centre on crown (plain grey-green on juvenile)

whitish around eye

buff to greenish underside

ADULT

Europe's smallest bird, the Goldcrest may sometimes be watched almost at arm's length as it feeds in lower branches of trees. It isn't so much bold or tame as simply oblivious to the presence of people: it generally ignores humans. The Goldcrest's succession of high-pitched, needle-thin but emphatic calls is a feature of many coniferous forests. The song is equally thin but remarkably penetrating, even audible from a fast-passing car. In winter, Goldcrests forage in a variety of places, including hedges, low thickets, and even clumps of gorse or brambles.

VOICE Call high, thin, sibilant but emphasized *see-see-seee*; song high, fast, rhythmic phrase with terminal flourish, complex at close range, at distance *seedli-ee seedli-ee seedli-ee seedli-ee seedli-i-didl-eeoo*.

NESTING Tiny cup of cobwebs, moss, and lichens, slung beneath branch; 7 or 8 eggs; 2 broods; April–July.

FEEDING Picks tiny insects, spiders, and insect eggs from foliage, often hovering briefly.

FLIGHT: quick, flitting; weak-looking whirr.

PIERCING SONG
The high-pitched song of the Goldcrest penetrates the noise of wind in the trees, and even land traffic noise.

OCCURRENCE
Breeds in most of Europe except Iceland, extreme N Scandinavia, and much of Mediterranean Europe. Present all year round in mixed and coniferous woodland, parks, and large wooded gardens; coastal migrants can be in very low scrub.

Seen in the UK
J F M A M J J A S O N D

SIMILAR SPECIES

FIRECREST see p.344
white stripe over eye
brighter
larger
plain wings
WILLOW WARBLER see p.339
plain head
plain wings
CHIFFCHAFF see p.342

Length **8.5–9cm (3¼–3½in)**	Wingspan **13–15.5cm (5–6in)**	Weight **5–7g (³⁄₁₆–¼oz)**
Social **Solitary**	Lifespan **2–3 years**	Status **Secure†**

Order **Passeriformes**	Family **Sylviidae**	Species *Regulus ignicapilla*

Firecrest

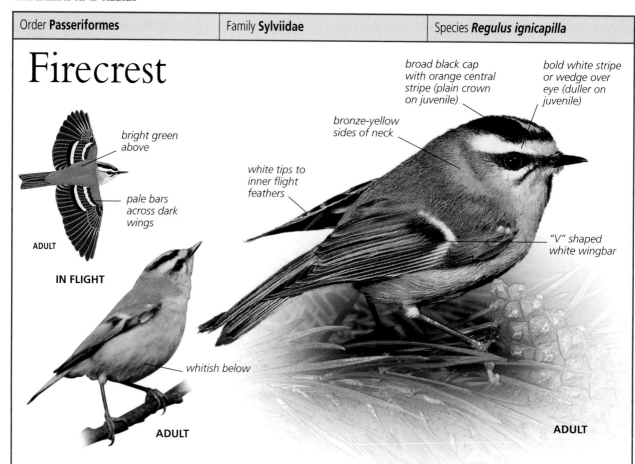

bright green above

pale bars across dark wings

ADULT

IN FLIGHT

broad black cap with orange central stripe (plain crown on juvenile)

bold white stripe or wedge over eye (duller on juvenile)

bronze-yellow sides of neck

white tips to inner flight feathers

"V" shaped white wingbar

whitish below

ADULT

ADULT

Less widespread than the Goldcrest, but in parts of Europe the more likely of the two to be seen, the Firecrest has an obviously close relationship with the slightly duller, plainer species. It has slightly firmer calls and a much less rhythmic, dynamic song, a useful distinction if a bird is seen as a silhouette against the sky at the top of a tall conifer (as so often happens). When it comes lower and allows a close view, it is revealed as one of the brightest of European birds.

VOICE High *zeet*; song sharp, quick, accelerating *zi zi zi zezezeeeee*.

NESTING Moss and lichen cup beneath branch, usually in conifer; 7–11 eggs; 2 broods; April–July.

FEEDING Takes tiny insects and spiders from foliage, slipping through leaves with ease and often hovering briefly.

FLIGHT: short, quick, weak flitting action, usually over very short distances.

SPRUCE NESTER
Firecrests usually nest in conifers; they are typically difficult to see clearly amidst the foliage.

OCCURRENCE
Breeds in extreme S UK, south to Spain and east to Baltic States and Balkans. Found all year in coniferous, broadleaved, and mixed woodland, shrubberies, parks, evergreen scrub, and bushy slopes with many hollies, yews, or similar bushes.

Seen in the UK
J F M A M J J A S O N D

SIMILAR SPECIES

GOLDCREST ♂♀; see p.343 — no white over eye — plainer face

CHIFFCHAFF see p.342 — plain wings

PALLAS'S WARBLER yellow rump in flight; see p.455 — long yellow stripe over eye

Length **9cm (3½in)**	Wingspan **13–16cm (5–6½in)**	Weight **5–7g (³⁄₁₆–¼oz)**
Social **Solitary**	Lifespan **2–3 years**	Status **Secure**

| Order **Passeriformes** | Family **Muscicapidae** | Species *Muscicapa striata* |

Spotted Flycatcher

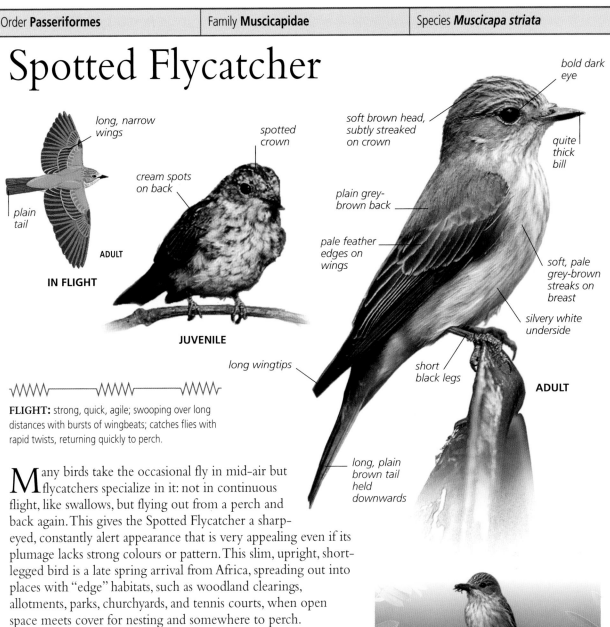

long, narrow wings

plain tail

IN FLIGHT

ADULT

spotted crown

cream spots on back

JUVENILE

long wingtips

bold dark eye

soft brown head, subtly streaked on crown

quite thick bill

plain grey-brown back

pale feather edges on wings

soft, pale grey-brown streaks on breast

silvery white underside

short black legs

ADULT

long, plain brown tail held downwards

FLIGHT: strong, quick, agile; swooping over long distances with bursts of wingbeats; catches flies with rapid twists, returning quickly to perch.

Many birds take the occasional fly in mid-air but flycatchers specialize in it: not in continuous flight, like swallows, but flying out from a perch and back again. This gives the Spotted Flycatcher a sharp-eyed, constantly alert appearance that is very appealing even if its plumage lacks strong colours or pattern. This slim, upright, short-legged bird is a late spring arrival from Africa, spreading out into places with "edge" habitats, such as woodland clearings, allotments, parks, churchyards, and tennis courts, when open space meets cover for nesting and somewhere to perch.

VOICE Short, slightly metallic or scratchy, unmusical *tzic* or *tzee*, *tzee-tsuk tsuk*; song of similar quality, short, scratchy, weak warble.

NESTING Cup of grass, leaves, moss, and feathers in creeper, old nest, cavity in wall, or open-fronted nest box; 3–5 eggs; 1 or 2 broods; June–August.

FEEDING Mostly catches insects in air, after flight from perch (from near ground level to treetop height); usually returns to same perch.

OPEN PERCH
A perch with a view of insects that catch the light as they cross sunlit clearings lets this flycatcher find a good meal.

SIMILAR SPECIES

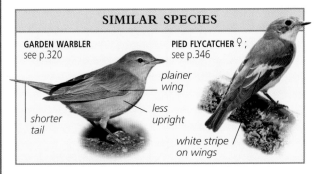

GARDEN WARBLER see p.320

shorter tail

plainer wing

PIED FLYCATCHER ♀; see p.346

less upright

white stripe on wings

OCCURRENCE
Breeds almost throughout Europe except in Iceland, present from May to September and often a late arrival in spring. In open woodland, parkland, gardens with bushes and trees, and similar places.

Seen in the UK
| J | F | M | **A** | **M** | **J** | **J** | **A** | **S** | **O** | N | D |

| Length **14cm (5½in)** | Wingspan **23–25cm (9–10in)** | Weight **14–19g (½–$^{11}/_{16}$oz)** |
| Social **Solitary** | Lifespan **3–5 years** | Status **Declining** |

| Order **Passeriformes** | Family **Muscicapidae** | Species *Ficedula hypoleuca* |

Pied Flycatcher

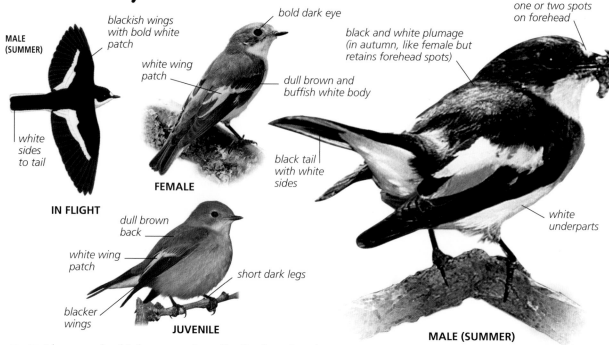

MALE (SUMMER)

blackish wings with bold white patch

white wing patch

bold dark eye

dull brown and buffish white body

white sides to tail

IN FLIGHT

FEMALE

black and white plumage (in autumn, like female but retains forehead spots)

one or two spots on forehead

black tail with white sides

white underparts

dull brown back

white wing patch

short dark legs

blacker wings

JUVENILE

MALE (SUMMER)

Neither a garden bird nor as universally distributed as the Spotted Flycatcher, the Pied Flycatcher is a forest species, preferring space under the canopy in which it can feed, flying out for flies or dropping to the ground. Such places often have Redstarts (see p.304), Wood Warblers (see p.340), and Pied Flycatchers as a characteristic trio of small birds in summer. All become elusive after nesting, Pied Flycatchers almost "disappearing" for a time, although they are frequent migrants in coastal areas later in autumn.

VOICE Sharp *whit* or *whit-tic, wheet*; song brief, simple, musical phrase with notes clearly separated, slightly hesitant, ending with trill, *see, see, see sit, see-sit sitip-seweee*.

NESTING Cup of leaves and moss, in tree hole, old woodpecker hole or, by preference, nest box; 5–9 eggs; 1 brood; April–May.

FEEDING Catches flies in air and picks insects from foliage and from ground; also eats seeds and berries.

REMARK Subspecies *F. h. iberiae* (Spain) has pale rump, bigger forehead spot, bigger wingbar and primary patch.

FLIGHT: strong, quite bounding; often drops to ground, catches flies in air but usually goes on to different perch.

NEST BOX
A male feeds his chicks in a box specially provided: numbers are increased by nest box schemes in suitable woods.

OCCURRENCE
Breeds in UK and across most of mainland Europe. Seen from April to August in broadleaved woodland with clear space beneath canopy, often where there are Wood Warblers. Migrants often on coasts in autumn.

| Seen in the UK |
| J F M **A M J J A S O** N D |

SIMILAR SPECIES

COLLARED FLYCATCHER ♀ similar to ♂ ♀; paler rump; see p.456

white collar

more white on wings

SEMI-COLLARED FLYCATCHER ♂ similar to ♂; paler rump; see p.456

small upper wingbar

SPOTTED FLYCATCHER similar to ♀; see p.345

thin buff streaks on wings; no white

| Length **13cm (5in)** | Wingspan **21–24cm (8½–9½in)** | Weight **12–15g (⁷⁄₁₆–⁹⁄₁₆ oz)** |
| Social **Solitary** | Lifespan **3–5 years** | Status **Secure** |

Families **Paridae, Aegithalidae, Timaliidae, Remizidae**

TITS AND ALLIES

IN THIS GROUP, there are the "true" tits, in the genus *Parus*, together with several "imposters": the Bearded Tit (really a parrotbill), the Long-tailed Tit, and the Penduline Tit. All are more or less social, the Penduline Tit least so; most are woodland birds, but Bearded and Penduline Tits live in or around reedbeds.

The true tits are rather small or very small birds (the Coal Tit is one of Europe's tiniest species), either green, blue, yellow, and white or mixtures of dull grey-brown, buff, white, and black. Several species come to garden feeders and are familiar favourites (especially the Blue and Great Tits, but even Crested Tits visit feeders where they are common).

These are primarily woodland species, timing their breeding to the sudden appearance of vast quantities of caterpillars on tree foliage (something that climate change is throwing out of synchronization, causing severe problems in places). Garden breeders do less well, but survive the winter better with artificial feeding. In winter, mixed groups of tits forage through woods, hedgerows, and gardens, typically mostly Blue and Great Tits with Coal, Marsh, and Willow Tits in ones and twos around the fringe. They take advantage of greater numbers, being better able to find food and also to spot approaching predators since many pairs of eyes are better than one.

SUSPENDED NEST
The nest of a Penduline Tit is a masterpiece of construction hung from a slender, swaying twig.

POPULAR BIRD
For many, the Blue Tit is the most typical, and favourite, garden visitor.

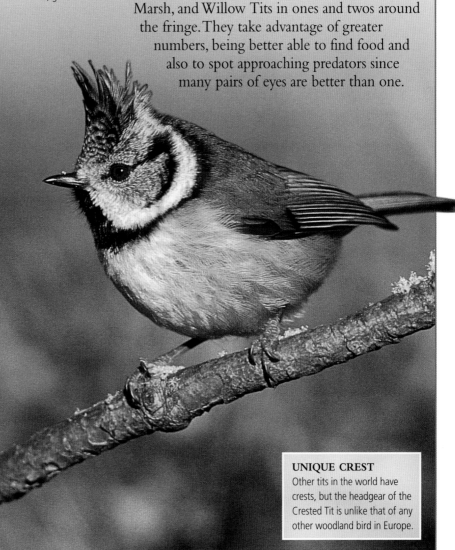

UNIQUE CREST
Other tits in the world have crests, but the headgear of the Crested Tit is unlike that of any other woodland bird in Europe.

| Order **Passeriformes** | Family **Paridae** | Species *Parus major* |

Great Tit 🔊 76

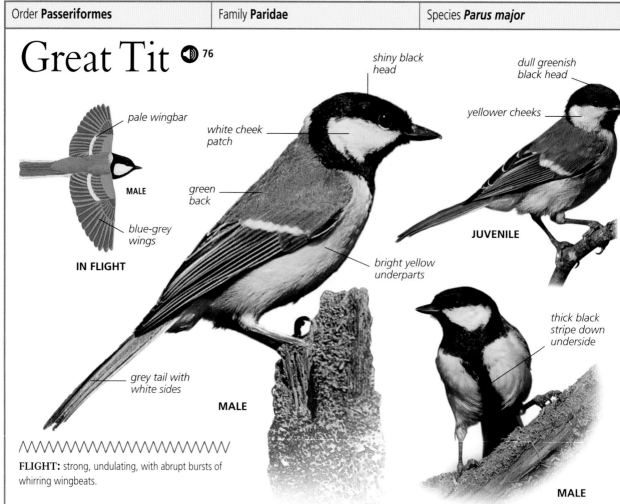

shiny black head

white cheek patch

green back

pale wingbar

MALE

blue-grey wings

IN FLIGHT

dull greenish black head

yellower cheeks

JUVENILE

bright yellow underparts

grey tail with white sides

MALE

thick black stripe down underside

MALE

Λ/\/\/\/\/\/\/\/\/\/\/\/\/\

FLIGHT: strong, undulating, with abrupt bursts of whirring wingbeats.

A big, colourful, bold, and aggressive tit, the Great Tit is well known almost everywhere and is one of the most familiar of garden birds; it is also common in woodland and on bushy hillsides. It feeds more on the ground than the smaller tits, lacking their extreme lightness and agility, but is still an acrobatic bird, moving more energetically and erratically than the woodland warblers. In spring, it has a simple but remarkably fine and appealing song.

VOICE Extremely varied, often confusing; calls include ringing *chink* or *pink*, piping *tui tui tui*, nasal *churrr*; song variation on repeated two-syllable phrase, sharp, metallic, strident, musical, or grating, with varying emphasis, *tea-cher tea-cher tea-cher* or *seetoo seetoo seetoo*.

NESTING Cup of moss, leaves, and grass in natural hole, woodpecker hole, or nest box; 5–11 eggs; 1 brood; April–May.

FEEDING Eats insects, seeds, berries, and nuts, especially tree seeds in autumn and winter, many from ground; commonly visits bird-tables and feeders.

narrower black stripe down underside

FEMALE

SIMILAR SPECIES

BLUE TIT ♂♀; white ring around nape; see p.350

smaller

pale blue cap

white on nape

no yellow or green

COAL TIT see p.349

OCCURRENCE
Breeds and all-year round resident almost throughout Europe except in Iceland. All-year in wide variety of mixed woodland, parks, and gardens; in S Europe, also on warm, scrubby hillsides.

| Seen in the UK |
| J F M A M J J A S O N D |

| Length **14cm (35in)** | Wingspan **22–25cm (9–10in)** | Weight **16–21g (9/16–3/4oz)** |
| Social **Loose flocks** | Lifespan **2–3 years** | Status **Secure** |

Order **Passeriformes**	Family **Paridae**	Species ***Periparus ater***

Coal Tit 🔊 77

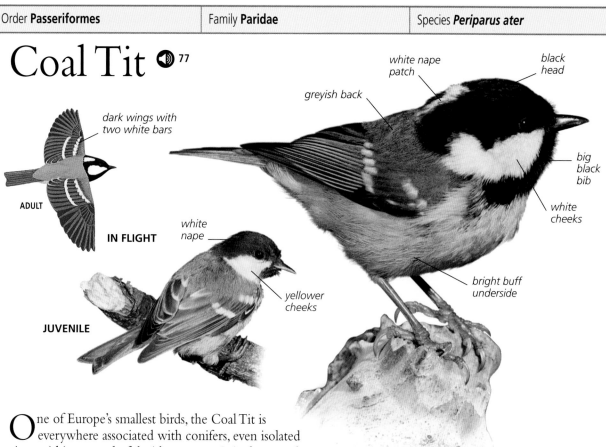

dark wings with
two white bars

ADULT

IN FLIGHT

white nape
patch

greyish back

black
head

big
black
bib

white
cheeks

white
nape

yellower
cheeks

JUVENILE

bright buff
underside

ADULT

One of Europe's smallest birds, the Coal Tit is everywhere associated with conifers, even isolated pines within a wood of deciduous trees. It is also a garden bird in many places. In autumn and winter, it regularly joins other tits in large, shapeless, roaming flocks that wander through woods and gardens in search of food. Woods often seem birdless until such a flock comes by, when suddenly there is too much to see at once. Coal Tits typically exploit their minute weight by searching the thinnest twigs.

VOICE Call high, sweet, sad *tseu* or *tsoooo*, thin *tseee*, bright *psueet*; song bright, quick, repetitive, high *wi-choo wi-choo wi-choo* or *sweetu sweetu sweetu*.

NESTING Hair-lined small cup of moss and leaves in hole in stump, tree, wall, or ground, or in small-holed nest box; 7–11 eggs; 1 brood; April–June.

FEEDING Finds tiny insects, spiders, and their eggs in foliage; eats many seeds and nuts; visits feeders frequently, often dashing off with food to eat nearby; hides much food in tufts of pine needles.

REMARK Subspecies *P. a. ledouci* (N Africa) has yellow cheeks and underside.

FLIGHT: weak, flitting, with whirring wingbeats, with sudden "stop" on perch.

TINY BUT FEARLESS
Coal Tits take very little notice of people and may forage through shrubberies almost within arm's length if one keeps still and quiet.

OCCURRENCE
Breeds through all of Europe except Iceland and extreme N Scandinavia. Lives all year round in mixed but mainly coniferous woodland, wooded parks, and gardens close to conifer woods.

Seen in the UK
J F M A M J J A S O N D

SIMILAR SPECIES

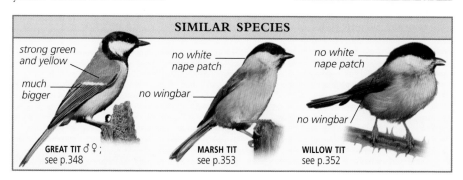

strong green
and yellow

much
bigger

GREAT TIT ♂♀;
see p.348

no white
nape patch

no wingbar

MARSH TIT
see p.353

no white
nape patch

no wingbar

WILLOW TIT
see p.352

Length **11.5cm (4½in)**	Wingspan **17–21cm (6½–8½in)**	Weight **8–10g (⁵⁄₁₆–³⁄₈oz)**
Social **Loose flocks**	Lifespan **2–3 years**	Status **Secure**

Order **Passeriformes**	Family **Paridae**	Species *Cyanistes caeruleus*

Blue Tit 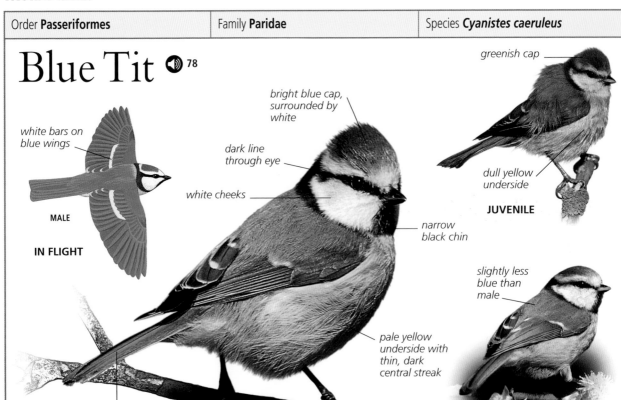 🔊 78

greenish cap

JUVENILE

dull yellow underside

white bars on blue wings

MALE

IN FLIGHT

bright blue cap, surrounded by white

dark line through eye

white cheeks

narrow black chin

pale yellow underside with thin, dark central streak

blue tail (brightest in spring male)

MALE

slightly less blue than male

FEMALE

Common, noisy, colourful, and tame, the Blue Tit is a favourite garden bird, coming to feeders of all kinds. It also nests in boxes in larger gardens, but is generally not very successful there as broods of young require prodigious numbers of caterpillars to thrive. Only large woodland areas provide sufficient supplies. Even there, in recent years, Blue Tits have had reduced breeding success as the chicks hatch when food supplies have declined, caterpillars having appeared earlier due to climate change.

VOICE Thin, quick, *tsee-tsee-tsee*, harder *tsee-see-sit*, scolding *churrrrr*; song trilled, slurred *tsee-tsee-tsee-tsisisisisisi*.

NESTING Small, mossy cup, lined with hair and feathers, in hole in tree or wall or nest box; 7–16 eggs; 1 brood; April–May.

FEEDING Takes many seeds, nuts, insects, and spiders; visits garden feeders and bird-tables frequently in large numbers.

FLIGHT: fast, undulating over long distance; bursts of whirring wingbeats; sudden stop on perch.

AT NUT BASKET
The Blue Tit uses its quick actions and surefootedness to dash in to a peanut basket and hang, often upside down, to reach its food.

OCCURRENCE
Present almost throughout Europe except in N Scandinavia and Iceland, all year. In woods of all kinds, parks, gardens, and bushy places. In winter, quite often in reedbeds and even wandering around edges of salt marshes.

Seen in the UK
J F M A M J J A S O N D

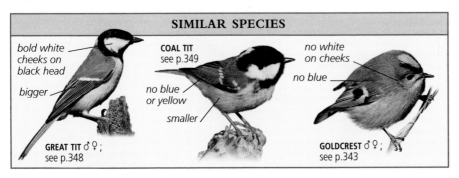

SIMILAR SPECIES

bold white cheeks on black head

bigger

GREAT TIT ♂♀; see p.348

COAL TIT see p.349

no blue or yellow

smaller

no white on cheeks

no blue

GOLDCREST ♂♀; see p.343

Length **11.5cm (4½in)**	Wingspan **17–20cm (6½–8in)**	Weight **9–12g ($^{11}/_{32}$–$^7/_{16}$oz)**
Social **Loose flocks**	Lifespan **2–3 years**	Status **Secure**

Order **Passeriformes**	Family **Paridae**	Species *Lophophanes cristatus*

Crested Tit

brown tail

brown wings

warm brown back

IN FLIGHT

pointed crest, mottled black- and white

white face with black edge to cheek

plain wings

black bib

buff underside

∧∧∧∧∧∧∧∧∧∧∧∧∧∧∧∧∧∧∧∧∧∧∧∧∧∧∧∧∧∧

FLIGHT: weak, flitting, quite quick, with bursts or flurries of wingbeats.

There are titmice with crests elsewhere in the world but this one is unique in Europe and thus easy to identify even in silhouette. It is a pine forest specialist, in the UK restricted to northern Scotland and more numerous in ancient pine forest than in newer plantations. It seems to require some variation, with clearings and forest edge, as well as dead or dying tree stumps in which it can nest. It is easily located by its distinctive stuttering call. Like other titmice, the Crested Tit is almost oblivious to the presence of people and can be watched feeding from very close range.

VOICE Quick, low, rather soft trill or stutter, *b'd-rrrr-rup*, also usual thin, high tit *zit* or *zee*.

NESTING Soft cup in hole in decaying tree stump; 5–7 eggs; 1 brood; April–June.

FEEDING Eats small insects and spiders; in winter, takes seeds, many from stores made in spring; visits feeders in wooded gardens.

PINE SPECIALIST
Although found in mixed woods in Europe, most Crested Tits prefer old pine forest, with dead trees and stumps to excavate a nest-hole in.

OCCURRENCE
Breeds in N Scotland and most of mainland Europe except extreme N Scandinavia, Italy, and most of Balkans. Present all year round mostly in conifer forest, and locally in deciduous woods in mainland Europe.

Seen in the UK
J F M A M J J A S O N D

SIMILAR SPECIES

black cap without crest

wingbars

COAL TIT
see p.349

no crest

MARSH TIT
see p.353

no crest

WILLOW TIT
see p.352

Length **11.5cm (4½in)**	Wingspan **17–20cm (6½–8in)**	Weight **10–13g (⅜–⁷⁄₁₆oz)**
Social **Loose flocks**	Lifespan **2–3 years**	Status **Secure**

Order **Passeriformes**	Family **Paridae**	Species ***Poecile montanus***

Willow Tit 🔊 79

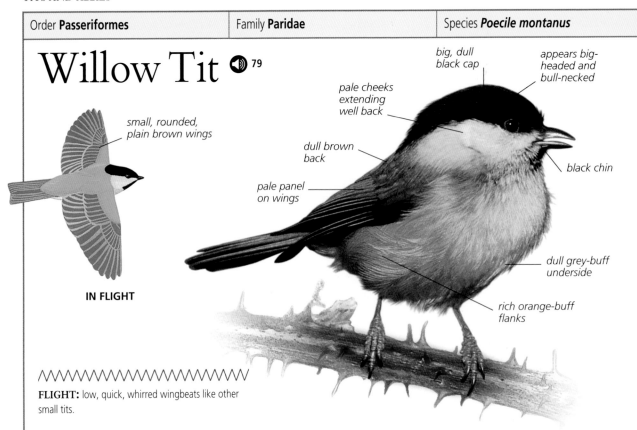

small, rounded, plain brown wings

IN FLIGHT

big, dull black cap

appears big-headed and bull-necked

pale cheeks extending well back

dull brown back

black chin

pale panel on wings

dull grey-buff underside

rich orange-buff flanks

/\

FLIGHT: low, quick, whirred wingbeats like other small tits.

Much like a Marsh Tit, the Willow Tit is more often found in places with few mature trees but plenty of lower bushes, such as old hedgerows and extensive willow carr over peat bogs. It is, however, also found in woods and the two often overlap. It often visits gardens but, like the Coal Tit, tends to take a morsel of food and fly away with it to eat elsewhere, so its visits are short. The Willow Tit appears big-headed and bull-necked, and uses its distinctive low, harsh, buzzy calls frequently, helping to separate it from the Marsh Tit. It requires patience and experience to learn how to separate the two on sight.

VOICE Thin *zi zi* combined with distinctive deep, nasal, buzzing *airr airr airr* or *charr charr charr*; song rarely varied warble, more commonly full, piping *tyoo tyoo tyoo*.

NESTING Excavates own hole in rotten stump; 6–9 eggs; 1 brood; April–June.

FEEDING Agile and acrobatic but generally quite sluggish, taking insects, seeds, and berries; comes to feeders in gardens for nuts and sunflower seeds.

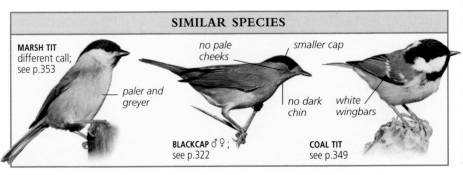

PEANUT RAIDER
The Willow Tit is quite a frequent visitor to hanging feeders in gardens. The characteristic pale wing panel is visible in this picture.

OCCURRENCE
Breeds in N and E Europe, west to UK and E France, and south to C Italy and Balkans, present year round. Occupies coniferous and birch forest, mixed woods, thickets and hedgerows, and often visits gardens.

Seen in the UK
J F M A M J J A S O N D

SIMILAR SPECIES

MARSH TIT different call; see p.353

paler and greyer

no pale cheeks

smaller cap

no dark chin

white wingbars

BLACKCAP ♂♀; see p.322

COAL TIT see p.349

Length **11.5cm (4½in)**	Wingspan **17–18cm (6½–7in)**	Weight **9–11g ($^{11}/_{32}$–$^3/_8$oz)**
Social **Loose flocks**	Lifespan **2–3 years**	Status **Secure†**

Order **Passeriformes**	Family **Paridae**	Species ***Poecile palustris***

Marsh Tit 🔊 80

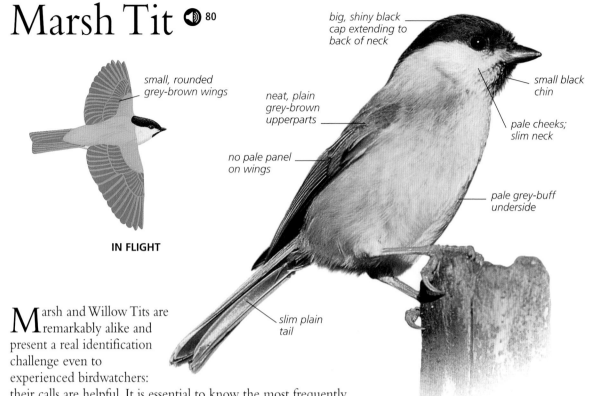

big, shiny black cap extending to back of neck

small, rounded grey-brown wings

neat, plain grey-brown upperparts

small black chin

pale cheeks; slim neck

no pale panel on wings

pale grey-buff underside

IN FLIGHT

slim plain tail

Marsh and Willow Tits are remarkably alike and present a real identification challenge even to experienced birdwatchers: their calls are helpful. It is essential to know the most frequently used ones to tell the two apart: a distinct *pit-chew* call is the best clue to a Marsh Tit, quite unlike any call used by the Willow. Both birds visit gardens but much less persistently than the Blue Tits and Great Tits. Marsh Tits like the vicinity of mature deciduous trees, especially beeches and oaks, although they often forage at a low level among thick undergrowth. They join mixed winter tit flocks, but usually only one or two hang around at the edges. Like most tits, Marsh Tits use existing holes in which to nest, while Willow Tits excavate their own.

VOICE Loud calls, often *titi-zee-zee-zee, tchair*, most distinctive a unique loud, bright, *pit-chew!*; song infrequent, quick, rippling *schip-schip-schip-schip*.

NESTING Grass and moss cup in existing hole in tree or wall, not often in nest box; 6–8 eggs; 1 brood; April–June.

FEEDING Mostly feeds on insects and spiders in summer; takes seeds, berries, and nits in autumn and winter, often from ground.

/\/\/\/\/\/\/\/\/\/\/\/\/\/\/\/\/\

FLIGHT: low, weak, flitting, with bursts of wingbeats, similar to close relatives.

NEAT APPEARANCE
A glossy cap and uniform wings give the Marsh Tit a neat look, and are good identification clues to distinguish it from the Willow Tit.

OCCURRENCE
Breeds in S UK, S Scandinavia, and east across middle Europe, south to Italy and Balkans. In deciduous woodland and parkland with tall trees, sometimes visiting gardens to use feeders especially in winter.

Seen in the UK
J F M A M J J A S O N D

SIMILAR SPECIES

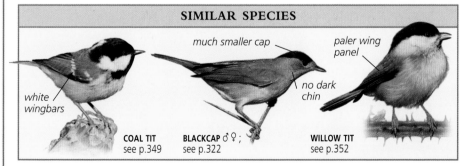

much smaller cap

paler wing panel

white wingbars

no dark chin

COAL TIT see p.349

BLACKCAP ♂♀; see p.322

WILLOW TIT see p.352

Length **11.5cm (4½in)**	Wingspan **18–19cm (7–7½in)**	Weight **10–12g (³/₈–⁷/₁₆oz)**
Social **Loose flocks**	Lifespan **2–3 years**	Status **Secure**

Order **Passeriformes**	Family **Aegithalidae**	Species *Aegithalos caudatus*

Long-tailed Tit 🔊 81

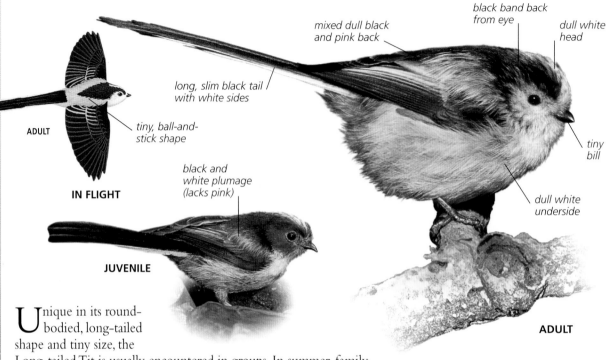

mixed dull black and pink back

black band back from eye

dull white head

long, slim black tail with white sides

tiny, ball-and-stick shape

ADULT

IN FLIGHT

black and white plumage (lacks pink)

tiny bill

dull white underside

JUVENILE

ADULT

Unique in its round-bodied, long-tailed shape and tiny size, the Long-tailed Tit is usually encountered in groups. In summer, family parties move noisily through bush tops or undergrowth; in winter sometimes much larger parties tend to string out as they feed, often crossing a gap between trees in a thin, erratic stream. Their high calls resemble those of other tits and Goldcrests (see p.343), but have a particularly shapeless, needle-like character, intermixed with low, abrupt notes that are immediately distinctive.

VOICE High, thin, colourless *seee seee seee* without emphasis or fuller quality of Goldcrest; short, abrupt, low *trrp*, longer *zerrrp* or *tsirrup!*

NESTING Unique rounded and domed nest with side entrance into soft, springy, elastic ball of lichen, moss, cobweb, and feathers, in low, thorny bush; 8–12 eggs; 1 brood; April–June.

FEEDING Groups move about, often in single file, picking tiny spiders and insects from twigs and foliage; eat a few seeds; increasingly visit feeders in gardens.

FLIGHT: weak, quick; whirring wingbeats; often in groups, single file, flitting from bush to bush, tail bouncing along behind.

AMAZING NEST
The Long-tailed Tit's globular or bottle-shaped nest, coated with lichen, is a remarkable structure. It expands as the chicks grow.

OCCURRENCE
Breeding bird in all of Europe except Iceland, present all year. Occupies mixed or deciduous woods with bushy undergrowth, scrub, and tall old hedgerows; increasingly visits gardens.

Seen in the UK
J F M A M J J A S O N D

LONG AND SLIM
A Long-tailed Tit looks quite slender in summer; it is in cold winter conditions that it looks like a round ball with a tail attached.

Length **14cm (5½in)**	Wingspan **16–19cm (6½–7½in)**	Weight **7–9g (¼–¹¹⁄₃₂oz)**
Social **Flocks**	Lifespan **2–3 years**	Status **Secure**

Order **Passeriformes**	Family **Timaliidae**	Species *Panurus biarmicus*

Bearded Tit

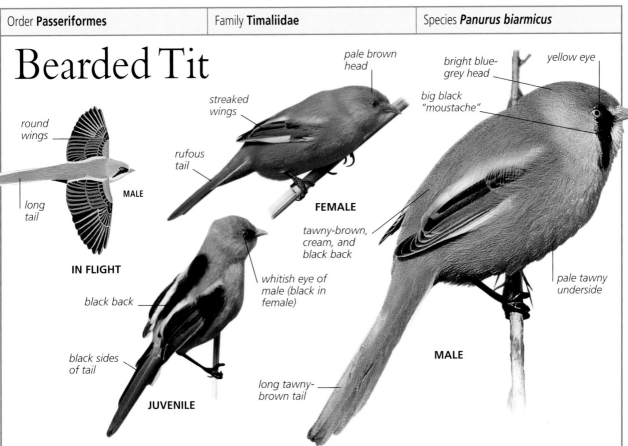

round wings

long tail

MALE

IN FLIGHT

pale brown head

streaked wings

rufous tail

FEMALE

bright blue-grey head

yellow eye

big black "moustache"

tawny-brown, cream, and black back

whitish eye of male (black in female)

black back

black sides of tail

JUVENILE

long tawny-brown tail

pale tawny underside

MALE

More closely related to the babblers and parrotbills of Asia than the tits, the Bearded Tit is one of Europe's most restricted birds in terms of habitat. It is entirely dependent on extensive reedbeds, although it will briefly occupy reedmace or tall, wet grass in winter when population pressure forces some to leave reedbeds to look for new sites. It can be hard to see, especially on windy days, but since it calls frequently it can usually be located quite easily. If nothing else, a glimpse of a tawny, long-tailed shape flitting across a gap in the reeds is usually forthcoming.

VOICE Variations on loud, metallic, "pinging" *psching*, *pink*, or *ping*, sometimes in loud, ringing chorus, often sporadic; quiet at times.

NESTING Deep cup of leaves, stems, and reed flower heads in reed litter under standing reeds in water; 5–7 eggs; 2 or 3 broods; April–August.

FEEDING Takes caterpillars from reed stems and reed seeds from flower heads and leaf litter or mud below.

FLIGHT: low, fast, over reeds; whirring, trailing long tail.

REEDBED INHABITANT
Patience and calm weather are needed for a view like this of a Bearded Tit in its reedbed habitat, but they are sometimes surprisingly tame.

SIMILAR SPECIES

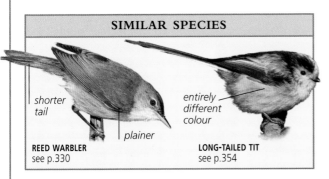

shorter tail

plainer

entirely different colour

REED WARBLER
see p.330

LONG-TAILED TIT
see p.354

OCCURRENCE
Extremely local, breeding in reedbeds in E UK, N and S France, Low Countries, Baltic area, E Spain, S Portugal, Italy, and SE Europe. Resident in winter, occasionally spilling into other wetland habitats.

Seen in the UK
J F M A M J J A S O N D

Length **12.5cm (5in)**	Wingspan **16–18cm (6½–7in)**	Weight **12–18g ($^{7}/_{16}$–$^{5}/_{8}$oz)**
Social **Loose flocks**	Lifespan **2–3 years**	Status **Secure†**

Order **Passeriformes**	Family **Remizidae**	Species *Remiz pendulinus*

Penduline Tit

deep red-brown band across wings

MALE

narrower black mask

IN FLIGHT

plain head gradually develops black

uniform, plain, pale brown back

FEMALE

JUVENILE

plain dark tail

pale grey head

sharp, narrow, triangular bill

red-brown back

broad black mask

buffish underside

MALE

FLIGHT: quick, erratic, bounding undulations with bursts of wingbeats.

A small, neat, well-patterned bird, the Penduline Tit can be hard to spot (even though easily heard) in tall riverside treetops; in winter, it is often in lower bushes in and around reedbeds and may be easier to find. It is usually close to water, although sometimes several fields away in lines of trees along little more than a ditch or beside a damp meadow. It is common in southeast Europe, but spreading in the west, with increasing appearances in the UK.

VOICE Distinctive high, far-carrying, pure whistle, *psieeee*, longer than similar Reed Bunting note (see p.405); song simple mix of trills and calls.

NESTING Remarkable hanging nest of plant down and cobwebs with tubular entrance high on side, dangling from slim twig; 6–8 eggs; 1 brood; May–June.

FEEDING Eats small insects and reed seeds, in acrobatic tit-like manner.

BOTTLE NEST
The remarkable flask-shaped nest of the Penduline Tit has a short entrance tube high up on one side.

OCCURRENCE
In summer, widespread north to Baltic; in winter, in Mediterranean area, rare in UK. Breeds in and around wetlands with tall trees, especially willows and poplars, and in reeds or reedmace; in winter, mostly in reedbeds.

Seen in the UK
J F M A M J J A S O N D

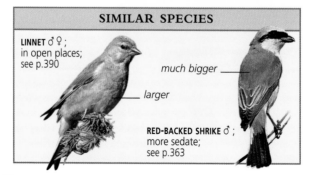

SIMILAR SPECIES

LINNET ♂♀; in open places; see p.390

larger

much bigger

RED-BACKED SHRIKE ♂; more sedate; see p.363

Length **10–11cm (4–4¼in)**	Wingspan **20cm (8in)**	Weight **8–10g (⁵⁄₁₆–³⁄₈oz)**
Social **Small flocks**	Lifespan **3–5 years**	Status **Secure†**

Families **Sittidae, Tichodromadidae, Certhiidae**

NUTHATCHES, WALLCREEPERS, AND TREECREEPERS

THESE ARE ALL BIRDS that find their food while creeping and climbing over hard surfaces: tree bark, walls, or rocks. There are two species pairs and one totally unique species.

NUTHATCHES

Nuthatches are agile, using the strength of their legs and toes to grip, and able to cling underneath branches or overhang, and as easily able to move head-down as right-way up. The Nuthatch is a woodland bird but also feeds on the ground; the Rock Nuthatch is a bird of rocks, walls, and ruins.

STRONG GRIP
Nuthatches can more or less cling to a branch at any angle, head-down or head-up.

WALLCREEPERS
Nothing else even suggests a Wallcreeper: it is a stunning bird of mountain cliffs and gorges, sometimes coming to quarries, bridges, and large buildings lower down in winter. It is elusive, hard to spot against grey rock, but occasionally gives breathtaking views at close range, which is always a memorable encounter. Wallcreepers creep in a rather crouched stance, bobbing as if mounted on springs, with frequent outward flicks of their wingtips.

TREECREEPERS
Treecreepers literally creep on trees: they can hang beneath a branch, but use the tail as a support, so never descend head-first. Identification is difficult, unless a bird is definitely outside the range of one or other, or it is singing. Treecreeper and Short-toed Treecreeper songs are usually distinctive, but the latter may sometimes sing confusingly like the former. Close examination, preferably of photographs, is necessary to identify a stray outside its normal range. Treecreepers join roving bands of tits in winter, when woods seem empty until, suddenly, trees are "full of birds" for a few minutes, before they move on.

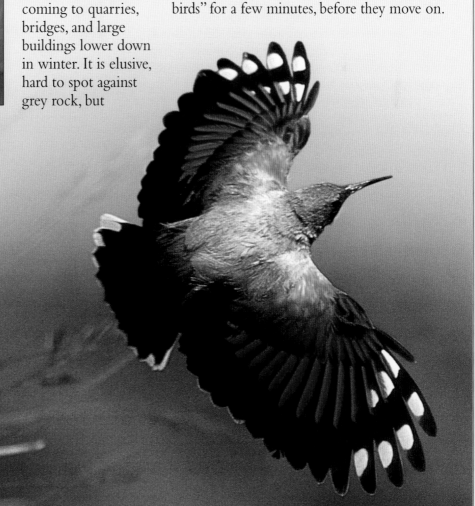

FLOATING FLIGHT
Wallcreepers in flight, despite their small size, are absolutely spectacular. At a distance the white spots are more evident than the deep red on the wings.

Order **Passeriformes**	Family **Sittidae**	Species *Sitta europaea*

Nuthatch 🔊 82

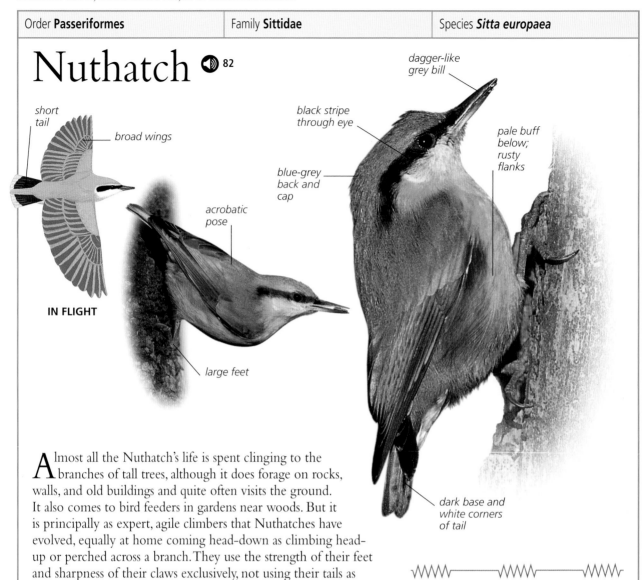

short tail

broad wings

IN FLIGHT

acrobatic pose

large feet

dagger-like grey bill

black stripe through eye

blue-grey back and cap

pale buff below; rusty flanks

dark base and white corners of tail

Almost all the Nuthatch's life is spent clinging to the branches of tall trees, although it does forage on rocks, walls, and old buildings and quite often visits the ground. It also comes to bird feeders in gardens near woods. But it is principally as expert, agile climbers that Nuthatches have evolved, equally at home coming head-down as climbing head-up or perched across a branch. They use the strength of their feet and sharpness of their claws exclusively, not using their tails as props as do woodpeckers and treecreepers.

VOICE Various loud, full, liquid whistles, *pew pew pew pew*, *chwee chwee* and fast ringing trills, loud *chwit*.

NESTING Uses old woodpecker hole or nest box, lined with bark and leaves, typically plastering mud around entrance; 6–9 eggs; 1 brood; April–July.

FEEDING Eats variety of seeds, berries, nuts, acorns, and beech-mast, often carried to be wedged in bark for easier manipulation; visits peanut baskets.

FLIGHT: bounding, slightly undulating; fast wingbeats.

OCCURRENCE
Breeds in most of Europe, except Iceland, N UK, N Scandinavia, and S Spain. Occupies mixed and deciduous woodland, parkland, and large gardens with big old trees all year round, rarely moving far.

Seen in the UK
J F M A M J J A S O N D

SIMILAR SPECIES

ROCK NUTHATCH
different habitat; see p.457

paler below

plain tail

GROUND FORAGER
Nuthatches frequently drop to the ground to seek fallen nuts and berries, hopping jerkily over the leaf litter.

Length **12.5cm (5in)**	Wingspan **16–18cm (6½–7in)**	Weight **12–18g (7/16–5/8oz)**
Social **Loose flocks**	Lifespan **2–3 years**	Status **Secure**

Order **Passeriformes**	Family **Tichodromadidae**	Species *Tichodroma muraria*

Wallcreeper

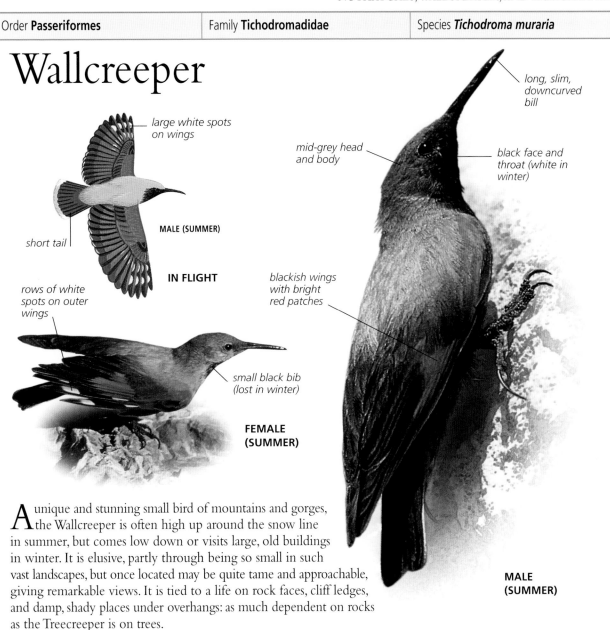

large white spots on wings

MALE (SUMMER)

short tail

IN FLIGHT

rows of white spots on outer wings

small black bib (lost in winter)

FEMALE (SUMMER)

long, slim, downcurved bill

mid-grey head and body

black face and throat (white in winter)

blackish wings with bright red patches

MALE (SUMMER)

A unique and stunning small bird of mountains and gorges, the Wallcreeper is often high up around the snow line in summer, but comes low down or visits large, old buildings in winter. It is elusive, partly through being so small in such vast landscapes, but once located may be quite tame and approachable, giving remarkable views. It is tied to a life on rock faces, cliff ledges, and damp, shady places under overhangs: as much dependent on rocks as the Treecreeper is on trees.

VOICE Long, rising and falling series of thin, whistled notes.
NESTING Untidy nest in hole in cliff or deep in crevice between tumbled rocks; 4 eggs; 1 brood; May–July.
FEEDING Searches rocks, especially wet spots and earthy ledges, and also buildings for insects and spiders, probing with its bill and fluttering constantly.

FLIGHT: hesitant, fluttery, but quite strong, undulating over long distances; remarkable bounding when feeding; moves butterfly-like over short distances.

EXCELLENT CAMOUFLAGE
The red of this juvenile Wallcreeper's wing is not obvious at long range: it often looks dark grey and is easily lost against a rocky background.

OCCURRENCE
Mostly rare and local; breeds in Pyrenees, Alps, and Balkans, typically up close to snow line. Little more widespread in S Europe in winter, coming to lower altitudes. On rocks, cliff faces, in gorges and quarries, but only rarely moving far from breeding range.

Seen in the UK
J F M A M J J A S O N D

Length **15–17cm (6–6½in)**	Wingspan **30–35cm (12–14in)**	Weight **25g (⅞oz)**
Social **Family groups**	Lifespan **3–5 years**	Status **Secure†**

Order **Passeriformes**	Family **Certhiidae**	Species *Certhia familiaris*

Treecreeper

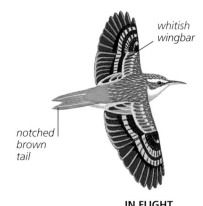

whitish wingbar

notched brown tail

IN FLIGHT

fine, curved bill

whitish stripe over eye

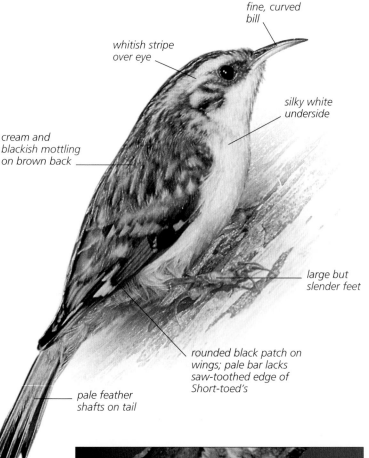

silky white underside

cream and blackish mottling on brown back

large but slender feet

rounded black patch on wings; pale bar lacks saw-toothed edge of Short-toed's

pale feather shafts on tail

FLIGHT: weak, low, undulating; typically from high in one tree to base of next.

Even more closely associated with the bark of trees than the Nuthatch, the Treecreeper can cling beneath a branch, hanging freely by its toes, but usually sits upright, propped up on its tail. It sometimes forages on the twigs of smaller bushes, more rarely on stone walls. Typically, Treecreepers work their way upwards on tree trunks and larger branches, often spiralling, before flying down to the next to begin the upward search for food once more. They are often on the edges of mixed tit flocks in autumn and winter.

VOICE Call thin, long, high *seee* and more vibrant *srreee*; song frequent, high, musical, like thin Willow Warbler's in pattern, falling trill with final flourish.

NESTING Untidy nest behind loose bark or ivy stem, sometimes in nest box; 5 or 6 eggs; 1 brood; April–June.

FEEDING Takes insects, spiders, and other tiny items from bark, probing with bill as it shuffles up or around trunks and branches; also forages on walls, and occasionally rocks.

REMARK Subspecies *C. f. familiaris* (Scandinavia) is whiter over eye and very white below.

STRONG GRIP
Treecreepers use their sharp claws and strong toes to grip tightly on rough bark, the tail adding stability and balance.

SIMILAR SPECIES

duller underside

SHORT-TOED TREECREEPER different call and song; see p.361

OCCURRENCE
Breeding bird and year-round resident in Great Britain and Ireland, local in France, N Spain and east across Europe. In mixed, deciduous, or coniferous woods, parks, along tall hedges, and sometimes in well-wooded gardens.

Seen in the UK
J F M A M J J A S O N D

Length **12.5cm (5in)**	Wingspan **18–21cm (7–8½in)**	Weight **8–12g ($^5/_{16}$–$^7/_{16}$oz)**
Social **Mixed flocks**	Lifespan **2–3 years**	Status **Secure**

| Order **Passeriformes** | Family **Certhidae** | Species **Certhia brachydactyla** |

Short-toed Treecreeper

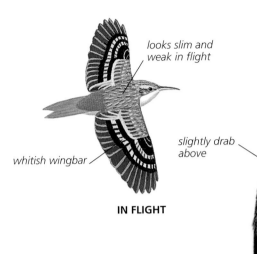

looks slim and weak in flight

whitish wingbar

IN FLIGHT

long, slender, slightly downcurved bill

slightly drab above

clean white throat

saw-tooth pattern across wings

plain tail

FLIGHT: quite direct but weak, undulating, with bursts of quick wingbeats.

Few species pairs are as difficult as the two treecreepers: the Short-toed is best told by its calls and song. Even held in the hand, the two can be near impossible to separate on plumage and measurements alone. The Short-toed has more obvious white tips to the wingtip feathers and a slightly different pattern across the closed wing. In general, the Short-toed is a touch duller, a little browner underneath, with a more contrasted white throat; sometimes it may look a little rounder, with its tail angled in more steeply to the bark, but such impressions are of little real value. It is equally dependent on trees, but does clamber on rocks at times.

VOICE Call quite strong, short, clear *tsoit*, sometimes longer *sreet*; song stereotyped, with discrete notes (not flowing like Treecreeper's), *stit-stit-steet, stit-it-steroi-tit*.

NESTING Cup of grass and feathers in crevice, like Treecreeper; 5 or 6 eggs; 1 brood; April–June.

FEEDING Like Treecreeper, creeps about branches and tree trunks, probing and picking (but not chipping away bark) for insects and eggs; sometimes forages on rocks.

BARK SPECIALIST
The Short-toed Treecreeper spends its whole life clambering on tree bark searching for food.

OCCURRENCE
Breeds locally in Spain, Italy, France, Low Countries, Italy, and Balkans. Typically in lowland, often deciduous woods, but also in pine forest in hills. Present all year, rare vagrant outside its breeding range.

| Seen in the UK |
| J F M A M J J A S O N D |

SIMILAR SPECIES

whiter below

TREECREEPER
different call and song; see p.360

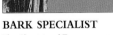

| Length **12.5cm (5in)** | Wingspan **18–21cm (7–8½in)** | Weight **8–12g ($^{5}/_{16}$–$^{7}/_{16}$oz)** |
| Social **Mixed flocks** | Lifespan **2–3 years** | Status **Secure** |

Family **Laniidae**

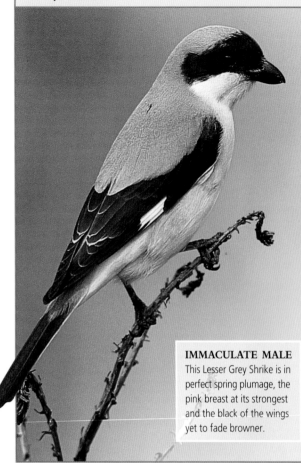

SHRIKES

THRUSH-LIKE IN SHAPE and general form, shrikes have stout, sharp, hooked bills and strong feet, and they are every bit as predatory as the small falcons. They drop to the ground onto prey, from a perch, or catch insects and birds in flight: a shrike will pursue and catch a bird almost as big as itself.

Shrikes are migratory, the Great Grey Shrike moving to western Europe in winter, others going to Africa. Most species are suited to warmer parts of southern and eastern Europe, where there are abundant large insects. Intensive farming in many areas has reduced their numbers and the Red-backed Shrike has only recently been lost as a breeding bird in parts of its original range.

Some species have obvious sexual differences in plumage, others are more or less the same. Identification is likely to pose problems only with migrant juveniles in autumn. Then precise details of bill, head, wing, and tail patterns are necessary to confirm more general impressions of size and shape.

IMMACULATE MALE
This Lesser Grey Shrike is in perfect spring plumage, the pink breast at its strongest and the black of the wings yet to fade browner.

Family **Oriolidae**

ORIOLES

SEVERAL SPECIES look vividly coloured in books; some may disppoint a little in real life. The male Golden Oriole, however, is always a wonderful sight if seen well, a vivid buttercup yellow and black. Strangely, it is remarkably elusive.

The song is loud and obvious, always an easy clue to the presence of an oriole, but seeing it is still difficult most of the time. Orioles live in dense foliage, typically in poplars or oak wood-land, and even their bright colours are hard to spot in the dappled light and shade of a wind-swept leafy canopy.

Male and female usually differ but old females become almost as bright as males. In winter, orioles migrate to Africa, where they come into contact with several other similar species. In Europe, nothing else is similar except for a poorly seen Green Woodpecker in flight, which recalls the female oriole, and no other bird is remotely so yellow and black as the adult male.

ELONGATED SHAPE
A Golden Oriole is rather thrush-like in form but longer-bodied and longer-winged, and with much shorter legs.

| Order **Passeriformes** | Family **Laniidae** | Species *Lanius collurio* |

Red-backed Shrike

black mask

pale powder-blue head

rufous-brown back

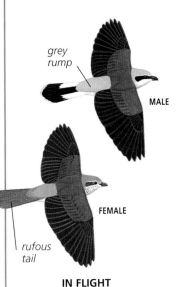

grey rump

MALE

rufous tail

FEMALE

IN FLIGHT

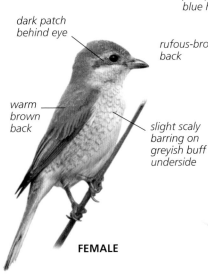

dark patch behind eye

warm brown back

slight scaly barring on greyish buff underside

FEMALE

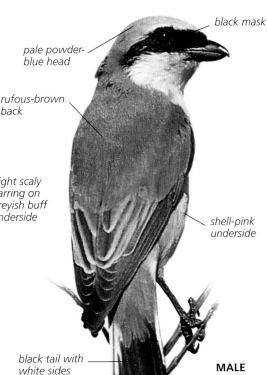

shell-pink underside

black tail with white sides

MALE

FLIGHT: jerky, bounding; bursts of wingbeats, tail sometimes waved.

Sadly diminished in much of its range, and gone from the UK as a breeding bird, the Red-backed Shrike is still moderately common in places where traditional farming leaves plenty of hedges, bushes, and rough grassland with an abundance of large insects. It perches prominently, looking for prey, which it catches in a sudden flurry on the ground. Large items are brought back up to a perch, sometimes to be impaled on a thorn for easy manipulation or for storage.

VOICE Harsh *hek*, harder *chek*; song low, rambling, some bright warbling and mimicry.

NESTING Untidy nest of grass, moss, feathers, and refuse in bush; 5 or 6 eggs; 1 brood; May–June.

FEEDING Watches from perch, and drops to ground to catch beetles and other large insects; catches some insects in flight; also feeds on small lizards and small rodents.

HIDDEN FEMALE
While males often perch on bush tops, the females, which are drabber, tend to be inconspicuous when breeding, perching low down on hedges or bushes.

OCCURRENCE
Breeds in mainland Europe, except in N Scandinavia and S Spain; now rare migrant in UK (where it was breeding species earlier). In farmland with hedges, thorn bushes, and bushy slopes, from April to October, when some migrants linger near coasts.

Seen in the UK

| J | F | M | A | M | J | J | A | S | O | N | D |

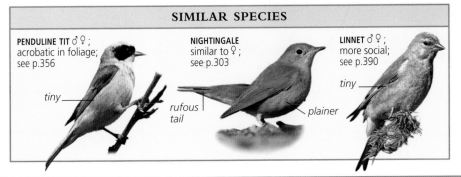

SIMILAR SPECIES

PENDULINE TIT ♂♀; acrobatic in foliage; see p.356

tiny

NIGHTINGALE similar to ♀; see p.303

rufous tail

plainer

LINNET ♂♀; more social; see p.390

tiny

| Length **16–18cm (6½–7in)** | Wingspan **24–27cm (9½–10½in)** | Weight **25–30g (⅞–1¹/₁₆oz)** |
| Social **Solitary** | Lifespan **3–5 years** | Status **Declining†** |

Order **Passeriformes**	Family **Laniidae**	Species *Lanius senator*

Woodchat Shrike

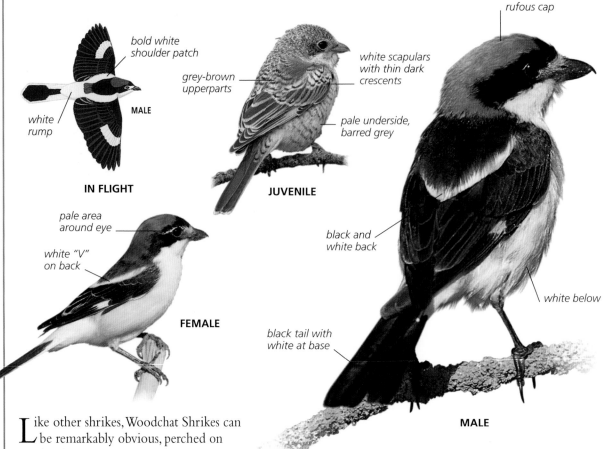

bold white
shoulder patch

MALE

white
rump

IN FLIGHT

grey-brown
upperparts

white scapulars
with thin dark
crescents

pale underside,
barred grey

JUVENILE

rufous cap

white scapulars
with thin dark
crescents

black and
white back

white below

pale area
around eye

white "V"
on back

FEMALE

black tail with
white at base

MALE

Like other shrikes, Woodchat Shrikes can be remarkably obvious, perched on overhead wires, trees, or bush tops, or frustratingly difficult to find as they skulk in thick cover. They are strikingly patterned and easy to identify. In parts of southern Europe, they are common and many can be seen, for example, on a long journey by road. They feed on insects and small birds, watching for these from a perch and chasing or diving on them from above.

VOICE Short, chattering, hard notes in alarm; song loud, quick, varied jumble of squeaks and warblers.

NESTING Untidy nest of grass and stems in low bush; 5 or 6 eggs; 1 brood; April–July.

FEEDING Takes big insects from ground or in air, after watching from open perch; also catches small birds, rodents, and lizards.

FLIGHT: strong, quick, low, undulating; swoops up to perch.

BOLD PERCH
A feeding Woodchat Shrike keeps a keen eye out for large insects and other potential prey. It may chase and capture smaller birds.

OCCURRENCE
Breeding bird in Spain, Italy, S France, east to Balkans, and locally in C Europe. Seen from April to October, in bushy areas, open countryside, orchards, overgrown old gardens, and other generally bushy places.

Seen in the UK
J F M A M J J A S O N D

SIMILAR SPECIES

much larger

RED-BACKED SHRIKE
juvenile, similar to juvenile; see p.363
• warmer coloration
• browner scapulars

MAGPIE
see p.369

Length **17–19cm (6½–7½in)**	Wingspan **25–30cm (10–12in)**	Weight **25–35g (⅞–1¼oz)**
Social **Solitary**	Lifespan **3–5 years**	Status **Vulnerable**

Order **Passeriformes**	Family **Laniidae**	Species *Lanius excubitor*

Great Grey Shrike

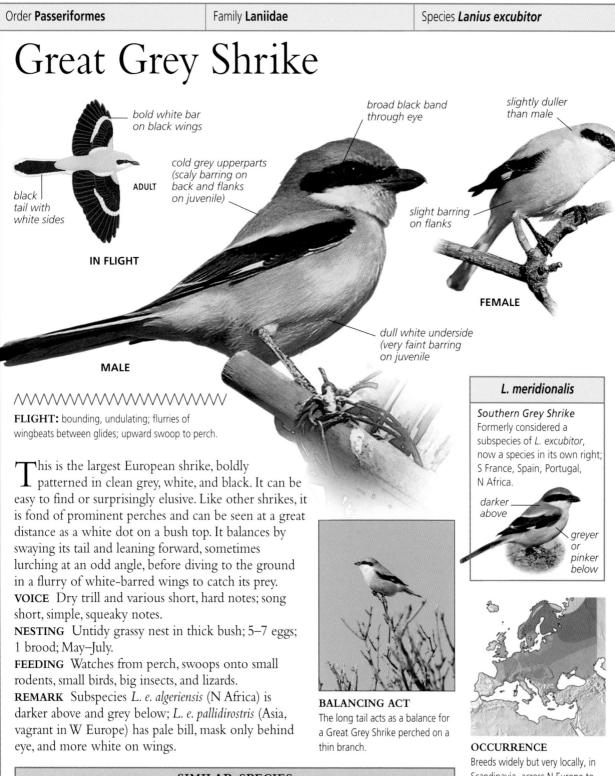

bold white bar
on black wings

black
tail with
white sides

ADULT

IN FLIGHT

broad black band
through eye

cold grey upperparts
(scaly barring on
back and flanks
on juvenile)

slight barring
on flanks

slightly duller
than male

FEMALE

dull white underside
(very faint barring
on juvenile)

MALE

FLIGHT: bounding, undulating; flurries of
wingbeats between glides; upward swoop to perch.

This is the largest European shrike, boldly
patterned in clean grey, white, and black. It can be
easy to find or surprisingly elusive. Like other shrikes, it
is fond of prominent perches and can be seen at a great
distance as a white dot on a bush top. It balances by
swaying its tail and leaning forward, sometimes
lurching at an odd angle, before diving to the ground
in a flurry of white-barred wings to catch its prey.
VOICE Dry trill and various short, hard notes; song
short, simple, squeaky notes.
NESTING Untidy grassy nest in thick bush; 5–7 eggs;
1 brood; May–July.
FEEDING Watches from perch, swoops onto small
rodents, small birds, big insects, and lizards.
REMARK Subspecies *L. e. algeriensis* (N Africa) is
darker above and grey below; *L. e. pallidirostris* (Asia,
vagrant in W Europe) has pale bill, mask only behind
eye, and more white on wings.

BALANCING ACT
The long tail acts as a balance for
a Great Grey Shrike perched on a
thin branch.

L. meridionalis

Southern Grey Shrike
Formerly considered a
subspecies of *L. excubitor*,
now a species in its own right;
S France, Spain, Portugal,
N Africa.

darker
above

greyer
or
pinker
below

OCCURRENCE
Breeds widely but very locally, in
Scandinavia, across N Europe to
France, Spain, and Portugal;
N European birds winter west to
UK, south to N Italy. Breeds in
birch woods, wooded bogs; in dry,
hotter, scrubby areas in S Europe;
in winter, on bushy, heathy, or
boggy ground.

Seen in the UK
J F M A M J J A S O N D

SIMILAR SPECIES

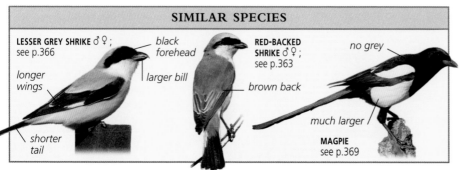

LESSER GREY SHRIKE ♂♀;
see p.366

longer
wings

shorter
tail

black
forehead

larger bill

**RED-BACKED
SHRIKE** ♂♀;
see p.363

brown back

no grey

much larger

MAGPIE
see p.369

Length **22–26cm (9–10in)**	Wingspan **30cm (12in)**	Weight **30–40g (1¹/₁₆–1⁷/₁₆oz)**
Social **Solitary**	Lifespan **3–5 years**	Status **Declining**

Order **Passeriformes**	Family **Laniidae**	Species *Lanius minor*

Lesser Grey Shrike

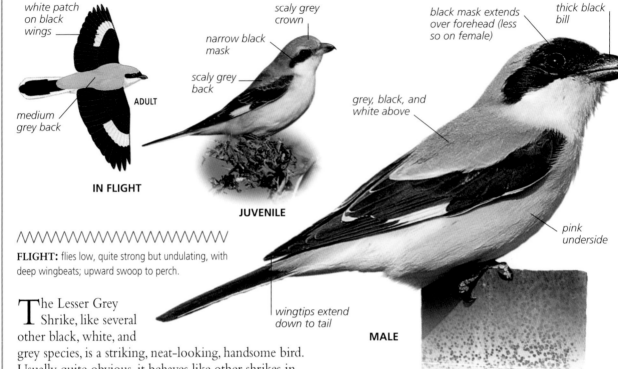

white patch on black wings

medium grey back

ADULT

IN FLIGHT

scaly grey crown

narrow black mask

scaly grey back

JUVENILE

black mask extends over forehead (less so on female)

thick black bill

grey, black, and white above

pink underside

wingtips extend down to tail

MALE

/\/\/\/\/\/\/\/\/\/\/\/\/\/\/\/\/\/\/\

FLIGHT: flies low, quite strong but undulating, with deep wingbeats; upward swoop to perch.

The Lesser Grey Shrike, like several other black, white, and grey species, is a striking, neat-looking, handsome bird. Usually quite obvious, it behaves like other shrikes in perching on open perches much of the time (but, like them, can be frustratingly elusive on occasions). It frequently flies out to chase prey, or drops to the ground with a flurry of white-barred wings. It is the southeastern counterpart of the Great Grey Shrike, preferring warm, dry summer climates and migrating to Africa in winter. In parts of eastern Europe, migrants follow long lines of trees beside roads in areas that are otherwise open, treeless croplands. Shrikes have strong claws to catch and hold prey and use their hooked bills to kill and tear up small birds and voles. Food may be impaled on thorns to make it easier to deal with.

VOICE Short, hard *tchek tchek*; brief, bright, screaming note serves as song often given in hovering flight.

NESTING Untidy structure of grass and twigs high in bush or tree; 5–7 eggs; 1 brood; May–June.

FEEDING Watches from high perch such as overhead wire and drops onto lizards, beetles, and small birds.

SPRING MALE
The male Lesser Grey Shrike looks handsome with his bold mask and pink underside.

SIMILAR SPECIES

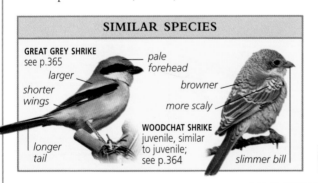

GREAT GREY SHRIKE
see p.365
larger
shorter wings
longer tail

pale forehead

browner

more scaly

WOODCHAT SHRIKE
juvenile, similar to juvenile; see p.364

slimmer bill

OCCURRENCE
Breeds in extreme S France, Italy, and more widely in Balkans and E Europe. Seen from March to September, chiefly in open places with scattered trees, bushes, orchards, and avenues, and in woodland edges.

Seen in the UK
J F M A M J J A S O N D

Length **19–21cm (7½–8½in)**	Wingspan **30cm (12in)**	Weight **30g (1¹⁄₁₆oz)**
Social **Solitary**	Lifespan **3–5 years**	Status **Declining†**

Order **Passeriformes**	Family **Oriolidae**	Species *Oriolus oriolus*

Golden Oriole 🔊 83

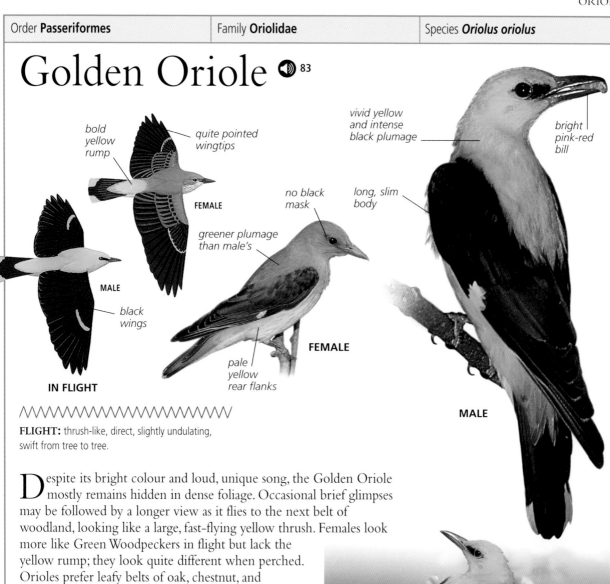

bold yellow rump

quite pointed wingtips

FEMALE

vivid yellow and intense black plumage

bright pink-red bill

no black mask

long, slim body

greener plumage than male's

MALE

black wings

FEMALE

pale yellow rear flanks

IN FLIGHT

MALE

FLIGHT: thrush-like, direct, slightly undulating, swift from tree to tree.

Despite its bright colour and loud, unique song, the Golden Oriole mostly remains hidden in dense foliage. Occasional brief glimpses may be followed by a longer view as it flies to the next belt of woodland, looking like a large, fast-flying yellow thrush. Females look more like Green Woodpeckers in flight but lack the yellow rump; they look quite different when perched. Orioles prefer leafy belts of oak, chestnut, and especially poplars.

VOICE Hoarse, strained, Jay-like or cat-like *meeaik*, fast *gigigi*; song far-carrying, loud, short phrase, very full-throated and fluty with yodelling quality, such as *wee-dl-eyo, wee-weo-we-weedl*, or *weeeoo*.

NESTING Shallow nest of grass and strips of bark, slung beneath horizontal fork in branch, high in tree; 3 or 4 eggs; 1 brood; May–June.

FEEDING Takes caterpillars and other invertebrates from foliage within dense tree canopy; also feeds on berries in late summer and autumn.

STUNNING COLOURS
One of Europe's most striking birds, good views of an adult male reveal a bird of brilliant yellow and intense black.

SIMILAR SPECIES

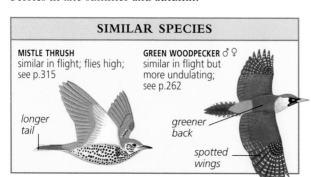

MISTLE THRUSH
similar in flight; flies high; see p.315

longer tail

GREEN WOODPECKER ♂♀
similar in flight but more undulating; see p.262

greener back

spotted wings

OCCURRENCE
Breeds in extreme E England, more commonly in Europe north to S Finland. From April to September, in open or dense woodland, poplar plantations, riverside forest, wooded parks, and similar places with airy, leafy trees.

Seen in the UK											
J	F	M	**A**	**M**	**J**	**J**	**A**	**S**	O	N	D

Length **22–25cm (9–10in)**	Wingspan **35cm (14in)**	Weight **55g (2oz)**
Social **Solitary**	Lifespan **Up to 5 years**	Status **Secure**

Family **Corvidae**

CROWS

THERE IS CONSIDERABLE VARIATION in the crow family within Europe. The Jay is colourful and strongly-patterned. Like most crows, it is heavily persecuted and very shy, but where unmolested it becomes much bolder. The Siberian Jay has quite different colours: it is a bird of far northern forests.

Magpies are striking, long-tailed, pied birds. They are generally disliked because of their liking for small birds' eggs and chicks. They are, nevertheless, fascinating and handsome.

The Alpine Chough is a high-altitude species, coming lower in winter, and often mixing with the Chough, itself a social bird where common. Choughs are also found on coastal cliffs in north-west Europe.

The world's largest crow is the Raven. The all-black Carrion Crow is widely spread but replaced in parts of Europe by the grey-and-black Hooded Crow.

MAGPIE
A highly social bird, the Magpie has increased in suburban areas, where ornamental shrubberies and parks provide ideal habitat. It is immediately distinctive.

RAUCOUS CALLS
The loud, rough, cawing calls of Rooks fit in well with a rural setting, above the treetops of a country churchyard or park.

Family **Sturnidae**

STARLINGS

TWO SPECIES ARE MOSTLY dark, shiny, quarrelsome birds; the third is paler when juvenile and pink and black when adult.

All the starlings are rather squat, sharp-billed, short-tailed birds that walk and run in a quick, shuffling fashion and fly quickly, often in dense flocks. Starlings also gather to roost in woods, reedbeds, and on structures such as piers and bridges, in gigantic flocks, although numbers have recently declined dramatically in many areas.

HIGHLY SOCIAL
Starlings are much more ready to rub shoulders than most birds.

Order **Passeriformes**	Family **Corvidae**	Species *Pica pica*

Magpie 84

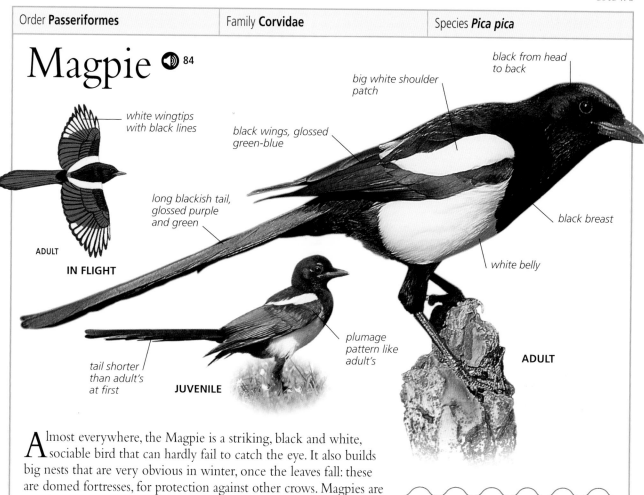

white wingtips with black lines

black wings, glossed green-blue

big white shoulder patch

black from head to back

black breast

white belly

long blackish tail, glossed purple and green

ADULT

IN FLIGHT

tail shorter than adult's at first

JUVENILE

plumage pattern like adult's

ADULT

Almost everywhere, the Magpie is a striking, black and white, sociable bird that can hardly fail to catch the eye. It also builds big nests that are very obvious in winter, once the leaves fall: these are domed fortresses, for protection against other crows. Magpies are usually seen in pairs but often form small groups and occasionally fill whole trees with flocks of 20–40 at a time, when gathering to roost. There is no other similar-looking bird in Europe.

VOICE Hard, chattering, mechanical rattle, *tcha-tcha-tcha-tcha-tcha* or *chak-ak-ak-ak-ak*; some squeaky, musical notes.

NESTING Big, domed nest of sticks with solid mud inner core, lined with roots and scraps; 5–8 eggs; 1 brood; April–June.

FEEDING Mostly takes insects, grain, and scraps in a wide range of habitats, from fields to car parks and roadsides; eats eggs and chicks in summer.

FLIGHT: straight, mostly direct, laboured; fluttering or rowing action, sometimes swooping down or swerving.

EYE-CATCHING
Long tails and pied plumage make Magpies handsome birds.

OCCURRENCE
Breeding bird in all of Europe except for Iceland, and seen all year. In farmland with hedges, at edges of woodland, in towns and parks; increasing recently in suburbs, often visiting gardens with hedges and shrubs.

Seen in the UK
J F M A M J J A S O N D

SWOOPING FLIGHT
Magpies look laboured in long-distance flight, but are agile enough in tight spaces and quick to dive from a high perch to snatch up a scrap of food.

Length **44–46cm (17½–18in)**	Wingspan **52–60cm (20½–23½in)**	Weight **200–250g (7–9oz)**
Social **Small flocks**	Lifespan **10–15 years**	Status **Secure**

| Order **Passeriformes** | Family **Corvidae** | Species *Garrulus glandarius* |

Jay 🔊 85

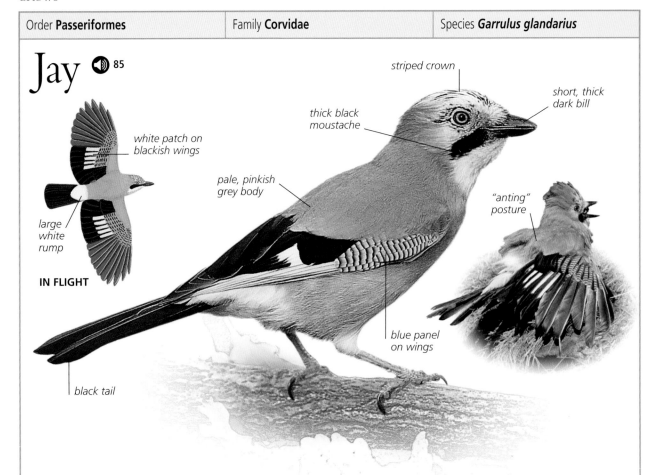

striped crown

short, thick dark bill

thick black moustache

white patch on blackish wings

pale, pinkish grey body

"anting" posture

large white rump

IN FLIGHT

blue panel on wings

black tail

A woodland bird that also ventures into parks and large gardens, the Jay is usually shy and not easy to watch for long periods: a harsh call may be the only clue to its presence. It may become much tamer, however, when it is left undisturbed in parks, and can be watched feeding on the ground under trees, or perhaps collecting acorns, which it does with great industry every autumn. It can carry several in a pouch under the throat, plus one in the bill, and buries hundreds each year for consumption in the winter and spring. It has an exaggerated, bouncy action while hopping on the ground. Jays sometimes deliberately place ants on their feathers, a behaviour called anting. The purpose of this is unclear but it probably helps to rid them of parasites.
VOICE Nasal, mewing pee-oo, short barking call; main call loud, tearing-cloth sound, harsh skairk!
NESTING Bulky nest of sticks, low down in thick bush; 4 or 5 eggs; 1 brood; April–June.
FEEDING Eats anything from caterpillars to small rodents: chiefly insects in summer with some eggs and small chicks and acorns (collected and stored) in winter.

FLIGHT: slow, laboured, rowing action of broad wings; often quite high over woodland in autumn when collecting acorns.

ACORN COLLECTOR
The Jay collects acorns every autumn, buries them, and usually digs them out to eat late in the winter or spring, when other food is scarce.

SIMILAR SPECIES

HOOPOE see p.259

long, curved bill

barred wings

OCCURRENCE
Breeds in almost all of Europe, except in N Scotland, Iceland, and N Scandinavia. In parks with extensive lawns and various woodland, especially with oak; also visits large gardens. N European birds move southwest in winter.

Seen in the UK
J F M A M J J A S O N D

| Length **34–35cm (13½–14in)** | Wingspan **52–58cm (20½–23in)** | Weight **140–190g (5–7oz)** |
| Social **Small flocks** | Lifespan **Up to 5 years** | Status **Secure†** |

Order **Passeriformes**	Family **Corvidae**	Species *Perisoreus infaustus*

Siberian Jay

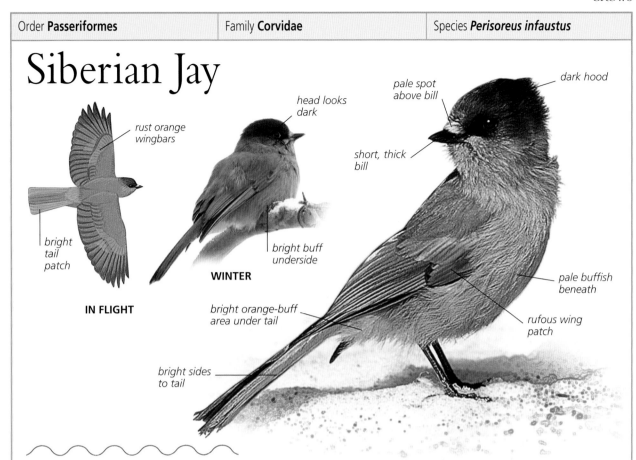

rust orange wingbars

head looks dark

pale spot above bill

dark hood

short, thick bill

bright tail patch

bright buff underside

pale buffish beneath

WINTER

rufous wing patch

IN FLIGHT

bright orange-buff area under tail

bright sides to tail

ADULT

FLIGHT: smooth, fast, silent, acrobatic in tight spaces.

A small jay, with a marked resemblance to the common Jay, especially in the expression of its face and bill, the Siberian Jay is a bird of the far north, often seen around camps and near villages in forest areas. It is usually bold and tame in the presence of people and eager to feed on scraps. It is, nevertheless, a rather elusive bird in many parts of its range until a family party appears nearby and seems to inspect human intruders, with quiet, soft, clucking calls. Only when an adult feeds its young can the two be separated easily.

VOICE Mostly silent, but occasional weak mewing or feeble screaming calls, especially from small groups.

NESTING Nest a loose platform of twigs and lichens close to trunk of conifer; 3–4 eggs; 1 brood; May–July.

FEEDING Eats almost anything of suitable size, from insects and small mammals to birds' eggs, seeds, berries, and scraps from human camps. It hides food in crevices in bark and under piles of pine needles for winter use.

CAMP FOLLOWER
Often tame or oblivious of human presence, the Siberian Jay frequently forages around woodland camp sites in the summer, taking whatever edible scraps it can find.

SIMILAR SPECIES

JAY
see p.370

paler, pinker body

white rump

OCCURRENCE
N Scandinavia; a resident in deep pine and spruce forest, especially older trees with an abundance of lichen and some undergrowth. Almost unknown outside its breeding range.

Seen in the UK
J F M A M J J A S O N D

Length **30cm (12in)**	Wingspan **40–45cm (16–18in)**	Weight **80–100g (2⅞–3⅝oz)**
Social **Small flocks**	Lifespan **Up to 10 years**	Status **Secure**

Order **Passeriformes**	Family **Corvidae**	Species ***Nucifraga caryocatactes***

Nutcracker

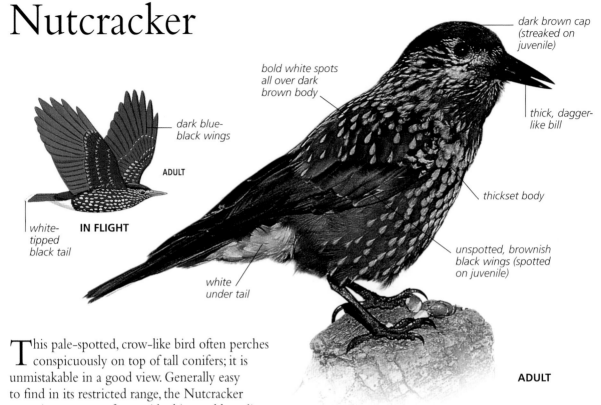

dark brown cap (streaked on juvenile)

bold white spots all over dark brown body

thick, dagger-like bill

thickset body

unspotted, brownish black wings (spotted on juvenile)

dark blue-black wings

ADULT

IN FLIGHT

white-tipped black tail

white under tail

ADULT

This pale-spotted, crow-like bird often perches conspicuously on top of tall conifers; it is unmistakable in a good view. Generally easy to find in its restricted range, the Nutcracker sometimes appears far outside this usual breeding distribution. It is subject to occasional population booms which, if they combine with a local food shortage, trigger large-scale movements, or irruptions, as birds are forced to fly far and wide in an effort to survive. Many do not survive these long journeys and the population quickly subsides. These invaders are nearly all of the slender-billed eastern race from Russia, although a few northern thick-billed birds are involved. These birds, far from their usual home, are often surprisingly tame.

VOICE Occasional long, drawn out, hard rattle in spring and summer; otherwise silent.

NESTING Nest of twigs lined with grass and moss, near trunk of tree, usually spruce; 3 or 4 eggs; 1 brood; May–July.

FEEDING Eats some large insects but mainly seeds of hazel, pine, and spruce, constantly collected and stored in summer and re-found with great accuracy (even under snow) in winter.

FLIGHT: rather Jay-like on broad wings but short-tailed, strong, direct, with upward swoop to treetop perch; drops steeply from perch.

UNIQUE BIRD
The Nutcracker is unique-looking, but novice birdwatchers may at times mistake Starlings and young Mistle Thrushes for the rarer, larger bird.

SIMILAR SPECIES	SUBSPECIES	OCCURRENCE

STARLING winter; see p.380

much smaller

N. c. macrothyncus
(NE Europe, Asia); more white on tail; slimmer bill

OCCURRENCE
Breeds in S Scandinavia, east from Baltic and in mountain areas of C and E Europe. In forests with spruce, hazel, and pine. Resident except when seed crops fail: birds then move south and west to find food, rarely in mass emigrations.

Seen in the UK
J F M A M J J A S O N D

Length **32–35cm (12½–14in)**	Wingspan **49–53cm (19½–21in)**	Weight **120–170g (4–6oz)**
Social **Small flocks**	Lifespan **Up to 5 years**	Status **Secure†**

Order **Passeriformes**	Family **Corvidae**	Species *Pyrrhocorax pyrrhocorax*

Chough

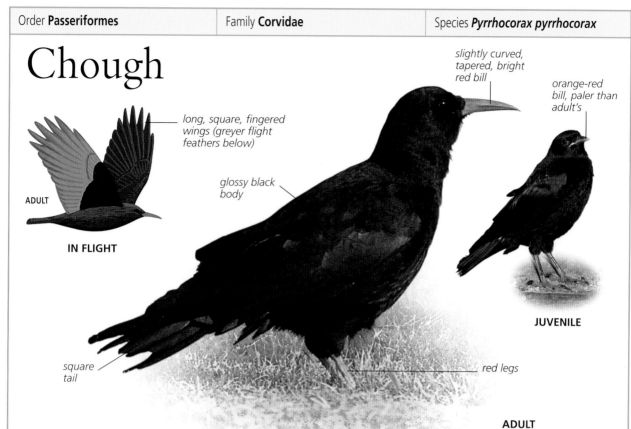

long, square, fingered wings (greyer flight feathers below)

ADULT

IN FLIGHT

slightly curved, tapered, bright red bill

orange-red bill, paler than adult's

glossy black body

JUVENILE

square tail

red legs

ADULT

Superficially like a Jackdaw (see p.375), the Chough is blacker, glossier, and altogether more showy. It is also more acrobatic in the air. It is usually found in small groups; where Choughs are common, much bigger flocks form, often mixed with Alpine Choughs. These big flocks may roam widely over mountain pastures or through green valleys below when peaks are in snow. In northwest Europe, Choughs are more coastal and always scarcer than in the mountains.

VOICE Loud calls distinctive, with explosive, ringing, piercing quality, *pee-yaa* or *chia*, some shorter *chuk* and *kwarr* sounds.

NESTING Nest of sticks lined with wool and hair, in sea cave and cavity in cliff or old ruin; 3–5 eggs; 1 brood; May–July.

FEEDING Eats ants from old pastures, insects dug up from beneath soil, and lichen on rocks, prised up with bill.

FLIGHT: exuberant, bouncy, aerobatic; soars well and often; deeply undulating at times; dives into caves or to cliff ledge with wings angled back.

AGILE BIRD
The aerobatic Chough makes long, steep, rapid descents and fast, upward swoops, in pairs or small flocks in concert.

OCCURRENCE
Breeds very locally on coasts of Ireland, W Britain, N and W France, and uplands of Spain, Portugal, S France, Italy, and Balkans. Frequents gorges, crags, high altitude pastures and coastal cliffs, quarries, and grassland; on beaches in winter.

Seen in the UK
J F M A M J J A S O N D

SIMILAR SPECIES

ROOK
see p.376

thick, black bill

larger

whitish face

larger

CARRION CROW
see p.377

thick, dark bill

ALPINE CHOUGH
rounder wings;
see p.374

yellow bill

rounder tail

Length **37–41cm (14½–16in)**	Wingspan **68–80cm (27–32in)**	Weight **280–360g (10–13oz)**
Social **Flocks**	Lifespan **5–10 years**	Status **Vulnerable**

| Order **Passeriformes** | Family **Corvidae** | Species **Pyrrhocorax graculus** |

Alpine Chough

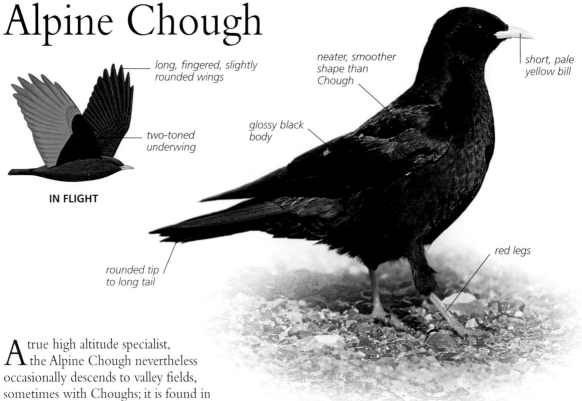

long, fingered, slightly rounded wings

two-toned underwing

IN FLIGHT

neater, smoother shape than Chough

glossy black body

short, pale yellow bill

rounded tip to long tail

red legs

A true high altitude specialist, the Alpine Chough nevertheless occasionally descends to valley fields, sometimes with Choughs; it is found in some rugged coastal areas as well, especially in winter. Its calls while it is circling about mountain peaks are distinctive. The Alpine Chough's wings are less rectangular and less straight-edged than the Chough's: the two choughs can be distinguished by their shape at distances which make fine details, such as bill colour, impossible to see.

VOICE Strange, rippling or sizzling *zirrrr* or hissy *chirrish*, penetrating *zeee-up*.

NESTING Bulky nest of stems in cliff cavity; 3–5 eggs; 1 brood; May–July.

FEEDING Forages on grassland; eats insects, other invertebrates, berries, seeds, and scraps from around ski lifts.

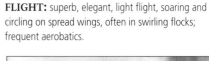

FLIGHT: superb, elegant, light flight, soaring and circling on spread wings, often in swirling flocks; frequent aerobatics.

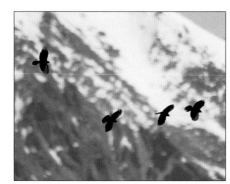

CIRCLING FLOCKS
This bird is often seen in swirling flocks, circling and crossing against a backdrop of mountain peaks.

FORAGING
The Alpine Chough typically forages on alpine grassland, often in large, active flocks.

SIMILAR SPECIES

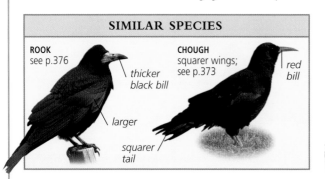

ROOK
see p.376

thicker black bill

larger

CHOUGH
squarer wings;
see p.373

red bill

squarer tail

OCCURRENCE
Breeding bird and resident all year in Pyrenees, Alps, Italy, and Balkans. From coasts in winter to highest peaks, on cliffs and alpine pasture. Often found around ski resorts and lifts.

| Seen in the UK |
| J F M A M J J A S O N D |

| Length **36–39cm (14–15½ in)** | Wingspan **65–74cm (26–29in)** | Weight **250–350g (9–13oz)** |
| Social **Flocks** | Lifespan **5–10 years** | Status **Secure†** |

Order **Passeriformes**	Family **Corvidae**	Species ***Corvus monedula***

Jackdaw 🔊 86

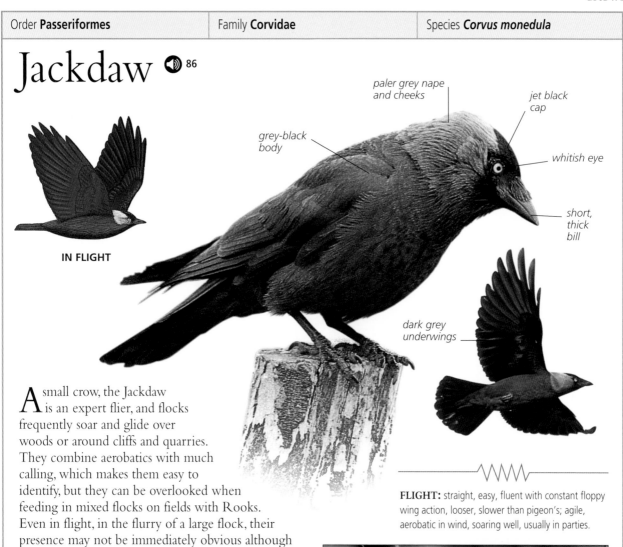

paler grey nape and cheeks

jet black cap

grey-black body

whitish eye

short, thick bill

IN FLIGHT

dark grey underwings

A small crow, the Jackdaw is an expert flier, and flocks frequently soar and glide over woods or around cliffs and quarries. They combine aerobatics with much calling, which makes them easy to identify, but they can be overlooked when feeding in mixed flocks on fields with Rooks. Even in flight, in the flurry of a large flock, their presence may not be immediately obvious although the size difference is marked. Jackdaws are often quite tame and frequently perch on buildings, large and small. Small parties often fly off, high and straight, with sudden bursts of speed.

VOICE Noisy; many calls based on short, sharp, yapping sound, *kyak* or *tjak!*, with slightly squeaky, bright quality, some longer calls like *chee-ar*.

NESTING Pile of sticks lined with animal dung, mud, roots, moss, and hair, in hole in tree or building, or old chimney; 4–6 eggs; 1 brood; April–July.

FEEDING Forages on ground, taking earthworms, seeds, and scraps; also takes caterpillars from foliage, and berries.

FLIGHT: straight, easy, fluent with constant floppy wing action, looser, slower than pigeon's; agile, aerobatic in wind, soaring well, usually in parties.

WOODLAND CROW
Jackdaws like cliffs and old buildings but are equally at home in treetops in mature woodland.

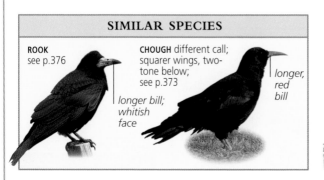

SIMILAR SPECIES

ROOK see p.376

CHOUGH different call; squarer wings, two-tone below; see p.373

longer bill; whitish face

longer, red bill

OCCURRENCE
Breeds in most of Europe except Iceland and N Scandinavia. In NE Europe only in summer, but resident elsewhere. In towns, parks, woods, farmland with scattered woodland, and gardens around old houses with open chimneys.

Seen in the UK
J F M A M J J A S O N D

Length **33–34cm (13–13½in)**	Wingspan **67–74cm (26–29in)**	Weight **220–270g (8–10oz)**
Social **Flocks**	Lifespan **5–10 years**	Status **Secure†**

Order **Passeriformes**	Family **Corvidae**	Species *Corvus frugilegus*

Rook 🔊 87

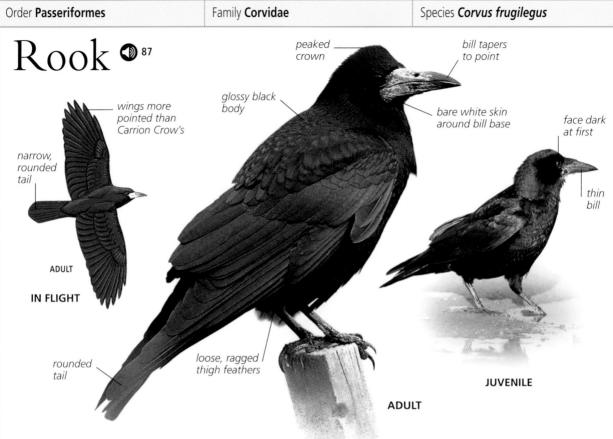

wings more pointed than Carrion Crow's

narrow, rounded tail

ADULT

IN FLIGHT

peaked crown

glossy black body

bill tapers to point

bare white skin around bill base

face dark at first

thin bill

rounded tail

loose, ragged thigh feathers

ADULT

JUVENILE

Where common, the Rook is one of the familiar birds of farmland and village, part of the traditional rural scene. It is a big crow, and a very social one, often mixed with Jackdaws, Stock Doves (see p.235) and Black-headed Gulls (see p.208). It nests in colonies in treetops, its big, stick nests always easy to see except at the height of summer when foliage conceals them. Occasionally, a pair or two will nest in more isolated situations, inviting confusion with Carrion Crows; the two species can sometimes be quite difficult to tell apart.

VOICE Loud, raucous, relaxed cawing, *caaar, grah-gra-gra*, variety of higher, strangled or metallic notes especially around colony.

NESTING Big nest of sticks in tree, lined with grass, moss, and leaves; 3–6 eggs; 1 brood; March–June.

FEEDING Eats worms, beetle larvae, seeds, grain, and roots from ground, especially ploughed fields or stubble, usually in flocks; also forages along roadsides for insects and large road casualties.

FLIGHT: direct, steady, evenly flapping; aerobatic around colony, twisting and diving; often soars.

AT COLONY
Typically, scores of Rook nests may be seen close together near tops of trees in a visually obvious colony.

OCCURRENCE
Absent from Iceland, Scandinavia, and Mediterranean area, but resident across W and C Europe and summer visitor to NE Europe. Typically in farmland with scattered trees, parks, large gardens, and villages with spinneys of tall trees.

Seen in the UK
J F M A M J J A S O N D

SIMILAR SPECIES

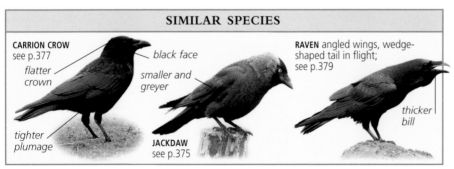

CARRION CROW see p.377

flatter crown

black face

tighter plumage

JACKDAW see p.375

smaller and greyer

RAVEN angled wings, wedge-shaped tail in flight; see p.379

thicker bill

Length **44–46cm (17½–18in)**	Wingspan **81–99cm (32–39in)**	Weight **460–520g (17–19oz)**
Social **Flocks**	Lifespan **5–10 years**	Status **Secure**

| Order **Passeriformes** | Family **Corvidae** | Species **Corvus corone** |

Carrion Crow 88

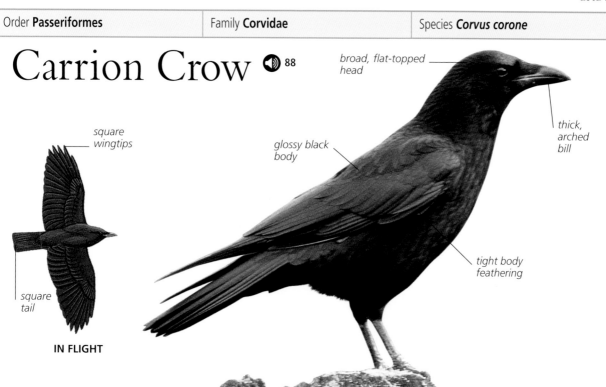

broad, flat-topped head

square wingtips

glossy black body

thick, arched bill

tight body feathering

square tail

IN FLIGHT

The all-black Carrion Crow is easily confused with the larger Raven and especially the Rook, which may be almost inseparable at long range. Carrion Crows tend to be more solitary than Rooks, but will often roost in scores, even hundreds, together and occasionally feed in flocks. More usefully, crows nest solitarily while Rooks breed in colonies or, at least, small clusters of nests. Carrion Crows are often wary in open countryside but can become bold in gardens and town parks if not persecuted.

VOICE Loud, harsh, grating *caw, krra krra krra*, metallic *konk, korr*, and variants.

NESTING Big stick nest, shallower than Rook's, in tree or bush; 4 or 6 eggs; 1 brood; March–July.

FEEDING On ground, takes all kinds of invertebrates, eggs, grain, and various scraps; often in pairs, sometimes big flocks on fields spread with manure.

FLIGHT: direct, steady wingbeats with few glides; soars occasionally.

JAUNTY AIR
A bold, upright stance and confident, long-striding walk are characteristic of the Carrion Crow.

OCCURRENCE
Breeds in Great Britain and east to Denmark and C Europe; Hooded breeds in Ireland, Scotland, Isle of Man, and N and E Europe; winter visitor to North Sea coasts. In all kinds of open areas from upland moors to farmland and suburbs.

Seen in the UK

| J | F | M | A | M | J | J | A | S | O | N | D |

SIMILAR SPECIES

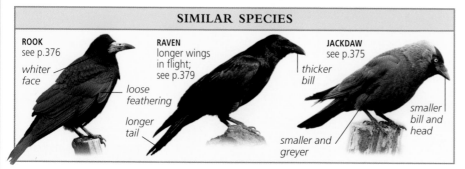

ROOK
see p.376

whiter face

loose feathering

longer tail

RAVEN
longer wings in flight;
see p.379

smaller and greyer

JACKDAW
see p.375

thicker bill

smaller bill and head

| Length **44–51cm (17½–20in)** | Wingspan **93–104cm (37–41in)** | Weight **540–600g (19–21oz)** |
| Social **Occasional flocks** | Lifespan **5–10 years** | Status **Secure** |

Order **Passeriformes**	Family **Corvidae**	Species *Corvus cornix*

Hooded Crow

heavy black bill

black hood

flattish head similar to Carrion Crow

IN FLIGHT

bold grey and black pattern

pale grey body

black tail and wings

ADULT AT NEST

Hooded Crows are familiar birds of open landscapes and also suburban areas, such as refuse tips, in much of Europe, replacing the Carrion Crow with just a very narrow line of hybridization where they meet in places such as northern Scotland. They have recently been treated as separate species. Hooded Crows have much the same seemingly intelligent character as Carrion Crows, being wild and shy where (as is often the case) they are persecuted, but bold, opportunistic, and approachable around towns and villages.

VOICE Loud, harsh, grating *caw, krra krra krra*, metallic *konk, korr*, and variants.

NESTING Big stick nest, shallower than Rook's, in tree or bush; 4 or 6 eggs; 1 brood; March–July.

FEEDING On ground, takes all kinds of invertebrates, eggs, grain, and various scraps; often in pairs, sometimes big flocks on fields spread with manure.

FLIGHT: direct, easy, with regular wingbeats, few glides.

OPPORTUNISTIC FEEDER
Hooded Crows eat almost anything edible, including rabbits and birds killed by road traffic, refuse from tips, and many large insects.

SIMILAR SPECIES

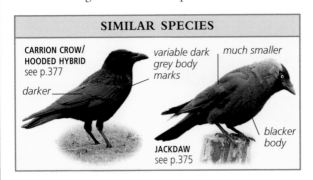

CARRION CROW/ HOODED HYBRID see p.377

darker

variable dark grey body marks

much smaller

JACKDAW see p.375

blacker body

OCCURRENCE
Breeds in open countryside, E Europe from Italy and Scandinavia eastwards, Scotland, Ireland, Isle of Man; more widespread but local in winter in NW Europe.

Seen in the UK
J F M A M J J A S O N D

Length **44–51cm (18–20in)**	Wingspan **93–104cm (37–41in)**	Weight **540–600g (19–21oz)**
Social **Small flocks**	Lifespan **5–10 years**	Status **Secure**

Order **Passeriformes**	Family **Corvidae**	Species ***Corvus corax***

Raven 🔊 89

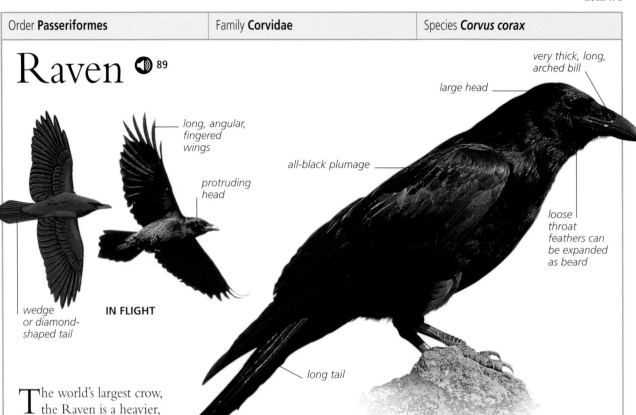

very thick, long, arched bill

large head

long, angular, fingered wings

protruding head

all-black plumage

loose throat feathers can be expanded as beard

IN FLIGHT

wedge or diamond-shaped tail

long tail

The world's largest crow, the Raven is a heavier, longer-winged, and longer-tailed bird than the Carrion Crow. Its heavier, longer bill is evident at close range. At long range, it is best identified by its shape, manner of flight, calls, and often the situation that it is in. Ravens are often found over the wildest and craggiest country, even over high, barren peaks, although they also frequent softer, wooded or farmed land where Carrion Crows are equally likely. Where they are unmolested they may be seen flying over coastal towns, and rarely they even nest on tall buildings.

VOICE Important clue: loud, abrupt, echoing *crronk crronk crronk* or *prruk prruk*, metallic *tonk*; various clicking, rattling or quiet musical notes, sometimes in rambling subsong audible at close range.

NESTING Huge nest of thick sticks, wool, grass, and heather, used for many years, under overhang on cliff, or in tall tree; 4–6 eggs; 1 brood; February–May.

FEEDING Eats almost anything; catches small mammals and birds, eats meat from dead sheep and road-killed rabbits; forages for scraps on shore or at refuse tips; eats invertebrates and grain.

FLIGHT: bold, strong, acrobatic, wings often angled; unique roll onto back and back again; soars easily.

LARGE HEAD
The feathers of the crown, chin, and throat can be raised to exaggerate the size of a Raven's head.

SIMILAR SPECIES

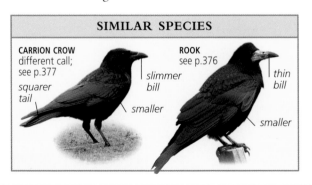

CARRION CROW different call; see p.377
squarer tail

slimmer bill

smaller

ROOK see p.376

thin bill

smaller

OCCURRENCE
In most of Europe except lowland Britain, France, Low Countries, and east to Denmark; year-round resident in large forests, mountain regions, open moorland, and hills with crags and isolated trees.

Seen in the UK
J F M A M J J A S O N D

Length **54–67cm (21½–26in)**	Wingspan **1.2–1.5m (4–5ft)**	Weight **0.8–1.5kg (1¾–3⅓lb)**
Social **Pairs/Small flocks**	Lifespan **10–15 years**	Status **Secure†**

Order **Passeriformes**	Family **Sturnidae**	Species *Sturnus vulgaris*

Starling 🔊 90

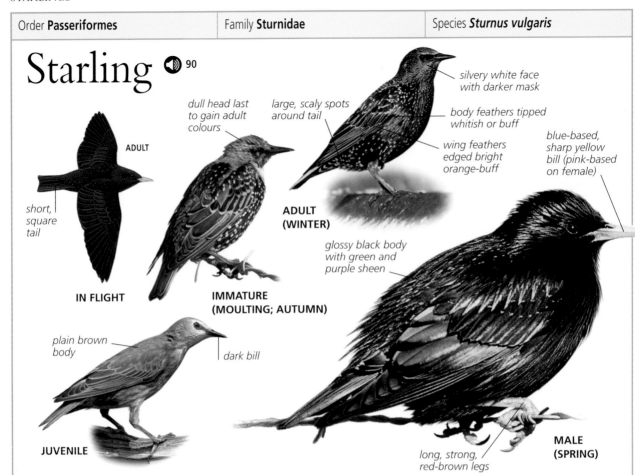

ADULT

short, square tail

IN FLIGHT

dull head last to gain adult colours

IMMATURE (MOULTING; AUTUMN)

large, scaly spots around tail

ADULT (WINTER)

silvery white face with darker mask

body feathers tipped whitish or buff

wing feathers edged bright orange-buff

glossy black body with green and purple sheen

blue-based, sharp yellow bill (pink-based on female)

plain brown body

dark bill

JUVENILE

long, strong, red-brown legs

MALE (SPRING)

Generally abundant, Starlings form dense, noisy flocks: no other small bird, apart from shoreline waders, creates such vast flocks that look like clouds of smoke at a distance. However, with widespread declines, flocks have been much reduced. They are found in many habitats, urban, suburban, and rural, many moving west within Europe in winter. In spring, Starlings sing loudly, with characteristic wing-waving actions.

VOICE Loud, slightly grating *cheer*, musical, twangy, whistled *tswee-oo*, variety of clicks, gurgles, squawking notes; song fast mixture of gurgles, rattles, trills, and whistles, some mimicry.

NESTING Loose, bulky nest of grass and stems, lined with roots, moss, wool, and feathers, in tree hole, cavity in building or wall, or large nest box; 4–7 eggs; 1 or 2 broods; April–July.

FEEDING In small to large flocks, finding invertebrates, seeds, and berries on ground; catches flying ants.

/\/\/\/\/\/\/\/\/\/\/\/\/\/\/\/\/\

FLIGHT: direct, fast, short glides and rapid flicked wingbeats; often in dense flocks, rising and falling.

WINTER FLOCK
Starling flocks in flight are marvellous examples of skilful coordination and close control.

SIMILAR SPECIES

SPOTLESS STARLING ♂♀; see p.381

BLACKBIRD ♂♀; see p.317

unspotted

longer body plumes

unmarked in summer

longer tail

OCCURRENCE
Breeds in all Europe except Spain, Portugal, and S Italy, where it is a winter visitor; only summer in N and E Europe. Breeds in woods, gardens, and towns; in winter, in forest, city centres, and industrial sites, on bridges and piers.

Seen in the UK
J F M A M J J A S O N D

Length **21cm (8½in)**	Wingspan **37–42cm (14½–16½in)**	Weight **75–90g (2⅝–3¼oz)**
Social **Flocks**	Lifespan **Up to 5 years**	Status **Secure**

Order **Passeriformes**	Family **Sturnidae**	Species ***Sturnus unicolor***

Spotless Starling

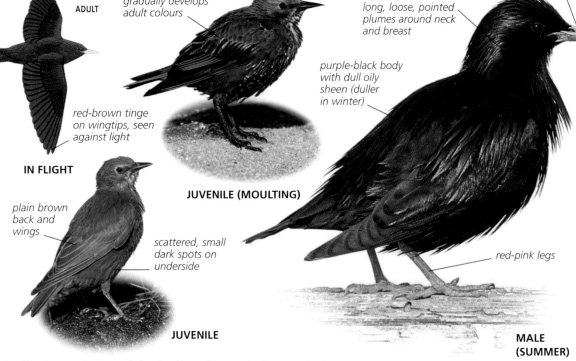

ADULT

gradually develops adult colours

blue-based yellow bill (pink-based on female)

long, loose, pointed plumes around neck and breast

purple-black body with dull oily sheen (duller in winter)

red-brown tinge on wingtips, seen against light

IN FLIGHT

JUVENILE (MOULTING)

plain brown back and wings

scattered, small dark spots on underside

red-pink legs

JUVENILE

MALE (SUMMER)

The Iberian equivalent of the Starling, this species has an obvious resemblance and close relationship with the more widespread species: in winter especially, they can be difficult to separate. In summer, however, as groups line the roofs of ancient buildings in Spain, or fly down to feed in the fields, they seem to look and sound a little different, with a subtle character of their own. In winter, Starlings join them across Spain and increasingly they stay to breed south of the Pyrenees, increasing the identification challenge.

VOICE Starling-like squawling and quarrelling notes; song has loud, musical, long-drawn *py-eeeew* and parrot-like sounds.

NESTING Bulky, untidy nest in roof spaces and cavities in walls; 4–7 eggs; 1 brood; April–June.

FEEDING Forages on ground for all kinds of invertebrates and seeds.

FLIGHT: like Starling but tends to look slightly bulkier, broader-winged, slightly slower.

HABITAT
The Spotless Starling is found in similar habitats as the Starling but is more often associated with old buildings and tiled roofs.

SIMILAR SPECIES

STARLING ♂♀; larger spots overall in winter; see p.380

pale spots under tail in summer

SUBTLE SHEEN
Unless seen closely, this bird looks solidly black. It has a more purplish sheen overall than a Starling.

OCCURRENCE
Breeds in Spain, Portugal, and extreme S France, Corsica, Sicily, and Sardinia. All year round in towns and villages, feeding on adjacent farmland; in winter, may mix with common Starlings.

Seen in the UK
J F M A M J J A S O N D

Length **21cm (8½in)**	Wingspan **37–42cm (14½–16½in)**	Weight **75–90g (2⅝–3¼oz)**
Social **Flocks**	Lifespan **Up to 5 years**	Status **Secure**

Family **Passeridae**

SPARROWS

R ELATED MORE CLOSELY to the African weavers than to the similar finches, sparrows are adaptable and widespread birds, the House Sparrow being closely associated with people wherever they are.

Male and female plumages are markedly different in House and Spanish Sparrows, but identical in the Tree Sparrow (both looking more like a House Sparrow male). Rock Sparrows, in another genus altogether, are quite different, but have no obvious variations in their plumage.

All sparrows are social. Spanish Sparrows are especially gregarious where they are common.

House Sparrows used to gather in hundreds to feed on grain and weed seeds in winter stubbles, but have declined in most places in recent years. Breeding birds may be in loose colonies, using a variety of sites including the base of White Stork nests, thickets, and dense creepers on walls, but House Sparrows mostly occupy holes or cavities of some sort in roofs and under eaves. Renovation of wooden eaves with plastic cladding has often been blamed for local declines. Even inside a small cavity, the nest is a mass of grass and other stems, feathers, and scraps, with an overall rounded effect that recalls the weavers, but lacking the neatness and precision of construction that characterizes their nests. Both House and Tree Sparrows are suffering a widespread decline in western Europe.

FEEDING FLOCK
Sparrows burst from a stubble field with a loud roar of wings. They feed in tight-packed flocks, often mixed with Greenfinches and Linnets, which also pack closely together in many situations, while other finches and buntings form loose groups.

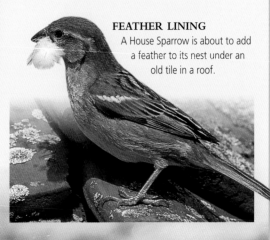

FEATHER LINING
A House Sparrow is about to add a feather to its nest under an old tile in a roof.

VIGOROUS BATHING
Sparrows bathe regularly, in water as well as in dust, helping to keep their plumage in good condition and free of parasites.

| Order **Passeriformes** | Family **Passeridae** | Species *Passer domesticus* |

House Sparrow 🔊 91

whitish wingbar

MALE

IN FLIGHT

grey cap with red-brown sides

thick black bill

red-brown back

pale greyish rump

black bib (bigger in spring)

unmarked grey underside (grey-buff on female)

MALE (SUMMER)

plain plumage

IMMATURE (AUTUMN)

yellow-brown cap

pale stripe behind eye

plain brown tail

FEMALE

Recent declines have seen numbers in gardens and town parks reduce and farmland flocks disappear but House Sparrows remain almost as widespread as ever. They are familiar in towns and gardens and even in farmland concentrate around buildings. Males are easily recognized, although they look quite like Tree and Spanish Sparrows. Females lack the bold patterns and can be taken for some finches, but in reality are equally distinct. House Sparrows are typically social and noisy birds.

VOICE Basic lively, simple *chirrup, chilp*; loud chattering chorus from flocks; series of chirps forms simple song.

NESTING Untidy nest of grass and feathers, in roof space, cavity in wall, in House Martin nest (see p.282), tree cavity, or more openly in creepers and around wires; 3–7 eggs; 1–4 broods; April–August.

FEEDING Usually on ground, taking seeds, buds, roots, berries, and many insects for young; catches some insects clumsily in flight; visits bird-tables for nuts, seed mixtures, and kitchen scraps.

FLIGHT: fast, whirring, with bursts of rapid wingbeats; often in noisy flocks.

WINTER MALE
In winter, the red-brown band behind the eye and dark bib are partly obscured by pale feather tips.

OCCURRENCE
Resident almost throughout Europe, but only very local in Iceland. Thrives in villages, around farms, and in all kinds of habitats close to human habitation, but has declined recently on farmland, in towns, and in suburban gardens.

| Seen in the UK |
| J F M A M J J A S O N D |

SIMILAR SPECIES

CHAFFINCH ♀
similar to ♀ ;
see p.388

duller

SPANISH SPARROW ♂
similar to ♂ ; see p.384

big white cheeks

white wingbars

streaked below

SUBSPECIES

P. d. italiae
(Italy, Crete)

brown crown

white cheeks

| Length **14cm (5½in)** | Wingspan **20–22cm (8–9in)** | Weight **19–25g ($^{11}/_{16}$–$^{7}/_{8}$oz)** |
| Social **Flocks** | Lifespan **2–5 years** | Status **Secure** |

Order **Passeriformes**	Family **Passeridae**	Species *Passer hispaniolensis*

Spanish Sparrow

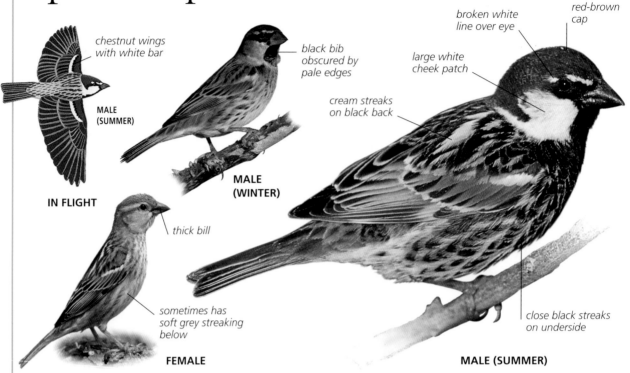

chestnut wings with white bar

MALE (SUMMER)

IN FLIGHT

black bib obscured by pale edges

MALE (WINTER)

broken white line over eye

red-brown cap

large white cheek patch

cream streaks on black back

thick bill

sometimes has soft grey streaking below

FEMALE

close black streaks on underside

MALE (SUMMER)

Much like the House Sparrow but, in summer, more brightly and strikingly patterned, the Spanish Sparrow is essentially a southeast European bird, and not actually common in Spain. Where House Sparrows are sparse it may take over that species' role in towns, but in many areas, it is a bird of farmland and damp places with willow thickets. It is highly social, sometimes found in large flocks and breeding in colonies. In Italy, the sparrows seem to be a constant form of hybrid between Spanish and House Sparrows.
VOICE Slightly higher and more metallic than House Sparrow's; loud chirruping, fast chorus from flock or colony.
NESTING Bulky nest of grass, in thicket, or in base of stick nest of stork or heron, often in tall willows or other wetland thicket, in colony; 3–7 eggs; 1 or 2 broods; April–July.
FEEDING Eats seeds and berries, mostly from ground; feeds insects to chicks.

FLIGHT: quick, low, whirring, like House Sparrow, with occasional momentary closures of wings.

DIFFICULT TEST
This female is clearly streaked, but most female Spanish Sparrows are very difficult to distinguish from female House Sparrows.

OCCURRENCE
Local breeding bird in Spain, Sardinia, and Sicily, more frequent (but in summer only) in Balkans. In farmland, villages, and wet places with willow thickets and tall trees.

Seen in the UK
J F M A M J J A S O N D

SIMILAR SPECIES

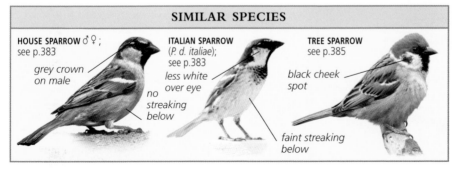

HOUSE SPARROW ♂♀; see p.383
grey crown on male
no streaking below

ITALIAN SPARROW (*P. d. italiae*); see p.383
less white over eye
faint streaking below

TREE SPARROW see p.385
black cheek spot

Length **14–16cm (5½–6½in)**	Wingspan **20–22cm (8–9in)**	Weight **20–25g (¹¹⁄₁₆–⅞oz)**
Social **Flocks**	Lifespan **2–5 years**	Status **Secure†**

Order **Passeriformes**	Family **Passeridae**	Species ***Passer montanus***

Tree Sparrow

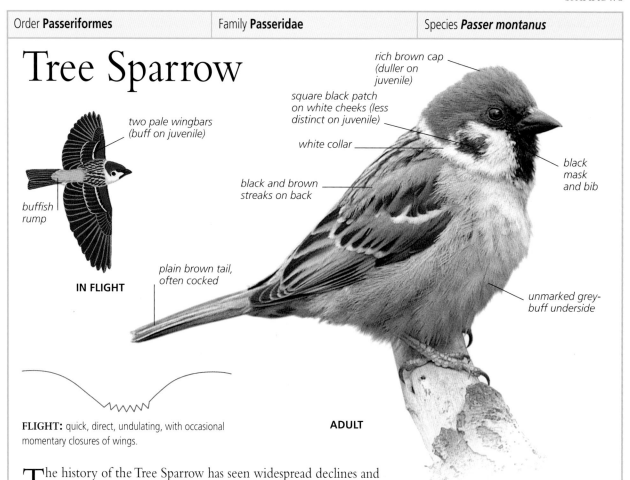

two pale wingbars (buff on juvenile)

buffish rump

IN FLIGHT

rich brown cap (duller on juvenile)

square black patch on white cheeks (less distinct on juvenile)

white collar

black and brown streaks on back

plain brown tail, often cocked

black mask and bib

unmarked grey-buff underside

ADULT

FLIGHT: quick, direct, undulating, with occasional momentary closures of wings.

The history of the Tree Sparrow has seen widespread declines and increases through Europe. By the end of the 20th century it was, in many areas, in the depths of a severe decline, and is now absent from large regions where it was quite recently common. Unlike House and Spanish Sparrows, male and female Tree Sparrows look alike. It is sometimes a suburban bird but is most suited to woodland with scattered clearings and farmland with mature trees.

VOICE Loud chirruping and cheeping calls like House Sparrow; a disyllabic *tsu-wit*; hard, short *tek tek* in flight.

NESTING Rounded or domed nest of straw and grass, in hole in tree or building, or in nest box; 4–6 eggs; 2 or 3 broods; April–July.

FEEDING Mostly picks seeds from ground; also eats some insects, buds, and scraps around farms; visits bird-tables and feeders for seeds and nuts.

FLUFFIER IN WINTER
The Tree Sparrow keeps warm by fluffing its flank feathers over its wings; details such as its wingbars are then obscured.

SIMILAR SPECIES

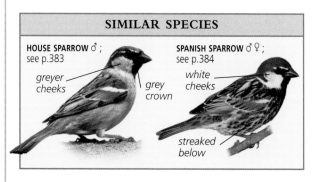

HOUSE SPARROW ♂; see p.383

greyer cheeks

grey crown

SPANISH SPARROW ♂♀; see p.384

white cheeks

streaked below

OCCURRENCE
Breeds in most of Europe but very local in UK, and absent from Iceland and N Scandinavia. Bird of farmland with scattered trees, parks, woodland, and woodland edge, but also town bird in much of S and E Europe.

Seen in the UK
J F M A M J J A S O N D

Length **14cm (5½in)**	Wingspan **20–22cm (8–9in)**	Weight **19–25g (11/16–7/8oz)**
Social **Flocks**	Lifespan **2–5 years**	Status **Secure**

Order **Passeriformes**	Family **Passeridae**	Species *Petronia petronia*

Rock Sparrow

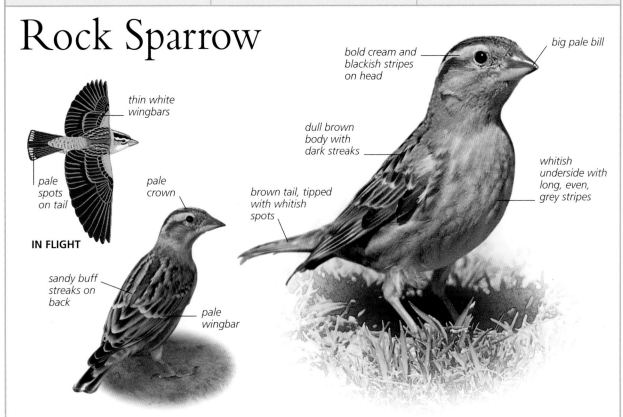

thin white wingbars

pale spots on tail

IN FLIGHT

pale crown

sandy buff streaks on back

pale wingbar

bold cream and blackish stripes on head

big pale bill

dull brown body with dark streaks

brown tail, tipped with whitish spots

whitish underside with long, even, grey stripes

R ock Sparrows need broken ground with cavities in which to nest. This requirement may be met by cliffs and gorges in mountains, lower slopes with scattered rocks, farmed land with earth cliffs, road cuttings, old buildings, or hollow poles which provide nesting places. The birds are best located by following up their distinctive nasal calls but can be elusive as they remain perched on rocky ledges, inconspicuous with their dull, pale colours and lack of any strong pattern.

VOICE Distinctive twangy, nasal, oft-repeated note, *tyeoo*, *tee-vit*, or *peoo*.

NESTING Domed nest of grass and feathers in cavity in old building, hollow post, and earth bank, or in crag, often loosely colonial; 5 or 6 eggs; 2 or 3 broods; May–July.

FEEDING Finds seeds and invertebrates on ground, in grass, or among stones and boulders on open ground.

FLIGHT: low, quick, whirring, undulating over a distance; tail often fanned.

DRINKING POOL
A small pool in a dry region is usually a good place to sit in wait for Rock Sparrows and other birds that come to drink.

OCCURRENCE
Breeds in Spain, Portugal, S France, S Italy, and Balkans; typically in dry, stony, or sandy areas with cliffs or road cuttings; in rocky places, gorges, and mountainous regions, present all year.

Seen in the UK
J F M A M J J A S O N D

SIMILAR SPECIES

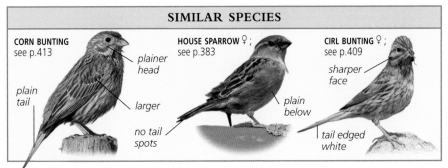

CORN BUNTING see p.413

plain tail

plainer head

larger

HOUSE SPARROW ♀; see p.383

no tail spots

plain below

CIRL BUNTING ♀; see p.409

sharper face

tail edged white

Length **15–17cm (6–6½in)**	Wingspan **21–23cm (8½–9in)**	Weight **20–28g (¹¹⁄₁₆–1oz)**
Social **Small flocks**	Lifespan **2–5 years**	Status **Secure**

Family **Fringillidae**

FINCHES

THERE ARE TWO MAIN groups of finches, the *Fringilla* species (Chaffinch and Brambling) and the Cardueline finches. The Chaffinch and Brambling are clearly closely related, their different colours arranged in very similar patterns; they have the same basic shape and behaviour, and frequently mingle in winter.

The others, however, are a very diverse group. Their shapes and behaviour are strongly determined by their food. The crossbills have remarkable beaks with crossed, hooked tips, specially adapted to extracting seeds from conifer cones. The Hawfinch has a massive bill for cracking open tough seeds and stones, such as olive and cherry, while the Bullfinch has a softer, rounded bill for manipulating buds and soft fruits. The Greenfinch has a big bill, used for dealing with strong seeds and for tearing open tough fruits such

SOCIAL FEEDERS
Goldfinches feed on seeds that tend to be abundant in small areas, so can afford to gather in large flocks.

as hips, while the Goldfinch and Siskin have delicate, pointed bills for extracting seeds from fruiting plants such as thistles and teazels and from cones of trees such as larch and alder.

Some species, such as the redpolls, are acrobatic and light enough to feed while perching on plants, while others are much less agile and feed while standing on the ground by pulling seed-heads down with their bills.

Most finches are gregarious but flock behaviour varies: Chaffinches form loose aggregations, while Twites, Redpolls, and Siskins dash about in flight in tight, coordinated parties.

SEED-EATERS
Living on a diet of weed seeds, these seed-eaters unusually feed seeds, not insects, to their chicks.

THIRSTY WORK
Crossbills eat an abundance of dry seeds and must frequently pause to drink from a puddle before flying off to another conifer.

| Order **Passeriformes** | Family **Fringillidae** | Species *Fringilla coelebs* |

Chaffinch 🔊 92

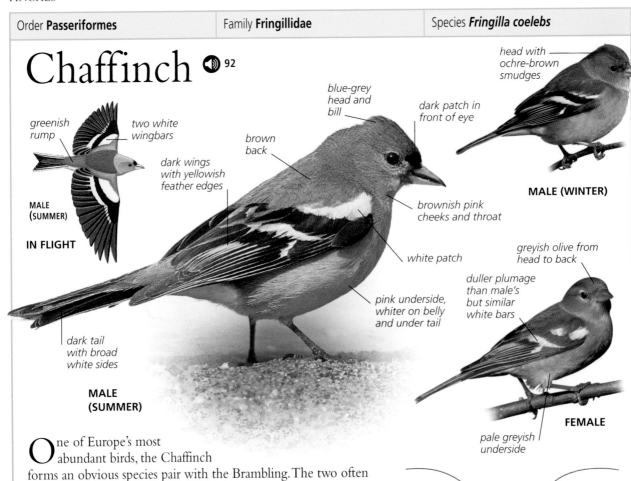

head with ochre-brown smudges

MALE (WINTER)

greenish rump

two white wingbars

dark wings with yellowish feather edges

MALE (SUMMER)

IN FLIGHT

dark tail with broad white sides

MALE (SUMMER)

blue-grey head and bill

brown back

dark patch in front of eye

brownish pink cheeks and throat

white patch

pink underside, whiter on belly and under tail

greyish olive from head to back

duller plumage than male's but similar white bars

pale greyish underside

FEMALE

One of Europe's most abundant birds, the Chaffinch forms an obvious species pair with the Brambling. The two often feed together outside the breeding season; their general shape, pattern, and behaviour are very similar. Chaffinches breed in separate territories, proclaimed by males singing loudly from prominent perches, but they are social birds at other times. They are often very tame, coming for food in car parks and picnic sites and frequently visiting gardens.

VOICE Flight call short, single, soft *chup*, frequent loud *pink!* in spring, loud *hweet, jilip*; song bright, cheery, rattled phrase with a flourish, *chi-chip-chip, chirichirchiri cheeip-tcheweeoo.*

NESTING Neat, perfectly camouflaged cup of grass, leaves, moss, cobweb, and lichen, against trunk of tree or bush; 4 or 5 eggs; 1 brood; April–May.

FEEDING Eats insects in summer, mostly caterpillars from foliage; otherwise takes seeds, shoots, and berries; visits bird-tables for seed mixtures, especially sunflower seeds.

FLIGHT: direct, quite quick, undulating; bursts of wingbeats between glides with wings closed.

SINGING MALE
The cheerful, rattling, and far-carrying song of the Chaffinch is an early sign of spring.

OCCURRENCE
Summer visitor in N and E Europe; all year in W and S (absent from Iceland); breeds in woods (extensive pine forest or conifer plantations to deciduous stands), parks, and gardens. Under beeches, in fields, and gardens in winter.

| Seen in the UK |
| J F M A M J J A S O N D |

SIMILAR SPECIES

BRAMBLING ♀ winter, similar to ♀; white rump; see p.389

orange upper wingbar

BULLFINCH ♂ similar to ♂ summer; white rump; see p.398

thick black bill and black cap

no white on tail

HOUSE SPARROW ♀ similar to ♀; see p.383

| Length **14.5cm (5¾in)** | Wingspan **25–28cm (10–11in)** | Weight **19–23g (¹¹⁄₁₆–¹³⁄₁₆oz)** |
| Social **Flocks** | Lifespan **2–5 years** | Status **Secure** |

Order **Passeriformes**	Family **Fringillidae**	Species *Fringilla montifringilla*

Brambling

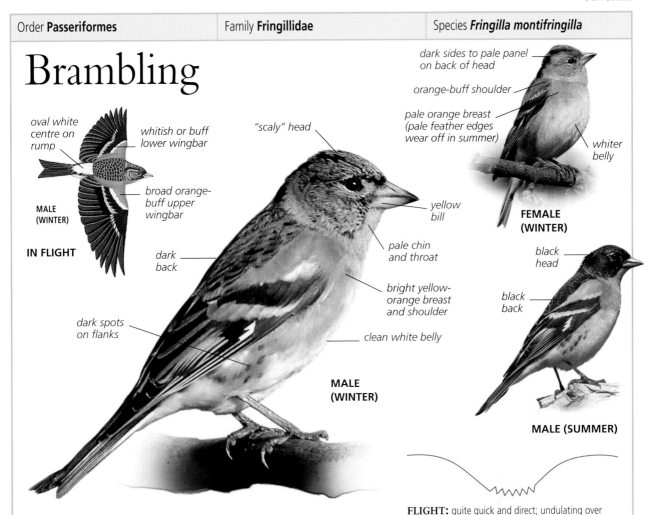

oval white centre on rump

whitish or buff lower wingbar

broad orange-buff upper wingbar

MALE (WINTER)

IN FLIGHT

"scaly" head

dark back

dark spots on flanks

yellow bill

pale chin and throat

bright yellow-orange breast and shoulder

clean white belly

MALE (WINTER)

dark sides to pale panel on back of head

orange-buff shoulder

pale orange breast (pale feather edges wear off in summer)

whiter belly

FEMALE (WINTER)

black head

black back

MALE (SUMMER)

FLIGHT: quite quick and direct; undulating over long distance.

Generally less common and not nearly so ubiquitous as the Chaffinch, the Brambling can nevertheless gather in gigantic flocks in winter, especially in central Europe. In the west, their numbers fluctuate from year to year with the food supply, especially tree seeds such as beech-mast. Spring males can often be seen in fine summer plumage in their winter quarters before they migrate.

VOICE Flight call slightly harder than Chaffinch, single *tchek*, distinctive nasal *tsweek*; song includes deep, nasal, buzzing *dzeeee* note like Greenfinch.

NESTING Cup of lichen, bark, roots, and stems, lined with hair and feathers; 5–7 eggs; 1 brood; May–June.

FEEDING Eats insects in summer, seeds at other times; often on ground feeding on beech-mast.

VERY LARGE FLOCKS
Bramblings may form huge flocks in winter. Millions have been noted in central Europe but scores or hundreds are more usual in most areas.

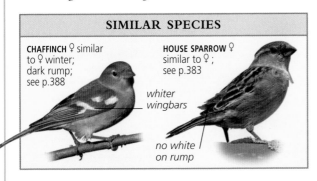

SIMILAR SPECIES

CHAFFINCH ♀ similar to ♀ winter; dark rump; see p.388

HOUSE SPARROW ♀ similar to ♀; see p.383

whiter wingbars

no white on rump

OCCURRENCE
Breeds in Scandinavia and NE Europe, in northern forest. In winter, throughout Europe, in farmland, parks, especially areas with beech, birch, and spruce, at times in gigantic concentrations where tree seeds are abundant.

Seen in the UK
J F M A M J J A S O N D

Length **14.5cm (5¾in)**	Wingspan **25–28cm (10–11in)**	Weight **19–23g (11/16–13/16oz)**
Social **Flocks**	Lifespan **2–5 years**	Status **Secure**

Order **Passeriformes**	Family **Fringillidae**	Species *Carduelis cannabina*

Linnet 🔊 93

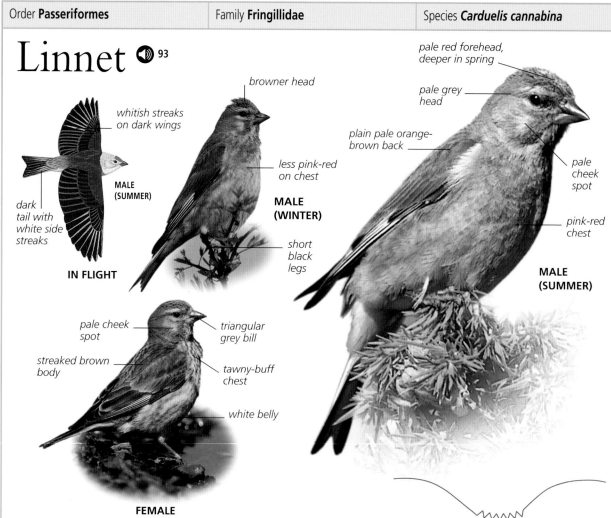

IN FLIGHT

whitish streaks on dark wings

MALE (SUMMER)

dark tail with white side streaks

browner head

less pink-red on chest

MALE (WINTER)

short black legs

pale red forehead, deeper in spring

pale grey head

plain pale orange-brown back

pale cheek spot

pink-red chest

MALE (SUMMER)

pale cheek spot

triangular grey bill

streaked brown body

tawny-buff chest

white belly

FEMALE

A small, lively, sociable finch, the Linnet breeds in small colonies and feeds in flocks all year round. Flocks move together, tightly coordinated, unlike the looser aggregations formed by Chaffinches. They are ground feeders, while Redpolls and Siskins are mostly tree feeders and Goldfinches feed on tall herbs; at times most finches can be found together in mixed flocks. Linnets prefer waste ground with plentiful seeding plants and bushes, or hedgerows, in which to nest.
VOICE Light, twittering, chattering flight call *tidit tidititit*, nasal *tseeoo*; song musical, quite rich, varied warbling with chattering intermixed, often chorus from flocks.
NESTING Neat little nest of stems and roots, lined with hair; 4–6 eggs; 2 or 3 broods; April–July.
FEEDING Often feeds in groups all year, on seeds, taken from ground; young fed on insects; rarely comes to gardens.

FLIGHT: light, dancing, jerky undulations; flurries of wingbeats; sudden drop to ground to feed.

SWIRLING FLOCK
Linnets fly in tight, lively, bouncy flocks, with well-coordinated movements.

SIMILAR SPECIES

TWITE ♂♀; see p.391

streaked tawny body

buff throat

streaked tawny-brown body

pale wingbar

REDPOLL ♂♀; see p.392

OCCURRENCE
Found locally on heaths, rough grassland, commons, farmland, and upland meadows, in most of Europe except N Scandinavia and Iceland. Present only in summer in N and E Europe, but resident elsewhere.

Seen in the UK
J F M A M J J A S O N D

Length **12.5–14cm (5–5½in)**	Wingspan **21–25cm (8½–10in)**	Weight **15–20g (⁹⁄₁₆–¹¹⁄₁₆oz)**
Social **Flocks**	Lifespan **2–3 years**	Status **Secure**

Order **Passeriformes**	Family **Fringillidae**	Species ***Carduelis flavirostris***

Twite

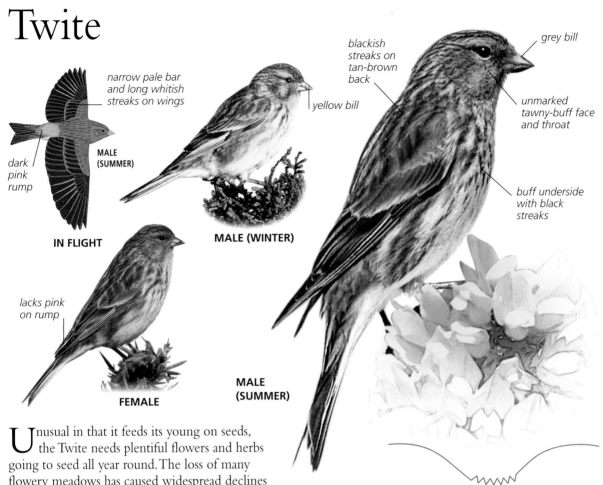

narrow pale bar and long whitish streaks on wings

MALE (SUMMER)

dark pink rump

IN FLIGHT

yellow bill

MALE (WINTER)

blackish streaks on tan-brown back

grey bill

unmarked tawny-buff face and throat

buff underside with black streaks

lacks pink on rump

MALE (SUMMER)

FEMALE

Unusual in that it feeds its young on seeds, the Twite needs plentiful flowers and herbs going to seed all year round. The loss of many flowery meadows has caused widespread declines and contractions in its range. Twites resemble Linnets but share characteristics with the Redpoll. They are, however, ground feeders, not treetop feeders like Redpolls. Like other smaller finches, they move in tight, coordinated flocks, rising from the ground, and circling and dropping again as one.

VOICE Flight call little harder than Linnet's, main call nasal, twanging, rising *twa-eeet*; song quick with buzzing notes and trills intermixed.

NESTING Deep cup of twigs, grass, and moss, lined with hair, in bush or bank; 4–6 eggs; 1 or 2 broods; May–June.

FEEDING Eats seeds; unlike most finches, also feeds young on seeds.

FLIGHT: bounding, fast, energetic with deep undulations; dives rapidly into cover.

ATTRACTED TO WATER
Twites use shallow pools for drinking and bathing, and are often easier to see then than when they are feeding in tall weeds.

SIMILAR SPECIES

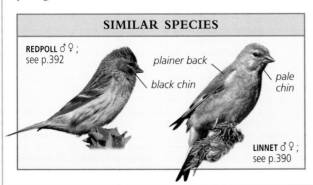

REDPOLL ♂♀; see p.392

plainer back

black chin

pale chin

LINNET ♂♀; see p.390

OCCURRENCE
Breeds in N Great Britain and Scandinavia, in weedy fields, at edges of moorland, and around upland farms. Winters around North Sea and Baltic coasts, mostly on salt marshes along coasts but declining. Scarce inland.

Seen in the UK
J F M A M J J A S O N D

Length **12.5–14cm (5–5½in)**	Wingspan **21–25cm (8½–10in)**	Weight **15–20g (⁹⁄₁₆–¹¹⁄₁₆oz)**
Social **Flocks**	Lifespan **2–3 years**	Status **Secure**

Order **Passeriformes**	Family **Fringillidae**	Species *Carduelis flammea*

Redpoll

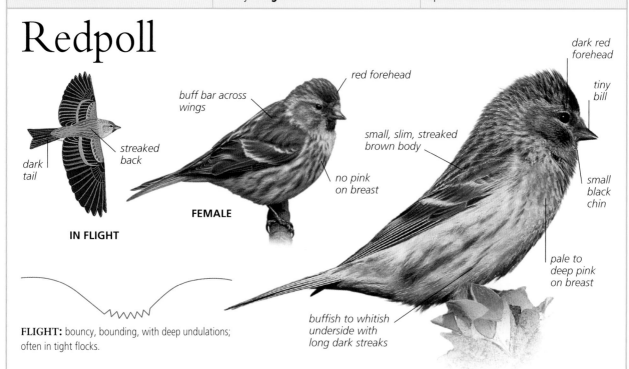

IN FLIGHT

dark tail

streaked back

FEMALE

buff bar across wings

red forehead

no pink on breast

small, slim, streaked brown body

MALE (SUMMER)

dark red forehead

tiny bill

small black chin

pale to deep pink on breast

buffish to whitish underside with long dark streaks

FLIGHT: bouncy, bounding, with deep undulations; often in tight flocks.

Typically a treetop bird, the Redpoll can also be found with Linnets in weedy fields, or feeding on the ground under birches where vast amounts of seeds have fallen. Most often, however, Redpoll groups feed, frequently with Siskins, in trees and move between treetops in noisy, well-coordinated flocks, circling together and often returning to the same tree after being disturbed. They may effectively "disappear" instantly on settling, becoming quiet and unobtrusive as they feed.

VOICE Flight call particularly hard, staccato chattering, metallic *chuchuchuchuchuchuchuch*, loud twangy *tsooeee*; song in flight combines chatter with fast, thin, reeling trill, *trreeeeee*.

NESTING Cup of twigs and grasses, lined with hair or wool, in bush or tree; 4–6 eggs; 1 or 2 broods; May–July.

FEEDING Mostly feeds in trees, on seeds, such as birch, alder, and larch, but also on or near ground in weedy fields and under birch trees.

FEEDING FLOCK
The outer twigs of seeding birch trees can be decorated with Redpolls hanging upside down and perched at all angles, reaching their preferred food.

see p.459 · see p.391 · see p.390

SUBSPECIES

whiter band over eye

paler

C. f. flammea
(Scandinavia); whiter wingbar

OCCURRENCE
Breeds with fluctuating numbers and range in Iceland, Ireland, Alps, Great Britain, Low Countries, and NE through Scandinavia. In winter to S France and Italy. In birch woods, larch, and bushy heaths; on ground under birch in spring.

Seen in the UK
J F M A M J J A S O N D

SIMILAR SPECIES

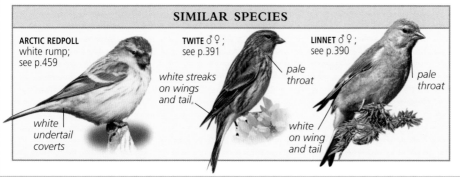

ARCTIC REDPOLL white rump; see p.459

white undertail coverts

TWITE ♂♀; see p.391

white streaks on wings and tail

LINNET ♂♀; see p.390

pale throat

white on wing and tail

pale throat

Length **11–14.5cm (4¼–5¾in)**	Wingspan **20–25cm (8–10in)**	Weight **10–14g (⅜–½oz)**
Social **Flocks**	Lifespan **2–3 years**	Status **Secure†**

| Order **Passeriformes** | Family **Fringillidae** | Species *Carduelis carduelis* |

Goldfinch 🔊 94

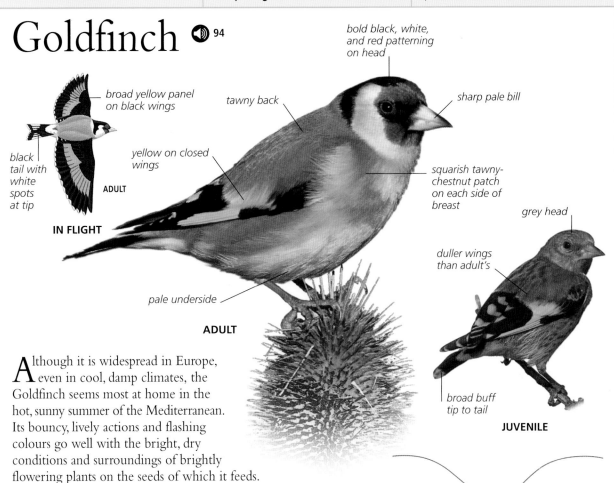

broad yellow panel on black wings

bold black, white, and red patterning on head

tawny back

sharp pale bill

black tail with white spots at tip

yellow on closed wings

ADULT

IN FLIGHT

squarish tawny-chestnut patch on each side of breast

grey head

duller wings than adult's

pale underside

ADULT

broad buff tip to tail

JUVENILE

Although it is widespread in Europe, even in cool, damp climates, the Goldfinch seems most at home in the hot, sunny summer of the Mediterranean. Its bouncy, lively actions and flashing colours go well with the bright, dry conditions and surroundings of brightly flowering plants on the seeds of which it feeds. It is, however, also found farther north in farmland with scattered woods and plenty of rough, open ground. Such places tend to be labelled "waste" and are all to often tidied up and stripped of the seed-bearing herbs and shrubs on which so many finches depend.

VOICE Calls are highly distinctive variations on usual finch theme: chattering, skipping flight call, *skip-i-lip* or *tililip* with liquid, lilting quality, rough *tschair*; song musical and varied, mixture of call notes and liquid trills.

NESTING Neat nest of roots, grass, and cobwebs, in tree or shrub; 5 or 6 eggs; 2 broods; May–July.

FEEDING Feeds on soft, half-ripe seeds on low-growing to medium-height plants, less often on ground; also eats tree seeds from alder and birch.

FLIGHT: particularly light and skipping, dancing, bouncy action with flurried beats of long wings.

FLASHING WINGS
A flock of Goldfinches in flight becomes a blur of yellow stripes; these, plus the bouncy, undulating action, make identification simple.

SIMILAR SPECIES

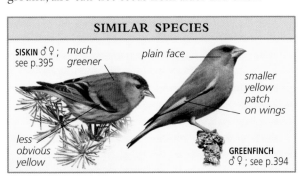

SISKIN ♂♀; see p.395

much greener

plain face

less obvious yellow

smaller yellow patch on wings

GREENFINCH ♂♀; see p.394

OCCURRENCE
Breeds in most of Europe except Iceland and N Scandinavia; only in summer in NE Europe, resident elsewhere, common in S. Likes weedy places with tall, seed-bearing flowers such as thistles, teasels; also alders and larch.

| Seen in the UK |
| J F M A M J J A S O N D |

| Length **12.5–13cm (5in)** | Wingspan **21–25cm (8½–10in)** | Weight **14–17g (½–⅝oz)** |
| Social **Flocks** | Lifespan **2–3 years** | Status **Secure†** |

Order **Passeriformes**	Family **Fringillidae**	Species ***Carduelis chloris***

Greenfinch 🔊 95

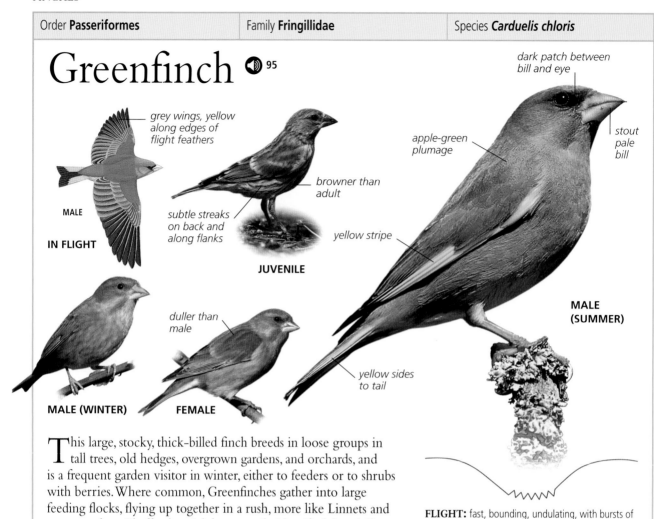

grey wings, yellow along edges of flight feathers

MALE

IN FLIGHT

subtle streaks on back and along flanks

browner than adult

JUVENILE

dark patch between bill and eye

apple-green plumage

stout pale bill

MALE (SUMMER)

yellow stripe

yellow sides to tail

duller than male

MALE (WINTER)   **FEMALE**

This large, stocky, thick-billed finch breeds in loose groups in tall trees, old hedges, overgrown gardens, and orchards, and is a frequent garden visitor in winter, either to feeders or to shrubs with berries. Where common, Greenfinches gather into large feeding flocks, flying up together in a rush, more like Linnets and sparrows than Chaffinches. Adults are easily identified, but duller juveniles can be more troublesome at times.

VOICE Flight call fast, light, tinny chatter, *tit-it-it-it-it*, loud, nasal *tzoo-eee*, hard *jup-jup-jup*; fine song series of staccato trills of varying pace and quality, some metallic and thin, others full, musical, with droning, buzzy *dzweee* intermixed; often in flight *chup-chup-chup, chip-ipipip chr'r'r'r'r'r, tit-it-it-it-it chup-up*.

NESTING Bulky nest of grass and twigs, lined with finer stems, hair, and feathers, in thick bushes or trees; 4–6 eggs; 1 or 2 broods; April–July.

FEEDING Eats seeds, from trees to short plants, many taken from ground; also feeds on berries and nuts; visits bird-tables and feeders.

FLIGHT: fast, bounding, undulating, with bursts of quick wingbeats between closed-winged swoops; display flight slower, with stiff, wavy wingbeats.

GARDEN VISITOR
The Greenfinch often visits bird-tables and feeders for sunflower seeds, seed mixes, and peanuts.

OCCURRENCE
In all of Europe except Iceland, but in summer only in extreme north. Does best in open deciduous woods, parks, big gardens of country houses, bushy areas, orchards, or around farmsteads with tall, dense hedges.

Seen in the UK
J F M A M J J A S O N D

SIMILAR SPECIES

grey head

yellow wingbars

dark tail

CITRIL FINCH ♂♀; ♀ has grey breast; see p.396

SERIN ♂♀; ♀ streaked; yellow rump; see p.397 ♂

yellow forehead of male

black and yellow wingbars

SISKIN ♂♀; see p.395

Length **15cm (6in)**	Wingspan **25–27cm (10–10½in)**	Weight **25–32g (⅞–1⅛oz)**
Social **Flocks**	Lifespan **2–3 years**	Status **Secure**

| Order **Passeriformes** | Family **Fringillidae** | Species *Carduelis spinus* |

Siskin

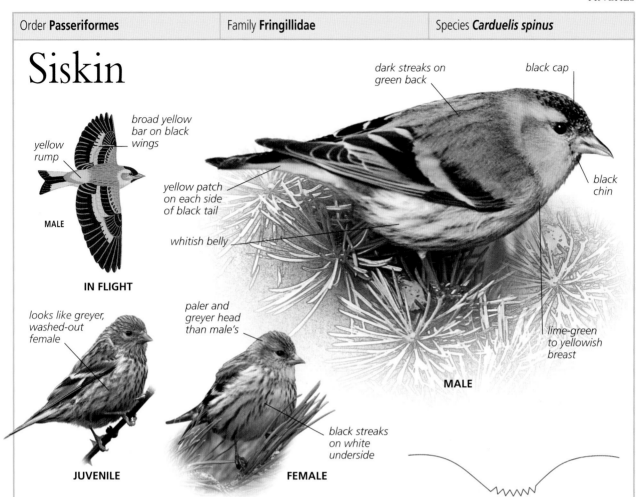

yellow rump

broad yellow bar on black wings

yellow patch on each side of black tail

whitish belly

MALE

IN FLIGHT

dark streaks on green back

black cap

black chin

lime-green to yellowish breast

MALE

looks like greyer, washed-out female

paler and greyer head than male's

black streaks on white underside

JUVENILE

FEMALE

A tree-seed feeder, the Siskin is particularly associated with conifers, but also feeds in birch and alder trees in winter. It visits gardens to eat peanuts and sunflower seeds, but is not usually a ground-feeder. In winter, it associates in flocks, which share a bounding, tight-packed sociability with the Redpoll. Males sometimes separate out from the flocks in spring to sing from treetops. When feeding, these tiny finches are acrobatic, almost tit-like in their actions.

VOICE Flight calls loud, whistled, clear, with slightly squeaky or metallic quality, *tsy-zee* or *tsu-ee*; feeding birds give low, hoarse buzz or purr; song mixes calls and fast trills with hard twittering notes, from tree or in flight.

NESTING Tiny nest of twigs and stems, lined with plant down and hair, high in tree; 4 or 5 eggs; 1 or 2 broods; May–July.

FEEDING Eats seeds of pine, larch, and various other trees.

FLIGHT: dashing, darting, undulating; often in tight-packed, coordinated flocks.

NUT BASKET FEEDER
Siskins come to gardens in spring, when natural supplies of seed are low; they like the reddish peanuts especially.

OCCURRENCE
Breeds locally in N and E Europe, Alps, Pyrenees, UK, and Ireland, in forest of spruce and pine. In winter, more widespread and found especially in stands of larch, spruce, and alders along rivers; visits gardens for peanuts.

Seen in the UK
| J | F | M | A | M | J | J | A | S | O | N | D |

SIMILAR SPECIES

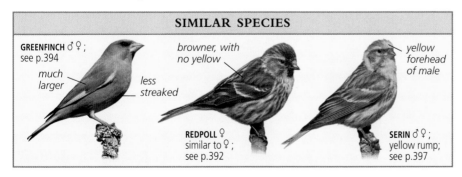

GREENFINCH ♂ ♀; see p.394

much larger

less streaked

browner, with no yellow

REDPOLL ♀
similar to ♀;
see p.392

yellow forehead of male

SERIN ♂ ♀;
yellow rump;
see p.397

| Length **12cm (4¾in)** | Wingspan **20–23cm (8–9in)** | Weight **12–18g (⁷⁄₁₆–⅝oz)** |
| Social **Flocks** | Lifespan **2–3 years** | Status **Secure** |

Order **Passeriformes**	Family **Fringillidae**	Species *Serinus citrinella*

Citril Finch

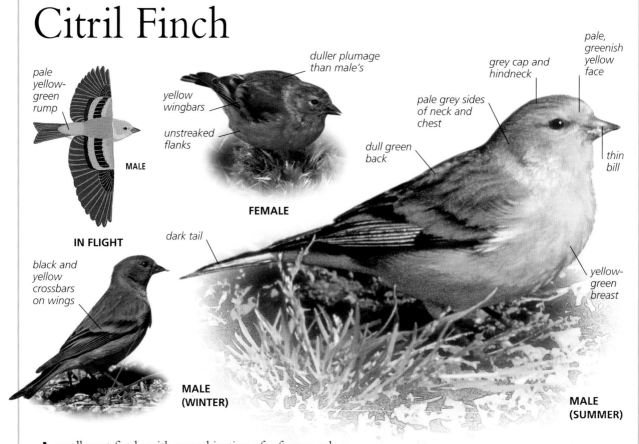

pale yellow-green rump

MALE

IN FLIGHT

duller plumage than male's

yellow wingbars

unstreaked flanks

FEMALE

dark tail

black and yellow crossbars on wings

MALE (WINTER)

grey cap and hindneck

pale, greenish yellow face

pale grey sides of neck and chest

dull green back

thin bill

yellow-green breast

MALE (SUMMER)

A small, neat finch, with a combination of soft grey, pale lemon-yellow, and apple-green on its body and boldly barred wings, the Citril Finch is a bird of high altitude forest-edge habitats. It feeds on the ground or in trees in clearings or around grassy Alpine meadows within easy reach of spruce trees. It is usually found in small groups or family parties, looking puzzlingly like subtly marked Siskins or small, dull Greenfinches at first.

VOICE Various quick flight calls, short *tek* or *te-te-te*; song quick, varied, rambling warble with wheezy notes and buzzy trills.

NESTING Nest of grass and lichens, lined with plant down, high in tree; 4 or 5 eggs; 1 or 2 broods; May–July.

FEEDING Feeds on seeds, both from trees and on ground beneath.

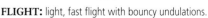

FLIGHT: light, fast flight with bouncy undulations.

MOUNTAIN SPECIALIST
Citril Finches can be spotted high up, close to the tree line around rocky Alpine pastures.

OCCURRENCE
Bird of mountain forests and adjoining high level pastures, and spruce woods at tree line, in N Spain, S France, Alps, Corsica, and Sardinia, rarely moving far from breeding areas.

Seen in the UK
J F M A M J J A S O N D

SIMILAR SPECIES

SERIN ♂♀; yellower rump; see p.397 — *smaller bill*

yellow tail sides

SISKIN ♂♀; yellower rump; see p.395

black cap on male

yellow streak on wing edges

bigger

GREENFINCH ♂♀; see p.394

Length **11–12cm (4¼–4¾in)**	Wingspan **18–20cm (7–8in)**	Weight **12–15g (7/16–9/16oz)**
Social **Flocks**	Lifespan **2–3 years**	Status **Secure**

Order **Passeriformes**	Family **Fringillidae**	Species *Serinus serinus*

Serin

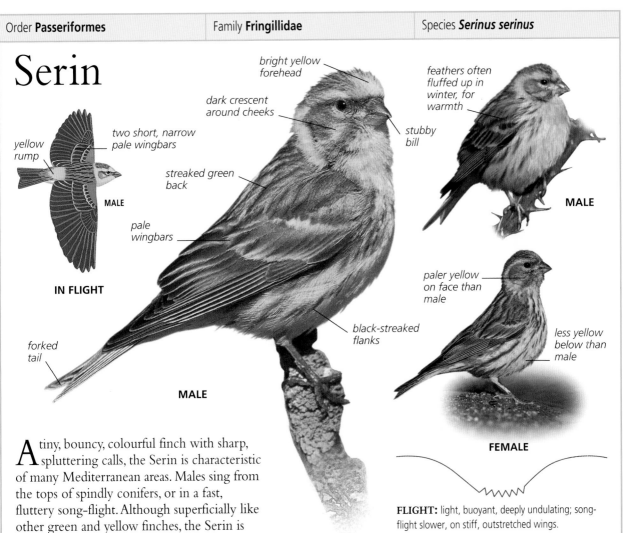

bright yellow forehead

dark crescent around cheeks

feathers often fluffed up in winter, for warmth

stubby bill

MALE

yellow rump

two short, narrow pale wingbars

streaked green back

pale wingbars

MALE

IN FLIGHT

forked tail

black-streaked flanks

MALE

paler yellow on face than male

less yellow below than male

FEMALE

A tiny, bouncy, colourful finch with sharp, spluttering calls, the Serin is characteristic of many Mediterranean areas. Males sing from the tops of spindly conifers, or in a fast, fluttery song-flight. Although superficially like other green and yellow finches, the Serin is generally easily identified in its usual range. However, various possible escaped cage birds have to be ruled out when identifying a potential out-of-range vagrant, including dull, streaky young Canaries.

VOICE Silvery, rapid trill, *zirr-r-r-r-r*; rising *tuweee*; song very quick, sharp, jingling or breaking glass quality, trills and twitters, often in stiff-winged song-flight.

NESTING Tiny, hair-lined cup of grass and moss in tree or bush; 4 eggs; 2 or 3 broods; May–July.

FEEDING Eats tiny seeds, mostly from ground or on low-growing plants.

FLIGHT: light, buoyant, deeply undulating; song-flight slower, on stiff, outstretched wings.

SIZZLING SONG
Males drop their wings to show off their yellow rumps as they sing their fast, high-pitched song.

OCCURRENCE
Resident in Spain, Portugal, S and W France, and Mediterranean area; summer visitor north to Baltic; only rare vagrant outside this range in W Europe. In villages, orchards, vineyards, olive groves, town parks, gardens, wooded areas, and along roadsides.

Seen in the UK											
J	F	M	A	M	J	J	A	S	O	N	D

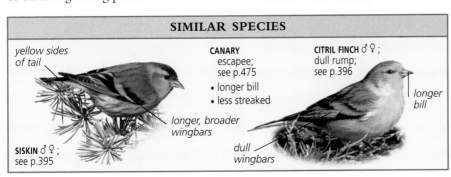

SIMILAR SPECIES

yellow sides of tail

CANARY escapee; see p.475
• longer bill
• less streaked

CITRIL FINCH ♂♀; dull rump; see p.396

longer bill

SISKIN ♂♀; see p.395

longer, broader wingbars

dull wingbars

Length **11–12cm (4¼–4¾in)**	Wingspan **18–20cm (7–8in)**	Weight **12–15g (⁷⁄₁₆–⁹⁄₁₆oz)**
Social **Flocks**	Lifespan **2–3 years**	Status **Secure**

| Order **Passeriformes** | Family **Fringillidae** | Species *Pyrrhula pyrrhula* |

Bullfinch 🔊 96

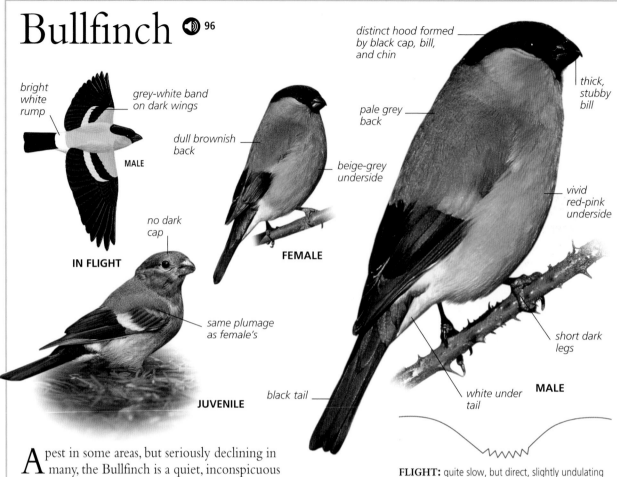

bright white rump

grey-white band on dark wings

MALE

dull brownish back

distinct hood formed by black cap, bill, and chin

pale grey back

beige-grey underside

thick, stubby bill

vivid red-pink underside

no dark cap

IN FLIGHT

FEMALE

same plumage as female's

short dark legs

black tail

white under tail

MALE

JUVENILE

FLIGHT: quite slow, but direct, slightly undulating over a distance.

A pest in some areas, but seriously declining in many, the Bullfinch is a quiet, inconspicuous bird despite its bold plumage. It uses its round bill to feed on soft buds, flowers, and shoots rather than hard seeds, usually feeding in pairs or family groups. If disturbed, it moves out of sight through a thicket or hedge. Its whistled calls are then highly distinctive. It does not visit bird-tables or feeders, although it may come to gardens in spring to raid flowering fruit trees.
VOICE Call low, soft, clear whistles, slightly descending, *peuuw, deu,* or *phiu*; song infrequent, creaky pea-whistle quality, with calls intermixed.
NESTING Cup of twigs, lined with moss and grass, in bush or tree; 4 or 5 eggs; 2 broods; April–June.
FEEDING Eats soft buds, seeds, berries, shoots, and some invertebrates, from low bushes and shrubs, occasionally on ground.

MALE CALLING
Usually inconspicuous, despite its bright colours, the Bullfinch's piping, whistled call is the best clue to its presence in a shrubbery or hedgerow.

SIMILAR SPECIES

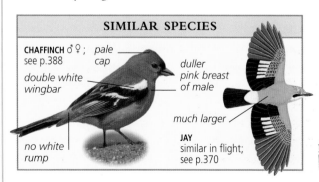

CHAFFINCH ♂♀; see p.388

pale cap

double white wingbar

duller pink breast of male

no white rump

much larger

JAY similar in flight; see p.370

OCCURRENCE
Breeds in most of Europe except Iceland, most of Spain, Portugal, and S Balkans; visits S Spain and Greece in winter. In woodland, farmland with hedges, thickets, parks, gardens with thick shrubberies and similar dense, low cover.

Seen in the UK
J F M A M J J A S O N D

| Length **15cm (6in)** | Wingspan **22–26cm (9–10in)** | Weight **21–27g (³⁄₄–¹⁵⁄₁₆oz)** |
| Social **Small flocks** | Lifespan **2–3 years** | Status **Secure** |

| Order **Passeriformes** | Family **Fringillidae** | Species ***Coccothraustes coccothraustes*** |

Hawfinch

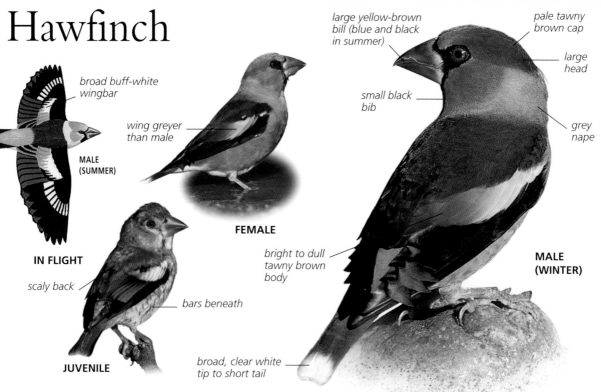

broad buff-white wingbar

wing greyer than male

MALE (SUMMER)

IN FLIGHT

scaly back

bars beneath

JUVENILE

broad, clear white tip to short tail

FEMALE

bright to dull tawny brown body

large yellow-brown bill (blue and black in summer)

small black bib

pale tawny brown cap

large head

grey nape

MALE (WINTER)

In much of Europe, this is one of the most elusive finches, but in southern Europe it can be remarkably approachable, even in suburban trees and orchards or clumps of cherries or olives. It is not, even then, very obvious, but can be located by its quiet, clicking calls. Where the Hawfinch is more typically shy, it may provide little more than a glimpse as it flies up through trees and away over the canopy. It may sometimes be seen perched high on treetops, its size and stocky build then unlike other finches except for the Crossbill.

VOICE Call Robin-like, short, sharp, metallic *tik* or *tzik*, thin *tzree*, *tikitik*; weak, unmusical, scratchy song.

NESTING Nest of twigs, roots, and moss, lined with rootlets, in old tree; 4 or 5 eggs; 1 brood; April–May.

FEEDING Mostly takes large tree seeds, berries, cherries, and other fruit stones from trees; also picks hornbeam, sycamore, beech, and other seeds from ground in late winter.

FLIGHT: strong, fast, direct, swooping with undulations and bursts of powerful, whirring wingbeats.

SEED CRUSHER
The big bill of the Hawfinch deals easily and neatly with small seeds and can cope with tough stones of cherries and olives.

OCCURRENCE
Widespread but very localized, breeding in deciduous woodland, parks, large gardens, orchards, and olive groves. In winter, in similar places with plentiful tree seeds. Absent from Iceland, Ireland, and N Scandinavia.

SIMILAR SPECIES

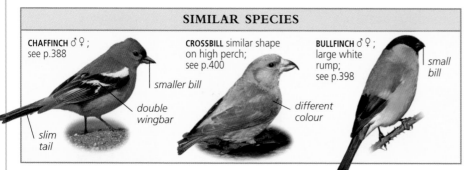

CHAFFINCH ♂♀; see p.388

smaller bill

double wingbar

slim tail

CROSSBILL similar shape on high perch; see p.400

different colour

BULLFINCH ♂♀; large white rump; see p.398

small bill

Seen in the UK
J F M A M J J A S O N D

| Length **18cm (7in)** | Wingspan **29–33cm (11½–13in)** | Weight **48–62g (11¹¹⁄₁₆–2¼oz)** |
| Social **Small flocks** | Lifespan **2–5 years** | Status **Secure** |

| Order **Passeriformes** | Family **Fringillidae** | Species *Loxia curvirostra* |

Crossbill 97

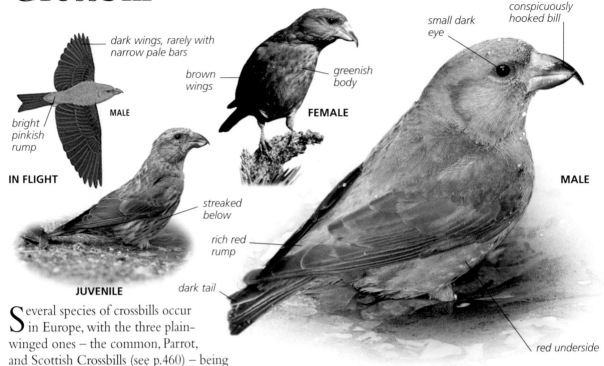

dark wings, rarely with narrow pale bars

brown wings

greenish body

MALE

small dark eye

conspicuously hooked bill

bright pinkish rump

FEMALE

IN FLIGHT

streaked below

rich red rump

MALE

JUVENILE

dark tail

red underside

S everal species of crossbills occur in Europe, with the three plain-winged ones – the common, Parrot, and Scottish Crossbills (see p.460) – being the most difficult to separate. The common Crossbill feeds on spruce seeds but also survives quite well in areas where larch or pine predominate (trees favoured by the smaller Two-barred and larger Scottish or Parrot Crossbills). It is subject to periodic irruptions when large numbers travel far and wide in search of food: almost any clump of pines may then host Crossbills for a time. They feed quietly but may burst out of a treetop with loud flight calls.

VOICE Loud, abrupt calls, similar to young Greenfinch but louder, more staccato, *jup-jup-jup* or *chip-chip-chip*; quiet conversational notes while feeding; song mixes buzzy notes, calls, and bright warbles and trills.

NESTING Small nest of twigs, moss, and bark, lined with hair or wool; 3 or 4 eggs; 1 brood; January–March.

FEEDING Eats seeds of spruce, larch, pine, and other conifers, using crossed bill to prise them from cones on twigs; also eats some berries, buds, and insects.

FLIGHT: strong, direct, bursting from treetops in sudden noisy flurry; fast wingbeats between glides with closed wings.

THIRSTY FINCH
Crossbills eat dry seeds and need easy access to pools for frequent bouts of drinking.

OCCURRENCE
Scattered over most of Europe except in Iceland, but erratic, not present in most years in many areas. Core areas in extensive woods of spruce, larch, and pine, with variety of more or less distinct local populations.

Seen in the UK
J F M A M J J A S O N D

SIMILAR SPECIES

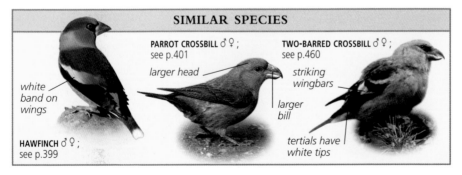

PARROT CROSSBILL ♂♀; see p.401

larger head

TWO-BARRED CROSSBILL ♂♀; see p.460

striking wingbars

white band on wings

larger bill

HAWFINCH ♂♀; see p.399

tertials have white tips

| Length **16 cm (6½in)** | Wingspan **27–30cm (10½–12in)** | Weight **34–38g (1³⁄₁₆–1⁶⁄₁₆oz)** |
| Social **Small flocks** | Lifespan **2–5 years** | Status **Secure** |

Order **Passeriformes**	Family **Fringillidae**	Species *Loxia pytyopsittacus*

Parrot Crossbill

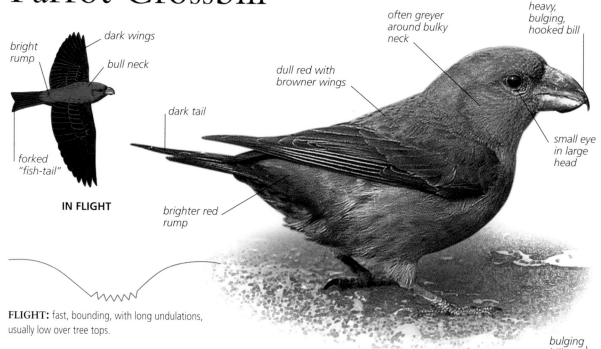

bright rump

dark wings

bull neck

dark tail

forked "fish-tail"

IN FLIGHT

often greyer around bulky neck

heavy, bulging, hooked bill

dull red with browner wings

small eye in large head

brighter red rump

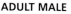

FLIGHT: fast, bounding, with long undulations, usually low over tree tops.

ADULT MALE

Oone of three exceedingly similar crossbill species in northern Europe, the Parrot Crossbill is the largest and biggest-billed. It is adapted to pine forests with tough pine cones, but others also feed in pines (especially the Scottish Crossbill) and identification is seldom easy. Like the Common Crossbill, it may 'erupt' from breeding areas in years when food is scarce and numbers are high, and moves south and west. Small groups are then sometimes briefly seen in unexpected places, including small clumps of pines in coastal areas.

VOICE Like Common Crossbill but a tendency to be deeper, harder, less clicking: *toop-toop-toop*; song includes call notes, warbles, trills, and buzzing sounds.

NESTING Untidy nest of thin twigs and moss, high in a pine tree; 3 or 4 eggs; 1 brood; March or April.

FEEDING Eats pine seeds, prised from cones with the crossed bill; often drinks at nearby pools on ground; also a few berries, insects, and other seeds.

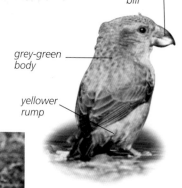

bulging bill

grey-green body

yellower rump

FEMALE

THIRSTY WORK
Like other crossbills, the Parrot Crossbill drinks frequently between bouts of feeding on dry pine seeds, repeatedly coming to favourite pools or rainwater puddles in the forest.

SIMILAR SPECIES

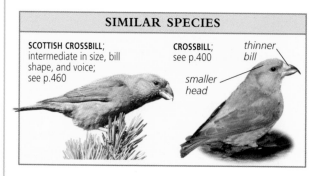

SCOTTISH CROSSBILL; intermediate in size, bill shape, and voice; see p.460

CROSSBILL; see p.400

thinner bill

smaller head

OCCURRENCE
Mostly resident in old coniferous forest in Scandinavia; rare visitor to the UK and probably breeds regularly in tiny numbers in Scotland. True status hard to define due to identification problems.

Seen in the UK
J F M A M J J A S O N D

Length **16–17cm (6½ in)**	Wingspan **30cm (12in)**	Weight **35–40g (1¼–1⁷⁄₁₆ oz)**
Social **Small flocks**	Lifespan **2–5 years**	Status **Secure**

| Order **Passeriformes** | Family **Fringillidae** | Species *Pinicola enucleator* |

Pine Grosbeak

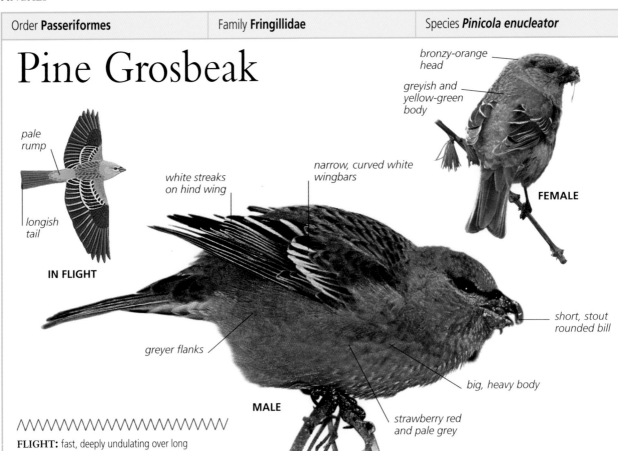

bronzy-orange head

greyish and yellow-green body

FEMALE

pale rump

white streaks on hind wing

narrow, curved white wingbars

longish tail

IN FLIGHT

greyer flanks

short, stout rounded bill

big, heavy body

MALE

strawberry red and pale grey

ᴧᴧᴧᴧᴧᴧᴧᴧᴧᴧᴧᴧᴧᴧᴧᴧᴧᴧᴧᴧ

FLIGHT: fast, deeply undulating over long distances, fluttery between branches.

One of Europe's largest finches, the Pine Grosbeak gives the impression of being a gentle, but fearless bird, often almost oblivious of human presence. It is hard to find in summer when it breeds in northern forests, but may be seen feeding close to houses, even in ornamental trees in town centres, at other times, when it sometimes allows itself almost to be touched. It is restricted to forests and trees with berries and soft seeds all year round, so is unlikely to be seen outside its usual range.

VOICE Clear, single or multi-syllabic ringing notes with a loud, fluty quality; short, clear song.

NESTING Close to the trunk of a conifer, typically a spruce; 3–4 eggs; 1 brood; May–July.

FEEDING Eats seeds, buds, and shoots; some insects in summer, from trees, bushes, and shorter herbaceous plants, often in shady forest undergrowth.

BERRY SPECIALIST
Soft berries and buds are essential to the winter survival of this large, confiding finch; it often finds a good supply in towns and suburbs.

SIMILAR SPECIES

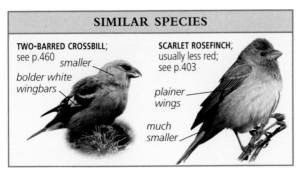

TWO-BARRED CROSSBILL; see p.460
smaller
bolder white wingbars

SCARLET ROSEFINCH; usually less red; see p.403
plainer wings
much smaller

OCCURRENCE
Breeds in old, extensive mixed or coniferous forest in extreme NE Europe and C Scandinavian mountain forests; in winter a little more widespread, rare in southern Scandinavia.

| Seen in the UK |
| J F M A M J J A S O N D |

| Length **19–22cm (8–9in)** | Wingspan **30–35cm (12–15in)** | Weight **50–65g (1¾–2⅜oz)** |
| Social **Small flocks** | Lifespan **Up to 5 years** | Status **Secure** |

Order **Passeriformes**	Family **Fringillidae**	Species ***Carpodacus erythrinus***

Scarlet Rosefinch

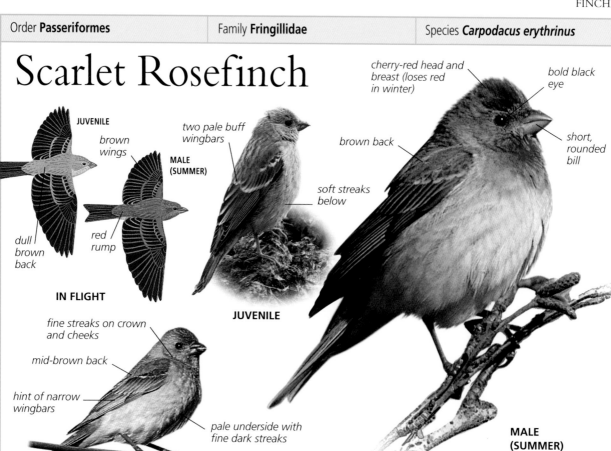

cherry-red head and breast (loses red in winter)

bold black eye

brown back

short, rounded bill

JUVENILE

brown wings

MALE (SUMMER)

two pale buff wingbars

soft streaks below

dull brown back

red rump

IN FLIGHT

JUVENILE

fine streaks on crown and cheeks

mid-brown back

hint of narrow wingbars

pale underside with fine dark streaks

FEMALE

MALE (SUMMER)

Several species of Rosefinches are widespread across Asia but only this one breeds in Europe. It is a bright, sturdy finch with a thick, bulky bill and small dark eyes in a plain face, giving a distinctive expression in all plumages. It has shown a tendency to spread westwards in recent years, with sporadic breeding even in Great Britain; singing males may turn up in early summer in unexpected places. This may or may not lead to long-term colonization; other species, such as the Serin, have shown a similar pattern without properly establishing themselves.

VOICE Short, ascending whistle, *vuee* or *tsoee*; song soft, rhythmic, whistling sequence.
NESTING Small neat grass nest low in bush; 4 or 5 eggs; 1 or 2 broods; May–July.
FEEDING Feeds on seeds, buds, shoots, and some insects, found in bushes or on ground.

FLIGHT: quite weak, soft; whirring wingbeats and slight undulations.

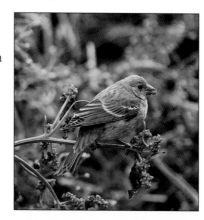

JUVENILE
The pale wingbars and dark, round eyes are conspicuous on this juvenile.

OCCURRENCE
Present from May to August from C Europe eastwards, north to Scandinavia, breeding in deciduous woodland and bushy places, often in wetland areas near lakes or rivers. In autumn, rare migrant on W European coasts.

Seen in the UK
J F M A M J J A S O N D

SIMILAR SPECIES

BULLFINCH ♂♀; see p.398

dark cap

grey back

grey cap

CHAFFINCH ♂♀; see p.388

white wingbars

CROSSBILL ♂♀; different habitat; see p.400

thicker bill

larger

Length **15cm (6in)**	Wingspan **22–26cm (9–10in)**	Weight **21–27g (¾–¹⁵⁄₁₆oz)**
Social **Small flocks**	Lifespan **2–3 years**	Lifespan **2–3 years**

Family **Emberizidae**

BUNTINGS

A BUNTING LOOKS MUCH like a finch: in general, buntings are a little slimmer and longer-tailed, and the structure of the bill is more constant, with a small upper mandible fitting neatly into a deeper, broader lower one that has a curiously curved cutting edge.

Most buntings have dark tails with white sides, but some, such as the Corn Bunting, have plainer tails. They show a variety of head patterns. Males are much like females in winter, with these patterns obscured by dull feather edges, but the dull colours crumble away in spring to reveal striking breeding plumage colours.

Females and juveniles, lacking these patterns, are more difficult to identify and some require care. Habitat, location, and time of year may be useful. Calls also help: several much rarer species visit western Europe in the autumn and look rather like Reed

PRE-ROOST GATHERING
Corn Buntings get together before flying to a roost in a thicket or reed-bed. Their flight calls often give them away.

Buntings, but a hard, sharp "tik" call concentrates attention, as the Reed Bunting does not have any corresponding call note. Songs are mostly brief, not especially musical, and repetitive, although some, such as the Yellowhammer's all-summer-long song phrase, have a particularly pleasing and evocative character. Most buntings are seed-eaters outside the breeding season and have suffered declines in areas where intensive modern farming has reduced the opportunities for birds to find weed seeds in winter. The Cirl Bunting has also declined with a lack of grasshoppers, which it feeds to its young in summer.

SPRING PERFECTION
This male Reed Bunting is at his best, having lost the dull feather fringes of winter. His plumage gradually turns paler in summer.

DRINKING POOL
Corn Buntings and other species often have a favourite pool where they drink.

| Order **Passeriformes** | Family **Emberizidae** | Species *Emberiza schoeniclus* |

Reed Bunting

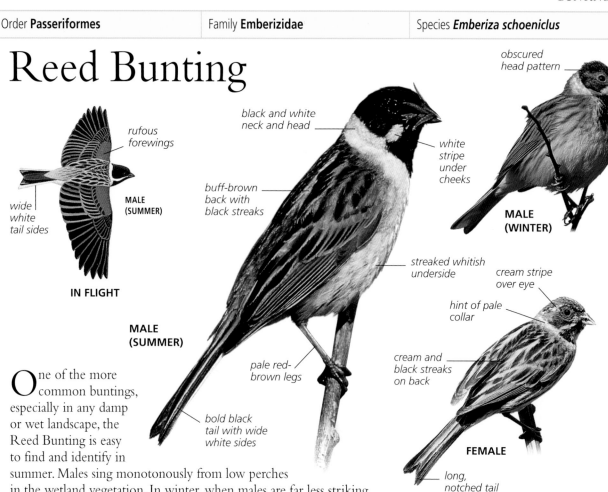

IN FLIGHT

rufous forewings

wide white tail sides

MALE (SUMMER)

black and white neck and head

white stripe under cheeks

buff-brown back with black streaks

streaked whitish underside

MALE (SUMMER)

pale red-brown legs

bold black tail with wide white sides

obscured head pattern

MALE (WINTER)

cream stripe over eye

hint of pale collar

cream and black streaks on back

FEMALE

long, notched tail

One of the more common buntings, especially in any damp or wet landscape, the Reed Bunting is easy to find and identify in summer. Males sing monotonously from low perches in the wetland vegetation. In winter, when males are far less striking, Reed Buntings are not so easily identified and also spread widely over all kinds of open ground and in thickets of willow, young conifers, and farmland hedgerows. They visit gardens at times.

VOICE Typical call quite full, loud, high *tseeu* or *psiu*, high, thin, pure *sweee*; *zi zi*; song short, stereotyped, simple, jangly phrase, two or three groups of notes clearly separated, *srip srip srip sea-sea-sea stitip-itip-itipip*.

NESTING Bulky nest of grass, sedge, and other stems, lined with roots and hair, on or close to ground in thick cover; 4 or 5 eggs; 2 broods; April–June.

FEEDING Mostly feeds on insects in summer, seeds at other times, taken low in bushes or on ground, often on open grass near water.

FLIGHT: slightly erratic, bounding, with flicking tail; dives into cover with flourish.

WINTER DRABNESS
Brown feather tips in winter obscure the male's head pattern. However, in spring, they wear away to reveal the full colours.

OCCURRENCE
Breeds in C and N Europe except for Iceland; seen in winter only in S Europe. Inhabits wet places with reeds, sedge, rushes, willow thickets, and fringes of lakes and rivers; also drier heathy slopes and heathland bogs. Sometimes visits gardens in winter, especially in hard weather.

Seen in the UK
J F M A M J J A S O N D

SIMILAR SPECIES

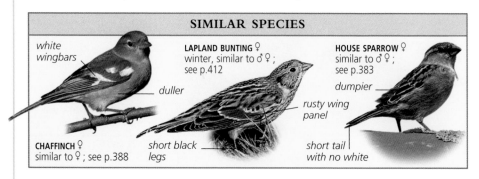

white wingbars

CHAFFINCH ♀
similar to ♀; see p.388

duller

LAPLAND BUNTING ♀
winter, similar to ♂♀;
see p.412

short black legs

rusty wing panel

HOUSE SPARROW ♀
similar to ♂♀;
see p.383

dumpier

short tail with no white

| Length **15cm (6in)** | Wingspan **21–26cm (8½–10in)** | Weight **15–22g (9/16–13/16oz)** |
| Social **Small flocks** | Lifespan **2–3 years** | Status **Secure** |

Order **Passeriformes**	Family **Emberizidae**	Species ***Emberiza pusilla***

Little Bunting

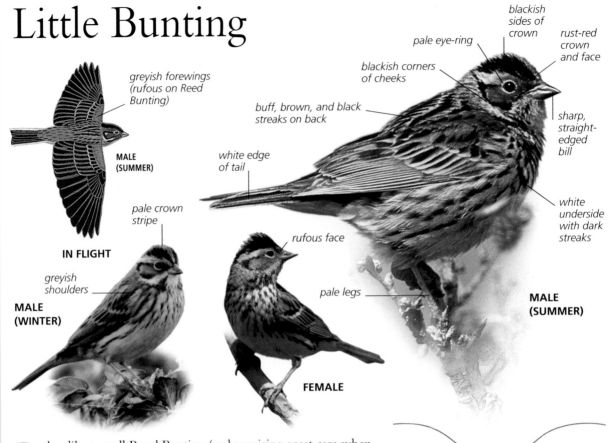

greyish forewings (rufous on Reed Bunting)

MALE (SUMMER)

IN FLIGHT

pale crown stripe

greyish shoulders

MALE (WINTER)

buff, brown, and black streaks on back

white edge of tail

rufous face

pale legs

FEMALE

blackish sides of crown

pale eye-ring

rust-red crown and face

blackish corners of cheeks

sharp, straight-edged bill

white underside with dark streaks

MALE (SUMMER)

Rather like a small Reed Bunting (and requiring great care when identifying migrants in autumn), the Little Bunting is a bird of the far north. It breeds in the vast taiga zone with mixed coniferous and birch forest. Rarely, one or two may winter in western Europe. It is, like many buntings, very much a ground bird most of the time, scuttling about on or very close to ground level even when disturbed. Generally rather quiet and unobtrusive, it is easy to overlook.

VOICE Call short, sharp, ticking *zik*; song short, high, mixed warble with clicking, rasping, and whistled notes.

NESTING Nest of grass and moss, in hollow on ground under bush; 4 or 5 eggs; 1 brood; May–June.

FEEDING Eats insects in summer; picks seeds from ground in autumn.

FLIGHT: quick, weak, light flitting action with flicked tail and short bursts of wingbeats.

SPRING MALE
The rufous colouring over the entire crown, face, and cheeks makes a summer adult eye-catching.

OCCURRENCE
Breeds in extreme NE Europe in open spaces in conifer forest. Autumn migrants rare on NW European coasts and islands, even rarer inland, often in damp places with weedy growth.

Seen in the UK
J F M A M J J A S O N D

SIMILAR SPECIES

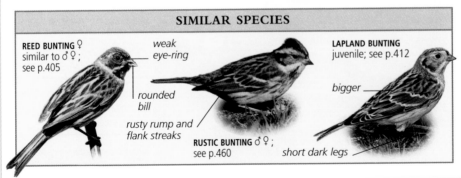

REED BUNTING ♀ similar to ♂♀; see p.405

weak eye-ring

rounded bill

rusty rump and flank streaks

RUSTIC BUNTING ♂♀; see p.460

LAPLAND BUNTING juvenile; see p.412

bigger

short dark legs

Length **12–13cm (4¾–5in)**	Wingspan **18–20cm (7–8in)**	Weight **15–18g (⁹⁄₁₆–⅝oz)**
Social **Small flocks**	Lifespan **2–3 years**	Status **Secure†**

| Order **Passeriformes** | Family **Emberizidae** | Species *Emberiza hortulana* |

Ortolan Bunting

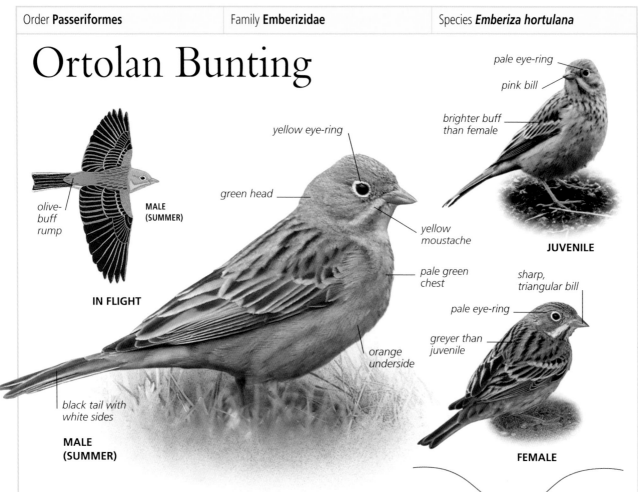

pale eye-ring

pink bill

brighter buff than female

JUVENILE

sharp, triangular bill

pale eye-ring

greyer than juvenile

FEMALE

yellow eye-ring

green head

yellow moustache

pale green chest

orange underside

IN FLIGHT

olive-buff rump

MALE (SUMMER)

black tail with white sides

MALE (SUMMER)

M ale Ortolans sing from bushes or trees on warm open slopes or in areas of upland pasture with hedges, walls, and copses. Their persistence makes up for a lack of real musical quality. Ortolan Buntings are also scarce but regular migrants in many coastal areas. They are usually quite shy and quick to fly off but tend to feed in open, grassy places where they can be watched from a distance. They are slim, pale buntings with sharp pink bills and obvious pale eye-rings.
VOICE Call thick, metallic, *dl-ip* and *chu*; song fluty, simple, ringing phrase, often repeated several times then changed to higher pitch, *sia sia sia si sia sru sru sru sru*.
NESTING Simple, hair-lined nest of grass and straw, on or near ground; 4–6 eggs; 2 or 3 broods; April–July.
FEEDING Eats insects in summer, and seeds from ground at other times, often from short grass clearings in dunes or fields.

FLIGHT: flitting, undulating, with bursts of relatively weak wingbeats; straighter over long distance with longer, shallow undulations.

STREAKY FEMALE
The general colour and pattern of the male are evident but subdued and faintly streaked on the female.

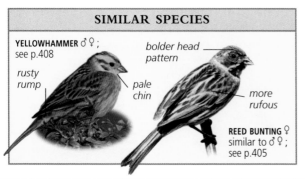

SIMILAR SPECIES

YELLOWHAMMER ♂♀; see p.408

rusty rump

bolder head pattern

pale chin

more rufous

REED BUNTING ♀ similar to ♂♀; see p.405

OCCURRENCE
Breeds across most of Europe except for UK, Iceland, and N Scandinavia, in variety of places from warm, bushy, stony slopes to semi-alpine pasture. Migrates to Africa in winter; rare on NW European coasts in spring and autumn.

| Seen in the UK |
| J F M **A M** J J **A S** O N D |

| Length **15–16cm (6–6½in)** | Wingspan **22–26cm (9–10in)** | Weight **21–27g (¾–15/16oz)** |
| Social **Small flocks** | Lifespan **2–3 years** | Status **Vulnerable†** |

Order **Passeriformes**	Family **Emberizidae**	Species ***Emberiza citrinella***

Yellowhammer 98

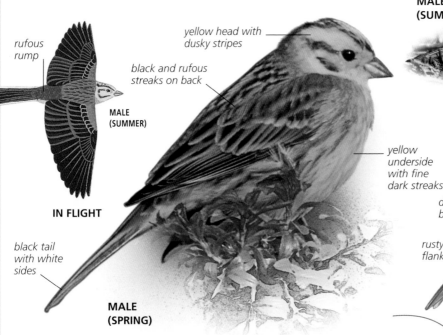

mixed rufous, buff, and black back

MALE (SUMMER)

rufous rump

yellow head with dusky stripes

black and rufous streaks on back

MALE (SUMMER)

IN FLIGHT

yellow underside with fine dark streaks

less yellow on head

pale cheek spot

darker back

more streaked below

rusty flanks

black tail with white sides

MALE (SPRING)

FEMALE

The common bunting of farmland and bushy heaths, the Yellowhammer is typical of warm, sunny days when the males sing non-stop. In winter, they gather in small groups, or mix with other buntings and finches, roaming weedy fields or ploughed land, searching for seeds. Small parties of Yellowhammers draw attention to themselves by their sharp calls. In flight, they show the typical long, white-edged black tail of buntings.

VOICE Call sharp, quick, metallic, spluttering *tsik, tzit,* or *twitik*; song sharp, thin, metallic trill with one or two longer, higher or lower notes at end, *ti-ti-ti-ti-ti-ti-ti-ti-teee-tyew*, or simpler quick trill.

NESTING Hair-lined nest of grass and straw on ground in base of bush or below bank; 3–5 eggs; 2 or 3 broods; April–July.

FEEDING Eats some insects in summer, otherwise mostly takes seeds from ground.

FLIGHT: undulating, quite fast; steep rise from ground when disturbed; bursts of wingbeats.

SINGING MALE
The Yellowhammer's sharp song is characteristic of warm summer days on gorsy heaths.

WINTER FLOCK
Seeds attract Yellowhammers in winter, and they feed in dense groups where they are still common.

OCCURRENCE
Breeds in most of Europe except for Iceland, N Scandinavia, S Spain, and S Portugal. Widespread in S and W Europe in winter. On upland pastures, heaths, farmland with hedges, and coastal grassland.

Seen in the UK
J F M A M J J A S O N D

SIMILAR SPECIES

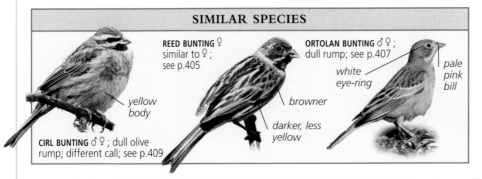

REED BUNTING ♀ similar to ♀; see p.405

ORTOLAN BUNTING ♂♀; dull rump; see p.407

yellow body

browner

darker, less yellow

white eye-ring

pale pink bill

CIRL BUNTING ♂♀; dull olive rump; different call; see p.409

Length **16cm (6½in)**	Wingspan **23–29cm (9–11½in)**	Weight **24–30g (⅞–1¹/₁₆oz)**
Social **Flocks**	Lifespan **2–3 years**	Status **Secure†**

| Order **Passeriformes** | Family **Emberizidae** | Species *Emberiza cirlus* |

Cirl Bunting

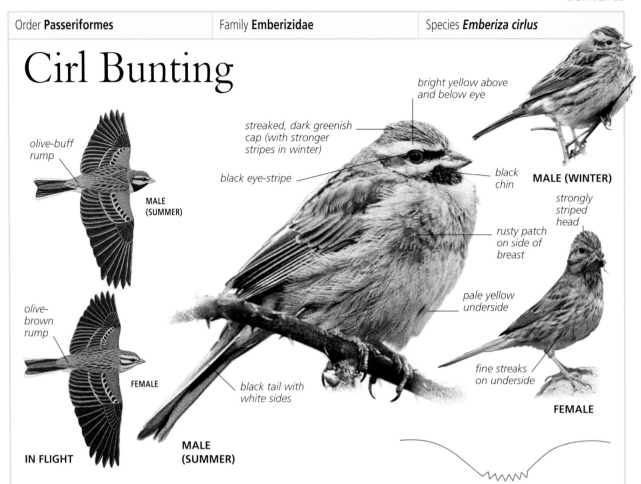

olive-buff rump

MALE (SUMMER)

olive-brown rump

FEMALE

IN FLIGHT

streaked, dark greenish cap (with stronger stripes in winter)

bright yellow above and below eye

black eye-stripe

black chin

MALE (WINTER)

rusty patch on side of breast

strongly striped head

pale yellow underside

fine streaks on underside

FEMALE

black tail with white sides

MALE (SUMMER)

With a song that recalls both Yellowhammer and Bonelli's Warbler (see p.341), the Cirl Bunting is a common bird of open, bushy slopes and well-treed farmland with hedges and thickets. It needs old, unimproved grassland, especially with a great many grasshoppers, so is suffering in the face of agricultural intensification. Males sing from bush tops but also from inconspicuous perches part way up trees, quite difficult to spot and likely to sit quite still for minutes on end.

VOICE Call very simple, short, high, thin *sip*; song fast, rattling trill on one note, or slower, lighter, more bubbling variant, *t-r-r-r-r-r-r-r-r-r-r* or *ti-ti-ti-ti-ti-ti-ti-ti-ti-ti-ti*.

NESTING Rough nest of grass and stalks, low in shrub or hedge; 3 or 4 eggs; 2 broods; April–July.

FEEDING Needs to eat grasshoppers and similar insects in summer; otherwise takes seeds from ground.

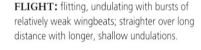

FLIGHT: flitting, undulating with bursts of relatively weak wingbeats; straighter over long distance with longer, shallow undulations.

FEMALE BIRD
The female Cirl Bunting has a strongly striped pale yellow and blackish head. The wings have rusty patches and the breast is pale yellowish.

SIMILAR SPECIES

YELLOWHAMMER ♂♀; rusty rump; see p.408

pale chin

REED BUNTING ♀ similar to ♂♀; see p.405

bolder head pattern

more rufous

OCCURRENCE
Breeds in extreme SW England, France, Spain, Portugal, and east to Balkans. Found all year on warm, bushy, often stony slopes, around tall, leafy orchard edges, and in olive groves. In winter, in weedy or grassy fields and gardens.

| Seen in the UK |
| J F M A M J J A S O N D |

| Length **15–16cm (6–6½in)** | Wingspan **22–26cm (9–10in)** | Weight **21–27g (¾–¹⁵/₁₆oz)** |
| Social **Small flocks** | Lifespan **2–3 years** | Status **Secure** |

Order **Passeriformes**	Family **Emberizidae**	Species *Emberiza cia*

Rock Bunting

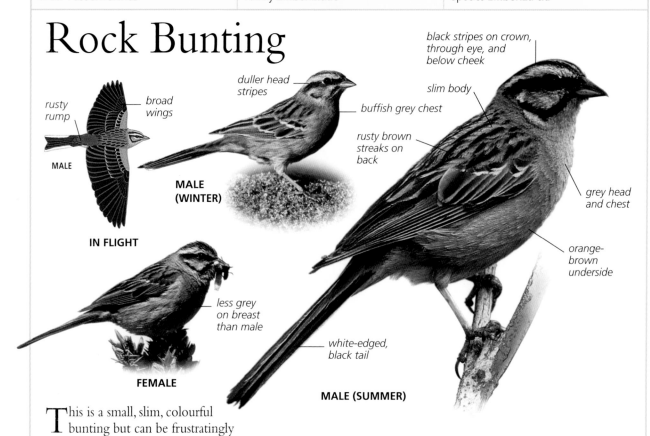

rusty rump · broad wings

MALE

IN FLIGHT

duller head stripes

MALE (WINTER)

black stripes on crown, through eye, and below cheek

slim body

buffish grey chest

rusty brown streaks on back

grey head and chest

orange-brown underside

less grey on breast than male

FEMALE

white-edged, black tail

MALE (SUMMER)

This is a small, slim, colourful bunting but can be frustratingly difficult to see. It tends to sit somewhere on a stony slope, often among thick bushes, calling frequently with a short, very thin, high note that is hard to pinpoint. In winter, it gathers in small flocks, often in grassy or weedy fields. It may be seen foraging beside roads in stony cuttings, or around archaeological sites with plenty of fallen stones and rough grass.

VOICE Call very thin, short, high *sip*, monotonous and elusive; song high, clear, erratic warbling phrase.
NESTING Nest of grass, roots, and bark on ground in thick cover; 4–6 eggs; 2 broods; April–June.
FEEDING Feeds on insects in summer; takes seeds from or near ground at other times.

FLIGHT: quite slow, low, erratic, with bursts of wingbeats; also flitting between bushes.

GROUND FEEDER
Rock Buntings feed on grassy clearings, among low rocks and shrubs, around tumbled boulders, and often along roadside cuttings.

OCCURRENCE
Breeds throughout Spain and Portugal, in Mediterranean region, and locally in Alps and C Europe. In rocky areas with dry, bushy slopes and crags and boulders, in alpine meadows and grassy places alongside road cuttings. Seen all year in majority of range.

Seen in the UK
J F M A M J J A S O N D

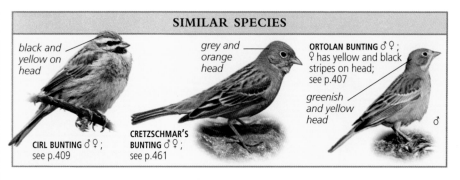

SIMILAR SPECIES

black and yellow on head

CIRL BUNTING ♂♀; see p.409

grey and orange head

CRETZSCHMAR'S BUNTING ♂♀; see p.461

ORTOLAN BUNTING ♂♀; ♀ has yellow and black stripes on head; see p.407

greenish and yellow head

♂

Length **15cm (6in)**	Wingspan **22–26cm (9–10in)**	Weight **21–27g (3/4 – 15/16 oz)**
Social **Small flocks**	Lifespan **2–3 years**	Status **Vulnerable**

Order **Passeriformes**	Family **Emberizidae**	Species *Plectrophenax nivalis*

Snow Bunting

small white wing patch

IMMATURE

black tail with white sides

dark grey head and back

white wings

MALE (WINTER)

black wingtips

IN FLIGHT

white head

black back and wingtips

white below

MALE (SUMMER)

stocky body with short legs

red- or orange-brown cap and cheeks

JUVENILE

dark-tipped yellow bill

sandy brown back

red-brown breast sides

MALE (WINTER)

white underside

short black legs

brown cap

black and brown streaks on back (plumage greyer in summer)

FEMALE (WINTER)

In summer, Snow Buntings are in the far north or on the highest peaks, usually where snow is still present. In winter, they roam widely over high ground, from ski resorts to barren, exposed mountainsides, but are more easily seen where they winter on the coast. Flocks prefer shingle banks and sheltered, muddy or gravelly marshes just inland of the beach, sometimes mixed with other buntings, finches, and larks. Their complex face and chest patterns may be confusing but the extensive white areas seen when they fly are good clues.

VOICE Loud call deep, clear *pyew* or *tsioo*, frequent lighter, trilling, rippling *tiri-lil-il-il-il-ip*; song short, clear, ringing phrase.
NESTING Nest of moss, lichen, and grass stems in cavity among rocks; 4–6 eggs; 1 or 2 broods; May–July.
FEEDING Takes insects in summer, mainly seeds and strandline invertebrates on beaches in winter.

FLIGHT: bouncy, erratic, as if swept by wind, with flurries of wingbeats and deep undulations; long wings.

ATTRACTED BY SEEDS
Snow Buntings can be attracted to patches of seeds scattered on the ground at the edge of a shingle beach in winter.

SIMILAR SPECIES

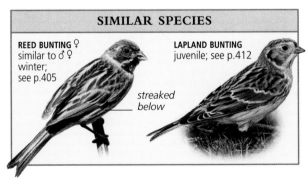

REED BUNTING ♀
similar to ♂♀ winter;
see p.405

LAPLAND BUNTING
juvenile; see p.412

streaked below

OCCURRENCE
Breeds very locally in N Scotland, Iceland, and N Scandinavia, on tundra or similar mountain top habitat. In winter, on coasts in S to N France and inland E Europe, at fringes of breeding range.

Seen in the UK
J F M A M J J A S O N D

Length **16–17cm (6½in)**	Wingspan **32–38cm (12½–15in)**	Weight **30–40g (1 1/16–1 7/16 oz)**
Social **Flocks**	Lifespan **2–3 years**	Status **Secure†**

| Order **Passeriformes** | Family **Emberizidae** | Species *Calcarius lapponicus* |

Lapland Bunting

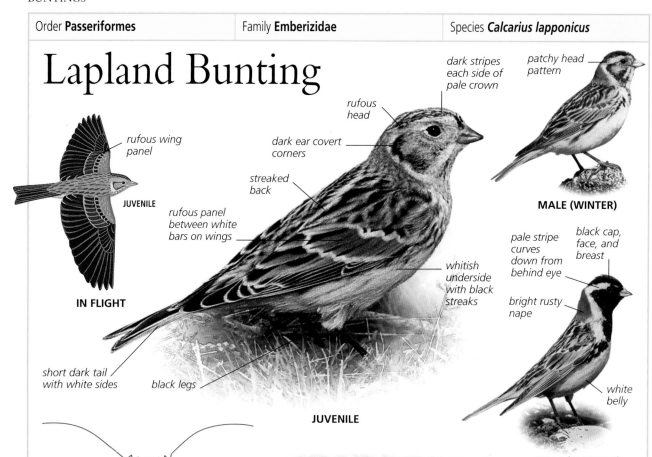

rufous wing panel

JUVENILE

rufous panel between white bars on wings

IN FLIGHT

short dark tail with white sides

black legs

dark stripes each side of pale crown

rufous head

dark ear covert corners

streaked back

whitish underside with black streaks

JUVENILE

patchy head pattern

MALE (WINTER)

pale stripe curves down from behind eye

black cap, face, and breast

bright rusty nape

white belly

MALE (SUMMER)

FLIGHT: quite direct, shallow undulations; bursts of fast wingbeats between glides.

In summer, a bird of remote, wild places, the Lapland Bunting is more familiar as a winter bird or autumn migrant. It appears near the coast, on grassy places such as golf courses, in dunes, and around grassier parts of salt marshes. It tends to creep inconspicuously until flushed from almost underfoot, or is noticed flying overhead with its distinctive calls. Its plumage patterns are superficially like those of a Reed Bunting, although more complex and richly marked, but its shape and actions recall a Snow Bunting.

VOICE Calls typically hard, quick, staccato rattle and clear whistle, *t-r-r-r-r-ik teu* or *tikikikiktik teu*; song in flight like short bursts of Skylark's song.

NESTING Nest of moss, lichens, and grass on ground, in hollow in tussock, or among rocks; 5 or 6 eggs; 1 brood; May–June.

FEEDING Shuffles on ground, finding seeds; feeds on insects in summer.

HARD TO SEE
This female Lapland Bunting, feeding among long grassy vegetation at the edge of coastal salt marshes, is hard to spot.

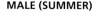

OCCURRENCE
Breeds in N Scandinavia, in tundra and high plateaux. In winter, mostly on salt marsh and short, wet grassland close to coasts, around North Sea and Baltic. Quite rare inland.

| Seen in the UK |
| J F M A M J J A S O N D |

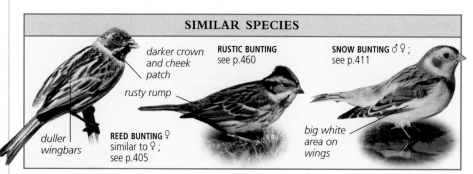

SIMILAR SPECIES

darker crown and cheek patch

rusty rump

duller wingbars

REED BUNTING ♀ similar to ♀; see p.405

RUSTIC BUNTING see p.460

SNOW BUNTING ♂♀; see p.411

big white area on wings

| Length **14–15cm (5½–6in)** | Wingspan **25–28cm (10–11in)** | Weight **20–30g ($^{11}/_{16}$–1$^{1}/_{16}$oz)** |
| Social **Small flocks** | Lifespan **2–3 years** | Status **Secure†** |

Order **Passeriformes**	Family **Emberiza**	Species ***Emberiza calandra***

Corn Bunting 🔊 99

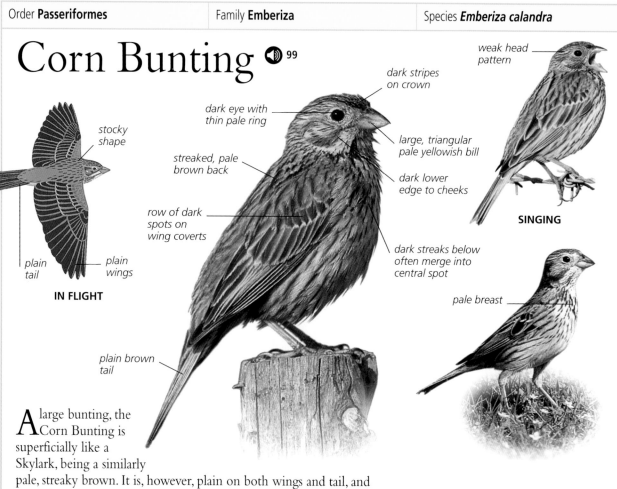

weak head pattern

SINGING

dark stripes on crown

dark eye with thin pale ring

streaked, pale brown back

large, triangular pale yellowish bill

dark lower edge to cheeks

row of dark spots on wing coverts

dark streaks below often merge into central spot

pale breast

stocky shape

plain tail

plain wings

IN FLIGHT

plain brown tail

A large bunting, the Corn Bunting is superficially like a Skylark, being a similarly pale, streaky brown. It is, however, plain on both wings and tail, and it perches on wires, fence posts, clumps of earth, or bushes, singing a short, simple phrase repeated with little variation. It feeds on the ground like other buntings, hopping and creeping rather than walking like a lark. It can often be seen flying over in small groups, calling distinctively, towards dusk, heading for communal roosts which may be scores or even hundreds strong.

VOICE Call short, abrupt, clicking *plip* or *quit*; song jangling, dry, fast rattled phrase like rattled keys or broken glass, *ti-ti-ti-tchee-irirrirr*.

NESTING Nest of grass and roots, lined with finer material, on ground; 3–5 eggs; 1 or 2 broods; April–June.

FEEDING Picks insects and seeds in summer, seeds in winter, from ground.

FLIGHT: long undulations; powerful bouts of wingbeats between looping glides with closed wings; in display, sometimes flies off with legs lowered.

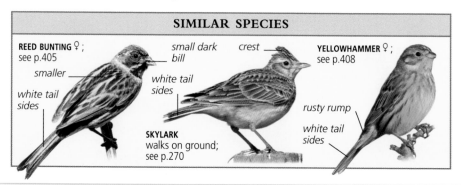

WINTER FLOCKS
Where they remain common, Corn Buntings feed in small groups or even larger flocks in winter, resorting to hedges when disturbed.

OCCURRENCE
Breeds locally in UK, across Europe north to Baltic, most commonly in S Europe. Around meadows, cereal prairies, and farmland with hedges and scattered trees. Present all year except in E Europe, where summer visitor only but declining in many areas.

Seen in the UK
J F M A M J J A S O N D

SIMILAR SPECIES

REED BUNTING ♀; see p.405

smaller

white tail sides

small dark bill

crest

white tail sides

SKYLARK walks on ground; see p.270

YELLOWHAMMER ♀; see p.408

rusty rump

white tail sides

Length **18cm (7in)**	Wingspan **26–32cm (10–12½in)**	Weight **38–55g (1⅜–2oz)**
Social **Small flocks**	Lifespan **2–3 years**	Status **Secure†**

RARE SPECIES

Europe has a remarkably wide variety of habitats and extends over a huge geographical spread from the Arctic to the Mediterranean, from the Atlantic to the Black Sea. There are regular European species that breed only in very small areas of this range (for example, the Pied Wheatear along the Black Sea shores), or appear only as migrants in small parts of the continent (for instance, the Great Shearwater that regularly sweeps past the southwest of Ireland on its oceanic migrations). These are, nevertheless, seen every year in the right areas. Some, for example, Mediterranean Shearwaters that are numerous in the Mediterranean in summer, but rare elsewhere, are relatively numerous. Others, with abbreviated treatment here, such as the Pied-billed Grebe from North America, are really rarities, properly belonging to the avifauna of other continents. A few individuals stray far from their breeding range to turn up in Europe, some species every year, others not so regularly. They are always, however, recorded in very small numbers.

The birds on the following pages include some that are rare everywhere in Europe and always unpredictable, most of which one cannot really plan to see, and others that are rare or restricted in range, but easily seen if one visits the right place at the right time of year.

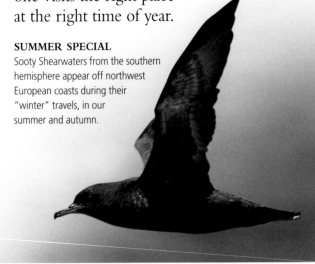

SUMMER SPECIAL
Sooty Shearwaters from the southern hemisphere appear off northwest European coasts during their "winter" travels, in our summer and autumn.

Family **Gaviidae**	Species **Gavia adamsii**

White-billed Diver

If anything, this massive diver is even bigger than a Great Northern Diver (see p.58), similarly chequered in summer but with an uptilted, yellowish white bill. The bill lacks a complete dark ridge and tip in winter, when the sides of the face are also paler than a Great Northern Diver's. In flight, its heavy head and longer feet are sometimes noticeable.

OCCURRENCE Rare in summer in Arctic Europe; in winter, very few south into North Sea.

VOICE Silent in winter; loud wailing and laughing notes in summer.

uptilted, yellowish white bill

WINTER

pale cheeks

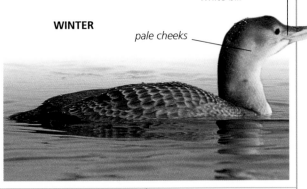

Length **80–90cm (32–35in)**	Wingspan **1.35–1.5m (4½–5ft)**

Family **Podicipedidae**	Species **Podilymbus podiceps**

Pied-billed Grebe

This stocky, big-headed grebe is like a large Little Grebe (see p.59) with a much stouter bill, which is plain yellowish in winter, but uniquely white with a black band in summer. In summer, it also has a black throat. Juveniles have dark head stripes. Rare visitors from North America may remain for some weeks on a suitable lake or reservoir. They tend to keep quite close to well-vegetated shores.

OCCURRENCE Rare in W Europe in autumn/winter, from Americas.

VOICE Silent when not breeding.

stout white bill with black band

ADULT (SUMMER)

black throat

Length **31–38cm (12–15in)**	Wingspan **50cm (20in)**

Family **Procellariidae**	Species *Puffinus gravis*

Great Shearwater

Breeding in the southern oceans and migrating north in the northern summer and autumn, the Great Shearwater is a master of its challenging marine environment. It banks steeply and often to a great height, gliding at speed with few flaps. Its dark brown cap looks black at a distance, and the brown back, narrow white collar, white over the tail, and dark patches under the wing all aid identification.

OCCURRENCE Rare to moderately common well out at sea off W Europe, from August to October.

VOICE Silent.

brown back

dark brown cap

narrow white collar

Length **43–51cm (17–20in)**	Wingspan **1.05–1.22m (3½–4ft)**

Family **Procellariidae**	Species *Puffinus assimilis*

Little Shearwater

The Little Shearwater is like a small, slightly dumpy Manx Shearwater (see p.67), often with a paler grey inner wing/black outer wing contrast and with more extensive white on its face quite easy to see at moderate range. It must nevertheless be watched with care in order to prove its identity, especially outside its normal range. It flies with rather fast wingbeats and few, short glides.

OCCURRENCE Breeds in Azores, Madeira, and Canaries; rare off NW Europe, in summer and autumn.

VOICE Rhythmic laughing notes at colony at night.

dark upperparts

extensive white on face

Length **25–30cm (10–12in)**	Wingspan **58–67cm (23–26in)**

Family **Procellariidae**	Species *Puffinus yelkouan*

Mediterranean Shearwater

Mediterranean "Manx" shearwaters are now separated as a full species or even split into two species. East Mediterranean birds (Yelkouan) are like small, more flappy Manx Shearwaters with feet projecting slightly beyond the tail, while the western ones (Balearic) are browner both above and below, but paler and smaller than Sooty Shearwaters. These birds may be seen on or low over the sea off Mediterranean shores in summer.

OCCURRENCE Breeds in coast and islands in Mediterranean; a few north to North Sea.

VOICE Strangled, yodelling notes over colonies at night.

 brownish above

Length **34–39cm (13½–15½in)**	Wingspan **78–90cm (31–35in)**

Family **Procellariidae**	Species *Puffinus griseus*

Sooty Shearwater

One of the southern ocean seabirds that migrates north in the European summer, the Sooty Shearwater is regularly seen off some headlands and ferry routes in West European seas. It is slightly pot-bellied, with long, narrow, angular wings, and appears all dark except for a variably pale underwing panel that typically looks like a soft, silvery white central patch. The Sooty Shearwater is quite noticeably larger than a Manx Shearwater (see p.67) when they are seen together, and can resemble a dark skua at times.

OCCURRENCE Biscay, Irish and British coasts, from August to October.

VOICE Silent.

all-dark appearance

Length **40–50cm (16–20in)**	Wingspan **0.95–1.1m (3–3½ft)**

Family **Procellariidae**	Species **Oceanites oceanicus**

Wilson's Storm-petrel

Abundant in Antarctic seas, Wilson's Storm-petrels rarely stray north of the equator. They remain well out at sea, sometimes with Storm Petrels (see p.68), feeding on floating offal and sometimes approaching fishing vessels or following ships. The white rump is very broad, the upperwing has a pale band but the underwing is all-dark. The long wings and legs give a particularly buoyant action.

OCCURRENCE Very rare off NW Europe in late summer.

VOICE Silent.

long legs

Length **16–18cm (6½–7in)**	Wingspan **38–42cm (15–16½in)**

Family **Procellariidae**	Species **Oceanodroma castro**

Madeiran Storm-petrel

Very like Leach's Petrel (see p.69), the Madeiran Storm-petrel is distinguished with difficulty by its broader white rump, extending well around the sides, and less forked tail. It is an entirely marine bird except when visiting nesting colonies at night; it is rather solitary at sea and does not follow ships. It breeds in burrows and crevices on rocky islands.

OCCURRENCE Breeds off Portugal and in Madeira; rare at sea north of this range.

VOICE Cooing purrs and squeaky notes from burrow at night.

pale band on inner wings

Length **19–21cm (7½–8½in)**	Wingspan **43–46cm (17–18in)**

Family **Pelecanidae**	Species **Pelecanus onocrotalus**

White Pelican

Huge and contrasted black and white, the White Pelican is rose-pink in summer (the juvenile is duller). It has an orange-yellow bill pouch and a dark eye in a patch of pink. Overhead it shows black trailing edges and tips to the wings, like a White Stork (see p.85), but it lacks the stork's long legs and slender neck. Flocks circle and soar in a more coordinated fashion than storks.

OCCURRENCE Breeds in Balkans and E Europe, on large lakes and marshes.

VOICE Various grunts at nest.

dark eye in pink area

orange-yellow bill pouch

black under-wings

ADULT

Length **1.4–1.75m (4½–5¾ft)**	Wingspan **2.45–2.95m (8–9¾ft)**

Family **Pelecanidae**	Species **Pelecanus crispus**

Dalmatian Pelican

Globally rare and endangered, the Dalmatian Pelican is one of the world's largest birds. Its obvious pelican form, greyish head and body, reddish bill pouch in summer, and dull wings (with no sharp black and white contrast) identify it. Close views reveal a pale eye in a whitish area (dark on pink on the White Pelican). In flight, it is a magnificent sight, soaring effortlessly in warm air.

OCCURRENCE Breeds in Greece and Danube Delta, on large reedy lakes and swamps.

VOICE Silent.

ADULT

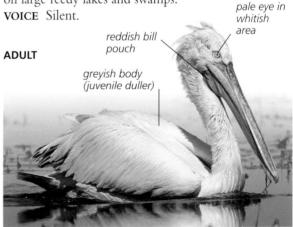

pale eye in whitish area

reddish bill pouch

greyish body (juvenile duller)

Length **1.6–1.8m (5¼–6ft)**	Wingspan **2.7–3.2m (8¾–10ft)**

Family **Phalacrocoracidae**	Species *Phalacrocorax pygmeus*

Pygmy Cormorant

A typical cormorant, the Pygmy Cormorant is nevertheless stocky, round-headed, short-billed, and thick-necked. Close views reveal a brown head and neck; in winter the throat is pale and the head less brown. The juvenile is paler below. When perched, or in flight, a rather long and rounded tail is evident. Groups often swim amongst vegetation or perch in overhanging trees or reeds, sometimes visiting coasts in winter.
OCCURRENCE Balkans and Black Sea coasts, on rivers and deltas.
VOICE Croaks and grunts at colonies.

long, rounded tail

ADULT (SUMMER)

Length **45–55cm (18–22in)**	Wingspan **75–90cm (30–35in)**

Family **Ardeidae**	Species *Egretta gularis*

Western Reef Egret

Like a thick-billed Little Egret (see p.80), the Western Reef Egret is typically dark grey with a white chin in West Africa, but white with pale grey or dark irregular marks in the Red Sea. Its legs are dull and brownish, the bill brown or blackish, with a yellower base. It is generally seen on the coast (but Little Egrets also frequent rocky shores), and often on piers and quays and associated structures.
OCCURRENCE Sinai and Red Sea; very rare in Morocco.
VOICE Silent.

white chin

dark grey body

Length **55–68cm (22–27in)**	Wingspan **88–112cm (35–44in)**

Family **Threskiornithidae**	Species *Plegadis falcinellus*

Glossy Ibis

Extremely slender but round-winged in flight, and elegant, round-bodied, but long-necked on the ground, the Glossy Ibis looks almost black unless seen closely in good light. Then it shows reflections of bronze and deep coppery red. Its slim, downcurved bill is distinctive as it wades and probes for food at the water's edge. Flocks tend to fly in wavy lines.
OCCURRENCE Rare in S Europe; more in Balkans and Middle East.
VOICE Mostly silent.

coppery red and bronze body

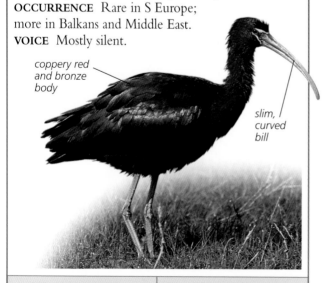

slim, curved bill

Length **55–65cm (22–26in)**	Wingspan **88–105cm (35–41in)**

Family **Anatidae**	Species *Anser caerulescens*

Snow Goose

Appearing especially brilliant white, even in the company of swans, the Snow Goose has a grey patch adjacent to bold black wingtips, a thick reddish bill, and deep pink legs. Some are grey-brown, bluer on the wings, with a white head, sometimes called "blue geese". Hybrid Canada x Greylag Geese are much bigger but may have a similar pattern, and "farmyard" white geese occasionally fly free.
OCCURRENCE Rare visitor to NW Europe from N America, or escapee.
VOICE Soft, rising, cackling notes.

ADULT

reddish bill

brilliant white body (juvenile duller and greyer)

black wingtips

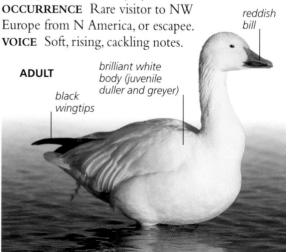

Length **65–75cm (26–30in)**	Wingspan **1.33–1.56m (4¼–5ft)**

| Family **Anatidae** | Species *Anser erythropus* |

Lesser White-fronted Goose

Now extremely rare, numbers of this goose are being boosted by birds "fostered" under other geese, blurring the true wild pattern. In a winter goose flock, its faster action, long wingtips, neat round head, and very short, shocking-pink bill help to identify it; other useful features are the bold white blaze over the crown and bright yellow eye-ring. Juveniles lack the white blaze.

large white forehead blaze

OCCURRENCE Very rare breeder in N Scandinavia; rare in W Europe in winter.
VOICE High, quick, yelping notes.

ADULT

long wingtips

| Length **56–66cm (22–26in)** | Wingspan **1.15–1.35m (3¾–4½ft)** |

| Family **Anatidae** | Species *Branta ruficollis* |

Red-breasted Goose

Uniquely patterned black, white, and deep red, the Red-breasted Goose is an easy bird to identify but is sometimes surprisingly difficult to spot in a dense flock of slightly larger Brent or Barnacle Geese (see pp.99, 98). Strong sunlight makes even White-fronted Geese (see p.93) very contrasty, and the Red-breasted can be hard to find among them.

white spot on face

OCCURRENCE Large flocks in winter around Black Sea; very rare in W Europe.
VOICE Loud, sharp, double *pik-wik*.

ADULT

striking black, white, and red plumage

| Length **54–60cm (21½–23½in)** | Wingspan **1.1–1.25m (3½–4ft)** |

| Family **Anatidae** | Species *Tadorna ferruginea* |

Ruddy Shelduck

Clearly a shelduck in shape and actions, the Ruddy Shelduck is instantly identifiable by its mostly rich rust-orange plumage. The males have a pale head and narrow black collar; females have whiter faces. In flight, the forewing is strikingly white. Other shelduck species that may escape from collections look similar but differ in head and neck details. Periodic appearances of Ruddy Shelducks in the UK in late summer may involve truly wild birds.

OCCURRENCE Rare in E Greece and Turkey; vagrant in W Europe.
VOICE Nasal honking calls.

pale face

MALE

rust-orange body

narrow black collar

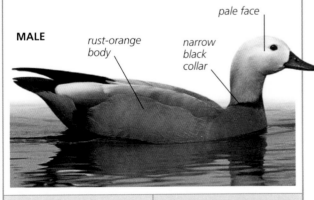

| Length **58–70cm (23–28in)** | Wingspan **1.1–1.35m (3½–4½ft)** |

| Family **Anatidae** | Species *Alopochen aegyptiaca* |

Egyptian Goose

Introduced as an ornamental bird to England, the Egyptian Goose has established itself in the wild but not spread far beyond eastern England. It looks a little like a pale brown Shelduck (see p.100), with a short pink bill, a brown eye patch, and big white wing patches. Some look quite rufous, others greyer.

brown eye patch

OCCURRENCE E England; occasional wanderers elsewhere.
VOICE Loud, raucous, staccato cackling.

ADULT

large white wing patch

long pink legs

| Length **63–73cm (25–29in)** | Wingspan **1.1–1.3m (3½–4¼ft)** |

| Family **Anatidae** | Species **Aix galericulata** |

Mandarin

Suitably exotic-looking for a duck of Southeast Asian origin, the Mandarin has been introduced into south Great Britain. Drakes have bushy orange "whiskers" and triangular orange "sails" on the back, and a black chest; females are dark grey-brown, mottled paler on the sides, with fine white "spectacles". They often perch in trees near freshwater lakes and rivers.

OCCURRENCE Locally in Great Britain, around wood-fringed lakes and slow rivers.

VOICE Short, rising whistling note.

orange "sails"

bushy orange whiskers

white on head

MALE

| Length **41–49cm (16–19½in)** | Wingspan **65–75cm (26–30in)** |

| Family **Anatidae** | Species **Aix sponsa** |

Wood Duck

Rather like the Mandarin, the Wood Duck has escaped into the wild but is far less well-established. Males have a long, dark, drooped crest, bold white face marks, and a white band between the dark chest and orange flanks; females look like female Mandarins but with a dark-tipped (not pale-tipped) bill and shorter and broader "spectacles".

OCCURRENCE Very rare in Iceland, from North America; scattered escapees in UK.

VOICE Mostly silent.

dark, drooping crest

MALE pale orange flanks

| Length **43–51cm (17–20in)** | Wingspan **68–78cm (27–31in)** |

| Family **Anatidae** | Species **Anas rubripes** |

Black Duck

Clearly related to the Mallard (see p.101), the Black Duck is like a plainer, darker female Mallard with a contrasted pale head, blue hindwing patches lacking the white edges shown by a Mallard, and a bold white underwing that is viewed when flying or flapping its wings. The bill is greenish yellow and the legs rich orange. Various farmyard Mallard derivatives may look superficially similar.

OCCURRENCE Rare vagrant from North America in NW Europe.

VOICE Mallard-like quacks.

pale bill

plain dark wings

dark overall

ADULT

| Length **53–61cm (21–24in)** | Wingspan **80–90cm (32–35in)** |

| Family **Anatidae** | Species **Anas americana** |

American Wigeon

Bearing an obvious resemblance to the European Wigeon (see p.105), the male American Wigeon is moderately easy to identify by the white forehead and broad dark green band across a pale, speckled face and a dusky pinkish body. Females, however, are very difficult, but a contrasted greyer head and dark eye patch sometimes help in identification; white "wingpits" are diagnostic if seen clearly.

OCCURRENCE Regular but rare visitor from North America to W Europe, in autumn/winter.

VOICE Drake has Wigeon-like whistle.

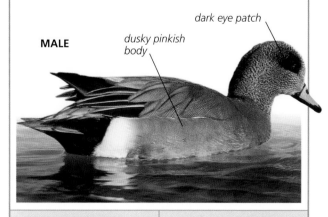

dark eye patch

MALE dusky pinkish body

| Length **48–56cm (19–22in)** | Wingspan **75–85cm (30–34in)** |

Family **Anatidae**	Species ***Anas discors***

Blue-winged Teal

This small, long-billed surface-feeding duck is usually seen in immature plumage which is dark, mottled, and Teal-like (see p.106), with a broken pale line over the eye and whitish spot near the bill, pale blue forewings, and yellowish legs. Males have a bold, vertical white blaze on the face and bright blue on the wings; females are duller. The face pattern is echoed by summer male Shovelers (see p.104), a species with which Blue-winged Teals at times associate. Occasionally one may remain for some time on a suitable lake in Europe.

OCCURRENCE Rare autumn/winter vagrant from North America.

VOICE Mostly silent.

vertical white blaze on face

MALE

dark, mottled body

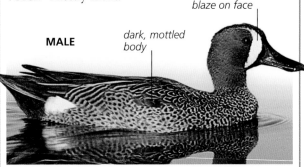

Length **37–41cm (14½–16in)**	Wingspan **55–65cm (22–26in)**

Family **Anatidae**	Species ***Marmaronetta angustirostris***

Marbled Duck

Rare and local, the Marbled Duck is a pale, mottled grey-brown bird with a distinctive dark mask running into a slight tuft on the nape. The bill looks dark, the tail and rear end of the bird pale. In flight, the wings show little pattern except for darker tips and an almost-white trailing edge. Pale spots on the flanks are distinctive if seen at close range. Most Marbled Ducks found in NW Europe are suspected to be escaped birds from collections.

OCCURRENCE Very rare, in S Spain, Morocco, and Turkey.

VOICE Silent.

dark mask

slight tuft at nape

ADULT pale spots on flanks

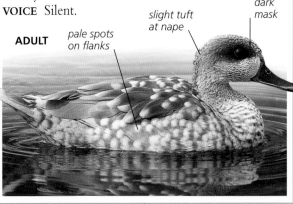

Length **39–42cm (15½–16½in)**	Wingspan **63–70cm (25–28in)**

Family **Anatidae**	Species ***Aythya nyroca***

Ferruginous Duck

A fast-declining bird, the Ferruginous Duck is a sleek, rich mahogany-red diving duck, with broad, dazzling white wing stripes. Drakes have white eyes and dark grey bills fading to whitish before a black tip. Females are duller and brown-eyed. All have a pure white patch under the tail and peaked heads. Hybrid diving ducks may look very similar and require close attention to features such as eye and bill colours.

OCCURRENCE Declining breeder in C and E Europe; rare visitor in NW Europe.

VOICE Quiet; occasional purring growls.

dark grey bill with black tip

white eye

white patch under tail

MALE

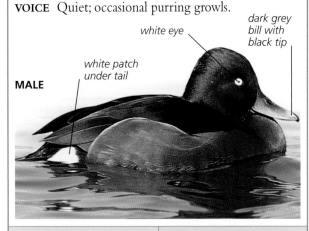

Length **38–42cm (15–16½in)**	Wingspan **60–67cm (23–26½in)**

Family **Anatidae**	Species ***Aythya collaris***

Ring-necked Duck

This is a close relative of the Tufted Duck (see p.108), identified by a more pointed head shape with no tuft, and grey wingbars. Drakes have grey flanks with a white "peak" at the front, brown females a Pochard-like (see p.110) pale face and white "spectacle". Hybrid ducks with similar patterns cause identification problems. A whitish ring behind the black bill tip is the sign of a true Ring-necked Duck.

OCCURRENCE Very rare but regular vagrant from North America to W Europe.

VOICE Low growling notes.

whitish ring behind black bill tip

pointed head

white "peak" on grey flanks

MALE

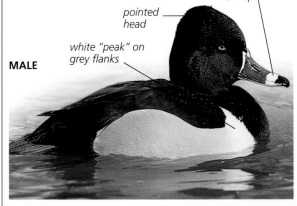

Length **37–46cm (14½–18in)**	Wingspan **65–75cm (26–30in)**

Family **Anatidae**	Species **Aythya affinis**

Lesser Scaup

A black-fronted, pale-bodied diving duck (resembling Tufted Duck and Scaup, see pp.108, 109), this rare bird has a rounded head with a very slight bump on the nape but no tuft. Its bill is pale blue-grey with a tiny black tip. The back is quite coarsely marked with wavy grey bands (greyer and more thickly marked than Scaup). The white flanks are sullied with pale grey, and faintly barred, unlike the pure white of an adult Scaup. Females are like female Scaup with a peaked nape.

OCCURRENCE Very rare vagrant to W Europe in autumn/winter, from N America.

VOICE Mostly silent.

blue-grey bill with small black tip

small bump on nape

wavy grey bands on back

MALE

Length **38–45cm (15–18in)**	Wingspan **70cm (28in)**

Family **Anatidae**	Species **Somateria fischeri**

Spectacled Eider

A rare and elusive northern species, this is a large duck but smaller than the Eider (see p.114); the drake is similarly white above and black below, and has a wedge-shaped face with a pale green head marked by a large whitish disc around the eye. The brown female has a pale buff version of this pattern. Unlike the King Eider, this species has not been found accompanying Eider flocks in NW Europe and remains a very difficult bird to see.

OCCURRENCE Breeds in Siberia and Alaska; very rare in Norway.

VOICE Silent in winter.

wedge-shaped head

large whitish disc around eye

black and white plumage

MALE

Length **50–58cm (20–23in)**	Wingspan **80–95cm (32–37in)**

Family **Anatidae**	Species **Polysticta stelleri**

Steller's Eider

This is a small and unusual eider, with a "normal" head and bill shape. The drake is largely pale, with a black stern and collar and bold black eye-spot. Females and immatures are dark, with two narrow white bars on the hindwing and white under the wing; the thick bill is grey, the head rather square with a slight bump on the nape.

OCCURRENCE Arctic breeder, regular in N Norway, rare in Baltic in winter.

VOICE Mostly silent.

slight bump on nape

thick grey bill

black and white wing feathers

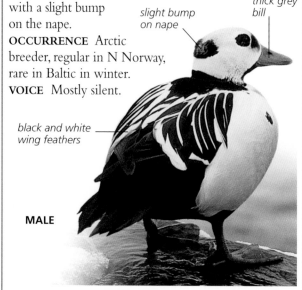

MALE

Length **42–48cm (16½–19in)**	Wingspan **68–77cm (27–30in)**

Family **Anatidae**	Species **Melanitta perspicillata**

Surf Scoter

Big, bulky, and almost Eider-like (see p.114) in its deep bill and wedge-shaped head, the Surf Scoter is worth looking for in large scoter flocks offshore. Very similar to Coots (see p.161) when asleep, drakes show a bold white nape patch and multi-coloured bill, but females are difficult to identify, looking like Velvet Scoters (see p.113) with all-dark wings. The deep, dark bill is distinctive only at close range.

OCCURRENCE Rare but regular vagrant from North America; exceedingly rare inland.

VOICE Silent.

multi-coloured bill

white nape patch

MALE

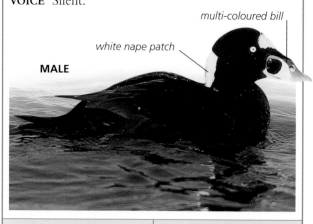

Length **45–56cm (18–22in)**	Wingspan **85–95cm (34–37in)**

Family **Anatidae**	Species *Netta rufina*

Red-crested Pochard

This large, bulky duck behaves more like a surface-feeder than a diving duck. Drakes have obvious "fuzzy" ginger heads, red bills, and black chests; females are plain brown with a dull whitish lower face. Both have very broad white wingbars. They tend to turn up amongst flocks of Tufted Ducks (see p.108) and Pochards (see p.110) on fresh water.

OCCURRENCE Breeds locally in S and E Europe; elsewhere occasional (usually escapees).

VOICE Various quiet barking notes.

MALE
(SUMMER)

ginger head

red bill

white flanks

Length **53–57cm (21–22½in)**	Wingspan **85–90cm (34–35in)**

Family **Anatidae**	Species *Histrionicus histrionicus*

Harlequin Duck

Harlequin Ducks prefer rushing rivers, moving to coasts and lakes in winter, but rarely travelling far. Drakes are boldly patterned but look essentially dark, with strange white stripes and spots on the head, neck, and chest. Females are dark brown, dumpy diving ducks, with a diffuse white face patch and bright white ear-spot.

OCCURRENCE Iceland; exceedingly rare vagrant in NW Europe.

VOICE Mostly silent.

MALE

pointed tail

brown flanks

blue-grey body with white stripes

white face patch

Length **38–45cm (15–18in)**	Wingspan **63–70cm (25–28in)**

Family **Anatidae**	Species *Bucephala islandica*

Barrow's Goldeneye

Like a large Goldeneye (see p.116), this Icelandic species has a squarer, bigger head, marked on the drake by a long, kidney-shaped white patch where the Goldeneye has a rounder spot. The back is more solidly black. Females are much harder to tell, with a rounder crown, bulkier nape, and more yellow on the bill in summer.

OCCURRENCE Breeds and winters in Iceland; rare vagrant elsewhere.

VOICE Deep growling notes from female.

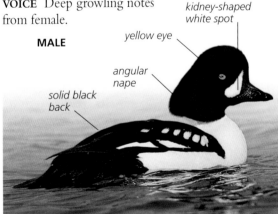

MALE

kidney-shaped white spot

yellow eye

angular nape

solid black back

Length **42–53cm (16½–21in)**	Wingspan **67–82cm (26–32in)**

Family **Anatidae**	Species *Oxyura leucocephala*

White-headed Duck

Stiff-tailed ducks include the introduced Ruddy Duck (see p.120) and native White-headed Duck in Europe. The latter is bulkier, paler, and less rich red in colour: drakes have more white on the head and swollen, pale sky-blue bills, while females have grey bills with a swollen base and black and whitish bands across the cheek. Immatures have black heads.

OCCURRENCE Rare in S Spain and Turkey, on large freshwater lakes.

VOICE Mostly silent.

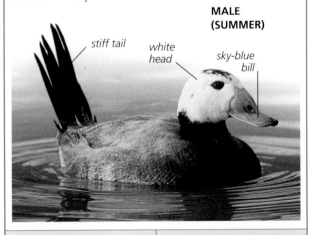

MALE
(SUMMER)

stiff tail

white head

sky-blue bill

Length **43–48cm (17–19in)**	Wingspan **60–70cm (23½–28in)**

Family **Accipitridae**	Species *Gypaetus barbatus*

Lammergeier

One of Europe's most spectacular birds, the Lammergeier is a massive, long-tailed vulture, flying with occasional deep, slow wingbeats but mostly with long, flat-winged, magnificent glides. Adults have white heads and rusty underparts and look shiny charcoal-grey above. Immatures are more uniformly grey or dark-hooded and paler-bellied. The long, wedge-shaped tail is most obvious on males.

OCCURRENCE Rare in Pyrenees, Crete, and Balkans; reintroduced in Alps.

VOICE Silent.

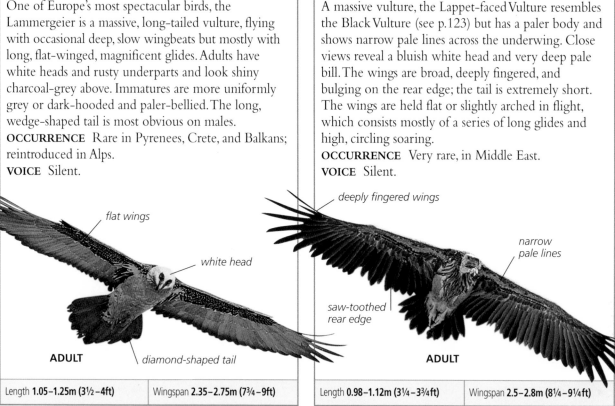

flat wings

white head

ADULT

diamond-shaped tail

Length **1.05–1.25m (3½–4ft)**	Wingspan **2.35–2.75m (7¾–9ft)**

Family **Accipitridae**	Species *Torgos tracheliotus*

Lappet-faced Vulture

A massive vulture, the Lappet-faced Vulture resembles the Black Vulture (see p.123) but has a paler body and shows narrow pale lines across the underwing. Close views reveal a bluish white head and very deep pale bill. The wings are broad, deeply fingered, and bulging on the rear edge; the tail is extremely short. The wings are held flat or slightly arched in flight, which consists mostly of a series of long glides and high, circling soaring.

OCCURRENCE Very rare, in Middle East.

VOICE Silent.

deeply fingered wings

narrow pale lines

saw-toothed rear edge

ADULT

Length **0.98–1.12m (3¼–3¾ft)**	Wingspan **2.5–2.8m (8¼–9¼ft)**

Family **Accipitridae**	Species *Aquila heliaca*

Imperial Eagle

This large, dark eagle has a pale grey base to the tail and white marks on the shoulders. Immatures are paler, with a bold pale rump, white upperwing bands, and contrasted underwings with a pale patch behind the angle. They have buffish bodies, with heavy, dark streaks. The wings are held flat or drooped in a glide, unlike the Golden Eagle (see p.126).

OCCURRENCE Rare in upland forests in Balkans.

VOICE Loud, barking notes.

dark brown streaks on breast

dark hindwings

JUVENILE

pale window on inner primaries

Length **70–80cm (28–32in)**	Wingspan **1.75–2.05m (5¾–6¾ft)**

Family **Accipitridae**	Species *Aquila adalberti*

Spanish Imperial Eagle

One of Europe's big eagles, the Spanish Imperial Eagle is a bird of lowlands and forested areas. It flies on rather flat wings, unlike the Golden Eagle (see p.126), adults showing a bold white front edge, a pale head, and a two-tone, dark-tipped tail. Juveniles are ginger-brown with dark wingtips, hindwings, and tail, a pale rump, and a whitish band along the upperwing.

OCCURRENCE Rare resident in C and S Spain.

VOICE Deep, barking notes.

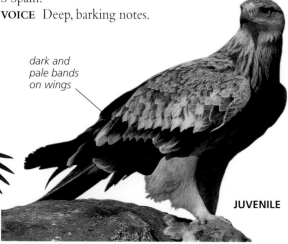

dark and pale bands on wings

JUVENILE

Length **72–85cm (28–34in)**	Wingspan **1.8–2.1m (6–7ft)**

Family **Accipitridae**	Species *Aquila pomarina*

Lesser Spotted Eagle

This eagle migrates in large flocks into Africa for the winter. It is plain brown when adult except for a pale mark at the base of the primary feathers; the forewing is paler than the hindwing (often uniform, or reversed, on Spotted Eagle). Juveniles have a single line of white across the upperwings, a white band above the tail, and pale patches on the outer wings.

OCCURRENCE Breeds in SE Europe north to E Baltic; migrates to Africa through Middle East.

VOICE High-pitched yapping barks.

pale spots on wings

plain brown body

JUVENILE

Length **55–65cm (22–26in)**	Wingspan **1.43–1.68m (4¾–5½ft)**

Family **Accipitridae**	Species *Aquila clanga*

Spotted Eagle

Of the big brown eagles, this is the stockiest and broadest-winged in silhouette. Adults are very dark except for a small pale patch at the base of the primaries and a paler patch above the tail; immatures are marked by rows of pale feather tips across the wings and a white crescent over the tail. The strong legs are heavily feathered.

OCCURRENCE Rare in summer in E Europe.

VOICE Occasional low barking notes.

strong, yellow-based bill

pale feather tips across wings

IMMATURE

Length **59–69cm (23–27in)**	Wingspan **1.53–1.77m (5–5¾ft)**

Family **Accipitridae**	Species *Aquila nipalensis*

Steppe Eagle

One of the massive, heavy eagles of Asia, migrating into Africa for the winter, the Steppe Eagle is closely related to the Tawny Eagle. It flies on flat or drooped wings, and immatures have a broad white band along the middle of the underwings, gradually lost over several years until the all-dark adult plumage is attained. It has a particularly long, protruding head compared with the chunkier spotted eagles.

OCCURRENCE Migrant in Middle East.

VOICE Silent on migration.

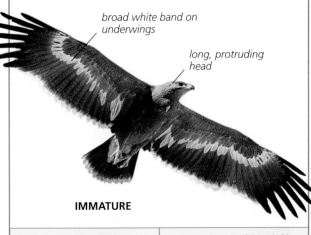

broad white band on underwings

long, protruding head

IMMATURE

Length **62–74cm (24–29in)**	Wingspan **1.65–1.9m (5½–6¼ft)**

Family **Accipitridae**	Species *Elanus caeruleus*

Black-shouldered Kite

A medium-sized, blunt-headed, broad-winged bird of prey with a short, narrow tail, the Black-shouldered Kite is often seen hovering towards dusk, like a big, clumsy Kestrel (see p.140). It is uniquely grey with black shoulder patches and a white underside, the wingtips grey above but black beneath. Juveniles are duller with pale scaly feather edges on a darker grey back.

OCCURRENCE Rare in S and W Spain and Portugal, common in Egypt, near marshland.

VOICE Sharp, high *kree-ak* sound.

broad head

black shoulder patch

ADULT

Length **31–36cm (12–14in)**	Wingspan **71–85cm (28–34in)**

Family **Accipitridae**	Species *Circus macrourus*

Pallid Harrier

Of the harriers, the male Pallid Harrier is the palest and most ghost-like, identified by its white breast and narrow dark wedge-shaped wingtip patch. Females are like Montagu's Harriers (see p.132) with darker hindwings and a pale collar, while juveniles have a bolder whitish collar beneath dark cheeks and a dark band around the hind neck. All have white rumps.
OCCURRENCE Rare migrant in SE Europe.
VOICE High, whinnying, trilling chatter.

very pale grey body

dark, wedge-shaped wingtip patch

MALE

Length 40–50cm (16–20in)	Wingspan 0.97–1.18m (3¼–3¾ft)

Family **Accipitridae**	Species *Buteo rufinus*

Long-legged Buzzard

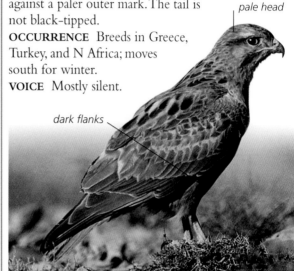

A big, bright buzzard with a pale cinnamon or rusty tail and whitish flight feathers with narrow black tips, the Long-legged Buzzard often hovers over open ground. It has a long-winged, eagle-like appearance. The belly or at least flank patches are dark and the upperwing has a dark wrist patch against a paler outer mark. The tail is not black-tipped.
OCCURRENCE Breeds in Greece, Turkey, and N Africa; moves south for winter.
VOICE Mostly silent.

pale head

dark flanks

Length 50–60cm (20–23½in)	Wingspan 1.3–1.5m (4¼–5ft)

Family **Accipitridae**	Species *Accipiter brevipes*

Levant Sparrowhawk

Clearly a long-tailed, broad-winged, bird-eating hawk, Levant Sparrowhawk is more sociable than the Sparrowhawk (see p.138) and migrates in flocks. Males have black-tipped, rather pointed wings, which are mostly white beneath; females also show dark wingtips. Both have dark eyes (Sparrowhawk's are yellow) and a black chin stripe, while males have grey cheeks (rusty on Sparrowhawk).
OCCURRENCE Breeds in Balkans and E Europe; migrates to Africa in autumn.
VOICE Shrill, repeated *ke-wik*.

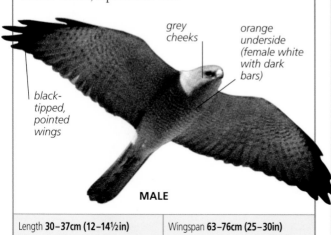

grey cheeks

orange underside (female white with dark bars)

black-tipped, pointed wings

MALE

Length 30–37cm (12–14½in)	Wingspan 63–76cm (25–30in)

Family **Falconidae**	Species *Falco vespertinus*

Red-footed Falcon

Small, delicate, slightly rounded in its contours, the Red-footed Falcon is between a Hobby and Kestrel (see pp.142, 140) in shape and behaviour. It hovers, but also swoops gracefully in pursuit of insects. Old males are smoky grey with paler wingtips, young ones grey with dark wingtips and reddish belly patches. Females are barred grey and brown, and pale buff on the crown and underside.
OCCURRENCE Breeds in E Europe, regular but rare in spring/summer in W Europe.
VOICE High, quick, staccato chatter.

smoky grey body

paler wingtips

MALE

Length 28–34cm (11–13½in)	Wingspan 65–76cm (26–30in)

Family **Falconidae**	Species *Falco eleonorae*

Eleonora's Falcon

This is a large, rakish, long-tailed, sharp-winged falcon of Mediterranean regions. One form is all-dark and blackish, and another has a white collar, dark moustache, and rufous underside. The underwing is two-toned, dark in front. Juveniles are plainer with narrow bars and pale cheeks. Eleonora's Falcons catch small migrant birds over the sea or big insects over lakes and marshes.

OCCURRENCE Scarce on Mediterranean islands and coasts.
VOICE Sharp, nasal, grating chatter.

white neck

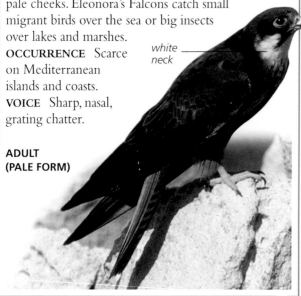

**ADULT
(PALE FORM)**

Length **37–42cm (14½–16½in)**	Wingspan **87–104cm (34–41in)**

Family **Falconidae**	Species *Falco rusticolus*

Gyr Falcon

The biggest and most heavily built falcon, the Gyr Falcon may be dark brownish (juveniles), slaty grey, or almost pure white according to age and location: the grey birds breed in N Europe, while the white ones visit mostly in late winter or spring from Greenland. The outer wing has paler areas underneath and the forewing is rather darker than the trailing edge.

OCCURRENCE Rare vagrant in W Europe, and rare breeder in Iceland and N Norway.
VOICE Deep, hoarse, rattling chatter.

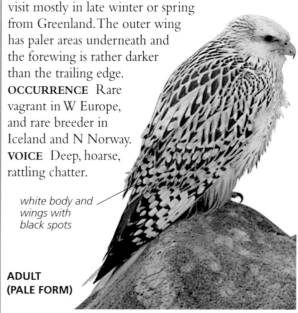

white body and wings with black spots

**ADULT
(PALE FORM)**

Length **53–63cm (21–25in)**	Wingspan **1.09–1.34m (3½–4½ft)**

Family **Falconidae**	Species *Falco cherrug*

Saker

A massive, powerful, broad-winged falcon, equal to a male Gyr Falcon in size, and paler and browner than a Peregrine (see p.143), the Saker has a pale buff head with only a thin dark moustache, and usually dark thigh feathers. The underwing is strongly two-toned. Juveniles are darker, blackish on the flanks, and dark under the tail unlike a young Lanner.

OCCURRENCE Rare in SE Europe, in hills, forests, and semi-arid grassland.
VOICE Loud, harsh, ringing chattering calls.

pale buff head

brownish upperparts

ADULT

dark thigh feathers

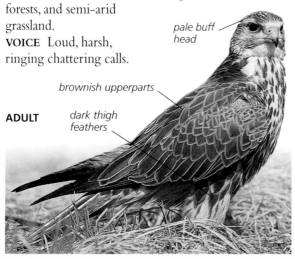

Length **47–55cm (18½–22in)**	Wingspan **1.05–1.29m (3½–4¼ft)**

Family **Falconidae**	Species *Falco biarmicus*

Lanner

This is one of the big falcons, longer-tailed and slimmer-winged than a Peregrine (see p.143), and darker and greyer than a Saker. It has a paler breast than a Peregrine and its head is marked with buff or rufous. The juvenile is browner, heavily striped below, but paler under the tail. All have a dark forewing band underneath the wing, most obvious on young birds.

buff or rufous head

OCCURRENCE Rare in S Italy and Balkans, in semi-arid areas and mountains.
VOICE Harsh, loud, rasping chatter.

blue-grey back

ADULT

Length **43–50cm (17–20in)**	Wingspan **95–105cm (37½–41¼in)**

Family **Phasianidae**	Species *Alectoris graeca*

Rock Partridge

A rare partridge of mountains and rocky slopes, best identified by distribution and habitat, the Rock Partridge has a pure white throat, black curving down beside the bill, and very little white behind the eye. It is a plain-backed, barred-flanked bird, like a Chukar or Red-legged Partridge (see pp.427, 152) in general appearance, with a short red bill and red legs and a rufous tail showing in flight.

black stripe through eye

OCCURRENCE Scarce on alpine slopes, in Alps, Italy, and Balkans.

VOICE Short, hard, choking notes in long series, more varied than Chukar's.

barred flanks (less regular on juvenile)

ADULT

Length **33–36cm (13–14in)**	Wingspan **46–53cm (18–21in)**

Family **Phasianidae**	Species *Alectoris barbara*

Barbary Partridge

A rare bird very restricted in range in Europe, the Barbary Partridge has striped flanks, a mostly whitish grey face without a dark eye-stripe, and a spotted, reddish brown collar. Its breast is grey, the belly pale orange, and legs pale reddish. A dark central stripe shows on the crown. It is very like a Red-legged Partridge (see p.152) when seen flying off and its general behaviour is similar.

OCCURRENCE Gibraltar, Sardinia, Atlantic islands, and N Africa.

VOICE Series of quick, rhythmic, hoarse notes.

whitish grey face

reddish brown collar

striped flanks (less neatly patterned on juvenile)

ADULT

Length **32–34cm (12½–13½in)**	Wingspan **46–49cm (18–19½in)**

Family **Phasianidae**	Species *Alectoris chukar*

Chukar

A large, pale, rather plain partridge with bold flank stripes, the Chukar is characterized by black on the forehead but not beside the bill, a creamy throat sometimes spotted at the base, and a broad pale line behind the eye. Only when introduced birds are encountered do these subtle points matter too much as distribution is usually sufficient to identify it.

broad white line behind eye

OCCURRENCE Common in Middle East; rare in NE Greece.

VOICE Loud, rhythmic, hollow *cha-cha-cha-chaker chaker chaker.*

bold stripes on flanks

ADULT

Length **32–35cm (12½–14in)**	Wingspan **47–52cm (18½–20½in)**

Family **Phasianidae**	Species *Chrysolophus amherstiae*

Lady Amherst's Pheasant

This striking pheasant is very difficult to see in dense undergrowth beneath dark conifer forest. Males are uniquely patterned black and white with yellow on the rump; they have long red feathers beside the extremely long tail. Females are dark rufous, closely barred black, with a paler, unbarred belly unlike the Golden Pheasant; at 60–80cm (23½–32in) long, they are much smaller than the males.

OCCURRENCE Introduced but rare resident in C England.

VOICE Loud, strident *aaahk-aik-aik* at dusk.

very long tail

striking black and white plumage

long red feathers

MALE

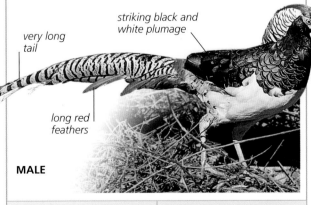

Length **1.05–1.2m (3½–4ft)**	Wingspan **70–85cm (28–34in)**

Family **Phasianidae**	Species **Chrysolophus pictus**

Golden Pheasant

Introduced but not spreading far from old release sites, the Golden Pheasant is difficult to see, despite its bright colours. Males are strikingly red and yellow, with long, marbled, golden-brown tails. Females, which are much smaller at 60–80cm (23½–32in) long, are pale brown with black barring all over, and much less spotted than a Pheasant (see p.155).
OCCURRENCE Rare; very local in S Scotland and S and E England.
VOICE Loud, shrieking *eh-aik*.

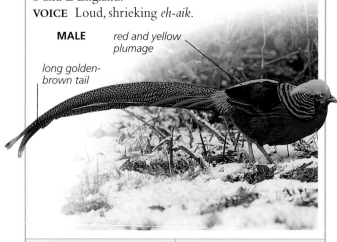

MALE
red and yellow plumage
long golden-brown tail

Length **90–105cm (35–41in)**	Wingspan **65–75cm (26–30in)**

Family **Turnicidae**	Species **Turnix sylvatica**

Small Button-quail

This tiny bird is an enigma and may even be extinct in Europe, but is common in Africa. It may survive in dry, heathy places with palmetto scrub. If flushed, it reveals a tiny, Quail-like form (see p.154) with obvious pale upperwing patches. On the ground, its pale greyish face with no dark stripes would be distinctive. The Small Button-quail calls at dusk and dawn.
OCCURRENCE Very rare in S Spain; scarce in Morocco.
VOICE Deep, booming *hoooo hoooo hoooo* notes.

spots on orange breast
ADULT

Length **15–17cm (6–6½in)**	Wingspan **25–30cm (10–12in)**

Family **Rallidae**	Species **Porzana parva**

Little Crake

A tiny, elusive bird of dense waterside vegetation and ditches, sometimes emerging onto open mud or weed, the Little Crake looks like a tiny Water Rail (see p.158) with a short bill. Males are blue-grey and unmarked below, and brown with blackish streaks and a few long buff lines above. Females are pale brown, buff beneath, with a few blackish streaks on top.
OCCURRENCE Sporadic across C and E Europe; vagrant in W.
VOICE Nasal, yapping notes accelerate into fast trill.

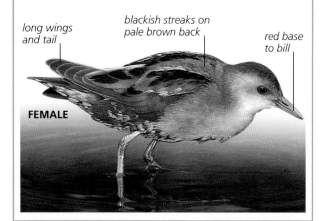

long wings and tail
blackish streaks on pale brown back
red base to bill
FEMALE

Length **17–19cm (6½–7½in)**	Wingspan **34–39cm (13½–15½in)**

Family **Rallidae**	Species **Porzana pusilla**

Baillon's Crake

Compared with the Little Crake, this is a rounder, dumpier, short-winged, and short-tailed bird. Sexes are alike: brown above with black-edged white flecks, grey below with white bars on the flanks; the bill is green (red at base on Little and Spotted Crakes, see p.159) and the legs greenish. Juveniles are greyer and more barred than paler young Little Crakes.
OCCURRENCE Rare and very local in W Europe; vagrant in NW.
VOICE Quiet, short, soft, dry rattle.

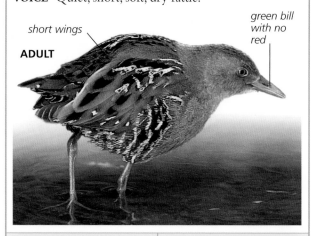

short wings
green bill with no red
ADULT

Length **16–18cm (6½–7in)**	Wingspan **33–37cm (13–14½in)**

Family **Rallidae**	Species *Fulica cristata*

Crested Coot

Rare in Europe, this bird is very like a Coot (see p.161). It is best distinguished by a duller bill against the white facial shield, a rather more rounded shape to the black face against the bill base, often a "bump" near the tail when swimming, and a plainer upperwing with no pale trailing edge. The small red knobs on the forehead which give it its name are usually hard to see but can be quite obvious in spring.

OCCURRENCE Very rare in SW Spain, Morocco.

VOICE Shrill double note, unlike Coot, and hollow, nasal *ka-hah*.

ADULT (SPRING)

red knobs on forehead

bulging rump

greyish body

Length **39–44cm (15½–17½in)**	Wingspan **75–85cm (30–34in)**

Family **Rallidae**	Species *Porphyrio porphyrio*

Purple Gallinule

This huge Moorhen-like (see p.160) bird is often elusive in thick, reedy swamps, but comes into the open at times. It is immediately obvious: large and purplish blue (in Egypt, with a green back and turquoise face). The massive red bill and shield and long pink-red legs are easy to see, as is the bold white patch under the short tail.

OCCURRENCE SW Spain, Sardinia, Egypt.

VOICE Loud, abrupt, bleating and hooting calls, hardly bird-like in tone.

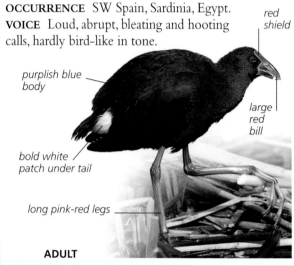

red shield

purplish blue body

large red bill

bold white patch under tail

long pink-red legs

ADULT

Length **45–50cm (18–20in)**	Wingspan **90–100cm (35–39in)**

Family **Gruidae**	Species *Anthropoides virgo*

Demoiselle Crane

Obviously a crane, this large grey bird is not always easy to tell from the common Crane (see p.162), especially in flight. Good views reveal a white head plume, long black breast feathers, and neat, narrow feathers (not bushy) cloaking the tail; in flight, the upperwing is less contrasted than on the Common Crane but wear increases the contrast as a pale grey "bloom" fades, and the smaller size is not obvious. Demoiselles are mainly Middle Eastern birds, regular in Cyprus, but very rare farther west.

OCCURRENCE Rare in extreme E Europe.

VOICE High, sharp trumpeting notes.

ADULT

long black breast feathers

Length **85–100cm (34–39in)**	Wingspan **1.55–1.8m (5–6ft)**

Family **Burhinidae**	Species *Burhinus senegalensis*

Senegal Thick-knee

This is a close relative of the Stone-curlew (see p.169) and can be distinguished only with care in a close view by a broad greyish band across the closed wing (narrow black and white bands on Stone-curlew). In flight, the white wingtip spots are slightly larger. Senegal Thick-knees are often seen on buildings or in groups on muddy riverbanks, unlike Stone-curlews.

OCCURRENCE In delta, along Nile, and Cairo, Egypt.

VOICE Loud, ringing whistles varying in pitch and volume.

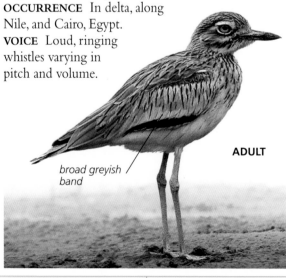

ADULT

broad greyish band

Length **38–45cm (15–18in)**	Wingspan **76–88cm (30–35in)**

Family **Glareolidae**	Species *Cursorius cursor*

Cream-coloured Courser

This is a desert bird, only rarely straying beyond this harsh environment. It is hard to spot on the ground, on which it moves in quick, jerky runs, head high, but striking in flight with black wingtips above and solidly black underwings. Pale grey-buff or pinkish buff, except for a grey nape and black and white stripes behind the eye onto the nape, it has long, pale whitish-grey legs. Juveniles have soft dark mottles above and the head stripes are duller, the nape pale grey-brown.

OCCURRENCE Breeds in Middle East, North Africa; rare vagrant farther north.

VOICE Short, high, sharp flight calls.

long pale legs

ADULT

Length **24–27cm (9½–10½in)**	Wingspan **70cm (28in)**

Family **Glareolidae**	Species *Glareola nordmanni*

Black-winged Pratincole

Pratincoles are beautiful, elegant, aerial birds, although they spend much time hunched on the ground. The Black-winged Pratincole is rather dark, with little red on the bill, quite extensive black on the face, and a tail shorter than the wingtips (unlike Collared Pratincole, see p.177). It is easier to identify in flight, but lighting effects demand care: the underwings are solidly blackish, and the upperwing dark with no pale trailing edge (Collared shows a white line).

OCCURRENCE Breeds around Black Sea; rare migrant/vagrant in W Europe mostly in summer.

VOICE Hard, grating flight call, *kettek* or *kit-i-kit*.

ADULT (SUMMER)

Length **24–28cm (9½–11in)**	Wingspan **60–70cm (23½–28in)**

Family **Glareolidae**	Species *Glareola maldivarium*

Oriental Pratincole

While obviously a pratincole, this is not an easy species to identify, sharing characteristics with both Collared Pratincole (see p.177) and Black-winged Pratincole. It looks short-tailed (with only a shallow fork and no streamers), and combines the dark upperwing and lack of a white trailing edge of Black-winged with the chestnut-red underwing coverts of Collared. A worn or moulting Collared is the likeliest source of confusion. It is similarly elegant in the air, and a proficient hunter of flying insects.

OCCURRENCE Very rare vagrant to W Europe, from Asia, mostly in late summer.

VOICE Strident and tern-like.

ADULT

short tail

Length **23–27cm (9–10½in)**	Wingspan **50–60cm (20–23½in)**

Family **Charadriidae**	Species *Charadrius semipalmatus*

Semipalmated Plover

Very much like the Ringed Plover (see p.170), it is unlikely that a vagrant Semipalmated Plover will usually be noticed. In summer, it has less white behind the eye and a thinner black breast-band than a Ringed. In winter or immature plumages, the shorter bill, narrow breast-band, and fractionally smaller size are useful; suspicions need to be confirmed by the call.

OCCURRENCE Very rare vagrant to W Europe, from North America.

VOICE Bright, rising, double whistle, *chi-weee*, more clearly articulated than a Ringed Plover's.

dark bill

ADULT (WINTER)

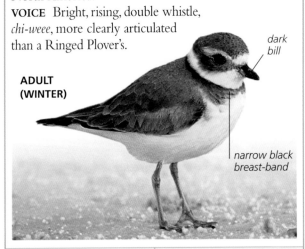

narrow black breast-band

Length **16–17cm (6½in)**	Wingspan **33–38cm (13–15in)**

Family **Charadriidae**	Species *Charadrius vociferus*

Killdeer

The Killdeer is larger than a Ringed Plover (see p.170) and has a long tail, a tall but horizontal stance, and an obvious double black breast-band. Its legs are dull, the rather long bill black. In flight, it is striking because of its long tail and contrastingly rusty rump, unlike any other ringed plover type, and bold white stripe on almost black wings. It may turn up almost anywhere on open, flat, sandy or wet or derelict ground.

OCCURRENCE Rare vagrant to W Europe in autumn or winter, from North America.

VOICE Loud, fluty whistle, *klu-eee* or *kil-deeee*.

double black breast-band

long black bill

long tail

ADULT

Length **23–26cm (9–10in)**	Wingspan **45–50cm (18–20in)**

Family **Charadriidae**	Species *Charadrius mongolus*

Lesser Sand Plover

In summer, this species has a more solidly dark reddish breast-band than the Greater Sand Plover. It is also stockier, with a broad, round head that is not so disproportionately large, and a slightly shorter, more tapered bill. It has blackish or dark grey-green legs. In winter and immature plumages, it shows a neat dark patch on each side of the breast and a rather narrow pale stripe over the eye.

OCCURRENCE Rare vagrant in Europe, from Asia, nowhere regular.

VOICE Hard, short, trilled or repeated *trrrk* or *tirrik*.

ADULT (WINTER)

narrow pale stripe over eye

blackish or dark grey-green legs

thick black bill

Length **17–19cm (6½–7½in)**	Wingspan **45–58cm (18–23in)**

Family **Charadriidae**	Species *Charadrius leschenaultii*

Greater Sand Plover

Much bigger than a Ringed Plover (see p.170), the Greater Sand Plover is also longer-legged, more upright, larger-billed, and has a big, broad, bulbous head. In summer, it is rusty red on the head and chest; in winter, it is plain with dusky chest sides on the white under-side. Young birds have pale scaly feather edges on the back. Care is needed to separate this from the Lesser Sand Plover.

OCCURRENCE Rare vagrant in Europe; regular in Israel and Egypt.

VOICE Trilling *trr-rr*, often repeated quickly.

JUVENILE

large black bill

pale, scaly feather edges

dusky chest sides

long, dull green legs

Length **19–22cm (7½–9in)**	Wingspan **57–64cm (22½–25in)**

Family **Charadriidae**	Species *Charadrius asiaticus*

Caspian Plover

This small- to medium-sized plover is long-legged, small-billed, and elegant. Pale brown above and white below, it has a broad chestnut breast-band in summer; winter birds and immatures have pale earthy buff across the chest, more extensively dark than on a sand plover. The legs are greenish, the wings show a white stripe, and the rump is all-dark in flight.

OCCURRENCE Rare vagrant in Europe from Asia; scarce migrant in Middle East.

VOICE Short *chup*.

ADULT (WINTER)

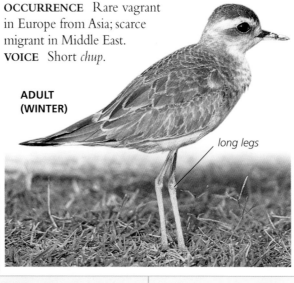

long legs

Length **19–21cm (7½–8½in)**	Wingspan **57–64cm (22½–25in)**

Family **Charadriidae**	Species *Pluvialis fulva*

Pacific Golden Plover

More similar to the Golden Plover (see p.174) than the American Golden Plover, this slightly smaller, longer-legged plover is hard to detect. In summer, it has bolder black chequering above and more black below than the Golden Plover. In winter, it is similar to the American species but less grey, longer-billed, and longer-legged. The dusky underwing is visible in flight. It has longer tertials than the American bird.

OCCURRENCE Very rare vagrant from Siberia to W Europe, mostly late summer.

VOICE Sharp, whistled *chu-wit* like Spotted Redshank (see p.191).

long bill

short wingtips beyond tertials

long legs

JUVENILE

Length 21–25cm (8½–10in)	Wingspan 45–50cm (18–20in)

Family **Charadriidae**	Species *Pluvialis dominica*

American Golden Plover

Difficult to find in Golden Plover flocks (see p.174), a winter American Golden Plover tends to look greyer, with a bolder head pattern, slightly longer legs, and longer wingtips. In summer, it is less yellow above, more extensively black beneath, with bold white chest sides. In flight, the dusky grey underwing is a crucial clue. Grey Plovers (see p.175) are larger and much bigger-billed; Pacific Goldens are more difficult to separate.

OCCURRENCE Regular but very rare vagrant in W Europe, from North America, in autumn-winter.

VOICE *Klu-i*, stressed on first syllable.

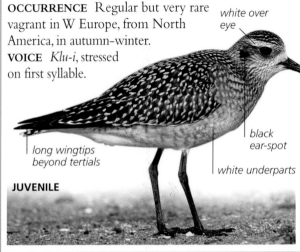

white over eye

black ear-spot

long wingtips beyond tertials

white underparts

JUVENILE

Length 24–27cm (9½–10½in)	Wingspan 50–55cm (20–22in)

Family **Charadriidae**	Species *Vanellus spinosus*

Spur-winged Lapwing

A big and boldly marked plover, scarcely reaching Europe, this is a common species along riversides and on sandy places in the Middle East. It is easily distinguished by its black cap and breast, bold white neck, and grey-brown back. It often stands in pairs or forms noisy groups. In flight, the wings show black tips and a broad white diagonal band on top.

OCCURRENCE Rare in Greece; common in Israel, Egypt, especially along Nile.

VOICE Loud, metallic, repeated, high *titi-tirik* and similar notes.

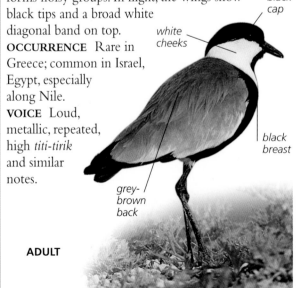

black cap

white cheeks

black breast

grey-brown back

ADULT

Length 25–28cm (10–11in)	Wingspan 60–65cm (23½–26in)

Family **Charadriidae**	Species *Vanellus gregarius*

Sociable Lapwing

A rather large, bulky plover, typically associating with Lapwings, the Sociable Lapwing looks grey with a dark belly and a black and white striped face in summer. In winter, the body is more uniform sandy grey and the head less boldly marked, but still showing a dark cap and pale stripes over the eye. In flight, the wings reveal a broad white triangular patch and black tips; the tail has a black band.

OCCURRENCE Rare vagrant to W Europe from Asia, sometimes in winter; rare migrant in SE Europe.

VOICE Harsh, chattering notes in flight, but usually silent.

dark cap

white over eye

JUVENILE

Length 27–30cm (10½–12in)	Wingspan 60–65cm (23½–26in)

Family **Charadriidae**	Species *Vanellus leucurus*

White-tailed Lapwing

More upright, long-legged, and elegant than other lapwings, this species is identified by its white tail with no black band, and long yellow legs that extend well behind the tail in flight. It may show a dark grey breast-band against a whiter belly. The wings have a neat black-edged white band and large black tips. Young birds are spotted above.

OCCURRENCE Very rare in Romania; very rare vagrant in W Europe in late summer.

VOICE Usually silent.

pale grey-brown head

dark grey breast-band

long yellow legs

ADULT

Length **26–29cm (10–11½in)**	Wingspan **60cm (23½in)**

Family **Scolopacidae**	Species *Limicola falcinellus*

Broad-billed Sandpiper

A small, short-legged wader, this bird has a contrasting dark back and white belly. In spring, it has a "frosty" look, fading to darker brown with coppery edges in late summer, with long whitish stripes on the back. In winter, it is much paler and plainer grey. The best feature is then the two white lines over each eye that become bolder in summer. The bill is rather heavy, faintly kinked down, and thinner at the tip.

OCCURRENCE Breeds in Scandinavia, migrates through E Europe; rare in west, mostly in late spring.

VOICE A high, buzzing trill, *bree-eeet*.

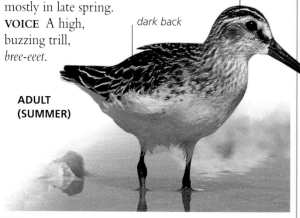

double white line over eye

dark back

ADULT (SUMMER)

Length **15–18cm (6–7in)**	Wingspan **30–34cm (12–13½in)**

Family **Scolopacidae**	Species *Xenus cinereus*

Terek Sandpiper

Disproportionately large-billed, this rare, short-legged sandpiper has a rather low, forward-leaning carriage that is exaggerated as it lurches and runs over muddy shores. It is plain dull greyish brown with a whiter underside, marked by a white trailing edge to the wing (but the rump is grey). In summer, it has blackish bands along the back. The legs are pale to rich orange-yellow.

OCCURRENCE Rare migrant in E Europe, very rare vagrant in W Europe, from Asia.

VOICE Soft notes in short, rapid series in flight.

large, upturned bill

ADULT (SUMMER)

yellow legs

Length **22–25cm (9–10in)**	Wingspan **38–40cm (15–16in)**

Family **Scolopacidae**	Species *Calidris subminuta*

Long-toed Stint

A small, long-legged, long-toed, slightly curve-billed stint, the Long-toed Stint tends to creep about like a tiny crake, or stretch upwards and look very upright. It is like a bright Least Sandpiper or a tiny Wood Sandpiper (see p.189), with yellowish legs, a dark cap reaching the bill, dark cheeks, a pale bill base, and bright upperpart "V"s on autumn juveniles.

OCCURRENCE Very rare vagrant from E Siberia.

VOICE Short trill, *chrrip*.

ADULT

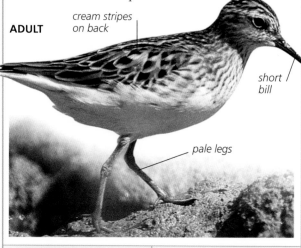

cream stripes on back

short bill

pale legs

Length **14–15cm (5½–6in)**	Wingspan **25–30cm (10–12in)**

Family **Scolopacidae**	Species *Calidris minutilla*

Least Sandpiper

Rather like a tiny Pectoral Sandpiper (see p.436), the Least Sandpiper is distinguished from the Little Stint (see p.183) by its pale legs and from Temminck's (see p.182) by its streakier back, darker breast, and fine pale "V" on the upperparts on juveniles. Pale legs instantly indicate something quite rare; the tiny (barely sparrow) size and angular shape are also distinctive. The Long-toed Stint is very similar but even rarer.

OCCURRENCE Rare vagrant in W Europe, from North America.

VOICE Sharp, abrupt *keek, ki-keek* or *tree-eep*.

streaked back

ADULT

pale legs

tiny bill

Length **13–14cm (5–5½in)**	Wingspan **25–30cm (10–12in)**

Family **Scolopacidae**	Species *Calidris tenuirostris*

Great Knot

With some resemblance to the Knot (see p.181), especially in winter, the Great Knot is nevertheless larger, with a small head, longer bill, slightly longer legs, and a longer, more tapered rear end. Juveniles are browner than young Knots, with dark scaly upperparts; they have dark breasts with rows of neat dark spots. Winter adults are grey but have darker breast spots, unlike a Knot. The bill is thick-based, tapered, and slightly downcurved; the rump is grey, like a Knot's.

OCCURRENCE Very rare vagrant in NW Europe and Middle East, from Siberia.

VOICE Vagrants mostly silent.

tapered rear end

short legs

spotted underside

ADULT (SUMMER)

Length **24–27cm (9½–10½in)**	Wingspan **40cm (16in)**

Family **Scolopacidae**	Species *Calidris bairdii*

Baird's Sandpiper

Of the vagrant small North American sandpipers, Baird's Sandpiper is the buffiest and longest-tailed, looking low-slung and tapered, with a short black bill and short blackish legs. Immatures have particularly well-marked pearly white, scaly feather edges on the upperparts and a buff breast above very white underparts. In flight, the rump is mostly dark and the wings have a thin white stripe.

OCCURRENCE Rare vagrant from North America, mostly in autumn.

VOICE Short, purring trill, *trreeet*.

short black bill

scaly back

JUVENILE

very long wings

short legs

Length **14–17cm (5½–6½in)**	Wingspan **30–33cm (12–13in)**

Family **Scolopacidae**	Species *Calidris fuscicollis*

White-rumped Sandpiper

Almost as slim and tapered as Baird's Sandpiper, the juvenile White-rumped Sandpiper in autumn is told by its less scaly upperside, with more rufous and black, a tiny pale bill base, a whiter stripe over the eye, and white "V" lines on the back. Adults are plain and grey in winter, also with long, tapered wingtips. In flight, the white patch above the tail is an obvious feature.

OCCURRENCE Very rare in W Europe, in autumn, from North America.

VOICE Thin, sharp, squeaky *tzeet*.

ADULT (WINTER)

short bill

long wings

black legs

Length **14–17cm (5½–6½in)**	Wingspan **30–33cm (12–13in)**

Family **Scolopacidae**	Species *Calidris pusilla*

Semipalmated Sandpiper

This is like a dull Little Stint (see p.183) with less clear pale "V"s above, a thicker, blunter bill, and with tiny webs between the toes. Bright juveniles have some gingery rufous on the head and back, others are greyer with a little buff around the neck and chest sides. Western Sandpipers are very similar, with slightly longer bills and more distinct streaks on the sides of the breast.

OCCURRENCE Rare vagrant from North America.

VOICE Short, muffled *tchrp*, stint-like *tip*.

JUVENILE

greyish or gingery rufous back

thick, blunt bill

partly webbed toes

Length **13–15cm (5–6in)**	Wingspan **25–30cm (10–12in)**

Family **Scolopacidae**	Species *Calidris mauri*

Western Sandpiper

Very rare in Europe, and very difficult to tell from a Semipalmated Sandpiper or Little Stint (see p.183), the Western Sandpiper is a tiny, stint-like wader with long legs and a slim, quite long, slightly curved bill. It has a slight pale "V" on its back in autumn, with a band of rufous feathers on each side, a broad pale band over the eye, and tiny webs between its toes.

OCCURRENCE Very rare vagrant in W Europe, in autumn, from North America.

VOICE High, thin, rough *jeet*.

ADULT

long, slightly curved bill

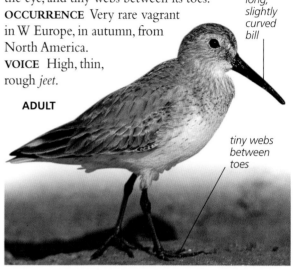

tiny webs between toes

Length **14–17cm (5½–6½in)**	Wingspan **28–31cm (11–12in)**

Family **Scolopacidae**	Species *Calidris ruficollis*

Red-necked Stint

In summer, the largely rust-red neck and upper chest of the Red-necked Stint are distinctive, although larger Sanderlings (see p.179) look similar in late summer. However, autumn vagrants are confusingly like Semipalmated Sandpipers and Little Stints (see p.183), requiring close study for identification. The very short bill, unwebbed feet, short legs, and deep body may help; grey wings against the brighter back, and a lack of white "V"s above are also useful.

OCCURRENCE Very rare in Europe, from E Siberia.

VOICE High, hoarse *chrit*.

ADULT (SUMMER)

rust-red neck

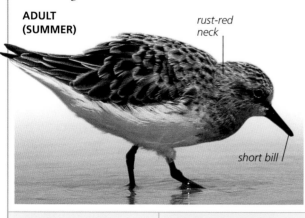

short bill

Length **13–16cm (5–6½in)**	Wingspan **25–30cm (10–12in)**

Family **Scolopacidae**	Species *Tryngites subruficollis*

Buff-breasted Sandpiper

Although often near water on migration, this sandpiper is as likely to be seen on open, dry ground where it runs in short, quick bursts. It is small, rounded, with long yellow legs and a short black bill, rather like a tiny Ruff (see p.187). The upperparts are spangled dark with scaly pale fringes. The whole neck and breast area is a warm, rich buff, slightly spotted at the sides. In flight, the rump looks dark, the wings have just a diffuse paler central band.

OCCURRENCE Regular but rare vagrant to NW Europe, from North America.

VOICE Mostly rather silent.

scaly pattern on back

buff breast

JUVENILE

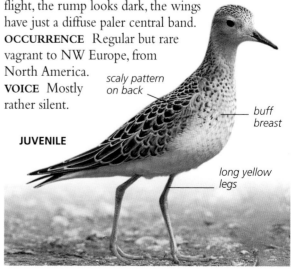

long yellow legs

Length **18–20cm (7–8in)**	Wingspan **35–37cm (14–14½in)**

Family **Scolopacidae**	Species *Calidris melanotos*

Pectoral Sandpiper

One of the commoner North American birds in Europe (but still rare), this Ruff-like (see p.187) wader is quite small, with bright buff feather edges above and a white "V" on the back, a dark cap, and, most usefully for identification, a closely streaked breast sharply defined against the white belly. In flight, the rump shows oval white sides. The legs are yellow.

OCCURRENCE Rare but regular in W Europe in autumn, from North America.

VOICE Short, quite deep, throaty trill, *trrr't*.

bright buff feather edges on upperparts

JUVENILE

closely streaked breast

dark cap

defined breast-band

Length **19–23cm (7½–9in)**	Wingspan **38–44cm (15–17½in)**

Family **Scolopacidae**	Species *Calidris acuminata*

Sharp-tailed Sandpiper

A smallish wader, the Sharp-tailed Sandpiper is like the rather less rare Pectoral Sandpiper without the closely streaked breast-band. Adults have a cap that is streaked dark and pale rufous, and a streaked breast petering out in a scattering of loose spots; immatures have a plain peachy breast, finely marked at the sides. All have greenish yellow legs and a yellowish base to the short, slightly curved bill.

OCCURRENCE Very rare vagrant in NW Europe, from NE Asia (E Siberia), early autumn.

VOICE Soft, quiet *wheep*.

streaked rufous cap

short bill

JUVENILE

diffuse breast-band

Length **17–21cm (6½–8½in)**	Wingspan **40cm (16in)**

Family **Scolopacidae**	Species *Tringa flavipes*

Lesser Yellowlegs

This looks like a small, delicate, greyer, slender Redshank or small Greenshank, and is also similar to the smaller, rounder Wood Sandpiper (see pp.190, 192, 189). It has long, bright, pale yellow to orange-yellow legs and, in flight, reveals plain wings and a square white rump. The bill is thin and straight (Greater Yellowlegs has a thicker bill, faintly upturned). It often wades quite deeply and so may be confused with Wilson's Phalarope (see p.438).

OCCURRENCE Regular but rare vagrant from North America to W Europe.

VOICE High, clear *tew*, sometimes repeated at same pitch.

thin, straight bill

yellow legs

JUVENILE

Length **23–25cm (9–10in)**	Wingspan **45–50cm (18–20in)**

Family **Scolopacidae**	Species *Tringa melanoleuca*

Greater Yellowlegs

More Greenshank-like (see p.192) than the Lesser Yellowlegs, the Greater Yellowlegs is nevertheless not always easy to distinguish from the Lesser. The bill is thicker, slightly paler-based, and faintly upturned, and, in most birds, there are more obvious white spots on the upperparts (which are browner than a summer Greenshank's or Lesser Yellowlegs'). The square white rump differs from the "V"-shaped wedge on a Greenshank.

OCCURRENCE Very rare vagrant to W Europe, from North America.

VOICE Loud, often with three notes, with third note at lower pitch, *tew-tew-tew*, but sometimes very like Lesser.

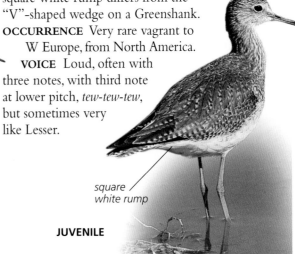

square white rump

JUVENILE

Length **30–35cm (12–14in)**	Wingspan **53–60cm (21–23½in)**

Family **Scolopacidae**	Species *Tringa solitaria*

Solitary Sandpiper

A small *Tringa* sandpiper, much like the Green Sandpiper (see p.188), this species is distinguished by its dark rump. It has a less obvious white face stripe but a bolder white eye-ring than the Green Sandpiper, and is darker, duller, and shorter-legged than a Wood Sandpiper (see p.189). Its long, tapered rear end is often bobbed up and down, as with the Green Sandpiper and the smaller, browner Common Sandpiper (see p.186).

OCCURRENCE Rare vagrant to NW Europe, from North America.

VOICE Rich *tewit-weet*.

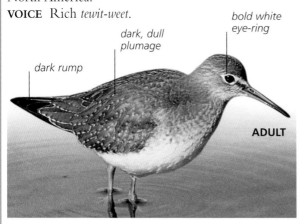

dark rump

dark, dull plumage

bold white eye-ring

ADULT

Length **18–21cm (7–8½in)**	Wingspan **35–39cm (14–15½in)**

Family **Scolopacidae**	Species *Actitis macularia*

Spotted Sandpiper

Very like a Common Sandpiper (see p.186), the shorter-tailed Spotted Sandpiper is distinguished in summer by a scattering of small or large black spots underneath. In autumn or winter, adults are plainer, greyer, with brighter yellow legs and a sharper call. Juveniles are plainer, less spotted on the edges of the longer wing feathers, but more contrastingly barred on the wing coverts.

OCCURRENCE Very rare visitor from North America, sometimes winters.

VOICE Sharp, thin *peet* or *peet-weet*.

short tail

plain greyish upperparts

ADULT (WINTER)

Length **18–20cm (7–8in)**	Wingspan **32–35cm (12½–14in)**

Family **Scolopacidae**	Species *Bartramia longicauda*

Upland Sandpiper

An unusual, slim-necked, long-tailed wader of dry ground, the Upland Sandpiper looks rather like a slim, young Ruff (see p.187) with shorter legs, a thin bill, and a dark-capped crown. The dark eyes stand out well on its pale face. The Upland Sandpiper is all-dark on wings and tail, and the underwing is dark and closely barred.

OCCURRENCE Very rare in autumn, from North America.

VOICE Whistling, bubbling note, *quip-ip-ip-ip* in flight.

dark crown

dark eye

thin bill

JUVENILE

long tail

Length **28–32cm (11–12½in)**	Wingspan **50–55cm (20–22in)**

Family **Scolopacidae**	Species *Micropalama himantopus*

Stilt Sandpiper

In water, when its long green legs are hidden, this species is often mistaken for a grey Ruff, Redshank (see pp.187, 190), or some other medium/small wader in winter plumage. Its long, thick, slightly downcurved bill is a useful clue. In summer, the barred underparts and a rusty cheek patch are obvious. Juveniles are marked with rufous above, streaked on the flanks, and show a dark cap and pale stripe over the eye (dowitcher-like). A square white rump shows in flight.

OCCURRENCE Rare vagrant to NW Europe from North America.

VOICE Soft, chirrupy *trrr-p*.

pale stripe over eye

long, thick bill

ADULT (WINTER)

Length **18–23cm (7–9in)**	Wingspan **37–42cm (14½–16½in)**

Family **Scolopacidae**	Species **Limnodromus scolopaceus**

Long-billed Dowitcher

This wader looks something like a cross between a Redshank and a Snipe (see pp.190, 200): it is typically quite pale and rather plain in autumn or winter, with a dark cap edged by a bold white line over each eye (an obvious "V" from the front). The bill is long, thick, and snipe-like, the legs short and greenish. In flight, it reveals a white wedge or long oval on the back and a whitish trailing edge to the wing. Good views reveal broad black and narrow white bars on the tail.

OCCURRENCE Regular but still rare vagrant to W Europe from North America.

VOICE Short, sharp *kik* or *keek*, often repeated in series such as *kip-ip-ip-ip*.

long, thick bill

close dark bars on tail

relatively short, green legs

JUVENILE

Length **27–30cm (10½–12in)**	Wingspan **42–49cm (16½–19½in)**

Family **Scolopacidae**	Species **Gallinago media**

Great Snipe

Difficult to identify when out of its usual range, the Great Snipe is a big, dark, heavy snipe with a rather thick bill and heavy, dark underpart barring. The closed wing shows lines of white feather tips. In flight, the adult shows big white tail sides, reduced on a juvenile. The upperwing is a better clue, with a central dark band, edged with white, right across to the outer edge. Its low, heavy, quiet flight is also a fair clue.

OCCURRENCE Breeds in Scandinavia, Baltic area, and eastwards; rare migrant in E Europe, vagrant in W.

VOICE Occasional deep croaks.

ADULT

thick bill

dark barring on underparts

white tips to coverts

Length **26–30cm (10–12in)**	Wingspan **43–50cm (17–20in)**

Family **Scolopacidae**	Species **Phalaropus tricolor**

Wilson's Phalarope

The largest phalarope, and most prone to feed on mud, Wilson's is slender but short-legged, less elegant on land than when swimming. In summer, a striking dark band curves back from the eye and down the neck. In winter, the back is pale grey, and there is only a hint of the neck stripe. Immatures have dark feathers with buff edges on the upperparts, and yellowish legs. All have a long, fine, straight bill and a white rump in flight. Yellowlegs and Wood Sandpipers (see p.189) are very similar.

OCCURRENCE Vagrant to W Europe from North America, in late spring and autumn.

VOICE Short, nasal *vit* in flight.

long, fine bill

ADULT (WINTER)

pale legs

Length **22–24cm (9–9½in)**	Wingspan **38–44cm (15–17½in)**

Family **Laridae**	Species **Larus genei**

Slender-billed Gull

This looks very like the Black-headed Gull (see p.208), except for the fact that it has a white head: there is no trace of a hood. It has a rather thick, long, orange-red to blackish bill and long, orange-red legs. Juveniles have weak brown markings on the wings and a narrow tail band. A close view reveals a pale eye (unlike any similar gulls), but this is hard to see at any distance.

OCCURRENCE Rare breeder, locally along Mediterranean coastal area; vagrant elsewhere.

VOICE Low, strained version of Black-headed Gull calls.

white head

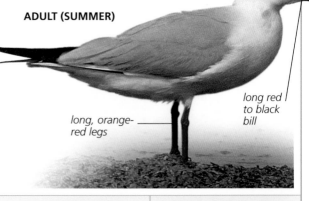

ADULT (SUMMER)

long, orange-red legs

long red to black bill

Length **37–42cm (14½–16½in)**	Wingspan **90–102cm (35–40in)**

Family **Laridae**	Species *Larus philadelphia*

Bonaparte's Gull

Resembling a small Black-headed Gull (see p.208), this gull has a slim, black bill like a Little Gull's (see p.218) and a light, airy flight like a tern's. Its upperwing is like a Black-headed's (a white outer triangle and black trailing edge), but the underwing is pure white except for a sharp, thin, black edge towards the tip. Adults in summer have slaty-black hoods; in winter and on immatures, the head is white with a dark ear-spot. Juveniles have a darker diagonal band across the wing coverts and darker trailing edge than a Black-headed Gull.

OCCURRENCE Rare vagrant to W Europe from North America.

VOICE High, sharp, tern-like notes and squealing calls.

black hood

slim black bill

ADULT (SUMMER)

Length **31–34cm (12–13½ in)**	Wingspan **79–84cm (31–33in)**

Family **Laridae**	Species *Larus delawarensis*

Ring-billed Gull

Like a stocky Common Gull (see p.214), but paler above, the Ring-billed Gull has less white between the grey of the back and black wingtip, a pale eye (looking dark at a distance), and a thicker bill, with a black band near the tip. The legs are greenish to yellow. One-year olds are more spotted on the neck and flanks, the black tail band less clear-cut.

OCCURRENCE Rare vagrant in NW Europe, regular in SW Britain, from North America.

VOICE Raucous, squealing calls.

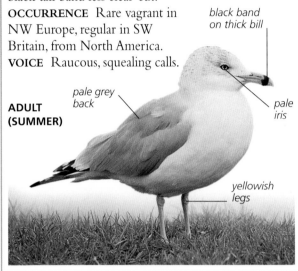

black band on thick bill

pale grey back

ADULT (SUMMER)

pale iris

yellowish legs

Length **41–49cm (16–19½ in)**	Wingspan **1.12–1.24m (3¾–4ft)**

Family **Laridae**	Species *Larus audouinii*

Audouin's Gull

Once very rare, now increasing, Audouin's Gull is slimmer-winged, narrower-tailed, and stubbier-billed than the Herring Gull (see p.211). Adults are very pale grey, their wingtips extensively black with tiny white spots on the feather tips. They have grey or greenish legs and dark red bills, banded black and tipped yellow. The dark eye and long white face shape are distinctive. Young birds are dark, with mostly black tails, very long wings, and blackish legs.

OCCURRENCE Breeds in E Spain, Balearics, Morocco, and Mediterranean islands, rare in Atlantic.

VOICE Low, nasal calls.

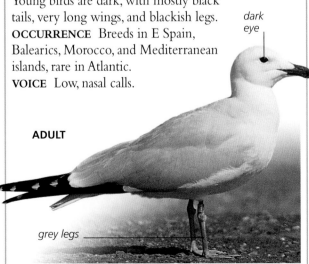

dark eye

ADULT

grey legs

Length **44–52cm (17½–20½ in)**	Wingspan **1.17–1.28m (3¾–4¼ft)**

Family **Laridae**	Species *Larus ichthyaetus*

Great Black-headed Gull

In summer, this huge gull has a black hood, pale grey back, white outer wings, and small black wingtips, set off by yellow legs and a long yellow bill banded black and red. In winter, the hood is lost and immature birds have a grey smudge through the eye. Often confused with Herring Gulls (see p.211), the flat forehead and long bill profile are useful for identification.

OCCURRENCE Very rare in Europe, regular in Middle East outside breeding season.

VOICE Deep, nasal, throttled call in flight but mostly silent.

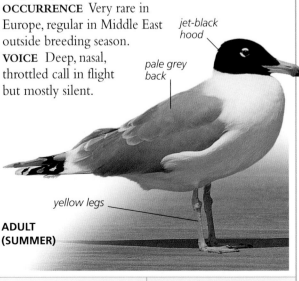

jet-black hood

pale grey back

yellow legs

ADULT (SUMMER)

Length **58–67cm (23–26in)**	Wingspan **1.46–1.62m (4¾–5¼ft)**

Family **Laridae**	Species *Larus sabini*

Sabine's Gull

This rare autumn migrant is brought close inshore in northwest Europe by Atlantic gales. It resembles a juvenile Kittiwake (see p.215) but the wing pattern is composed of three sharp triangles, dark (grey on adults, grey-brown on juveniles) in front, black at the tip, and pure white at the back, with no diagonal black band. Unlike immature Kittiwakes, which lose most of their black and look dull and scruffy, Sabine's Gull looks very neat.

OCCURRENCE Regular in autumn off W Europe, rare in North Sea.

VOICE Tern-like calls unlikely to be heard from migrants.

short dark bill with yellow tip

dark head (pale in autumn, winter)

ADULT (SUMMER)

black legs

Length **30–36cm (12–14in)**	Wingspan **80–87cm (32–34in)**

Family **Laridae**	Species *Larus pipixcan*

Franklin's Gull

A small, dark, short-legged gull, Franklin's Gull looks like a Laughing Gull but has a white band crossing the wing near the black and white tip. The bill is typically short, less tapered, and less drooping in appearance than a Laughing Gull's, but some are difficult to separate on the ground. Young birds have white on the breast and flanks where Laughing Gulls are dark, and dark outer primaries unlike the much paler Black-headed Gulls (see p.208). Common Gulls are paler and much larger (see p.214).

OCCURRENCE Very rare in NW Europe, from North America.

VOICE Soft nasal calls, but usually rather silent.

dark hood (jet-black in summer)

pale eye-ring

ADULT (WINTER)

Length **32–36cm (12½–14in)**	Wingspan **80–87cm (32–34in)**

Family **Laridae**	Species *Larus atricilla*

Laughing Gull

A long-winged, sharp-featured gull with a long black bill and black legs, the Laughing Gull is usually easy to identify. Summer adults have jet-black hoods with thin white eyelids. In winter, the head has only dusky smudges. The back is a deep mid-grey. Young birds are browner on the wings with black along the hind edge, have black tail bands, and are smoky grey across the breast and along the flanks, looking very contrasty with their white rump and underside.

OCCURRENCE Rare vagrant in W Europe, from North America.

VOICE Loud, squealing notes.

black bill

IMMATURE (1ST WINTER)

long wings

black legs

Length **36–41cm (14–16in)**	Wingspan **0.98–1.1m (3¼–3½ft)**

Family **Laridae**	Species *Pagophila eburnea*

Ivory Gull

Almost pigeon-like with its dumpy form and short legs, the Ivory Gull is longer and more tapered at the back and longer-winged in flight. It has black legs, dark eyes, and a grey bill with a yellow tip. Juveniles are lightly spotted with black and smudged dark on the face. Albino Kittiwakes and Common Gulls (see pp.215, 214) may cause identification problems: the bill colours are then important.

OCCURRENCE Rare vagrant in W Europe; breeds in Svalbard and high Arctic islands.

VOICE Loud, shrill tern-like calls but mostly silent in winter.

white body with dark spots

IMMATURE (1ST WINTER)

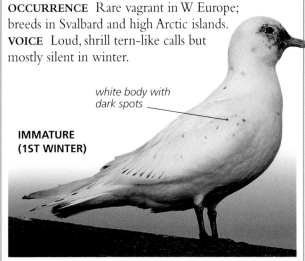

Length **41–47cm (16–18½in)**	Wingspan **1–1.13m (3¼–3¾ft)**

Family **Laridae**	Species *Rhodostethia rosea*

Ross's Gull

A rare Arctic species, Ross's Gull is pigeon-like in form, with rather broad-based but long wings and a wedge-shaped tail. Its very short bill is black, the short legs red or pinkish. Summer adults are flushed bright pink and have a thin black collar; winter birds are duller and the black is reduced or replaced by smudges of grey. Young birds have a Little Gull-like (see p.218) dark zigzag pattern but the hindwing is all white; they show a dark ear-spot and a smoky grey hindneck.

OCCURRENCE Rare vagrant, mostly in winter, sometimes spring, from Arctic.

VOICE Mostly silent.

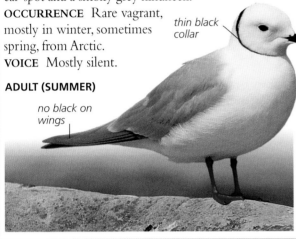

thin black collar

ADULT (SUMMER)

no black on wings

Length **29–32cm (11½–12½in)**	Wingspan **73–80cm (29–32in)**

Family **Sternidae**	Species *Sterna maxima*

Royal Tern

This is a large, magnificent tern, almost the size of a Caspian Tern (see p.225) but more elegant. A very pale bird, it has white underwings marked only by narrow dark feather tips (Caspian Tern has a big black patch) and a white rump (the smaller Lesser Crested Tern is greyer). It is white-headed with a black nape, but has a black cap in summer; the bill is dagger-like, and rich orange. Immatures have dark primaries and hindwing bars, like a young Common Gull (see p.214).

OCCURRENCE Very rare vagrant in NW Europe, from North America and/or Africa.

VOICE Rather weak, strident, scratchy calls.

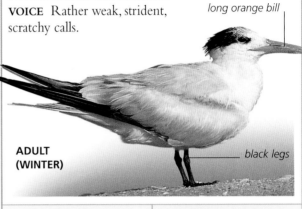

long orange bill

ADULT (WINTER)

black legs

Length **42–49cm (16½–19½in)**	Wingspan **86–92cm (34–36in)**

Family **Sternidae**	Species *Sterna bengalensis*

Lesser Crested Tern

Large and elegant, like a slightly darker-backed Sandwich Tern (see p.220), the Lesser Crested has a grey rump (hard to see), black legs, and a long, slim, dagger-like, bright orange bill. In summer, it has a ragged black crest, in winter a white forehead and crown. It is difficult to separate in isolation from the Royal Tern which is bigger, thicker-billed, and whiter-rumped. Immatures have dark wing markings like a young Common Gull (see p.214), but less bold than on a Royal Tern.

OCCURRENCE Occasional birds in Sandwich Tern colonies in summer, but a rare vagrant.

VOICE Loud, grating, Sandwich Tern-like *kirrik*.

orange bill

ADULT (SUMMER)

Length **33–40cm (13–16in)**	Wingspan **76–82cm (30–32in)**

Family **Sternidae**	Species *Sterna fuscata*

Sooty Tern

A large black and white tern, the Sooty Tern is a tropical bird, spending most of its time well out over the sea. It looks boldly pied, with a long and deeply forked tail, the streamers tipped with a blob of white; feather textures differ, causing slight variations in some lights. The forehead has a deep, wide white patch that reaches to just above the eye. Young birds are dark above with pale bars, and mostly very dark brown below.

OCCURRENCE Rare vagrant in summer and autumn; breeds in Red Sea, Caribbean.

VOICE Mostly silent away from breeding areas.

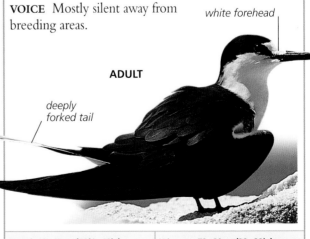

white forehead

ADULT

deeply forked tail

Length **42–45cm (16½–18in)**	Wingspan **72–80cm (28–32in)**

Family **Sternidae**	Species *Sterna anaethetus*

Bridled Tern

Like the Sooty Tern, the Bridled Tern is a tropical seabird that looks very dark above and white below, with a long, forked, white-edged, dark tail. Good views reveal a contrast between the brownish grey back and black cap and wingtips; the white forehead tapers back into a point behind the eye. Care is required to rule out the larger, blacker Sooty Tern, which is also a rare vagrant in Europe. Juveniles are dark and barred above, paler below.

OCCURRENCE Rare vagrant mostly in late summer; breeds in Red Sea, W Africa.

VOICE Mostly silent.

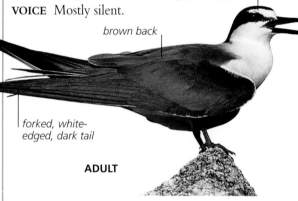

white over eye

brown back

forked, white-edged, dark tail

ADULT

Length **37–42cm (14½–16½in)**	Wingspan **65–72cm (26–28in)**

Family **Sternidae**	Species *Sterna forsteri*

Forster's Tern

Very like a Common Tern (see p.222), Forster's has paler wingtips (all frosty-white or pearly grey in winter) and white underparts in summer. In winter, it shows a bold blackish mask and a black bill (like the Gull-billed Tern, see p.221); the bill is shorter than on a Sandwich Tern (see p.220) and slimmer than a Gull-billed's. Juveniles have a black mask and dusky grey centres to the tertials. The shape, size, and behaviour are much the same as for the Common Tern.

OCCURRENCE Rare vagrant to W Europe, mostly late autumn or winter, from North America.

VOICE Mostly silent in winter.

ADULT (WINTER)

black ear patch

Length **33–36cm (13–14in)**	Wingspan **64–70cm (25–28in)**

Family **Sternidae**	Species *Chlidonias leucopterus*

White-winged Black Tern

The three *Chlidonias* terns, Black, Whiskered (see pp.226, 227), and White-winged Black, are the "marsh" terns; this is the smallest and dumpiest, with a slightly quicker flight action than the other two. In summer, it is boldly black with white wings and tail; autumn juveniles have a dark back, pale wings, whitish rump, and clean white breast sides (no dark spot as on Black); winter adults are much paler, with whitish rumps.

OCCURRENCE Breeds in E Europe, rare migrant elsewhere, mostly in autumn.

VOICE Short, simple, squeaky *kek* notes in flight.

black upper-parts

white forewings

white tail

ADULT (SUMMER)

Length **20–24cm (8–9½in)**	Wingspan **50–56cm (20–22in)**

Family **Alcidae**	Species *Uria lomvia*

Brünnich's Guillemot

Extremely like a Guillemot (see p.231), Brünnich's is more thickset and thicker-billed, with a white streak along the gape and a pointed white breast against the dark foreneck (rounded on Guillemot). Its flanks are pure white, not streaked. In winter, the head is dark to below the eye, without the dark eye-stripe of a Guillemot or the white patch behind the eye of a Razorbill (which it otherwise resembles, see p.232). It looks the most solid, short-necked, and deep-bellied of the auks in flight.

OCCURRENCE Breeds in Iceland, far N Scandinavia; vagrant in NW Europe.

VOICE Crow-like growling notes.

ADULT (SUMMER)

white stripe on black bill

Length **40–44cm (16–17½in)**	Wingspan **64–75cm (25–30in)**

Family **Pteroclididae**	Species *Pterocles orientalis*

Black-bellied Sandgrouse

Sandgrouse are pigeon-like in form, partridge-like in plumage, with tiny bills, short legs, long, tapered wings, and long tails. The Black-bellied has a short tail, and is chunky, with an obvious bold black underside and white underwings with black tips. On the ground, the male's plain face and breast (one narrow bar at the lower edge) are distinctive; the back is spotted on the male and closely barred in a complex pattern on the spotted female. Black-bellied Sandgrouse are shy; they fly long distances each morning to drink.

OCCURRENCE Breeds in C and S Spain, Turkey, in wide open, dry plains.

VOICE Rolling, bubbling flight call, fast trill slowing to stutter.

FEMALE

black underside

Length **30–35cm (12–14in)**	Wingspan **60–65cm (23½–26in)**

Family **Pteroclididae**	Species *Pterocles alchata*

Pin-tailed Sandgrouse

Slimmer than the Black-bellied Sandgrouse, the Pin-tailed has a fine tail spike, a bright white belly, and white underwings with bold black tips (like Black-bellied). On the ground, the face looks rufous with a black eye-stripe, the breast narrowly banded with black, the back beautifully spotted (male) or barred (female) with buff in a delicate and complex pattern. Large flocks visit pools to drink each morning.

OCCURRENCE Rare breeder in C and S Spain, very rare in S France, in arid, stony areas.

VOICE In flight, rhythmic, grating, descending *cata-cata* or *rrria-rrria*.

spotted back

MALE

Length **28–32cm (11–12½in)**	Wingspan **55–63cm (22–25in)**

Family **Cuculidae**	Species *Clamator glandarius*

Great Spotted Cuckoo

This unusual-looking bird is quite unlike the Cuckoo (see p.239). In flight, it is long and slim, with broad-based, tapered, slightly rounded wings and a long, narrow tail, its head small and held up, the chest rather deep. Adults are grey above, with white spots, whitish below, and grey on the crown. Juveniles have a black cap, darker back with pale spots, and a rusty outer wing. The yellowish chest and white belly are striking. It perches with wings and tail drooped.

OCCURRENCE Breeds in Spain, Portugal, and S France; rare in Italy; vagrant farther north.

VOICE Loud, rattling or cackling trill often given from cover.

white below

white-spotted, grey upperparts

ADULT

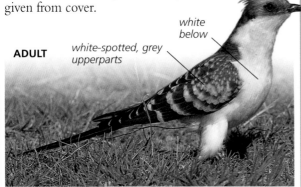

Length **35–39cm (14–15½in)**	Wingspan **55–65cm (22–26in)**

Family **Cuculidae**	Species *Coccyzus americanus*

Yellow-billed Cuckoo

A small, neat, white-breasted cuckoo, the Yellow-billed Cuckoo is pale brown above with rusty wingtips and black tail sides with big white spots. The white tail feather tips may be obvious when perched. The small eyes are dark, and the bill short and slightly curved. In flight the long wings and tail and the slender, raised head give a typically cuckoo appearance: it usually swoops upwards to a perch. Yellow-billed Cuckoos rarely survive more than a day or so when they reach Europe.

OCCURRENCE Very rare vagrant to NW Europe in late autumn, from North America.

VOICE Vagrants are silent.

black-tipped yellow bill

pale brown above

white spots on tail when spread

Length **29–32cm (11½–12½in)**	Wingspan **48–52cm (19–20½in)**

Family **Psittacidae**	Species *Psittacula krameri*

Ring-necked Parakeet

This introduced bird to Europe and the Middle East thrives in very localized areas. The typical long-tailed parakeet form, with a short bill and bright green plumage, as well as the loud calls, are distinctive (but other species escape at times and could be confused). Males have a black chin and dark neck-ring (red on the nape); females have a plain green head.

OCCURRENCE
Various populations from SE England to Istanbul and Cairo, mostly in towns and suburbs.
VOICE Loud, squealing, squawking calls.

red nape

black chin of male

MALE — long tail

Length **39–43cm (15½–17in)**	Wingspan **42–48cm (16½–19in)**

Family **Strigidae**	Species *Strix nebulosa*

Great Grey Owl

Sitting upright in a tree this owl looks enormous; in flight it is very impressive. It is very large-headed with a grey facial disc and white marks between the eyes. The outer wings have buff patches and dark bars. Young birds look dark grey; watching them may attract dangerous attacks from angry parents.

white crescents between small yellow eyes

broad grey facial disc

OCCURRENCE
Breeds in boggy northern forests, in NE Sweden and Finland; rare vagrant elsewhere.
VOICE Deep, growling notes; song is series of slow, booming hoots.

ADULT

massive body

Length **59–68cm (23–27in)**	Wingspan **1.28–1.48m (4¼–4¾ft)**

Family **Strigidae**	Species *Strix uralensis*

Ural Owl

This big, grey-brown owl has a longer tail than a Tawny (see p.241) or Great Grey Owl, a plainer, pale grey-buff face, and small dark eyes (with no white crescents). The back has two lines of pale spots; the underside is white with dark streaks. The wings are more uniform than a Great Grey's, although the tips are closely barred. Young birds are paler-faced and browner than young Great Greys, distinguished by their eye colour.

OCCURRENCE Rare breeder in mountain forest in E Scandinavia, NE Europe, and E Europe.
VOICE Deep, cooing hoots, two, then two, then three with pauses.

ADULT

dark streaks on pale underside

long tail

Length **50–59cm (20–23in)**	Wingspan **1.03–1.24m (3½–4ft)**

Family **Strigidae**	Species *Nyctea scandiaca*

Snowy Owl

A huge owl, big-headed and broad-winged, with a tiny hint of ear tufts, the Snowy Owl is nearly all-white (male) or white with narrow dark bars (female). Young birds are mostly grey-brown. Barn Owls (see p.249) in car headlights can look big and white but Snowy Owls are giants, with a distinctive fast-up, slow-down wingbeat and a liking for remote landscapes.

OCCURRENCE Rare breeder in Iceland and N Scandinavia; vagrant elsewhere.
VOICE Grating, chattering, and barking notes.

yellow eye

all-white body

MALE

Length **53–65cm (21–26in)**	Wingspan **1.25–1.5m (4–5ft)**

Family **Strigidae**	Species *Surnia ulula*

Hawk Owl

As it perches on a treetop or, more especially, flies across a forest clearing, this owl gives a hawk-like effect. It has a much bigger head, with a bold black "frame" to the white face and fierce yellow eyes; the back is dark, broadly smudged and spotted with white. Young Hawk Owls are darker and more uniformly grey. No other owl has the same big-headed, long-tailed, upright shape of the Hawk Owl.

OCCURRENCE Breeds in N Scandinavia in boggy areas or clearings in forest.

VOICE Long, rapid, bubbling song and fast, chattering calls.

black "frame" to white face

white underside with grey bars

long tail

ADULT

Length **35–43cm (14–17in)**	Wingspan **69–82cm (27–32in)**

Family **Caprimulgidae**	Species *Caprimulgus ruficollis*

Red-necked Nightjar

This nightjar is restricted in range and habitat and best separated from the common Nightjar (see p.250) by its call. Its rusty collar is distinctive in good light; both sexes have white wing and tail spots and usually a large white throat patch. The shape and actions are the same as a Nightjar's, very short- and broad-headed, long-tailed, and long-winged; the tail is often fanned and broad, almost like a third wing.

OCCURRENCE Breeds almost throughout Spain and Portugal, rare in S France; rare vagrant elsewhere.

VOICE Repetitive, wooden, hollow, slightly squeaky double tap, *ko-tok ko-tok ko-tok ko-tok*.

rusty collar

Length **30–34cm (12–13½in)**	Wingspan **60–65cm (23½–26in)**

Family **Apodidae**	Species *Apus caffer*

White-rumped Swift

Overhead the White-rumped Swift is a fast-moving, narrow-winged, shapely swift, very dark except for paler marks on the hindwing and sometimes a paler midwing band. It has narrow, swept-back, scythe-shaped, stiff wings and a narrow, forked tail, often held closed in a single spike. The white rump is a narrow, curved band barely visible from below (unlike the broad, easily seen rump of the Little Swift).

OCCURRENCE Breeds very locally in SW Spain; winters in Africa.

VOICE Short, hard notes running together as fast trill.

stiff dark wings

crescentic white rump

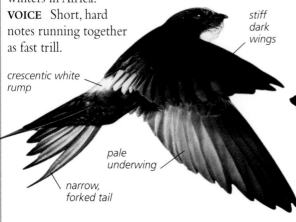

pale underwing

narrow, forked tail

Length **14–15cm (5½–6in)**	Wingspan **33–37cm (13–14½in)**

Family **Apodidae**	Species *Apus affinis*

Little Swift

With straight, blade-like wings and a short, square tail, the Little Swift looks paler-winged and darker-bodied overhead, with a dull white throat, but in any other view the square white rump is very obvious. In comparison, House Martins (see p.282) are less stiff- and narrow-winged, and white beneath as well as on the rump; White-rumped Swifts have scythe-like wings, a narrow white rump, and a deeply forked tail. Flocks of Little Swifts are often seen over towns and villages in areas where this species is common.

OCCURRENCE Very rare vagrant from N Africa and Middle East.

VOICE Fast, twittering sounds.

dull white throat

broad white rump

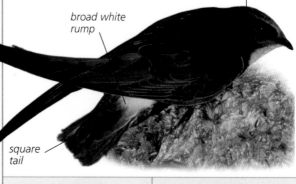

square tail

Length **12–13cm (4¾–5in)**	Wingspan **32–34cm (12½–13½in)**

Family **Picidae**	Species *Dendrocopos syriacus*

Syrian Woodpecker

This is the most similar woodpecker to the common Great Spotted Woodpecker (see p.265). Male (red nape), female (black nape), and juvenile (red crown) variations are like Great Spotted but the red under the tail is replaced by pale pink-red on Syrian. The black face-stripe does not join the black hind-neck (hard to tell when the bird is hunched), and the bill is rather long.

OCCURRENCE Common in SE Europe, scarce but spreading northwest into E Europe.

VOICE Soft *kik*; drumming slightly longer and less abrupt than Great Spotted's.

pale pink-red under tail

FEMALE

Length **23–25cm (9–10in)**	Wingspan **38–44cm (15–17½in)**

Family **Picidae**	Species *Dendrocopos leucotos*

White-backed Woodpecker

A rare, large woodpecker of undisturbed forest, this obvious pied type has barred wings (no white shoulder patch) and a white rump. Close views are difficult, but show a red crown on males and buffish underparts deepening to pinkish red under the tail. A white band between the dark back and cheek patches is distinctive. Old woodland is important for this declining species.

OCCURRENCE Very rare in Pyrenees; scattered resident in E Europe and S Scandinavia.

VOICE Dull, throaty *kik*, sometimes repeated; drumming accelerates.

red crown

pinkish red under tail

MALE

Length **25–28cm (10–11in)**	Wingspan **40–45cm (16–18in)**

Family **Alaudidae**	Species *Calandrella rufescens*

Lesser Short-toed Lark

This small, pale, streaky lark is much like the Short-toed Lark (see p. 274), but distinguished by a gorget of fine, dark streaks; it also has more uniform wings (less contrasted rows of dark feather centres). In some ways it looks more like an undersized Skylark (see p. 270), but lacks the pale hind edge to the wings. Close views should show a longer wingtip point. The calls are important in helping to make identification certain.

OCCURRENCE Rare in S and E Spain and Turkey, Middle East, and N Africa.

VOICE Dry, buzzing trill, *drrrrt*; song rich, varied, quick, with buzzy calls intermixed.

streaked breast

long wing point

Length **13–14cm (5–5½in)**	Wingspan **24–32cm (9½–12½in)**

Family **Alaudidae**	Species *Chersophilus duponti*

Dupont's Lark

In its hot, sandy, open, often saline habitat, Dupont's Lark is usually difficult to see: it prefers to run rather than fly when disturbed. This streaky lark stands upright, showing a closely streaked breast and white underside. In flight, the wings look plain above, pale below (unlike Skylark or Calandra Lark, see p.270, 275), and the tail a little longer than on Crested Lark (see p.271).

OCCURRENCE Rare and local in E Spain and North Africa, in short, sparse, vegetation.

VOICE Call thin *choo-chee*; song short, whistling, fluty notes.

flattish crown

curved bill

long, narrow neck

Length **17–18cm (6½–7in)**	Wingspan **30cm (12in)**

Family **Motacillidae**	Species *Anthus richardi*

Richard's Pipit

This is a large pipit, Skylark-like (see p.270) in its size, bulk, and general plumage. It often stands upright, breast pushed out, on long, thick legs, its bold, strong bill quite distinct. There is no trace of a crest. The face is marked by a bold whitish area around the eye with a dark mark beneath; there is a thick black line on each side of the throat (less marked on a Tawny Pipit, see p.289). The long tail is often bobbed.

OCCURRENCE Regular, but rare, late autumn migrant in NW Europe, from Asia.

VOICE Loud, rasping *schreep* and quieter variations.

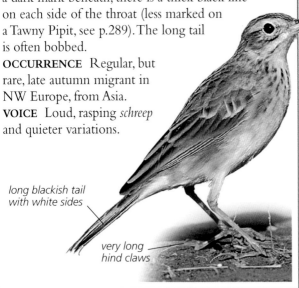

long blackish tail with white sides

very long hind claws

Length **17–20cm (6½–8in)**	Wingspan **29–33cm (11½–13in)**

Family **Motacillidae**	Species *Anthus godlewski*

Blyth's Pipit

Only recently observed with any regularity in Europe, Blyth's Pipit is difficult to identify, resembling Richard's and juvenile Tawny Pipits (see p.289). It is fractionally smaller than Richard's, with a shorter tail, a slightly richer underside colour, a slightly shorter, pointed bill, and shorter hind claws. It may look more like a small pipit species and more wagtail-like than Richard's, but only close observation and several clearly heard calls can separate them for certain.

OCCURRENCE Very rare vagrant in NW Europe, from Asia.

VOICE Slightly higher than Richard's, less explosive, with fading, breathy quality, *psh-eee*.

short tail

wagtail-like shape

Length **15–17cm (6–6½in)**	Wingspan **28–30cm (11–12in)**

Family **Motacillidae**	Species *Anthus hodgsoni*

Olive-backed Pipit

Looking rather dark and uniform above or bright and streaked in front in a brief view, this pipit reveals a subtle pattern on closer examination. It is greenish, with very soft streaking above, and has a dark cap, a broad, bright cream stripe above the eye, a dark stripe through the eye, and a cream spot on the ear coverts. The underside is bright yellow-buff to buff with bold black streaks. It frequently walks in longish vegetation, bobbing its tail, but flies into trees if disturbed.

OCCURRENCE Rare vagrant in NW Europe from Asia, mostly in late autumn.

VOICE Tree Pipit-like hoarse or buzzing *spees* or *tees*.

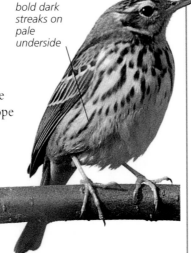

bold dark streaks on pale underside

Length **14–15cm (5½–6in)**	Wingspan **24–27cm (9½–10½in)**

Family **Motacillidae**	Species *Anthus gustavi*

Pechora Pipit

Slim and streaky like most pipits, the Pechora Pipit has bolder pale stripes on the back (edged black), striking white wingbars, a buff breast, a white belly streaked with black, and a pinkish-based bill. It is difficult to see well and crouches when disturbed. The breast/belly contrast, wingbars, and longer wingtips help separate it from a juvenile Red-throated Pipit (see p.288).

OCCURRENCE Rare vagrant in autumn in NW Europe, from Asia.

VOICE Short, slightly buzzed, clicking *dzep*, not often heard.

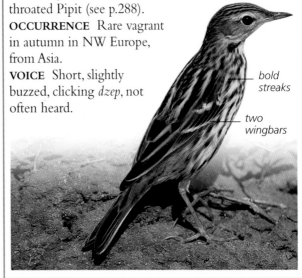

bold streaks

two wingbars

Length **14–15cm (5½–6in)**	Wingspan **23–25cm (9–10in)**

Family **Motacillidae**	Species *Motacilla citreola*

Citrine Wagtail

In spring, male Citrine Wagtails look like Yellow Wagtails (see p.291), but with a greyer back and a narrow black band between the back and yellow head. Females lack the black, have less yellow, but show yellow around dark cheeks (which have a paler centre). Autumn juveniles are like young Pied Wagtails (see p.290), with a plainer chest; they have pale-centred cheeks, and are pale buffish between the eye and bill.

OCCURRENCE Regular in Middle East, rare in SE Europe, vagrant (mostly autumn) in NW Europe.

VOICE Like Yellow, but harsh, distinctly buzzed *tzsip*.

black collar

yellow underside

MALE (SPRING)

Length **16–17cm (6½in)**	Wingspan **24–27cm (9½–10½in)**

Family **Turdidae**	Species *Cercotrichas galactotes*

Rufous Bush Robin

Bush robins are small, long-tailed chats, often raising and fanning their tails and bounding along in leaping hops on the ground. This species is bright buff, with a ginger-orange tail tipped with narrow black and big white spots. A bold white line over the eye and black eye-stripe are distinct. In SE Europe and the Middle East, birds have dull sandy brown on the head and back, with a contrasted rufous rump. The tail spots are especially obvious in flight.

OCCURRENCE Scarce breeder in S Spain, Balkans, Middle East, and North Africa.

VOICE Clicking and buzzing calls; high, clear, thrush-like song.

bold white line

rufous tail with white spots

Length **15–17cm (6–6½in)**	Wingspan **22–27cm (9–10½in)**

Family **Turdidae**	Species *Tarsiger cyanurus*

Red-flanked Bluetail

This rare bird inhabits dense northern forests. Males are slaty blue above, brighter on the crown, with a white chin and pale underside edged orange. Females and immatures are browner, with dusky chests and orange flanks; the tail is dull steel-blue. The white throat stands out as a well-defined wedge. In general, the form and behaviour resemble the Robin (see p.300), but it is a shy bird. It frequently flicks its wings and tail.

OCCURRENCE Breeds in extreme NE Europe; very rare vagrant in NW Europe in autumn.

VOICE Short whistle and hard, short *tak*; song short, bright, melancholy phrases.

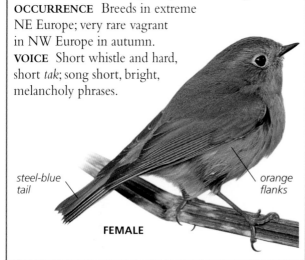

steel-blue tail

orange flanks

FEMALE

Length **13–14cm (5–5½in)**	Wingspan **21–24cm (8½–9½in)**

Family **Turdidae**	Species *Oenanthe isabellina*

Isabelline Wheatear

A pale, female or young Wheatear (see p.306), especially of the large Greenland race, can look very much like this rarer species. Greyish brown above, with slightly darker and weakly marked wings, it has a tapering whitish stripe over the eye (less broad and flared than on Wheatear). The tail has a broad black band with a very short central "T" stem, leaving a squarish, slightly creamy white rump.

OCCURRENCE Breeds in NE Greece, Turkey, and Middle East; rare vagrant in NW Europe.

VOICE Short, hard call; song includes short, repeated whistles.

thick, long bill

dark spot on wings

creamy buff underside

black tail

Length **15–16cm (6–6½in)**	Wingspan **27–31cm (10½–12in)**

| Family **Turdidae** | Species *Oenanthe cypriaca* |

Cyprus Wheatear

Earlier regarded as a race of the Pied Wheatear, this bird is now treated as a species. It likes rocky areas with short, often sparse, vegetation. Males have dusky grey caps outlined with white, against a largely dark body, except for buff and white underparts and a vivid white rump and tail base; females are browner, rich buff beneath with a dark throat. The tail has a broad black band at the tip.

OCCURRENCE Except as a migrant through the Middle East to Africa, confined to Cyprus, March to October.

VOICE A sharp *tsak* and upswept *tsuee*, often in combination; buzzy, repetitive song.

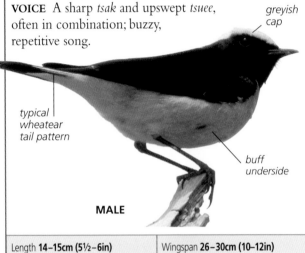

greyish cap

typical wheatear tail pattern

buff underside

MALE

| Length **14–15cm (5½–6in)** | Wingspan **26–30cm (10–12in)** |

| Family **Turdidae** | Species *Catharus minimus* |

Grey-cheeked Thrush

Several North American thrushes are small, like softly marked miniature Song Thrushes (see p.313). The Grey-cheeked Thrush is dull olive-brown, with a greyer face marked by a thin, weak eye-ring and cold greyish chest marked by rounded, blurry, dark spots. The underwing (usually hard to see) has several dark and whitish bands. This is a shy bird, usually remaining on or close to the ground in thick bushes.

OCCURRENCE Very rare late autumn vagrant in NW Europe, from North America.

VOICE Shrill *tsee*.

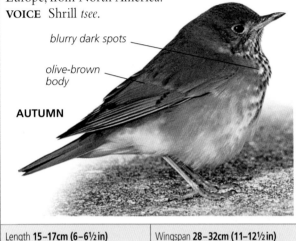

blurry dark spots

olive-brown body

AUTUMN

| Length **15–17cm (6–6½in)** | Wingspan **28–32cm (11–12½in)** |

| Family **Turdidae** | Species *Zoothera dauma* |

White's Thrush

Only a juvenile Mistle Thrush (with bright, pale speckling above and pale wingbars; see p.315) looks much like a White's Thrush. The latter is a difficult bird to observe, being wary and flighty and keeping to low cover where it creeps and shuffles secretively. It is a pale, sandy buff bird with black crescents below; the back has black-edged buff spots. In flight, the tail looks dark with pale sides and the underwing flashes striking black and white stripes (Mistle Thrush has plain white underwings).

OCCURRENCE Rare vagrant, typically in late autumn, in NW Europe, from Asia.

VOICE Silent bird on migration.

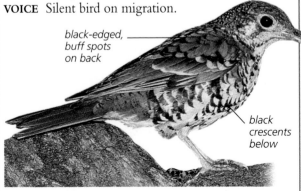

black-edged, buff spots on back

black crescents below

| Length **27–31cm (10½–12in)** | Wingspan **40–45cm (16–18in)** |

| Family **Turdidae** | Species *Zoothera sibirica* |

Siberian Thrush

Like the other *Zoothera* species, White's Thrush, this bird has bold black and white bands under the wings, sometimes visible as it flies off. Males are slate-grey, blacker on the face, with a white stripe over each eye, a white belly, and white tips to the outer tail feathers; immature males are duller. Females are brown, barred with black crescent-shaped marks below, with a buff line over the eye and a broader buff band under the cheeks. The white tail corners and banded underwings are distinctive.

OCCURRENCE Very rare vagrant in NW Europe in autumn/winter, from Asia.

VOICE Thin, simple call, *tsee*.

buff band under cheeks

dark crescent-shaped marks below

FEMALE

| Length **20–21cm (8–8½in)** | Wingspan **34–36cm (13½–14in)** |

Family **Turdidae**	Species **Turdus ruficollis**

Dark-throated Thrush

The two forms, the Black-throated and the Red-throated, are both Blackbird-like (see p.317) with pale grey-brown backs and dull white underparts with dusky streaking. The face and chest are black on male Black-throateds and dusky rust-red on Red-throateds. Immatures are streaked on the face and breast, with a hint of the black or red colour developing in males. The rump is a paler grey than the tail.
OCCURRENCE Both very rare in W Europe, in autumn/winter, from Asia.
VOICE Fieldfare-like (see p.316) chacking calls.

grey back

dark chest

JUVENILE MALE (BLACK-THROATED)

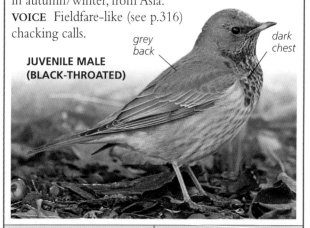

Length **23–26cm (9–10in)**	Wingspan **37–40cm (14½–16in)**

Family **Turdidae**	Species **Turdus obscurus**

Eyebrowed Thrush

A neat, smallish thrush, the Eyebrowed Thrush shares the pale stripe over the eye with a Redwing (see p.314). It has a white spot under the eye, and orange flanks and breast-band. The bill is yellowish at the base and the legs look dull orange-yellow. The underside is more uniformly orange than any Redwing's and entirely lacks streaks or spots. Adults have a grey hood, more contrasted than the autumn immatures.
OCCURRENCE Rare autumn vagrant in NW Europe, from Siberia.
VOICE Thin, Redwing-like *tseeee* note.

pale stripe over eye

white spot under eye

AUTUMN

Length **21–23cm (8½–9in)**	Wingspan **36–38cm (14–15in)**

Family **Turdidae**	Species **Turdus naumanni**

Dusky Thrush

The two forms of this species are very different: the "Dusky Thrush" has rich, dark upperparts, bold black and white face stripes, and white underparts spotted black (concentrated in a breast-band and flank spots), and "Naumann's Thrush" has orange-buff on the face, orange spots on the underside, and a rusty rump and tail. Both are obvious medium-large thrushes, bold and upright like a Song Thrush (see p.313), but shy and likely to fly off low and fast if approached.
OCCURRENCE Very rare vagrant in W Europe, from Siberia, mostly in autumn/winter.
VOICE Rather hard, sharp alarm note.

white stripes on face

DUSKY FORM

Length **20–23cm (8–9in)**	Wingspan **36–39cm (14–15½in)**

Family **Sylviidae**	Species **Sylvia hortensis**

Orphean Warbler

A big warbler of olive groves and bushy slopes, the Orphean Warbler is rather like a massive Lesser Whitethroat (see p.323). Males have dark grey heads, somewhat blacker on the cheeks, with big white throats and whitish eyes. Females and immatures are slightly browner above and slightly buffer on the chest (not so white beneath or pure grey above as the male), and have dark eyes. The long dark tail has white sides, unlike a Blackcap's (see p.322).
OCCURRENCE Breeds in Mediterranean region and N to C France; very rare outside this range.
VOICE Hard *tak*; simple/repetitive in SW, more prolonged in SE Europe.

pale eye

long tail

buff chest

MALE

Length **15–16cm (6–6½in)**	Wingspan **20–25cm (8–10in)**

Family **Sylviidae**	Species *Sylvia melanothorax*

Cyprus Warbler

A typical *Sylvia* warbler in its spiky-billed, capped appearance with an inquisitive expression, bulky body, and slim, sometimes raised tail, this is a Sardinian Warbler-like (see p. 324) bird with dusky markings beneath. Males show a white streak between the black head and dark-spotted throat; the underparts are spotted blackish. Females are greyer, the chest more subtly mottled. Both have a red orbital ring and a thin white outer eye-ring. All have dark spots under the white-edged tail.

OCCURRENCE Breeds in Cyprus; rare migrant through Middle East.

VOICE Dry, ticking notes and rattling alarm call.

black head

spotted underparts

MALE (SPRING)

Length **13cm (5in)**	Wingspan **15–18cm (6–7in)**

Family **Sylviidae**	Species *Sylvia rueppelli*

Rüppell's Warbler

Bigger than a Sardinian Warbler (see p.324), Rüppell's Warbler is even more striking, with its black face, grey nape, white moustachial stripe, and big black throat. A red eye-ring is also obvious. Females have a grey face and a pale throat with darker spots. Juveniles are paler still, grey-faced, with a faint reddish eye-ring; they share the adults' dark-centred, pale-edged wing feathers and at least a hint of a white moustache. All have pale reddish brown legs.

OCCURRENCE Breeds in SE Europe; very rare vagrant elsewhere; winters in Africa.

VOICE Sharp, hard *zak* and rattle.

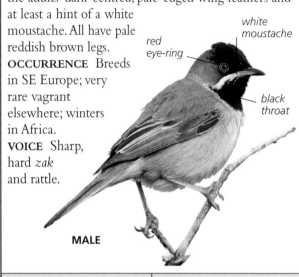

red eye-ring

white moustache

black throat

MALE

Length **13cm (5in)**	Wingspan **18–21cm (7–8½in)**

Family **Sylviidae**	Species *Sylvia conspicillata*

Spectacled Warbler

This warbler looks very like a small Whitethroat (see p.325). The male has a grey head with a white throat (greyer in the centre) and a black patch between the eye and the bill; the eye is encircled by white. The back is grey-brown, and the wings have a rusty patch; the breast is darker pinkish than a Whitethroat's. The female is browner-headed, like the female Whitethroat, but the wing is more uniform rust-brown, the wingtip projection shorter. Juveniles in autumn are similar.

OCCURRENCE Breeds in Spain east to Italy and in the Canaries; very rare vagrant farther north.

VOICE Distinctive buzzing *dzz* or *d-rrr*, sometimes longer, dry, hesitant rattle.

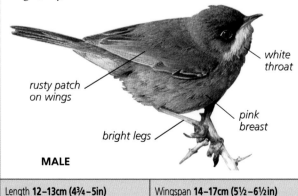

rusty patch on wings

white throat

pink breast

bright legs

MALE

Length **12–13cm (4¾–5in)**	Wingspan **14–17cm (5½–6½in)**

Family **Sylviidae**	Species *Sylvia sarda*

Marmora's Warbler

Similar to a Dartford Warbler (see p.327) in size, shape, behaviour, and general character, Marmora's Warbler is a much more restricted bird in range. It is a greyer bird, the male rather plain smoky grey except for a paler throat, red bill base, red eye, and red legs. Females are paler, duller but equally grey, with no trace of brown; immatures are just slightly tinged with olive-brown above, a little less so on the wings than a juvenile Dartford Warbler, and a little paler, purer grey, on the throat than the commoner bird.

OCCURRENCE Scarce breeder in Balearics, Corsica, and Sardinia; very rare vagrant elsewhere.

VOICE Dull, buzzy *tshek* or *tsak* notes; song quite soft, fast rattling warble with brighter trill at end.

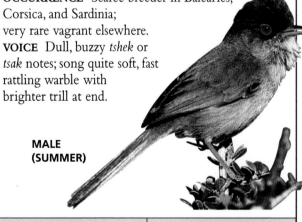

MALE (SUMMER)

Length **13–16cm (5–6½in)**	Wingspan **13–17.5cm (5–7in)**

Family **Sylviidae**	Species *Acrocephalus paludicola*

Aquatic Warbler

Rare and declining, the Aquatic Warbler is much like a bright, strongly patterned Sedge Warbler (see p.328), especially the immature Sedge that tends to have a pale crown stripe and some faint breast streaks resembling the marks on Aquatic. A peach-buff bird with streaks of black and cream, it has a striped head with a sharply defined pale crown stripe. Fine streaks on the chest and flanks are distinctive in summer. A cream "V" on the back is characteristic.

OCCURRENCE Rare breeder south of Baltic; regular but very rare migrant in reedbeds in W Europe.

VOICE Short, metallic *tak*; song varied, less energetic than that of Sedge Warbler.

ADULT

black and cream stripes on body

Length **12–13cm (4¾–5in)**	Wingspan **17–19cm (6½–7½in)**

Family **Sylviidae**	Species *Locustella fluviatilis*

River Warbler

Small warblers with rounded tails, very long undertail coverts, and rounded outer edges to the closed wings, the *Locustella* species have a thick, tapered rear end and a sharp bill. Their songs are insect-like, prolonged trillings: that of the River Warbler is the best way to locate it. This is a dark brown bird, with whitish tail feather tips and a gorget of soft, brown streaks (unlike Reed, Savi's, or Cetti's Warblers; see pp.330, 335, 336) but a plain back (unlike Grasshopper or Sedge Warblers; see pp.334, 328).

OCCURRENCE Breeds in NE Europe from Baltic south to Black Sea; rare in summer in W Europe.

VOICE Song has rhythmic, fast, hissing, mechanical quality, *tsi-tsi-tsi-tsi-tsi-tsi-tsi-tsi*.

plain back

ADULT

rounded edge of wings

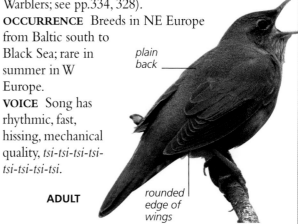

Length **15–16cm (6–6½in)**	Wingspan **19–22cm (7½–9in)**

Family **Sylviidae**	Species *Locustella lanceolata*

Lanceolated Warbler

The most-streaked *Locustella* species, this is a particularly secretive bird, creeping and hiding in the sparsest cover and very difficult to watch. It looks like a small, dark Grasshopper Warbler (see p.334) with striped underparts (or in autumn at least a gorget of diffuse streaks) and quite distinct, narrow dark spots under the tail (softer, longer marks on Grasshopper). Narrower, more defined pale edges to the tertials may aid identification but, while typical ones are distinctive, there is a problem with overlapping features with these two species.

OCCURRENCE Very rare but regular vagrant in NW Europe, from Siberia, in autumn.

VOICE Short clicking call note, rarely heard.

pale edges to tertials

ADULT

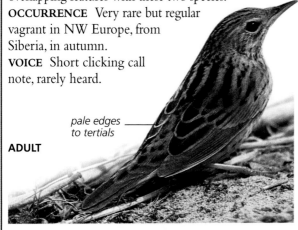

Length **12cm (4¾in)**	Wingspan **15–16cm (6–6½in)**

Family **Sylviidae**	Species *Acrocephalus dumetorum*

Blyth's Reed Warbler

This species is dull and plain in appearance, with markedly uniform wings. It has a long bill and a pale stripe from the bill to the eye (less clear behind the eye). Its wingtips are short and its legs dark (Marsh Warbler's are long and pale, respectively; see p.331). The wingtips are plain dark (Marsh has sharp pale feather edges) and the bill has a pale base, the lower mandible tipped darker (completely pale on Marsh).

OCCURRENCE Breeds in NE Europe, rare vagrant in W Europe in summer and autumn.

VOICE Short, hard, clicking call; song rich, varied, each phrase slowly repeated several times.

pale stripe from bill to eye

short wingtips

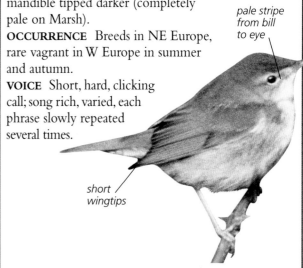

Length **13–14cm (5–5½in)**	Wingspan **17–19cm (6½–7½in)**

Family **Sylviidae**	Species *Acrocephalus agricola*

Paddyfield Warbler

This small, pale, reed-type warbler is marked by a strong pale stripe over the eye, edged darker above and below. Its bill is quite short and pale, with a dark tip. A rufous rump may be obvious (less so on autumn juveniles). The short wings, with quite strongly patterned tertials (dark centres and pale edges), help to separate it from Blyth's Reed Warbler. The unrelated Booted Warbler can also look very similar.

OCCURRENCE Breeds around Black Sea; very rare vagrant in W Europe.

VOICE Short, hard *tack* and *chek* notes; fast, varied song with much mimicry.

short wingtips

strong pale stripe over eye

Length **12–13cm (4¾–5in)**	Wingspan **15–17cm (6–6½in)**

Family **Sylviidae**	Species *Hippolais olivetorum*

Olive-tree Warbler

The largest of the *Hippolais* group, the Olive-tree Warbler is one of Europe's largest warblers, typically seen moving heavily through olive, almond, or holm oak foliage. It has a pale, strong, dagger-like bill, thick dark legs, and a long, square, white-edged dark tail. Its wingtip projection is particularly long. It appears very grey (less so on more olive-hued juveniles) with a marked pale wing panel. There is a short white line from the bill to just above (not behind) the eye.

OCCURRENCE Scarce breeder in Balkans and Middle East; winters in Africa.

VOICE Short, hard *tack*; harsh, grating, repetitive song.

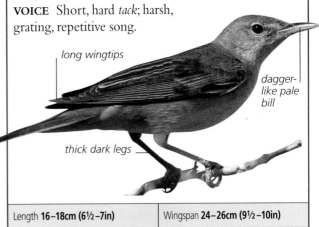

long wingtips

dagger-like pale bill

thick dark legs

Length **16–18cm (6½–7in)**	Wingspan **24–26cm (9½–10in)**

Family **Sylviidae**	Species *Hippolais languida*

Upcher's Warbler

A rather large *Hippolais* warbler, with a pale, broad-based, dagger-like bill, Upcher's Warbler has short undertail coverts and long, square tail with whitish sides. The wings have a paler central panel when closed, formed by pale feather edges. Strong dark legs and a habit of swaying its tail from side to side are helpful identifying features. It is slightly larger and rounder-headed than the very similar Olivaceous Warbler.

OCCURRENCE Rare summer visitor in Middle East; winters in Africa.

VOICE Hard, metallic *tack* note; energetic warbling song.

pale sandy grey above

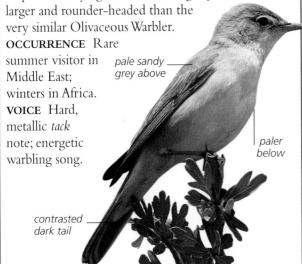

paler below

contrasted dark tail

Length **14–15cm (5½–6in)**	Wingspan **20–23cm (8–9in)**

Family **Sylviidae**	Species *Hippolais pallida*

Olivaceous Warbler

The neat, long, flat-headed, long-billed, pale coloured Olivaceous Warbler is distinguished as much by its lack of marked features as anything else. It has an all-pale lower mandible and greyish legs. The wings are plain although the feather tips are paler. The wingtip point is short (longer on Icterine, p.305, shorter on Booted). It frequently dips its tail, like a Chiffchaff (see p.342).

OCCURRENCE Scarce breeder in Spain, more common in SE Europe; rare vagrant in NW Europe.

VOICE Sparrow-like twitter and hard, dry *tack* calls; song unmusical, fast warble with recurring pattern.

narrow whitish sides of tail

Length **12–14cm (4¾–5½in)**	Wingspan **18–21cm (7–8½in)**

Family **Sylviidae**	Species *Hippolais caligata*

Booted Warbler

This *Hippolais* warbler is like a Willow Warbler (see p.339) in general form, and also recalls the Paddyfield Warbler in pattern. Pale sandy grey or warmer brown, it has a spiky, dark-tipped pale bill and a slight dark stripe through the eye and a thin pale line above it, sometimes quite marked. The broad-based bill, short undertail coverts, and long, slim, square-tipped tail (bobbed upwards but not flicked down) help to identify it.

OCCURRENCE Breeds in extreme NE Europe; rare vagrant in W Europe in autumn.

VOICE Dry, hard, tapping *tak* or *tek*.

dark sides to crown

long, slim tail

pale sandy grey body

Length **11–12cm (4¼–4¾in)**	Wingspan **18–20cm (7–8in)**

Family **Sylviidae**	Species *Phylloscopus fuscatus*

Dusky Warbler

Stockier than a Chiffchaff (see p.342), the Dusky Warbler is browner, tinged grey or olive, with a broad, long pale stripe over the eye (whitest in front, buff behind), pale orange-brown legs, and pale underparts with slightly brighter, buffer flanks. The dark eye-stripe often sharpens the effect of the line over the eye.

OCCURRENCE Rare but annual vagrant in NW Europe, from Asia, in late autumn.

VOICE Hard *tchuk* or *tak* notes, or repeated *tek tek*.

dark eye-stripe

broad pale stripe over eye

fine, pointed bill

pale underparts

Length **11–12cm (4¼–4¾in)**	Wingspan **14–20cm (5½–8in)**

Family **Sylviidae**	Species *Phylloscopus swarzi*

Radde's Warbler

A rare and highly prized warbler, skulking and elusive but calling often, Radde's Warbler looks dark, bulky, and strong-billed. Its legs are thick and bright pinkish. A long, slightly kinked pale stripe runs over each eye, edged darker above and below. The back is olive green, less brown than the Dusky Warbler's, and the underside more brightly flushed with orange-buff on the flanks and rusty-buff on the undertail coverts.

OCCURRENCE Very rare but regular late autumn vagrant to NW Europe, from Asia.

VOICE Soft, repeated, slightly chuckling *chup* or *chep*.

pale stripe over eye

thick pale legs

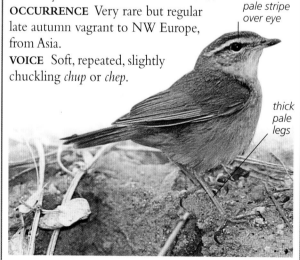

Length **12cm (4¾in)**	Wingspan **15–20cm (6–8in)**

Family **Sylviidae**	Species *Phylloscopus borealis*

Arctic Warbler

The *Phylloscopus* warblers, including the Willow Warbler (see p.339), are greenish, delicate, and quick-moving birds. The Arctic Warbler is rather thickset and solid with a stout bill (pale lower mandible with a dark tip), a thick, dark stripe through the eye and a long cream line above it, and a thin cream wingbar (sometimes two). Larger than the Greenish Warbler, it has longer wingtips, and pinker legs in autumn.

OCCURRENCE Breeds in extreme N Scandinavia; very rare migrant/vagrant in autumn in NW Europe.

VOICE Call hard, sharp *dzit*; song low, fast trill.

AUTUMN

thin wingbar

long wingtips

Length **12–13cm (4¾–5in)**	Wingspan **16–22cm (6½–9in)**

Family **Sylviidae**	Species ***Phylloscopus trochiloides***

Greenish Warbler

This delicate, fast-moving warbler is grey-green above and silvery white below. The yellowish stripe over the eye typically reaches the top of the bill (unlike Arctic Warbler). A single narrow cream wingbar is usual, a second short one occasional. Whiter flanks help to give it a lighter look than the Arctic Warbler; but it may be confused with some Chiffchaffs with a pale wingbar.

OCCURRENCE Breeds in NE Europe; rare migrant in late summer; occasional in late spring in W Europe.

VOICE Loud, sweet, disyllabic *schu-weet* or *tshi-li*; quick, trilling song.

pale wingbar

AUTUMN

Length **10cm (4in)**	Wingspan **15–21cm (6–8½in)**

Family **Sylviidae**	Species ***Phylloscopus inornatus***

Yellow-browed Warbler

A very small, strongly patterned, beautiful warbler, the Yellow-browed Warbler is clear grey-green or olive-green above, whiter beneath, with black-centred, white-tipped tertials and two yellowish cream wingbars; the upper one is thin and short, the lower longer and broad, edged dark green and black, catching the eye in the briefest view. It is an elusive, active little bird, often hard to see well against the sky in leafy trees.

OCCURRENCE Rare but regular migrant in NW Europe, in late autumn, from Asia.

VOICE Penetrating, sharp, rising *sweeet* or *chi-weet*.

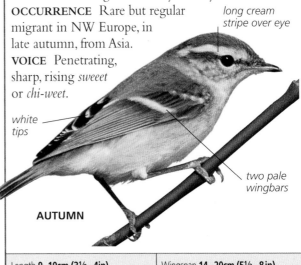

long cream stripe over eye

white tips

two pale wingbars

AUTUMN

Length **9–10cm (3½–4in)**	Wingspan **14–20cm (5½–8in)**

Family **Sylviidae**	Species ***Phylloscopus humei***

Hume's Leaf Warbler

A very close and very similar relative of the Yellow-browed Warbler, Hume's is another tiny, but slightly duller, warbler. It is dusky grey-green, whiter below, with a long, cream stripe over the eye, an all-dark bill (no pale base), and two pale wingbars, one broad and obvious, the upper one short, weak, and often inconspicuous. Its tertials are dull with pale tips, less blackish than on the Yellow-browed.

OCCURRENCE Very rare vagrant in NW Europe, from Asia.

VOICE Loud, cheeping *tsee-oo*, falling at end, or flatter *tsweeet*.

dark bill

AUTUMN

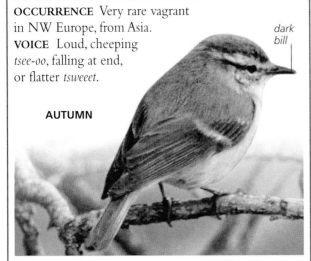

Length **9–10cm (3½–4in)**	Wingspan **14–20cm (5½–8in)**

Family **Sylviidae**	Species ***Phylloscopus proregulus***

Pallas's Warbler

The tiniest and most boldly patterned leaf warbler, Pallas's Warbler is eye-catching but not easy to separate from the Yellow-browed unless the crown and rump are visible. It is brighter green and neckless, its head boldly striped yellow and dark green-black, with a long central crown stripe. Its rump is pale, lemon-yellow or cream, best seen as it hovers briefly while feeding.

OCCURRENCE Very rare but regular late autumn vagrant in NW Europe, from Asia.

VOICE Rising, soft *chuee* call.

boldly striped head

broad lower wingbar, edged darker

AUTUMN

Length **9cm (3½in)**	Wingspan **12–16cm (4¾–6½in)**

Family **Muscicapidae**	Species *Ficedula parva*

Red-breasted Flycatcher

This delightful, tiny flycatcher is best identified by its black tail with a long rectangle of white on each side at the base. Males have a grey hood and a small orange-red throat patch. Females and juveniles have plainer heads, with marked pale eye-rings, and smudgy marks beside the throat. The legs are short and black, the tail often cocked upwards. Migrants can be very tame.

OCCURRENCE Breeds in E and NE Europe; rare but regular autumn migrant in NW Europe.

VOICE Short, dry, Wren-like *trr-r-rt* and *tut*; song high, sharp, rhythmic, falling away in purer cadence.

pale eye-ring

long wings

JUVENILE

white on tail

Length **11–12cm (4¼–4¾in)**	Wingspan **18–21cm (7–8½in)**

Family **Muscicapidae**	Species *Ficedula albicollis*

Collared Flycatcher

This is very similar to the Pied Flycatcher (see p.346), plumages other than the adult male's being difficult. Females are greyer than Pied, with a greyish rump; the wing patch is thinner, but there is a larger white patch on the primaries. Juveniles may have a short upper wingbar. Confusions arise with hybrids, as well as Semi-collared Flycatchers.

OCCURRENCE Breeds in E Europe, north to Baltic islands; rare vagrant in W Europe in spring.

VOICE Thin *tseeeep* and short *tek*; song slow, harsh whistles of varying pitch.

bold white patch near bill

white collar

MALE large white wing patch

Length **12–13cm (4¾–5in)**	Wingspan **22.5–24.5cm (8¾–9¾in)**

Family **Muscicapidae**	Species *Ficedula semitorquata*

Semi-collared Flycatcher

A difficult bird of restricted range, the Semi-collared Flycatcher is best identified when breeding, by the adult males: the white throat hooks around under the ear coverts in a half collar, the wings have a lot of white with a very big primary patch, and the rump is pale grey; Iberian Pied Flycatchers (see p.346), however, look very similar. Females have very thin white wing marks, but a strong upper wingbar.

OCCURRENCE Breeds in Balkans and Turkey; migrates through Middle East in spring and autumn.

VOICE Call low, piping whistle; song slow, like Collared Flycather's, more rhythmic like Pied's.

white half collar

upper wingbar

MALE (SUMMER)

Length **12–13cm (4¾–5in)**	Wingspan **23–24cm (9–9½in)**

Family **Paridae**	Species *Parus cyanus*

Azure Tit

A rare bird of remote places, this is a little-known species in Europe. It has a basic Blue Tit-like look (see p.350), but lacks yellow and green entirely, and has a longer tail with broad white sides. The crown is all white (no blue cap), the back pale grey, and wings blue with broad white bands. The underside is all white. Hybrids of Azure and Blue Tits have a pale blue cap and bluer tails with less white at the corners.

OCCURRENCE Breeds in extreme NE Europe in damp woods and willow stands.

VOICE Most calls very like Blue Tit's; song more stuttering.

all-white crown

long tail

Length **12–13cm (4¾–5in)**	Wingspan **19–21cm (7½–8½in)**

Family **Paridae**	Species *Parus cinctus*

Siberian Tit

With a pattern recalling a Willow Tit (see p.352), this bigger bird also has a richer, brighter brown back and rusty flanks, contrasting with grey wings, white cheeks, and a dark brownish cap and bib. The cap is often dull, washed grey or grey-brown. From the front, the bib makes a broad wedge under the large, almost bulbous cheeks. In very cold conditions in northern conifer forest, it is often fluffed out, looking unexpectedly large.

OCCURRENCE Breeds in N Scandinavia in old, remote forest and birch wood.

VOICE Basic *zi-zi-tah tah tah* much like Willow but less emphatic; song more nasal and buzzing.

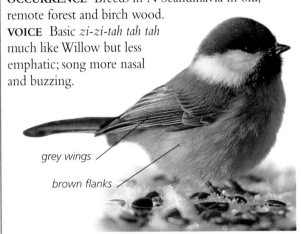

grey wings

brown flanks

Length **13–14cm (5–5½in)**	Wingspan **20–21cm (8–8½in)**

Family **Paridae**	Species *Parus lugubris*

Sombre Tit

The same size as a Great Tit (see p.348), the Sombre Tit's basic pattern is more like a Willow Tit's (see p.352). It has a deep, grey-black cap, a very large, wide black bib, and a restricted wedge of white between these across the cheeks. It is a rather heavy little bird, with a thick bill. Relatively quiet, it does not draw attention to itself unless calling.

OCCURRENCE Breeds in woods or on bushy slopes, in Balkans, Turkey, and Middle East.

VOICE Like Blue Tit (see p.350), plus Great Tit-like grating churrs.

white wedge on cheeks

grey back

pale streak on wings

pale, dull grey below

Length **13–14cm (5–5½in)**	Wingspan **21–23cm (8½–9in)**

Family **Sittidae**	Species *Sitta whiteheadi*

Corsican Nuthatch

A tiny nuthatch of pine forest in Corsica, this unmistakable bird has a typical stout, tapered nuthatch form, with a spike-like bill, short legs but strong feet, and short, square tail held well clear of its perch. Males have a blackish cap and eye-stripe separated by a long white line. Females have the black replaced by grey, but the white line over the eye is equally distinctive.

OCCURRENCE Only found in Corsica, in mature pine forest in high mountain valleys.

VOICE Throaty, harsh call, repeated at intervals; song an even, fast, high trill.

spiky bill

grey above

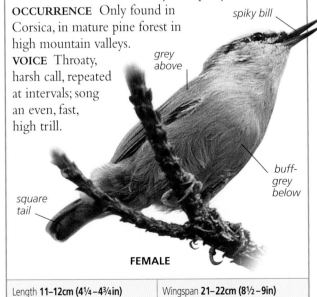

buff-grey below

square tail

FEMALE

Length **11–12cm (4¼–4¾in)**	Wingspan **21–22cm (8½–9in)**

Family **Sittidae**	Species *Sitta neumayer*

Rock Nuthatch

The best places to see this bird are archaeological sites in Greece and Turkey, where it often flits about the ruins, drawing attention to itself by its bold behaviour and voice. It looks like a large, washed-out Nuthatch (see p.358), but has a plain grey tail (no dark and white marks) and whitish flanks (no rust-orange). It often perches very upright, breast pushed out, bobbing, almost like a slim Dipper (see p.295).

OCCURRENCE Breeds in Balkans and Turkey, in rocky areas.

VOICE Rising and falling, far-carrying, strident whistling notes.

long black eye-stripe

long bill

plain tail

Length **14–15cm (5½–6in)**	Wingspan **23–25cm (9–10in)**

Family **Laniidae**	Species *Lanius isabellinus*

Isabelline Shrike

A close relative of the Red-backed Shrike (see p.363), the Isabelline Shrike is similar in basic appearance but paler, more sandy-brown, with a pale, rusty tail. Males have a black mask and dark wings; females are plainer. Immatures look like rusty-tailed, sandy-backed young Red-backed Shrikes, with paler, plainer upperparts; the tail may be entirely pale rufous or darker with rufous edges and a rufous rump.
OCCURRENCE Very rare vagrant in W Europe, from Asia, mostly in late autumn.
VOICE Migrants are generally silent.

rusty tail

IMMATURE

Length **16–18cm (6½–7in)**	Wingspan **26–28cm (10–11in)**

Family **Laniidae**	Species *Lanius nubicus*

Masked Shrike

The small, slender, and well-marked Masked Shrike is mostly black and white with peachy orange flanks and is easily identifiable. Males are brighter than females. Juveniles look like young Woodchat Shrikes (see p.364), but have slim, blacker tails, greyer upperparts with at least some scaly whitish shoulder marks making more of a patch than on Woodchat, and a bigger white patch on the primaries.
OCCURRENCE Breeds in Balkans and Turkey; winter migrant in Africa.
VOICE Scratchy, hoarse note and rough rattling call.

white forehead

black eye-stripe

large white shoulder patch

orange flanks

MALE

Length **17–18cm (6½–7in)**	Wingspan **24–26cm (9½–10in)**

Family **Corvidae**	Species *Cyanopica cyanus*

Azure-winged Magpie

This striking bird is a magpie in form (see p.369), with an upright, short body, short wings, long tail, and stout bill and legs, but quite different from the familiar pied bird in plumage. It has a deep black cap and a white throat; the back is pale fawn, the underside a paler shade, while the wings and tail are pale, dusty blue. Small flocks roam through pine woods, calling frequently.
OCCURRENCE Breeds in S Spain and Portugal; resident.
VOICE High, nasal, calls with bright, whining quality, and deeper, grating notes.

pale blue wings

fawn body

long, pale blue tail

Length **31–35cm (12–14in)**	Wingspan **38–40cm (15–16in)**

Family **Sturnidae**	Species *Sturnus roseus*

Rose-coloured Starling

This exotic-looking starling is usually seen in western Europe in immature plumages, but adults occur in southeast Europe at times. Adults are pale pink (dusky in winter) with a black hood, wings, and tail; whitish feather tips obscure some of the black in winter. Immatures are like sandy grey young Starlings (see p.380) except for a shorter yellowish bill, more contrast between pale body and dark wings, and a pale rump.
OCCURRENCE Rare migrant in SE Europe, vagrant in W Europe, in summer and autumn.
VOICE Short, harsh calls and varied, unmusical, rattling song.

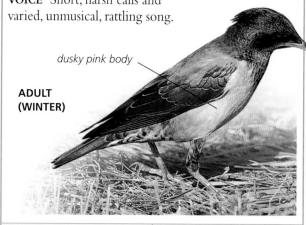

dusky pink body

ADULT (WINTER)

Length **19–22cm (7½–9in)**	Wingspan **37–40cm (14½–16in)**

| Family **Vireonidae** | Species *Vireo olivaceus* |

Red-eyed Vireo

Vireos are like rather large, stocky warblers with quite thick bills. The Red-eyed Vireo has a strong head pattern (grey cap edged black, broad white stripe over the eye, and black eye-stripe), a dark red eye, and a basic green above, whitish below pattern. The greenish tail is short and square, helping to give it a slightly different look from European warblers with green upperparts. It tends to be quite slow and heavy in its movements through foliage.

OCCURRENCE Very rare but annual vagrant in NW Europe, in autumn, from North America.

VOICE Short, nasal *chway*.

white over red eye

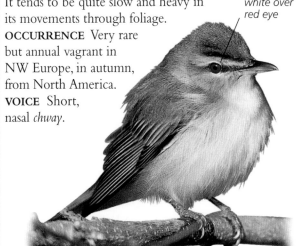

| Length **14cm (5½in)** | Wingspan **23–25cm (9–10in)** |

| Family **Parulidae** | Species *Dendroica striata* |

Blackpoll Warbler

In summer, this is a black and white bird, but in autumn immatures are dull-looking: greenish with soft dark streaks on the back and pale greyish yellow underparts with soft dusky streaks. They have a pale stripe above and pale marks below the eye, white under the tail, and dark wings with two long, narrow, diagonal wingbars. The white under the tail and streaked chest are important points to eliminate even rarer species.

OCCURRENCE Very rare vagrant in NW Europe in late autumn, from North America.

VOICE Liquid, sharp, short *chip*.

two curved white wingbars

IMMATURE (AUTUMN)

| Length **12–13cm (4¾–5in)** | Wingspan **15cm (6in)** |

| Family **Parulidae** | Species *Dendroica coronata* |

Yellow-rumped Warbler

While some autumn plumages are very difficult to identify, most North American wood warblers are striking birds, at least in summer. Yellow-rumped Warblers are small, neat, active birds, distinguished by a yellow patch on each side of the chest, and a bright yellow rump. They are streaky brown above, and whitish with blacker streaks below in autumn. Two long, diagonal wingbars are clearly visible. The head is not strongly patterned but has white crescents above and below the eye.

OCCURRENCE Very rare vagrant in NW Europe in late autumn, from North America.

VOICE Frequent, hard, single notes, *chik* or *twip*.

two white wingbars

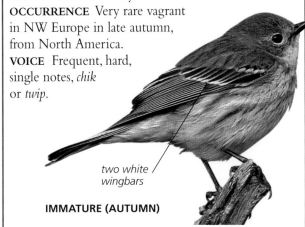

IMMATURE (AUTUMN)

| Length **12–13cm (4¾–5in)** | Wingspan **15cm (6in)** |

| Family **Fringillidae** | Species *Carduelis hornemanni* |

Arctic Redpoll

Redpolls are split into several races or species; the Arctic Redpoll is usually recognized as a species but can be hard to distinguish. Males have a large white rump, white underparts, and unmarked undertail coverts; a broad whitish wingbar, small red forehead patch, and a short yellow bill aid identification. Females and immatures are more streaked, but the rump is unstreaked white, the wingbar white, and the undertail area unmarked white.

OCCURRENCE Breeds in extreme N Scandinavia; winters in Scandinavia and vagrant in W Europe.

VOICE Calls like Redpoll's, not safely distinguishable.

unmarked under tail

broad wingbar

white underparts

MALE

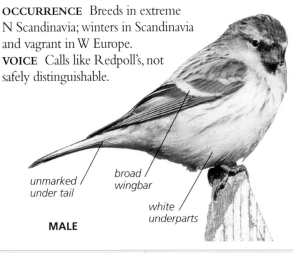

| Length **12–14cm (4¾–5½in)** | Wingspan **21–27cm (8½–10½in)** |

Family **Fringillidae**	Species *Loxia leucoptera*

Two-barred Crossbill

A smallish crossbill, the Two-barred Crossbill is typically marked by two broad white wingbars (unlike the Crossbill, see p.400, which may only occasionally have wingbars) and white spots on the tertial tips. Males are rather deep cherry-red with blacker wings (Crossbills tend to be more orange-red with browner wings); females are green and brown, with yellow-green rumps. Dark back spots are distinctive. Juveniles are duller, browner, with much thinner wingbars, and are difficult to identify with absolute certainty.

OCCURRENCE Rare breeder in extreme NE Europe; vagrant elsewhere.

VOICE Weaker than Crossbill's.

MALE

two broad wingbars

Length **16cm (6½in)**	Wingspan **26–29cm (10–11½in)**

Family **Fringillidae**	Species *Loxia scotica*

Scottish Crossbill

If Parrot and common Crossbills (see p.400) are hard to distinguish, the Scottish Crossbill, being intermediate between the two, can seem impossible to identify. It is restricted to pine forest in Scotland, but the other two can be found there, too. It has bulging cheeks, a thick neck, and a deep, hefty bill; its plumages are like those of the other species and its calls are confusingly difficult unless recorded and analysed technically. Research continues into the relationship of all these forms.

OCCURRENCE Resident in N Scotland, presumably does not move elsewhere.

VOICE Much as Crossbill's, sometimes deeper, thicker notes.

bulging cheeks

becomes increasingly red with age

IMMATURE MALE

Length **16–17cm (6½in)**	Wingspan **27–37cm (10½–14½in)**

Family **Passeridae**	Species *Montifringilla nivalis*

Snowfinch

The Snowfinch is large, long-winged, and short-legged with black-tipped white wings recalling a Snow Bunting (see p.411). The head is grey (black face and bib on summer male), the back dull grey-brown, and the tail white with a narrow black centre. In summer, the male has a black bill; otherwise the bill is yellow.

OCCURRENCE Sparse breeder, at high altitude, in Pyrenees, Alps, Italy, and Balkans.

VOICE Wide variety of sharp, hoarse, or mewing calls; trilling, sparrow-like song.

black bill

dull grey-brown back

MALE (SUMMER)

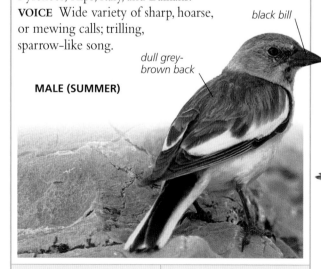

Length **17–19cm (6½–7½in)**	Wingspan **34–38cm (13½–15in)**

Family **Emberizidae**	Species *Emberiza rustica*

Rustic Bunting

In summer, males are boldly marked black and white on the head, reddish above, and white below with a red-brown breast-band. Females and autumn males have a paler central crown stripe on a duller head; both sexes raise their crown feathers at times. Immatures are streaked yellow-brown, with a broad pale stripe over the eye, a white ear-spot edged black, and a cream band under the cheek. The rump is rust-brown; two thin white wingbars are usually obvious.

OCCURRENCE Breeds in Sweden, Finland, and Russia; rare migrant to E Europe and vagrant in W Europe; in wet forested areas; May to September.

VOICE Short, sharp, penetrating *tic* or *zit*; song short, rhythmic, rattling phrase.

MALE (AUTUMN)

rufous rump

Length **12–13cm (4¾–5in)**	Wingspan **14–17cm (5½–6½in)**

Family **Emberizidae**	Species *Emberiza caesia*

Cretzschmar's Bunting

This is very like an Ortolan Bunting (see p.407) but rust-red on the throat and moustache where the Ortolan is yellow. The head and chest are blue-grey, the back rufous-brown, and the underside a rich rust-orange. Females are duller; both sexes have a white eye-ring. The immature shows the eye-ring, black-streaked upperparts and broad, bright rusty edges to the tertials; it is a richer, more rufous bird than a young Ortolan.

OCCURRENCE Breeds in Greece, Crete, Turkey, and some Greek islands; very rare vagrant elsewhere.

VOICE Sharp, short *tsip* note, very like Ortolan Bunting's.

blue-grey head

streaked rufous-brown above

MALE

Length **14–15cm (5½–6in)**	Wingspan **23–26cm (9–10in)**

Family **Emberizidae**	Species *Emberiza leucocephalos*

Pine Bunting

Difficulties arise with intermediates between the Pine Bunting and Yellowhammer (see p.408) but most pure birds are identifiable. Males are easy, with their white crown and cheek, edged black and rufous; the back is rusty with black streaks and the underside whitish. Females are greyer, with a less marked head; immatures have white underparts streaked grey, a white spot on the ear coverts, a white eye-ring, and white feather edges on the wings (yellowish on Yellowhammer).

OCCURRENCE Vagrant in NW Europe, late autumn and winter, from Asia.

VOICE Metallic ticking notes, like Yellowhammer's.

MALE (WINTER)

streaked, rusty back

white cheeks

Length **16–17cm (6½in)**	Wingspan **26–30cm (10–12in)**

Family **Emberizidae**	Species *Emberiza melanocephala*

Black-headed Bunting

This big bunting has easily identifiable males with a black head, yellow chin, rufous back, and yellow underside; females and immatures are difficult to distinguish from vagrant or escaped Red-headed Buntings. Females have large grey bills, hooded grey-brown heads, and pale yellow underparts, with some rufous above (unlike Red-headed); immatures are slightly more streaked, especially on the crown (more than Red-headed) and rather bright above (Red-headed typically dull).

OCCURRENCE Breeds in S Italy and Balkans; rare late summer vagrant in NW Europe.

VOICE Various metallic, ticking calls; fuller accelerating song.

black head

yellow underside

MALE

Length **16–17cm (6½in)**	Wingspan **26–30cm (10–12in)**

Family **Emberizidae**	Species *Emberiza aureola*

Yellow-breasted Bunting

The summer males of this small, neat bunting are distinctive, with a black and chestnut head, upperparts, and breast-band, against bright yellow on the chest and belly, and a white shoulder patch. In autumn, immatures are streaked brown, rather yellower or buff beneath, finely streaked, with two white wingbars; they have a pale central stripe on the top of the head, a broad pale stripe over each eye, a pale band under the cheek, and a pale spot at the rear of the dark-edged ear coverts.

OCCURRENCE Breeds from E Finland into Russia; rare migrant/vagrant in NW Europe in autumn.

VOICE Short, ticking *tsik* note.

pale stripe over eye

two wingbars

yellow or buff below

FEMALE

Length **15–16cm (6–6½in)**	Wingspan **21–24cm (8½–9½in)**

Family **Emberizidae**	Species *Pheucticus ludovicianus*

Rose-breasted Grosbeak

Very rare in Europe, this is an unmistakable bird by virtue of its large size for a finch, very large bill, and striking pattern. Males are black and white with red on the breast; immatures brown and streaked, males with red under the wings. These, and adult females, are boldly marked with a dark cap, very broad white band over the eye, dark cheeks, and white throat; two bars of white spots cross the wing. The breast is buff, streaked with wavy black lines.

OCCURRENCE Very rare vagrant in autumn in NW Europe, from North America.

VOICE Short, hard, *chik* call.

white spots on wings

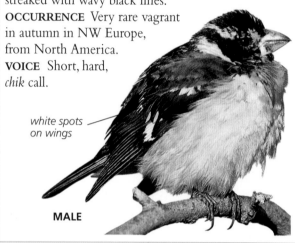

MALE

Length **18–20cm (7–8in)**	Wingspan **30–32cm (12–12½in)**

Family **Emberizidae**	Species *Junco hyemalis*

Dark-eyed Junco

This small American bunting is sparrow-like, rather inconspicuous and quiet. Males are smoky grey, blacker around the face, with an oval white belly patch, white tail sides, and a pale pinkish bill. Females are tinged browner, especially on the wings, and a little sullied below (less pure white) but share the same basic pattern, which is unlike any European species.

OCCURRENCE Very rare vagrant, sometimes remaining all winter, in NW Europe, from North America.

VOICE Short, ticking note, sometimes repeated.

pale pink bill

smoky grey body

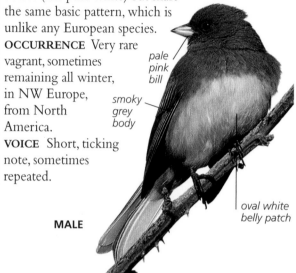

oval white belly patch

MALE

Length **14cm (5½in)**	Wingspan **25–30cm (10–12in)**

Family **Emberizidae**	Species *Zonotrichia albicollis*

White-throated Sparrow

American sparrows are more like European buntings. Adult White-throated Sparrows have a thin white crown stripe edged black, a broad white band over the eye (yellow at the front), grey cheeks, and a white chin patch. Immatures are duller, with a greyish and less clear-cut chin and throat. The body plumage, streaked brown above and grey beneath, as well as the general stance and behaviour, recall a Dunnock (see p.297).

OCCURRENCE Rare vagrant in NW Europe, mostly in spring, from North America.

VOICE Call a sharp, persistent, thin *zit*, and thicker *chink* notes.

white band over eye with yellow in front

streaked brown upperparts

ADULT

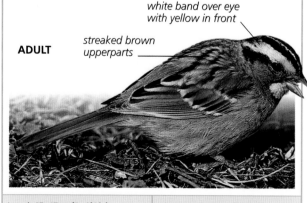

Length **15–17cm (6–6½in)**	Wingspan **20–25cm (8–10in)**

Family **Icteridae**	Species *Dolichonyx oryzivorus*

Bobolink

Bobolinks visiting Europe in autumn are rather yellowish birds, striped with black and cream; they are dumpy and heavy-bellied, with a narrow, tapered head and tail. The bill is sharply triangular, and the head shows a central yellow-buff crown stripe edged black and broad buff stripes over each eye. The back has two long straw-coloured lines; the underside is creamy with faint streaks only on the flanks. A short, narrow, spiky tail helps to separate it from a common bunting or sparrow.

OCCURRENCE Very rare vagrant in autumn in NW Europe, from North America.

VOICE Short, sharp *pink*.

black and cream stripes on upperparts

creamy below

long, narrow tail

ADULT (AUTUMN)

Length **16–18cm (6½–7in)**	Wingspan **30cm (12in)**

VAGRANTS

The list that follows consists of birds that occur only very rarely in Europe, known as vagrants or accidentals. It also looks a little further beyond Europe, to list those birds whose normal range is the Middle East and North Africa, so covering a total faunal area known as the Western Palearctic.

Vagrants to Europe arrive from Asia and North America (and fewer from Africa). Western Europe, especially the UK, is well placed to receive birds that are blown off course from eastern North America and cross the Atlantic. It was thought that such birds cross the ocean on board ship, but it is now accepted that even small birds can, with a following wind, survive a flight across the Atlantic, although they probably do not survive long afterwards. Larger species, however, such as some wildfowl, may live for years in Europe and a few (that have been trapped, ringed, and released in order to follow their movements) have even returned to North America in subsequent years. These are not, in any true sense, European birds, but are included here to complete the range of species that have been recorded. Many appear again, others may not: by their nature these "accidentals" are unpredictable.

Common Name	Scientific Name	Family/Scientific Name	Description
Ostrich			
Ostrich	*Struthio camelus*	Ratites/Struthidae	Vagrant in North Africa, from southern Africa
Albatrosses			
Shy Albatross	*Diomedea cauta*	Albatrosses/Diomedeidae	Large seabird from southern oceans
Yellow-nosed Albatross	*Diomedea chlororhynchos*	Albatrosses/Diomedeidae	Large seabird from southern oceans
Black-browed Albatross	*Diomedea melanophris*	Albatrosses/Diomededae	Long-winged seabird from South Atlantic
Wandering Albatross	*Diomedea exulans*	Albatrosses/Diomedeidae	Large seabird from southern oceans
Petrels and Shearwaters			
Black-capped Petrel	*Pterodroma hasitata*	Petrels and Shearwaters/Procellariidae	Large petrel from Caribbean
Atlantic Petrel	*Pterodroma incerta*	Petrels and Shearwaters/Procellariidae	Large petrel from South Atlantic
Soft-plumaged Petrel	*Pterodroma mollis*	Petrels and Shearwaters/Procellariidae	Large petrel from South Atlantic
Fea's Petrel	*Pterodroma feae*	Petrels and Shearwaters/Procellariidae	Large, rare petrel from Madeira
Zino's Petrel	*Pterodroma madeira*	Petrels and Shearwaters/Procellariidae	Large, rare petrel from Madeira
Bulwer's Petrel	Bulweria bulwerii	Petrels and Shearwaters/Procellariidae	Dark, long-tailed petrel from mid-Atlantic islands
Streaked Shearwater	*Calonectris leucomelas*	Petrels and Shearwaters/Procellariidae	Vagrant in Middle East, from tropical oceans
Flesh-footed Shearwater	*Puffinus carneipes*	Petrels and Shearwaters/Procellariidae	All-dark shearwater from Indian Ocean
Audubon's Shearwater	*Puffinus lherminieri*	Petrels and Shearwaters/Procellariidae	Small shearwater from Indian Ocean

Common Name	Scientific Name	Family/Scientific Name	Description
Petrels and Shearwaters *continued*			
Wedge-tailed Shearwater	*Puffinus pacificus*	Petrels and Shearwaters/ Procellariidae	Large dark shearwater from Indian Ocean
White-faced Storm-petrel	*Pelagodroma marina*	Petrels and Shearwaters/ Procellariidae	Small petrel from South Atlantic
Swinhoe's Storm Petrel	*Oceanodroma monorhis*	Petrels and Shearwaters/ Procellariidae	Small, dark, oceanic petrel from Pacific
Gannets and Cormorants			
Masked Booby	*Sula dactylatra*	Gannets/Sulidae	Gannet-like seabird from tropical oceans
Brown Booby	*Sula leucogaster*	Gannets/Sulidae	Dark brown gannet, in Red Sea
Cape Gannet	*Morus capensis*	Gannets/Sulidae	Black and white gannet from southern Africa
Double-crested Cormorant	*Phalacrocorax auritus*	Cormorants/Phalacrocoracidae	Large black waterbird, vagrant in UK, from North America
Darters and Anhingas			
African Darter	*Anhinga rufa*	Darters and Anhingas/ Anhingidae	Sharp-billed, cormorant-like waterbird, vagrant in North Africa, from southern Africa
Frigatebirds and Tropicbirds			
Lesser Frigatebird	*Fregata ariel*	Frigatebirds/Fregatidae	Large, fork-tailed seabird from tropical oceans
Red-billed Tropicbird	*Phaethon aethereus*	Tropicbirds/Phaethontidae	White seabird from tropical oceans
Bitterns and Herons			
Black-headed Heron	*Ardea melanocephala*	Herons/Ardeidae	Dry-ground heron, vagrant in North Africa, from southern Africa
Goliath Heron	*Ardea goliath*	Herons/Ardeidae	Very large heron, vagrant in Middle East, from Africa
Black Heron	*Egretta ardesiaca*	Herons/Ardeidae	Small dark heron from Africa
Intermediate Egret	*Egretta intermedia*	Herons/Ardeidae	White egret from Africa, Asia
Snowy Egret	*Egretta thula*	Herons/Ardeidae	White egret from North America
Schrenck's Bittern	*Ixobrychus eurhythmus*	Herons/Ardeidae	Small bittern from Asia
Least Bittern	*Ixobrychus exilis*	Herons/Ardeidae	Small bittern from North America
Dwarf Bittern	*Ixobrychus sturmii*	Herons/Ardeidae	Small bittern from Africa
American Bittern	*Botaurus lentiginosus*	Herons/Ardeidae	Stripe-necked bittern from North America
Mangrove Heron	*Butorides striatus*	Herons/Ardeidae	Small dark heron, in North Africa and Middle East
Storks			
Yellow-billed Stork	*Mycteria ibis*	Storks/Ciconiidae	White stork with red mask, vagrant in Middle East, from Africa

Common Name	Scientific Name	Family/Scientific Name	Description
Ibises			
Bald Ibis	*Geronticus eremita*	Ibises/Threskiornithidae	All-dark ibis, rare breeder in North Africa
Wildfowl			
White-faced Whistling Duck	*Dendrocygna viduata*	Wildfowl/Anatidae	Large, noisy duck, vagrant in North Africa, from southern Africa
Lesser Whistling Duck	*Dendrocygna javanica*	Wildfowl/Anatidae	Small duck from Africa
Bar-headed Goose	*Anser indicus*	Wildfowl/Anatidae	Pale grey goose from Asia
Spur-winged Goose	*Plectropterus gambensis*	Wildfowl/Anatidae	Large goose from Africa
Cotton Pygmy-goose	*Nettapus coromandelianus*	Wildfowl/Anatidae	Small duck, vagrant in North Africa, from southern Africa
Baikal Teal	*Anas formosa*	Wildfowl/Anatidae	Colourful surface-feeding duck from Asia
Cape Teal	*Anas capensis*	Wildfowl/Anatidae	Surface-feeding duck, vagrant in North Africa, from southern Africa
Red-billed Teal	*Anas erythrorhyncha*	Wildfowl/Anatidae	Surface-feeding duck, vagrant in North Africa, from southern Africa
Cape Shoveler	*Anas smithii*	Wildfowl/Anatidae	Surface-feeding duck, vagrant in North Africa, from southern Africa
Southern Pochard	*Netta erythrophthalma*	Wildfowl/Anatidae	Diving duck, vagrant in North Africa, from southern Africa
Redhead	*Aythya americana*	Wildfowl/Anatidae	Pochard-like diving duck, vagrant in UK, from North America
Canvasback	Aythya valisineria	Wildfowl/Anatidae	Large, pale Pochard-like duck from North America
Birds of Prey			
Crested Honey Buzzard	*Pernis ptilorhyncus*	Hawks/Accipitridae	Medium-sized bird of prey, vagrant in Middle East, from Asia
American Swallow-tailed Kite	*Elanoides forficatus*	Hawks/Accipitridae	Fork-tailed kite from North America
Bald Eagle	*Haliaeetus leucocephalus*	Hawks/Accipitridae	Massive eagle from North America
Pallas's Fish Eagle	*Haliaeetus leucoryphus*	Hawks/Accipitridae	Huge eagle from Asia
Rüppell's Vulture	*Gyps rueppellii*	Hawks/Accipitridae	Distinctive vulture, vagrant in Middle East, from Africa
Bateleur	*Terathopius ecaudatus*	Hawks/Accipitridae	Acrobatic eagle, vagrant in Middle East, from Africa
Dark Chanting Goshawk	*Melierax metabates*	Hawks/Accipitridae	Large grey hawk, vagrant in Middle East, from East Africa
Shikra	*Accipiter badius*	Hawks/Accipitridae	Small pale sparrowhawk, in Middle East
Swainson's Buzzard	*Buteo swainsoni*	Hawks/Accipitridae	Large hawk from North America

Common Name	Scientific Name	Family/Scientific Name	Description
Birds of Prey *continued*			
Tawny Eagle	*Aquila rapax*	Hawks/Accipitridae	Big brown eagle, rare in North Africa
Verreaux's Eagle	*Aquila verreauxii*	Hawks/Accipitridae	Large black eagle, rare in North Africa
Amur Falcon	*Falco amurensis*	Falcons/Falconidae	Red-footed falcon from Asia
Barbary Falcon	*Falco (peregrinus) pelegrinoides*	Falcons/Falconidae	Peregrine-like falcon, in Middle East and North Africa
Sooty Falcon	*Falco concolor*	Falcons/Falconidae	Large grey falcon from Middle East
American Kestrel	*Falco sparverius*	Falcons/Falconidae	Tiny falcon from North America
Gamebirds			
Caucasian Grouse	*Tetrao mlokosiewiczi*	Grouse/Tetraonidae	Sleek black grouse, in Middle East
Caspian Snowcock	*Tetraogallus caspius*	Gamebirds/Phasianidae	Large mountain grouse, in Middle East
Caucasian Snowcock	*Tetraogallus caucasicus*	Gamebirds/Phasianidae	Large mountain grouse, in Middle East
Double-spurred Francolin	*Francolinus bicalcaratus*	Gamebirds/Phasianidae	Brown gamebird, in North Africa
Black Francolin	*Francolinus francolinus*	Gamebirds/Phasianidae	Blackish gamebird, rare in Middle East
Helmeted Guineafowl	*Numida meleagris*	Guineafowl/Numididae	Dark, white-spotted gamebird, in North Africa
Cranes			
Hooded Crane	*Grus monacha*	Cranes/Gruidae	Dark-headed crane from Asia
Siberian White Crane	*Grus leucogeranus*	Cranes/Gruidae	Large crane from Asia
Sandhill Crane	*Grus canadensis*	Cranes/Gruidae	Grey crane from North America
Rails, Crakes, and Coots			
Striped Crake	*Porzana marginalis*	Rails,Crakes, and Coots/ Rallidae	Small pale crake, rare in North Africa
Sora	*Porzana carolina*	Rails,Crakes, and Coots/ Rallidae	Dark crake from North America
Allen's Gallinule	*Porphyrula alleni*	Rails,Crakes, and Coots/ Rallidae	Moorhen-like bird from Africa
American Purple Gallinule	*Porphyrula martinica*	Rails,Crakes, and Coots/ Rallidae	Moorhen-like bird from North America
American Coot	*Fulica americana*	Rails,Crakes, and Coots/ Rallidae	Coot from North America
Bustards			
Arabian Bustard	*Ardeotis arabs*	Bustards/Otididae	Very large, pale bustard, in Middle East

Common Name	Scientific Name	Family/Scientific Name	Description
Waders			
Painted Snipe	*Rostratula benghalensis*	Waders/Scolopacidae	Snipe-like wader from Africa
Crab Plover	*Dromas ardeola*	Plovers/Charadriidae	Heavy-billed, black and white wader, in Middle East
Egyptian Plover	*Pluvianus aegyptius*	Plovers/Charadriidae	Small wader from Africa
Black-headed Lapwing	*Vanellus tectus*	Plovers/Charadriidae	Striking plover from Africa
Red-wattled Lapwing	*Vanellus indicus*	Plovers/Charadriidae	Eye-catching plover from Asia
Chestnut-banded Plover	*Charadrius pallidus*	Plovers/Charadriidae	Small sand plover from southern Africa
Three-banded Plover	*Charadrius tricollaris*	Plovers/Charadriidae	Small plover from Africa
Kittlitz's Plover	*Charadrius pecuarius*	Plovers/Charadriidae	Small, compact plover, vagrant in Middle East, from Africa
Short-billed Dowitcher	*Limnodromus griseus*	Waders/Scolopacidae	Long-billed wader from North America
Hudsonian Godwit	*Limosa haemastica*	Waders/Scolopacidae	Large, long-billed wader from North America
Eskimo Curlew	*Numenius borealis*	Waders/Scolopacidae	Medium-sized wader (possibly extinct) from North America
Little Curlew	*Numenius minutus*	Waders/Scolopacidae	Whimbrel-like wader from Asia
Grey-tailed Tattler	*Heteroscelus brevipes*	Waders/Scolopacidae	Medium to small grey wader from SE Asia
Willet	*Catoptrophorus semipalmatus*	Waders/Scolopacidae	Godwit-like wader from North America
Swinhoe's Snipe	*Gallinago megala*	Waders/Scolopacidae	Dark snipe from Asia
Pin-tailed Snipe	*Gallinago stenura*	Waders/Scolopacidae	Snipe-like bird from Asia
Skuas, Gulls, and Terns			
South Polar Skua	*Stercorarius maccormicki*	Skuas/Stercoraridae	Large skua from southern oceans
Brown-headed Gull	*Larus brunnicephalus*	Gulls/Laridae	Small gull, vagrant in Middle East, from Asia
Glaucous-winged Gull	*Larus glaucescens*	Gulls/Laridae	Large gull, vagrant in North Africa, from North America
Sooty Gull	*Larus hemprichii*	Gulls/Laridae	Large dusky gull, in Red Sea
Grey-headed Gull	*Larus cirrocephalus*	Gulls/Laridae	Vagrant in North Africa, from southern Africa
White-cheeked Tern	*Sterna repressa*	Gulls/Laridae	Black-capped dark tern, in Middle East
Aleutian Tern	*Sterna aleutica*	Terns/Sternidae	Grey tern from Arctic Pacific
American Little Tern	*Sterna antillarum*	Terns/Sternidae	Little Tern from North America
Crested Tern	*Sterna bergii*	Terns/Sternidae	Large tern from Indian Ocean

Common Name	Scientific Name	Family/Scientific Name	Description
Skuas, Gulls, and Terns *continued*			
Elegant Tern	Sterna elegans	Terns/Sternidae	Long-billed tern from Caribbean
Brown Noddy	*Anous stolidus*	Terns/Sternidae	Dark, tern-like seabird from tropical oceans
Skimmers			
African Skimmer	*Rynchops flavirostris*	Skimmers/Rynchopidae	Long-billed bird, vagrant in Middle East, from Africa
Auks			
Ancient Murrelet	*Synthliboramphus antiquus*	Auks/Alcidae	Small, Little Auk-like seabird from N Pacific
Parakeet Auklet	*Cyclorrhynchus psittacula*	Auks/Alcidae	Small auk-like seabird from N Pacific
Crested Auklet	*Aethia cristatella*	Auks/Alcidae	Small Puffin-like seabird from N Pacific
Tufted Puffin	*Lunda cirrhata*	Auks/Alcidae	Large dark puffin from N Pacific
Sandgrouse			
Pallas's Sandgrouse	Syrrhaptes paradoxus	Sandgrouse/Pterocliidae	Partridge-like bird, vagrant in W Europe, from Asia
Lichtenstein's Sandgrouse	*Pterocles lichtensteinii*	Sandgrouse/Pteroclididae	Small, barred sandgrouse, in Middle East
Spotted Sandgrouse	*Pterocles senegallus*	Sandgrouse/Pteroclididae	Large pale sandgrouse, in Middle East
Crowned Sandgrouse	*Pterocles coronatus*	Sandgrouse/Pteroclididae	Pale sandgrouse, in Middle East
Chestnut-bellied Sandgrouse	*Pterocles exustus*	Sandgrouse/Pterocliidae	Large sandgrouse, in Middle East
Pigeons and Doves			
Yellow-eyed Dove	*Columba eversmanni*	Pigeons and Doves/ Columbidae	Small pigeon from Asia
Bolle's Pigeon	*Columba bollii*	Pigeons and Doves/ Columbidae	Dark pigeon, endemic to Canary Islands
Laurel Pigeon	*Columba junoniae*	Pigeons and Doves/ Columbidae	Dark pigeon, endemic to Canary Islands
Trocaz Pigeon	*Columba trocaz*	Pigeons and Doves/ Columbidae	Dark pigeon, endemic to Madeira
Laughing Dove	*Streptopelia senegalensis*	Pigeons and Doves/ Columbidae	Small dark dove, in Middle East
Oriental Turtle Dove	*Streptopelia orientalis*	Pigeons and Doves/ Columbidae	Dark dove from Asia
African Collared Dove	*Streptopelia roseogrisea*	Pigeons and Doves/ Columbidae	Brown and pinkish dove, vagrant in Middle East, from Africa
Namaqua Dove	*Oena capensis*	Pigeons and Doves/ Columbidae	Tiny, long-tailed dove, in Middle East
Mourning Dove	*Zenaida macroura*	Pigeons and Doves/ Columbidae	Sharp-tailed, Collared Dove-like species from North America

Common Name	Scientific Name	Family/Scientific Name	Description
Cuckoos and Coucals			
Didric Cuckoo	*Chrysococcyx caprius*	Cuckoos/Cuculidae	Green and white cuckoo, vagrant in Middle East, from Africa
Oriental Cuckoo	*Cuculus saturatus*	Cuckoos/Cuculidae	Small cuckoo from Asia
Black-billed Cuckoo	*Coccyzus erythrophthalmus*	Cuckoos/Cuculidae	Small cuckoo from North America
Senegal Coucal	*Centropus senegalensis*	Coucals/Centropodidae	Black-capped, rufous cuckoo, in North Africa
Owls			
Pale Scops Owl	*Otus brucei*	Owls/Strigidae	Small eared owl, rare in Middle East
Brown Fish Owl	*Ketupa zeylonensis*	Owls/Strigidae	Large, eared owl, in Middle East
Hume's Tawny Owl	*Strix butleri*	Owls/Strigidae	Small, pale desert owl, in North Africa and Middle East
Marsh Owl	*Asio capensis*	Owls/Strigidae	Small Short-eared Owl-like bird, in North Africa
Nightjars			
Nubian Nightjar	*Caprimulgus nubicus*	Nightjars/Caprimulgidae	Small nightjar, rare in Middle East
Egyptian Nightjar	*Caprimulgus aegyptius*	Nightjars/Caprimulgidae	Pale nightjar, rare in Middle East
Swifts			
White-throated Needletail	*Hirundapus caudacutus*	Swifts/Apodidae	Large swift from Asia
Chimney Swift	*Chaetura pelagica*	Swifts/Apodidae	Dumpy swift from North America
Plain Swift	*Apus unicolor*	Swifts/Apodidae	All-dark swift, in Canary Islands
Pacific Swift	*Apus pacificus*	Swifts/Apodidae	Large swift from Asia
Kingfishers			
Belted Kingfisher	*Ceryle alcyon*	Giant Kingfishers/ Cerylidae	Big kingfisher from North America
Pied Kingfisher	*Ceryle rudis*	Giant Kingfishers/ Cerylidae	Large, black and white kingfisher, in Middle East
White-throated Kingfisher	*Halcyon smyrnensis*	Halcyon Kingfishers/ Dacelonidae	Big, red-billed kingfisher, in Middle East
Bee-Eaters			
Blue-cheeked Bee-eater	*Merops persicus*	Bee-eaters/Meropidae	Greenish bee-eater from Middle East
Little Green Bee-eater	*Merops orientalis*	Bee-eaters/Meropidae	Small, bright bee-eater, in Middle East
Rollers			
Indian Roller Middle	*Coracias benghalensis*	Rollers/Coracidae	Colourful roller, vagrant in East, from South Asia

Common Name	Scientific Name	Family/Scientific Name	Description
Woodpeckers			
Northern Flicker	*Colaptes auratus*	Woodpeckers/Picidae	Colourful woodpecker from North America
Levaillant's Green Woodpecker	*Picus vaillantii*	Woodpeckers/Picidae	Large, scarce green woodpecker, in North Africa
Yellow-bellied Sapsucker	*Sphyrapicus varius*	Woodpeckers/Picidae	Small woodpecker from North America
Larks			
Hoopoe Lark	*Alaemon alaudipes*	Larks/Alaudidae	Large pale lark, in Middle East
Thick-billed Lark	*Rhamphocoris clotbey*	Larks/Alaudidae	Heavy desert lark, in North Africa
Bimaculated Lark	*Melanocorypha bimaculata*	Larks/Alaudidae	Large lark, rare in Middle East
White-winged Lark	*Melanocorypha leucoptera*	Larks/Alaudidae	Large lark from Asia
Black Lark	*Melanocorypha yeltoniensis*	Larks/Alaudidae	Stocky lark from Asia
Hume's Short-toed Lark	*Calandrella acutirostris*	Larks/Alaudidae	Small lark, vagrant in Middle East, from Asia
Oriental Skylark	*Alauda gulgula*	Larks/Alaudidae	Plain lark from Middle East
Chestnut-headed Sparrow-lark	*Eremopterix signata*	Larks/Alaudidae	Small, sparrow-like lark from Africa
Black-crowned Sparrow-lark	*Eremopterix nigriceps*	Larks/Alaudidae	Small, finch-like lark, in Middle East
Dunn's Lark	*Eremalauda dunni*	Larks/Alaudidae	Small plain lark, rare in Middle East
Temminck's Lark	*Eremophila bilopha*	Larks/Alaudidae	Pale, horned, desert-living lark, in Middle East and North Africa
Martins and Swallows			
Tree Swallow	*Tachycineta bicolor*	Swallows/Hirundinidae	Glossy green and white swallow from North America
Plain Martin	*Riparia paludicola*	Swallows/Hirundinidae	Small brown martin, in North Africa
Ethiopian Swallow	*Hirundo aethiopica*	Swallows/Hirundinidae	Long-tailed swallow from Africa
Wire-tailed Swallow	*Hirundo smithii*	Swallows/Hirundinidae	Slender swallow from Africa
Rock Martin	*Ptyonoprogne fuligula*	Swallows/Hirundinidae	Small, pale Crag Martin-like bird, in Middle East
Pipits			
Buff-bellied Pipit	*Anthus rubescens*	Pipits and wagtails/Motacillidae	Dark-legged pipit from North America
Berthelot's Pipit	*Anthus berthelotii*	Pipits and wagtails/Motacillidae	Small pipit, in Canary Islands and Madeira
Long-billed Pipit	*Anthus similis*	Pipits and wagtails/Motacillidae	Large, pale, mountainside pipit, in Middle East

Common Name	Scientific Name	Family/Scientific Name	Description
Shrikes			
Black-crowned Tchagra	*Tchagra senegala*	Shrikes/Laniidae	Boldly patterned shrike, in North Africa
Brown Shrike	*Lanius cristatus*	Shrikes/Lanidae	Dull shrike from Asia
Long-tailed Shrike	*Lanius schach*	Shrikes/Lanidae	Brownish shrike from Asia
Bulbuls			
White-eared Bulbul	*Pycnonotus leucotis*	Bulbuls/Pycnonotidae	Black and brown bulbul, vagrant in Middle East, from Asia
Waxwings			
Cedar Waxwing	*Bombycilla cedrorum*	Waxwings/Bombycillidae	Yellow-bellied waxwing, vagrant in UK, from North America
Grey Hypocolius	*Hypocolius ampelinus*	Waxwings/Bombycillidae	Shrike-like bird, in Middle East
Mockingbirds			
Northern Mockingbird	*Mimus polyglottus*	Mockingbirds/Mimidae	Thrush-like bird from North America
Brown Thrasher	*Toxostoma rufum*	Mockingbirds/Mimidae	Rusty, thrush-like bird from North America
Catbird	*Dumetella carolinensis*	Mockingbirds/Mimidae	Chat-like bird from North America
Accentors			
Black-throated Accentor	*Prunella atrogularis*	Accentors/Prunellidae	Dunnock-like bird, vagrant in Middle East, from Siberia
Siberian Accentor	*Prunella montanella*	Accentors/Prunellidae	Dunnock-like bird from Siberia
Radde's Accentor	*Prunella ocularis*	Accentors/Prunellidae	Dunnock-like bird from Siberia
Chats and Thrushes			
Siberian Blue Robin	*Luscinia cyane*	Chats/Saxicoliidae	Vagrant in NW Europe, from Siberia
Siberian Rubythroat	*Luscinia calliope*	Chats/Saxicoliidae	Colourful chat from Siberia
White-throated Robin	*Irania gutturalis*	Chats/Saxicoliidae	Large greyish chat from Middle East
Eversmann's Redstart	*Phoenicurus erythronotus*	Chats/Saxicolidae	Large redstart from Asia
Moussier's Redstart	*Phoenicurus moussieri*	Chats/Saxicoliidae	Brightly patterned chat, in North Africa
Güldenstädt's Redstart	*Phoenicurus erythrogaster*	Chats/Saxicoliidae	Striking chat from Asia
Blackstart	*Cercomela melanura*	Chats/Saxicoliidae	Small, grey, black-tailed chat, in Middle East
Fuerteventura Stonechat	*Saxicola dacotiae*	Chats/Saxicoliidae	Small chat, endemic to Canary Islands

Common Name	Scientific Name	Family/Scientific Name	Description
Chats and Thrushes *continued*			
Desert Wheatear	*Oenanthe deserti*	Chats/Saxicoliidae	Black-tailed brownish wheatear from North Africa and Middle East
Finsch's Wheatear	*Oenanthe finschii*	Chats/Saxicoliidae	Large wheatear, in Middle East
White-crowned Wheatear	*Oenanthe leucopyga*	Chats/Saxicoliidae	Blackish wheatear from Middle East
Mourning Wheatear	*Oenanthe lugens*	Chats/Saxicoliidae	Piebald wheatear, in Middle East
Pied Wheatear	*Oenanthe pleschanka*	Chats/Saxicoliidae	Small dark wheatear from Middle East and extreme E Europe
Red-rumped Wheatear	*Oenanthe moesta*	Chats/Saxicoliidae	Large wheatear, in Middle East
Hooded Wheatear	*Oenanthe monacha*	Chats/Saxicoliidae	Large wheatear, in Middle East
Persian Wheatear	*Oenanthe xanthoprymna*	Chats/Saxicoliidae	Dark wheatear, in Middle East
Varied Thrush	*Zoothera naevia*	Thrushes/Turdidae	Small thrush from W North America
Wood Thrush	*Hylocichla mustelina*	Thrushes/Turdidae	Small, spotted thrush from North America
Veery	*Catharus fuscescens*	Thrushes/Turdidae	Tiny spotted thrush from North America
Hermit Thrush	*Catharus guttatus*	Thrushes/Turdidae	Small spotted thrush from North America
Swainson's Thrush	*Catharus ustulatus*	Thrushes/Turdidae	Small spotted thrush from North America
Tickell's Thrush	*Turdus unicolor*	Thrushes/Turdidae	Colourful thrush from Asia
American Robin	*Turdus migratorius*	Thrushes/Turdidae	Large thrush from North America
Babblers			
Fulvous Babbler	*Turdoides fulvus*	Babblers/Timaliidae	Thrush-like bird, in North Africa
Arabian Babbler	*Turdoides squamiceps*	Babblers/Timaliidae	Pale, thrush-like bird, in Middle East
Warblers and Allies			
Graceful Prinia	*Prinia gracilis*	Warblers/Sylviidae	Small, long-tailed warbler, in Middle East
Scrub Warbler	*Scotocerca inquieta*	Warblers/Sylviidae	Small, long-tailed warbler, in Middle East
Gray's Grasshopper Warbler	*Locustella fasciolata*	Warblers/Sylviidae	Shy warbler from Asia
Clamorous Reed Warbler	*Acrocephalus stentoreus*	Warblers/Sylviidae	Large reed warbler, in Middle East
Thick-billed Warbler	*Acrocephalus aedon*	Warblers/Sylviidae	Large reed warbler-like bird from Asia
Basra Reed Warbler	*Acrocephalus griseldis*	Warblers/Sylviidae	Rare reed warbler, in Middle East

Common Name	Scientific Name	Family/Scientific Name	Description
Warblers and Allies *continued*			
Desert Warbler	*Sylvia nana*	Warblers/Sylviidae	Pale, sandy warbler from N Africa and Middle east
Tristram's Warbler	*Sylvia deserticola*	Warblers/Sylviidae	Small, Whitethroat-like warbler, in North Africa
Ménétrie's Warbler	*Sylvia mystacea*	Warblers/Sylviidae	Rare migrant warbler, in Middle East
Arabian Warbler	*Sylvia leucomelaena*	Warblers/Sylviidae	Dark-headed warbler, in Middle East
Two-barred Greenish Warbler	*Phylloscopus (trochiloides) plumbeitarsus*	Warblers/Sylviidae	Small warbler (like Greenish Warbler) from Asia
Green Warbler	*Phylloscopus (trochiloides) nitidus*	Warblers/Sylviidae	Small warbler from Asia
Eastern Crowned Leaf Warbler	*Phylloscopus coronatus*	Warblers/Sylviidae	Small leaf warbler from Asia
Plain Leaf Warbler	*Phylloscopus neglectus*	Warblers/Sylviidae	Small leaf warbler from Asia
Ruby-crowned Kinglet	*Regulus calendula*	Kinglets/Regulidae	Tiny Goldcrest-like bird from North America
Flycatchers			
Brown Flycatcher	*Muscicapa dauurica*	Flycatchers/Muscicapidae	Plain flycatcher from Asia
Acadian Flycatcher	*Empidonax virescens*	Tyrant Flycatchers/Tyrannidae	Greenish flycatcher from North America
Eastern Phoebe	*Sayornis phoebe*	Tyrant Flycatchers/Tyrannidae	Small, dull flycatcher from North America
Nuthatches			
Red-breasted Nuthatch	*Sitta canadensis*	Nuthatches/Sittidae	Small, stripe-headed nuthatch from North America
Eastern Rock Nuthatch	*Sitta tephronota*	Nuthatches/Sittidae	Large nuthatch, in Middle East
Krüper's Nuthatch	*Sitta krueperi*	Nuthatches/Sittidae	Small, dark-capped nuthatch, in Middle East
Sunbirds			
Nile Valley Sunbird	*Anthreptes metallicus*	Sunbirds/Nectariniidae	Long-tailed nectar-eater, in Middle East
Palestine Sunbird	*Nectarinia osea*	Sunbirds/Nectariniidae	Tiny, dark nectar-eater, in Middle East
Crows			
Fan-tailed Raven	*Corvus rhipidurus*	Crows/Corvidae	Short-tailed raven, in North Africa and Middle East
Brown-necked Raven in	*Corvus ruficollis*	Crows/Corvidae	Somewhat thinner-billed raven, North Africa and Middle East
House Crow	*Corvus splendens*	Crows/Corvidae	Grey and black crow, introduced in Middle East from India
Daurian Jackdaw	*Corvus dauuricus*	Crows/Corvidae	Pied jackdaw from Asia

Common Name	Scientific Name	Family/Scientific Name	Description
Starlings			
Tristram's Starling	*Onychognathus tristramii*	Starlings/Sturnidae	Dark, red-winged starling, in Middle East
Tanagers			
Scarlet Tanager	*Piranga olivacea*	Tanagers/Thraupidae	Large finch from North America
Summer Tanager	*Piranga rubra*	Tanagers/Thraupidae	Finch-like bird from North America
Buntings			
Rufous-sided Towhee	*Pipilo erythrophthalmus*	Buntings/Emberizidae	Thickset finch-like bird from North America
Lark Sparrow	*Chondestes grammacus*	Buntings/ Emberizidae	Streaky-headed bunting-like bird, vagrant in UK from North America
Fox Sparrow	*Passerella iliaca*	Buntings/Emberizidae	Rufous bunting from North America
Song Sparrow	*Melospiza melodia*	Buntings/Emberizidae	Streaky bunting from North America
White-crowned Sparrow	*Zonotrichia leucophrys*	Buntings/Emberizidae	Sparrow-like bird from North America
Black-faced Bunting	*Emberiza spodocephala*	Buntings/Emberizidae	Dark bunting from Asia
Cinnamon-breasted Bunting	*Emberiza tahapisi*	Buntings/Emberizidae	Dark-coloured bunting from Africa
Grey-necked Bunting	*Emberiza buchanani*	Buntings/Emberizidae	Slender bunting from Asia
Yellow-browed Bunting	*Emberiza chrysophrys*	Buntings/Emberizidae	Small bunting from Asia
Pallas's Reed Bunting	*Emberiza pallasi*	Buntings/Emberizidae	Small bunting from Asia
Red-headed Bunting	*Emberiza bruniceps*	Buntings/Emberizidae	Yellowish bunting from Asia
Cinereous Bunting	*Emberiza cineracea*	Buntings/Emberizidae	Dull bunting from Asia
House Bunting	*Emberiza striolata*	Buntings/Emberizidae	Small bunting, in North Africa and Middle East
Black-faced Bunting	*Emberiza spodocephala*	Buntings/Emberizidae	Dark bunting from Asia
Savannah Sparrow	*Passerculus sandwichensis*	Buntings/Emberizidae	Sparrow-like bunting, vagrant in NW Europe, from North America
Indigo Bunting	*Passerina cyanea*	Buntings/Emberizidae	Dark bunting from North America
New World Warblers			
Blackburnian Warbler	*Dendroica fusca*	New World Warblers/ Parulidae	Colourful warbler from North America
Yellow Warbler	*Dendroica petechia*	New World Warblers/ Parulidae	Small warbler from North America
Yellowthroat	*Geothlypsis trichas*	New World Warblers/ Parulidae	Stocky warbler from North America
Ovenbird	*Seiurus aurocapillus*	New World Warblers/ Parulidae	Woodland warbler from North America

Common Name	Scientific Name	Family/Scientific Name	Description
New World Warblers *continued*			
Northern Waterthrush	*Seiurus novaeboracensis*	New World Warblers/ Parulidae	Streaked warbler from North America
Tennessee Warbler	*Vermivora peregrina*	New World Warblers/ Parulidae	Plain warbler from North America
Yellow-throated Vireo	*Vireo flavifrons*	Vireos/Vireonidae	Small, warbler-like bird from North America
Philadelphia Vireo	*Vireo philadelphicus*	Vireos/Vireonidae	Small, warbler-like bird from North America
Finches			
Blue Chaffinch	*Fringilla teydea*	Finches/Fringillidae	Large blue finch, endemic to Canary Islands
Canary	*Serinus canaria*	Finches/Fringillidae	Greenish finch, endemic to Canary Islands
Red-fronted Serin	*Serinus pusillus*	Finches/Fringillidae	Small finch, in Middle East
Syrian Serin	*Serinus syriacus*	Finches/Fringillidae	Small, greenish, upland finch, in Middle East
Crimson-winged Finch	*Rhodopechys sanguinea*	Finches/Fringillidae	Thickset mountain finch, in Middle East
Mongolian Finch	*Bucanetes mongolicus*	Finches/Fringillidae	Large finch from Asia
Trumpeter Finch	*Bucanetes githagineus*	Finches/Fringillidae	Small, pale pinkish finch, in Middle East
Sinai Rosefinch	*Carpodacus synoicus*	Finches/Fringillidae	Pale, pink-tinged finch, in Middle East
Long-tailed Rosefinch	*Uragus sibiricus*	Finches/Fringillidae	Small finch from Asia
Evening Grosbeak	*Hesperiphona vespertina*	Finches/Fringillidae	Large finch from North America
Desert Finch	*Rhodospiza obsoleta*	Finches/Fringillidae	Pale finch, in Middle East
Sparrows			
Dead Sea Sparrow	*Passer moabiticus*	Sparrows/Passeridae	Small, colourful sparrow, in Middle East
Desert Sparrow	*Passer simplex*	Sparrows/Passeridae	Pale, dark-billed sparrow, in North Africa
Hill Sparrow	*Carpospiza brachydactyla*	Sparrows/Passeridae	Pale sparrow, in Middle East
Chestnut-shouldered Sparrow	*Gymornis xanthocollis*	Sparrows/Passeridae	Pale sparrow, in Middle East
New World Orioles			
Brown-headed Cowbird	*Molothrus ater*	New World Orioles/ Icteridae	Black bird, vagrant in NW Europe, from North America
Yellow-headed Blackbird	*Xanthocephalus xanthocephalus*	New World Orioles/ Icteridae	Glossy black bird from North America
Northern Oriole	*Icterus galbula*	New World Orioles/ Icteridae	Colourful oriole from North America

GLOSSARY

Many of the terms defined here are illustrated in the general introduction (pp. 8–53). For anatomical terms see also pp.10–11.

• **ADULT** A fully mature bird, able to breed, showing the final plumage pattern that no longer changes with age.
• **BARRED** With marks crossing the body, wing, or tail.
• **BROOD** Young produced from a single clutch of eggs incubated together.
• **CALL** Vocal sound often characteristic of a particular species, communicating a variety of messages.
• **COLONY** A group of nests of a highly social species, especially among seabirds but also others such as the Sand Martin and Rook.
• **COVERT** A small feather in a well-defined tract, on the wing or at the base of the tail, covering the base of the larger flight feathers.
• **CRYPTIC** Describes plumage pattern and colours that make a bird difficult to see in its favoured habitat.
• **DABBLE** To feed in shallow water, with rapid movements of the bill, sieving water through fine comb-like teeth to extract food.
• **DECLINING** Populations undergoing a steady decline over a number of years.
• **DIMORPHIC** Having two forms: sexually dimorphic means that the male and female of a species look different; otherwise indicates two colour forms.
• **DRUMMING** Sound made by woodpeckers with rapid beats of the bill against a hard object, or by a snipe, diving through the air with vibrating tail feathers.
• **EAR TUFT** A bunch of feathers on the head of an owl, capable of being raised as a visual signal and perhaps to assist camouflage.
• **ECLIPSE** The plumage of male ducks that is adopted during the summer, when they moult and become flightless for a short time.
• **ENDANGERED** Found in very small numbers, in a very small area or in a very restricted and declining habitat, so that the future security of the species is in doubt.
• **ESCAPEE** A bird that has escaped into the wild from a collection of some kind, such as a zoo or wildlife park.
• **EYE PATCH** An area of colour around the eye, often in the form of a "mask", broader than an eye-stripe.
• **EYE-RING** A more or less circular patch of colour, usually narrow and well-defined, around the eye.
• **EYE-STRIPE** A stripe of distinctive colour running in front of and behind the eye.

• **FAMILY** A category in classification, grouping species or genera that are closely related; ranked at a higher level than the genus.
• **FLIGHT FEATHER** Any one of the long feathers on the wing (primaries and secondaries).
• **FOREWING** The front part of a wing, including the outer primaries, primary coverts, and secondary coverts.
• **GAPE** A bird's mouth, or the angle at the base of the bill.
• **GENUS (pl. GENERA)** A category in classification: a group of closely related species, whose relationship is recognized by the same first name in the scientific terminology, e.g. *Larus* in *Larus fuscus*.
• **HINDWING** The rear part of the wing, including the secondary feathers, especially when it has a distinctive colour or pattern.
• **HYBRID** The result of cross-breeding between two species; usually infertile. Rare in the wild.
• **IMMATURE** Not yet fully adult or able to breed; there may be several identifiable plumages during immaturity but many small birds are mature by the first spring after they have fledged.
• **INNER WING** The inner part of the wing, comprising the secondaries and rows of coverts (typically marginal, lesser, median, and greater coverts).
• **JUVENILE** A bird in its first plumage, that in which it makes its first flight, before its first moult in the autumn.
• **LEK** A gathering of birds at which males display communally, with mock fighting, while females choose which one to mate with.
• **LOCALIZED** More than 90 per cent of the population occurs at ten sites or less.
• **MOULT** The shedding and renewing of feathers in a systematic way; most birds have a partial moult and a complete moult each year.
• **MIGRANT** A species that spends part of the year in one geographical area and part in another, moving between the two on a regular basis. (See also p.26.)
• **ORDER** A category in classification: families grouped to indicate their close relationship or common ancestry; usually a more uncertain or speculative grouping than a family.
• **OUTER WING** The outer half of the wing, comprising the primaries, their coverts, and the alula, or bastard wing (the "thumb").
• **ORBITAL RING** A thin, bare, fleshy ring around the eye, sometimes with a distinctive colour.
• **PRIMARY** Any one of the long feathers, or quills, forming the tip and trailing edge of the outer wing, growing from the "hand".

• **RACE** *See* SUBSPECIES.
• **RARE** Found in small numbers or very low densities, although not necessarily at risk.
• **SCAPULAR** Any one of a group of feathers on the shoulder, forming a more or less oval patch each side of the back, at the base of the wing.
• **SECONDARY** Any one of the long flight feathers forming the trailing edge of the inner wing, growing from the ulna or "arm".
• **SECURE** The population is under no current threat.
• **SONG** Vocalization with character particular to the individual species, used to communicate a claim to a breeding territory and attract a mate.
• **SONG-FLIGHT** A special flight, often with a distinctive pattern, combined with a territorial song.
• **SPECIES** A group of living organisms, individuals of which can interbreed to produce fertile young, but do not normally breed, or cannot produce fertile young, with a different species.
• **SPECULUM** A colourful patch on a duck's hindwing, formed by the secondary feathers.
• **STREAKED** With small marks that run lengthwise along the body.
• **SUBSPECIES** A race; a recognizable group within a species, isolated geographically but able to interbreed with others of the same species.
• **SUPERCILIARY STRIPE** A stripe of colour running above the eye, like an eyebrow.
• **TERTIAL** Any one of a small group of feathers, sometimes long and obvious, at the base of the wing adjacent to the inner secondaries.
• **UNDERWING** The underside of a wing, usually visible only in flight or when a bird is preening.
• **UPPERWING** The upperside of the wing, clearly exposed in flight but often mostly hidden when the bird is perched.
• **VAGRANT** An individual bird that has strayed beyond the usual geographic range of its species.
• **VENT** The area of feathers between the legs and the undertail coverts.
• **VULNERABLE** Potentially at risk due to a dependence on a restricted habitat or range, or to small numbers.
• **WINGPIT** A group of feathers – the axillaries – located at the base of the underwing.
• **WINGBAR** A line of colour produced by a tract of feathers or feather tips, crossing the closed wing and running along the spread wing.
• **YOUNG** An imprecise term to describe immature birds; often meaning juveniles or nestlings.

INDEX

ACKNOWLEDGMENTS

THE AUTHOR would like to thank: the team at Dorling Kindersley for their hard work and patience; Marcella for her encouragement and forbearance at home; Chris Gomersall for his dedication in the pursuit of photographs; and Richard Thewlis for the research on the maps.

DORLING KINDERSLEY would like to thank: Sean O'Connor, Rachel Gibson, Kim Bryan, Simon Maugham, Peter Frances, and Rick Morris for getting the project started; Carolyn Clerkin for compiling the acknowledgments. We would also like to thank Roland Fiala for the use of his sound recordings and his help in putting together the audio CD.

The publisher would like to thank the following for their kind permission to reproduce their photographs: (Key: a=above; c=centre; b=below; l=left; r=right; t=top).

Aquila Wildlife Images: Darren Frost 428bl; Hanne and Jens Erikson 126tr; Mike Wilkes 394tr; Paul Harris 446tr.

Ardea London Ltd: Chris Knights 392cb; Hans D. Dossenbach 251tr; John Daniels 197tc; Peter Steyn 415tr, 428tr; Uno Berggren 243tc.

BBC Natural History Unit: Dietmar Nill 240tr, 367cr; Elio Della Ferrera 122cra; Hans Christoph Kappel 240br; Jose B Ruiz 240cr; Klaus Nigge 122crb; Rico & Ruiz 333tr, 381tr, 445tl; Warwick Sloss 223tc.

Richard Brooks: 180cra, 210tr, 361crb, 427tr.

Laurie Campbell Photography: 260bl, 280cbl, 293bc, 368bl.

R.J. Chandler: 58cra, 154tr, 172tr, 175cra, 221tc, 297cla, 390cla, 430bl, 432bl, 433bl, 433br, 434bl, 435bl, 446bl.

Robin Chittenden: 11br, 18br, 119tr, 214cla, 252cca, 306ccb, 342crb, 450tl, 454br, 459br, 460tl, 461br

Corbis: Eric and David Hosking 317tcr.

David Cotteridge: 34br, 64crb, 68cra, 68crb, 80tc, 88cr, 97tc, 136ca, 151cl, 168tc, 172tc, 177tr, 180tc, 183cla, 188tr, 204cb, 216cr, 231tr, 252tr, 255tr, 262cla, 266ccr, 268tr, 281cra, 284tr, 285tc, 287cr, 287tr, 289cbr, 301cra, 301bcr, 303tc, 305tla, 306tc, 308ccb, 312tr, 321cra, 321ccb, 324tc, 325tc, 341cra, 362tl, 384ccb, 397ccb, 401ctr, 407tc, 413tr, 443br, 449br, 451tl, 451br, 453tr, 453bl, 457bl, 459tr, 461tr.

Goran Ekström: 253c, 285bcr, 302car, 402crb, 455bl.

Hanne and Jens Eriksen: 107cra, 121tr, 129crb, 159cla, 198tr, 199cra, 284cb, 312tc, 366tr, 392tr, 406tr, 407crb, 423tr, 423bl, 430tl, 432br, 433tr, 434tr, 434br, 438tl, 439br, 441bl, 444br, 447tl, 448br, 456bl, 458tl, 458br.

FLPA – Images of nature: 94bcl, 97cr, 162cr, 168cla, 210tc, 261tr, 272c, 321tr, 323cra, 328br, 354cr, 383bcr, 396tr, 406ccb, 444tl; E & D Hosking 415br; E Coppola/A Petretti/Panda 426tl; Foto Natura Stock 66cra; Fritz Polking 242tc; H Hautala 436br; Hans Dieter Brandl 267cla, 446tl; John Holmes 450bl; John Watkins 118tc; Lee Rue 106cbr; M Melodia/Panda 66tr; Martin B Withers/ FLPA 237cla; P Harris/Panda Photo 374cr; Panda Photo 66tc, 234cr; Peter Steyn 445bl; R Wilmshurst 103ca; Richard Brooks 73cl, 279tr, 311tc, 311tr, 326ccb, 336ccb, 409cra; Robin Chittenden 397tr; Roger Tidman/FLPA 86cl; S C Brown 227ccb; Silvestre 147tr; Silvestria 299br; Silvestris 329tc; Tony Hamblin 116crb; W S Clark 129tc, 425bl; W Wisniewski 62cl; Yossi Eshbol 72c, 76tr, 427tl.

Bob Glover: 210cbl, 212tc, 213cla, 218tr, 219tc, 219ccb, 235cr, 235cb, 279clb, 285cb, 320ccb, 323cb, 387cla, 390crb, 404tr.

Chris Gomersall Photography: 1, 4, 5, 8tr, 9bcla, 10cr, 18tc, 18trb, 18cl, 18cr, 21cl, 54c, 56crb, 57cb, 58tr, 58crb, 61cr, 64bc, 64cca, 65c, 67tr, 67ca, 70bl, 71crb, 74cra, 75tc, 75c, 77cr, 81c, 81cr, 82tc, 82bc, 85tr, 85cr, 89tr, 89bc, 91crb, 91ccb, 92c, 97tr, 97cl, 98cr, 98bcr, 99clb,

100cr, 100bl, 101ca, 101c, 102cr, 105cb, 108cra, 108crb, 110cla, 110cra, 110crb, 114crb, 116clb, 119cr, 120bc, 145tc, 145tr, 145cra, 122cr, 125ca, 125cb, 126tc, 126cb, 130tc, 130crb, 141cb, 141crb, 144tr, 144crb, 146tr, 146cra, 146bc, 148crb, 149tr, 149crb, 150tr, 150bc, 151c, 152tr, 153c, 156cla, 156cra, 156bc, 157cr, 160tc, 160cra, 161crb, 163tr, 163cra, 163bc, 165cra, 165cl, 165br, 166tr, 166crb, 167cra, 169tr, 169c, 174bc, 176cra, 178tc, 181crb, 184bcr, 185ccb, 186tc, 186cr, 189cr, 188crb, 190tr, 190cra, 190tcr, 192tr, 192cra, 192crb, 194tc, 194cla, 195cla, 196cla, 196ccb, 200tr, 203cra, 203cl, 203br, 208tc, 211tr, 215ccb, 216tr, 220cb, 220cra, 223cra, 224cra, 224cbr, 229cca, 229ccb, 230cb, 231tc, 231crb, 231trb, 232tr, 233cra, 234tr, 236c, 237c, 244ccb, 245tc, 251bc, 252ccb, 254ccb, 256cra, 259tr, 259cra, 262tr, 273ccb, 274tr, 275tc, 275tr, 275ccb, 277bc, 280tc, 280cra, 287cb, 290tr, 293clb, 293crb, 294cla, 295br, 296tr, 296cla, 297ccb, 299cra, 299clb, 300tc, 300ccr, 303cra, 303cr, 305tc, 305tr, 309tc, 313tc, 314tr, 315ccb, 319cla, 319cra, 327ccb, 328ccb, 328ca, 330cb, 350ccb, 351ccb, 368tc, 368cr, 369tr, 370crb, 373tc, 376tc, 376cbr, 377tr, 377ccb, 379tcl, 380tc, 380cra, 382cr, 383tc, 383cra, 383ccb, 386tr, 386ccb, 387bc, 388cb, 394ccb, 395crb, 395cca, 404crb, 408ccr, 409tc, 4090tr, 409crb, 413cra, 415tl, 416bl, 422br, 429tl, 439tr, 441tr, 441br, 443bl.

Mark Hamblin: 9bca, 56tc, 72tc, 82cr, 91cra, 99c, 103tc, 104ca, 109ca, 111cr, 113tc, 116crb, 138tr, 161ca, 161cr, 167tc, 170cra, 175c, 186tr, 239tr, 241tr, 246tr, 249tr, 250cra, 257tc, 257cbr, 260br, 265tr, 266tr, 266cca, 283bc, 291tc, 293tr, 297tr, 304cla, 306cal, 310tr, 315cla, 345crb, 345, 347bc, 350tc, 351tc, 352tr, 370cra, 378cr, 388cra, 391cla, 398tc, 398tr, 398cla, 405tr, 405cra, 408cra.

Huttenmoser: 357bc, 358tr, 358cla, 359bl.

Pentti Johansson: 264cb.

Rob Jordan: 55bc, 382bc.

Arto Juvonen: 147cal, 263cb.

Steve Knell: 228crb.

Chris Knights: 90cr, 93tr, 118crb, 169tc, 169cr, 246tc, 278ccb, 316cb, 362br, 382cl, 389crb, 393crb.

Mike Lane: 8ra, 9tcb, 9bcl, 12bl, 13bl, 16tr, 19tc, 55cca, 57ca, 59ca, 60tr, 61tr, 61cl, 61bc, 62tr, 68cca, 71tr, 73tc, 73crb, 89cra, 93tc, 94tr, 95tc, 96c, 102c, 106tr, 109tr, 108tc, 111tc, 120tc, 134cr, 134crb, 136tr, 148cra, 149cla, 149ca, 154tc, 155tc, 156tc, 158tr, 161c, 166tc, 171tr, 170tc, 170tc, 172cra, 172cra, 172crb, 172crb, 174tr, 176tr, 179tr, 179ca, 184tr, 187tr, 194tr, 197tr, 207tc, 207tr, 207crb, 208cla, 214c, 222tr, 224tr, 229tr, 230tr, 255ccl, 270tr, 274tc, 278tc, 283tr, 290crb, 292tr, 301tc, 302cb, 308tr, 309cca, 310tc, 313tr, 316tr, 316cla, 317tr, 317cla, 319bl, 322ccr, 324cra, 327cla, 328tc, 331tc, 332tr, 332ca, 332cr, 334tr, 302cb, 303tr, 303cr, 304tr, 308tc, 309ccb, 314tr, 321tr, 322tr, 326ca, 332cla, 347tr, 352tr, 357tc, 357cra, 373tc, 380cra, 382br, 390bl, 393br, 399tl, 399tr, 436tl, 439tl, 439bl, 442tr, 442bl, 444tl, 444tr, 448tr, 451tr, 452tl, 458bl.

Gordon Langsbury: 57cr, 71cra, 78tc, 78cr, 79cr, 151cr, 191crb, 225cca, 374tr, 412tr, 417tr, 417bl, 418tl, 418br, 425tr, 425tr, 429br, 430br, 437tr, 437br, 438tl.

Wayne Lankinen: 419bl, 419br.

Sampo Laukkanen: 378tcl.

Henry Lehto: 162tc, 396cla, 455tl.

Tim Loseby: 80tr, 98tc, 103cb, 112crb, 116tr, 193crb, 198crb, 217tr, 289ca, 290tc, 309cla, 321cla, 345, 386cla, 392cla, 396ccb, 403tr, 403cla, 403ccb, 407cra, 410cla, 410ccb, 453tl, 460br.

George McCarthy: 9bra, 9bc, 73tr, 76cr, 76cr, 77tc, 77cl, 78tr, 79tr, 79cla, 81tc, 88bl, 100cra, 114tr, 114ca, 135tc, 148cb, 155tr, 155cra, 159tr, 185tr, 191tr, 193cla, 195tr, 206tr, 213crb, 223cla, 227tr, 248tr, 267tc, 282ccb, 291bcra, 292ca, 355tr, 358tr, 363tc, 363tr, 419tl, 427bl, 435tr, 436br, 448tr, 451tr, 457tr.

Anthony McGeehan: 66crb, 67crb, 415bl.

Juan Martin Simon: 423br.

Dick Newell: 449cal.

Philip Newman: 133cl.

Natural History Museum: 8bl, 9bl, 16cla, 16ca, 16cca, 16cr, 16cl, 16c, 16cc, 16bl, 16bc, 16br.

Natural Picture Library: Rico & Ruiz 9tr.

N.H.P.A.: 344cb; Bill Coster 143tc; Nigel J Dennis 225cla; Ralph and Daphne Keller 446bl; Roger Tidman 69tr.

Oxford Scientific Films: Chris Knights 152cb; Mike Brown 317cla; Paolo Fioratti 262cr

Anders Paulsrud: 147cb.

Jari Peltomaki: 243crb, 261c, 402car.

Benjamin Pontine: 456tl.

Rene Pop: 232tc, 455tr, 458tr.

Mike Read: 90tr, 176crb, 342cb, 371bl, 460l.

Matti Rekila: 247cb, 247tr, 247tc, 378crb.

George Reszeter: 244ca.

RSPB Images: Andy Hay 14tr, 15cl, 176tcl, 200crb, 385tr, 385crb; Barry Hughes 170crb, 170bcl, 302tcl, 329car, 417tl; Bill Paton 17br, 88tr, 354cb, 375crb; Bob Glover 14ac, 19bl, 21c, 138crb, 142tc, 153cb, 175tc, 185cr, 190crb, 195crb, 238crb, 273tl, 355cr, 380crb, 413ccb; Carlos Sanchez Alonso 86cb, 122tr, 130tr, 131cb, 132cra, 142tr, 162tr, 163cb, 242ccb, 248tc, 305bc, 364cbr; Chris Gomersall 17bl, 19bc, 20bl, 104cr, 125tr, 143crb, 167crb, 188cla, 194crb, 223cb, 239tcr; Chris Knights 13crb, 15cr, 150c, 152bcr, 152ccr, 196cca, 235cla, 290ccr, 296tc, 331tr, 367ca, 387tr, 400tr, 403bcr, 426bl; David Hosking 75cr; David Kjaer 138cra, 144tc, 206ccb, 244cra, 271cra, 309ccb, 347cla, 350cra, 391tr, 411crb; David Tipling 21tl, 154cr, 187tc; Dusan Boucny 17cb, 247tr, 366cr; E A Janes 179crb; George McCarthy 14cl, 15ca, 17cr, 81bc, 189tr; Gerald Downey 135cb, 291cra, 408tr; Gordon Langsbury 140cb, 191tc, 286ccb, 300tr; Jan Halady 318cb; Jan Sevcik 39ccb, 226cca, 250tr, 408ccl; John Lawton Roberts 257tc, 262c, 346cb; Leslie J Borg 78ccb; Malcolm Hunt 180crb, 323cla, 343tr, 416tl; Mark Hamblin 133cra, 138tc, 265c, 295bc, 297tc, 314crb, 318tr, 348cra, 348crb, 370tr, 391tc, 394cla, 398crb; Maurice Walker 16cr, 239cb, 348bcl, 349tr, 349tr; Michael Gore 78cca, 87clb, 311ccb, 361tc; Mike Lane 65cr, 87cla, 135tr, 136cr, 177crb, 178crb, 197cr, 258tc, 269tr, 301cb, 330cla, 376tr, 395cla, 403tr; Mike McKavett 294cr; Mike Read 168crb; Mike Richards 250crb; Paul Doherty 137tr; Peter Perfect 369bl; Philip Newman 14bl, 313ccr, 325ccb; Raymond Franklin 90br; Richard Brooks 10bl, 153cla, 265tc, 288cra, 317tcl, 356tc, 373ccr, 380cla, 390tr, 399ccb; Robert Horne 353cb; Robert Smith 257bc, 311cbl, 312crb; Roger Tidman 139tr; Roger Wilmshurst 14br, 17cla, 18tr, 21tr, 62crb, 155cr, 160c, 315tc, 318tc; Stanley Porter 202cr; Steve Austin 15br, 149trb, 173cr, 173bcr, 228tr; Steve Knell 199bc, 241tc, 339ccb, 346tc, 392tc; Tony Hamblin 18ccl, 150cla, 343ccb.

Carlos Sanchez: 339tc, 356cla.

Carlo Sanchez: 272tr.

Chris Schenk: 115cla, 115cbr, 440tl, 441tl.

Science Photo Library: Andrew Syred 11cc.

Ran Schols: 335tcr, 337car, 337cb.

K. Taylor: 229cr.

Richard Tibbits: 11bla, 11ba, 24ca.

Roger Tidman: 8br, 9tlb, 9br, 11tl, 12cra, 18bl, 18bc, 20tr, 55tr, 56cra, 59cr, 62cr, 71tc, 76tc, 77tr, 79cb, 82tr, 83tcl, 84cla, 85cr, 86tr, 86cr, 88cr, 91cla, 91tcr, 92tc, 92tr, 92cb, 95cra, 95crb, 96bl, 98tr, 99tr, 100tr, 101ca, 103cr, 106cra, 106ccb, 112tc, 112c, 115tc, 115tr, 117ca, 119ca, 120ca, 123tr, 124tr, 124crb, 127tr, 127cr, 128tr, 129tr, 130cla, 131tc, 131cra, 132tc, 132tr, 132bcr, 134tc, 134ca, 139tc, 140tc, 141tc, 141cra, 141br, 164tc, 164tr, 164cr, 166cra, 167cl, 168cra, 173tr, 173cl, 174cl, 175cl, 176bl, 180tr, 180cb, 181tc, 182ca, 182bcr, 183tr, 184cla, 184cra, 185cla,

187cra, 191cla, 195tr, 196tc, 198tc, 198ca, 199tr, 200cla, 201tr, 201crb, 202tr, 205tr, 205cla, 205bcr, 208cra, 209tr, 209cla, 210cbr, 212tcl, 219tr, 219cla, 220tc, 220ccb, 221cra, 221ccr, 222cb, 225tr, 225ccb, 227ccr, 228ca, 230tc, 234cb, 235tr, 236tr, 237tr, 238cla, 239cla, 253tr, 257cra, 258tr, 262bl, 270cbr, 272cla, 274ccb, 276tc, 278tr, 281tr, 281crb, 282tc, 282ca, 282cra, 288cla, 288crb, 291bcr, 296bc, 298tr, 298bc, 303tr, 304tc, 306tr, 307tc, 307cca, 315tr, 320tr, 322tr, 322cra, 325tr, 326tr, 326cla, 330tr, 341tr, 342tc, 346cla, 348tr, 350tr, 358bc, 364tc, 364tr, 365tc, 367tr, 370tr, 372tr, 380tcl, 381tc, 381cla, 381crb, 381bcl, 383tr, 384tr, 384cla, 388tc, 391crb, 394tc, 397tc, 397cra, 399tc, 399tr, 399cla, 400cla, 400ccb, 401tr, 402tr, 404bl, 410tc, 411tc, 411tr, 413tc, 416br, 417bl, 418bl, 419tr, 420tr, 421tr, 422tr, 423tl, 424tl, 426br, 428tl, 428br, 433tl, 434tl, 435tl, 438tl, 440br, 446br, 450br, 452bl, 453br, 455br, 457br.

David Tipling: 115tc, 263tr, 264tr, 352cb.

Ray Tipper: 87cl, 159crb, 182tr, 290crb, 295cla, 324ccb, 338ccb, 429br, 431bl, 431br, 432tl.

Roni Vaisannen: 371tcl.

Colin Varndell: 59tr, 72cra, 143cla, 160tr, 171cb, 327tr, 342ccb, 349cca, 360crb.

Halli Veerinder: 11bl, 11b.

Marcus Veresvuo: 263ca, 323tr, 356tr, 382bc.

Roger Wilmshurst: 8cr, 8crb, 65tr, 102tc, 104tc, 105tr, 107cla, 110tc, 142c, 143tr, 153tc, 160crb, 176tcr, 180cla, 196tr, 206cca, 209trb, 213tc, 214tr, 215cra, 231cbl, 256tc, 256cra, 267tr, 271c, 273tr, 285tr, 304tr, 306cbl, 307tr, 310cla, 325cla, 375tr, 379crb, 390tc, 393tc, 420bl, 456tr, 461tl, 461bl.

Windrush Photos: 401cb; A Morris 459bl; A. Morris 73bl; Alan Petty 158cla, 236tc; Andy Harmer 280cbr; Arnaud B van den Berg 94cb, 414bl; Arnoud B. van den Borg 396tc; Arthur Morris 220tr, 224tc, 421br, 445bl; B. Hughes 111crb; B. R. Hughes 170tr; B.R Hughes 170tr; Chris Schenk 111cra, 148tr; Chris Shenk 70tr; David Tipling 15tr, 18cc, 19tr, 57tr, 60cl, 69cra, 74bc, 82bl, 83cr, 87c, 90tc, 96tr, 96cr, 98cla, 99cra, 99crb, 101tr, 105cr, 109cra, 109cr, 111cl, 119tc, 120tr, 142cr, 161tr, 162cl, 174tc, 178cla, 183clb, 186tc, 187cla, 199cla, 204tr, 211tc, 211ca, 212cra, 212tr, 213tr, 215trb, 216tc, 216ca, 218cra, 234cla, 238tr, 243tr, 245c, 258tc, 260tr, 264ca, 265cr, 268tc, 268cbr, 269bc, 271tc, 276tr, 288tr, 289tr, 291c, 300cra, 307cbr, 333c, 334tc, 340ccb, 347tr, 355tc, 371tr, 372bcl, 373tr, 374ccl, 388tr, 389tr, 394cca, 395tr, 406cca, 406tr, 418tr, 420tl, 420tl, 421bl, 422tl, 424tl, 424tr, 427br, 429bl, 432tr, 438bl, 447tr, 447bl, 448tl, 449br, 454tr, 454bl, 456ct; George McCarthy 16cl; Goran Ekström 113crb, 128crb, 366tc, 369bcr, 445br; Ian Fisher 73cra; J Hollis 365tr; Jari Peltomaki 356ccb; Kevin Carlson 164c, 355cla, 410tr; Paul Doherty 21r, 137cl, 137bcr, 375cra; Pentti Johansson 13tl, 60crb, 261tc, 372crb; Peter Cairns 351tr; R. H. de Heer 119crb; Richard Brooks 80cr, 182tc, 279ccr, 304cb, 365cra, 430tr; Roger Wilmhurst 13br; Tom Ennis 56cl, 179cra, 217cb, 436tr, 435br.

Steve Young: 12c, 13cb, 18bcl, 19rc, 57cl, 59tc, 60cra, 67tc, 68tr, 69cla, 69crb, 72tr, 72, 75bcr, 87tr, 93tr, 100tcl, 102tr, 104tr, 105cl, 106tc, 107tc, 107tr, 108tc, 109tc, 109cr, 110tr, 110cr, 111tr, 114tc, 114cr, 116ca, 116cra, 118tr, 118ca, 171cla, 178cla, 181tr, 181cla, 193tr, 205cla, 207cra, 208tr, 208cr, 211cr, 211ccr, 212crb, 212trb, 213ca, 214ca, 214cl, 215tr, 217tc, 218tc, 218cla, 218ccb, 222cla, 222cra, 226tr, 226cla, 226ccb, 276crb, 281tc, 290cla, 291tr, 292tc, 294tr, 301tr, 307cla, 309tr, 310ccb, 321tc, 323tc, 331cb, 336cca, 338tc, 343tc, 356tr, 363cb, 365ccr, 369ca, 405cb, 411cca, 412tc, 412c, 421tl, 436bl, 438br, 440tr, 449tr, 449, 450tr, 451bl, 452br, 454tl, 459bl, 460tl.

Front jacket and spine: ImageStage/Alamy: Frank Krahmer

Back jacket: below right RSPB Images/A Moffatt

All other images © Dorling Kindersley.

For further information see: www.dkimages.com